AN INTELLECTUAL
HISTORY OF
MODERN CHINA

Edited by

MERLE GOLDMAN
Boston University

LEO OU-FAN LEE
Harvard University

CAMBRIDGE
UNIVERSITY PRESS

CAMBRIDGE
UNIVERSITY PRESS

32 Avenue of the Americas, New York NY 10013-2473, USA

Cambridge University Press is part of the University of Cambridge.

It furthers the University's mission by disseminating knowledge in the pursuit of education, learning and research at the highest international levels of excellence.

www.cambridge.org
Information on this title: www.cambridge.org/9780521797108

© Cambridge University Press 2002

First published 2002

A catalogue record for this publication is available from the British Library

Library of Congress Cataloguing in Publication data

An intellectual history of modern China / edited by Merle Goldman, Leo Ou-Fan Lee.
    p.   cm.
   Includes bibliographical references and index.
   ISBN 0-521-80120-6- ISBN 0-521-79710-1 (pbk.)
    1. China-Intellectual life-20th century.   1. Goldman, Merle. II. Lee, Leo Ou-Fan.

DS775.2 .I58 2001
951 .05-dc21   2001043168

ISBN 978-0-521-80120-1 Hardback
ISBN 978-0-521-79710-8 Paperback

AN INTELLECTUAL HISTORY OF MODERN CHINA

An Intellectual History of Modern China is the only comprehensive book on modern China's intellectual development from the nineteenth to the end of the twentieth century. While existing studies tend to focus on individual Chinese thinkers, this book includes all the major Chinese thinkers, as well as political figures who have influenced China's modern history.

Merle Goldman and Leo Ou-Fan Lee introduce and set the contemporary, scholarly context for this collection of essays, drawn from the later volumes (Volumes 12, 13, 14, 15) of *The Cambridge History of China*. The chapters, authored by eminent historians and social scientists in the field of Chinese studies, together trace the transformation of Confucian ideas, the introduction of Western views, and the resulting, uniquely Chinese view of the world. By linking key intellectual developments and figures to emerging political movements, they explain the profound impact of changing ideas and values on Chinese politics and revolution. Merle Goldman brings the history up to date with a new, concluding chapter on the post-Mao era and China's intellectual scene at the end of the twentieth century. Her analysis explains the changes and continuities across the pre-1949, Mao, and post-Mao periods.

This book offers a summation of classic scholarship on the intellectual life of modern China. Scholars and students will find useful general background, incisive analysis, and inspiration for future research on China's intellectual history.

Merle Goldman is Professor of Chinese History at Boston University. Her recent books are *Sowing the Seeds of Democracy: Political Reform in the Deng Xiaoping Era* (1994) and *China: A New History* (Enlarged Edition, 1998), coauthored with the late John K. Fairbank.

Leo Ou-Fan Lee is Professor of Chinese Literature at Harvard University. He is the author of *Shanghai Modern: The Flowering of a New Urban Culture in China, 1930–1945* (1999).

In memory of our beloved teacher and mentor,
Benjamin Schwartz

CONTENTS

Introduction: The Intellectual History of Modern China   *page* 1
by LEO OU-FAN LEE, Harvard University
AND MERLE GOLDMAN, Boston University

1   Intellectual Change: From the Reform Movement to the May
Fourth Movement, 1895–1920   13
CHARLOTTE FURTH, University of Southern California

2   Themes in Intellectual History: May Fourth and After   97
BENJAMIN I. SCHWARTZ, Professor Emeritus, Harvard University

3   Literary Trends: The Quest for Modernity, 1895–1927   142
LEO OU-FAN LEE

4   Literary Trends: The Road to Revolution, 1927–1949   196
LEO OU-FAN LEE

5   Mao Tse-tung's Thought to 1949   267
STUART SCHRAM, Fairbank Center for East Asian Research,
Harvard University

6   The Party and the Intellectuals: Phase Two   349
MERLE GOLDMAN

7   Mao Tse-Tung's Thought from 1949–1976   395
STUART SCHRAM

8   A New Relationship between the Intellectuals and the
State in the Post-Mao Period   499
MERLE GOLDMAN

Bibliography   539

Index   567

INTRODUCTION: THE INTELLECTUAL HISTORY OF MODERN CHINA

Leo Ou-Fan Lee and Merle Goldman

The English term 'intellectual history' is most unfortunate since it seems to imply an exclusive concern with the intellect in the narrow sense of the term and hence also seems to imply an exclusive concern with the history of those called intellectuals. Intellectual history, as here defined, involves the totality of conscious life – the life of the intellect, the emotions, the imagination, and every variety of sensibility – and not simply the realm of conceptualization. Furthermore, we are by no means exclusively concerned with the intellectual life as a self-subsistent realm – as the so-called 'history of ideas' – but with human consciousness as related to the historical situations in which we find ourselves.[1]

These words of Benjamin Schwartz in his essay "A Brief Defense of Political and Intellectual History," written in 1971, are as valid and insightful now as they were then. They were meant as a defense of the study of political and intellectual history, the two main areas of Schwartz's research focus. Yet, even in the early 1970s they did not seem to "enjoy high esteem in many sectors of the historical profession."[2] The situation has not much improved, especially in the case of the intellectual history of modern China. With a few exceptions not much major work has been done according to Schwartz's interpretation. Of course, what Schwartz calls for – the totality of conscious life – is a daunting task. Moreover, as China opened up to outside scholars beginning in the mid-1970s, the mainstream scholarship on modern China concentrated on rural and local histories or on institutional case studies. As a consequence, scholarship revolving around "the man (but seldom woman) and his ideas" that was prevalent in doctoral dissertations until the 1970s was largely jettisoned in the last few decades of the twentieth century.

This state of affairs reveals both a paradigm shift in methodology and a different way of interpreting modern Chinese history. Instead of focusing on a few or a group of individuals, scholars in the China field seek to encompass the larger pictures of locality, region, and nation. In part, this

---

[1] Benjamin I. Schwartz, "A Brief Defense of Political and Intellectual History: The Case of China," in his *China and Other Matters* (Cambridge, MA: Harvard University Press, 1996), 36–37. The essay was first published in 1971.

[2] Ibid., 30.

shift is in reaction to the fact that because Western scholars before the opening up of China in the mid-1970s had little direct contact with China and no direct access to Chinese archives and colleagues since China's 1949 revolution, they were dependent almost exclusively on the written word. Consequently, they concentrated on historic individuals and their writings. With the availability of new archival sources, as well as on-site field research and interviews, Western scholars since the mid-1970s have sought to gain a wider understanding of China in its various forms of collectivity rather than through the individual views of its leading representatives. Accompanying the virtual abandonment of intellectual history is a comparable scarcity of biographical studies. In short, the study of China at the end of the twentieth century was dominated by social and economic history. And political and institutional history fared only slightly better than intellectual history.

In reality, however, Schwartz's defense of intellectual and political history — and the close connection between them — also reflects modern China's own historical course. Looking back on the two centuries of foreign invasions, wars, chaos, and revolutions, it is practically impossible *not* to see these events in political terms. Given the materials at hand in midcentury, it was not surprising that Western scholars saw intellectual history as a history of ideas of a small number of prominent individuals who sought to deal with the political crises of the time. At its best, this approach to intellectual history has yielded some great results. As Schwartz's own classic work on Yan Fu has demonstrated,[3] the study of one man's ideas need not be confined to his own ideas alone; it can go beyond the narrow biographical scope and shed new light on both the Qing intellectual tradition and the strains of Western liberalism entering China through the prism of Yan Fu's translations.

Under Schwartz's influence, a number of scholars have followed suit: The work of Chang Hao and Lin Yu-sheng have likewise sought to rise beyond the biographical confines. Chang delineates a whole spectrum of ideas of the late Qing intellectual transition in his study of Liang Qichao.[4] Lin uses the ideas of a few May Fourth intellectuals to explore and expose their common totalistic mode of thinking.[5] To these might be added the works of Jerome Grieder (on Hu Shi), Charlotte Furth (on Ding Wenjiang),

[3] Schwartz, *In Search of Wealth and Power: Yen Fu and the West* (Cambridge, MA: Harvard University Press, 1964).
[4] Hao Chang, *Liang Ch'i-ch'ao and Intellectual Transition in China, 1890–1917* (Cambridge, MA: Harvard University Press, 1971).
[5] Yu-sheng Lin, *The Crisis of Chinese Consciousness: Radical Anti-Traditionalism in the May Fourth Era* (Madison: University of Wisconsin Press, 1978).

Lawrence Schneider (on Gu Jiegang), Guy Alitto (on Liang Shuming), and a host of others who have focused on the ideas of single intellectuals in order to shed some light on larger issues.[6] Most of these works appeared in the 1970s, in the wake of Schwartz's Yan Fu book and the work of another distinguished intellectual historian, Joseph Levenson, also a close colleague of Schwartz. Still, even these significant works fall short of Schwartz's original conception of intellectual history, which calls for a larger vision and more interdisciplinary effort. Built into his own work is a comparative sweep that encompasses both China and other cultures, both their past traditions and their present manifestations. What is suggested in the paragraph quoted above is an approach which combines intellectual history not only with political history but with cultural and literary history as well.

A RENEWAL OF INTELLECTUAL HISTORY

With this compilation of essays on intellectual history drawn from *Cambridge History of China* volumes, written in the 1980s, plus a new article by Merle Goldman on intellectual developments in the post-Mao era, the time has come to renew Schwartz's defense of intellectual history with reflections drawn from a more recent perspective. These chapters are strictly speaking not exclusively concerned with intellectual history as Schwartz has defined it. Rather, they represent a summation of scholarship that is related to a broad range of intellectual history. They provide a general background that serves as points of departure for new scholarship in this much neglected field. These chapters also vindicate Schwartz's defense of political and intellectual history. In Charlotte Furth's chapter on intellectual change from the late Qing to the May Fourth period, she analyzes the ideas of Kang Youwei (K'ang Yu-wei), Yan Fu (Yen Fu), Liang Qichao (Liang Ch'i-ch'ao), and Tan Sitong (T'an Ssu-t'ung) within the framework of the reform movement. She shows their crucial connection with and shaping impact on the political movement of late Qing politics. In addition, Furth gives attention to the "neo-traditional" strains of the "national essence" school, specifically a few seminal intellectual figures – Zhang Binglin (Chang Ping-lin), Zhang Dongsun (Chang Tung-sun), Liang Shuming – as a way to delineate the intellectual transition from late Qing reformism to the May Fourth movement.

---

[6] Jerome B. Grieder, *Hu Shih and the Chinese Renaissance: Liberalism in the Chinese Revolution, 1917–1937* (Cambridge, MA: Harvard University Press, 1970); Charlotte Furth, *Ting Wen-chiang: Science and China's New Culture* (Cambridge, MA: Harvard University Press, 1970); Laurence A. Schneider, *Ku Chieh-kang and China's New History* (Berkeley: University of California Press, 1970); Guy S. Alitto, *The Last Confucian: Liang Shu-ming and the Chinese Dilemma of Modernity* (Berkeley: University of California Press, 1978).

Schwartz's chapter on the May Fourth period focuses on several crucial themes that can only be understood within the framework of political history. Likewise, Stuart Schram's two chapters on Mao's thought, from his student days until his death in 1976, trace the complexities of Mao Zedong's political thought within the context of his political activities and ideological debates. Merle Goldman's two chapters on the Party and intellectuals also trace the zigzag courses of a relationship whose full significance cannot be understood without the political background of the Party's own history and policies. Even Leo Lee's two chapters on literary trends are written, following the standard literary histories done in China, within a framework of political and intellectual history. In virtually all the chapters in this volume, the role of the Chinese intellectuals as both individuals and members of groups involved in various forms of political action are in the forefront. In this regard, the study of intellectual history in modern China is tantamount to the study of intellectuals involved in the major political issues of their time.

Such an approach is appropriate given the tremendous impact of the May Fourth Movement. It was during the May Fourth period that the role of modern intellectuals, including most writers and artists, became firmly entrenched as the embodiment of enlightenment. In May Fourth discourse, the modern intellectual stands in a privileged position vis-à-vis Chinese society and the Chinese people – as the former's moral conscience and reformist advocate and the latter's voice. Despite the May Fourth's revolutionary nature, the intellectuals' elite position vis-à-vis society resonated with that of their literati ancestors. Like them, they saw themselves as the rejuvenators of Chinese culture, which they believed was the key to China's salvation.

From historical hindsight, however, we can see that this discourse was clearly a case of self-empowerment of a new group of educated elite who created a new self-image of their own importance precisely at the time when the traditional channels of political advancement (in particular, the civil service examination) were no longer available. In this respect, in contrast to traditional literati, this new "intelligentsia" also sought to enhance what they considered to be "new knowledge" and values as opposed to old morality and scholarship. Accentuating the ideological polarity between "Tradition versus Modernity," which was also critiqued by Schwartz, was largely a May Fourth invention. Nevertheless, like their predecessors, the May Fourth intellectuals had put themselves on the central stage of modern Chinese history and created new "cultural capital" out of their new status and educational background. As a consequence, the study of modern

Chinese intellectual history henceforth focused on "an exclusive concern with the history of those called intellectuals."[7]

The May Fourth intellectual project, however, was never completed. Intellectual enlightenment supposedly was to promote the cause of what the May Fourth's leading intellectual Chen Duxiu called Mr. Science and Mr. Democracy. These two reigning slogans, which Chen apparently coined to impart an appeal of human drama, became involved in such intellectual and political intricacies that for the next half century they were the focus of constant debate and reaffirmation. Though they have become part of the official ideology of both the Guomindang and Chinese Communist Party, in the Communist Party's official celebration of the eightieth anniversary of the May Fourth Movement in 1999, President Jiang Zemin set the new ideological tone by focusing only on two themes – science and patriotism – but not on democracy, which had been the clarion-call of the Tiananmen student movement of 1989, the tenth anniversary of which also occurred in 1999. While some scholars and intellectuals both inside and outside China see democracy as part of the liberal tradition of individualism and human rights, few question the increasing relevance of science especially in its utilitarian meaning of technology. Moreover, in this familiar narrative both science and democracy have been interpreted in connection with nationalism, whose political significance has far outweighed its intellectual validity in modern China.

From historical hindsight it is also clear that the dominance of the May Fourth discourse has imposed a set of value systems and interpretive frameworks on later generations of Chinese intellectuals whose own intellectual origins need to be examined. Chief among them is the May Fourth leaders' optimistic embrace of a Western-derived concept of modernity as truth without questioning its negative consequences. Leo Lee has written elsewhere on this modern mode of consciousness as developing from an evolutionary faith which in turn gave rise to a new consciousness of time and history as teleological progress toward a future utopia.[8] Its seeds were first sown in Kang Youwei's vision of the world of "great harmony"; its ethos was manifested in the May Fourth discourse of enlightenment, and its programmed activity reached a peak in the Chinese Communist Revolution.

---

[7] See Benjamin Schwartz's essay, "The Limits of 'Tradition' versus 'Modernity': The Case of the Chinese Intellectuals," included in *China and Other Matters*, 45–64.

[8] Leo Ou-fan Lee, "In Search of Modernity: Reflections on a New Mode of Consciousness in Modern Chinese Literature and Thought," in *Ideas across Cultures: Essays in Honor of Benjamin Schwartz*, Merle Goldman and Paul A. Cohen eds. (Cambridge, MA: Harvard East Asian Monographs, 1990), 110–111.

For all his nativist reactions – carefully delineated in Schram's chapter –
Mao continued to maintain this modern notion of progress, though as
Schwartz has pointed out, in his revolutionary vision Mao renounced the
"technocratic" aspects of modernity in favor of a revolutionary "reign of
virtue" derived from Rousseau.[9]

The ideological manifestation of Chinese modernity was nationalism. As
is well known, the May Fourth was named after the date in 1919 on which
students at several Beijing universities demonstrated against the Treaty of
Versailles, at which Japan as one of the victorious allied nations was given
the German-occupied area of the Shandong peninsula without prior consent by the Chinese delegation. Japan's imperialistic move provided the
immediate political background for the burgeoning sentiment of patriotism, which became equated with nationalism. To counter imperialism,
this simple sentiment implores all citizens to love their nation, for better
or worse. In the words of the French thinker, Ernest Renan, the modern
nation is "a soul, a principle," the creation of a collective moral conscience[10] – very much as the May Fourth intellectuals would have defined
it. At the same time, however, the fervent idealism of the May Fourth intellectuals led them to believe that a modern nation could be constructed
by moral emotion alone.

Thus, nationalism became an ideological conviction sustained by emotions. The political demand for "national survival," according to the famous Chinese scholar Li Zehou, replaced the intellectual project of enlightenment as the central task for intellectuals.[11] For the May Fourth
intellectuals, instilling the patriotic sentiment of national survival became
a more pressing issue than dealing with the technical problems of nation-
building, which were left to the politicians and other professionals under
the Guomindang regime. As the Guomindang government became increasingly authoritarian in the 1930s, however, most intellectuals became radicalized as opponents of the state, which they deemed corrupt, ineffectual,
and a continuation of the precarious warlord government. Their sense of
urgency and disillusionment soon led to a revolutionary imperative calling
for total change in place of the reformist agendas first initiated by their

---

[9] See Schwartz's two classic essays, "The Reign of Virtue: Leader and Party in the Cultural Revolution" and "The Rousseau Strain in the Contemporary World," both included in *China and Other
Matters*, 169–87, 208–26.

[10] Ernest Renan, "What Is a Nation?" included in Homi Bhabha ed., *Nation and Narration* (London:
Routledge, 1990), 8–22.

[11] These ideas are also discussed in Vera Schwarcz, *The Chinese Enlightenment: Intellectuals and the Legacy
of the May Fourth Movement of 1919* (Berkeley: University of California Press, 1986).

predecessors in the late Qing. They replaced the old alternatives of reform or revolution with a linear scheme – from reform to revolution. For the next half century, these two master narratives – nationalism and revolution – dominated the modern Chinese imagination. Their "truth" was deemed self-evident and hence taken for granted without any critical reflection. The proper faculty of intellectuals – their capacity for critical reflection – was pushed to the background.

Scholarly interest also developed in the post-Mao era in a number of figures who once resisted or challenged this dominant May Fourth discourse. Some may be called "conservatives" who are described in the chapters by Furth and Schwartz. But their significance goes beyond any narrowly defined intellectual category. For instance, the publication of the diaries of the literary critic Wu Mi aroused considerable interest.[12] Wu, together with his friend Mei Guangdi, had founded the journal *Xueheng* (Critical Review) in the May Fourth period which advocated a conservative brand of humanism under the influence of Irving Babbitt. Another eminent figure is Chen Yinque, a scholar of traditional Chinese literature and history who, in addition to his scholarly works, wrote a number of classical poems that apparently contained arcanely coded references to his own frustrations under the Maoist regime.[13] The scholarship on the history of Chinese philosophy of Feng Youlan, the Neo-Confucian philosopher whose checkered career under Mao bespeaks the tragic poignancy of the "true believers," has survived in spite of the vicissitudes of his political fate.

A revival of interest at the close of the twentieth century in these figures, who were primarily scholars, is not surprising. It signifies a longing, if not nostalgia, among a considerable number of Chinese intellectuals for a bygone era in which, despite wars and revolution, it was still possible to define one's intellectual status in terms of scholarship, not politics, even though their reaction to politics had led them to their particular form of intellectual endeavor. After half a century of ideological turmoil, both the regime and the intellectuals desire a much needed respite from political campaigns. The one-hundredth anniversary of the founding of Beijing University in 1998 became the occasion for both scholarly commemoration and official patronage. The historical connection between Beijing University and May Fourth, coupled with the rediscovery of the scholarly intellectuals mentioned above, reinforces the impression that genuine scholarly en-

---

[12] *Wu Mi riji* (Beijing: Shenghuo, tushu, xinzhi sanlian shudian, 1998), ten volumes.
[13] Lu Jiandong, *Chen Yinque de zuihou ershinian* (*The Last Twenty Years of Chen Yinque*) (Beijing: Sanlian shudian, 1996).

deavor, which was marginalized from the May Fourth Movement until the post-Mao era, is now receiving renewed attention.

Nevertheless, the motivations of the Party and the intellectuals diverge. The former gave tacit consent to the relative autonomy of scholarship as one way to divert intellectuals from political activities and improve China's image in the world; the latter used scholarship to recover a certain intellectual dignity which had long been denied them as a result of the Party's insistent persecution of intellectuals and politicalization of intellectual and cultural life since the Yan'an period. The tragic story of the victimization of Chinese intellectuals by the Party has been documented by Merle Goldman in her two chapters included in this volume and in her other works. She shows that as Mao and the Party launched successive, intensifying political campaigns against China's intellectuals, their elitist status was completely demolished; from the height of their self-inflated glory during the May Fourth era they were relegated ideologically to the bottom of the new society. After Mao's death in 1976, however, intellectuals regained some of their past status, as the Party gradually withdrew its control of most areas of life except from such areas as politics, birth control, and sectarian groups such as the Buddhist meditation movement Falun Gong, which it perceived as potentially political. Thereby it left sufficient public spaces for what Tang Tsou has called "zones of indifference" in which intellectuals could maneuver for some degree of freedom.[14]

Deng Xiaoping's economic reforms, beginning in the late 1970s, largely dissipated the revolutionary ethos of the earlier era with the spread of a market economy and capitalist consumption. As a result, the relationship between the intellectuals and the state underwent further drastic changes. The increasing commercialization of culture in post-Mao China triggered several crises among intellectuals themselves: Some renounced their calling and went into business; others retreated into the universities and became professional academics; still others denounced the materialistic values that accompanied China's move to the market. The Chinese intellectuals' traditional sense of self-importance and historical mission was deflated if not entirely abandoned. Chinese intellectuals at the end of the twentieth century had turned themselves into scholars, technocrats, cultural producers, business people, and entertainers, but they were no longer social prophets, the agents of national salvation, or visionary leaders of change as they had been throughout most of Chinese history and even into the Mao era until Mao brutally suppressed them.

[14] See Goldman's final chapter, "A New Relationship between the Intellectual and the State in the Post-Mao Period."

THE INTERACTION BETWEEN POPULAR
AND ELITE CULTURES

In the essay which included the paragraph quoted at the beginning of this Introduction, Schwartz emphatically stated that "one of the barriers to a broadly conceived intellectual history of China has been the facile acceptance of the distinction between 'folk culture' and 'high culture'." "There is no reason whatsoever," he asserted, "why the study of conscious life of the masses should not also be subsumed under the category of intellectual history." And he further faulted intellectual historians of China for having devoted "too little attention to movements of popular religion, to the 'ideologies of rebellion,' to the interweaving of mythology and cosmological thinking on the popular level, and a host of other subjects."[15] Moreover, the "conscious life of the masses" is manifested not only in popular religious beliefs and practices but also in works of literature and other forms of print culture. The few studies of popular culture in imperial China have fully demonstrated that there were always elements of highbrow Confucian values or intellectualized Buddhist or Daoist doctrines which became transformed into popular forms.[16] At the same time, the educated elite has always been interested in the assimilation of popular forms, especially in works of literature, both poetry and fiction. Popular inspirations have enriched the heritage of Chinese literature for at least two millennia before Hu Shi put its history in a new framework that emphasized the "living" tradition of vernacular literature.

Due to the dominance of May Fourth ideology, however, Chinese as well as Western scholarly attention slighted the close interactions between the popular and elite cultures that continued throughout the twentieth century.[17] In fact, before the May Fourth intellectuals appeared on the scene, the popular press had embraced a set of cultural imaginaries derived from Western modernity. They are found in the massive translations of Western fiction which were first serialized in the late Qing newspapers and journals, in the pictorial narratives published in the famous *Dianshizhai huabao* (a pictorial journal from the Dianshi studio), and in the voluminous novels written by Bao Tianxiao, Zhou Shoujuan, Zhang Henshui, and many others, some of whom were later ridiculed by May Fourth leaders as belonging to the Saturday School of "Butterflies and Mandarin Ducks." Whereas their

---

[15] Schwartz, *China and Other Matters*, 38.
[16] See David Johnson, Evelyn Rawski, and Andrew Nathan eds., *Popular Culture in Late Imperial China* (Berkeley: University of California Press, 1985).
[17] An exception is E. Perry Link, *Mandarin Ducks and Butterflies: Popular Fiction in Early Twentieth-Century Cities* (Berkeley: University of California Press, 1981).

language may have been more traditional (written mostly in a simple form of *wenyan* or classical style), the contents were by no means traditional. Schwartz should be gratified that a number of scholars of a younger generation have taken up his challenge to work on popular culture and ideologies of rebellions as seen in books by Perry Link, Elizabeth Perry, Jeffrey Wasserstrom, and those of their students.

The popular cultural landscape of the late twentieth century has changed even more drastically than that of the early decades of the twentieth century. The new communication technologies have created new forms and modes of cultural production and circulation – from the print-based media to visual and electronic media to the computer – which are quickly and persistently changing the nature and function of popular culture. Moreover, such a landscape is no longer based on a single national setting but has become increasingly "transnational" – a landscape which includes Mainland China, Taiwan, Hong Kong, Singapore, as well as the "diasporic" communities in Southeast Asia and North America.[18] As Hong Kong movies, American television series, and Taiwan rock stars become widely popular everywhere, popular culture already cuts across narrowly defined political boundaries. Production and consumption – from literary texts to movies and name-brand clothing – have become the new rules of the game. Ideological propaganda at century's end had become increasingly marginalized and intellectual creativity globalized.

These changed circumstances may also change the perception of China's recent past. They encourage a reconsideration of modern Chinese intellectual history within a broader spectrum and exploration of topics and sources which have been largely neglected because of the dominance of May Fourth elitism. Scholars in both China and the West have begun to pay increasing attention to the period immediately before 1919 – from about 1895 to 1915 – as a pivotal era of transition in which the beginnings of a Chinese modernity can be traced. In addition to the elitist theories of new fiction as advocated by Liang Qichao and Yan Fu, attention is paid to various forms of urban print culture: newspapers, journals, as well as the numerous genres of writing (satirical prose, poetry, translations, and stories and serialized novels) published in these media. In these new print spaces, ideas about a new literature and a new vernacular language were first presented. The emergence of these new mediums was a reflection of the thriving publishing industry centered in Shanghai. Some of the largest publishers, such as the famous Commercial Press, launched huge publica-

---

[18] See Leo Lee, "Trans-Chinese: Notes on Language and Sensibility," *Venue* 1 (September 1997), 160–172.

tion projects such as textbooks for new schools, dictionaries, and compendia of miscellaneous items – all in the name of promoting new knowledge. In this transitional period, the host of "cultural producers" – journalists, editors, translators, booksellers, as well as writers and painters – contributed to a new culture industry and popularized the ideas of reform and new learning. Without their efforts the May Fourth New Culture Movement would not have succeeded so readily.

The May Fourth leaders – Chen Duxiu in particular – were especially adept in turning the print space first carved out by the practitioners of popular culture to their own advantage. Chen's ideological polemic with the editors of the *Dongfang zazhi* (Eastern miscellany), the flagship publication of the Commercial Press, in the early 1920s demonstrates this adeptness.[19] But in seizing the high ground in this cultural war, the May Fourth leaders also erected a new wall that separated their New Culture from the popular print arena, whose intellectual significance was purposefully downgraded. The most obvious case is their ideological dismissal of the so-called "Butterfly and Mandarin Duck" school of writers, who research now shows were never totally opposed to the values of New Literature. In fact, we can trace a direct genealogy from late Qing journalism to the Butterfly school in terms of the forms and genres of their writing as well as the background of their personnel. The neglect of this and other forms of popular writing must be attributed to the May Fourth elitist legacy.

Renewed interest in these popular sources before May Fourth and new interest in rich popular culture of the post-Mao era do not mean, however, an end to the study of elite intellectuals. Rather, they compel us to do intellectual history in a new way by combining the study of "the life of the intellect" (or intellectuals) with the study of "the emotions, the imaginations, and every variety of sensibility" – in other words, to do full justice to Schwartz's original formulation. If we are concerned with "human consciousness as related to the historical situations in which we find ourselves," we must not limit ourselves to the study of ideas of intellectual leaders but should extend our concern to the minds of other social groups as well. The study of popular culture should be a part of intellectual history and not subsumed only under the disciplines of sociology, cultural anthropology, or social history.

In his essay, Schwartz quotes a variety of French thinkers (Sartre, Merleau-Ponty, and above all Levi-Strauss) whose ideas were much discussed in the

---

[19] This debate is discussed in detail in Leo Lee, "Belated Modernity: Reflections on the May Fourth Intellectual Project," included in the collection *The Appropriation of Cultural Capital,* edited by Milena Doleželová-Velingerová and Oldřich Král, (Cambridge, MA: Harvard University Asia Center, 2001).

1970s, but he does not choose to comment on specific methodologies. He also alludes to the possibility that "ideas themselves may be concerned with matters which are entirely material," but he does not explain what he means by "material" matters. Schwartz saw ideas as produced against a "material" background by people who wish to relate to the concrete environment in which they find themselves. Such "materials" can be studied not merely as historical documentation but as cultural artifacts and in *context* – the milieu in which ideas are produced and circulated. Likewise, the empirical research for "historical materials" as sheer "evidence" no longer suffices, because materials, like ideas, are subject to interpretation: They are made to speak by the interpretive act of the researcher and scholar.

Consequently, intellectual history stands to benefit from a number of other disciplines – in particular, literary analysis and anthropology as well as history and political science. From a literary perspective, we can look at historical context itself as constructed by "texts" and "textuality," which in turn involve the problem of reading and interpretation.[20] And there is no reason why the areas of concern for contemporary cultural anthropology – and for that matter contemporary cultural studies – cannot be given a historical dimension. As Schwartz has said: "An intellectual history of China, as here conceived, should be concerned not simply with 'Chinese thought' but with Chinese thinking and thinking within the framework of their historical situations."[21] Such "thinking" must be studied in a framework that encompasses both ideas and behavior, both individuals and collectivities, that are situated in China's multifarious cultural traditions, both past and present. This volume of intellectual history begins the process of the study of modern Chinese intellectual history as proposed by our teacher Benjamin Schwartz.

[20] This literary and theoretical turn is already fully manifested in the works of some Western intellectual historians (Hayden White and Dominic LaCapra) and institutionalized as programs (e.g., "the history of consciousness" program at the University of California at Santa Cruz).
[21] Schwartz, *China and Other Matters*, 43.

CHAPTER 1

INTELLECTUAL CHANGE: FROM THE REFORM MOVEMENT TO THE MAY FOURTH MOVEMENT, 1895 – 1920

EVOLUTIONISM IN REFORM THOUGHT

The years 1898 and 1919 are usually thought of as two watersheds in the history of China's intellectual break with the values of Confucian civilization. The 1898 reform movement was an effort at institutional change on the part of ranking literati close to the throne. It began as a response to military defeat by Japan in 1895, but ended in the abandonment of the traditional Sinocentric world-view and a large-scale effort to assimilate the 'new learning' (*hsin-hsueh*) of the West. The movement bore fruit in the late Ch'ing modernization drive and in the collapse of the imperial system in 1911, bringing in its wake a wave of still more sweeping intellectual re-evaluation. Where the cutting edge of reform in 1898 had been directed at the inherited political order, the intellectual campaign for a totally 'new culture', which was symbolized by the May Fourth demonstrations of 1919, was seen as an attack upon the traditional moral and social orders as well. The leadership of the later movement came from China's newly modernized universities and schools. In addition to anti-imperialism, its goal was the establishment of a scientific and democratic 'new culture' purged of all relics of China's feudal past. In a generation China's intellectuals had apparently moved from the questioning of core traditional values to their total repudiation.

Moreover, in this same generation the intellectual elite as a class had undergone a number of important structural changes. It had created novel modes of communication and association, in the form of newspapers and periodical press on the one hand, and various types of study societies and political parties on the other. The classical examination system had ended, and had been replaced by a system of schools, leading to the erosion of traditional career opportunities in the civil service and the rapid professionalization and specialization of intellectual work. Centres of culture, historically urban to a degree in China, were subjected to the influence of a different kind of urbanism: that of the cosmopolitan industrializing city. If the intellectual class moulded by these shifts was developing a new cohesiveness, it was also threatened by a new estrangement from the rest of Chinese society. No longer educated for office, intellectuals more and more stood outside the mainstream of political power; educated more and more according to foreign models, they risked losing the inherited language which could form a bridge to the common people.

The discovery of the West: reformist evolutionary cosmology

Intellectual change after the 1890s must first of all be studied in the light of the Chinese 'discovery of the West' – not merely as the source of imperialist aggression or technological wizardry, but as a world civilization in its own right. At first this discovery was the result of the transmission to a broader elite of knowledge accumulated by a few pioneers after the 1800s. The important reform study societies of the years 1895–8 began by propagating the works of treaty-port publicists and compradores like Wang T'ao and Cheng Kuan-ying, or of early envoys to Europe like Hsueh Fu-ch'eng and Kuo Sung-tao; or of Christian missionary education societies and the early Chinese arsenal schools for technological 'self-strengthening'. However, compared with the flood of energy aroused by the reform movement itself, these early explorations of Western learning soon seemed limited indeed. Pushed by political exile and pulled by the lure of the new education, thousands lived and studied abroad after 1900, and returned to China to claim positions as intellectual leaders. For those who remained at home, translations – especially of works on world history, geography, politics and law – were increasingly available, at first mainly from Japanese but later from European languages as well. Pioneer Chinese translators like Yen Fu, who specialized in British and French social and political philosophers, and Lin Shu, who was famous for European romantic fiction, were among the most popular authors of their generation. In Peking in 1895 members of the radical Study Society for Self-Strengthening (Ch'iang-hsueh hui) organized by K'ang Yu-wei had not been able to find a world map in any bookshop in the city. By 1919 the capital's reorganized Peking University under the chancellorship of Ts'ai Yuan-p'ei (trained both at the Hanlin Academy and at Leipzig University) employed graduates of Western universities, and included courses in European literature, history, science and philosophy.

Facts like these have led to a widespread assumption that the reform generation was stamped by the Chinese 'response to the West', and must be analysed in terms of the impact of foreign ideas upon native systems of thought. Fung Yu-lan, a leading neo-traditional scholar, has typically characterized the period between the 1890s and the 1920s as one of Chinese infatuation with the 'spiritual civilization of the West' – to be distinguished from both the Sinocentrism of the dynastic era and the critical neo-traditionalism of the 1920s and 1930s.[1] Chinese Marxist historians like Hou Wai-lu have linked this presumed infatuation with the West to structural changes in the society – the drive for industrialization of an emerging bourgeoisie, which, like its European counterpart, found the scientific and democratic ideology of the Enlightenment a fit form to express their socio-economic aspirations.[2] The American scholar Joseph Levenson was more impressed with evidence suggesting that Chinese reformers viewed the West and its intellectual claims with a good deal of ambivalence, but interpreted the latter as an expression of tension between their commitment to universal values – which dictated the necessity of adopting new beliefs from abroad – and their particularistic sense of national cultural identity, which tugged them towards the comforts of tradition.[3]

The notion of 'response to the West' does indeed call attention to the critical importance of Western imperialism as an external force motivating the desire to change, and to the enormous stimulus, both positive and negative, generated by this first serious Chinese exploration of dominant nineteenth-century Western traditions of science and socio-political thought. One danger in the concept, however, is its tendency to suggest that the process was one of linear substitution of 'Western' ideas for native ones; and that Chinese played an intellectually passive role. Another is to foster the assumption that once the process of Westernization had occurred, it was impossible for Chinese thereafter to maintain any authentic commitment to traditional values. The notion that the Chinese moved reactively from the assertion of traditional values before 1890 to their denial in the course of the campaign for a 'new culture' in 1919 has been a consequence of this explanatory model.

An alternative perspective is first suggested when one distinguishes the political occasion behind the reform movement from its intellectual content, and so can recognize native sources of inspiration for the latter. Increasingly scholars have noted that comparatively heterodox movements of traditional thought – whether the anti-despotism of the late Ming loyalists of the seventeenth century, the individualism of the Lu-Wang tradition of Neo-Confucianism, the social humanitarianism of Mahayana Buddhism, the libertarian strands in Taoism, or the pragmatic and utilitarian approach to statecraft of a Mo-tzu, a Yen Yuan, or even the

---

1 Fung Yu-lan, *Hsin shih lun* (New culture and society).
2 Hou Wai-lu, *Chin-tai Chung-kuo ssu-hsiang hsueh-shuo shih* (Interpretive history of modern Chinese thought).
3 Joseph R. Levenson, *Confucian China and its Modern Fate*.

Legalists – were all *points d'appui* upon which many reformers built their cases. The imperial orthodoxy had concealed the diversity of the Chinese tradition more than it had destroyed it, and not all native traditions – elite or popular – were conservative ones. On the other hand, it is also increasingly understood that China's own neo-traditional philosophers and their Maoist adversaries alike have been correct in saying that commitment to Confucian values survived the iconoclastic onslaught of the 'New Culture' and May Fourth movements, and has continued to guide the social behaviour and spiritual life of many Chinese down to post-Liberation times.

Nonetheless, the 'response to the West' model of intellectual change is only partially challenged by an analysis which perceives continuities, like discontinuities, as historically linear. A more fruitful approach may be to recognize that the leading thinkers of the reform generation were trying to understand how both continuities and discontinuities fit into significantly altered structures of meaning. The socio-political struggle for reform was not articulated in isolation, but within the framework of a new evolutionary cosmology. This was a systemic conception of the universe, in which natural, spiritual and social phenomena were perceived as manifestations of a single cosmic reality. The external source of this new cosmology lay in the Chinese discovery of what they took to be new truths of nature and facts of history revealed by the West. On the one hand there was the discovery of a world history encompassing a plurality of high civilizations in dynamic interaction with one another as well as with a 'barbarian' perimeter; on the other, there was the exploration of the implications of Western scientific law – particularly the laws of evolution based upon Darwinian biology, but also those of Newtonian physics as well. Internally the cosmology relied upon the Confucian-Taoist tradition which taught that socio-political phenomena and natural cosmic patterns are linked in a process of interdependent causation. There resulted from the new cosmology a world-view which took away from Chinese their self-image as the sole source of world civilization, and exposed them as members of one culture and one nation among many. But at the same time the consequent relativization of China was no simple cutting down to size – rather it implied the relativization of all cultures, all social stages, and all points in historical time. It resulted in a new faith in world-historical progress among Chinese, but one which stressed both the moral teleology of the historical process and its relative incompleteness at any given temporal stage. This in turn led to a reemphasis upon time itself, in the classic sense of 'change' (*i*) as a metaphysical reality – the cosmic energies at work directing all the structures of existence in their ultimately interacting motions. Finally, it created a heightened sense of certain problems of human moral action in a cosmos now considered remarkable for its dynamism – which would have either to create human beings in its own Faustian image, or leave them helpless before an externally determinative process.

Not surprisingly, the first to express the new affirmation of change in a relativized world were a few men whose early personal contact with Europe had been relatively sustained. Hsueh Fu-ch'eng, a member of the Chinese diplomatic mission to London between 1890 and 1894, his writings on reform first stimulated by the Japanese seizure of the Ryūkyūs in 1879, offered a typical early sketch of the new world history. Between the dawn of humanity and today 10,000 years have elapsed, he believed, a fact known by the inherent law of alternation which governs the speed of world change. Hsueh's internal periodization of that 10,000 years followed standard traditional historiography, but he assessed the present as a fundamental turning-point: the end of the era of separation between Chinese and barbarian and the coming of an age of association among states. Importantly, Hsueh saw these transformations as simply necessary, independent of human desire: 'The reason for its happening is not that people love change; it is time and circumstance'.[4]

This sense of necessity was more subtly and affirmatively underscored by Yen Fu, the great translator of European social classics, in his famous essay of 1895, 'On the speed of world change', which offered the first definitive reform analysis of the idea of progress. Yen Fu was also impressed by parallels between the present and the Ch'in-Han era, the great watershed in traditional Chinese institutional history, but he confessed that the causes behind such historical transformations remained mysterious:

Using forced language we speak of a cosmic-historical process of Change [*yun hui*]. When such a process is at work, even sages have no power over it.... To say they can take hold of it and move it is false. The sage's role is merely to know its origins and foresee its movements.[5]

Convinced that their moment in history was a turning-point so basic it could only be the result of some cosmic principle at work, reformers first saw evolutionary time as patterned according to deeply satisfying

4 Hsueh Fu-ch'eng, *Ch'ou-yang ch'u-i* (Preliminary proposals on foreign affairs, 1886), reprinted in Yang Chia-lo, ed. *Wu-hsu pien-fa wen-hsien hui-pien* (Documentary collection of the literature of the 1898 reform movement), 1. 159–61.
5 Yen Fu, 'Lun shih-pien chih chi' (On the speed of world change), reprinted in *Yen Chi-tao shih wen-ch'ao* (Essays and poems of Yen Fu, preface 1916), chüan 1.1.
6 Wang T'ao, 'Pien fa' (Reform), reprinted in Yang Chia-lo, *Wu-hsu pien-fa wen-hsien hui-pien*, 1.133–5.

traditional beliefs, and their own role in 'serving the times' as that of regulators of cosmic order. In the words of the pioneer treaty-port journalist Wang T'ao, 'The Way honours institutions which suit the times, and no more'.[6] In this context the political reform movement in China was less an end in itself than an accommodation to a new stage in world historical development; and the known institutions of the industrialized Western world provided intimations, the more exciting because dimly outlined, of utopian future possibilities for human society as a whole.[7]

As the foregoing suggests, evolutionary cosmology took shape less as the insight of one individual than as a set of common conceptions arrived at among many. Nonetheless, in its mature form it is best examined here through the thought of the major reform intellectuals who were in part its creators. The senior partner of the group was certainly K'ang Yu-wei, whose works, *The false classics of the Hsin period* (*Hsin hsueh wei-ching k'ao*; 1891), and *Confucius as a reformer* (*K'ung-tzu kai-chih k'ao*; 1897) had supported the canonical claims of the long submerged New Text School of Confucianism in a provocative effort to make tradition serve reform. Shortly after the collapse of the imperially sponsored Hundred Days reform effort of 1898, which K'ang had personally led, he put together his major utopian synthesis, *The book of the great commonwealth* (*Ta-t'ung shu*) – a work which although never completely published in his lifetime was known in draft and outline among his more influential disciples.[8]

Of these, T'an Ssu-t'ung was certainly the boldest and most provocative thinker, whose philosophical originality rivalled that of K'ang himself. His execution at the age of 33 by the Ch'ing authorities after the counter coup of September 1898 was a martyrdom deliberately sought on his own part, and it canonized his spirit in the minds of his surviving comrades, making his posthumously published book, *On humanity* (*Jen hsueh*; 1901) a talismanic legacy.[9] Liang Ch'i-ch'ao, who served as K'ang's close political ally, together with K'ang virtually created the study society movement through which reform ideas swept the country after 1895. Already a pioneer journalist as editor of the study society vehicle, *Shih wu pao* (Current affairs; The China progress), in 1896 and 1897, he attained

7 The new optimism has been analysed against the background of Neo-Confucian political culture in Thomas Metzger, *Escape from predicament: Neo-Confucianism and China's evolving political culture*.
8 K'ang Yu-wei, *Ta-t'ung shu* (Book of the great commonwealth). English translation by Laurence G. Thompson, *Ta Tung Shu: book of the great commonwealth*.
9 T'an Ssu-t'ung, *Jen hsueh* (On humanity), first published in *Ch'ing-i pao* (1899), and reprinted four times in the next 15 years. My study of T'an has been greatly aided by David Wile, 'T'an Ssu-t'ung: his Life and Major Work, the Jen Hsueh' (University of Wisconsin, Ph.D. dissertation, 1972).

the peak of his influence as the editorial voice of the reform opposition in Japanese exile after 1899.

If the foregoing three men had all staked their careers upon winning reform under the monarchy in 1898, paying for their failure with exile or death, Yen Fu, the fourth great inspirer of the movement, maintained a more temperate stand on the edge of events. Ostensibly the superintendent of a naval academy in Tientsin, he was a rare British-trained 'foreign expert' in engineering. Rarer still, and unique to his generation, was his synthetic view of contemporary Anglo-European civilization, which he developed in a series of remarkable translations of major works of Herbert Spencer, T. H. Huxley, J. S. Mill, Adam Smith, Montesquieu, and others. Here he utilized the scholar's traditional convention of commentary and the resources of the classical Chinese philosophical vocabulary to present a dazzlingly interpretive rendition of his originals.

The complex intellectual relations among these four may be represented by seeing K'ang and T'an as drawing most deeply upon native roots for their philosophical synthesis, by contrast with the Western inspired Social Darwinism of Yen Fu and Liang Ch'i-ch'ao. Such an analysis sees K'ang and T'an tending to internationalism, reminiscent of the *t'ien-hsia* ideal of a Sinocentric cosmos; to utopianism, as they projected the canonical golden age on to the future, and to faith in the Confucian idea of *jen* (goodness) as a cosmic-moral principle. By contrast Yen Fu and Liang Ch'i-ch'ao appear encouraged by their Social Darwinist orientation to take more nationalistic, pragmatic and secular perspectives. However, before 1903 or 1904 the writings of all four displayed an underlying optimism about China's long-range prospects which belied the indignant and anxious tones of their anti-imperialist, anti-court polemics, and which is best understood as based upon a shared belief in the benign nature of the metahistorical process as a whole, leading to a progressively realized world community.

The major contribution of both the *Ta-t'ung shu* and the *Jen-hsueh* was to present the idea of evolution integrated into a cosmology which linked the process of evolutionary unfolding with social change. Both works recognized the transvaluation of social values which the new stage of world history portended, while remaining confident that Confucian spiritual truth would continue to be the metaphysical source of the pattern of change.

Originally New Text Confucianism had provided K'ang Yu-wei with a Chinese *schema* of advancing historical stages which could be accommodated to a full-scale Western theory of progress. By means of this he embraced unilinear historical change with the enthusiasm of a discoverer. However, a parallel – although in a formal sense devolutionary – analysis of the metahistorical process found in a text attributed to the classic Confucian school was even more important as a source of the *Ta-t'ung shu*. This text, *Evolution of the Rites* (*Li yun*), described the doctrine of the 'three ages', beginning with the golden age of antiquity 'when the great Tao prevailed' – an era of 'Great Peace' (*Ta-t'ung*) unsullied by the institutions of familism or private property. According to the *Li yun* the historical sage rulers of the Three Dynasties had presided over a second era of 'lesser tranquility', a devolution away from the golden age to a world marked by both military power and ritual morality: 'the empire became a world of families where people love only their own parents and their own children [and] goods and labor are used only for private advantage'.[10] When K'ang located the present as transitional between the third 'age of disorder' which had begun in the times of Confucius, and a coming 'age of rising peace' which would lead the world back towards Great Peace, he was prophesying a transition away from a social system based on patriarchal clans and tribes and a corresponding political system based on the despotic authority of rulers over people or nobles over commoners. Instead would emerge a world where the hierarchical distance between peoples and their rulers and between different individuals in their social relations would be markedly diminished. The political form embodying this new relationship among people would be the nation-state and constitutional monarchy. In the immediate sense, these were the 'institutional reforms' (*pien-fa*) which would bring China to a level of parity with Japan and Europe and effect her transition to the social system of rising peace. The final stage of Great Peace was still several centuries distant, K'ang believed, although the political systems of Switzerland and the United States, as republican nations, already exhibited in embryo the egalitarianism which would then permeate all social relationships. Such a world, sketched in the *Ta-t'ung shu*, would be without any social distinctions based on property, class, race or sex. Here the nation-state itself would be superseded by a global parliamentary government, and all people would accept common customs and be united in common faith.

K'ang's *ta-t'ung* seemed to break with the fundamentals of Confucian belief by its assertion that the perfectly moral society should have no hierarchical social distinctions; it arrived at this position through a development of the classic Mencian idea that the 'extension' of benevolence in the world springs from the nurture of natural human capacities for sympathy with others. Thus, extended and universalized human goodness

---

10 Quoted in Fung Yu-lan, *A history of Chinese philosophy*, 1.378.

becomes 'love' (*jen*), which in K'ang's version was conceived as a dynamic cosmic-moral energy. As such, it evinced itself in what he saw as the power of attraction and repulsion inherent in the motions of the external cosmos as well as in the surges of spontaneous 'attractive' sentiment which underlie the moral life of conscious beings. During the age of rising peace social norms, or *li*, still permitted a limited or 'partial' expression of human solidarity, by allowing for ethical distinctions between near and far, or high and low; in the age of the great community social customs would have cast off all such 'selfishness', and would perfectly reflect a spirit of undifferentiated universal love (*jen*).

Thus K'ang's model of natural and social evolution took off from the historical transition from barbarism to civilization, and included a secular vision of advanced democratic and affluent societies suggested by Western examples. Yet fundamentally he believed that the whole process was an odyssey of human spiritual perfection. Underpinning his prophecy of a utopia through modernization lay the traditional Neo-Confucian vision of an organismic cosmos transformed through the self-actualization of the sage's sincere mind. Yet K'ang's version suggested a novel relationship between the poles of that organism: that is, between the sage on the one hand and the external cosmos of 'Heaven and Earth' on the other. Rather than placing sages in the centre as the source of cosmic transformations, K'ang imagined them almost as spectators before the awesome panorama of the universe. *Jen*, though still playing its role as the source of the moral consciousness of the individual, manifested itself most potently in the external sphere – in the starry heavens, in the dynamism of change itself. From this came his orientation towards materialism, the seeds of cosmological determinism, and a radical moral optimism. Gone was the common Neo-Confucian tendency to anxiety over cosmic deficiency and moral failure; instead K'ang breathed confidence that spontaneous human desires are in harmony with *jen*, and that personal enjoyment, pleasure, abundance – all these as well as enlightenment were to be expected bounties of the utopia of the future. The sage would not create social utopia; history itself would. If the attainment of spiritual perfection would come through the collapse of social barriers to human community, K'ang imagined this less as the result of human struggle than as a gift of liberation.

Therefore, this dream of the human conquest of selfishness appeared devoid of any strong sense of the necessity of internal struggle to overcome it. Indeed K'ang usually explained the obstacles to moral success as arising from environmental and ritual 'barriers' external to the self. But he also defined moral action in practice as requiring in fact acceptance of these barriers, that is, as action suited to the times in which one happens to live. As such the evolution of the spirit becomes a deterministic cosmic unfolding: 'When the proper time arrives, the changes suited to it take place of themselves'. Only a seer's foreknowledge might be said in part to determine the future even in reflecting it; the true moral action of the sage, then, lies in prophecy.

Presented in this context, K'ang's specific social ideals, though modern and even 'Westernized' in detail, still lacked a truly secular autonomy within his system of belief. The imagery he preferred (that of the 'nine barriers' to human community) echoed that of classic statements of the mystical experience – Confucian and otherwise – where the ordinary boundaries between the self, the external world and the numinous are at least fluid, at most obliterated entirely. K'ang's social ideal emphasized the elimination of political, racial, sexual and national barriers, not so much because such hierarchies were evil as because all differentiation of phenomena obscures the truth that on the level of philosophic truth 'reality' is 'one'. On the psychosocial level, the *Ta-t'ung shu* did express K'ang's own protest against the constraints of familism. These barriers he indeed keenly felt as evils, but here too K'ang was bypassing the intermediate sphere of social relations. For him barriers were seen as either concrete constraints upon individuals in their personal lives, or as abstract illusions due to an imperfect metaphysical understanding.

In this way K'ang's adaptation of Confucian metaphysics shifted the balance between sage and cosmos: as a teleological force K'ang's external cosmos had more purposeful dynamism than the traditional view easily allowed; as a limited foreknower of the process of change, the sage had correspondingly less. T'an Ssu-t'ung's work redressed the balance. In reasserting the ideal of the sages' power, he created a politicized sage as secular hero. He offered a dialectical model of external cosmic forces of enlightenment and resistance as the necessary theatre for the drama of sagely self-actualization. Put together, the two views made evolutionary cosmology evoke both cosmic mechanisms and human powers at play in an expanding universe.

If K'ang's book reflected its author's self-image as a prophet T'an's might be said to suggest his finally chosen destiny as a martyr. In its moral activism religious saviours were seen as the key agents of world historical change; at the same time T'an imagined the final culmination of that change would be the transcendence of selfhood itself. Where K'ang did not look far beyond an earthly paradise, T'an made the final goal of evolution secondary to a stage when even human consciousness as presently conceived would cease to exist.

Like K'ang, T'an posited cosmic-moral energies which, by regulating their own motions, are presumed to create the structures of the 'things' in which they inhere. This view implied a criticism of the Neo-Confucian dualism of 'principle' (*li*) and 'material force' (*ch'i*), and was bolstered by physical notions borrowed from Western science; but his model of the motions of 'matter' was more heavily indebted to Buddhist-Taoist pheno-menology. Where K'ang identified *ch'i* (material force) with 'electricity', T'an started with the idea that 'ether' was the unitary material substance permeating, inhering and connecting all the realms of phenomena, space and living things. But while the basic substance was defined as material, the all-important mode of its active functioning was moral: '*jen* is the function of ether'. Thus, the transformations of ether are generated through the activity of moral energy, and the identifying characteristic of this activity, T'an called *t'ung*.

'Pervasiveness', 'communication', 'permeability', 'circulation': *t'ung* eludes translation least when juxtaposed with its opposite, *sai* or 'obstruc-tion', 'stoppage'. By means of this key concept T'an achieved a comple-mentarity K'ang had missed between the structure of his cosmology and the structure of his ideal social relations. The moral functioning of ether is most apparent when the boundaries of things are permeable. In the realm of society they may be boundaries of culture, nationality, custom; or the economic boundaries which inhibit trade and communication among peoples. In the realm of interpersonal relations they are the bar-riers of selfishness which prevent moral community. On the natural level they are boundaries which organize the psycho-physical continuum into discrete phenomena bounded by time and space, distinguished relationally in terms of their opposites, defined imperfectly as 'objects' by individuated human egos. In its most truly perfected form, then, the moral activity of ether in its unimpeded flow would reveal the interconnected unity of everything: the truth of the Confucian metaphysical axiom, 'the great man regards Heaven, Earth, and the myriad things as one body.'

In this way, T'an derived the socially revolutionary prescription to 'break through the nets' of the existing Confucian order. T'an saw tradi-tional Chinese as enslaved to the 'doctrine of names' (*ming-chiao*). Lin-guistic 'naming' – a primary human tool used to identify phenomena of experience according to their discrete characteristics – historically had been understood in China as Confucius' method of rendering moral judgments and so defining moral norms. Therefore, for T'an, it became the symbol for the formal hierarchical norms of personal and political conduct prescribed as the *li* or 'five relationships'. T'an's theory of pro-gress envisaged the overthrow of the current social system based upon *li*

under the influence of the quickening activity of *jen*. This can be interpreted as the inner message of the book's title: as the human 'learning of
love' is perfected, human beings will come to enjoy a more lively and
abundant material life, quicker, more natural and spontaneous emotional
experience, more egalitarian political and personal relationships, and
an ever broadening spiritual consciousness.

T'an's projection of evolution extended from the original generation
of the cosmos to a final age of 'Great Peace'. He combined the New Text
schema of the 'three ages', the facts of geological and biological evolution
as he understood them, and aspects of traditional Taoist cosmology. Thus
he proceeded from the primary differentiation of existence from non-
existence, through the formation of the solar system and the presumed
march of the Darwinian evolutionary process towards higher and higher
forms of organic life. For the future he predicted the eventual uniform
distribution over the globe of a human population hundreds of times its
present size, yet protected from threats to health and sustenance by the
achievements of science and medicine. The advance of science would
be aided by an innate evolutionary tendency of successive generations of
living beings to assume ever more refined and spiritual forms, leading
eventually to a race of 'pure intelligences', able to live on air and water,
and to escape the confines of the earth itself.

However, at the most general level, T'an believed that the pattern of
all these changes was to be discerned, fittingly, in the *I ching* or *Book of
changes* itself. T'an's final cosmic myth of evolution depended for its logic
on the numerological symbolism of the primary *I ching* hexagram, *ch'ien*,
and on a biological metaphor of stages of the life-cycle as traditionally
associated with the spiritual development of Confucius. He envisaged six
stages, the first three a devolution from the primitive 'great peace' of
archaic tribal society to Confucius' own 'world of disorder'; the second
three an ascension through the disorder of the later empire to the 'ascend-
ing peace' of the near future, culminating in the final 'great peace' where,
like Confucius in his old age, people would 'follow [their] heart's desire
without transgressing what is right'. For T'an the structure of each age
was determined by the role of political rulers and religious teachers in
society – proceeding from the gradual emergence of these forms of leadership to their unification on a global scale, which in turn would prepare
the way for a world in which 'everyone possesses the virtue of a religious
teacher and so the religious teacher is eliminated; everyone possesses the
power of a ruler and so the ruler is eliminated'.[11]

---

11 T'an Ssu-t'ung, *Jen hsueh*, reprinted in *T'an Ssu-t'ung ch'üan chi* (The complete works of
   T'an Ssu-t'ung, 1966), 88.

Unlike K'ang Yu-wei, T'an Ssu-t'ung was not content with a teleology devoid of any central human mechanism, and his theory included a model of the role of moral action in the cosmic process. This model formed a bridge between conventional Neo-Confucian models of self-cultivation and an ethic which defined the good both instrumentally in terms of future goals, and subjectively by the psyche's experience of internal struggle to attain them. At the beginning of the reform movement T'an had spoken of the commitment to change as requiring 'daily renewal'. However, in the *Jen hsueh* he introduced another, more original concept, 'psychic energy' (*hsin-li*) with the message that the psyche capable of working in tandem with the energies of the cosmos moves in an open-ended, developmental direction, and finds its expression in active struggle to change the world. Fully developed, 'psychic energy' would be expressed in actions combining the spontaneous empathy of Mencian mind (*hsin*) with the salvationist compassion of the Bodhisattva. Here of course T'an was constructing a theory of the self which could correspond to his cosmology of circulating ether. However, it was critical to his conception that psychic energy, as a form of ether in motion, was seen as stimulated to its characteristic activity in proportion as it met forces of resistance. For its own self-perfection, sincere mind required obstacles to overcome. 'The more we progress, the greater the obstacles, and this continues ceaselessly without rest'.[12] Further, psychic energy is 'what people rely upon to perform tasks',[13] that is, an instrument used to attain goals analytically separable from its own activity, and so containing a morally ambiguous potential. In the final pages of the *Jen hsueh*, T'an chose to return to the religious saviour as his preferred human agent of evolutionary change. But his sensitivity to the Faustian ideal of human action in a progress-oriented cosmos linked his own philosophy and that of the Social Darwinian, Yen Fu.

Yen Fu advocated the infusion of Anglo-Saxon liberalism into Chinese politics, because he saw its characteristic 'individualism' as the 'psychic energy' driving the movements of advanced scientific and industrial civilization. Since that civilization took its shape from these Faustian energies of striving individuals acting in and upon the world, the key to his underlying cosmology lay in the theories of Herbert Spencer. 'He has explained all transformations in terms of evolution. He has written books and composed treatises which embrace Heaven, earth and humanity under one principle'.[14]

12 *Ibid.* 74.
13 *Ibid.* 80.
14 The basic study of Yen Fu in English is Benjamin Schwartz, *In search of wealth and power: Yen Fu and the West.* The excerpted quotation is on p. 111.

Most deeply satisfying in Spencer's philosophy was its underlying monistic view of natural and social evolution as a unilinear progression from the simple and homogeneous ,to the heterogeneous and complex. The agent of evolution was the Darwinian mechanism of struggle for survival among species and the elimination of the weak by the strong. In Yen Fu's view this process was benign both because it served the ends of civilization, and because the 'strength, intelligence and morality'[15] of successful competitors in the social evolutionary process was itself in his eyes an admirable thing. Successful human groups 'begin in mutual antagonism; they end by completing one another.'[16] His major book on Darwinism, the translation of Huxley's *Evolution and ethics* (published in Chinese as *T'ien-yen lun*), argues in favour of Spencer as opposed to Huxley in that human ethics and the natural forces of evolutionary selection are seen as complementary parts of an overall cosmic process. *Ch'ün hsueh*, Yen Fu's term for Spencer's sociology, is an allusion to the idea of 'groups' in the naturalistic philosophy of Hsun-tzu, in which it is claimed that human beings owe their position at the top of the hierarchy of living things to their social 'grouping' instinct. Yen Fu believed that human groups which excel in ever more complex forms of social organization would create the culture that eventually inherits the earth.

In his selection of European classics which would acquaint his compatriots with nineteenth-century liberalism – in his view the Western value system *par excellence* – Yen Fu proved most sensitive to the historicist and sociological themes of his originals. Looking at Adam Smith, he stressed the utilitarian 'invisible hand' by which the action of individual enlightened self-interest worked to serve the long-term economic needs of society. In Mill's *On Liberty* he was impressed with the role of freedom in providing an arena for impartial truth-seeking, so that in the long run society might be united on the basis of correct commonly-held principles. To explain the importance of law in European politics, Yen Fu turned to Montesquieu, yet even here his affinity lay with Montesquieu's doubts about legislated 'natural rights', and with his contrasting sense that strong social determinants shape political institutions. Throughout, Yen Fu interpreted the European liberal tradition in ways which pointed to a natural complementarity between self-assertive individual action and the needs of the social organism.

Like the evolutionary theorists of the New Text School, Yen Fu had an overview of human history, which envisaged a unilinear march of progress to a future democratic and industrial world marked by abundance

15 Yen Fu, 'Yuan ch'iang' (On strength). For reprint see *Yen Chi-t'ao hsien-sheng i-chu* (Posthumous works of Yen Fu), 101.
16 *Ibid.* 107.

and enlightenment. However, in analysing its stages, he focused less on the utopian distance and more on the present national task of transition to a level of parity with the West in 'wealth and power'. Spencer had laid down the path of progress as moving from tribal and patriarchal forms of society to the 'military state' of early modern nationhood, and beyond. Yen Fu believed the Chinese present represented an uneasy turning-point between these first two. As the pioneer modern theorist of Chinese backwardness, he argued China had enjoyed the political form of the military state since Ch'in, but that its natural development had been stunted by the continuing influence of 'patriarchal' Confucian cultural norms, absolutized as a code of ritual morality (*li*). Progress would come through the psychological transformation of great numbers of individual Chinese who were to cultivate in themselves the 'strength, intelligence and morality' the nation needed to build a powerful enlightened modern culture. Here Yen Fu's belief in the determining power of culture, which is of human making, counterbalanced much of his pessimism concerning China's backwardness. Dependent upon an effort of national spirit rather than upon material constraints, China's prospects were directly correlated with the people's capacity for self-transformation.

If to be a Confucianist one must embrace its humanistic metaphysics, Yen Fu would scarcely qualify, even in the unconventional manner in which K'ang Yu-wei and T'an Ssu-t'ung did. His method of moralizing the cosmos was otherwise: it was not some inner altruistic core of sincere mind which defined those human actions which truly led to progress, but rather the capacity of such action impersonally to serve the times itself. In this way Yen Fu shifted the balance even further from the transforming power of virtue as an internal quality of the sage personality and towards the adaptive power of the insightful intelligence as a response to socio-historical forces. Yet even this seemingly more deterministic ideal of human action in an evolutionary cosmos was substantially counterbalanced by another consequence of Yen Fu's detachment from the Confucian sage personality ideal in ethics. His emphasis upon individualism was inextricably linked with a belief that 'the people are true lords of the world'. His conception of nationalism was built upon this conviction that the collective energy of a whole people constitutes the critical mass which makes cultural development possible. When K'ang and T'an spoke of universal moral ends for which the nation state could only be a transient vehicle, they pointed inwards to personal salvation as the means embracing the paradox – in T'an's words – that 'in saving the world one may fail to save oneself; in saving only oneself one may yet save the world'.[17]

17 *T'an Ssu-t'ung ch'üan chi*, 89.

In solidly resting his hopes on a progressive enlightened people, Yen Fu was a pioneer of the populist interpretation of Chinese nationalism.

However, in spite of these differences all three saw evolution organically as a total process linking natural, social and spiritual forces in an interdependent whole. All believed that this interdependence extended over time as well, enabling the mind of the philosopher to encompass the whole from the experience of any one of its stages. Most important, all were equally convinced that an ineffable metaphysical 'unknowable', itself lying outside the process, still constituted the ground against which it developed. Where the first two grounded their theories in the Confucian humanist's faith in *jen* as a cosmic force, Yen Fu's metaphysics was more Taoist. He identified Spencer's 'unimaginable' with the mystical scepticism of Lao-tzu, and his acceptance of evolutionary necessity was deeply informed by that sage's anti-anthropomorphic mystical naturalism. Above all, the cosmos envisaged by all these reformers possessed an open-ended dynamism which implied fundamental social change, and which in the case of T'an and Yen, incorporated the idea of struggle in and of itself as the characteristic function of virtuous 'mind'. This introduced into Chinese cosmological thought a sense that the expanding universe of scientific law was matched in the Faustian energies of human actions. Such in sum were the evolutionary laws constantly referred to in reform literature as '*kung-li*' – the 'universal principles of nature and society'.

Of the four great reform leaders, Liang Ch'i-ch'ao strayed least from the political issues of the immediate present, and the imperatives for action these created. His journalistic immediacy was an important source of his enormous popularity and influence, even as the variability of mood and opinion it entailed aroused criticism as well. But it was his historical perspective, in fact, which made him look for the key to broad patterns of evolutionary change in contemporary events. Yen Fu and the Japanese thinker Katō Hiroyuki were the sources of Liang's knowledge of Social Darwinism, in the latter's hands given a heightened nationalist and racialist interpretation. However, even as he analysed the modern era of imperialism in which Asians and Westerners were locked in struggle for hegemony, he was sketching out a philosophy of history and a theory of human action whose cosmological underpinnings recall T'an Ssu-t'ung, and which developed the Faustian implications of Yen Fu's interpretation of Western individualism.

Cosmologically, Liang's structures were comparatively simple. He coalesced T'an's 'ether' and 'psychic energy' into a single concept: 'dynamism' (*tung-li*), or the kinetic energy in material and spiritual phenomena. 'Where there is dynamism [*tung*] there is interpenetration [*t'ung*];

where there is interpenetration there is *jen*, so all mutually sympathetic things cannot remain apart like Ch'in and Yueh, but must be activated by consciousness and create the new without end.'[18] However, by introducing a 'dialectic' element into this framework Liang suggested that the socio-historical pattern of change is based on the alternation of cosmic 'motive forces' of action and resistance In concrete terms, the recent past in Europe and China was one in which repressive forces of autocracy had given rise to an inevitable counter-movement of resistance in the form of a rising social demand for people's rights.

By linking historical movements with an account of the metahistorical forces presumed to be responsible for them, Liang presented both a moralized version of Darwinian evolution, and a conception of liberty as the attribute of those found 'fit' in the Darwinian struggle. By people's rights (*min-ch'üan*), Liang was explicit that he did not mean the 'natural rights' of Western Enlightenment political theory, but rather something closer to effective capabilities, won by striving individuals through the successful exertion of their energies. 'Rights' are really a kind of 'power' (*ch'üan-li*), Liang declared, though insisting that this did not invalidate the moral basis of the political ideal. 'This doctrine [of *ch'üan-li*] seems the negation [of people's rights] but actually is the perfection of it'.[19] Implicitly then, 'rights' are a manifestation of the psychic energies of the self maximally extended beyond the mind to the outside world. Histori-cally, Europe's ancient liberties had been aristocratic privileges forcibly preserved, while modern democratic liberties had been won through popular struggle and revolution. Further, since the psychic energies of individuals are characterized by inherent powers of mutual attraction, an ever broader consolidation of 'groups' would appear the natural result of evolutionary struggle. Liang's famous call for the emergence of a 'new people' (*hsin min*) in China pointed the liberated individual in this same collectivist direction. Thus, the progress of human liberty was described as the spread of the collective human power of dynamism to wider and wider groups of humanity – a process exhibited in primitive times through the struggle between tribes, and expected to culminate in the distant future as a result of the successful assertion of 'rights' by the weakest members of the human race – the common people (*p'ing-min*) and women.

As in T'an Ssu-t'ung, Liang's theory of human action in the historical

---

18 Liang Ch'i-ch'ao, 'Shuo tung' (On dynamism), first published 1898, reprinted in *Yin-ping-shih wen-chi* (Collection from the ice drinker's studio; hereafter *YPSWC*), *ts'e* 2. 37–40. See also Chang Hao, *Liang Ch'i-ch'ao and intellectual transition in China, 1890–1907*.

19 Jen-kung [Liang Ch'i-ch'ao], 'Lun ch'iang ch'üan' (On power), *Ch'ing-i pao*, no. 31 (1899).

process assigned a positive value to reactionary forces (such as autocracy and imperialism) – as necessary to motivate the reactive dynamism of the generators of progress. He also asserted that the psyche's inborn power of movement in struggle itself led to more human self-actualization through the creation of higher forms of social 'grouping'. From the cosmic perspective the dynamism which generated historical change exhibited something like a principle of entropy. Liang believed that human equality would finally be achieved when the energies of domination and those of resistance were evenly balanced throughout the world. The utopian great community (*ta-t'ung*) would be undifferentiated – its social manifestation would be equally shared power; its historical manifestation, stasis or the end of history.[20]

Unlike T'an Ssu-t'ung, Liang Ch'i-ch'ao in 1902 specifically denied that his philosophy of historical evolution had a Confucian core. *Jen*, he said, was too 'yielding' a virtue to be the motive force of the self-development of a modern nation. Nonetheless the definitive statement of his philosophy of history written the same year remained rooted in assumptions about the evolutionary process itself which substantially overlapped those of the others. He asserted that 'humanity is the pivot [*chi-tse*] of evolution, the inexhaustible source of its transformations.' When he asked that his 'new history' be based upon study of the evolution of social 'groups' (*ch'ün*), he acknowledged their common organicism. He saw race as a key source of group cohesion and therefore a basis for competition between contemporary 'groups' or nations. But nonetheless Liang believed that the psychic energies expressed through the total manifestations of a culture were the dominant agents of change in individual social systems. In claiming that history would serve the nation by disclosing the directions of social change, he was making a common claim for the existence of a historical teleology known to scholars through their intuition of the metahistorical 'spirit' (*ching-shen*) presumed to inform and guide it. In claiming a legitimate place for the 'subjective' in historical writing, he was not simply giving licence to interpretive opinion, but pointing to the creative contribution of those with foresight whose subjective mind is capable of grasping the total historical continuum in a synthesis.[21]

All in all, the evolutionary cosmologies of the major reform thinkers form a spectrum: from a more cosmic to a more human-centred concept of the forces underlying world change, from comparatively static to more

20 Liang Ch'i-ch'ao, 'Shuo ch'ün hsu' (Preface to 'groups'), *YPSWC*, *ts'e* 2. 3–4.
21 See the following essays by Liang Ch'i-ch'ao: 'Chung-kuo shih hsu-lun' (Sketch of Chinese history), *YPSWC*, *ts'e* 3. 1–12; 'Kuo-chia ssu-hsiang pien-ch'ien i-t'ung lun' (On similarity and difference in alterations in national thought), *ibid. ts'e* 3. 12–22; 'Kuo-tu shih-tai' (A transitional age), *ibid. ts'e* 3. 27–32.

dialectical models of them, and from less to more emphasis upon the modern nation as a positive factor in the evolutionary process. All of these marked a shift away from Confucian-Taoist metaphysics towards a more naturalistic, historicized and secular model of the evolutionary process. Liang Ch'i-ch'ao demonstrated both his understanding of this spectrum and the limits he set on it when he offered his view of the function of the philosophy of history in the modern world. It should, he said, provide a substitute for religious dogma: by which he meant a complete explanatory system concerning human society, the causal patterns underlying events, and the moral purposes implicit in them. For Liang, as for the other reformers, evolutionism provided for a new ethic of personal striving in association with a philosophy of modernization. At the same time, evolutionism endowed the future with cosmically grounded moral purposes, allowing him like the other reformers to hope their innovations would serve to perfect a traditionally recognized kingdom of ends.

Ta-t'ung and Western models for institutional change

Evolutionary cosmology supplied the framework for the Chinese reformers' interpretation of the strengths of Western civilization, powerfully influencing the way European and American nations were taken as models of progress. Western accounts too often assume that Asian reformers' admiration of the West was simply a belated appreciation of the West's true achievements. This neglects both the limits and biases in reformers' sources of information, and the implications given to that information at Chinese disposal by the overarching value system within which it was assimilated. Both the Protestant missionaries and the anglicized Chinese of the treaty ports, who were the early tutors of the reform leadership, certainly spoke as apostles and apologists for Victorian civilization. In Meiji Japan, Chinese reformers had an alternate model for successful Westernization already filtered through East Asian cultural adaptations. However, in responding to the optimistic picture of Western economic and political institutions these accounts suggested, Chinese were combining a genuine sense of discovery with their own utopian projections. The 'West' in this sense served not only as a 'real' model of civilized alternatives, but also as a repository for ideal images projected out of the historical imagination of the Chinese themselves. Filtered through the interpretive matrix of reform cosmology, science and democracy appeared to be the material and social manifestations of a total cosmic order linked to the ultimate ends of ta-t'ung. Science and technology offered a vision of a materialist universe whose secrets would yield wealth and power such as had eluded generations of imperial rulers. Democracy suggested institutions by which Chinese might revitalize their political community, bringing it closer to the perennial ideal of 'public-mindedness'.

The first major contribution of Western science to Chinese reform thought was as the theoretical underpinning of evolutionary cosmology itself. In using concepts of physics as building blocks for their philosophy, both K'ang Yu-wei and T'an Ssu-t'ung communicated a new kind of certainty that truths of nature were reliably known. They thought that science demonstrated the relativity of all phenomena, an ideal more revolutionary to them in its cultural and social application than in its theoretical essentials. Confucian philosophy did not make humanistic values dependent upon a cosmological divide between spirit and matter. Nor had these values historically been associated with the notion of a spatially fixed, anthropocentric world, or a taxonomically fixed human species marked off from nature by a unique capacity for transcendence.

Because of this – and all the more because nineteenth-century missionaries themselves typically taught science as a kind of natural theology, proof of Heavenly Design – the reformers found in science a confirmation of Buddhist-Taoist phenomenology untainted by the corrosion of scepticism. For K'ang the instruments of scientific measurement showed the relativity of our ordinary perceptions: we 'see' the light of a dead star but do not see the swirling molecules which make up a drop of water. For T'an scientific theories of the underlying construction of matter 'come close to destroying relativity' as a final – as opposed to an initial – truth of experience. Both drew the analogy with Buddhist cosmology, and exuberantly gave way to a Mahayana sense of possible worlds – of 'world seas' beyond the galaxies, and 'lotus seas' beyond the 'world seas'; of 'unimaginable realms' where the 'divine sages play'. Thus science reinforced their belief in an external, determinative cosmos which was in and of itself a source of God-like power relatively independent of human will.

Obviously neither K'ang nor T'an understood how definitions of scientific truth must be controlled by experimental verification. They felt free to incorporate into their cosmologies as science the traditional constructs of speculative reason. Nonetheless, they believed in scientific truth the more because empirical observation on the one hand, and mathematics on the other appeared to support it. K'ang was a keen astronomical observer, and T'an experimented with classical mechanics; both were fascinated by mathematics as a kind of deductive reasoning capable of expressing the truths of nature they thought they discerned. For T'an algebra supplied an abstract method of stating the universal cosmological relationships of relatives and the constant. K'ang, an ethical relativist in the sense that he saw social morality as historically conditioned, tried to prove that final moral truths are best expressed in the axioms of Euclidian geometry.

By contrast Yen Fu's appreciation of science rested more on a belief in a methodology of verification. This led him to translate first J. S. Mill's *Logic*, and then Stanley Jevons, in an effort to introduce to China principles of induction as the foundation of all solid truth-seeking. Even so, in spite of this pioneering role in introducing positivistic philosophy of science, as a 'social scientist' Yen Fu was like the others in his belief that the facts of science – here in particular Darwinian biology – confirmed the authority of his entire evolutionary cosmology.

A keen practical appreciation of Western technology had been commonplace in statecraft circles since the early days of the 'self-strengthening' movement in the 1860s; however, the reformers' new faith in science as a kind of true cosmology made it easier for them to welcome the coming of technological civilization. The 1898 reform leaders took the basic step of accepting the socially transformative potential of industrialization. Almost equally important, they came to see that technological change is open-ended, both necessitating a continued flow of invention, and holding open the possibility that problems of human health and welfare deemed intractable today might be solved by methods to be developed in the future. The view that economic development and scientific progress were valuable as a means to the nationalist ends of independence and state power was a staple of reform propaganda, but the leaders went significantly beyond this to present the fruits of development as human goods in their own right.

They not only submitted plans for developing strategic industries like railways and mines; they also offered classic meliorative arguments for the mechanization of production: it would create jobs and increase leisure too; scientific agriculture would augment the food supply; modern communications would facilitate the world-wide spread of enlightenment. If these views suggest a Chinese version of a classic nineteenth-century faith in industrial progress, equally typical of such a faith was the Chinese reformers' conviction that they did not face any insurmountable material obstacles to success. To Western scepticism about China's ability to modernize, Liang Ch'i-ch'ao replied by echoing the Europeans' own confidence in the resources of science and invention to overcome problems of population and food supply. He and others imitated Europe's own confidence in the inexhaustible resources of nature by assuming that a nation of China's size and diversity must enjoy a full measure of these waiting

to be exploited. Consciousness of backwardness was there, but counterbalanced by a 'great leap' mentality which showed up most strikingly
in the summer of 1898. All reformers, even the sober Yen Fu, spoke of
overtaking Europe in decades at the most, observing that Europe's own
economic pre-eminence was recent, and that latecomers to development
have the advantage of being able to learn from their precursors' mistakes.

The social costs of industrialism, so visible in Europe itself, were
little discussed in the early years of reform. When K'ang Yu-wei or
Liang Ch'i-ch'ao noted in passing that the growth of industrial capitalism
in Europe so far had not eliminated, and might even have widened, the
gap between the rich and the poor, they saw this as Europe's moral failure,
but neither an inevitable nor a permanent feature of the development
process. T'an Ssu-t'ung offered an arresting ethical defence of capitalist
behaviour by comparing the liberality of extravagance with the stinginess
of thrift. His conclusion was that by contrast with traditional agrarian
habits of frugality – hoarding and saving – the capitalist modes of spending
and investing expressed the spirit of 'permeability' (*t'ung*) in the economic
sphere. This does not mean that he or the other reformers understood
consumer capitalism as the end of development. T'an rather believed that
the attainment of material abundance would liberate people from enslave-
ment to their desires for things; while K'ang prophesied that in the
world of the 'great community' wealth would be shared publicly by all.
Capitalist development represented the inevitable, indeed the only model
at hand, but in light of the altruistic moral ideal of *ta-t'ung* it was perceived as only a stage. From the other end, Liang Ch'i-ch'ao, on being
exposed to the ideal of socialism in 1902, heartily approved of it, seeing
it as the natural direction for advanced economic systems to take towards
a pre-established goal.

While Western science and technology promised to transform society
materially, democracy aroused hopes for political renewal. Here the
reformers had both an immediate target of criticism in the imperial
autocracy, and a long-term ideal of 'public' government which had eluded
centuries of bureaucratic practice.

Historically, Chinese practitioners of statecraft had seen the goal of
'public' government as a moral spirit of politics. In organizing public
administration and recruiting leaders they had posed two broad alternatives, each with unacceptable costs. One was a 'feudal' model of hereditary
local self-government, which was believed to foster a commonality
(*kung*) of ties between the ruling group and the people at the grass-roots
level, but at the cost of privatizing rulership in local hereditary families.
The other was a 'bureaucratic' model of an impersonal centralized civil

service, which was more effective in enforcing a commonality (*kung*) of impartial regulation, but at the cost of estranging the governing elite from the people. Exposure to Anglo-Saxon politics and the 'spirit of public morality' widely believed to prevail among the citizens of parliamentary democracies gave reformers hope for a resolution of this ancient dilemma. 'Public assemblies' (*i-yuan*) seemed capable of resolving the tension between the values of community and those of impartiality, and so realizing the Confucian-Legalist synthesis in the political ideal of 'public mindedness'.

Since reformers contrasted the 'public' rule of constitutional assemblies with the 'private' rule of imperial autocrats, people looked to parliamentary politics as a corrective to typically bureaucratic evils, tipping their interpretation of the ideal in the 'feudal' communitarian direction. Some in the K'ang-Liang group felt that public assemblies would rectify just about every widely recognized defect of the imperial administrative system, from its over-centralization to its stress on seniority or duplication of office. As an alternative to bureaucracy, rather than, as in the West, to hereditary class rule, parliaments were imagined to provide a finely articulated system of *communication* among all levels of participation in the political process. Confucianism assumed that correct political action must be based upon commonly recognized principles, and so assemblies were valued not for mediating among a plurality of interests, but rather as educative and expressive instruments for achieving a common consensus. Thus they were conceived as a corrective to the moral evils of officialism: estrangement papered over by commandism on high; submission accompanied by covert criticism from below. The goal was less to create a formal equality of status between rulers and ruled than to create a community of understanding and purpose among them.

Thus idealized, the Chinese reformers viewed constitutional systems as the political form naturally appropriate to highly evolved social groups. T'an Ssu-t'ung stated the organic collectivist interpretation of such democratic political forms in a particularly forceful way. Instead of having purely political assemblies, he proposed that the problems of the reform agenda be attacked by a network of voluntary 'study societies' (*hsueh-hui*), representing functional groupings in society: farmers, artisans, merchants, students, officials, and so forth. These would provide a forum for the common pursuit of enlightenment among persons with a natural unity of purpose in a context linking learning with action. 'In this way,' he dreamed, 'people who are distant will be brought close, what is bogged down will move forward; the stopped-up will flow, the separate will unite, the obscure become clear, and the weak strong; moreover, broad publicity will lead people to speak, allowing no concealment'.[22]

Viewed in this harmonious light, democracy suggested to the reformers analogies with utopian models of politics drawn from antiquity. K'ang and T'an believed that Confucius was a reformer not only because he understood the principle of adaptation to change, but also because he upheld a 'democratic' ideal of rule by the virtuous, exemplified in the ancient sage kings Yao, Shun and the Duke of Chou. Liang Ch'i-ch'ao made still more forceful claims for a 'democratic spirit' in Mencius' view that the mandate of Heaven finally lay with the people; while some others even conjectured that public assemblies had actually existed in the Chou dynasty. For Yen Fu, Lao-tzu was the antique source of a democratic spirit of personal independence and social 'yielding'.

Western scholars have commonly viewed such analogies as inspired by cultural nationalism: the desire to find native Chinese 'equivalents' for admired aspects of Western culture. Among conservative Chinese at the time they were denounced as efforts to gain respectability for new ideas by cloaking them in native dress, while later Chinese radicals dismissed them as disguised traditionalism. However, within the K'ang-Liang group itself there was recognition of evolution even as reformers found these classical analogies compelling. What they admired in antiquity, they said, was the latent essence in incipient form of an essential moral ideal that history would realize and complete. Yen Fu and Liang Ch'i-ch'ao combined explicit recognition that Mencius' populism, for example, was more paternalistic than participatory with the conviction that whatever the 'germs' of 'ancient democracy' may have been in China or in Greece, they were organically linked by the logic of historical evolution with the full-blown democratic political systems only just presently coming into being in the modern world.

The original Chinese discovery of the West had led to the emergence of evolutionism as a reform philosophy in China. Evolutionism itself, by identifying the West with the future and the teleology of moral ends that symbolized, encouraged utopian thinking about Western institutions. Science and democracy remained the most admired aspects of Western civilization for most Chinese down through the May Fourth movement of 1919. At the same time the goals of development continued to be associated with the native utopian ideal of *ta-t'ung*: as entailing not only the creation but also the common sharing of wealth; as bringing the

22 T'an Ssu-t'ung, 'Chih shih p'ien' (Essay on public affairs), reprinted in Yang Chia-lo, ed. 3. 83–92. See p. 86.

elimination of status hierarchies, if not literally, then through the formation of new psychological bonds of community; as making possible the moral self-actualization of the individual.

It was a paradox that the 'West' as a total civilization was the object of this admiration during a period of its unprecedented imperialist encroachments on China. The same reform journals which sketched out the new cosmopolitan world-view also analysed the dangerous shifts in the Far Eastern power balance since 1895. Here the 'West' stood for the expansionist 'scramble for concessions' – in anything but a friendly light – and the K'ang-Liang group was deeply involved in the politics of national resistance.

Nonetheless reformers' accounts of imperialism were more self-critical than anti-Western. Domestically, the reformers wished to discredit the militant 'expel the barbarian' policies of the conservative '*ch'ing-i*' faction at court, which were held responsible for the recent military defeats. Even beyond this, however, there was no way to avoid the logical connection between pro-Westernism in culture and appeasement in foreign affairs, holding Chinese rather than foreigners as basically responsible for the crisis. Reform nationalist propaganda hammered away at the object lessons to be drawn from the history of fallen empires like Persia or Turkey, and of 'lost' peoples like the Poles, the Irish or the American Indians – all social organisms seen as having failed in the evolutionary struggle. The underlying message was that China's problems lay within.

In 1895 Yen Fu said simply that Westerners had not originally come to China with an intent to do harm. T'an Ssu-t'ung offered a subtle contamination theory of imperialism, pointing out that the 'strong and righteous' nations of the West, in their impatience to cure an ailing China, were resorting to methods of fraud and coercion which risked becoming their habitual mode of conduct, first abroad, but then also at home. Yet even this penetrating account of the dynamics of power's corruption was offered along with criticism of the weak, who, as targets of opportunity, had to acknowledge their own complicity in the occasion of crime. If the union of 'strength, morality and intelligence' which Yen Fu saw as the mark of powerful peoples was recognized as a synthesis subject to internal fluctuation, still to most reformers the interdependence of all parts was axiomatic. Confucianism taught that virtue and power come from a single source. Western strength was linked to the level of culture presumably attained by Western peoples. Blaming themselves for their powerlessness, Chinese reformers sought the remedy in the inherent momentum of evolution on the one hand, and on the other in their own efforts of psychological self-renewal.

Furthermore, after the 1898 'scramble for concessions' and the 1900 Boxer catastrophe had passed, the empress dowager finally committed the court to reform in 1901, making the prospects for internal development appear hopeful at long last. In spite of continued dangers from the Western powers, the nation appeared embarked upon the serious pursuit of its own modernization along lines pioneered in Meiji Japan. While the reading public was always more or less impatient with the pace of change as directed by the Manchu court, it exhibited through the new popular press growing enthusiasm for modern 'enlightenment' (wen-ming). A widely read serialized novel of 1903 affirmed the spirit of 'modern times':

Just look at what has happened over the past few years . . . people's minds have been stimulated and all levels of society have been roused to action. Are these not indications, like the sea and the wind, that the sun is about to rise and the rain to fall? Whether these people have succeeded or failed, flourished or declined, been public-minded or selfish, genuine or false, they eventually will be recognized as men of merit in a civilized world. . . . 'The vile and the beautiful are mutually transformed by change'. With these words I felicitate the future.[23]

And so the continued political disgrace and exile of Liang Ch'i-ch'ao, K'ang Yu-wei and many of their followers did not prevent the ideas they had pioneered from acquiring an influential constituency. By 1903 or 1904 evolutionism as a 'bland religion of modernization' was rapidly passing into the mainstream of elite culture.

The erosion of reformist evolutionary optimism

However, even as the reform consensus hardened, it began to be exposed to a new kind of attack. After 1905 reform gradualism was attacked by the revolutionary T'ung-meng hui. Reformers' appeasement of the West and of the court was now challenged by a new anti-imperialist and anti-Manchu militancy. Reform pro-Westernism in culture had to face a nativist backlash, the 'national essence' movement visible from about 1904. Finally, reform utopianism was vulnerable to the inevitable fear of failure – as evidence mounted suggesting Chinese backwardness was a more intractable burden than originally hoped.

The attitudes of Liang Ch'i-ch'ao, who abandoned 'revolution' for 'reform' between 1903 and 1911, display an underlying consistency when

23 Li Po-yuan, Wen-ming hsiao-shih (A little history of modern times), translated by Douglas Lancashire, Renditions: a Chinese-English translation magazine, 2 (Spring 1974) 128.

seen in this context.[24] Like Yen Fu, Liang had always tied the progressive evolution of Chinese politics to the spread of modern cultural enlightenment among the people. For this reason his populist ideal of 'the new citizen' was less organically holistic than it seemed. It incorporated a social distinction quite traditional in China between the civilized and the barbarian, the educated and the ignorant, and made confidence in progress depend upon the triumph of the former over the latter. Again like Yen Fu, Liang was from his first exposure to the Enlightenment concept of 'natural rights' generally sceptical of it. That the people might be sovereign through some form of abstractly legislated *a priori* rights was an idea incompatible with his own belief that political utopia would be arrived at through a historical process of human self-actualization.

With these assumptions, Liang's faith in the populist politics of the 'new citizen' was steadily undermined by what he took as evidence of continued moral backwardness in Chinese society. In practice these evils were identified more with the activities of the emerging revolutionary left after 1903 than with the traditional masses, as the new spirit of politics seemed to be leading to the 'backward' phenomenon of an anarchic breakdown of order.

In accommodating his belief system to the new requirements of gradualism, Liang simply adjusted evolutionary cosmology to a distopian interpretation. Instead of rapid advance, such an interpretation stressed cosmic reversals. Instead of emphasizing voluntarism – that success in the evolutionary struggle is the direct consequence of the exercise of human psychic powers – it stressed all of the historical determinants inhibiting people from changing themselves or society. Instead of holding out hope of moral success, it was haunted by the spectre of moral failure. This distopian version of evolutionary cosmology did not require a basic shift in assumptions, only a more pessimistic appraisal of the 'times' themselves, since evolutionism made events themselves the only source of interpretation.

Ironically, though evolutionary cosmology had explained the Chinese historical situation during a great political reform movement, it eventually came to suggest a sharply diminished role for 'politics' as an autonomous source of change. In the culminating event of the generation – the Revolution of 1911 – Chinese intellectuals had a powerful lesson in the impotence of groups of conscious political actors to accomplish their desired goals, a lesson which helped distopian evolutionism achieve wide currency. As the respected Shanghai organ of the constitutionalist movement, *Tung-fang tsa-chih* (Eastern miscellany), noted in 1914, a prin-

24 For Liang's political career see Philip Huang, *Liang Ch'i-ch'ao and modern Chinese liberalism.*

ciple of Spencerian sociology is that 'living organisms and social systems gradually change in order to maintain forms in harmony with their environment and circumstances'.[25] Their conclusion was that the Chinese national psychology must be recognized as ill-adapted to modern political forms. To Yen Fu the lesson of the new democracy was that 'the level of civilization of our masses cannot be forced'.[26] Liang Ch'i-ch'ao acknowledged that the revolution as an event was irreversible, but drew the lessons of a conservative historicism: 'the [imperial] political authority, once trampled, cannot recover its mystery'.[27]

If after 1911 a deterministic emphasis upon China's historical situation meant resignation to backwardness, stress on the human factor spelled acceptance of moral responsibility for failure. Evolutionary cosmology had balanced the determinism of cosmic forces with a complementary emphasis upon the Faustian human spirit as contributing to the process of change. Consequently the failure of the republic implied not merely fate but also moral blame. In the mood of disillusionment that swept the country, intellectuals freely castigated new republican office-holders, but their overall focus was not just on corruption of leadership, but on the cultural backwardness of the race which they thought it illustrated. Even as indignation poured forth, with it seeped the poison of self-accusation. Critical evaluations of the Chinese 'national character', and of 'national psychology' became stock essay themes after 1912. Inasmuch as these assumed that the people as a whole are the activating agents in the social organism, they carried on the voluntaristic tradition of reform thought, but in a context which inescapably compromised the reformers themselves.

Liang Ch'i-ch'ao's historiographical principles did not change, but the lessons he drew from history did. When in 1916 he looked back over the first five years of the republic, he still saw his own generation as a 'transitional age' whose 'motive force' had been the external stimulus of the West, causing the old doctrines to lose their credibility. The problem was, he thought, that China's 'reactive force' had dissipated itself in a single violent spasm of revolution and restorationist backlash. He still believed that human psychic energies move history in a long-term arc of progress, but for the present time in China he saw these as depleted by habituation to novelty, and feared that in the immediate future 'there will be no more thunder and lightning available for use'. Such exhaustion of

25 Ch'ien Chih-hsiu, 'Shuo t'i-ho' (On adaptation), Tung-fang tsa-chih, 10. 10 (1 Jan. 1914).
26 Quoted in Schwartz, In search of wealth and power, 218–19.
27 Liang Ch'i-ch'ao, 'Fu-ku ssu-ch'ao p'ing-i' (Critique of the restorationist thought tide), Ta Chung-hua, 1. 7 (20 July 1915).

spirit was seen as both cause and consequence of the fact that 'we are not in accord with the pattern of world cultural progress'.[28]

With such a conclusion, evolutionary cosmology among the reformers reached the end of the road. Reform discovery of the West – of the ideas of natural science and historical progress – had first stimulated what almost might be called a resurgence of organismic metaphysical theory. Evolution came to be imagined as a self-generating cosmic process, its dynamism and direction guided by 'dialectical' forces inherent within it. Then, as its teleology of moral ends was envisaged in the form of a social utopia identified with modernization, it became necessary for reformers to judge the system by the achievements of their own history itself. As the power of the cosmos was imagined in ways that dwarfed the role of the traditional sage, reformers tried to recreate him as a Faustian hero, or to collectivize human psychic energy as the 'spirit' (*ching-shen*) of the people. Each step constituted a *de facto* secularization, as the metaphysically grounded moral purposes which presumably constituted the 'motive force' of change were tested by people and events themselves. When moral teleology was no longer credibly perceived as at work in the world, evolutionary cosmology became a purely naturalistic system of belief, which maintained the integration of the social and cosmic orders at the cost of, in the Confucian sense, 'dehumanizing' men and women themselves. Beyond the resulting crisis of faith, which by the time of the May Fourth movement had touched all the surviving reform leaders, there had to emerge a different conceptual framework for understanding the relationship of historical process and spiritual value.

NATIONAL ESSENCE AND THE FUTURE OF CONFUCIANISM: THE EMERGENCE OF NEO-TRADITIONAL ALTERNATIVES

In the thinking of the original reform generation, evolutionary cosmology had first embraced change's possibilities and then increasingly justified adaptation to its necessities. However, whether a thinker stressed the moral ends embodied in the movements of the cosmos, or, alternatively, thought primarily of the naturalistic and social processes of history, neither pole of emphasis implied denial of linkage with the other. As the dissolution of China's traditional political order, anticipated since the 1890s, became a fact of revolutionary politics in 1911, these organicist assumptions became increasingly burdensome to their adherents. However much the monarchy may have been castigated for its political failures,

28 Liang Ch'i-ch'ao, 'Wu-nien-lai chih chiao-hsun' (Lessons of the past five years), *Ta Chung-hua*, 2. 10 (20 Oct. 1916).

it had been a sacred institution, symbolizing the interdependence of the Chinese value system and the socio-political order. The break-up of this unitary institution, and even more its apparent sequel in a rudderless, unprincipled and ineffective republic, was profoundly dispiriting.

As the links between the Confucian spiritual order and the socio-political system were thus seen to weaken, many intellectuals shifted from a philosophical language based upon the assumptions of evolutionary cosmology to one which more resembled evolutionary naturalism. The first was syncretic: it embraced science but also assumed Confucian-Taoist processes underlying nature were metaphysically prior and fundamental to science's functioning. The second was Westernized: it opted for contemporary physical models of the universe. The first saw consciousness as linked to the human spirit, and imagined it microcosmically – embodying the same forces that move the cosmos at large and capable, because of this, of interacting harmoniously with them. The second saw consciousness as psychology, and imagined human beings as purely biological and social organisms, so denying that human history can reflect ontology. Where the first balanced determinative cosmic processes against human heroes able to save society by activating the spirit of a 'new people', the second saw individuals and the realm of politics itself as determined by underlying sociological forces. Although the pull of such a naturalistic and sociological view of evolution was powerfully felt by men like Liang Ch'i-ch'ao, its secularist implications were in the final analysis unacceptable to surviving reformers.

Rather, evolutionary naturalism became the preserve of more radical thinkers. These included the extremist fringe among the republican revolutionaries, the anarchists. Their ideology, developed in the years immediately preceding the 1911 Revolution, glorified the institutional destabilization accompanying revolutionary moments in history, and also identified social revolution as the fundamental agent of progress. They also included the Westernizers of the emerging New Culture movement after 1911,[29] who began to construct a Marxist-derived critique of the 'feudal' social institutions responsible for China's backwardness. Such radicals did not entirely abandon metaphysical thinking about change based on traditional cosmological notions. But their debts to Confucianism were unacknowledged, papered over by a programmatic embrace of science not only as a naturalistic cosmology, but also as a positivist method of verification justifying the rejection of all tradition. The cumulative effect of these radical departures was to make their opponents identify

29 The classic study of intellectual radicalism in the May Fourth period is Chow Tse-tsung, *The May Fourth movement.*

the negative direction of republican politics and society squarely with an amoral secular rationalism of Western origin.

In this way, the erosion of the Confucian spiritual order and its invasion by the West could be seen as a secular erosion of all value. Those who thought this could not help being stirred by deep feelings of spiritual crisis. Born of this crisis, neo-traditionalism eventually forged an alliance between those who had been suspicious of late Ch'ing modernization from a very early stage, and those original reformers like Liang Ch'i-ch'ao and K'ang Yu-wei who were increasingly depressed by the distopian evolutionism which seemed to offer the only consistent explanation of the moral failures of the revolution.

In seeking a way out, however, neither K'ang-Liang nor any other neo-traditionalists began with a wholesale repudiation of evolutionary principles. In seeking to adapt tradition to contemporary needs, all assumed that traditions do change. In the effort to explain the relationship between 'essential' traditional values and contemporary cultural expression of them, all took advantage of the fact that Confucian-Taoist cosmology had not analytically distinguished the essential Way from the process of Change. Nonetheless, their philosophical assertion of organic unity was continually juxtaposed with an analysis of contemporary socio-political conditions that belied it. As a result two alien philosophical vocabularies coexisted uneasily in neo-traditionalist writings. One was based on the old assumptions of the interdependence of society and value in a dynamic cosmos; the other vocabulary reflected a newly perceived discontinuity between the socio-political realm on the one hand, where modernization was generally accepted as necessary, and the spiritual-moral realm of value on the other. 'Spiritual East' and 'materialist West': these commonplaces of neo-traditionalist rhetoric owed their vast popularity to the double and contradictory message conveyed. On the one hand they suggested a seemingly organicist evaluation of total cosmic and world orders; on the other they did not suggest two parallel entities, but metaphorically or symbolically mapped a dualistic universe in which spiritual values must abide above and apart from socio-political fact. The history of neo-traditionalism down through the May Fourth period saw the gradual supplanting of the first connotation by the second.

Between the 1898 reform and the May Fourth movement three neo-traditional currents may be discerned, each with its own strategy for adapting Confucianism and the classical heritage to modern conditions.[30] One was the National Essence (*kuo-ts'ui*) movement among classical

---

30 See Wing-tsit Chan, *Religious trends in modern China*, and Charlotte Furth, ed. *The limits of change: essays on conservative alternatives in republican China*.

scholars and political activists. Well before the Revolution of 1911, they were interested in an analysis of Chinese history which explored the origins and development of national traditions from archaic roots in land, race and culture – and which would validate the current struggle for sovereignty and independence. Since they made history serve nationalist ideology, and justified nationalism as the essential means for the survival of the Chinese cultural heritage, the National Essence group gravitated toward the anti-Manchu, anti-imperialist political movement. However, their effort to recast the Confucian classical canon as national history also reflected late Ch'ing educational change which had disassociated classical knowledge and office-holding, necessitating new roles for learning and new social functions for the learned.

The second neo-traditional current was led by Liang Ch'i-ch'ao upon his return to the mainland as a prestigious elder statesman after the 1911 Revolution. Liang still focused on the collective psychology of the Chinese people as he had in his call for a 'new people' in 1902. Now, however, he attempted to define and defend a historically rooted 'national character' (*kuo-hsing*) – a presumably still vital social morality to be found in unique Chinese norms of interpersonal relations and spiritual self-cultivation. Like 'national essence' history, the 'national character' was subject to evolutionary law, but its value derived from its organic links with the past, and change was now to be judged by compatibility with its temper. His post-revolutionary journals, *Yung-yen* (Justice) and *Ta Chung-hua* (Great China) became forums for debate in which admirable and faulty qualities of the national psychology were extrapolated from contemporary social evidence.

Third, a concern for the modern relevance of the central spiritual symbols of Confucianism still preoccupied many. Some of these followed K'ang Yu-wei who had advocated since the original 1898 reform period that Confucianism become institutionalized as a state cult. During the first years of the republic this idea attracted an organized following which lobbied for a 'religion clause' in the constitution. More philosophically inclined Confucianists looked for support in an evolutionary sociology of religion – defending the faith as an historically advanced one, free of the superstition and super-naturalism of more primitive beliefs. In this debate, of course, both sides shared a common goal: to see Confucianism as a functionally modern belief system.

All three of these neo-traditional currents shared some underlying characteristics. All were suspicious of dominant Western values – identified as competitive individualism, materialist profit seeking and utilitarianism. All implicitly defined core Chinese values reactively as the antitheses of these. Since they opposed 'Westernization' in culture, neo-traditionalists made a special contribution to anti-imperialist and nationalist sentiment. Second, in each movement evolutionism was balanced by a revisionist essentialism, as the presumed dross of heritage was dismissed in favour of some core of truth. Sometimes the criteria for such truth were historically fundamentalist, as when National Essence scholars pruned the classics of the accumulation of 2,000 years of imperially-sponsored commentaries. Sometimes the criteria were evolutionary, as when the present 'national character' was detached from the ritual morality of the recent past and presented as functionally compatible with modernization. In this way neo-traditionalists shared in the contemporary penchant for sociological reasoning, making the functional utility of traditional systems of belief the basis for justifying faith. But they also felt a need to see contemporary Confucian value from a perspective outside history, as immune to its fluctuations. So where imperial Confucianism had merged sacred and secular institutions, diffusing religious and moral sentiment in the practices of daily life, neo-traditionalists were gradually forced to regard value as a distinctly autonomous sphere.

When at the height of the May Fourth movement two 'choice souls' in the younger generation, the philosophers Liang Sou-ming (Liang Shu-ming) and Hsiung Shih-li, experienced emblematic conversions to Confucianism, the sacred-secular polarization was at last explicitly acknowledged by Confucianists themselves. Rather than justifying their new belief on evolutionary or utilitarian grounds, Liang and Hsiung said they valued Confucianism for its capacity to order and express the uniquely spiritual side of their personal experience, and to answer questions about the meaning of existence as a whole. This, then, was a classic modernist defence of the special genius of 'religion': its capacity to provide symbolic resources for dealing with aspects of the human condition for which secular philosophy has no answer. Following this, evolutionist and functionalist defences of faith, always ambiguous, rapidly gave way to 'intuitionist' ones.

National essence

A Japanese neologism of the Meiji period, the term '*kuo ts'ui*' (national essence) began to appear in the writings of Chinese intellectuals around 1903, when the reform of the educational system and the secularization, if not abolition, of the monarchy were first clearly delineated as goals of the Ch'ing reform movement. In the broadest sense, 'national essence' was the slogan of scholars who were looking for an alternative to Confucian learning in the service of the imperial orthodoxy and examination system.[31] Interest in a modern 'national learning' (*kuo-hsueh*) first surfaced among Chang Chih-tung, Lo Chen-yü and other central government bureaucrats in charge of new educational policies, who wanted to limit foreign influence on curriculum and establish Chinese ethics as a streamlined department of study in the new school system.[32] However, many classical scholars saw the issue as not merely one of adapting to new conditions, but in a spirit of resistance to Western-oriented change, making the movement to 'preserve the national essence' a vehicle for militant nationalists and critics of the reform movement.

Beginning about 1904 leadership gravitated to a clique of brilliant eccentrics who found in anti-Manchu politics a strategy for revolution as the restoration of the spirit of the Ming, T'ang or even pre-Han era, and also a rationale for a Darwinist influenced historiography glorifying the unique Han race and culture. The Association for the Preservation of Classical Chinese Learning (Kuo-hsueh pao-ts'un hui), founded in Shanghai in January 1905 by Teng Shih, Huang Chieh and Liu Shih-p'ei, preached anti-Manchu revolution as an attractive alternative to reform modernism and accommodation with the West. Although national essence advocates acknowledged that the West was a source of world civilization in its own right, and that some interrelation between centres of civilization was a necessary pattern of world history, much of their scholarship, in fact, appeared motivated by a search for historically rooted native alternatives to the crumbling imperial Confucian orthodoxy. Here they drew primarily on the Confucian and non-Confucian 'one hundred schools' (*chu-tzu pai-chia*) of the classical Chou era, but also on the Ming loyalists, Buddhism, and on the 'knight errant' tradition of heroic violence.[33] Finally, within the movement there was a strong undercurrent of solidarity with China's common people, who were like these neo-traditionalists in being the natural victims, rather than beneficiaries, of modernization programmes dominated by the court and provincial elite. The archaic populist rhetoric of secret societies and dynastic revolts, basic to anti-Manchu polemic, was well suited to inspire cultural conservatives to support political strategies based on violence, and to express sympathy with the more backward common people against the so-called 'enlightened' and pro-Western privileged.[34]

Initial efforts at revisionist history by 'national essence' historians were

31 'Pei-ching ta-hsueh t'ang chih kuo-hsueh wen-t'i' (The problem of national learning at Peking University), *Hsin-min ts'ung-pao* 34 (July 1903) 61-2.
32 Marianne Bastid, *Aspects de la réforme de l'enseignement en Chine au début du 20e siècle*, 64-5.
33 Furth, *Limits of change*, pt 2, 'National Essence', 57-168.
34 See Joseph Esherick, *Reform and revolution in China: the 1911 Revolution in Hunan and Hupeh*.

heavily influenced by political anti-Manchuism. Chang Ping-lin's *Book of raillery*, Liu Shih-p'ei's *Book of the expulsion* and Huang Chieh's *Yellow history*, all published between 1901 and 1906,[35] constituted a scholarly attack on the legitimacy of Manchu rule. All of these works defined the Chinese nation (*min-tsu*) in terms of racial myth: the presumed common descent of the Chinese people from the legendary Yellow Emperor (2697–2597 BC). The implication was that on racial grounds the Manchus should be excluded from the national community. These works broke decisively with canonical tradition by emphasizing the primitive and archaic nature of the earliest stages of Chinese history. Chang and Liu drew upon the Darwinist sociology of Herbert Spencer for a comparatively based evaluation of ancient China and other cradle civilizations and so-called savage peoples. For a time they were even impressed with the ideas of the Belgian Sinologist Terrien de la Couperie, who had posited a common 'cradle' for both Chinese and Middle Eastern antiquity.[36] Nonetheless, the strongest single influence upon these works remained the *Yellow book* (*Huang shu*) of the seventeenth-century Ming loyalist historian, Wang Fu-chih.

As 'national history', these works transcended their anti-Manchu polemical purpose. They offered a definition of the Chinese people as a 'nation' (*min-tsu*) – an organic collectivity based upon common ties of place, blood, custom and culture. All of them pointed to some antique point of origin for the complex of national values which might provide a key to the restoration of polity and culture today. Melding Rousseau and Wang Fu-chih, Liu Shih-p'ei hypothesized that an original social contract between sage ruler and people had led to the creation of unique, Confucian social and ritual forms by the early sage kings. For Chang Ping-lin, the family system and its formal genealogical lines established China's racial unity, while language itself concentrated the essence of Chinese thought, and legalist statecraft of the Ch'in-Han era had shown the way to serve the needs of national wealth and power. None denied the existence of an evolutionary pattern in history, but as organicists all stressed origin over development, affirming essential identity over evolutionary continuity between past and present values.

In their message concerning value, 'national essence' scholars had signi-

---

35 *Ch'iu shu* (Book of raillery), reprinted in Lo Chia-lun, ed. *Chung-hua min-kuo shih-liao ts'ung pien* (Collection on the history of the Chinese republic); *Jang shu* (Book of expulsion), first published 1903, reprinted in *Liu Shen-shu hsien-sheng i-shu* (Collected works of Mr Liu Shen-shu [Liu Shih-p'ei]), 1. 762 ff.; *Huang shih* (Yellow history), first published in *Kuo-ts'ui hsueh-pao* (National essence journal) (1905), 1–9.
36 Selections from de la Couperie's *Western origins of Chinese civilization* were published in *Hsin-min ts'ung-pao* between Sept. 1903 and Jan. 1905.

ficantly shifted their focus from the Confucian classical tradition, to a more abstract idea of the totality of the culture as essence – the accumulated spiritual legacy of a particular people. Moreover, this new view of the inherited classical culture went hand in hand with a distinctive critique of earlier forms of classicism, which built upon the established 'school of Han learning' (*Han-hsueh*). Since the seventeenth century this school had promoted understanding of the classics through careful philological and textual analysis of surviving documents, and in the nineteenth century had led to a revival of interest in long buried and heterodox systems of thought. However, 'national essence' scholars transcended these traditional approaches to strip the classics of their authority as the sacred repositories of normative ideals, re-evaluating them as a section of the vast, heterogeneous corpus of ancient Chinese literature, now seen simply as documents for the study of history. This also made possible a historical methodology which established a bridge between the traditions of careful evidentiary analysis of Ch'ing dynasty textual scholars of 'Han learning' and a twentieth-century critical approach to evidence identified with the Western scientific method.

At the same time the 'national essence' approach to learning took shape not just as an alternative to both canonical Confucianism and straight-arrow 'Westernization'. A basic concern of the greatest 'national essence' historian, Chang Ping-lin, was to criticize the cultural programme of K'ang Yu-wei's reform group. Opposing what he saw as reform evolutionary modernism with anti-Western, anti-imperialist cultural essentialism, Chang popularized his ideas between 1906 and 1908 as editor of the T'ung-meng hui's revolutionary *People's Journal* (*Min pao*), and presented them in more academic form in his acclaimed *Critical essays on antiquity* (*Kuo-ku lun-heng*) published in 1910.[37] Politically the Chang-K'ang polemic was associated with the rivalry of 'reform' and 'revolutionary' factions of politicians; intellectually, it was identified as the Old Text-New Text controversy over the classics, pitting rival versions of the Confucian legacy. The result was two contrasting modern ways of looking at the sage, both of which, by the standards of neo-Confucian and imperial orthodoxy, were equally heterodox, since neither allowed the traditionally received texts to be taken as a canonical legacy of a true Golden Age of antiquity.[38]

In the hands of K'ang Yu-wei, the early Han New Text tradition of oral transmission of the classics had suggested a radical interpretation of Confucius as a religious founder who had literally created the canon bet-

---

37 Chang Ping-lin, *Kuo-ku lun-heng* (Critical essays on antiquity).
38 Chou Yü-t'ung, *Ching ku-chin wen-hsueh* (Old and new text classical learning).

ween the sixth and fifth centuries BC as a vehicle for his own prophetic visions of *ta-t'ung*. K'ang's argument was technically complex, depending upon finding philological bases for thinking that the versions established as authoritative by Liu Hsin in the first century AD were politically inspired forgeries, and that their originals did not date earlier than Confucius' own lifetime. However, to say that the classics were prophecy made it impossible to believe in them as containing an objective core of historical truth concerning high antiquity. As K'ang's critics noted, 'if Liu Hsin was a forger, Confucius was also a forger'.[39] K'ang had posed a choice unprecedented in Confucian tradition between either a mystical faith in Confucius as a being transcending history, or doubt that there was any historical base for the Confucian Golden Age the classics recorded.

Moreover, this scepticism had a corollary: dethroned as canon, the classics would have to be understood in the historical context of the ages in which they were now thought to have been created, that is, as politically motivated inventions designed to bolster the legitimacy of the Chou dynasty 'later kings' or of their successors, the Western Han emperors. To his critics, K'ang Yu-wei's theories suggested both a false portrait of Confucius as a divine religious founder, and a true and lamentable evaluation of Confucian scholarship as the tool of state power throughout imperial history. Rather than interpret such scholarship as ideology, reflecting the values and priorities of an age, they saw it as distortion, revealing the compromised morality of generations of literati statesmen whose learning advanced careers more than truth, contributing ultimately to imperial decline. In this way, K'ang's philosophical and historical theses were turned against their author, to condemn the K'ang-Liang reform movement as a contemporary manifestation of the careerist 'practical statecraft' (*ching-shih*) tradition in Confucianism.[40]

In orchestrating this attack upon New Text Confucianism, Chang Ping-lin relied upon the more conventional 'Han learning' tradition that Confucius had been 'a transmitter, not a creator', and that 'the six classics are history' – that is, surviving remnants of the public records of the early Chou court. However, Chang used these precedents both to ridicule the idea that Confucianism could be a religion on the model of Christianity, and by extension to claim the Confucian school had no privileged message to convey concerning social morality. In denying Confucianism its historic role of ordering society, he rejected both its basic model of sagehood as linking 'sage within and king without', and the scholar-

39 Quoted in Hou Wai-lu, *Chin-tai Chung-kuo ssu-hsiang hsueh-shuo shih*, 789.
40 The impact of the New Text-Old Text controversy on early republican historiography is analysed in Laurence A. Schneider, *Ku Chieh-kang and China's new history*.

statecraft symbiosis which had characterized the traditional political culture. His own Confucius, instead, was a scholar who had created the first private, as opposed to court-sponsored, school of thought in Chinese history – a pioneer both of 'scientific' fidelity to facts in scholarly work, and of an admirable detachment of the intellectual vocation from the corruptions of power.

In their opposition to New Text utopian reformism, most early 'national essence' partisans did not follow Chang Ping-lin all the way to rejecting the idea of Confucius as China's foremost moralist. Rather, while branding K'ang as a fame-seeking corruptor of the sagely ideal, they remained within the more standard anti-superstition pole of Confucian humanism. Chang Ping-lin's thought went beyond such superficial rationalism and moralism, leading to the first fundamental neo-traditional criticism of the evolutionary principles underlying reform cosmology as a whole. In his repeated attacks on the reformers, published in a variety of anti-Manchu revolutionary periodicals between 1903 and 1908, Chang castigated the speculative New Text historical reasoning not only because K'ang did not 'seek truth from fact' and 'hid the failings of the ancients'[41] but also because the reform model of the cosmological process imposed a fixed law of natural and social evolution upon events which in fact defy such a deterministic analysis.[42]

In Chang's cosmos, change, rather than being predictable and regular, is marked by discontinuity, randomness and chance. Time, rather than presenting itself as a linear sequence of events towards a teleologically predetermined goal, appears without beginning or end, as 'movement and stasis in mutual opposition'.[43] Matter, when analysed philosophically, leads to epistemological scepticism concerning its own nature, and thus to the negation of 'materialism'. From Taoism Chang drew cosmological constructs which portrayed the universe as an undetermined flux, in which phenomenal forms continually take shape free from any external coercion or direction. From Wei-shih Buddhism he took the belief that this flow of phenomena itself must be acknowledged the creation of mind, 'perfuming' a monistic 'storehouse consciousness' with an unstable succession of dharmas in motion. In light of such a model of cosmic truth, Chang believed that reform evolutionists and their faith in *kung-li*, or

41 Quoted in Hou Wai-lu, *Chin-tai Chung-kuo ssu-hsiang hsueh-shuo shih*, 801–2.
42 See the following by T'ai-yen [Chang Ping-lin]: 'Chü-fen chin-hua lun' (Progress as differentiation), *Min-pao*, 7 (5 Sept. 1906) 1–13; 'She-hui t'ung-ch'üan shang-tui' (Discussion of the 'History of politics'), *Min-pao*, 12 (6 March 1907) 1–24; 'Wu-wu lun' (The five negatives), *Min-pao*, 16 (25 Sept. 1907) 1–22; 'Po shen-wo hsien-cheng shuo' (Against 'soul' as a foundation for constitutional government), *Min-pao*, 21 (10 June 1908) 1–11; 'Ssu-huo lun' (On four delusions), *Min-pao* 22 (Sept. 1906–July 1908) 1–22.
43 Chang Ping-lin, 'Ssu-huo lun', 10.

natural laws of progress, were absurd. When Yen Fu as a Spencerian outlined a world pattern of historical development from patriarchal to military state, he betrayed his ignorance of China's institutional history, a subject in which Chang was an expert. But more important he showed his insensitivity to the unique nature of any particular historical or human experience, and to the elusive nature of causal processes. When K'ang and Liang said that the human grouping instinct would lead to higher, more successful forms of material and moral community, they were imposing Darwinian laws of social cooperation on human beings whose life ideal should rather be the autonomous, detached and spontaneous 'natural' existence dictated by Chuang-tzu's doctrine of the 'equality of things' (ch'i wu).

In seeing reform cosmology as materialistic and deterministic Chang was responding to the established association between reform thought and Westernization, and also to the place of science in the cosmology itself, suggestive as it was of powerful external cosmic processes of nature and machine overshadowing human effort. But in his protest against determinism Chang mostly returned to an old debate on nature and society which had historically divided Warring States Confucianists and Taoists. In saying that human beings have no natural ties with others and that no social laws bind them as moral absolutes, he uttered the classic Taoist cry of individualist protest against Confucian social values – a cry which did not imply an assertion of the right to socially defined freedom, but rather the desire to align the self with the a-social, self-generating, spontaneous rhythms of the natural universe.

Chang Ping-lin, like the reform cosmologists, philosophized as if metaphysics maps out structures which harmonize with socio-historic processes; but given the nature of his cosmology, the linkages of interdependence were extremely difficult to maintain. Like the reformers, Chang turned to the traditional symbolism of cosmic 'barriers', which could express either external social and natural obstacles to human community, or internal psychological and spiritual barriers obstructing the true self's experienced identity with the cosmos as a whole. Yet where reform utopians imagined the breaking of barriers to lead to the moral community of ta-t'ung, Chang wanted to 'end the triple fusion of human kind, living things and the world'.[44] With the destruction of consciousness the world itself, product of the defective perceptions of living beings, would be obliterated. Tan Ssu-t'ung had employed very similar Buddhistic constructs to express a vision of the transcendence of consciousness; Chang Ping-lin's version saw annihilation.

44 Chang Ping-lin, 'Wu-wu lun', 22.

Buddhism as a 'life-negating' cosmology traditionally had the potential to be this kind of metaphysical alternative to Confucianism. In the reform generation, however, the appeal to such an alternative reflected something new – the emerging sacred-secular polarization which accompanied the broader revolution. In the Old Text–New Text controversy Chang maintained, as against K'ang Yu-wei, that Confucianism is not a religion – a surface formulation of his underlying assumption that socio-political order and cosmic truth occupy separate spheres. However, in this case rejecting Confucian spirituality was not a choice for secularism; it was a neo-traditionalist's search for spiritual alternatives to the old comforts of the moralized Confucian universe. On the level of private belief Chang turned to Buddhism and Taoism both for a native critique of Confucian errors, and for a harsh kind of existential understanding. In life as a 'national essence' man of learning he opted for the vocation of 'disinterested scholarship', implying that pure knowledge is a value outside society and in essence superior to it. In this way his personal cosmological beliefs complemented the more widespread national essence idealization of the spirit of Chinese culture, preserved in the classical legacy.

Moreover, as a critical theory, Chang Ping-lin's beliefs were adaptable to the emerging neo-traditional analysis of Eastern versus Western cultures. Staples of this analysis included such views as: that progress is an illusion and belief in it a kind of modern superstition; that pursuit of wealth and power in a Darwinian struggle for existence leads to perilous reliance upon externals at the expense of inner life; and that Chinese culture will perish if it does not rely upon its own internal spiritual powers of renewal.

During the May Fourth movement of 1919 the slogan 'national essence' was identified with opponents of vernacular language reform, and the movement appeared a clear loser in the battle over China's New Culture. Nonetheless, the national essence critique of Westernization and its model of national history focusing on the ethnic and territorial roots of a uniquely Chinese culture were carried on by Kuomintang scholars. The 'national essence' concept of a politically disinterested scholarly vocation found ready acceptance among many later republican academics. More important, the movement introduced a new way of looking at the concept of 'culture' itself, seeing it as an absolute, a repository of values which stands outside the socio-political processes of modernization, yet constitutes an evaluative standard against which that process must be measured. This concept, and the critique of evolutionary cosmology which complemented it, broke ground for a new style dualistic metaphysics based on the opposition of spirit to matter.

The national character

As might be expected, Liang Ch'i-ch'ao's post-1911 defence of tradition was the one which went furthest in accommodating evolutionism, a secularist approach to value, and concern for reforming social morality. As if the fall of the Manchu dynasty itself was a signal that protracted upheaval contains perils of social dissolution, Liang started the new journal *Yung-yen* (Justice) on his return to the mainland in 1912, and presented in the leading article of the first issue an affirmation of the 'national character' (*kuo-hsing*).[45]

Ever since his first call for a 'new people' in 1902 Liang's reformism had been based upon the assumption that the key to progress and social well-being lay in the health and vitality of an organically conceived spirit, expressed through the collective national psychology. Liang now renewed his hopes for the national psyche. The virtues of this 'national character' were relatively modest: it was neither eternally valid, nor directly in touch with the ontologically true. It was simply historically suitable. Yet in making his claim for suitability, Liang was here no longer making a concession to Chinese backwardness, but saying that certain fundamental features of Confucian social morality could and must outlive the old absolutized norms of the 'five relationships' to provide a basis for healthy, and therefore gradual, national development. He stated that nations have a nature (*hsing*) like people, and that their fate depends upon this intangible quality, visible in religion, customs and language. The 'nature' can change, but only gradually, as a body may alter its physical composition but cannot be totally overhauled without killing the organism. 'A gardener in pruning trees trims branches, and gets rid of leaves, but he is never willing to damage the trunk or root'. A nation's 'nature' is killed when not one of its traditions is sacred.[46]

In this way Liang came to idealize not an abstract historical 'objective geist' of culture, but a presumably living 'national character' (*kuo-hsing*), an attainable moral property of those millions of ordinary Chinese who he thought had not been spoiled by the events of the past 20 years. As against Western 'individualism' and 'hedonism', Liang offered the antidote of 'familism' (*chia-tsu chu-i*), identifying the fundamental familistic values as 'reciprocity' (*shu*), 'respect for rank' (*ming-fen*), and 'concern for posterity' (*lü hou*).[47] Of these three virtues the last two were seen as par-

---

45 Liang Ch'i-ch'ao, 'Kuo-hsing p'ien' (Essay on the national character), *Yung yen*, 1. 1 (Jan. 1913), 1–6 (sep. pag.).
46 *Ibid.*
47 Liang Ch'i-ch'ao, 'Chung-kuo tao-te chih ta-yuan' (Fundamentals of Chinese morality), *Yung-yen* 1. 2 (Dec. 1912) 1–8; 1. 4 (Feb. 1913) 1–8 (sep. pag.).

ticularly functional for modern nationalism. They encouraged a spirit of collective solidarity and self-sacrifice in building the future and confirmed the moral legitimacy of a political elite based on talent as against democratic levelling. In making 'reciprocity' the cardinal virtue of interpersonal relations, Liang opted for a moderate liberalization of generational and sexual relationships which would not threaten the underlying solidarity of the family. As against the unilateral virtue of 'filiality', 'reciprocity' had always called attention to the moral claims of inferiors without, however, fundamentally challenging the hierarchy of interpersonal roles.

This clear-cut revisionist interpretation of the Confucian social ethic did not break with the underlying concepts of evolutionary cosmology, but merely underscored reform evolutionism's assumption that core values shape and inform social change. 'I have advocated preserving the "national essence" all of my life', Liang said in 1916, 'but I mean by it something different from the common interpretation.'[48] His position was simply that if any particular historical Confucian customs were relative and partial, the Confucian idea of the moral personality (*jen-ko*) in itself was an intrinsic, not a contingent value, which would survive the era of nationalism in world politics.[49]

If Liang's theory of the 'national character' was in keeping with his underlying evolutionary beliefs, it also carried his stress on the priority of society and culture over politics. Concurrent with the discussion of the 'national character', *Yung-yen's* political analyses of the controversy over a monarchical restoration argued against it, but on relativistic grounds. Liang declared that the form of government (*cheng-t'i*) – that is, its actual system of representative and administrative organization – is a more fundamental index to the functioning of a political system than the form of the state (*kuo-t'i*) – that is, its seat of formal sovereignty. The implication was that, while China's 'state form' should now remain republican in recognition of the simple facts of recent history, its future 'form of government' properly ought to evolve compatibly with native norms of social relations.[50]

Both because it dealt with concrete norms of social ethics and because of the evolutionary model of change it entailed, Liang's theory of the 'national character' confronted the New Culture movement on common ground. While giving sharply different answers, the two sides asked the same kind of questions: given that the norms of interpersonal relations

48 Liang Ch'i-ch'ao in *Ta Chung-hua*, 1. 2 (Feb. 1915) 7.
49 *Ibid.*
50 See *Yung-yen*, 1. 3 (1913) 3–4 and *Ta Churg-hua*, 1. 8 (Aug. 1915) 13.

are cultural forces determining the evolution of political order, how do China's historical models serve, and do they need to be changed fundamentally? Answers took a common turn: for every article that praised a Chinese devotion to peace, inner contentment, familistic emotions, another savaged the presumed national predilections for passivity, conformity, dependency and slavishness to authority. The argument for the functional modernity of Chinese traditions of collectivism and public-mindedness was matched by the example of the functioning modernity of Western individualism, competitiveness and scientific rationality.

Not surprisingly, then, Liang's defence of the evolutionarily modernized 'national character' eventually met the same fate as his advocacy of the evolutionarily advanced 'rational' Confucius. Even during the early republican years, disappointments with republican politics had caused Liang to alternate his neo-traditional assertions of value with occasional outbursts of distopian pessimism.[51] Finally the experience of the First World War, which so gravely damaged the prestige of Western civilization in the eyes of Chinese intellectuals in general, taught Liang one final lesson of the times – that the assumptions of evolutionary cosmology itself must be abandoned. Returning from a humiliating, dispiriting assignment as a Chinese observer at the Paris Peace Conference which ignored China's national rights, Liang wrote his 'Reflections on a trip to Europe'.[52] It condemned contemporary Western civilization *in toto*. Liang no longer saw an organic vision of human historical progress, even if with twists and turns, but two starkly diametrical metahistorical systems. The first was a Western one dominated by the iron laws of a 'scientific view of humanity', generating an economic and social system based on the machine and given over to the pursuit of power and wealth, and to the corruptions of hedonism and greed. The contrasting Eastern civilization was now at a turning point, risking disaster if she followed Europe in infatuation with the idea of an omnipotent science. The limits of Liang's accommodation with a secular evolutionism had been reached. Once it appeared finally inhospitable to symbols of Confucian moral value, he abandoned evolutionary theory. Liang Ch'i-ch'ao's last cosmic myth of total civilizations was not a true organic cosmology, but a metaphor for a dualistic metaphysics of matter and spirit. Chinese spirit could be seen as embodied in a civilization only if that civilization stood apart from the process of modernization apparently engulfing the planet as a whole.

51 See supra, fn. 26.
52 Liang Ch'i-ch'ao, 'Ou yu hsin-ying lu chieh-lu' (Reflections on a trip to Europe), 1919 reprinted in *Yin-ping-shih ho-chi* (Combined writings), *chuan-chi, ts'e* 5. 1–152.

Confucianism as a religion

Historically Confucianism was a '*chiao*' (doctrine or teaching) and the English word 'religion' had no exact classical Chinese translation. As it was brought in by nineteenth-century missionaries, the concept itself was linked to Christian assumptions of a spirit-matter dualism which Confucianists did not share; institutionally it evoked the Christian separation of church and state which was irrelevant in a patriarchal society. Therefore when in the 1890s the New Text reform intellectuals began to raise the question whether Confucianism was, or should be considered as a religion, they had to import new language (beginning with the Japanese neologism for religion, *tsung-chiao*), propose new institutional structures and eventually suggest an altered definition of Confucianism's central meaning. At each step, however, the syncretic Confucian heritage, in which neither Confucian humanistic rationalists at one pole nor Confucian mystics at the other traditionally felt required to repudiate the other, provided a reservoir of symbols and concepts that could blur the sacred-secular polarization which the idea of 'religion' here implied. The notion that Confucianism was a 'religion' at all, then, was controversial, attacked by those who considered themselves within the tradition perhaps even more hotly than by secularists without.

The New Text Confucianism of K'ang Yu-wei and T'an Ssu-t'ung introduced the religion issue first of all in the form of a doctrinal influence. As self-styled syncretists, both K'ang and T'an held that all three of the world's great historic religions had a common core of truth – a position which gave Christianity an explicit contribution to make to ontology. To make Confucius a religious founder, to speak of *jen* as encompassing fraternal love, to exalt prophecy and martyrdom, and express hope for religious Messiahs to come and save the world – these things certainly bespoke syncretists who had been touched by the Christian drama even as they denied the exclusively Christian origin of such ideas. K'ang was further impressed with the Protestant ideal of an inner spiritual voice overriding doctrinal convention, and liked to compare his own role in China to Luther's leadership of the Reformation.[53] In T'an Ssu-t'ung's work Christian influence is suggested most directly in those passages of the *Jen hsueh* which see fundamental tension between the human spirit and body, and assert that the Confucian tradition had its own form of a doctrine of immortality.[54]

New Text reformers were led by this doctrinal syncretism to make their

53 See Hou Wai-lu, *Chin-tai Chung-kuo ssu-hsiang hsueh-shuo shih*, 704–27.
54 T'an Ssu-t'ung, *Ch'üan chi*, 24–35.

first claim that Confucianism has a 'religious' character. But the Christian theological impact upon reform cosmology probably had less to do with this claim in the short run than the example of the Christian church as an institution. K'ang Yu-wei's famous campaign to make Confucianism into a state religion, inaugurated in 1895 and doggedly pursued by him and others until the death of Yuan Shih-k'ai in 1916, in fact was a reflection of socio-political more than spiritual concerns.[55] Recognizing the extent to which a constitutional monarchy and new school system meant the secularization of politics, K'ang hoped to create a corps of religious specialists who would preside over a formal state cult. Separation of church and state appeared to him a key to the ability of strong nations of the West to 'drive a cart on two wheels', upholding social morality in a pluralistic polity. In this way, he said, 'religion maintains its awesome power, morality is honoured, even as dissension rages'.[56] K'ang's blue-print for Confucian religion was an accommodation to the break-up of the imperial Confucian synthesis and accompanying scholar-official rule. Nonetheless, it was only a social accommodation to China's contemporary needs, not a strategy conceived out of the conviction that Confucian truth required such forms of expression.

The utilitarian argument for faith as a prop to social morality attracted a certain kind of support. Gentry dismayed by what they saw as the moral collapse accompanying the revolution were ready recruits to the network of provincial Confucian societies which sprang up after 1911, and which campaigned heavily between 1912 and 1914 for a religious clause in the republican constitution. This movement had K'ang's blessing, and was formally led by his disciple, the Columbia educated economist Ch'en Huan-chang. However, officials under Yuan Shih-k'ai saw to it that changes in the republican government's official sacrifices tended towards civic plainness more than ritual elaboration, while Yuan disavowed that any of his regime's ceremonials constituted the establishment of a state religion. Here Yuan was adjusting his manipulation of traditional symbols to an educated public opinion which argued that a state cult was an historically regressive idea, since it substituted a more primitive Western style supernaturalism for the native humanistic faith which in fact marked China as an advanced civilization.

As a utilitarian proposal justified as suitable to the times, the state cult idea was vulnerable to alternatives whose claim to a suitable modernity

55 See Hsiao Kung-chuan, *A modern China and a new world: K'ang Yu-wei, reformer and utopian 1858–1927*, ch. 4, pp. 97–136.
56 K'ang Yu-wei, 'Chung-hua chiu-kuo lun' (On China's salvation), *Pu-jen tsa-chih*, 1 (March 1913) 21–2.

could be called superior. A more attractive intellectual defence of Confucianism, then, used the idea of the evolution of religion to evaluate China's lack of a Confucian church as the mark of advance, not regression. An early republican history of Chinese religion from such an evolutionary perspective was in Hsia Tseng-yu's *Textbook on Chinese History* (*Chung-kuo li-shih chiao-k'o shu*).[57] Hsia argued that China had moved from a primitive belief in the power of spirits to a higher level of religious consciousness with the emergence of Confucianism and Taoism in the 'Spring and Autumn' era. But, he continued with an indirect slap at the New Text movement, for political reasons superstitious elements were revived by the architects of the imperial cult in the Western Han. Hsia argued that the mystical content in an originally ethical Confucianism was the result of Taoist influence, leaving open the possibility that contemporary Chinese might follow Chang Ping-lin in looking to Taoism for ontological doctrine, while honouring Confucian morality. The more standard approach, however, was to reject this Taoist influence as also a 'superstitious' and negative one, and to agree with Liang Ch'i-ch'ao's original argument against K'ang in 1902 that 'to make Confucianism a religion is to distort the true spirit of Confucius.'[58] The Christian concept of 'religion' applied to the Confucian tradition had bred its opposite, a rationalistic model of the sage. Secular values such as intellectual tolerance, acceptance of the body and rejection of an after-life became, by such reasoning, hallmarks of the Confucian consciousness, and defence of faith rested upon its compatibility with the truths of science.

In 1913 a sophisticated compromise was suggested by the philosopher Chang Tung-sun in the form of a mild criticism of the early republican proliferation of Confucian societies.[59] Turning from analysis of Chinese doctrine to Western philosophy of religion in the abstract, Chang suggested that William James' definition of 'religion' left no doubt that Confucianism, having both ontology and ethics, should be included under the concept. At the same time he argued for the scientific rationality of advanced forms of religious belief, noting that the *I ching* teaches that the supraphenomenal world of the Great Ultimate (*t'ai-chi*) is unknowable, and that Tao is an evolutionary principle of the cosmos. As a corollary,

57 Hsia Tseng-yu, *Chung-kuo li-shih chiao-k'o-shu* (Textbook of the history of China). See the analysis in Ts'ai Yuan-p'ei, 'Wu-shih nien-lai Chung-kuo chih che-hsueh' (Chinese philosophy in the last fifty years), *Shen-pao* anniversary issue, *Tsui-chin wu-shih nien* (The last fifty years).

58 Liang Ch'i-ch'ao, 'Pao-chiao fei so-i tsun K'ung lun' (To 'save the faith' is not the way to honour Confucius), *Hsin-min ts'ung-pao*, 2 (22 Feb. 1902) 59-72.

59 Chang Tung-sun, 'Yü chih K'ung-chiao kuan' (My view of Confucianism), *Yung-yen*, 1. 15 (July 1913) 1-12.

Chang praised Confucian ethics as in harmony with the modern moral ideal of socialism.

These Confucian modernizers, then, whether they spoke for a state cult, for Confucius as a rationalist, or for 'rational religion', all used styles of reasoning that depended upon an evolutionary framework but paid the price of appearing utilitarian in nature. Even if their arguments lacked the crude instrumentalism of appeals to faith as a guarantee of social order, they all broadly viewed it as functional to evolving social systems, and so had to prove this functionality, not in terms of some distant world of *ta-t'ung*, but in the present. But to support Confucian humanism detached from Confucian mysticism or ritual was to make the core of faith rest in a socio-political morality already deeply compromised by change, and whose ethical norms Confucian reformers had themselves been early to attack. On the other hand, to identify Confucianism with contemporary ideals of scientific rationalism made faith vulnerable to challenge from the more thoroughgoing rationalism of science itself – from views of the cosmos based on atomic physics more than on the *I ching* and from models of truth derived from laboratory experiment more than traditionally validated belief. The sacred-secular polarization which had created the 'religious' and 'rational' versions of the sage in the first place, ended by rendering the 'rational' sage obsolete.

By the May Fourth period the debate over a modern form for Confucianism had led neo-traditionalists to a new consciousness of a 'problem of religion' in human life which the discussions of the previous decade had not adequately explored. In its light, all previous strategies for an evolved, modernized Confucianism were seen as equally tainted with utilitarianism. In the May Fourth discussions of the 'problem of religion', evolutionary assumptions became the monopoly of secularists, who argued that with the march of progress and gradual perfection of scientific knowledge, 'religion' would become socially obsolete. Western science, which suggested to earlier reformers a speculative model of the natural world's functioning in harmony with ideal values, now was recast as a positivistic method of verification challenging them. With this shift, the defence of faith also shifted ground. There was not only a retreat from evolutionism but also a new preoccupation with a Western-derived epistemological issue, in which scientific rationalist theories of verification would be countered by 'intuitive' models of truth.[60]

A leading intuitionist metaphysician was Liang Shu-ming, a young

---

60 Yen Chi-ch'eng, "'Shao-nien Chung-kuo" tsung-chiao wen-t'i hao p'i-p'ing' (Critique of the special issue on the religious question of *Young China Magazine*), *Min to* (People's tocsin), 3.2 (1 Feb. 1922) 1–12. See also Chow, *May Fourth movement*, 322–3.

Peking University philosopher, himself the product of the most advanced education the reform generation had to offer. He had experienced a crisis of faith in the first years of the republic which led him initially to a Buddhist and then increasingly to a Confucian commitment.[61] When members of the Young China Association, led by a group studying abroad in France, inaugurated a public debate on the 'problem of religion' in 1921, Liang spoke in the spirit of his own conversion, which had been preceded by bouts of suicidal depression, and had taken place in a mood of protest against all nationalistic or other utilitarian impulses to belief. Religion, Liang said, will always be humanly relevant because it alone deals with issues which 'lie outside the particular universe, if not outside its extension.'[62] In focusing upon death and suffering as the perennial human realities to which religion alone can give satisfactory meaning, Liang leaned heavily towards Buddhism – 'Indian religion' – as the model for a true religion of 'transcendence' (ch'ao-chueh). However, his own Confucian view, developed in the debate of 1921 and published in a book the next year, was concerned with the same fundamental issue in its central claim that Confucianism is an affirmation of the ontological reality of 'life' (sheng) itself.

Liang's book, Eastern and Western civilizations and their philosophies (Tung Hsi wen-hua chi ch'i che-hsueh) made him perhaps the most popular single neo-traditional thinker of the May Fourth period.[63] The book's success may be attributed to the fact that with remarkable emotional effect if not logical clarity it blended the neo-traditional thinker's rival impulses – on the one hand to continue the now familiar traditions of evolutionary cosmology, and on the other hand to express the new sense of estrangement between an a-historical world of value, understood through the intuitive human knowledge of the good, and natural and sociopolitical processes governed by science.

Eastern and Western civilizations first of all sketched an outline of human civilization evolving through metahistorical stages, each, according to Liang's vocabulary (which here was indebted to Schopenhauer), the product of the direction of a spiritual Will (ta i-yü). Liang identified the Will with life itself (sheng) and also with jen. Like T'an Ssu-t'ung Liang found in Wei-shih Buddhism and in Neo-Confucian cosmology based on the I ching the inspiration for a view of the total cosmos as a mind-created ceaseless flux of existence, taking shifting phenomenal form through the

61 See Guy Alitto, Liang Shu-ming.
62 Quoted in Yen Chi-ch'eng, 'Shao-nien Chung-kuo tsung-chiao wen-t'i'.
63 Liang Shu-ming, Tung Hsi wen-hua chi ch'i che-hsueh (Eastern and Western civilizations and their philosophies).

mediation of *yin* and *yang* forces. However, biology, as transmitted through the vitalism of Henri Bergson, let Liang assert that the universe is literally organic, a living structure. Where for an earlier reform-generation philosopher like T'an life and death were metaphors for a finally undifferentiated continuum, in Liang Shu-ming's cosmic myth they were sharply polarized. Where T'an blended physics, ethics and ontology in his concept of interpenetrating ether, Liang, in reaction against the science-inspired naturalistic models of causation, divided 'causal relationships' (*yuan*) from true 'causes' (*yin*). The first, he said, could be understood in terms of material forces like history or environment, while the second must be seen as proceeding from spirit (*ching-shen*).

Formally speaking, Liang's vision of human destiny presented an 'evolution' of humanity from a 'Western'-style world civilization where the Will's animating direction is towards mastery of the external environment, to a 'Chinese'-style civilization in which the Will moves to adjust and harmonize with the world, coming finally to rest in an 'Indian' civilization of the Will's mystical self-abnegation and rejection of life itself. Formally also, each stage of the metahistorical movement of cosmic Will was seen as giving rise to typical historical patterns of culture. First was a Western culture characterized since the Greeks by philosophical scepticism and utilitarianism, leading to science, democracy and industrial capitalism as the social and material manifestations of a spirit of rationalist self-seeking. By contrast, Chinese civilization since Confucius had been spiritually shaped by the living force of *jen*, and so in its social arrangements had been tolerant and flexible, frugal and agrarian, cooperative and nourishing of human sentiments.

However, this 'evolutionary' scheme was presented more as a set of autonomous ideal alternatives than as a literal temporal sequence. Basically, he presented China's as the only kind of civilization which could be seen as in harmony with the true nature of the cosmos, as 'life' itself. The heart of Liang's message was a defence of Confucian metaphysical values because they alone recognize that the living cosmos cannot be grasped by fixed categories of rationalist analysis, but dictate instead human acceptance of the fluid, intuitive (*chih-chueh*) nature of experience. Only the Confucianist doctrines of *jen* and of the mean (*chung-yung*) allow human life to move with, rather than against, these cosmic rhythms, making possible a truly living life, free and unimpeded in the flow of the inner spirit's intuitions, emotions and joy.

In Liang Shu-ming as in the original reformers there survived a Confucian metaphysical pathos: a traditional rendering of the true self as weakly bounded, capable of extending and transforming the world through mind, and also subject to invasion and loss at the hands of bad external cosmic forces. In terms of moral psychology, the movements of authentic inner mind are recognizable because these alone are truly spontaneous and so free; as opposed to the external calculating mind of self-interest. However, superimposed upon this moral metaphysic, and shifting its direction and meaning, was a new polarization derived not from Chinese tradition, but from the Western philosophical clash of science and metaphysics. Liang identified scientific rationalism with the amoral rationalism of the calculating mind. The deterministic universe, that he presumed was dictated by Western scientific law, was linked to the externally threatening cosmic forces which obstruct the work of potentially transforming mind. In this way the fluid inner-outer dualisms of the older metaphysics were now associated with structurally distinct spheres: matter versus spirit, rationality versus intuition, intellect versus emotion. Such spirit, intuition, emotion cannot gradually infuse and transform their opposites; they can only, if possible, displace them. The implication of this, if it does not lead the philosopher to a radical monism, must be dualistic: if through intuitive forms of consciousness one may be in touch with the structures of the cosmos, it will be with those of a special transcendent kind, operating above other more mundane processes of nature and thought. Liang acknowledged this clearly in his later work, where he dropped all preoccupation with the idea of a metahistorical cosmic continuum for a philosophy of '*li-hsing*', a Mencian kind of intuitive reason. But the direction of his new Confucianist defence of faith was already evident in 1921 and 1922, and later 'new Confucianists' of the 1920s and 1930s, like Chang Chün-mai and Fung Yu-lan, followed the same path.

In this way by 1919 neo-traditionalists who had seen evolutionary theory as maintaining the links between core Confucian values and socio-political change were in disarray. Liang Ch'i-ch'ao had abandoned his vision of a global modernization process compatible with China's moral revival; K'ang Yu-wei lost his bid for the institutionalization of Confucian religion in a republic; functionalist arguments for Confucian ethics and 'national essence' arguments for classical language and canon were alike on the defensive. Confucianists, to be persuaded, sought a new path. Here Confucian truth was seen as metaphysically detached from history, validated finally only by direct intuitive experience, and able to speak to theological problems of meaning more than social problems of choice. The 'spiritual East' had become a country of the heart.

Science and metaphysics

Ironically it might be said that the development of neo-traditionalism in early twentieth-century China is a story of the gradual 'Westernization' of Confucian philosophy. By 1919, even as the various movements to 'save the faith', 'preserve the national essence' and speak in favour of the 'national character' expressed increasingly urgent anti-Western views, the conceptual language they used reflected the impact of the secularist and scientific intellectual revolutions brought by the West. However, by 1919 the West had also provided ammunition to counter the programmatic scientism and secularism of new culture radicals. It presented stunning examples of the failure of its own liberal democratic institutions: the farce that was the constitutional republic of China at home and the catastrophe of the First World War abroad. Liang Shu-ming's *Eastern and Western civilization* and Liang Ch'i-ch'ao's *Reflections*, both bore the stamp of these events. They were the opening statement of a response to the high tide of intellectual radicalism of that year which fully utilized the resources of the new neo-traditional dualistic framework.

This response culminated in a sprawling debate on the subject of 'science and metaphysics', sparked by Liang's associate, the philosopher Chang Chün-mai, which took place in 1923, eventually drawing in dozens of partisans of metaphysics, including Liang himself, Chang Tung-sun, Lin Tsai-p'ing and Fan Shou-k'ang.[64] In that debate defenders of Confucian spiritual truth condemned Darwinian evolutionism, the idea of an authoritative social science, physiological models of psychology, and all positivistic theories of knowledge. In his lead article setting off the controversy, Chang Chün-mai contrasted naturalistic knowledge, governed by science, with 'a point of view based on living experience' (*jen-sheng kuan*). This latter he summarized as 'subjective, intuitive, synthetic, freely willed and unique to the individual.'[65] Like Liang Shu-ming, Chang associated the sphere of 'life' with the inner spirit's experiential consciousness of value, and he saw it threatened by the bad cosmic forces of the 'deterministic universe'. However he opposed the fluid inner sphere to a fixed and static outer sphere of experience. Then, he went on explicitly to identify this inner spiritual consciousness with the idea of 'intuitive knowledge' (*liang-chih*) in the doctrine of mind of the Lu-Wang school of Neo-Confucianism.

The choice of Lu-Wang doctrine marked a shift of emphasis among

64 *K'o-hsueh yü jen-sheng kuan* (Science and philosophy of life), prefaces by Hu Shih and Ch'en Tu-hsiu.
65 Chang Chün-mai, 'Jen-sheng kuan' (Philosophy of life), in *K'o-hsueh yü jen-sheng kuan*.

Confucian reformers and neo-traditionalists – away from the fundamentalist 'five classics' or the speculative cosmologists of the early Sung, and towards a central focus on the classical Neo-Confucian school which had stressed a metaphysic based on moral experience. Not only was this school potentially more adaptable to the needs of the new neo-traditional philosophical dualism, but also its preoccupation with understanding moral experience or moral knowledge suggested linkages with the alien Western epistemological issues in which the debaters quickly became embroiled, once scientific models of verification had to be challenged on their own philosophical ground. However, in spite of substantial debts to Kant, Bergson, Rudolph Eucken and Hans Dreisch, Chang and his supporters were less adept epistemologists than they were emotionally eloquent metaphysicians. On the subject of the moral sentiments, although Chang and others spoke in passing of their aim through the development of inner life to create a spiritual culture, by and large they neglected metahistorical system building for attempts to characterize subjective moral experience.

The liberal and radical partisans of science in the debate were the ones who embraced evolutionism in its naturalistic form, and did so moreover with a utopian optimism and speculative exuberance reminiscent of the old K'ang Yu-wei. Hu Shih, with a bow to Dewey and Russell, offered a prose poem of praise to the 'naturalistic universe', where human life, however frail, has a purpose and will succeed, through the action of 'creative intelligence' in constructing an affluent and rational world culture. Wu Chih-hui, the veteran anarchist, even conjured up the entire Confucian-Taoist cosmological continuum of the reformers – that ceaseless flow of Change carrying mankind in its bosom into the mists of an evolutionary future. In these presentations, the original reform conception of science as a kind of true cosmology, reliably mapping the natural universe while offering technological liberation that empowers human beings to work successfully for moral and material utopia, remained virtually unaltered.

As a full dress polemic (*lun-chan*) among intelligentsia, the 'science and metaphysics' debate could not end without the public's verdict on winners and losers. When metaphysicians were declared to have reaped the worst of it, this reflected the size of their following but not necessarily its staying power. In fact the first to fade from China's intellectual centre stage were the scientists, whose evolutionary naturalism had lost out to Marxism by the late 1920s. Since neo-traditionalism now offered intellectuals a well-defined modern alternative to the secularization of Chinese values, it had persistent powers of renewal. As an attitude of cultural resistance to the West, it had substantial social appeal in the succeeding two decades.

SOCIAL UTOPIA AND THE BACKGROUND OF THE MAY FOURTH MOVEMENT

Reform and revolution

Neo-traditionalism as a reaction against reform modernization began in China with the 'national essence' movement which gained a following between 1904 and 1907. A clearcut revolutionary movement, aimed at the overthrow of the Manchu dynasty and the establishment of a republic, emerged clearly around the same time. As part of a single historical trend the two currents quite naturally mingled for a while, particularly through the persons of anti-Manchu classical scholars who shared with revolutionary radicals a common hatred of the present. One such, Chang Ping-lin, was even the chief defendant at a political trial in Shanghai in 1903 which is often identified as the opening cannonade in the revolutionary faction's campaign.

In 1905 the radicals achieved a consolidation of sorts with the formation of the T'ung-meng hui (Revolutionary Alliance) under Sun Yat-sen, which based itself on a student constituency, while seeking allies among Overseas Chinese, secret societies and new army units on the mainland. Between 1905 and 1908 the Revolutionary Alliance's Tokyo-based periodical, *Min pao*, enjoyed wide attention as the voice of the Chinese revolutionary movement, engaged in a dramatic polemic with the reformers, personified by Liang Ch'i-ch'ao's *Hsin-min ts'ung-pao* (Journal of the new people). Yet even as the Alliance claimed victory in this polemic, dissatisfied voices from its own left criticized its ideology of political revolution as offering no important social alternatives to constitutionalist reformism. These were China's anarchists, a radical fringe intellectually significant out of all proportion to their tiny numbers. All revolutionaries were identified by their faith in political revolution itself as a necessary catalyst of institutional change. But the anarchists went on beyond politics to define revolution as the realization of utopian social alternatives associated with the ideal of *ta-t'ung*, not just as the eventual gift of the evolutionary process but as the right of youth today. Anarchist social utopianism, therefore, survived the political Revolution of 1911 to inspire the iconoclastic spirit of rebellion among a republican 'new youth' at war with the old social system.

Since reformers and revolutionaries all had assumed that social change is integral to the evolutionary process, between 1903 and 1907 when the distinction between the two groups was first coming into general use, their differences were not always easy to discern. While literary war raged in the pages of *Min pao* and *Hsin-min ts'ung-pao*, the questions dividing the two sides often appeared more tactical than strategic. The basic issue was the ability of the Ch'ing court to advance the nation towards common goals of modernization and national independence.[66] On potentially significant social issues the reformers, led by Liang Ch'i-ch'ao, did oppose Sun Yat-sen's principle of 'land nationalization' (part of his *min-sheng chu-i*) as economically irrational and a device for stirring up 'barbarous' elements among the common people against the more prosperous 'enlightened'. But social policy received limited attention in a politically oriented controversy, while Sun and Liang accepted a common overview of social evolution: imperial China had been spared the 'feudal' class divisions of Europe, while contemporary China would need a mixed economy accommodating some forms of capitalist enterprise in order to develop, yet happily might build upon native traditions of social harmony in a transition to a cooperative mode of industrialism in the future.[67]

In its earliest stage of development between 1903 and 1907 then, the revolutionary outlook appeared rather as an exaggeration of reform views than a repudiation of them – no more than a call for the speeding up of history, casting the new Faustian personality in the guise of a revolutionary hero. Revolutionaries were simply the latest mouthpieces for the original reform utopianism. Revolution was not only Chinese, but harbinger of a new world order of science and democracy. Moral progress goes hand in hand with material development: in casting off the old society, revolutionaries are abandoning a stifling and outmoded autocracy in politics, and the social forms that inhibit the development of wealth and power, the realization of the self and the attainment of *ta-t'ung*. Such attainment depends upon the moral success of the revolutionary person, whose activities must be free of all taint of utilitarian self-interest if they are to complement the forces of progress. These were staples of revolutionary faith as earlier they had been of reform faith.

By 1905 what separated Liang Ch'i-ch'ao and the reform faction from a truly revolutionary mentality was their unwillingness to believe in revolution as an inevitably progressive movement, a necessary agent of history. As a reformer Liang had been among the first to introduce the newly awakened Chinese public opinion to the idea that modern revolution (*ko-ming*) involves institutional change, as opposed to the mere re-

---

66 For analysis of the debate see Michael Gasster, *Chinese intellectuals and the Revolution of 1911.*
67 Martin Bernal, *Chinese socialism to 1907.*

moval of Heaven's mandate (the original meaning of *ko-ming*) from ruling houses as in past Chinese crises of dynastic succession. Further, Western history showed the revolutions of 1776 and 1789 as historical facts, climactic flashpoints in the clash of forces of action and resistance which drive history forward. Nonetheless, after 1905 Liang's own evaluation was that the spirit of the contemporary age of 'national imperialism' mandated Chinese adherence to strong government – either 'enlightened despotism' or constitutional monarchy.[68] For Liang, such political arrangements were the price to be paid for Chinese backwardness. With such a conclusion the reformers' evaluation of the primary agents of change implicitly shifted from the political to the cultural and social realms. Political leaders do not order culture and society; rather these in their lava-like flow slowly mould politics along channels grooved to withstand radical shifts of direction. So Liang began to contrast 'social reform, which recognizes present social organization and corrects it' and 'social revolutionism . . . [which] cannot be practised; or, if it can, only after a millennium.'[69] However, this conservatism did not imply a rejection of political violence, which Liang did not in principle condemn. Violence was a tactic like any other, adaptable to gradualist ends. In this way Liang's disagreement with the revolutionaries over the nature of the times came close to the classic division between radical as stage-leaper and conservative as guardian of existing arrangements.

If radicals first broke with reformers over the speeding up of history, this acceleration not only led to a theoretical celebration of socio-political struggle, but also forced the social goals of that struggle into the foreground of radical thought. *Ta-t'ung*, telescoped in time, was instead extended in space, inspiring in the anarchists an internationalism that sometimes literally took the present 'streets of Paris, markets of London, skyscrapers of New York'[70] as the reification of progress. Where K'ang Yu-wei dreamed of a future world parliament, Chinese anarchists linked their working organizations with European radical parties, chiefly the anarcho-communists, and associated *ta-t'ung* directly with the theory and practice of Western revolutionary socialism. Looking at China, anarchists were specially sensitive to social conflicts there, and offered a sharpened social criticism both of the feudal past and of the reformist present. Finally the anarchists took over the call for personal liberation from the constraints of Confucian social roles – a call that had first come from

---

68 Liang Ch'i-ch'ao, 'K'ai-ming chuan-chih lun' (On enlightened despotism), *Hsin-min ts'ung-pao* (1906), reprinted in YPSWC, *ts'e* 6. 13–83.
69 Quoted in Bernal, *Chinese socialism*, 158–9.
70 Min [Ch'u Min-i], 'Wu-cheng-fu shuo' (On anarchism), *Hsin shih-chi*, 40 (28 March 1908) 158. Pagination according to 1966 Tokyo reprint.

K'ang Yu-wei and T'an Ssu-t'ung – and made it the focal point of their social programme. Where K'ang and T'an had finally subordinated social emancipation to political reform in the present and to spiritual liberation in the future, the anarchists judged all other issues by this one. For them the emancipation of the individual from the 'net' of ritualism was the test by which the revolution should ultimately be judged.

If the first hallmark of a distinctly radical outlook was a focus on individual liberation and on revolutionary 'moments' as evolution's catalyst, the second was a scientism which associated utopia with the naturalistic version of evolutionary cosmology. Taking up from the original reformers the faltering banners of progress, the anarchists and later the group around the *New Youth* magazine (*Hsin ch'ing-nien*) proudly inscribed these with secular mottoes affirming the material bases of consciousness, the biological nature of life forces, and the sociological foundations of causal mechanisms in history. Their real intellectual debts to Confucian humanism and Confucian metaphysics went largely unacknowledged, as they reduced the tradition to a reactionary system of social ethics.

However, radical scientism did not provide an unbroken path to utopia. Distressed like everyone else by republican disorder, radicals turned to sociological analyses of the historical forces deemed responsible for China's backwardness: feudal customs which were a drag on politics; feudal cultural values underlying feudal customs; the economics of agrarianism interdependent with both of these. But by embracing a scientific world-view, they were paradoxically less paralysed than neo-traditionalists were by the spectre of sociological determinism. Liang Ch'i-ch'ao's 1902 call for a 'new people' was revived by *New Youth* in 1915 as a summons to cultural revolution. This time a personality ideal of individual autonomy and scientific intelligence was consciously opposed to a 'metaphysical' outlook, yet still seen as a moral agent of progress. Secularism and evolutionary cosmology were harmonized in a radical vision of social utopia.

Early anarchism: revolutionary nihilism

Chinese were interested in Western anarchism as early as 1902, but the first phase of this interest was in keeping with the early radicals' focus on political revolution.[71] The term 'anarchism' (*wu-cheng-fu chu-i*) referred to the 'nihilists' of Europe's 'extreme revolutionary' party – an ideology noteworthy for its use of terrorism as a political tactic. Its immediate foreign

71 For discussion of the nihilists see Don C. Price, *Russia and the roots of the Chinese revolution*, ch. 7; and Bernal, *Chinese socialism*, 198–226.

inspiration was the conspiratorial fellowships of the Russian revolutionary movement, which had carried out such spectacular assassination attempts against Czarist officials in the late nineteenth century, leading up to the revolution of 1905. In China the native popular tradition of 'knight errantry' supplied complementary models of idealistic outlaws like the Liang mountain band, or of sworn brotherhoods who, like the heroes of the Peach Garden Oath, took up arms for justice in an age of chaos.

Nonetheless, for Chinese radicals the essential fascination of the terrorist act was as an instrument of progress. Revolutionary violence was imagined as a kind of 'reactive force' – the only response to autocracy strong enough to outmatch its heavy weight of oppression. In the words of one student pamphleteer, 'revolutions in all nations stem from uprisings and assassinations, but the impact of assassinations is even greater than that of uprisings. . . . As the power of heroes grows, the power of monarchs must come to an end.'[72] The terrorist could thus be called a radicalized compatriot of the new citizen – one who makes the utmost possible outward assertion of personal powers and so stands for the most emphatic rejection of the passive psychology of tradition and the historical stagnation it complemented. The young hotheads who attempted political assassinations beten 1904 and 1907 acted as if, by some supremely self-disregarding history-making act, they could become both instruments of progress and the conscious embodiment of its moral goal of public community.

The terrorist's path, then, was an individualistic one, but those who thought of following it were perhaps even more concerned than the ordinary new citizen to moralize their self-assertion into conformity with the metahistorical process it was designed to serve. Here the enormity of violence directed against others could be balanced only by the risks it presented to the self. In demanding absolute 'sincerity' of the revolutionary, the nihilists put to new uses the neo-Confucian concept that the sage's power must be linked to the flow of 'sincere mind' pervading the self unimpeded. If 'sincerity' both sharpened the assassin's knife and validated its use, the best proof of this in practice would be the spontaneous ego-abandonment of one whose risk of life is total.

This heavy reliance on internalized neo-Confucian moral norms, while necessary to legitimize the revolutionary vocation, was also perhaps partly responsible for the ineptitude of nihilist attempts. Chang Chi, Yang Tu-sheng, Liu Shih-fu and Wang Ching-wei were all prominent radicals implicated in assassination plots, none of which succeeded in killing its

72 Quoted in Price, *Russia and the roots of the Chinese revolution*, 148.

intended victim. The movement's true heroes and heroines were less killers than martyrs: Ch'iu Chin, the woman warrior who allowed herself to be captured and executed after being implicated in an abortive rising in Anhwei in 1907;[73] or Wu Yueh, the high-school student who was killed in 1905 by the bomb he was trying to throw at a group of imperial ministers at the Peking railway station.

Ch'iu Chin's message to the world was that an exemplary self-sacrificing act can change society; Wu Yueh saw his nihilist's mission in terms of evolutionary cosmology. His 'testament', which with a photo of his shattered body was published in a memorial issue of *Min pao*, explained his act as part of an 'age of assassinations' historically necessary to activate the forces of repression, and so move the pendulum of revolution's dialectical advance. Where Ch'iu Chin saw the task of revolution as society's moral regeneration and so chose martyrdom in the style of T'an Ssu-t'ung, Wu Yueh intended his act to embody a 'reactive force' of change equal to autocratic 'motive force' which had provoked it.[74] Both showed the nihilist's debt to traditional Chinese ideals of moral heroism, but their acts were also an effort to balance the claims of social duty and those of self assertion. They offered an early and extreme solution to the problems lying in wait for radical Chinese who sought to develop the individualist potential of the new personality ideals in defiance of Confucian ideals of group interdependence. Thus the nihilists, while more political than social revolutionaries, raised moral problems of individualism which the later anarchist social utopians would have to face.

The Paris group and the Tokyo group

Two widely separated yet intellectually kindred anarchist groups appeared among overseas Chinese students in Paris and in Tokyo at almost the same time, the summer of 1907. Each grew out of a preliminary study society organized under the stimulus of direct contact between Chinese and foreign radicals – French and Japanese – who advocated anarchocommunism, then at the height of its pre-1914 European influence. Each group published a journal, the work of a small coterie of students clustered around one or two older, more prestigious scholars. Though half a world apart, the Paris and Tokyo anarchists kept in touch with each

73 Mary Backus Rankin, 'The emergence of women at the end of the Ch'ing: the case of Ch'iu Chin', in Marjorie Wolf and Roxane Witke, eds. *Women in Chinese society*, 39–66.
74 Wu Yueh, 'Wu Yueh i-shu' (Wu Yueh's testament), *T'ien t'ao: Min-pao lin-shih tseng-k'an* (Demand of heaven; Min-pao special issue), 25 April 1907. See also Price, *Russia and the roots of the Chinese revolution*, 150–1.

other's work, as well as with the activities of the T'ung-meng hui, which they considered at least temporarily allied to their own cause.[75]

In the nineteenth-century West, anarchist utopians were of two classic types: those looking to liberation through technological progress, evoking utopia through scientistic fantasies of the future in the manner of Saint Simon; and those more like Charles Fourier who sought happiness in the unspoiled simplicity and intimate community of arcadia. The two Chinese groups included both these imaginative poles.

As their journal's name of *New Century* (*Hsin shih-chi*) implied, the Paris group believed themselves on the most advanced frontier of modernism, in touch with industrial civilization, and with its social and moral vanguard in the anarcho-communist movement led by Peter Kropotkin, Elisee Reclus and Errico Malatesta. Li Shih-tseng, a founder of the group, was a student of biology at the Pasteur Institute and a friend of Paul Reclus, Elisee's nephew. *New Century*'s senior editor, Wu Chih-hui, had some training in paleontology and preached Kropotkin's 'mutual aid' as a scientific sociology superior to Yen Fu's Spencerian evolutionism, which dictated the support of rationalism versus superstition in culture, and internationalism and pacifism in politics. As self-styled scientific materialists, the Paris group captured some of the prophetic *élan* of the 1898 visionaries of *ta-t'ung*. Wu Chih-hui showed particular exuberance as a technological utopian. Praising the inventive, tool-making faculty as the root of human genius, he called for 'saving the world through machines' in a spirit of inspired play – half cosmological fantasy, half science fiction:

At that time of the most broadly developed [scientific] learning, engineering for the convenience of communication will be preeminent, seeking to facilitate free travel under sea and in the air. Further, there will be [substitute] materials to reform the barbaric habit of meat eating; while the refinement of health and medicine will prolong our years of life. As to chemistry, physics and all the progressive natural sciences . . . at that time due to the simplification and unification of written language . . . a hundred new methods will make them easy to learn and easy to understand. When travelling through parks and forests we may sit at ease among the flowers and beneath the trees, chatting and drawing, conversing with strangers met along the road, and drawing our study materials from our knapsacks. When difficult problems are solved like this, adolescent youngsters will be able to master all today's total of scientific knowledge.[76]

However, unlike K'ang Yu-wei, Wu's scientism took the Westernized

75 English language treatments of these two groups may be found in Robert A. Scalapino and George Yu, *The Chinese anarchist movement*, and in Agnes Chan, 'The Chinese anarchists' (University of California, Berkeley, Ph.D. dissertation, 1977).
76 X yü X [Wu Chih-hui], 'T'an wu-cheng-fu chih hsien-t'ien' (Casual talk on anarchism), *Hsin shih-chi*, 49 (30 June 1908) 191–2.

form of setting rationalism against religion. Insisting quaintly that his
was a naturalistic view of the universe purged of metaphysical ghosts,
Wu refused to acknowledge that his vision of 'the process of evolutionary
purification' through 'benevolence'[77] owed any debt to Confucian spiritual
symbolism. Following his lead, *New Century* insisted upon the sacred-
secular polarization, and used it to condemn Confucianism as no more
than reactionary superstition. In place of the reform tendency to see
modern ethics as a steady development of germs incipient from ancient
times, *New Century*'s account of the process of ethical change often relied
upon images of purgation, whereby in the catharsis of a revolutionary
'moment' an originally good state of nature is rid of accumulated impuri-
ties.

By contrast with the scientistic *New Century*, *Natural Morality* (*T'ien-i*),
the anarchist journal published in Tokyo, reflected the humanistic bent
of its editors, the classical scholar Liu Shih-p'ei and his wife Ho Chen.[78]
A founding member of the National Essence Preservation Association
and scion of a famous scholarly family, Liu found that his anti-Manchu
opinions made a sojourn abroad advisable in 1907. In Tokyo an acquaint-
ance with the Japanese radicals Kōtoku Shūshui and Kita Ikki just as
they were abandoning reform socialism to become anarcho-syndicalists
led Liu to his two-year experiment with anarchism. Ho Chen, apparently
equally affected by the Tokyo milieu, formed a Society for the Recovery
of Women's Rights and, as formal editor and publisher of *Natural
Morality*, made radical feminism an integral part of the anarchist message.

Natural Morality, then, blended an iconoclastic attack upon existing
institutions with a curious cultural conservatism. Rather than asserting
that modern Europe is closest to *ta-t'ung*, Liu Shih-p'ei and Ho Chen
argued that 'Europe, America and Japan have only pseudo-civilizations.'[79]
They imagined a utopia of farmer-scholars dwelling in small autarchic
agrarian communities, where 'none shall depend upon another nor be
the servant of another', and all would live in a state of 'non-interference'
(*fang jen*).[80] Although *Natural Morality* published the first Chinese translation of *The communist manifesto*, Liu Shih-p'ei gave equal place as precursors of anarchism to the fourth century A.D. Taoist philosopher Pao

77 Lai kao [Wu Chih-hui], 'T'ui-kuang jen-shu i i shih-chieh kuan' (On curing the world
    through the extension of the benevolent arts), *Hsin shih-chi*, 37 (7 March 1908), 147–8.
78 *T'ien-i* (Natural morality), nos. 3–19 (10 July 1907–15 March 1908). Pagination according
    to the 1966 Tokyo reprint.
79 Liu Shih-p'ei and Ho Chen, 'Lun chung-tsu ko-ming yü wu-cheng-fu ko-ming chih te-
    shih' (On the strengths and weaknesses of racial revolution as opposed to anarchist rev-
    olution), *T'ien-i*, 6 (1 Sept. 1907) 135–44.
80 Liu Shih-p'ei, 'Jen-lei chün-li lun' (On the equalization of human powers), *ibid*. 3 (10 July
    1907) 24–36.

Ching-yen (Pao P'u-tzu), and to the Warring States agronomist Hsu Hsing. Pao P'u-tzu was the author of a classic tract denouncing all government, while Hsu Hsing rejected Mencius' division of society into functional hierarchies of mental and manual labourers, and insisted instead that all without exception till the soil. Where *New Century* chose Kropotkin as their Western sage, *Natural Morality* especially revered Tolstoy, publishing his 'letter to the Chinese', which praised traditional China as the freest society in the world, and warned against the oppressive consequences of constitutional government, industrialism and military power.[81]

Both as a traditionalist and as an anarchist, Liu Shih-p'ei hated the modernizing direction of the late Ch'ing reforms, which he saw as leading to a society infected with evils of the contemporary West: the growth of militarism and the coercive apparatus of the state, the creation of new and deeper class divisions, and of a commercialized culture stained by materialism and greed.[82] For Ho Chen modernization programmes to end female seclusion and to foster women's education offered the same false illusion of reform, denying women the possibility of true economic and personal independence, while furthering new libertarian forms of male sexual exploitation.[83] Faced with the possibility that the coming political revolution might not lead to the abolition of all government, Liu and Ho made unfavourable comparisons of China's future with its past. If *ta-t'ung* is closer when there are few status barriers of wealth and rank, then traditional China was both post-feudal and pre-capitalist; its vaunted political despotism had been a facade, whose structural weaknesses had been successfully manipulated by the people 'to cast off the sphere of human government and guard their formless liberty.'[84] Although Liu Shih-p'ei did not mistake this nostalgic characterization of historical China for his utopian ideal itself, his revolt from modernity both inspired his radical thought and also motivated him in deciding to abandon the revolutionary cause late in 1908.

Like the reformers of 1898, both groups of anarchists saw themselves as internationalists. However, by 1907 internationalism was less simply a development of the traditional East Asian cosmopolitan ideal of 'all under heaven' (*t'ien-hsia*) and more a contemporary protest against both the anti-Manchu and anti-imperialist nationalist movements which had

81 *T'ien-i*, 11–12 and 16–19 (30 Nov. 1907 and 15 March 1908).
82 Liu Shih-p'ei, 'Lun hsin-cheng wei ping-min chih-ken' (On why the new politics injures the people), *T'ien-i*, 8–10 (30 Oct. 1907) 193–203.
83 Chih Ta, 'Nan-tao nü-ch'ang chih Shang-hai' (Shanghai, where men are robbers and women are whores), *T'ien-i*, 5 (19 Aug. 1907) 95–8.
84 Liu Shih-p'ei and Ho Chen, 'Lun chung-tsu ko-ming', 138.

grown up so powerfully since the 1890s. The anarchist rejection of 'wealth and power' as national defence priorities in the face of imperialism, more than any other single issue, provoked criticism from readers of both magazines. To answer, the anarchists drew upon Kropotkin against Darwin and Spencer, arguing that analogies from the group life of animals show that human social evolution is propelled by intra-species cooperation rather than by strife.

Yet a contrasting implication of their internationalism was that national enmities obscure other, deeper social cleavages. Where reformers saw class conflict, if at all, as largely external to China, the anarchists repeatedly discussed contradictions between rich and poor, bureaucrats and the people, the educated and the ignorant, city dwellers and country folk, and males and females. These deep-rooted antagonisms marring the past and present social orders were caused, they said, by the 'coercive power' of inherited systems of political authority.

On the theory that every political system serves the power interests of some elite group, *New Century* argued that the common people of China should recognize that a constitutionalist government would become the instrument of the gentry, just as abroad such governments served the capitalists. Ho Chen attributed female subordination to women's economic dependence on men, and saw female productive labour as the most menial in a general hierarchy of labour exploitation. Liu Shih-p'ei criticized the social costs of the Ch'ing reform programme: it was taxing the peasants in order to create schools, security organizations and 'self-government' assemblies for the political aggrandizement of the local elite. Analyses like these showed a class consciousness adaptable to Marxist perspectives, and so paved the way for the populist mass movements of the May Fourth period.

Sensitivity to the reality of social conflict was a function of the anarchist passion for equality. Class and status hierarchies were seen as imposed by the 'boundaries' (*chieh*) of all social distinctions, whether race, nationality, wealth, occupation, place of residence, or sex. Many extreme features of anarchist utopian blueprints were in fact strategies to overcome the subtlest differentials in the life situation of different individual human beings. Both *Natural Morality* and *New Century* proposed the rotation of sexual partners and of places of residence. Liu Shih-p'ei, following Hsu Hsing's criticism of Mencius, saw all functional divisions of labour as sources of social hierarchy. Trying to adapt Hsu Hsing's remedy of individual economic self-sufficiency to the modern scene, he proposed that each person in the course of a lifetime follow all the basic occupations seriatim:

road construction at age 21, mining and lumbering at age 22, manufacturing between 23 and 30, and so on.[85]

However, since group differences stratify even more sharply than individual ones do, the anarchists also saw 'boundaries' blocking equality in the existence of all social groups – whether family, clan, tribe, province or nation. All these create bonds of privatized attachment which pit one group collectively against all others. European anarcho-communists constantly spoke of how voluntary associations would provide a healthy structure of social organization once governments had vanished. But the Chinese anarchists were more likely to imagine either the autarchy of small, self-sufficient communities or a unitary world – in either case a system which locates the autonomous individual in a single undifferentiated collectivity. Only this could preserve the public character of utopian institutions from the corruption of private group or individual interests. Therefore it is not surprising to find that in their more original writings – those not directly abstracted from a Western model – the anarchists focused on the emancipation of the individual from all group attachment, and in particular from the most primary attachment of the family.

In the final analysis, for every anarchist the restructuring of family life was the most fundamental issue. Formulations varied: most saw the family as the root political structure that undergirds all other systems of authority. Others stressed that the family's special personal immediacy made it the place in the social system where change must begin. Others located the moral root of selfishness in the particularistic ties families create. All made clear the family's centrality to their own experience, and therefore to any utopian vision of an alternative mode of human happiness.

In asking for revolution in interpersonal relations the anarchists in fact were following K'ang Yu-wei and T'an Ssu-t'ung who had predicted the eventual 'breaking of the nets' of Confucian ritualism. K'ang Yu-wei's earliest philosophical manuscripts, which predated his evolutionary system of *ta-t'ung* by at least a decade, stressed personal 'autonomy' (*tzu-chu*) as an essential dimension of human nature which could find outer expression only within the framework of egalitarian interpersonal relationships.[86] In the chapters on the family in the *Ta-t'ung shu*, for which these manuscripts were a primary source, K'ang never denied that filial piety imposed upon children an absolute moral obligation to repay parents for their nurture. But he saw this obligation as the source of such

---

85 Liu Shih-p'ei, 'Jen-lei chün-li lun', 27–8.
86 Li San-pao, 'K'ang Yu-wei's iconoclasm: interpretation and translation of his earliest writings, 1884–87', (University of California at Davis, Ph.D. dissertation, 1978).

deep psychic pain as could be eased only when 'men will have the happiness of having abolished family, without the suffering of leaving the family.'[87] Many key institutions of K'ang's utopia, such as its public nurseries, hospitals, schools and old age homes, were substitute structures where services historically performed by the family would be provided in a way that would bypass private dependence, and therefore leave only a generalized public sense of debt. 'Having neither given favors nor received favors, there will naturally be no ingratitude.'[88]

K'ang Yu-wei believed that hierarchy in interpersonal relations came from morally binding if psychologically intolerable asymmetrical relations of owing and being owed. This was the meaning behind his condemnation of the Confucian cardinal virtue of 'duty' (*i*) as the source of all inequality.[89] T'an Ssu-t'ung, on the other hand, described the Confucian family simply as a system of oppression where 'those above . . . control those below'.[90] Both saw the interdependence of high and low within the family as morally corrupt, but for K'ang that corruption was based on guilt, while for T'an its source was tyranny. Between K'ang's appeal, which was for freedom from the burdens of reciprocal obligation, and T'an's, which was for emancipation from the dependency of slavery, there was the potential difference between psychological rebellion and political revolt.

Although both these elements were present in anarchist attacks on the family system, the later utopians tended to follow T'an's political model of family relationships. They claimed that family relationships, rather than being based on legitimate moral feelings, were purely practical arrangements. 'The father wishes his son to be filial and exacts this by fear and force, and the son becomes a slave and beast. So filial devotion is the father's personal gain. . . . The son wishes the father's benevolence only for his own benefit, . . . and parents become "ox and horse to posterity". . . . So parental benevolence is the son's personal gain.'[91] Such, according to Li Shih-tseng, was the utilitarian essence of relations that Confucianists habitually glossed over with sayings about 'reciprocity' (*shu*) and 'human sentiments' (*jen-ch'ing*). Moreover, these utilitarian arrangements of mutual dependence and servitude were based on 'fear and force'. So the politicized model of familism as a crucible of oppression had to be matched by a call for revolt, and by an assertion of faith

87 *Ta-t'ung shu*, Thompson trans., 184.
88 *Ibid.* 186.
89 Li San-pao, 'K'ang Yu-wei's iconoclasm', ch. 2.
90 T'an Ssu-t'ung, *Ch'üan-chi*, 14.
91 Chen [Li Shih-tseng], 'San-kang ko-ming' (Revolution against the three bonds), *Hsin shih-chi* 11 (31 Aug. 1907) 42.

that this 'coercive power' (*ch'iang-ch'üan*) is external and artificially imposed. In this way the present Hobbesian society where strong and weak are locked in a mutually brutalizing struggle for supremacy was seen as only the prelude to a time when 'human sentiments' might flower once more in a world irradiated by 'natural morality' (*kung-tao chen-li*) alone.

Every utopian who saw the transformation of the family as the most basic social goal was driven by the logic of this concern to advocate some feminism. Some like Li Shih-tseng followed T'an Ssu-t'ung, who had considered women the weakest of all persons in the familistic hierarchy, and so the purest victims of the system. As male radicals they wrote of women's sufferings as surrogates for their own as youth before the elders. They lectured upon women's need for self-improvement to overcome dependency with a paternalism tempered by their own sense of only relative superiority. Others in thinking of the problems of women were more affected by K'ang Yu-wei's reasoning: if the family as a biological continuum is to be abolished, its greatest vulnerability is in the marriage relationship. Preparing women for autonomy through education and work became the essential prerequisite to the detachment of childbearing from the nexus of family relationships. For Liu Shih-p'ei and Ho Chen, however, utopia most fundamentally required the abolition of the division of labour, a theoretical position which made the equality of the sexes the last and most difficult of uniformities to obtain, limited as it must be by irreducible differences in biological function. For this reason Ho Chen argued that women who did not wish to be servants of men must choose to work for a communist society where alone all forms of servitude can be eliminated.[92]

However, male utopians and women radicals differed significantly on the role of sexuality in the transvaluation of family values. From K'ang. Yu-wei to the *New Century* group, a typical male utopian ideal was a world where men and women would enjoy free sexual relations unburdened by obligation. Intellectually this was a quite natural extension of their defence of spontaneous human sentiment against ritualized morality, and their suspicion that all kinds of exclusive personal relationships are inherently selfish. But Ho Chen, like most other Chinese women feminists, was more puritan than libertarian about sexuality – her ideal being an end to polygamy and to women's oppression as sexual 'playthings'.[93]

92 Ho Chen, 'Lun nü-tzu tang chih kung-ch'an chu-i' (On how women should know about communism), *T'ien-i*, 8–10 (30 Oct. 1907) 229–37.
93 Ho Chen, 'Nü-tzu fu-ch'ou lun' (On women's revenge), *T'ien-i*, 3 (10 July 1907) 7–17. See also Rankin, 'The emergence of women at the end of the Ch'ing'.

Anarchist rhetoric was at its most militant when the social institutions of marriage and the family were being analysed as political systems, based on raw power. However, this political model of family relations was difficult to sustain when anarchists dwelt at any length upon the subjective feelings of individuals as family members. In Chinese funeral ceremonies pious Confucian children ritually blame themselves for their parent's death. 'How can the children be to blame?' cried Li Shih-tseng,[94] intending to lay blame for false social attitudes on a corrupt environment. But in the family slaves are also dependants; and the parents' external power is matched by the child's docile acceptance of weakness and need. Belief in false Confucian values, the 'superstition' that chains an individual to accept dependency became, then, an internal failure of the self, to be overcome by moral effort. In this way the anarchists' desire to revolutionize the Confucian family system led them to reaffirm the earlier reform belief in the human being's responsibility as a moral agent in the furtherance of progress.

Yet within this new individualist framework, the question of the nature of moral success posed ambiguities earlier reformers had not faced. 'Without autonomy (*tu-li*), one naturally loses the power of liberty (*tzu-yu*); without liberty one naturally loses the power of equality (*p'ing-teng*),'[95] said Liu Shih-p'ei. The Western neologism 'liberty', used here to refer to formal civil rights in a political community, is merely a link in the natural process which begins with the individual's inner self-definition (autonomy) and ends with his or her ideal experience of human relationships (equality). Yet in this sense the enemies of autonomy and equality are not the impersonal structures of the state, which threaten liberty, but those other individuals who in actual life are the usual source of the most intimate human ties. In opposing autonomy and equality to kinship, the anarchists suggested not a political ideal of the free citizen, but a moral ideal of the self-sufficient person. Its realization carried new psychic costs: rejection of the network of relationships which were both conventionally venerated and a primary source of security and gratification. The struggle for autonomy became not a straightforward search for personal liberation, but an arduous self-discipline where there was a heavy burden of responsibility for self and all too easily also a burden of guilt.

The demand for individual liberation from the constraints of Confucian ritualism was at the heart of what may be called the existential liberalism of the reform generation. The attack on the family swelled this movement, but it also showed the psychic costs of individualism when

94 Li Shih-tseng, 'San-kang ko-ming', 41–2.
95 Liu Shih-p'ei, 'Jen-lei chün-li lun', 25.

it was defined as detachment from all social relationships. Such detachment could be imagined as leading to happiness only on a mystical level where the individual as a discrete atom in equal relations with others, dissolves into the undifferentiated.

Individual liberation, then, was finally imagined in the utopian language of K'ang and T'an's evolutionary cosmology: a process whereby a whole complex system of 'boundaries' (*chieh*) would be broken. In New Text Confucianism, the idea of boundaries had evoked geographical, cultural and ethnic obstacles to unified human fraternity. Buddhist-Taoist metaphysics saw boundaries as the artificial grid of things imposed upon an undifferentiated continuum of reality; while Neo-Confucian tradition gave the concept a moral basis, stressing the multiple layers dividing the inner moral mind and bad external forces of the world – the permeable membranes, as it were, which form the battleground of moral effort.

So for the anarchists the symbolism of boundaries dissolved became a way of suggesting a possible human happiness transcending social utopia. *New Century* discussions of utopian liberation commonly drifted into metaphysical reflection on a self-forgetting which can lead to harmony with the unbounded cosmic flux:

When people lack the mind that distinguishes this from that, all living things in the world are equal. There is no means for creatures to struggle, no basis for nature to select . . . in mutual succour and mutual aid all trace a path towards peace. Such love is not born of feelings, but is the extreme of non-feeling.[96]

This is how Wu Chih-hui attempted to reconcile the humanly involving love of Christians (and Confucians) with the metaphysical detachment of the Buddhist-Taoist sage.

Even in his discussions of technology and utopia, Wu Chih-hui, like K'ang Yu-wei before him, described science's greatest gifts as fostering a life like Chuang-tzu's 'free and easy wandering', where everywhere becomes nowhere. Freed by science from laborious work and disease, the men and women in utopia are above all students and travellers. In study the goal is universal knowledge – an omnivorous grasping of the world in imagination. In travel, there are movable dwellings, inns and hostels, great ships, trains, balloons and sea diving bells, even mechanical conveyor belts between settlements. Such picturesque fantasies sketched out a style of living in which the loving permeability of one's effortless communication with the whole world implies also its opposite: detachment from any particular ties in that world.

96 Wu Chih-hui, 'T'ui-kuang jen-shu', 148.

If *New Century* writers symbolically represented liberation of the self as the individual's merging with the whole, Liu Shih-p'ei in *Natural Morality* imagined self-liberation through the play of cosmic forces leading humanity from autonomy to equality. The moral energies of self-assertion present in each individual would eventually be balanced constantly by exactly equivalent energies in all others, making the stasis of utopia dependent upon the fine tuning of a 'uniform distribution of power' (*chün li*). But in both cases the process of liberation begins with the self-assertion of the individual seeking to realize emancipation and ends with the nullification of social individuality.

A basic philosophical conflict between Confucianism and Taoism had revolved around the irreconcilability of Taoist individualist mystical detachment and Confucian humanistic social involvement. In refusing to choose between these alternatives the anarchists were saying that there should not be any deep-rooted contradictions between the psyche's search for spiritual enlightenment and its participation in the work of saving society. In this way, in spite of their affinity for Taoist-style egalitarian criticism of Confucian social ethics, the anarchists opted for a morally affirmative metaphysics more in harmony with Confucian myths of cosmic-human interdependence. Still, their denial that moral feelings can truly be expressed in particular human relationships allowed a Taoist spirit of detachment to infuse their discussion of social utopia. In this situation they could resolve the conflict between individual freedom and social community only by presenting the social equality (*p'ing*) of interrelated persons as an illusionary reflection of the cosmological equality (*p'ing*) of an undifferentiated ego-dissolving continuum of experience.

The social utopians had raised, if they did not answer, the question of whether individual emancipation ought to be considered an ultimate end, in light of a morality detached from all consideration of social involvement. When they were not engaged in mystical leaps, most social utopians drew back from this brink; the anarchists insisted that the realization of equality establishes public social relationships characterized by mutual aid. But such claims, tested in experience by those who followed the summons to struggle against the political authority of elders, left the youth of the early republican family revolution to consider in personal terms the rewards and the costs of autonomy. Though most New Youth later hastened as far as they could to justify their personal rebellion as furthering progress, by 1919 a few hardy souls were taking the stand that the only alternative to ritual culture is the unchecked assertion of a socially amoral self. Some were liberal academic scholars, like the historian Fu

Ssu-nien who chose personal 'spontaneity' over social 'obligation' as a private right.[97] Some were literary romantics, like the bohemians of the Creation Society, who pronounced their art to be a form of pure self-expression, requiring no social justification beyond its own beauty and interest. Even Lu Hsun told the New Youth that the 'way of the viper' was preferable to that of the sage, and proposed as a new culture hero the Nietzschian 'superman'.[98] All these rebels were expressing a desire to root action in a subjectivity that is a law unto itself, even if it brands its possessors with the status of madmen. In this way the anarchist call for personal emancipation contained the potential for a kind of pure individualism, but one which its followers themselves saw as demonic. Under the circumstances it is not surprising that few Chinese followed the utopian individualist path to the end.

In their commitment to social equality, which underlay both their call for the emancipation of the individual and their critique of familism, the anarchists broke new ground in Chinese social thought. Nonetheless this radical content was largely presented within the theoretical framework of reform evolutionary cosmology. The anarchists' emphasis upon the catalytic agency of revolutionary 'moments' was easily incorporated within an overall view of nature as the scientifically 'material', morally charged and dynamically developing cosmos of the reformers. Their reductionistic definition of Confucianism as a system of reactionary social practice simply left them with an unacknowledged debt to the Confucian metaphysical symbolism pervading their models of a slowly humanizing universe. Ch'u Min-i's formulation of these themes in New Century was particularly striking.[99] He saw a struggle between 'coercive power' and moral enlightenment pervading the world, in which the forces of creation and destruction acting on matter are interdependent, generating the 'negative power of progress' or 'revolution' hand in hand with the 'positive power of progress' or 'education'.[100] In this way, Ch'u said, the cosmos would progress in an open-ended cumulative fashion from the condition of 'existence' (yu) to one of 'non-existence' (wu): the first qualitatively enforced, seeming, ritualistic, false; the second spontaneous, genuine, benevolent, true. Belief in Kropotkin's mutual aid reinforced

97 David Reynolds, 'Iconoclasm, activism and scholarship: the tension between "spontaneity" and "obligation" in the thought of Fu Ssu-nien', paper presented at the Regional Seminar on Confucian Studies, University of California, Berkeley, 4 June 1976.
98 Lu Hsun, 'Wen-hua p'ien-chih lun' (On the pendulum movement of culture), and 'Mo-lo shih li shuo' (On the power of Mara poetry), in Fen (Graves). First published in Honan (Honan magazine), 1907.
99 Min [Ch'u Min-i], 'Wu-cheng-fu shuo' (On anarchism), Hsin shih-chi, 31–48 (21 Jan.–16 May 1908).
100 Ibid. 158.

Mencian teachings on human nature to produce in Ch'u an extravagant moral optimism that today a 'truly human world' is coming into being, and a faith in the prophetic role of those with a morally pure 'discerning mind' who alone can grasp the idea of revolution in its totality.

As a secularist scientific philosophy, the ideas of a Ch'u Min-i or a Wu Chih-hui were imperfect at best, distinguishable from reform versions of scientism only in the explicit claims that the sacred and the secular belong to distinct incompatible spheres of meaning. Their resulting commitment to scientific models of truth, derived as it was from alien Western controversies opposing science against religion, became an anarchist dogma without having much impact upon their actual cosmological thought. Rather, the latter continued along the reform path in its metaphysical assumptions of cosmic-human interdependence.

As theorists of revolution the anarchists followed T'an Ssu-t'ung and Liang Ch'i-ch'ao in developing the most dialectical of reform descriptions of the forces of change. Here, however, anarchist versions of evolutionary cosmology were linked to the significantly new elements in their social thought. Believing that human society is basically divided between oppressed and oppressing social groups, anarchists envisioned progress through the clash of these rather than simply via the harmonious spread of enlightenment from advanced to backward sections of the human community. Although they saw the gradualist processes of education and revolutionary flashpoints as interdependent in the historical process, they sought to educate oppressed groups, making the educative function a dialectical one: generator of resistance, not collaboration. In these ways anarchists did not simply develop a socially utopian vision of the future, but contributed to a socially revolutionary model of the political process.

Post-revolutionary anarchism and socialism

The founding of the republic in 1911 opened the way both for the free dissemination of anarchist ideas on the Chinese mainland and for new experiments in radical organization. Even in pre-revolutionary exile, the Paris and Tokyo groups had downgraded the sphere of politics but had looked upon agitational activities as education for social revolution. At the time of the 1911 Revolution, anarchists drew upon European radical experience to advocate all sorts of activities – from study societies to rallies, clubs, assassinations, strikes and tax boycotts – as propaganda, designed to raise Chinese public consciousness to the level of the European *avant-garde*. In this way China could be ready for the world-wide 'age of revolution' which they expected would be launched in Europe some time in the next generation.

Two groups led the way in propagandizing activity as soon as the old government had been overthrown. The first was the Conscience Society (Hsin she) of Liu Shih-fu, the second, Chiang K'ang-hu's Chinese Socialist Party (Chung-kuo she-hui tang).[101] Liu Shih-fu had been politically awakened in 1907 by reading *New Century* while serving a prison term in Canton for an anarchist assassination attempt, an ordeal which resulted in his declaring himself a disciple of Kropotkin. In February 1912, gathered with a few close followers on a retreat at the Buddhist White Cloud monastery near Hangchow, he dedicated his life to the propagation of the anarchist cause, and the Conscience Society was born. Chiang K'ang-hu had been exposed to anarchism and socialism on travels to Japan and Europe in 1907 and again in 1909, which had brought him into contact both with the Tokyo radicals and with the Paris *New Century* group. Back in China as administrator of several schools for women's education, he began to make speeches advocating socialism for China in the summer of 1911, and immediately took advantage of the revolution to organize a network of educational clubs for the dissemination of his ideas.

Both these movements saw their key programme as based on the abolition of the family and the creation of universal public institutions in its place, and on universal equal education. Together these were expected to end all class division and status hierarchies, and create a society of socially uniform individuals. Nonetheless, Chiang and Liu Shih-fu soon became adversaries, predictably reflecting their respective alliances with the European socialist Second International and with the International Anarchist Congress.

In the ensuing debate between them over the proper meaning of 'socialism', Liu Shih-fu objected both to Chiang K'ang-hu's acceptance of a role for state power in socialist society, and his tolerance of a degree of private enterprise in a socialist economy. With a purity of vision uncompromised by any utilitarian considerations, Liu Shih-fu projected a harmonious and atemporal total communism, where consumer as well as producer goods would be publicly owned, where money would be abolished and work rendered easy and enjoyable through the progress of science. Moreover, he insisted that anarcho-communism, based on the

101 For Liu Ssu-fu, in addition to Chan, 'Chinese anarchists', see also Edward Krebs, 'Liu Ssu-fu and Chinese anarchism 1905–15', (University of Washington, Ph.D. dissertation, 1977). For a discussion of Chiang and his party see Martin Bernal, 'Chinese socialism before 1913', in Jack Gray, ed. *Modern China's search for a political form*, 89–95; and Frederic Wakeman, *History and will: philosophical perspectives on Mao Tse-tung's thought*, 207–10.

principles of mutual aid innate in human nature, had nothing in common with any individualist interpretation of anarchism.[102]

Chiang K'ang-hu, on the other hand, remained a nationalist and a Darwinian of the Spencerian mould, believing that economic progress depends upon the utilization of human beings' natural competitive instincts in productive activities. As the means for achieving human equality, he advocated the abolition of the family, a transformation which he said centrally depended upon the complete emancipation of women; and the abolition of inherited wealth, which he thought would foster healthy economic competition and specialization of labour while ensuring that individuals nurtured by public institutions would repay these on their death.[103] Among Western social thinkers Chiang was particularly attracted by the ideas of August Bebel in *Women and socialism*, and by the Scottish Presbyterian evolutionary socialist, Thomas Kirkup, whose *History of socialism* he translated into Chinese.

Organizational as well as doctrinal differences separated the two groups. An energetic promoter, Chiang K'ang-hu saw his network of socialist clubs as preparatory to the organization of a political party. Although his claim that by 1913 the Chinese Socialist Party had 400,000 members and 400 branches was doubtless exaggerated, it reflected his hope to achieve a mass base. It also explains the Peking government proscription which resulted in his retirement to the United States late in 1913 and the movement's immediate decline thereafter.[104] Liu Shih-fu's Conscience Society, on the other hand, was built on close-knit, organic principles whose very personalism and intimacy made its suppression more difficult. It was the most devoted of a number of similar anarchist-inspired fellowships established right after the revolution when the symbolism of renewal inherent in that event suggested innovations in living to further the ideals of *ta-t'ung* in social practice. The dream of establishing an experimental rural community, harboured by Liu Shih-fu, Chang Chi and others, was never realized by any of these associations. However, the Conscience Society followed a pattern of collective self-help pioneered by the *New Century* group in Paris: members supported themselves out of a common fund raised in part from contributions and group-owned

102 Shang-hai wu-cheng-fu chu-i kung-ch'an t'ung-chih she kung-pu [Shih Fu], 'Wu-cheng-fu kung-ch'an-tang chih mu-ti yü shou-tuan' (Goals and methods of the anarchist-communist party), *Min-sheng* (Voice of the people), 19 (18 July 1914) (reprint edn by Lung-men shu-tien, Hong Kong, 1967), 222–225.

103 Chiang K'ang-hu, *Hung-shui chi: Chiang K'ang-hu san-shih sui i-ch'ien tso* (Flood tide: collection of writings by Chiang K'ang-hu before the age of thirty).

104 Bernal, 'Chinese socialism before 1907', 91.

productive enterprise, such as a restaurant or print shop, and shared a common residence.

More important than these tentative experiments in communal living, the association of utopia with the ideal of a morally perfected self bore fruit in ascetic and self-denying codes of personal conduct. A pledge to uphold the code in fact constituted the normal ritual establishing one's membership in an anarchist fellowship. The Conscience Society code showed a classic religious association of evil with pollution in its strictures against alcohol, tobacco and meat-eating; specifically anarchist goals were reflected in the rules against contracting a marriage, affiliating with a religion, or holding any kind of political office; while the emancipated personality ideals of autonomy and equality dictated prohibitions against employing servants or riding in rickshaws or sedan chairs. Other anarchist fellowships had more lenient codes than the Conscience Society. The largest, the Society to Advance Morality (*Chin-te hui*), founded in 1912 by the original *New Century* leadership, even allowed for degrees of membership according to the level of personal commitment. Such concessions to human weakness and the demands of existing social institutions were perhaps inevitable.

The Conscience Society's decline after 1915 was largely due to external events: Liu Shih-fu's premature death from tuberculosis that year, shortly after the group had been rocked by the outbreak of the First World War, which fatally tested the internationalist principles of the European parent organization led by Kropotkin. However, between 1912 and 1915, the Society published four anthologies of selections from *New Century*, a number of pamphlets and broadsheets, and a journal, *Min sheng* (Voice of the People), printed in Chinese and Esperanto;[105] and it had spawned affiliates in several cities. It was claimed that as late as 1919 loose successors of the Conscience Society were active in Peking, Shanghai, Nanking, Tientsin and in the province of Shansi, bearing such names as The Collective (Ch'ün she), Society of Anarchist Comrades (Wu-cheng-fu chu-i t'ung-chih she), Truth Society (Shih she), and Equality Society (P'ing-she).[106] The original *New Century* group also continued to be active after 1915. Although its leaders Li Shih-tseng and Wu Chih-hui remained based in Europe, it had a significant impact upon the Chinese student movement through its sponsorship of a series of innovative work-study programmes in France, where wartime mobilization had created a

---

105 *Min sheng* (Voice of the people) 1–33 (20 Aug. 1913–15 June 1921).
106 Yang Ch'üan, 'Chung-kuo chin san-shih nien lai chih she-hui kai-tsao ssu-hsiang' (Social reform thought in China in the last thirty years), *Tung-fang tsa-chih*, 21. 17 (10 Sept. 1924) 53.

labour shortage. By this means between 1912 and 1920 several hundred Chinese students pooled earnings to support themselves and their fellows while learning abroad.

After 1912 these groups of revolutionary socialists contributed to Chinese radicalism more through educational propaganda and social experiment than through doctrinal innovation. Compared with their predecessors, the post 1911 groups showed a heightened concern with social practice which stimulated closer attention to the organizational work of their European prototypes. This in turn produced, in addition to the native style anarchist fellowships, efforts at political party-building and popular education, and in Shanghai, attempts to organize urban workers. Expressions of sympathy for anarchism as the modern doctrine of *ta-t'ung* were commonplace among Chinese of radical temper in the years between the revolution and the May Fourth movement. After 1917 this sympathy extended to Peking University under the presidency of Ts'ai Yuan-p'ei, who encouraged free thought, revival of the Advance Morality Society and work-study programmes on the *New Century* model. A substantial number of the founding members of the Chinese Communist Party, including Mao Tse-tung, recalled that it was anarchism which had attracted them politically before their conversion to Marxism-Leninism after 1920. The very word 'communism' (*kung-ch'an chu-i*) was generally understood as an anarchist, not a Marxist term down to this time.[107]

Thus, before 1919 the Western socialist tradition was known to China chiefly in anarchist rather than Marxist guise. This exposure made Chinese familiar with the broad outlines of the history of the socialist movement in Europe and America, but with only a tiny corpus of original socialist literature, and that overwhelmingly from Kropotkin and his associates. Marxism, where it had been discussed in passing by reformers and revolutionaries alike before 1917, was associated with the European social democratic and labour movements in a context of parliamentary democracy and industrial production alien to the Chinese environment. The Chinese social-utopian stress on the revolution in family relationships made an un-Marxist claim for the transformation of personal life as a cause, rather than merely an effect, of other changes in the revolutionary process. Still, the anarchist exposure in some ways prepared Chinese for orthodox Marxism-Leninism later on. It acquainted people with a Marxist-style periodization of history to compete with the Spencerian one; and also with a dialectical view of change operating through a revolutionary process. It fostered a naïve but intensely felt class conscious-

107 Chow, *The May Fourth movement*, pp. 97–8, 224–5.

ness and a sympathetic concern for the common people as the agents of progress. In addition, certain persistent strands in later Chinese communist theory and practice may be better understood in light of the indigenous radical vision that the Chinese social utopians mobilized and developed. These include the Maoists' stress on cultural remoulding and rectification of personality as autonomous sources of revolutionary change; their dislike of urban-industrial economic rationalization in favour of rural-communal social mobilization; their suspicion that functional 'boundaries' create class differences; their cult of 'self-reliance'; and last but not least their need to rely on moralized human energy as the dynamo of change, which has produced both moments of utopian effort to leap forward into the millennium and recurrent haunting fears of historical reversal.

New youth

In September 1915 a magazine, New Youth (Hsin ch'ing-nien), was founded in Shanghai under the editorship of Ch'en Tu-hsiu, a well-known radical and professor of the humanities.[108] This publication, which officially inaugurated China's New Culture movement, drew together ideas which formed the third stage of thinking about evolutionary cosmology since the original reform movement of the 1890s. The original reformers had set forth the new progress-oriented world view between 1895 and 1905. The anarchists had then developed the reform utopian vision to stress revolutionary struggle to destroy social inequality and Confucian ritualism as the means to personal happiness and social utopia. Writers in New Youth described evolution in naturalistic scientific language, devoid of Confucian moral meaning. But at the same time they saw the energies of 'youth' itself propelling the process of change, infusing the universe with a new kind of moral optimism based on vitalist biology.

However, New Youth did not begin in 1915 with a straightforward affirmation of this optimistic philosophy of progress. Rather at first it was a vehicle for radical intellectuals anxious to counteract what they saw as retrogressive forces in politics and culture which were growing stronger as the experiment in republicanism faltered under the presidency of Yuan Shih-k'ai, and then fell hostage to contending militarists after his death. Still, the venture that opened as a defensive counter-thrust by beleaguered radical modernists gained momentum as large numbers of actual 'new youth', educated in the post-imperial environment, gathered

---

108 Hsin ch'ing-nien (New youth), Sept. 1915–July 1926, reprint edn in 14 vols. (Tokyo, 1962).

behind *New Youth*'s slogans advocating science, democracy, literary revolution, and the revolt of youth and women. By 1919 the militancy of the student movement and the apparent rout of conservatives from academic leadership at Peking and other universities gave grounds for belief that the New Culture was becoming a reality. The student-led May Fourth demonstrations of that year against foreign imperialism and the warlord government in Peking suggested the complementary appearance at last of a mobilized and awakened people as a progressive political force. This quickening of change at home had counterparts abroad in the end of the First World War, and above all in the Russian Revolution. By 1920 Ch'en Tu-hsiu and his close collaborator on *New Youth*, the philosopher and Peking University librarian Li Ta-chao, announced their conversions to Marxism and turned the magazine into a vehicle for the new Chinese communist movement. Utopian perspectives on Chinese and world history were now rekindled in a new ideology, and ground was laid for the Chinese communist revolution itself to give a retrospective imprimatur to the idea that the New Youth movement had in fact marked another great transformation of the times.

At *New Youth*'s inception in September 1915, Ch'en Tu-hsiu and his associates largely shared the pessimism about evolution that oppressed emerging neo-traditionalists and constitutionalists in the early years of the republic. Far from conjuring up anarchist-style ideal alternatives by leaps of pure imagination, *New Youth* was soberly preoccupied with the problem of China's cultural backwardness, and the dangers this posed to contemporary politics. Sharing the by then common sociological perspective on evolution, they reasoned that social custom, ethics and national psychology exercise a determinative influence upon political change. Like Liang Ch'i-ch'ao and other analysts of the 'national character', they were concerned how to overcome maladaptive disjunctions between parts of the social organism. So *New Youth*'s campaign against cultural backwardness was presented first of all instrumentally, as the way to combat a monarchic restoration in politics. Wu Yu, the magazine's best-known critic of familism, argued that China's historic inability to escape despotism was due to patriarchal mores, while Ch'en Tu-hsiu himself, in a running polemic with K'ang Yu-wei, lodged similar arguments against Confucian ethics as the tool of conservative political control under Yuan Shih-k'ai's dictatorship.[109]

However, this instrumentalist argument, which by 1915 was central

109 Siu-tong E. Kwok, 'The two faces of Confucianism: a comparative study of anti-restorationism of the 1910s and 1970s', paper presented to the Regional Seminar in Confucian Studies, University of California, Berkeley, 4 June 1976.

to the moderates' case for cultural reform, played only a secondary role in Ch'en Tu-hsiu's thinking. His point of departure was a new faith in science, not only in the reform manner as a form of natural philosophy, but as a positivistic method of verification controlling standards of truth about nature and society. Liang Ch'i-ch'ao in defending the 'national character' advocated cultural adaptation within the parameters of what he saw as Confucian ideals of moral personality, and viewed the naturalistic interpretation of evolution with increasing unhappiness. But Ch'en took science as a verification procedure which mandates accepting the naturalistic universe as both fact and value. Unlike most of the anarchists, who still saw consciousness as linked to an authentic 'mind' reflecting a spiritual dimension of experience, Ch'en Tu-hsiu spoke of consciousness as based on physiological psychology and imagined human beings as purely biological and social organisms. This denial that historical evolution is linked to cosmological process meant that Ch'en Tu-hsiu represented the extreme of his generation in secularism and detachment from the sage personality ideal. In consequence he and *New Youth* had the reputation of standing for 'total Westernization'.[110]

Of course Ch'en Tu-hsiu's scientistic world view was not as totally uprooted from inherited beliefs and mores as he would have had his audience believe. True, he was among the first to present his ideas in a vernacular vocabulary almost free of traditional philosophical concepts, thus avoiding the frequent reform and anarchist tactic of presenting traditional metaphysical beliefs in new rationalistic dress. Still, the personality ideal he offered to youth in 1915, for all its heightened secularism, remained in many ways a direct descendant of the 'new citizen' of 1902.

The reformers' 'new citizen' had been asked to be progress-oriented, self-assertive, dynamic and independent. K'ang Yu-wei had posited a cosmic base for the independent self, in that each individual partakes of the primordial essence of the universe. T'an Ssu-t'ung had made struggle an experiential dimension of moral personality, and Liang Ch'i-ch'ao had said that the striving individual as an agent of progress embodies the morality of its goals in the literal sense that combativeness, seen as refusal to yield to others' superior power, must contribute to the moral end of equality. Such Social Darwinism from the perspective of the weak reconciled the interests of the individual and the collective with relative ease, and allowed pragmatic, productive effort to claim moral value.

In Ch'en Tu-hsiu's lead essay, 'A call to youth', the animating energy in the human personality was seen as youth itself, not as a function of

110 For Ch'en Tu-hsiu's scientism see D. W. Y. Kwok, *Scientism in Chinese thought 1900–1950*, 59–81.

years but as the psychic attribute that makes individuals truly self-aware, and so capable of the powers of renewal that serve progress. 'Youth is like early spring, like the rising sun, like trees and grass in bud, like a newly sharpened blade!'[111] In this way naturalistic metaphors replaced cosmological ones as the thematic framework for a summons to adopt the attitudes of a modern person. 'Be progressive, not conservative'; 'Be aggressive, not retiring'; 'Be cosmopolitan, not isolationist'; these injunctions reflected basic goals of cultural renovation since the 1890s. 'Be autonomous, not servile' incorporated the social-utopian demand for radical emancipation from ritual personal relationships, but also in Ch'en's interpretation suggested the use of scientific reason as the criterion for independent thought and action. Here and in his call to 'Be practical, not formalistic,' and to 'Be scientific, not speculative,' Ch'en developed the pragmatic, task-oriented potential of the original 'new citizen' ideal in the light of his own advocacy of experimental models of verification and social decision-making.

Therefore, in accounts of the emancipated individual in *New Youth*, this scientistic secularism fostered a further shift towards defining self-realization through external social practice and away from the earlier model of personal liberation conceived of as an aspect of moral self-actualization. The individualist virtues – independence, self-reliance – were not associated in social-utopian style with a radical and essentially mystical emancipation from all entangling social relationships. Instead they suited a European model family system based upon free choice of marriage partner, the nuclear family and the economic independence of all adults. More important, these virtues were seen as functionally related to economic productivity: 'The pulse of modern life is economic and the basic principle of economic production is individual independence. . . . The independent individual in ethics and private property in economics bear witness to each other: this is unassailable. Social mores and material culture have advanced greatly because of it.'[112]

The same belief in the functional interrelationship of psychological attitudes and social consequences informed *New Youth* discussions of the problem of suicide, which had fascinated so many Chinese of the reform generation as they sought to understand and internalize new personality ideals. Nihilists earlier had condemned 'escapist suicide' in favour of 'suicidal assassination' on the grounds that only the second 'not only

111 Ch'en Tu-hsiu, 'Ching-kao ch'ing-nien' (A call to youth), *Hsin ch'ing-nien*, 1. 1 (September 1915).
112 Ch'en Tu-hsiu, 'K'ung-tzu chih tao yü hsien-tai sheng-huo' (Confucianism and modern life), *Hsin ch'ing-nien*, 2. 4 (1 Dec. 1916) 297.

saves oneself but also improves the world'.[113] When supporters of the New Youth movement denied the act of suicide its traditionally recognized message of moral affirmation or protest, their own withdrawal of the power to be moved in fact altered suicide's effective social meaning. But their intent was also to go beyond the nihilists' simple rejection of passivity in order to question the validity of any act based upon a Confucian moral ideal of exemplary inner self-abnegation, as well as the Confucian presumption of its resonance in a cosmic continuum extending beyond mortality. In the light of these beliefs, T'an Ssu-t'ung had chosen martyrdom, but 20 years later in the secular world of *New Youth*, the choice of death however nobly intended was seen simply as an evasion of social responsibility: 'Only the living can struggle.'[114]

For the evolutionary naturalists of *New Youth* life itself was both the source of human value and proof of evolution's moral teleology. During the May Fourth period the French philosopher Henri Bergson attracted attention from neo-traditional Confucianists as a Western sage whose doctrine of '*élan vital*' showed he understood the intuitive roots of moral experience inaccessible to scientific reason. But Bergson's 'creative evolution' made Ch'en and his associates think they had found a scientifically valid philosophical language that reaffirmed an evolutionary vision of natural human interdependence in a developing universe suffused with humanist purposes. Youth, by virtue of its comparative freedom from the backward drag of the inherited environment and its 'class' hostility to gerontocracy, was the social group most fit to act as the cutting edge of progressive change. Youth was also the symbol of the biological energies presumed to animate the forces of the universe as a whole.

By this route the scientific, pragmatic modernists of the New Youth movement came back to cosmological theories of the metahistorical process. In Li Ta-chao[115] the magazine had a metaphysician of youth who drew on Confucian-Taoist cosmic symbolism unaccompanied by Confucian moral symbolism to celebrate all the movements of the naturalistic universe as having the inherent value of life itself: 'The cascade of the great actuality continually arises from actuality without beginning and flows towards actuality without end. My own "I", my own life also is endlessly part of the flow of life in compliance with the flow of great actuality, and with its increase, continued movement, onward revolution

113 Quoted in Bauer, *China and the search for happiness*, 354.
114 T'ao Meng-ho, 'Lun tzu-sha' (On suicide), *Hsin ch'ing-nien*, 6. 1 (15 Jan. 1918) 22. See also Ch'en Tu-hsiu, 'Tui-yü Liang Chü-ch'uan [Liang Chi] hsien-sheng tzu-sha chih kan-hsiang' (Impressions of the suicide of Mr Liang Chü-ch'uan), *ibid.* pp. 25–26.
115 For a full-scale study of Li Ta-chao see Maurice Meisner, *Li Ta-chao and the origins of Chinese Marxism*.

and advance. Actuality is energy; life is its onward revolution.'[116] Li selected the moment of creation as the primary aspect of the metahistorical process. Within the universe of phenomena characterized by bipolar pairs of qualitative forces, youth, spring, birth, creation have existence only thanks to their relativistic dependence upon their opposites – death, winter, age and destruction. But beyond phenomena the universe as a whole must be seen under the aspect of time itself. Here time's phenomenal characteristics – differentiation, relativity and change – must be contrasted with its numinous aspects – the absolute, uniformity and constancy. Therefore 'youth', 'spring', 'now', are numinous reality: the energies of these moments vibrate through all others. 'Use the springlike self of today to kill the white-haired self of yesterday; . . . use the springlike self of today to prepare to kill the white-haired self who is coming.'[117] For Li Ta-chao the social message implied by such transcendent images was that conservatives must be recognized as out of tune with the energies of the cosmos, and that the only authentic human use of the present is to struggle to create the future. The biological and emotional lesson was the denial of death – either of the self, the nation, or the physical universe.

An euphoric impulse towards a poetry of celebration was basic to Li Ta-chao's temperament, visible as early as 1915 when in a widely read literary exchange he reproached his friend Ch'en Tu-hsiu for pessimism and misanthropy in face of the nation's difficulties.[118] But the spread of the New Culture movement at home and the quickening pace of world change in the closing years of the European war raised expectations in both men. Ch'en Tu-hsiu saw events confirming his belief in the power of acceleration in history generated by the complex interplay of cultural and institutional causes and effects: 'A kind of theory gives rise to a form of society; a form of society gives rise to a kind of theory. Complex influences shift with the times; the more complex the shifts and the shorter the time in which they occur, the higher the level of progress.'[119] So intent became their focus on contemporary affairs that in 1918 Li and Ch'en started a second magazine, *Weekly Critic* (*Mei-chou p'ing-lun*), devoted exclusively to the discussion of national and world politics.

At first it seemed as if the Allied victory in the world war was the climactic event which defined this great turning point in the times. Not only *New Youth*, which had identified history's goals with the advance of

116 Li Ta-chao, 'Chin' (Now), *Hsin ch'ing-nien*, 4. 4 (15 April 1918) 337.
117 Li Ta-ch'ao 'Ch'ing-ch'un' (Spring), *Hsin ch'ing-nien*, 2. 1 (1 Sept. 1916) 16.
118 Li Ta-chao, 'Yen-shih hsin yü tzu-chueh hsin' (On misanthropy and self awareness), *Chia-yin* (Tiger magazine), 1. 8 (10 Aug. 1915).
119 Ch'en Tu-hsiu, 'K'ung-tzu chih tao yü hsien-tai sheng-huo' *Hsin ch'ing-nien*, 296.

Western democracy and science, but all Chinese aware of the Wilsonian programme of self-determination expected the Allied victory to reverse the recent course of imperialist encroachments on China's sovereignty. But Li Ta-chao's 1918 salute to the Bolshevik Revolution turned out to be more significant. When he greeted the new year of 1919 as the dawn of a 'new era' (*hsin chi-yuan*), drawing upon the historical symbolism of renewal implied by a change of reign titles, Li made clear that the pattern of progress he now foresaw would be generated by systems of economic production as Marx foretold:

From now on all know that productive systems can be reformed, national boundaries can be as if struck down, and human kind can all enjoy opportunities for work, and that all kinds of sorrow, hardship, anxiety, strife, can all naturally vanish. . . . Now the productive system is giving rise to a great movement. The united working class and their comrades all over the world will make rational production unions, break down national barriers and overthrow the world capitalist class . . . these are the glories of our new era! Like ice exposed to spring sun, in the light of these glories the evils of the past will gradually melt away, the residues of history will as leaves blown by autumn wind fall to the ground.[120]

The interest in Marxism which spread rapidly among radical Chinese in 1919 and 1920 was stimulated by the same disillusionment with the victorious liberal democracies that prompted neo-traditionalists to unite behind a post-war critique of the 'materialistic West'. The Versailles Treaty, then, on all sides became a catalyst stimulating re-evaluation of the reform model of the West which had so powerfully influenced a whole generation's vision of Chinese and world progress. The trauma of republican politics, the First World War and China's betrayal at the Peace Conference made Liang Ch'i-ch'ao abandon faith in the moral teleology of evolution. Ch'en Tu-hsiu, who (through the war) had identified the Allied cause with the ideals of justice, in 1919 found the shock of the Versailles Treaty compounded by a five-month stay in prison for his role in the May Fourth demonstrations against it. By the middle of 1920 Ch'en was totally committed to the new revolutionary social science of Marxism. From all sides of the ideological spectrum many followed the direction of either Liang or Ch'en, giving vent to a criticism of the liberal West all the stronger for having been so long unexpressed. For a whole generation Chinese committed to their own national revival according to a pattern of world progress had tended to mask one of the two Janus faces the West presented to China. Either they had compartmentalized their anger at violations of Chinese sovereignty, dealing with these on a

120 Li Ta-chao, 'Hsin chi-yuan' (A new era), *Mei-chou p'ing-lun* (15 Jan. 1919).

purely non-theoretical practical level, or they had maintained belief in the unity of enlightenment and power at the price of blaming themselves for Chinese weakness. The Marxist perspective, like the neo-traditional one, permitted a release from the bitterness of silent humiliation, as the balance shifted back toward belief that external evils were responsible for many of China's problems.

The reform model of the liberal West never recovered its original lustre. In the immediate atmosphere of the May Fourth anti-imperialist movement, the liberal reform belief which suffered most in radical circles was that in gradualism itself. Instead, evolutionary and revolutionary methods of change were seen as increasingly incompatible alternatives. Where the earlier anarchists had argued that a long-range historical perspective united these two in a complementary dialectic, young Mao Tse-tung, as a student radical in the provincial capital of Changsha, was an opponent of those he called evolutionary believers in *ta-t'ung*. Rather, he called for a mobilization of 'a great union of the popular masses' which he claimed could quickly achieve a total transformation of Chinese society.[121] Hu Shih, a popular Peking University professor who had become a follower of John Dewey in the course of his American education, found in the fall of 1919 that his advocacy of a scientistic, problem-oriented approach to reform was now sharply challenged. In a polemic dubbed the 'problems versus isms' debate, his claim that change comes 'in inches and drops' was countered by Li Ta-chao, who replied that each age is characterized by a fundamental orientation of the times derived from its system of economic relations. In the light of this, Li said, all of its problems may be shown to be interrelated, the people's consciousness can achieve a common foundation, and a direction can be set for total change. Both sides understood the arguments for a 'problems' approach as an attempt to challenge revolutionary socialist ideology.[122]

By the end of the May Fourth period, in radical circles the concept of *ta-t'ung* was increasingly associated with the previous generation's reform ideology and with a passive, apolitical and elitist approach to change. Nonetheless, as the foregoing suggests, at least one factor in the intellectual appeal of Marxism for Chinese at this time was that, side by side with the model of political action the Bolshevik revolution supplied, it was possible to see in early Marxist interpretations of history and society a final revision of evolutionary cosmology. While Chinese disillusionment

121 Mao Tse-tung, 'Min-chung ti ta-lien-ho', first published in *Hsiang-chiang p'ing-lun* (Hsiang River review), 21 July-4 Aug. 1919. See annotated translation by Stuart Schram, 'The great union of the popular masses', *The China Quarterly*, 49 (Jan.-March 1972) 88-105.
122 Chow, *May Fourth movement*, 218-22; Meisner, *Li Ta-chao*, 105-12.

with the liberal democracies proved irreversible, the Chinese faith in 'democracy' and 'science' as reform utopians originally interpreted them could survive uprooting from the soil of contemporary Europe and America to be projected yet again onto the world's distant future. Li Ta-chao, as the first major Chinese Marxist theorist and Mao's early teacher, not only believed that Marxism was the true carrier of the Western scientific and democratic heritage, but also took up social-utopian themes of personal liberation and the natural ethic of mutual aid as part of his Marxist creed.[123]

As a Marxist, Li Ta-chao portrayed the class system as operating on a world-wide scale to make the labouring people the motive force of world progress, and their struggle an inevitable manifestation of the development of natural and social phenomena. Moreover, he believed that the common people's power to make revolution was derived from their autonomy: from their self-consciousness of their own power, and their knowledge that those who belong to themselves are those who can rise up to be useful to society. Li saw in the labouring masses a human agent of change dynamic enough to complement the impersonal forces of production without being overwhelmed by them. In this way even without developing a sophisticated Marxist theory of social practice, Li found the balance that evolutionary cosmologists had sought between the 'voluntarism' of inner human conscious activity and the 'determinism' of external metahistorical processes. Finally, just as evolutionary cosmologists had sought to harmonize Darwinian means of competitive struggle and Confucian ends of moral community, Li considered mutual aid to be a complement to class struggle: as the ethical goal of socialism mutual aid could not, he thought, be disassociated from the processes of class struggle to attain that goal.

Throughout the reform generation, those who took their intellectual orientation from evolutionary cosmology, whether in its more sacred or more secularized forms, had depended upon a few essential ideals. They had assumed that traditional Confucian-Taoist cosmological categories complemented rather than contradicted Western models of the natural universe. They had maintained an organicist assumption of the interdependence, above, of the natural-historical and the cosmic-spiritual spheres, and, below, of the social, cultural and political orders: even as all these parts were increasingly perceived as analytically distinct. They projected a utopian portrait of world-wide progress, leading, with whatever twists and turns, to the ideal world of *ta-t'ung*. And, while they had dethroned politics and political leaders as the primary agents of change, they had resisted deterministic alternatives which made progress subject to impersonal social and historical forces alone. Instead, they looked within humanity, first for moral energy conceptualized as a subjective spiritual force, then as an organic collective spirit of a whole people, and finally objectified in mass political movements. When Chinese Marxists no longer relied upon any Confucian-Taoist symbols to describe the universe at large, when they no longer linked the energies of the revolutionary working classes to a spirit of universal humanistic enlightenment developing within the people, and when they portrayed themselves as strict, secular scientific materialists, they had stepped outside the boundaries of evolutionary cosmology as a belief system. To the extent that the Marxist focus on mass political movements as agents of change demanded attention to social action, the intellectual energies of Chinese Marxists no longer went to evolutionary myth-making. Yet as the case of Li Ta-chao illustrates, this break was by no means always immediate or sharp, and evolutionary cosmology has left its imprint upon the structure of Chinese Marxist dialectics.

CHAPTER 2

THEMES IN INTELLECTUAL HISTORY: MAY FOURTH AND AFTER

THE MAY FOURTH INCIDENT

It goes without saying that many factors combined to create the great intellectual upsurge of 1919 and the early 1920s that in the Chinese fashion has been given a neutral numerical designation as the 'Five-four' (*Wu-ssu*, that is, fifth month, fourth day) movement. There were several necessary developments behind this phase of China's intellectual transformation, the first and foremost being the creation of Peking University (generally abbreviated as Peita) as a modern institution of higher learning. From 1917 it was under the leadership of a new president, Ts'ai Yuan-p'ei (1867–1940). Ts'ai's career spanned the old and the new eras. By the age of 25 he had distinguished himself in classical studies at the Hanlin Academy but he subsequently became a revolutionary in the T'ung-meng hui, studied Western philosophy in Germany for four years, and served as the Chinese Republic's first minister of education for six months in 1912. Taking control at Peita, he welcomed ideas from all over the world and collected a faculty of brilliant young men of diverse backgrounds.

This institutional development soon brought forth a major linguistic reform, namely *pai-hua*, the written vernacular. Ch'en Tu-hsiu (1879–1942), who became dean of letters, had studied in Japan and France, participated in the Revolutions of 1911 and 1913, and founded several magazines including *Hsin ch'ing-nien* (New youth) in 1915, which he continued to edit after becoming dean. Another classically-trained young scholar, Hu Shih (1891–1962) returned to Peita from study between 1910 and 1917 at Cornell and Columbia. Hu Shih soon had Ch'en Tu-hsiu's support in the promotion of *pai-hua*, as an essential tool both for modern thinking and for bringing education to the common people. The esoteric classical writing intelligible only to scholars was abandoned in favour of the expressions and vocabulary of everyday speech – the change made when Latin gave way to the national languages in the European Renaissance. By 1920 the Ministry of Education prescribed the use of *pai-hua* in the schools.

Meanwhile patriotic public concern over the fate of the country, although still superficial in numerical terms, had been increasingly exercised by Japanese encroachment. It was epitomized in the Twenty-one Demands of 1915 and by the tendency of warlords, especially of the Anfu Clique dominant in Peking, to conspire for their own gain with Japan's imperialists. In 1919 Chinese nationalism was at a new height of concern over the Shantung issue. At the Paris Peace Conference it was finally decided to honour the secret wartime agreements made by Japan with Great Britain, France and Italy by which Japan would retain the entitlements of Germany in Shantung province, from which the Japanese had expelled the Germans in 1914. This flagrant denial of the new Wilsonian principles of open diplomacy and self-determination touched off the May Fourth incident.

On that afternoon over 3,000 students from a dozen Peking institutions rallied at the Gate of Heavenly Peace (T'ien-an men) at the entrance to the palace to protest at the Paris decision and the complicity of the Anfu government that had itself in 1918 secretly agreed to let Japan remain in Shantung. Beginning peaceably, the demonstrators eventually beat a pro-Japanese official and burned a cabinet minister's residence. The Peking government used force to imprison hundreds of students, whose fellow students then became all the more active. The whole patriotic public was aroused. Student disturbances erupted in at least 200 other localities. Shanghai merchants closed their shops for a week and workers went on strike in some 40 factories. A student movement was born in which women participated, broad public support was enlisted, and the sanction of saving China was invoked to achieve an unprecedented degree of student organization and activism. This was a new political expression of nationalism, all the more significant because it was unpremeditated. Of the many consequences that flowed from the incident, the Peking government was obliged to give in, and some 1,150 students marched victoriously out of jail – a victory that was to be felt for a long time afterwards.

Because May Four as an incident occurred at a time when major developments in politics, thought and society were already under way, it was neither a beginning nor a culmination, even though its name is now used to cover an era. It follows that we must look before and after if we are to see the long-term trends of the time. We must also accept the fact that so broad and protean a period of China's history is most feasibly approached on one level at a time. Even on the plane of thought and culture, moreover, we must recognize limits.

The contributions to this volume concerned with modern China's intellectual history focus their attention for the most part on the intellectuals themselves. It is a focus which requires no apologies, for this stratum, small as it was, concerned itself with themes and issues of enormous, intrinsic significance for China and for the modern world in general. Yet the fact remains that in so directing our attention, we are not dealing with the conscious life of the vast majority of the Chinese population who, for the most part, continued at least until 1949 to live in a world still dominated by the categories of the traditional popular (and high) culture. To be sure, China in the twentieth century sees the emergence of a large urban population exposed to the world of the new popular press, new kinds of Western-influenced literature and even cinema; a population which participates in political events, and shares new ideas – and yet, a population which also continues to live deeply within the older traditions. Indeed, the world of popular religion and of 'superstition', the world of secret societies and religio-political sects, the world of Buddhist monks, Taoist priests and sect leaders, is a world which still lives on even now in Taiwan and other sectors of the Chinese cultural world outside of the People's Republic. There its fate still remains uncertain in spite of official suppression. It is a world which is only now beginning to receive serious scholarly attention in the West. Its twentieth-century history has yet to be written.

Within the Chinese intelligentsia itself, there have been scholars, politicians and novelists – men such as Ku Chieh-kang, Cheng Chen-to, Ch'ü Ch'iu-pai, Lu Hsun, and Shen Ts'ung-wen among others – who have concerned themselves with the world of popular culture. As we shall indicate below, they have tended to view that world in terms of particular concerns and preoccupations of their own, but their writings taken together with the work of pioneer Japanese scholars and some Western anthropologists will facilitate future work on this subject.

The main focus of this chapter is on themes and issues which were to dominate the discourse of the intellectual stratum during the May Fourth period (loosely defined) and after. Yet to begin our account with 4 May 1919, would be to begin *in medias res*. It is now clear to all students of twentieth-century intellectual history that some of the overarching themes which were to dominate the first half of our century (and beyond) in China were in fact already posed at the end of the nineteenth and beginning of the twentieth centuries. Since many of these themes have been analysed in the contributions to this volume of Charlotte Furth and Leo Ou-fan Lee, we can begin here with a brief recapitulation.

PROGRESS AND NATIONALISM

As the preceding chapter points out, the grandest and most enduring theme of all is the theme of historical or evolutionary progress as first interpreted in the writings of the great pioneers like K'ang Yu-wei, Yen Fu, and T'an Ssu-t'ung. It is in their writings that we meet the notion of a vast cosmic-social process leading mankind eventually to the realization of unimagined possibilities of human achievement or even to a utopian resolution of all human problems. Whether the idea was frankly accepted as Western or whether, as in the case of K'ang Yu-wei, one sought Chinese roots for it, it remained profoundly subversive in its implications for the conventional Confucian socio-political order which had prevailed for so many centuries.

While the idea itself is universalistic in its implications, its acceptance in China can be related to certain immediate pressing concerns of the last decade of the nineteenth century. The prospect of the possible imminent collapse of the polity was one which Chinese literati such as Yen Fu, K'ang Yu-wei, and Liang Ch'i-ch'ao could not accept. Their deeply ingrained sense of themselves as custodians and political leaders of the society made it unthinkable for them to accept the notion of the demise of China as an independent socio-political entity.

By the end of the century they finally confronted the crucial question of whether the survival of the established conventional Confucian order as a total system was any longer compatible with the survival of China as a socio-political entity (what Liang Ch'i-ch'ao called the 'ch'ün'). Having opted for the latter they had in effect opted for nationalism as the demand of the immediate future. Once the survival and prosperity of the nation was established as a paramount goal, the theme of nationalism was to remain dominant in spite of its involvement from the very outset with ideologies like social Darwinism which posited more universalistic goals. It was a burning question of national survival, which in the first instance led to an uninhibited examination of all those technologies, institutions, systems and ideas that had promoted the ascendancy of the Western nation-state. The revitalization of China as a socio-political entity was – at least in the short range – to remain a major object of progress.

Yet the idea of progressive evolution itself had a significance which went beyond this goal. What Yen Fu learned in the West was not simply the fact that new unimagined human possibilities had been realized in the West and might be emulated in China. What he had acquired was a new faith in the idea of progressive cosmic evolution. The West had progressed by somehow being in line with the soaring energies of the cosmic processes of evolution – a universal process which must somehow also be at work in China itself.

The notion of impersonal forces and configurations of history beyond the control of individual men was itself not a new idea in China. History had often been described in terms of the mysterious workings of Heaven or the 'Tao' within the cosmic-social 'outer realm' over which men exercised the most limited control. There was in fact a strand of Chinese thought represented by Shao Yung, Chang Hsueh-ch'eng and others which was much preoccupied with such historical patterns. On the whole, it was not one of the more sanguine strains in Chinese thought since it tended to stress the constraints imposed on human hopes by historical fate. What was new in Western nineteenth-century doctrines of progressive evolutionism and historicism was not the notion of the impersonal forces of history as such – but the notion that such forces inevitably tended in a direction favourable to human hopes. This idea itself – quite apart from the particular conception of the dynamic forces involved – was what united K'ang Yu-wei, who still employed traditional terminology, with Yen Fu, who used the language of social Darwinism.

What this implied on the negative side was nothing less than the historical relativization of the established conventional Confucian order. The kingship, the examination system, the immemorial structures of bureaucracy and the rituals of human relations, which had seemed to be part of an eternal order (even when the actual functioning of the order was subject to severe criticism), now belonged to their place in time. To be sure, Yen Fu, K'ang Yu-wei and Liang Ch'i-ch'ao remained monarchists throughout the first decade of the century, but this was now an instrumental monarchism. The Chinese people were woefully unprepared for a republic. Yet it was they who at one stroke had reduced the kingship to the humble status of a passing human institution.

What one perceives here is a radical sense of release from all prevailing structures – a 'breaking out of all the networks' in the vivid phrase of T'an Ssu-t'ung. On this level, we have something like a radical critique of the past. Why had the forces of history which had moved inexorably forward in the West been paralysed in China? To K'ang Yu-wei, Confucius' true message had been distorted by centuries of Old Text Confucianism. To Yen Fu, the sages and sage-kings had almost systematically repressed the creative energies of the people. Such explanations seem hardly consonant with a determinist doctrine of progressive evolution. They seem to suggest the power of the conscious will to retard the evolutionary forces. It is this theme, in fact, which already prefigures the 'unmasking' view later found in the writings of the New Culture and more vulgar Marxists – namely, the view that China's traditional elite culture had been a kind of deliberate device for suppressing the forces of progress. Whatever the inconsistencies of these doctrines, however, one could now hope that the forces of evolution or history would finally break through all the barriers, structures, and the negative repressive authoritarianism of the past. In all of this one perceives a pervasive mood of 'anti-structuralism' – a preference for reality conceived of in terms of a continuum of energy and transcendent formless forces rather than in terms of eternal orders and structures.

We have spoken here of the conventional Confucian order rather than of the entire heritage of the past, for the fact is that the pre-1911 generation did not carry out a 'totalistic' rejection of that heritage. It was deeply enough immersed in the culture to be acutely aware of its rich variety and inner conflicts. Alternative traditions were often invoked in order to find Chinese equivalents of Western ideas, and here the motives involved may well have been the need to salvage national pride at a time when what was 'valuable' no longer corresponded to history, as has been suggested by Joseph Levenson.[1] Yet the revival of Mahayana Buddhist philosophy[2] and 'philosophic' Taoism at the end of the century (and even before) cannot be completely disposed of in this way. The fact is that Buddhism and Taoism brought to bear a perspective which relativized and devalued Confucian concepts of eternal structures from the point of view of a transcendental realm of being beyond all forms and structures.

In the past this transcendance had not been subversive in any sociopolitical sense. The 'Buddha mind' of Yogacara Buddhism, the realm of non-being (*wu*) of Taoism, had provided places of refuge into which one could 'sink back' from all the sufferings of a corrupt world. To some of those involved in the Buddhist revival such as Yang Wen-hui, Ou-Yang Ching-wu and even the revolutionary Chang Ping-lin, the basic attraction of Buddhism still lay here. Yet what we note now is a kind of inversion in which the ultimate source of being is no longer viewed as a refuge but as the source of a kind of infinite propulsive energy breaking through all the confining structures of human history and finally leading men to an ultimate deliverance on both the societal and individual levels.[3] On the individual level, in the form of a quasi-Buddhist-Taoist pantheism,

---

1 See Levenson, Joseph R., *Liang Ch'i-ch'ao and the mind of modern China*; and also *Confucian China and its modern fate*.
2 See Chan Wing-tsit, *Religious trends in modern China*, for an English source on this subject.
3 This inversion was not entirely without historical precedent. The theme of the world-saving Bodhisattva who saves men not through religious compassion but through sociopolitical transformation can be found in Wang An-shih and others.

it could even become the inspiration of the variety of romanticism which would eventually lead to Kuo Mo-jo's rhapsodic cry, 'All nature is a manifestation of God. I am also a manifestation of God. Therefore I am God. All nature is a manifestation of myself.'[4] The invocation of these traditional strains meant that the kind of abyss between the human realm and the cosmic realm presupposed by so many modern Western versions of the idea of progress did not emerge as a major issue to these pioneer thinkers.

In all of this the pioneers confronted what might be called the Leninist dilemma. Like Lenin they had enthusiastically embraced the concept of a linear development of the 'objective forces' of history leading to a predictable future. Yet like Lenin, they also were exasperated by the failure of these forces to operate in China's living present. If history in the past could be ascribed to objective organic forces, the metaphor more applicable to the present was that of history as a kind of pre-existent path or ladder. The faith that the goal is pre-ordained remains an inspiring faith yet the responsibility for leading China along this path would fall to a new stratum of 'sages', 'foreknowers' and 'vanguards'.

Despite the common spirit of radical negation towards the immediate past, when we turn to the pioneer thinkers' positive visions of the future we note significant differences among them. They seem roughly in agreement concerning the requirements of the next historical stage – some programme of modernization pivoted on the monarchy roughly along the lines of Meiji Japan. Yet the orientations of K'ang Yu-wei and Yen Fu were profoundly different. Yen Fu was prepared to discern the universal republic of man in the distant future, but his present attention was firmly fixed on the concrete study of those mechanisms of material and social technology which had led the West – Great Britain in particular – to its present high estate. The tasks of the intellectual vanguard in China would be the sober scientific tasks of mastering the knowledge of those technologies, institutions and infrastructures which would lead to the release of the physical, intellectual and moral energies of the individual and the consolidation of these energies in the service of the nation-society. Involved in all this was the actual appropriation of many of the doctrines of Anglo-American liberalism. What was required was the creation of rationalized bureaucratic, legal, economic and educational systems which would create a 'new individual' (Liang Ch'i-ch'ao's 'new citizen') all of whose constructive energies and capacities would be developed in the service of the nation. By his translation of Adam Smith's *Wealth of nations*

4 Cited by Leo Ou-fan Lee, *The romantic generation of modern Chinese writers*, 183, from Kuo's preface to his translation of Goethe's *Sorrows of the young Werther*.

Yen even indicated that a capitalist economy would be an essential component of such a programme. The essential pathos is that of rational technocracy despite the fact that the pleas for liberty often take on a genuinely emotional tone.

When we turn to K'ang Yu-wei we find that his sweeping spiritual-moral imagination led him to quite a different pathos in spite of his acceptance of a programme of modernization for the next stage of history close to that just described. His utopian imagination quickly led him to leap beyond the model of the future provided by the contemporary West to his own quite different apocalyptic vision. When we now examine his utopian work (*Ta-t'ung shu*) (The book of the great harmony) we note that while it may well have been influenced by nineteenth-century Western socialist literature, there is a distinctly Buddhist-Taoist dimension in the text. The utopia of the future will be a universal republic of mankind in which all the structures of family, class and nation which divide men from each other will have been dissolved and along with them all the obligations which had burdened men's lives. Yet these structures are not dissolved in order to liberate the 'individual' from society. They are rather dissolved in order to fuse men into a common humanity no longer separated by obstacles and barriers. On an even more mystical level, this sinking into the ocean of humanity may ultimately involve a more cosmic liberation of suffering mankind from the trammels of individual existence as such. While K'ang Yu-wei and his disciple T'an Ssu-t'ung interested themselves in science and technology, their ultimate vision of history was that of a spiritual-moral drama leading to a spiritual-moral resolution. It is a theme which stands in striking contrast to Yen Fu's 'technocratic' vision of the foreseeable future.[5] The two contrasting visions are fraught with implications for the future.

It was, of course, Yen Fu and Liang Ch'i-ch'ao who introduced a striking new view of the dynamic principles of evolution – the gospel of social Darwinism. However questionable its relation to Darwinism as biological science, this new, shocking and exciting doctrine was now destined to become the source of a transformation of Chinese values. The processes of natural selection and the survival of the fittest, whether applied to the interactions of individuals or of national societies, required a new conception of man. Dynamism, aggressiveness, self-assertion, the realization of capacities – all the vitalities which had been suppressed by a morality which had fostered peace, harmony, passivity and resignation –

---

5 There is, to be sure, a somewhat different Taoist-Buddhist dimension in Yen Fu's own thought. See Benjamin Schwartz, *In search of wealth and power: Yen Fu and the West*, particularly ch. 10.

must now be exalted. Above all, what was required was the kind of economic competition and 'struggle for survival' among men of capacity and talent which seemed so compatible with liberal ideas. The idea assumed its more radical and lurid aspect when applied to the conflicts of nations. The theme of the struggle of collectivities as an engine of progress would, of course, eventually find a new and different embodiment in Marxism-Leninism.

Social Darwinism in China was by no means as favourable to the cause of economic individualism as one might suppose from its contemporary Western context. It did not inhibit an interest from the very outset in contemporary Western doctrines of socialism or the socialist critique of capitalism. K'ang Yu-wei's vision of utopia was certainly 'socialistic' in spirit. Liang Ch'i-ch'ao, who was to become the somewhat inconsistent spokesman of both his earlier master K'ang Yu-wei and of Yen Fu, was to be the first in China to discuss socialism and the socialist critique of capitalism. Yen Fu's own advocacy of Adam Smith's doctrine was not based on any passionate acceptance of the gospel of classical economics, but on a 'realistic' assumption that capitalism was evolution's engine for achieving industrial development. Liang Ch'i-ch'ao, who was eventually won back to this view after 1905 in the course of his debates with the revolutionaries, nevertheless entertained the idea that in the future a state socialism which controlled and consolidated the economy while diminishing economic inequality might make China a more effective combatant in the jungle of international affairs than a liberalism which in the end could only weaken the state by its emphasis on divisive individual and group interests.

One of the concomitants of the interest in socialism – whether combined or not combined with social Darwinism – was, in fact, to be the emergence of a somewhat more benign attitude towards the Chinese past – an attitude which seemed to run directly counter to the indictment of that past discussed above – coupled with the beginnings of the anti-capitalist critique of the contemporary West from a 'higher' standpoint. In China, as both Liang Ch'i-ch'ao and Sun Yat-sen insisted, it had always been assumed that the ruling class would concern itself with the people's livelihood. China had never known the sharp divisions of class which marked the truly Darwinian history of the West. China might in the future use 'the advantages of backwardness' (later echoed in Mao's conception of China's 'poverty and blankness') to avoid some of the most dire consequences of Western capitalism. Yen Fu, who remained more faithful to his Spencerian source of inspiration continued to insist that the harsher conflicts which had supposedly marked the history of the West, and even the individualistic competition of capitalism, were all proofs of that civilization's superior fitness. China required individual as well as collective dynamism.

REVOLUTION

The first decade of the twentieth century was also to witness the powerful impact of yet another theme – that of revolution. The concept of revolution as a kind of collective act marking a total qualitative break with the established socio-political order is, of course, based on the idea of progress, yet in some ways it seems more easily linked to Western eighteenth-century ideas than to nineteenth-century concepts of an incremental evolutionary or historical growth. Chinese revolutionaries such as Sun Yat-sen and the revolutionary students in Japan at the beginning of the century would speak in a rhetoric which mingled eighteenth-century Western ideas with the rhetoric of social Darwinism.

In dealing with the past Yen Fu and Liang Ch'i-ch'ao (who again is less consistent in his rhetoric) had evidenced a certain variety of populism. They had indignantly deplored the way in which the traditional culture had inhibited the creative energies and capacities of the people. Yet having been inhibited, the potentialities of the people could be cultivated only by a long and ordered process of evolutionary development under the guidance of a vanguard. There was no reason to believe that there was some latent popular wisdom just below the surface which would make itself manifest once the obstacle of the old society had been eliminated by a revolutionary transformation. The revolutionaries as a whole used a variety of arguments. Sun Yat-sen was prepared on one level to argue that the Chinese people had in fact developed roots of 'village democracy' which would provide a firm foundation of democracy once the incubus of the Manchus had been removed. Others argued that the forces of evolution could only be released by revolution. 'Revolution', states Tsou Jung in his *Ko ming chün* (Revolutionary army), 'is the law of evolution'. For them, the dichotomy perceived by later Marxists in both China and the West between 'positivistic evolutionism' and 'dialectic revolutionism' was quite blurred. It should be added that the outcome of the revolution was envisioned as a democratic republic – although very often as a democratic republic with a 'socialistic' dimension.

From the outset the Chinese revolutionaries confronted the same Leninist dilemma. Was a revolution an objective event which would simply happen when its time had come or did it require a vanguard of revolutionary activists and heroes? Like most of their revolutionary contemporaries in Russia and to some extent under their influence, they were, of course, speedily convinced that the revolution required revolutionary leaders. It was on this level that the young revolutionaries were to seek not only an answer to the needs of the nation but also a new image of themselves as individuals. The new individual of Yen Fu and Liang Ch'i-ch'ao would be a productive and disciplined 'modern man' – the self-confident engineer, industrialist and professional of the new society. Yet the same negation of the existing order which had made possible this image also made possible a more romantic view of individuality which emphasized the liberation of man's capacities for emotional experience. Lin Shu's translations of Western literature at the beginning of the century opened up new vistas of rich emotional experience – new images of love, adventure and heroism.[6] The assimilation of this new sensibility to the image of revolutionary heroism as a mode of self-realization can be readily seen in individuals such as the famous revolutionary martyrs Ch'iu Chin, Wu Yueh and Ch'en T'ien-hua.

As noted above, in the case of the revolutionaries as well as in the case of the reformers, this new ideal by no means involved a 'totalistic' rejection of the entire cultural heritage. The young revolutionaries still had strong roots in the broader heritage even as they rejected the established conventional Confucian order. The tradition of warrior heroes (*yu-hsia*), of the heroic martyrs of the Ming dynasty and non-collaborators of the early Ch'ing, blended in their minds with the examples of Russian populist terrorists and the image of poet-rebels like Lord Byron. One need not doubt their sincere devotion to the cause of revolution, but revolution had also become a mode of individual self-realization.

Not only do we find strong traditional elements in the outlooks of the revolutionaries. We even find that the revolutionary movement as a whole was to become the centre (although reformers also participated) of a movement of integral cultural nationalism which stood in marked contrast to the essentially iconoclastic nationalism of Yen Fu. Here we find the ubiquitous dilemma of modern nationalism. On the one hand, the achievement of national wealth and power may require a radical break with the constraints of tradition. On the other hand, a vital sense of national identity seems to require faith in the intrinsic worth of the nation's cultural accomplishments of the past.

In China the theme of anti-Manchuism as preached by the fiery scholar Chang Ping-lin seemed to provide an extraordinarily effective basis for an organic sense of nationhood. The Ch'ing dynasty was, in his view,

6 See Lee, *The romantic generation*.

not simply a dynasty in decline. It was the representative of an inferior 'race' which had for centuries kept in thrall the Han people which was in every way its superior. The revolution, once accomplished, would finally liberate the high creative powers of the Han race. The Han people is an organic entity with its own history, its own 'national essence', and its own path into the future. As in the case of the European organic notions of nationalism, with which he was certainly familiar, Chang vehemently insists that Chinese derive their categories of thought from their own tradition. Yet, paradoxically, this emphasis on the Chinese spirit does not seem to require a particular loyalty to any specific manifestation of that spirit as the embodiment of universal truth. As a famous scholar in the Ch'ing tradition, Chang Ping-lin was above all insistent that Chinese youth acquire a knowledge of and pride in their entire cultural heritage. Yet at another level, he himself had his own particular commitments within the heritage. This was equally true of other revolutionary cultural nationalists such as Liu Shih-p'ei, Liu Ya-tzu and others whose predilections within the national heritage tended to its more literary and aesthetic aspects. Organic 'cultural' nationalism was, to be sure, only one tendency within the revolutionary camp. Sun Yat-sen, whose personal life experience had been far removed from that of literati such as Liu Shih-p'ei and Chang Ping-lin, was indeed able to incorporate strong components of organic nationalism into the eclectic body of his Three People's Principles, but his fundamental orientation remained Western as did that of many in his entourage. Yet 'organic nationalism' as a theme was to play a significant role in the future history of the Kuomintang movement.

One more strain to be noted within the revolutionary camp is the strain of anarchism. Anarcho-syndicalism at the turn of the twentieth century was a dominant influence in the more radical wing of the European and American left. At the time, it was indeed the anarchists rather than the European socialists in general or Marxists in particular who represented the 'revolutionary left'. In this as in many other matters, translations from the Japanese and contacts with Japanese radicals were the main channel of communication.[7]

The acceptance of anarchism by some of the revolutionaries can be related to the vehement attack on the repressive, negative authority of the past which we already find in the pioneer thinkers. To be sure, they (as well as many of the revolutionaries) by no means drew the conclusion that all authority as such is inherently evil or dispensable. What China

---

7 Martin Bernal, 'The triumph of anarchism over Marxism 1906–1907', in Mary Wright, ed. *China in revolution, the first phase 1900–1913*. See also above, pages 391–6.

required in their view was a new type of constructive, nurturant authority which would foster the powers of the people. Some more apocalyptic minds were able to leap precisely to that conclusion, fortified by a faith nourished from abroad that a world anarchist revolution was imminent in the West. It is indicative of the kaleidoscopic interweavings of doctrine at this time that Liu Shih-p'ei, an enthusiastic advocate of 'national essence', was able to find in the book of Lao-tzu warrant for his belief that an anarchist revolution in China would restore the primeval state of a Taoist society of 'non-action'. Others, however, sought cosmological support in Kropotkin's benign 'mutual aid' version of Darwinian doctrine. Here one could find a cosmology more congenial to Chinese tradition allied to a doctrine of extreme political radicalism.

It should be added at this point that both before and after 1911 we find certain idiosyncratic temperaments who do not respond to the same drummer as most of the new literati. For whatever reason, they prove highly resistant to the overwhelmingly socio-political preoccupations of the twentieth century.

The complex figure of Chang Ping-iin, who was, on one level, deeply and passionately involved in socio-political conflicts and the rise of cultural nationalism, was on another 'existential' level deeply influenced by the revival of Mahayana Buddhist philosophy (particularly the consciousness-only, 'Vijnanavada' school) and the thought of Chuang-tzu. On this level, he found his ultimate solace in a mystic perspective which denied the intrinsic value of the entire phenomenal world. Freely accepting Darwinism as a paradigm of the world of fluctuating forms, he simply denied that it bore with it any hope of ultimate redemption. In effect he negated progress.

Another interesting instance is that of Wang Kuo-wei, whose personal temper and life experience led him to disclaim what he regarded as the shallow concerns with national 'wealth and power' or with any doctrine of political salvation. Having come into contact with the thought of Schopenhauer, he found a Western confirmation for his basic feeling that life itself is the problem, quite apart from the particular miseries of specific conditions. Having eventually been convinced, evidently by Nietzsche and the positivists, that Schopenhauer's metaphysics 'could not be believed' in spite of the promise it held for release from life's miseries, he then found solace in a kind of philosophically inspired literary criticism (as in his interpretation of the novel *The dream of the red chamber*) and finally in a life of creative scholarship which blended the Ch'ing and Western philological traditions.

THE 1911 REVOLUTION AND THE 'NEW CULTURE'

The Chinese Revolution of 1911 has often been considered 'superficial'. It produced no social revolution. Yet the fact remains that the end of the universal kingship and the collapse of the entire cosmology which legitimized it; the fragmentation and militarization of power and authority throughout the society often down to the local level; the loss of moral authority on many levels of that society; the convulsive insecurity of local holders of power and wealth both old and new; the failure of the new republic to establish its own bases of legitimacy – were all to have a traumatic impact on the intellectuals' perceptions of the themes treated above. Many of these trends had been underway before 1911. The end of the examination system had itself had an enormous effect on the social role of the literati. The cosmology of kingship had already been undermined by the evolutionary doctrines of K'ang Yu-wei, Yen Fu, Liang Ch'i-ch'ao and others, but in the apt words of Lin Yü-sheng, 'Over a long period the gate of the dike may be eroded; when it finally bursts nothing can hinder the thrust of the flood that spreads ruin and destruction in the natural order beyond.'[8] No doubt, an objective study of Chinese society in all its regional variations between 1911 and 1919 would reveal a variety of conditions and even some positive developments. Yet in the perception of most of the 'high' intellectuals, the total scene was one of deterioration, fragmentation, corruption and brutality. Somehow the stream of evolution in China seemed to have sunk into a slough of despond.

Yen Fu and K'ang Yu-wei now both felt confirmed in their conviction that 'evolution cannot be forced', and that a republican revolution at this stage of China's evolution was an enormous mistake. Liang Ch'i-ch'ao accepted the revolution and the irreversibility of the demise of monarchy as the decree of History. He was at first, on thoroughly consistent grounds, in favour of Yuan Shih-k'ai's efforts to create a 'republican' dictatorship which would be able to carry through the tasks of modernization. K'ang Yu-wei, again on thoroughly consistent evolutionary grounds, continued to believe that at this point only the symbols of monarchy could restore the centre that had collapsed.[9] A common tendency among all three during this period was a greater inclination to accept the premises of cultural nationalism. K'ang Yu-wei had of course long ad-

8 Lin Yü-sheng, *The crisis of Chinese consciousness: radical anti-traditionalism in the May Fourth era,* 17.
9 This was to lead to his support of the efforts of the queue-wearing warlord Chang Hsun to restore the Ch'ing dynasty in 1917.

vocated the need for his own version of a Confucian religion during the middle historical stage of 'lesser order' (*hsiao-k'ang*). Yen Fu and Liang Ch'i-ch'iao, in an environment of growing disintegration, were now increasingly convinced that China required minimal elements of a stabilizing common faith. It is in such circumstances that we find Yen Fu signing the petition of the 'society for Confucianism' that Confucianism be recognized as a state religion.[10] China, he argued, was still, alas, in a period of transition from a 'patriarchal' to a 'military' stage of society[11] and it still required a patriarchal faith.

The responses of the active revolutionaries were diverse. Many quickly demonstrated that their ideological commitments had been emphatic rather than profound. Soon they became embroiled with the politics of the unsavoury warlord era. Sun Yat-sen continued (actively, but without much effect) during the bleak years after the Second and Third Revolutions to seek for a base of political power. The adherents of the 'national essence' school soon found that the Han race did not automatically achieve a full 'restoration' once the corrupt Manchus had been removed. In the case of men such as Liu Shih-p'ei the preoccupation with the preservation of national cultural identity continued but the faith that it might be preserved through political means now faded. In the words of Laurence Schneider, 'the cultural mission of the group was now its sole source of solidarity.'[12] Its concept of culture tended to focus on literature and traditional scholarship, leading it to become a vehement source of opposition to both the linguistic and literary revolutions of the May Fourth period.

The most significance response to the discouragement of the post-revolutionary period was, however, to be the New Culture movement most prominently represented by the journal *New Youth*, founded by Ch'en Tu-hsiu in 1915. Characterizing this movement as a whole, what we find on the negative side is a much more radical – more 'totalistic' – attack on the entire cultural heritage. There is little novelty in Ch'en's exhortations 'be independent not servile, progressive not conservative, aggressive not passive',[13] but now these attacks are directed not simply against the conventional Confucian socio-political order but against the entire tradition with all its 'three teachings of Confucianism, Taoism and Buddhism' (not to speak of the superstitious culture of the masses).

10 Yen Fu *et al.* 'K'ung-chiao-hui chang-ch'eng' (The programme of the Society for Confucianism), *Yung-yen (Justice)*, 1. 14 (June 1913) 1–8.
11 Schwartz, *In search of wealth and power*, 234.
12 Laurence A. Schneider, 'National essence and the new intelligentsia' in C. Furth, ed. *The limits of change: essays on conservative alternatives in Republican China*, 71.
13 Ch'en Tu-hsiu, 'Ching-kao ch'ing-nien' (A call to youth), *Hsin ch'ing-nien* (New youth), 1. 1 (Sept 1915) 7.

The language of social Darwinist evolutionism is still invoked but in some sense the 'old society' and the 'old culture' are now treated as a kind of vast, inert incubus which had paralysed the soul of the nation. The revolution had proven that one could, after all, remove the entire traditional political structure without affecting the rot which permeated the whole society. Indeed, not only did the dead weight of the past have the power to persist. It seemed (as in the case of Yuan Shih-k'ai's attempts to restore the monarchy) to have the power to reconstitute itself. The task which lay ahead was thus nothing less than to transform the entire conscious life of a nation. The 'new cultural' leaders felt that this task was the absolutely necessary precondition of any political action or institutional reform. The resolve expressed by the young Hu Shih in 1917 upon his return from the United States 'not to talk about politics for twenty years' seemed to express the common sentiment of the entire New Culture group. As the title of their main organ indicated, they regarded their first and primary audience to be the educated youth who had not yet been entirely corrupted by 'the old and the rotten'.[14]

Here too there seems to be only a difference of degree between the New Youth outlook and that of the pioneer thinkers. In confronting what I have called the Leninist dilemma, the pioneers had come to stress the role of conscious ideas in changing society. Yet their educational approach was supported by the sense that changes were actually taking place or about to take place in the institutional infrastructure of society during the course of the Manchu reform movement. Evolution – with some conscious help – then seemed to be on the move. Similarly, the diagnosis of the New Culture group before 1919 led them to feel that nothing but a change of consciousness could move the society.

One aspect of the new cultural movement before 1919 which was to have continuing implications for the future was the sharp line it drew between politicians and intellectuals. This disassociation had been prefigured in the abolition of the examination system in 1905. It is also clear that in the past, in spite of the 'scholar-official' cliché, there had always been literati who were primarily intellectuals and others who were primarily politicians. Also, in the period after 1919, many intellectuals were to immerse themselves once more in political life. Yet the self-perception of the intellectuals (particularly the academic and literary intellectuals) as a separate stratum was to persist even after 1949 and was even to carry with itself a certain ongoing sense of the 'right' to autonomy in intellectual life.

Another vital aspect of the New Culture movement was the emergence

14 *Ibid.* 1–2.

of the 'New Literature' so ably treated elsewhere in this volume (see chapter 9). Here also we see the emergence of literature[15] as a major, autonomous area of human experience. Although poetry and belles-lettres had long been an organic part of the high culture of the literati ideally they had never been separated from the entire programme of self-cultivation. There had always been figures such as Ou-yang Hsiu who had been very 'literary' in orientation (*wen-jen*), but the notion of literature (in the sense of belles-lettres) as a high, autonomous vocation had not prevailed. Above all, the writing of fiction as a department of literature had not been a respected high cultural activity. Here, as in so many other areas, Liang Ch'i-ch'ao had been a pioneer in his advocacy of the employment of fiction as a powerful emotional medium for promoting his socio-political ideas. The young brothers Chou Shu-jen (Lu Hsun) and Chou Tso-jen had also been pioneers during their days in Japan before 1911 in their aspiration to use literature as a means of curing the deep spiritual ailments of the Chinese people. It was, however, the New Culture movement which effectively launched the new vernacular 'high cultural' literature. Yet if the new culture elevated the genre of fiction to a high cultural status, it did so for the most part by wedding it to the view that fiction must 'serve life'. To this extent, the new literature in China was in the main oriented from the outset to the view that literature must serve social ethical goals. This general orientation does not, of course, preclude an absorption of some of the greater writers in purely literary concerns, but the general goals were to retain their hold.

Even the romantic 'Creation' group of Kuo Mo-jo, Yü Ta-fu and others which had ostensibly adopted the slogan of 'art for art's sake' was deeply moved by concerns which were not strictly artistic.[16] Romanticism as a release from the repressive structures of traditional life had, as we have seen, emerged before 1911 and even then had been as much related to the search for individual meaning in life as to the romance of revolution. In the years after 1911 when the promise of political salvation dramatically receded, the concern of the younger intellectuals with the meaning of their own personal lives, in a world where faith in traditional values both public and private had sharply declined, was to become an important dimension of the new culture. In a sense, 'individualism' in both its liberal and romantic senses now seems to have had a direct impact on personal life to a degree which was certainly not true for the pioneer generation, who still lived quite comfortably within the confines of conventional Confucian family values. For a time, at least, the concern with individ-

15 See Lee, *The romantic generation* ch. 2.
16 Discussed in Lee, *The romantic generation*; also in David Roy, *Kuo Mo-jo: the early years*.

ualism as such seemed not to be entirely instrumental to socio-political goals. The translation of Ibsen's *A doll's house* in the Ibsen issue of *New Youth* sponsored by Hu Shih is symbolic of this concern. Similarly the rapt absorption of the romantic 'Creation Society' authors in their own unfulfilled emotional yearnings was anything but a concern for 'art for art's sake'. In the words of Leo Lee, 'Far from the French symbolist notion that art not only restructures life but also constructs a new edifice into which the artist can escape life, Ch'eng's (Fang-wu) arguments point in the other direction',[17] towards an overriding concern with 'life' whether this concern took the form of Yü Ta-fu's melancholy self-indulgence or Kuo Mo-jo's soaring narcissism.

Another development clearly associated with the New Culture movement is what might be called the 'higher criticism' of the traditional heritage represented by figures such as Hu Shih, Ku Chieh-kang, Ch'ien Hsuan-t'ung and others.

Conflicts regarding the validity and authenticity of various traditions and scriptures had been a feature of Chinese thought for ages. The great philological scholars of the empirical research (*k'ao-cheng*) school of the Ch'ing dynasty had also fostered the critical treatment of the great texts, although it is much to be doubted that their work had the sceptical-iconoclastic connotations ascribed to it by their twentieth-century admirers. K'ang Yu-wei – by no means a critical scholar – had attempted at the beginning of the century to use a systematic attack on the orthodoxy of certain Old Text scriptures to support his own New Text version of Confucianism.

Like the scholarship of K'ang Yu-wei the movement to 'reorganize the national heritage' (*cheng-li kuo-ku*), as it was designated by Hu Shih, had a deep ideological motive. The methods of 'science' could, in the words of Laurence Schneider, be used 'to undermine the credibility of orthodox histories and the historical foundations of scripture.'[18] One of the most effective ways of removing the dead hand of tradition was to dissolve the factual claims of the myths which supported that tradition. In the end this critical liberation of historical studies from the burden of certain fundamentalistic and conventional ways of viewing the past was to be taken up by many other scholars of 'national studies' – even by 'neo-traditionalist' scholars who did not necessarily share the iconoclastic preoccupations of Hu Shih and Ku Chieh-kang.

Even in the case of the iconoclastic 'new cultural' scholars, their intentions were not entirely destructive. Although Hu Shih, Ku Chieh-kang

17 Lee, *The romantic generation*, 22.
18 Laurence Schneider, *Ku Chieh-kang and China's new history*.

and Fu Ssu-nien committed themselves to a future whose model was to be found in the contemporary West, as Chinese nationalists they were by no means entirely free of the desire to find what Hu Shih called 'congenial stocks' in the Chinese past from which a modern culture might grow. The view of science advocated by Hu Shih's teacher John Dewey, with its notion of gradual, incremental evolution, encouraged the idea that the present must somehow grow out of the past. Both Ku Chieh-kang and Hu Shih were indeed able to find to their own satisfaction strands of Chinese thought which pointed towards modernity. There was the presumed 'scientific' method of Ch'ing scholarship, the beginnings of logic in China's ancient thought, and in the case of Hu Shih, the vital vernacular literature of the past which was in such striking contrast to the decadent, formalistic classical literature of the elite. This populist theme which contrasted the discredited and oppressive 'high culture' of the elite with the vital energy of the folk was eventually to lead Ku Chieh-kang to his extensive studies of folklore (see below). Hu Shih, who was equally concerned with both the new literature and the new scholarship, was later able to combine both interests in his scholarly investigations of the vernacular fiction of the past. All of these endeavours, whether literary, scholarly or simply publicistic, were thoroughly infused with the common premises of the New Culture movement.

Despite the shared premises of the movement, when we juxtapose the names of some of its major protagonists – Hu Shih, Ch'en Tu-hsiu, and Lu Hsun – we become acutely conscious of the profound differences among them. As a young student before 1911, Hu Shih had already been profoundly influenced by the social Darwinist ideas of Yen Fu and Liang Ch'i-ch'ao. His happy experiences as a student in the United States and his contacts with the philosophy of the earlier John Dewey then seem to have led him by a kind of smooth evolution to his own version of Ch'en Tu-hsiu's famous formula 'Mr Science and Mr Democracy', a formula which once it had been set forth was to remain essentially unchanged. Yen Fu's Bacon-Mill conception of science as a kind of simple inductionism was to provide a bridge to Dewey's experimentalistic concept, and Hu Shih's own life experience in early twentieth-century America was to provide him with a happy image of democracy in operation even though he also enthusiastically accepted Dewey's more advanced, critical view of true democracy.

In John Dewey, science and democracy were inseparable values. The experimental method of science in its reliance on tentative hypotheses applied to the study of 'problematic situations' represented a rejection of all spiritual authority and all pre-established dogma – whether religious, political or metaphysical. It thus was the very basis for the assertion of freedom. If men would cooperate together to apply the methods of science, which had been so successfully applied to nature, to the study of human social and cultural problems – an area still subjugated to the empire of dogma – the ends of true liberty and equality would be brought close to realization. The spread of scientific intelligence, thus conceived, through the whole society by education, would lead men to analyse and deal effectively with their collective problems and even to reconcile their clashing interests. In spite of Dewey's sharp criticism of mere formal 'political democracy' and constitutionalism, there seems little doubt that his whole outlook presupposed a common acceptance of constitutional democracy as 'the rules of the game'.

While Hu Shih seems to have accepted Dewey's view of science as methodology, the subtle epistemological issues raised by Dewey as a philosopher seem to have escaped him entirely, and he found it quite possible to combine Dewey's pragmatism with a simple dogmatic mechanistic-naturalistic metaphysics.[19] In this area he remained very much in the tradition of Yen Fu and Liang Ch'i-ch'ao, even though his naturalism is unencumbered by Taoist-Buddhist overtones. Again, Dewey's emphasis on 'scientific inquiry' and education in dealing with socio-political problems; his deprecation of 'mere politics' seems to have reinforced a preexistent tendency in Hu Shih to regard the disorderly and 'irrational' political conflicts of China as irrelevant to China's true progress.

Dewey's emphasis on scientific intelligence and education was entirely in keeping with the whole new cultural emphasis on the transformation of conscious life. It was thus entirely appropriate that when Hu Shih returned to China in 1917 he should have become closely associated with the movement. His deep interest in language reform was entirely in keeping with the broad educational goals of the movement. His interest in the New Literature reflected both a deep personal fondness for literature and a conviction that the affective power of literature provided a most powerful vehicle for communicating new ideas. When one surveys his life in retrospect, one cannot but feel that Hu's pronounced literary and scholarly concerns reflected personal inclinations as well as the no doubt sincere belief that 'reorganizing the national heritage' was a crucial cultural task. This does not mean that he did not devote a good deal of attention to social and political questions in his writings over the years, but, unable as he was for the most part to affect the actual course of poli-

19 Hu Shih's staunch support of this kind of metaphysics seems to have shielded him from any response to Dewey's later subtle discussions of religious and aesthetic experience.

tical affairs, he found that it was much more feasible to apply 'scientific intelligence' to the critique of the cultural heritage.

When we turn to Ch'en Tu-hsiu we find that while he actually created the formula 'Mr Science and Mr Democracy', his view of both these categories was different in subtle ways from that of Hu Shih. His temperament, unlike that of Hu, was passionate and impatient. The fact that the Western influence which had been predominant in his case had been French rather than Anglo-American was not insignificant. His view of science was basically that of a crude Darwinian metaphysic. Science was a corrosive which could be used to undermine traditional values. The fact that the forces of evolution seemed to have completely bogged down in China led him to moments of deep depression, yet like Hu Shih, he was basically able to combine his 'scientific' determinism with a strong faith in the powers of an intellectual elite. Unlike Hu Shih, the positive doctrine of science as a piece-meal experimental methodology did not penetrate the centre of Ch'en's consciousness and he was later able to transfer the use of the word science from Darwinism to Marxism without losing any sense of its apodictic certainty.

Similarly, Hu Shih's conception of scientific method seems to have rendered him impervious to the appeal of the notion of total revolutionary transformation, while Ch'en Tu-hsiu, who greatly admired the French Revolution as a fountainhead of modern democracy, was probably inherently more vulnerable to the appeal of revolutionary transformation in spite of his thoroughly anti-political 'cultural' approach during the period before 1919. Yet during the period of close collaboration between the two (1917–19) there was nevertheless a great resemblance in their views on the individual and on the ingredients of democracy.

Lu Hsun (Chou Shu-jen), who was to become modern China's most distinguished literary giant, was a man of quite different sensibilities. Throughout his life in his more literary persona, he seems to have had a peculiar sensitivity to the 'powers of darkness'. In his youth, he was easily converted to the evolutionary creed and yet his dark doubts began to emerge even before 1911. His own personal family experiences, his deep sense of the corruption and 'slave mentality' of the Chinese people, seem even before 1911 to have diminished his faith in the effectiveness of the forces of evolution in China. His contacts with Nietzsche's writings did not turn him into a true Nietzschean but provided him with the vivid image of the free, heroic, defiant spirit who sets himself against the 'slave mentality' of the mass of mankind. For a time, he indulged in the youthful dream of the Nietzschean-Byronic poetic hero who would be able to rouse mankind out of its spiritual slumbers. It may also have been Nietzsche and Byron who led him very early to a certain lack of sympathy for the prosaic, 'bourgeois' culture of Western Europe and America. In spite of Yen Fu's influence, Lu Hsun was to remain cool to the Western technocratic strain of thought as well as to the detached 'realism' of much Western literature with its over-complicated view of man's moral life.

The post-1911 revolutionary situation was to lead Lu Hsun to a blank wall of despair. His vision of the capacity of Nietzschean literary heroes to mould society seems to have faded rapidly. His 'totalistic' image of China's bad past and present was if anything more sombre than that of his 'new cultural' colleagues. The cruelty, corruption, servility and hypocrisy of contemporary China did not represent a decline of traditional values, but in some sense were actually a manifestation of those destructive values. In his 'Diary of a madman', he makes it clear that it is not only the actuality of Chinese society which makes it 'man-eating'. Its ideals are also 'man-eating' ideals. Even the young revolutionaries of the pre-1911 period had speedily succumbed to the poisonous influence of this incubus. Lu Hsun's decision to take up writing once more was a response to the 'educational' aims of the New Culture movement but it seems to have been a highly sceptical response.

In spite of his 'totalistic iconoclasm' it is nevertheless important to point out that on the level of his literary imagination, Lu Hsun continued to be fascinated by certain 'counter-traditional' aspects of the Chinese past. The past to which he looked was, however, entirely different from the past in which Hu Shih sought his 'congenial stocks'. It was the past of 'neo-Taoist' bohemians of the southern dynasties, of popular fantasy and fable and even the past of certain intimate personal values. Yet none of these attractions seems to have wrenched Lu Hsun from his rejection of the heritage as a whole.

MAY FOURTH AND ITS CONSEQUENCES

In dealing with the consequences of the events of May 1919, we shall not here dwell on the multiplicity of doctrines which were to find expression in a myriad of new periodicals. May Fourth simply marked an explosive stage in the expansion (already under way) of the audience for the themes of the New Culture – particularly its 'totalistic' rejection of the cultural heritage. It is now, however, quite clear that most of the doctrines embraced were not new.

One of the main consequences of these events for our purposes here is their implications for the purely cultural diagnosis of China's ills. May Fourth was a political act, a seemingly effective act of political protest

against foreign imperialism. It even led for a time to a kind of mass movement (albeit of students and urban strata only). The new cultural leaders
had in the past been mainly concerned with China's domestic ills. The
social Darwinist coloration of their thought had not on the whole led
them to moralistic judgments of the behaviour of the imperialist powers
or to attribute China's ills primarily to foreign causes. Yet the nationalistic impatience and sense of urgency of the students forced some of
their intellectual elders to turn their attention away for the moment from
their long-term cultural effort, to face the sad state of contemporary
politics in China.

Even the antipolitical Hu Shih was forced by the events of May Fourth
to reassess his posture. The immediate effect was to raise his hopes that
the cultural transformation which, to his delight, already seemed to have
taken place among young intellectuals, would flow not into politics but
into a 'social movement'. John Dewey, who was himself present in China
in 1919, encouraged this hope by his own observation that 'the students'
organizations have gone into popular education, social and philanthropic
service and vigorous intellectual discussion.'[20] Hu Shih spoke of 'masses
to educate, women to emancipate, schools to reform'.[21] The assumption
seems to have been at the outset that all these goals might be pursued
while by-passing the intractable facts of political-military power as they
existed in the China of 1919. Yet by the summer of 1922, Hu Shih, under
the proddings of his friend Ting Wen-chiang, was himself induced to
help found the journal *Nu-li chou-pao* (Endeavour), which was frankly
dedicated to political action.

Ting Wen-chiang, who, as an able geologist was one of the few actual
scientists among the new culture's 'scientific' intellectuals, had been
trained not in America but in Scotland.[22] There he had acquired a thoroughly British empiricist view of science (like Hu Shih he was an admirer
of the Ch'ing 'empiricists') but a type of empiricism not as implicated
with the gospel of democracy as was Dewey's version of experimentalism.
Accordingly, Ting was less inclined to indulge in the moralistic judgments
of militarists and politicians that figured so strongly in Hu Shih's outlook.
His attitude towards established power seemed to be – is it usable for our
purposes? Hu Shih had in the interim himself become painfully aware
of the power of political forces to interfere with the intellectuals' rights
of freedom of speech and action. He had also become aware of the rise
of new authoritarian '-isms' – prepared to pre-empt the arena of political

20 Jerome B. Grieder, *Hu Shih and the Chinese renaissance*, 179.
21 *Ibid.* 177.
22 On Ting see Charlotte Furth's study *Ting Wen-chiang: science and China's new culture.*

action. Hence one aspect of his political action was the liberal call for 'civil rights' as against the arbitrary acts of government. This was a cause to which he remained faithful ever after.

The other side of Hu Shih's political proposals – his call for a government of 'good men' and a 'government with a plan' – already pointed to the grave problem of how to relate 'science' to 'democracy' in China. Given his 'common-sensical' definition of science, Dewey allowed himself to hope that the methods of scientific inquiry would rapidly be propagated throughout American society, making science a weapon of an enlightened people through the new education. Given China's situation, Hu Shih could only hope that men of scientific enlightenment (who were 'good' by definition but also few in number) might bring their influence to bear on established centres of power. Hu Shih no less than the Communists and Nationalists felt himself forced to believe in an enlightened elite. The hope of being able to work with Wu P'ei-fu's government was of course to be short-lived, and Hu Shih was soon to return to his cultural view of China's problems.

One of the groups better able to take advantage of the nationalist political fervour which pervaded the young during May Fourth (a fervour which overrode all ideological differences) was Sun Yat-sen and his entourage. Whatever one may think of Sun's merits as a thinker or statesman, the fact is that during the whole bleak period from 1911 to 1919 he had not been diverted from his political goal of establishing a strong central government, however ineffective his methods. He did not succumb to the 'new cultural' obsession with the sickness of China's culture. On the contrary, even before 1911 his contacts with 'national essence' thinking had convinced him that national pride in the achievements of the past must be fostered and he had even developed definite ideas of what was to be prized.

One of the traditional values to be prized was the old stress on 'people's livelihood' which Sun had long since been able to link (like Liang Ch'i-ch'ao) to the 'socialist' critique of the sharp class antagonism in Western society. Like Liang he constantly stressed the relative lack of class antagonism, as he defined it, in traditional Chinese society. Also during the years of growing bitterness after 1911, he had devoted a good deal of attention to the problem of how to create a disciplined, unified vanguard party in China. In general his faith in constitutional democracy of the Western type gradually declined. It is thus not surprising that Sun and some of his closest disciples expressed an immediate and keen interest after the October Revolution in Lenin's views on party organization as well as in the Bolshevik formula for dealing with military power. Some of the younger men in Sun's entourage – such as Hu Han-min, Tai Chi-t'ao, Chu Chih-hsin – were indeed to prove remarkably receptive to the Leninist theory of imperialism as an analysis of Western behaviour.[23]

INTRODUCTION OF MARXISM-LENINISM

The doctrine of the Bolshevik revolution was to be one of the newer additions to the doctrinal storehouse of the May Fourth period which otherwise drew on older themes. The phraseology of the Leninist theory of imperialism very quickly became popular among many circles after the 'betrayal of Versailles', but the acceptance of Soviet communism as a total doctrine was to prove a much slower process as is amply proven by the small number of immediate converts. Thus in dealing with the appeals of Marxism-Leninism we must by no means confine ourselves to the early beginnings of the communist movement.

The first appeal of the October Revolution lay perhaps in the fact of revolution itself. The lively faith in a progressive evolutionary cosmology which had been the central creed of the pre-revolutionary period had lost its vigour. The new cultural leaders who still thought of the present West as China's future had felt obliged to fall back on their own resources as educators. Even those prepared to call themselves socialists and anarchists who had accepted the anti-capitalist image of the West could discern little sign of dramatic historic movement in what appeared to be an increasingly stable West.

The man who most vividly symbolized the response to the Bolshevik Revolution as a sign that world history was again on the move was Li Ta-chao.[24] One of the more idiosyncratic members of the new culture group, he had somehow managed to maintain a buoyant faith in his own poetic version of historical progress even during the bleak years. His own conception differed from the prevailing social Darwinist creed. Inspired by sources as diverse as Emerson, Bergson, Hegel, and a Taoist-Buddhist strain, he had conceived of history as a kind of unified, ever youthful World Spirit ever able to break through the static structures to which it gives rise. His readiness for a cosmic act of liberation thus made him extraordinarily responsive to the apocalyptic message of the Bolshevik Revolution as the harbinger of a new historic movement which would sweep away 'all national boundaries, all differences of classes, all barriers.' As Maurice Meisner points out, this more universal vision was combined in Li with a bone-deep Chinese nationalism which seemed to envisage

23 Their ideas found expression in the journal *Chien she* (Construction), 1920.
24 For a study of Li see Maurice Meisner, *Li Ta-chao and the origins of Chinese Marxism*.

the possibility that China would somehow be able to participate in this world drama as a 'people-nation'. The Leninist doctrine of imperialism with its positive attitude towards the provisional role of nationalism in the 'backward' world during a bourgeois democratic stage, provided a space for Li Ta-chao's vision although it is by no means clear that Li truly accepted the provisional nature of the nationalist component. As Joseph Levenson has, however, pointed out, this new vision of history – even before it involved any deep knowledge of the dynamics of Marxism – now would place China itself in the vanguard of an historic movement which would lead beyond the corrupt contemporary West. The West could be rejected from a higher yet iconoclastic point of view.

As has often been pointed out, the Marxist-Leninist revolution was also responsive to a problem we have met before and already described as the Leninist dilemma. The problem involved both a deep belief that History is 'on our side' and deep doubts whether the movement from the present into the future can be entrusted to impersonal forces. Lenin had faced the problem of the conscious vanguard – a problem faced not only by Yen Fu and Liang Ch'i-ch'ao in the past but by Sun Yat-sen and even Hu Shih and Ting Wen-chiang in the May Fourth era. But he had done so in a new way. The model of the communist party as the concentration of the general will of the industrial proletariat, the military metaphor of the party as a general staff of highly disciplined, monolithically united 'professional revolutionaries', who could analyse the temporal terrain of emerging objective historical situations just as generals can interpret the spatial terrain in which they operate – these notions were to become indispensable components of the Marxist-Leninist message.

In retrospect, however, it would appear that an even more important aspect of Leninism as a political strategy was another side of the military metaphor – its emphasis on mass mobilization as a source of political power. The organizational philosophy of the party could be borrowed by others (as the Kuomintang did after 1923). The essential, however, was the combination of the concept of the vanguard party with a concern for mass mobilization. Lenin no doubt sincerely believed that the Bolshevik party was the incarnation of the general will of the industrial proletariat, and this belief led him to relate himself aggressively (but not always successfully) to the organization of the party's 'class basis'. But beyond that he had a deep appreciation of the power to be derived from a linkage to immediately felt mass needs, as in his adoption of the slogan 'peace and land' in 1917. None of this implies that individuals who enter the movement are not directly moved in their organizational activities by immediate sentiments of compassion and indignation. It does mean that the leadership remains a 'general staff' whose strategies and perspectives are not in theory confused by the 'limited', short-term perspectives of the masses. The leadership is confident that it operates from a long-term historical perspective. Again the military metaphor also implies a determination to relate oneself not only to mass mobilization but to a constant realistic and detached assessment of the strength and disposition of political forces in the environment. By constantly interpreting these political forces as reflections of 'class relations' in the Marxist sense, one could maintain one's faith that one was relating practice to Marxist theory.

One should hasten to add that none of these abstract propositions guaranteed an ultimate communist victory in China. The question of how one was to acquire a mass base was not itself answered by the bare formula. The question of whether an effective party could be created without great leaders remained to be resolved. The emphasis on a 'realistic' political strategy provided no guarantees of the correctness of the strategies pursued either in China or in Moscow, nor could one ever discount the crucial decisiveness of unforeseen contingencies such as the Japanese intervention of later decades.

A word should be said at this point about the relative lack of attention to the political potential of mobilized mass energy before 1919. Certainly China had known the power of mass mobilization in the rebellions of the past. Yet despite the widespread older assumption that 'the people' would be the beneficiaries of progress, even the revolutionaries before 1911 did not, on the whole, think of mass organization as a source of political power[25] (with the somewhat questionable exception of their cooperation with secret societies[26]). One may speculate that in some sense the new Western ideas of the literati increased rather than diminished their distance from the masses, intensifying their perception of the people as a helpless entity sunk in ignorance and passivity.

Despite the fascination of the pre-1911 revolutionaries with Russian 'revolutionary heroism' the idea of 'going to the people' did not truly emerge until the May Fourth period in the 'social movement' of the times. The notion of direct contact between intellectuals and masses was to have a considerable future in the work of Yen Yang-ch'u, T'ao Hsing-chih, Liang Shu-ming and others, but again this was not to involve the

---

25 Edward Friedman in his book *Backward toward revolution: the Chinese Revolutionary Party* speaks of the 'mass' organizational activities of some of Sun's followers such as Chu Chih-hsin after 1911.

26 For a discussion of this cooperation see Mary Backus Rankin, *Early Chinese revolutionaries: radical intellectuals in Shanghai and Chekiang, 1902–1911.*

idea of mass mobilization as a source of political and military power. It need hardly be added that the 'new cultural' perspective of the period before 1919 was hardly oriented to mass political mobilization, however sincere its ultimate commitment to mass education.

PROBLEMS AND '-ISMS'

One of the more significant conflicts which emerged out of the winds of doctrine of the May Fourth period was the debate between Hu Shih, Li Ta-chao and others concerning the question of 'problems versus -isms'. In the textbook accounts of the intellectual history of China after the May Fourth period, often written under Marxist inspiration, one finds a series of debates, each leading to the clear victory of one side and gradually leading by a progressive ascent to the victory of Marxism and then within the Marxist camp to a victory of 'true' Marxism. A less triumphalist view of these debates does not lead to such confidence concerning the designation of clear winners and clear losers.

Hu Shih's articles in *Mei-chou p'ing-lun* (Weekly critic) of July and August 1919 on 'Problems and -isms' reflect his disturbance over the drift of his friends Ch'en Tu-hsiu, Li Ta-chao and others into the communist camp. As he was later to remark, 'Though the slaves of Confucius and Chu Hsi are fewer now, a new breed of slaves of Marx and Kropotkin has sprung up.'[27] In these articles Hu draws a sharp contrast between Dewey's scientific approach to society which directs its attention to concrete situations and problem areas, analyses them and provides concrete solutions for specific problems, on the one hand, and totalistic '-isms' which claim to provide total and 'fundamental solutions' for all the problems of a society on the other. As one might have expected, his opponents reply that all the separate problems of a society are related to a total structure or system and can be solved fundamentally only when the 'system' is changed as a whole. It is interesting to note that at this time Ch'en Tu-hsiu, who had not yet been won over to the communist camp, still tended to support Hu Shih's point of view. Yet Li Ta-chao and many of the students were yearning to find in anarchism and Marxism warrant for their ardent hopes that there might indeed be a 'fundamental solution' to China's overwhelming problems and that History would lead to such solutions. In post-1949 China, Hu Shih has, of course, been treated as the decisive loser of the debate.

One need not be a follower of John Dewey's 'scientific methodology'

27 Grieder, *Hu Shih and the Chinese renaissance* 189, cited from 'Wo ti ch'i-lu' (My crossroads), *Hu Shih wen-ts'un* (Collected works of Hu Shih), 3. 99–102.

to assert that any society, whatever its socio-political structure, tends to confront separate problems which must be considered separately no matter how much they may be enmeshed with other problems. While the rise of the People's Republic may indeed have solved some fundamental problems (among them the creation of a political order which seems to maintain its general legitimacy), it has, even in the view of its leadership, continued to be confronted by serious – even fundamental – problems, some old and some new, many of which are by no means easy to solve.

The fatal weakness of Hu Shih and the ultimate strength of his opponents was his notion that one could proceed to the solution of social-educational problems without confronting the tragic problems of political power. To involve oneself in an effort to create one's own base of political power in the current Chinese environment was, in his view, to become embroiled with all the irrational passions and selfish intrigues and violence of warlord politics. All this had little to do with the attitude of 'scientific' rationality required for the solution of these problems. To the extent that he did relate himself to politics he, like his scientist friend Ting Wen-chiang, could only hope to influence incumbent holders of power to accept his recommendations.

What is involved here is not the abstract question of whether those who possess social and political power can ever under any circumstances be persuaded to implement reforms. For a time, Ting Wen-chiang, who did not share Hu Shih's moralistic diffidence towards militarists, was actually able to influence the Kiangsu warlord Sun Ch'uan-fang to carry out certain judicious urban reforms in the Shanghai area.[28] In the brutal and desperately insecure political environment of this period in China, however, holders of power and privilege were not easily to be diverted from their narrow obsessions with political survival.

The communists (although not notably Li Ta-chao) were, on the other hand, prepared to address themselves to the problem of creating political (and ultimately) military power and to act in terms of existing intractable power realities, whether these realities did or did not ultimately conform to the class categories of Marxist analysis. This did not mean that in 1919 Li Ta-chao or any other self-professed communist had access to some 'fundamental solution' of all the current problems of China or even that the slogan 'revolution' had any immediate consequences for Chinese politics. The French and Russian Revolutions have been called social rather than simply political yet at their core lay the destruction of an established *ancien régime*. The destruction of the Peking government in the fragmented

28 See Charlotte Furth, ch. 7 of this volume.

China of 1919 would have had little consequence, and both Nationalists and Communists were to see their task in the next few years as that of dealing with the 'problem' of how one constructs the bases of a new political authority in China rather than the problem of destroying an *ancien régime*. The social could not be divorced from the political and the political task was one of building a new political order rather than that of destroying a firmly established old political order.

THE THEME OF POPULAR CULTURE

The May Fourth episode did not lead to immediate political results, and there were many in the intellectual stratum including Lu Hsun who were not particularly impressed with its significance. There were those such as Hu Shih, Ku Chieh-kang, Fu Ssu-nien and others who were to continue in their belief that the root of China's problem was cultural, and they must therefore 'reorganize the national heritage'.

One new tendency within this enterprise was the emergence of a positive attitude towards the study of popular culture. Even Hu Shih, in his insistence that the vernacular literature of the past had been much more vital and alive than the sterile 'classical' works of the high culture, had introduced a kind of populist theme into his outlook. He seemed willing to include the 'vernacular literature' of the past among the 'congenial stocks' to be preserved. None of this would involve interest in any aspect of the religious culture of the masses. Yet the theme of the greater vitality of popular culture led him to encourage Ku Chieh-kang and others in their efforts to explore folkways and regional customs and collect folktales and folksongs. Ku Chieh-kang had himself been touched by the new movement which had emerged among students since 1919 to 'go to the people' and he was able to relate this movement to his own thesis that while intellectuals in the past had allied themselves to the old aristocracy, they should now take advantage of their new found autonomy as intellectuals to relate themselves to the common people. To do this, one would, however, have to study the conscious life of the masses – their folklore, their customs and folksongs, always employing the methods of scientific inquiry.[29]

From the very outset of this effort there emerged the idea of using popular forms to convey new messages of enlightenment, such as the notion of composing popular ballads with new educational content. In the case of Ku Chieh-kang, however, his interest in folksongs, temples and

29 See Schneider, *Ku Chieh-kang and China's new history*, ch. 4.

festivals gradually took on a more positive aspect. He gradually came to find in the forms of popular culture the embodiment of aesthetic values. In an attack on the anti-superstition policies of the Nationalist Government in 1929 (which was, on the whole, fundamentally hostile to popular culture) Ku was to complain that 'the superstitions are not necessarily overthrown while the artistic legacy of earlier men is indeed overthrown.'[30] Appreciation of the positive aspects of the vital, creative popular culture went hand in hand with the growing bitterness of Ku's 'scientific' assault on the orthodoxy of the high culture. Here he again took up the 'unmasking' theme of the pioneer thinkers – that, from Ch'in to Ch'ing, this culture had been used to suppress the creative life of the people. In the course of his scholarly activity over the years in such journals as the *Ke-yao chou-k'an* (Folksong weekly) and *Min-su chou-k'an* (Folklore), Ku and other students of popular culture such as Cheng Chen-to and Chung Ching-wen were to produce an impressive corpus of research.

The interest in the 'creative, original' aspects of popular culture was not confined to the scholars. Lu Hsun's ambivalence towards various aspects of Chinese popular culture such as graphic arts and the folk theatre continued to colour all of his fictional writings, while Shen Ts'ung-wen, who had spent his youth in the frontier areas of West Hunan, wrote at great length about the life and customs of an area in which Chinese and Miao peoples lived side by side, again finding in this popular culture a source of unreflective vitality.

In all of this one finds little inclination on the part of intellectuals to regard with any sympathy the current 'action' movements among the non-Westernized population such as Buddhist or syncretic sectarian movements or secret societies. Political enlightenment it was felt must come from elsewhere.

This view is particularly marked in the case of the communist Ch'ü Ch'iu-pai who harshly criticized his fellow Marxist literateurs for their 'Western classicism'. His point was simple. If a revolutionary literature were to be written in China which would rouse the masses (and here his mind was focused mainly on the urban proletariat), it must be written in a language and using the forms of life which the masses understood. These popular forms were, however, to be used basically to serve a new content and not because of any intrinsic value of their own. In concentrating on urban working people, Ch'ü was quite convinced that he would be dealing with basically 'modern' common men. His criticism of the

30 *Ibid.* 152.

effort of the 'popular culture' scholars was, on the whole, harsh. The vernacular literature so highly praised by Hu Shih was in essence the work of literati, and the culture of the masses contained a mass of superstitions designed to keep the people in bondage. In the Yenan period Mao Tsetung would later take up the theme of using the forms of popular culture (now that of the peasant masses) for strictly modern political purposes. Yet the nationalistic emphasis in the Mao of Yenan was to lead him to a somewhat more favourable assessment of the value of popular culture of the past and to a broader sense of its contents. Like Hu Shih, he was prepared to admit vernacular Chinese fiction into the precincts of the people's culture, however suspicious the 'popular' credentials of its authors.

'NEO-TRADITIONALISM' – FINDING TRUTH IN THE HERITAGE

Another outcome of the May Fourth movement which until recently has received comparatively little attention in Western literature was the whole 'neo-traditionalist' reaction against the 'totalistic iconoclasm' of the movement. The neglect of the figures associated with this tendency has again been based on the premise that its presumed defeat in 1949 renders its ideas completely uninteresting. Let us note first that the figures to be dealt with here have little to do with the popular culture orientation just discussed. They were unabashedly oriented towards the high culture of the past even when they tended to identify this high culture with the 'Chinese spirit' in general. Also they were acquainted in varying degrees with modern Western thought and did not hesitate to employ Western ideas to support their positions. In the view of Joseph Levenson this search for support from the sages of the West indicated anew the 'traditionalistic' nature of their thought. It betrayed a lack of confidence that traditional Chinese thought could stand on its own merits. It was again a case of salvaging national pride by finding Chinese equivalents of Western ideas. However, while this kind of 'romantic' cultural nationalism is often present (most notably in the case of Kuomintang ideology after 1927), one cannot make the a priori assertion that this is inevitably the case.

Levenson's view probably holds true for the revolutionary 'national essence' circle of Liu Shih-p'ei, Liu Ya-tzu and others before the May Fourth period. Yet the successors of this older 'national essence' group after May Fourth represented an entirely different breed. Men such as Mei Kuang-ti and Wu Mi, who had studied at Harvard University under the eminent Irving Babbitt and who still continued their affiliations with the older 'national essence' group, adopted an entirely different approach which found expression in their periodical the *Hsueh heng* (Critical review). Through Irving Babbitt they came in contact with the Western tradition of the literary critic as the critic of life. Babbitt had erected the categories 'classical' and 'romantic' into the status of major life attitudes. The 'classical' represented metahistorical aesthetic and ethical standards, as well as the 'inner check' in the moral life of the individual. It represented order and structure. The 'romantic' represented the dissolution of all standards, the unbridled domination of passions in individual and collective life, and so forth. The *Critical Review* leaders were convinced that these were categories which cut across cultural differences and they were much encouraged by Babbitt himself to believe that the Confucian values and classical Chinese literature represented that which was most classical in China. Whether this represents 'cultural nationalism' or a genuine perception of spiritual affinities across cultures is a matter which cannot be clearly decided. The fact remains that this particular brand of 'neo-traditionalism' was not to prove very vital. Liang Shu-ming, who regarded himself as the bearer of authentic Confucianism, dismissed the scholastic and aesthetic focus of the whole 'national essence' group as representing the 'picking up of stiff rotten goods'.[31]

It is noteworthy that the man who points out the main line of 'neo-traditional' thought after the May Fourth period is again the ever voluble Liang Ch'i-ch'ao. Having made a trip to Europe as a non-official member of the Chinese delegation to the Paris Peace Conference, he felt the genuine sense of gloom and dismay among many European thinkers on the continent after the catastrophe of the First World War. These contacts led him to write his 'Reflections on a European journey' which is nothing less than a total reassessment of the essence of 'Eastern and Western civilizations'. Discussions of this type which had gone on before in the writings of Yen Fu, Ch'en Tu-hsiu and others had always led to the drastic reduction of those vast complexes called civilizations to simple, manageable dichotomies. The essence of Western civilization was to Liang essentially what it had been in the past – a 'materialistic' civilization (as he now called it) bent on the subjugation of nature through science and technology, a Darwinian universe of inexorable conflict among individuals, classes and nations. What was drastically reversed was his evaluation of this civilization. In the past he had enthusiastically accepted social Darwinism as a positive prescriptive ethic. Now it was the ethic which in the opinion of critical Western thinkers themselves had led to the

31 See Guy Alitto, *The last Confucian: Liang Shu-ming and the Chinese dilemma of modernity*, 118.

holocaust of the First World War. Since this was the essence of Western civilization (for its aggressive, belligerent nature had even earlier historical roots), wherever he now found in the West more spiritually oriented critics such as Eucken or Bergson, he now tended to detect the influence of the East.

More pertinent to our theme, however, is the question of where Liang now finds the locus of the Chinese spirit. He finds it not in those doctrines which had dwelt in the past on the so-called 'outer realm' – doctrines concerning rules of proper behaviour (*li*), institutions and social organization and doctrines concerning the structure of the natural world. Here China would have to continue to learn much from the material and social technology of the West. He rather finds it precisely in those modes of thought which had stressed the 'inner realm' – in the Sung-Ming Neo-Confucianism of Chu Hsi and Wang Yang-ming, and beyond that in the Mahayana Buddhistic philosophy to which he had been attracted as a youth. The core of China's unique culture lies in its faith that man has an inner intuition which unites him to the cosmic, ineffable source of all being, a source from which he derives the power of spiritual and moral self-transformation. The West thought of freedom only in terms of the satisfaction of creaturely needs – not in terms of a cosmically based moral autonomy.

In the case of Liang Ch'i-Ch'ao – man of many transformations – one can never be entirely sure of the springs of his thought. Joseph Levenson may be quite right to assume that he derived a good deal of ordinary nationalistic gratification from his new-found sense of China's spiritual superiority. Yet Liang's finding the core of Chinese thought in Neo-Confucianism prefigured the central tendency of the whole neo-traditional movement of the following period.

THE DEBATE ON SCIENCE AND HUMAN LIFE

Another important moment in the emergence of the new traditionalism, as well as in the clarification of the meaning of the term science in China, was provided by the 'debate on science and human life'[32] launched by Liang's young associate and student of German philosophy, Chang Chün-mai, in 1923. His contention that science could not explain man because human life was 'subjective, intuitive, freely willed and unique to the individual' reflected his neo-Kantian studies as well as the German debates on 'natural sciences and spiritual sciences' (Naturwissenschaft

---

32 See *K'o-hsueh yü jen-sheng-kuan* (Science and the philosophy of life), prefaces by Hu Shih and Ch'en Tu-hsiu. See also above, pages 372–3.

und Geisteswissenschaft). Unlike Liang, Chang was acutely aware of the German counter to the tradition of Anglo-American empiricism. Nevertheless, he seemed able to make a quick transition from Kant's epistemological scepticism to the cosmic intuitionism of Wang Yang-ming.

Ting Wen-chiang, who most concretely represented science among the intelligentsia, took up the challenge of Chang's attack on the universal claims of science. From the first discussions in the writings of Yen Fu the word 'science' in China had conveyed a sense of apodictic certainty. From the outset the prevailing concept of science was that of a Baconian inductionism which finds its most complete expression in Mill's *Logic* (translated by Yen Fu). John Dewey's scientific methodology with its focus on experience and experiment was clearly in this tradition in spite of his deep reservations concerning British sensationalist empiricism. From Yen Fu to Mao Tse-tung, however, there also seemed to be little questioning of the faith that systems such as Herbert Spencer's social Darwinism and Marxism were based on concepts derived by inductive observation. The recognition that the cutting edge of the natural sciences lay more in the power of mathematico-deductive hypotheses, rather than in simple procedures of observation and experiment, was not to gain many adherents in China.

Ting Wen-chiang's outlook was based on the positivist epistemology of Karl Pearson's *Grammar of science*, which insisted that science provides the only way man has of organizing and classifying the sense data which are the only link between him and a world beyond that he can never know 'in itself'. While this introduces a rare concern with Western epistemological scepticism, its view of science does not stray from the inductionist tradition. As Charlotte Furth has pointed out in chapter 7, Ting's science of geology was precisely an observational-classifying science. The other participants in the debate, such as Wu Chih-hui, Hu Shih and ultimately Ch'en Tu-hsiu, who was by now a Communist, tended to ignore Ting's epistemology (as well as Dewey's) and to maintain staunchly that science supported either the kind of fanciful mechanistic materialism interlaced with Taoist-Buddhist overtones advocated by Wu Chih-hui or the new true social science of Marxism. Hu Shih and Ch'en Tu-hsiu were to agree that science was a tool for controlling the world of nature and society and that it undermined Chang's faith in the 'inner' transformative spiritual and moral power of the individual. Beyond this, the debate simply laid bare the fact that the word science itself no longer provided any common ground of solidarity.

Chang Chün-mai's argument and his subsequent development demonstrated once more that the heart of the more vital new traditionalism would be Neo-Confucian thought in general and Wang Yang-ming in particular.

A word should be said at this point about the centrality of Wang Yang-ming in traditional thought after May Fourth. Without attempting an analysis of the Ming sage and his followers something must be said about his appeal to figures as diverse as Liang Shu-ming, Hsiung Shih-li and even Chiang Kai-shek. There is first of all the faith in the spiritual-moral inner intuition which links man to an ultimate ground of cosmic being as a source of spiritual-moral life. What we have here is a defiant rejection on intuitive grounds of Western post-Cartesian epistemological scepticism and the concept of a 'valueless' universe. While Wang's intuition led him to conclusions which were in harmony with Confucian moral-political values, his reliance on the 'inner light' bore within itself the possibility of a detachment from traditional Confucian views of the 'outer realm'. By contrast, Chu Hsi's insistence on the need to derive truths by the 'investigation of things' seemed to bind him irrevocably to the 'things' of the traditional order. Finally, Wang's insistence that intuitive moral insight could be gained only in the course of individual action in the world of concrete social situations gave some at least a strong motivation for action in the world.

One of the most notable figures in the neo-traditional movement has been Liang Shu-ming (still alive and flourishing at this writing). Having been exposed in his childhood to a thoroughly Westernized education on the lines proposed by Yen Fu and Liang Ch'i-ch'ao, Liang was not driven in the discouraging years after 1911 into the 'new culture' camp. The sterling example of his father, Liang Chi, who was a kind of living paradigm of Confucian virtue, would have been enough to make him reject Lu Hsun's totalistic negative view of tradition. Instead he sought solace first in Buddhism and then in the Neo-Confucian outlook of the Wang Yang-ming school.

We shall not dwell here on his famous work of 1921, *Eastern and Western cultures and their philosophies*,[33] except to remark that its image of the West was in broad strokes very much that of Liang Ch'i-ch'ao. The essence of Chinese culture lay in its early discovery that what is essentially human in man is his spiritual-moral nature which, when unimpeded, leads both to inner harmony and to unobstructed empathy among men. The achievement by Chinese culture of this insight so early in its history had had its costs. While the West's dynamic civilization had led it to what he saw as a monstrous capitalist-consumer society, it had also led it to

33 All these matters are superbly covered in *The last Confucian* by Guy Alitto.

discover the methods for coping with man's elemental needs. China required the benefit of these methods but not at the cost of losing its spiritual base. Liang fully accepted the activist implications of Wang Yang-ming's philosophy and also seemed to share Wang's conviction that Confucianism had definite implications for social as well as personal reality, that is, Confucianism had implications for the 'outer' as well as the 'inner' realm. It was this conviction which gradually led him to his interest in the 'rural reconstruction' movement already underway and supported by 'Westernizers' such as James Yen and T'ao Hsing-chih. The vast masses of China's countryside had in his view not yet been corrupted by the corrosive effects of urban capitalism but were nevertheless suffering from the myriad evils of poverty, corruption and instability.

Liang's educational and reform activities in Tsou-p'ing county, Shantung, after 1930 were based on a rejection of the political bureaucratic path. Chiang Kai-shek's effort to combine Wang Yang-ming notions of 'self-cultivation' with his own dream of a rationalized, modern bureaucratic-militarized state seemed to Liang to provide no solution. In the conditions of corruption, military coercion and violence which prevailed the sage could bring his moral influence to bear only through direct contact with the rural masses. In one respect there was some resemblance between Liang's ideas and those of Mao Tse-tung during the Yenan period. Guy Alitto has indeed argued that some of Liang's ideas on moral self-scrutiny or small group confessionals, and on the reorientation of rural education may indeed have significantly influenced his friend Mao after their famous interview of 1938.[34] Yet the differences were to remain significant. Liang's programme was based either on the by-passing of the established political structure or, *faute de mieux*, on the support of favourably inclined power-holders (in this but in no other way he resembled Hu Shih). Mao's was premised on the Marxist-Leninist whole-hearted acceptance of the brutal game of power. To Liang any effort to construct a political organization of his own would negate his own Confucian conception of the moral bases of authority. In this, of course, he was like Mencius before him who managed to disguise the fact of the violent origins of the 'sacred three dynasties' themselves. The Maoist use of 'rural reconstruction' as instrumental to the ulterior purpose of building a base of military and political power no doubt already suggested to Liang the possibilities of the future corruption of the communist effort in spite of his admiration of it. In 1953 he was indeed to charge that the adoption of a Stalinist model

34 *Ibid.* 283–92.

of development by the People's Republic was the expression of such a bureaucratic perversion. Yet he himself discovered no way of insulating his rural reconstructional activities from the vicissitudes of the political environment.

While Liang Shu-ming's Confucianism led him directly to the realms of action, the same was not true of Hsiung Shih-li and his disciples T'ang Chün-i, Mou Tsung-san, and others. Hsiung Shih-li (1885–1968) was a somewhat idiosyncratic 'marginal' personality whose educational formation had been largely within the framework of the traditional culture although he had briefly become involved in revolutionary politics. Like others before him he had first been attracted by 'consciousness-only' Buddhism and then was won back by Wang Yang-ming to a Confucian belief in the significance of man's moral life. Unlike Liang Shu-ming, neither he nor his disciples became committed to an immediate programme of action, even though they acknowledged the social implications of their doctrines. The defence and elucidation of the foundations of their intuitionist philosophy seemed to them to require all of their attention, unlike Liang Shu-ming, who seemed quite secure in his own 'sageliness'. Thomas Metzger has argued that the kind of religio-ethical optimism and faith in 'sagely' power found in the writings of T'ang Chün-i, when detached from the older external Confucian order, could become the basis of an ebullient faith in the possibility of a total social transformation.[35] He argues that on an unacknowledged level Mao Tsetung himself shared in this 'traditional' faith. Yet the fact remains that T'ang Chün-i, Mou Tsung-san and Hsiung Shih-li (who lived on in the People's Republic until his death in 1968) did not accept the People's Republic as the realization of their vision and continued to be deeply preoccupied with the relevance of their faith to the existential problems of personal life.

Quite another version of Neo-Confucianism is that represented by Fung Yu-lan who was trained as a philosopher in the United States. Like Mei Kuang-ti, he found his philosophic inspiration in the Anglo-Saxon West. If he is a 'neo-traditionalist' at all, his traditionalism is of a distinctly cosmopolitan variety. Having committed himself to the kind of Platonic 'neo-realism' which flourished for a time in early twentieth-century America and England, he felt confident that its categories could be applied to Chu Hsi's thought. Significantly, neo-realism represents a sharp reaction in the West against the dominant tradition of epistemological scepticism. Some of its adherents were indeed prepared to accept a Platonic

35 Thomas A. Metzger, *Escape from predicament: Neo-Confucianism and China's evolving political culture.*

account of mathematical and logical truth as objective, eternal forms. Fung seems to have been deeply impressed by the ancient Greek ideal of intellectual contemplation as the way to achieve a sense of sublimity and of detachment from the disorders of man's daily existence. Science, in this view, does not merely involve an effort to apply logico-mathematical ideas to an achievement of the mastery of the physical world. To the 'sagely' man science involves the contemplation of the beauty of mathematical and logical 'forms'. In Fung's view this involved intellectual contemplation but not mysticism. Thus, in seeking a Chinese equivalent of his outlook Fung was attracted precisely to what he perceived to be the intellectualism of Chu Hsi rather than to the 'anti-intellectual' intuitionism of Wang Yang-ming. Whether his interpretation of Chu Hsi's *li* as Platonic forms is valid remains a matter of great dispute. Yet one need not doubt that Fung believed he had found here a Chinese framework for his basic outlook.

None of this implied a rejection of the social and nationalistic concerns of his contemporaries. On the contrary Fung was quite ready in the 1930s to accept a quasi-Marxist determinist view of history. History like nature has its own presiding configurations – its own 'forms' of growth and Fung is quite prepared to think of these forms in terms of necessary stages of historical process based on a conception of economic determinism. Moral behaviour in this view means behaviour which conforms to the requirements of a given socio-historical stage of development. On the contemplative level of his being the 'sage' is above the vicissitudes of history. In his moral-practical life he is able to adjust to the requirements of history. This philosophy led him to a willing acceptance of the People's Republic but it did not shield him against future troubles.[36]

It should be added that all these varieties of traditional thought have continued to exercise their influence in Hong Kong, Taiwan and even among Chinese intellectuals abroad. They remain part of the larger intellectual scene of twentieth-century China.

THE ASCENDANCY OF MARXISM

Before we deal with the rise of Marxism to a position of dominance in the Chinese intellectual world, something should be said about those tendencies which are labelled liberal – often on doubtful grounds. Hu Shih continued after May Fourth to cling staunchly to his basic positions even though he was now assailed by enemies on all sides. The spectacular

36 See the unpublished dissertation of Michel Masson, 'The idea of Chinese tradition: Fung Yu-lan, 1939–1949', (Harvard University, Ph.D. dissertation, 1978).

events of the years 1924-7 and the passionate emotions which accompanied them did not sway him. Irrational political passion as ever remained irrelevant to truth. Although he, like his mentor Dewey, was by no means committed to capitalism, he remained convinced that China's basic ills were not due to foreign imperialism. He continued to attack the 'dogmas' of both Sun Yat-sen and the Marxists.

After the establishment of the Nationalist government, Hu continued to attack the traditionalistic components of the Kuomintang ideology, continued to call for the application of 'scientific intelligence' to national policies, continued to call for constitutionalism and civil rights and to advocate a 'modern' system of education which would create a new elite of enlightened and modern men. In the *Tu-li p'ing-lun* (Independent critic) published during the years 1932-7 under the shadow of the growing Japanese threat, Hu Shih was joined by such figures as Ting Wen-chiang and the historian Chiang T'ing-fu in their effort to influence the policies of the Nationalist government. It was soon to become apparent, however, that what they shared with Hu Shih was more his commitment to 'science' than his commitment to democracy.

Ting Wen-chiang had never been as committed to liberal values as Hu Shih and in the sombre decade of the 1930s he, like Chiang T'ing-fu, had come to feel (like Yen Fu and Liang Ch'i-ch'ao before them) that what China needed was a 'scientific' dictatorship – a technocracy which would modernize the bureaucratic, industrial and educational systems of the country. Ting had even been much impressed by Stalin's Russia as a model. They both had a rather poor opinion of the competence of the Kuomintang leadership despite the Nationalist government's professed commitment to the same goals. Yet they could only continue to hope that the Nationalist government, the only centre of organized power, would heed their advice. The rural revolutionary drama of the Chinese Communists in Hunan and Kiangsi and later in Yenan seemed to them utterly irrelevant to the nation's needs and further enfeebled the central power of the state. Hu Shih himself was torn between his attraction to their vision of a scientific elite and his faith in constitutional democracy. Like the others, however, he could only hope to bring his influence to bear on established power. In the end, with the polarization between what he regarded as totalitarian communism and the more limited albeit corrupt authoritarianism of the Kuomintang, which might eventually be pushed in a more liberal direction, he felt that he had to choose the lesser evil. To the end he proved unable as the spiritual leader of a political cause to cope with the tragic and intractable realities of political power in twentieth-century China.

The years between 1924 and 1927 were however, marked above all by the spectacular spread among the urban intelligentsia of certain versions of Marxism as a dominant intellectual outlook. It should nevertheless be noted that the spread of Marxism and the ultimate victory of the Chinese Communists remain two related but separable facts.

In the stormy years 1924–7, many of the younger generation of the May Fourth era, who had thoroughly internalized its totalistic anti-traditionalism, now had a concrete opportunity to participate in the dynamic political drama made possible by the Kuomintang-Communist alliance. From the very outset, the Leninist theory of imperialism and its image of the Western world was to win wide acceptance not only among those close to the Communist Party but even among Kuomintang-affiliated intellectuals and politicians. The events of 30 May 1925 seemed to confirm most graphically the link between foreign imperialism and the exploitation of China's new industrial proletariat. The activism of the urban population and the Communist Party's actual success in establishing a link to the urban working class seemed to confirm Marxist-Leninist views regarding the role of that class in history. The ability of P'eng P'ai, Mao Tse-tung[37] and others to create a link to the peasantry was again not inconsistent with Lenin's view of the role of the peasantry in a bourgeois democratic revolution. During the northern expedition of 1926–7 many intellectuals found themselves participants either in mass organization activities or in the organs of the newly founded Wuhan government. The experience kindled both their nationalist rage and their more universal hopes for the transformation of the world. The revolution would achieve both national unification and the transformation of China into a radically new society. To be sure, bitter conflicts in Moscow showed that Marxism-Leninism yielded no automatic illumination, but so long as the trajectory of revolution moved forward, the desire to believe that Moscow was the source of a higher universal wisdom remained strong.

Among the Marxist intellectuals the members of the romantic Creation Society (see page 474) and of the newly formed 'Sun' (T'ai-yang) Society were to play a prominent role. Having explored the ecstasies and despairs of romantic love and the expressive experience of the writer, Kuo Mo-jo, Chiang Kuang-tz'u and others felt that they now had significant heroic roles to play as revolutionary leaders. Their self-image was thus very similar to that of the romantic revolutionaries before 1911. They would inspire the ardour of the revolutionary masses through the vehicle of a new proletarian literature.

37 For a study of the beginnings of the communist peasant movement see Roy Hofheinz, Jr. *The broken wave: the Chinese communist peasant movement, 1922–1928.*

Lu Hsun's gravitation to Marxism-Leninism was much more painful and arduous. His deep despondency concerning the 'man-eating' power of the old culture had not really been shaken by the events of May Fourth.[38] His mordant reflections on what had happened to many of the young idealists of the pre-1911 period was, perhaps, a factor of some importance in his failure to respond. His hesitancy to accept the new theory of human progress may also have stemmed from his hostility to what he regarded as the romantic revolutionary posturings of his enemies in the Creation Society, who fancied that they could influence the course of history through their proletarian rhetoric. Even when he moved into the Marxist camp, he was to seek theoretical support from Plekhanov and others for his attack on their wild exaggeration of the causative role of literature in social revolution. His use of Marxist categories began before 1927, but it is characteristic of him that what finally drove him close to the Communist Party was the bitter rage roused by the Nationalist government's execution of young people in his immediate entourage. This was no doubt reinforced by a more positive and yet hesitant hope that the Marxist-Leninist analysis of history would prove more accurate than the evolutionary doctrines of the past.

An important element in the polarization of the urban intelligentsia towards Marxism was the abyss which arose between them and the faction within the Kuomintang led by Chiang Kai-shek. While Chiang had been influenced by the anti-imperialist aspect of Leninist rhetoric, his education in both Chekiang and Japan had early led him to the kind of cultural nationalism that rendered him immune to the totalistic iconoclasm of May Fourth. The military basis of his rise to power may have led him further to deprecate the usefulness and trustworthiness of urban intellectuals. It also gave him even after 1927 an unswerving conviction that the task of first priority in China was military unification. In all of these convictions, he seemed to feel that he remained a faithful disciple of Sun Yat-sen. By the same token, all his opponents both within the Kuomintang and outside the party saw in him the recrudescence of the older militarism. He was the symbol of the melancholy fact that the subordination of military to civil power had not yet taken place. Also, the gap between his cultural nationalism and 'totalistic iconoclasm' remained.

The débâcle of 1927 did not lead to a decline in the prestige of Marxism. The Leninist notion that a wrong political strategy basically reflects a wrong 'revolutionary theory' encouraged the view that with a correct theory the revolution would forge ahead. For many (but not for all) the

---

38 See Harriet C. Mills, 'Lu Xun: literature and revolution – from Mara to Marx' in Merle Goldman, ed. *Modern Chinese literature in the May Fourth era.*

continued existence of the Soviet Union as the headquarters of revolution provided valid reassurance that history would ultimately follow a Marxist-Leninist trajectory.

It is thus no accident that a major concern of many Marxist intellectuals during the next decade was to understand Chinese society in Marxist terms. The Leninist use of theory as 'a guide to action' encouraged the belief that the 'party line' of a given period must be based on a Marxist analysis of the disposition of class forces and on the determination of the historical stage. The 'debate on the social history of China'[39] was to be an expression of this concern. However, the determination of China's present 'mode of production' in Marxist terms was to prove to be no easy matter. Quite logically it led to a concern with the periodization of China's long social history. In probing all these questions the participants imperceptibly were driven from a consideration of 'theory as a guide to action' to the more deterministic aspects of Marxist doctrines as applied to the past. Some who participated in the debate were fundamentally interested in Marxism as social science *par excellence*. Thus T'ao Hsi-sheng, a leading figure in the debates, like some other participants was an adherent of the Kuomintang. He found no difficulty in placing his Three People's Principles ideology within the framework of Marxist categories or in drawing non-communist conclusions from his analyses. Other participants, however, represented Stalinist and Trotskyist factions.

At this point we can only note certain features of the debate. On the whole, it would appear that in attempting to use the Marxist concepts of capitalism and feudalism in the analysis of Chinese society, the participants simply illuminated certain unresolved obscurities in Marx's own doctrines on these matters. Is feudal society any agrarian society dominated by a ruling class which rules by 'extra-economic' power? Or do different 'relations of property' reflect different 'relations of production'? Is any type of landlord class feudal? Can the prevalence of commercial relations define the nature of society or is the role of the 'mode of production' crucial? Texts could be found supporting divergent answers to these and many other questions.

The Marxist concept of the 'Asiatic mode of production' was largely rejected by most of the participants, who opted for some version of the unilinear scheme of historical periodization which Marx had prescribed for the West. It was, after all, only within the framework of this scheme that he had actually described the dynamic dialectic of history. There

39 For a study of the debate see Arif Dirlik, *Revolution and history: origins of Marxist historiography in China 1919–1937*; also Benjamin Schwartz, 'Some stereotypes in the periodization of Chinese history', *Philosophic Forum*, I. 11 (Winter 1968) 219–30.

were some participants such as T'ao Hsi-sheng who envisioned other ways of describing and periodizing the unilinear view, but to accept for China Marx's view of a static 'Asian mode of production' was virtually to deny that Chinese social history had a dynamic of its own.

If the debate was won, it was won by fiat rather than by argument. The Mao Tse-tung of the Yenan period made no 'theoretical' contribution whatsoever to the debate. His own interest in high theory led him to another debate less prominent in Marxist circles concerning the philosophic interpretation of the dialectic and questions of Marxist epistemology.

In the 1930s Marxism was also to become a dominant force on the literary front. In the League of Left-wing Writers formed by Lu Hsun, Ch'ü Ch'iu-pai and others we find the emergence of stormy unresolved debates concerning the Marxist view of the role of literature as a 'superstructural' phenomenon. While Marxism seemed to be the culmination of the tendency to stress the moral-political function of literature, it by no means logically led all the participants to accept the subordination of the writer to the authority of shifting party lines. It was thus quite clear that Lu Hsun himself had not accepted the claim of such authority.

The decade of the 1940s was, of course, to witness the full assault of the Japanese war-machine. The vast disruption produced by the war and the emotional engagement of all allowed little energy for new intellectual trends. The pressures of the war did, it is true, tend to politicize even those who were least political such as Liang Shu-ming, who was to become a founder of the Democratic League. One noteworthy feature of this politicization, however, was that it revealed a kind of 'liberal' strain within the intellectual stratum as a whole, even though most of them were by no means liberals in some of their basic commitments. Over the course of the first half of the century, the intellectual stratum had, for better or worse, achieved a sense of its own autonomy as a separate intellectual (rather than political) element. The 'scholar' had up to a point been sundered from the 'official'. They had also grown accustomed to the free exchange of ideas. Often in responding to the claims of the nationalist and communist governing elites, they had perforce tended to stand on the grounds of civil rights. In the polarized world of civil war after 1945 a large part of the intelligentsia was drawn to the communist side. Yet subsequent events were to demonstrate that this 'liberal' strain would remain a problem.

Another significant development of the 1940s was, of course, the Yenan 'thought of Mao Tse-tung'. Without in any way derogating his political genius, we can be quite clear that many of the subjects with which he dealt were part of the general intellectual discourse of the period covered in these pages. The problems Mao considered had been considered by others before him.

Have all the issues raised by the intellectuals during the first half of the century been resolved since 1949? Some have undoubtedly been resolved, at least for our segment of time. A powerful centre of political authority has been created (some would say all too powerful). In spite of recurrent political causes, law and order has been re-established. A relatively equitable distribution of goods has been achieved within a very poor economy. Nationalist passions have been somewhat appeased. Public health has advanced and the status of women has been improved. Yet in spite of the claims of the '-ism,' many of the fundamental 'problems' considered above remain. What will be China's future relationship to its cultural heritage? Can one avoid the 'technocratic' approaches envisioned by Yen Fu and Ting Wen-chiang if one's aim is to achieve 'modernization'? Have the questions of bureaucracy and power been resolved? What about literature, art and the meaning of personal existence? Chinese must grope their way into the future like all the rest of us.

CHAPTER 3

LITERARY TRENDS I:
THE QUEST FOR MODERNITY, 1895–1927

In a seminal essay on modern Chinese literature, Professor C. T. Hsia delineates a 'moral burden' which tends to overhang the entire corpus of literary creation in the first half of the twentieth century. 'What distinguishes this modern phase of Chinese literature', Professor Hsia remarks, is its 'obsessive concern with China as a nation afflicted with a spiritual disease and therefore unable to strengthen itself or change its set ways of inhumanity.' This 'patriotic passion', which enkindles all the major writers of the period, also produces in Hsia's view, 'a certain patriotic provinciality': 'the Chinese writer sees the conditions of China as peculiarly Chinese and not applicable elsewhere.'[1] It is this obsession that dictates, in turn, a general preoccupation with content, rather than form, and a preponderance of 'realism' – as the modern Chinese writer's effort to make some sense of the socio-political chaos in his immediate environment. The study of modern Chinese literature is, therefore, burdened with China's modern history, and a generally historical approach – with due regard to intrinsic literary concerns – is both imperative and inevitable.

From a historical perspective, the theme of 'obsession with China' contains at least three major variations which may be regarded as further hallmarks of modern Chinese literature. First, the moral vision of China 'as a nation afflicted with spiritual disease' creates a sharp polarity between tradition and modernity: the disease is rooted in Chinese tradition, whereas modernity means essentially an iconoclastic revolt against this tradition and an intellectual quest for new solutions. In this sense, the rise of modern Chinese literature represents an integral part of the New Culture movement, as most students of the May Fourth movement have pointed out.[2] Second, this anti-traditional stance in modern Chinese literature is derived not so much from spiritual or artistic considerations (as

1 C. T. Hsia, 'Obsession with China: the moral burden of modern Chinese literature', in his *A history of modern Chinese fiction*, 2nd edn, 533–6.
2 See, for instance, Chow Tse-tsung, *The May Fourth movement: intellectual revolution in modern China*. See also Benjamin Schwartz, ed. *Reflections on the May fourth movement: a symposium*, esp. the Introduction.

in Western modernistic literature) as from China's socio-political conditions. It may be argued that modern Chinese literature arose as a result of the increasing gap between state and society: as the intellectuals became more and more frustrated with the state's failure to take initiatives, they turned away from the state to become radical spokesmen of Chinese society. Modern literature thus became a vehicle through which to voice social discontent. The bulk of modern Chinese literature is anchored in contemporary society and evinces a critical spirit vis-à-vis the writer's political environment. This critical stance has been the most enduring May Fourth legacy; its repercussions have been persistently felt down to the present day.

A third hallmark of modern Chinese literature is that, much as it reflects an overpowering sense of socio-political anguish, its critical vision is intensely subjective. Reality is perceived from the writer's individual point of view, which betrays, at the same time, an obsession with self. This prevalent tendency of what Professor Jaroslav Průšek calls 'subjectivism and individualism' – an 'orientation toward the author's own fate and own life', his 'own person and character' which is set 'in opposition to the whole society'[3] – thus gives rise to an aggravated ambivalence in the modern Chinese writer's conception of self and society. His obsessions with China are coupled with a feeling of personal disgust with her ills; he yearns for hope and commitment, while at the same time he suffers from a sense of loss and alienation. It is this subjective tension, born of largely unresolved ambivalence, which provides the basic impetus for three decades of literary creativity and movements and which marks off the 'modern' phase of Chinese literature from its traditional and communist phases.

LATE CH'ING LITERATURE, 1895–1911

The origins of modern Chinese literature can be traced to the late Ch'ing period, more specifically to the last decade and a half from 1895 to 1911, in which some of the 'modern' symptoms became increasingly noticeable. It is to this period that we shall first direct our attention.

The growth of literary journalism

The emergence of late Ch'ing literature – particularly fiction – was a by-product of journalism, which evolved out of a societal reaction to a series

3 Jaroslav Průšek, 'Subjectivism and individualism in modern Chinese literature', *Archiv Orientalni*, 25. 2 (1957) 266–70.

of deepening political crises.[4] China's humiliating defeat in the first Sino-Japanese war of 1894–5 finally shocked the intellectual elite into action. But their demands for change culminated only in the unsuccessful reform movement in 1898. Disillusioned with the prospect of change from above, the reform-minded of the literati turned away from the ineffectual state to become the radical spokesmen for Chinese society. Their efforts were concentrated on generating 'public opinion' with which to bring pressure to bear on the central government. And they found in treaty-port journalism a useful medium for their purposes.

Non-official newspapers had already appeared by the second half of the nineteenth century, mainly under the sponsorship of Western missionaries. But the rapid proliferation of such newspapers was led by the reform-minded of the intellectual elite. Liang Ch'i-ch'ao's *Ch'iang-hsueh pao* (Self-strengthening news) and *Shih-wu pao* (Current affairs) were founded in 1895 and 1896 as organs of K'ang Yu-wei's reform party. After their failure in 1898 Liang escaped to Japan where he continued his journalistic career by founding two newspapers, *Ch'ing-i pao* (Political commentary; 1898–) and *Hsin-min ts'ung-pao* (New People miscellany; 1901–), both of which were quickly to become authoritative. Liang's example was followed by Yen Fu, who helped publish *Kuo-wen pao* (National news; 1897–), and Ti Ch'u-ch'ing, who founded *Shih-pao* (The times; 1904–). The journalistic ranks were soon joined by revolutionaries with their own newspapers, notably Chang Ping-lin's *Su-pao* (Kiangsu tribune; 1897–) and *Kuo-min jih-jih pao* (National people's daily; 1903–). By 1906, according to two tabulations, a total of 66 newspapers had been published at Shanghai alone, and the total number of newspapers published in the entire period came to 239.[5]

In order to popularize their cause, it was standard practice for these newspapers to write trenchant news items, but also include poems and articles of an entertaining nature, which were later allocated to a special 'supplement' (*fu-k'an*). As the demand for these supplements increased they were expanded and published separately as independent magazines. Thus literary journalism was born. Edited by a hybrid group of journalist-littérateurs – men who had some knowledge of Western literature and foreign languages but a more solid background in traditional Chinese

4 Leo Ou-fan Lee, *The romantic generation of modern Chinese writers*, 3–7.
5 The figure of 66 was given by Li Pao-chia. Of these at least 32 are what A Ying calls 'little newspapers', which are less overtly political but more attuned to the leisurely amusements of the urban middle class. See A Ying, *Wan-Ch'ing wen-i pao-k'an shu-lueh* (A brief account of late Ch'ing literary journals and newspapers), 51. The figure of 239 is given in an article, 'Ch'ing-chi chung-yao pao-k'an mu-lu' (A catalogue of important newspapers and periodicals), in Chang Ching-lu, ed. *Chung-kuo chin-tai ch'u-pan shih-liao ch'u-pien* (Historical materials on modern Chinese publications, first collection), 77–92.

literature – these publications featured a plethora of pseudo-translations, poetry, essays and serialized fiction which, although claiming to awaken the social and political consciousness of the people, served also as mass entertainment. By the end of the period, four major magazines had formed the top rank of Shanghai literary journalism: *Hsin hsiao-shuo* (New fiction; 1902–), founded by Liang Ch'i-ch'ao; *Hsiu-hsiang hsiao-shuo* (Illustrated fiction; 1903–), edited by Li Pao-chia (Po-yuan); *Yueh-yueh hsiao-shuo* (Monthly fiction; 1906–), edited by Wu Wo-yao (Yen-jen) and Chou Kuei-sheng; and *Hsiao-shuo lin* (Forest of fiction; 1907–), edited by Huang Mo-hsi.

For at least two decades before the 'literary revolution' of 1917, urban literary journalism – a half-modernized form of 'mass literature' – had already established the market and the readership for the latter-day practitioners of New Literature. The editors and writers of these magazines wrote feverishly to meet deadlines, and profusely to make money. Their arduous efforts resulted in the establishment of a new profession: the commercial success of their works proved that the practice of literature could be an independent and potentially lucrative vocation. It remained, however, for their May Fourth successors to lend an aura of social prestige to the new profession.

A noteworthy feature of late Ch'ing literary journalism was the dominant position accorded to 'fiction' (*hsiao-shuo*) both in magazine titles and as an important genre of literature. The term *hsiao-shuo* still retained from traditional times its broad connotations of miscellaneous writings falling outside the domains of classical prose and poetry. Thus *hsiao-shuo*, as understood by the late Ch'ing practitioners, comprised all forms of popular narrative literature – the classical tale, the novel, the *t'an-tz'u*, (a form of oral story-telling), and even drama. But of these variegated forms, the serialized novel emerged as definitely the major form of late Ch'ing literature. This was due especially to the pioneering efforts of Liang Ch'i-ch'ao and other members of the literary elite to infuse this traditionally 'debased' literary genre with new intellectual vitality and political significance.

Theories of 'new fiction'

The crucial relationship between fiction and society – the socio-political function of *hsiao-shuo* – was articulated in three important manifestos. In the first issue of the Tientsin newspaper *Kuo-wen pao*, Yen Fu and Hsia Tseng-yu wrote an article entitled, 'Announcing our policy to publish a fiction supplement', in which the two men took pains to demonstrate the power of fiction among the masses in the past in order to underscore its vast potential as an educational instrument in the present. But traditional Chinese fiction, Yen warned with a touch of condescension typical of traditional literati, was also full of 'poison'. 'And because people of shallow learning are addicted to fiction, the world has suffered incalculably from the poison of fiction and it is difficult to speak of its benefit.' Thus, the Chinese people had to be re-educated with a new kind of fiction which had worked wonders in the West and in Japan.

Liang Ch'i-ch'ao followed basically this line of argument in his 1898 essay, 'A preface to our published series of translations of political fiction'. He agreed with Yen Fu on the educational potential of fiction but showed even greater contempt for the traditional product. Since most Chinese novels were imitations of either *Shui-hu chuan* (The water margin) or *Hung-lou meng* (Dream of the red chamber), Liang argued, they had earned the disapprobation of scholars for their 'incitement to robbery and lust'. What was urgently needed, then, was a 'revolution in the novel' whereby public interest in old fiction could be switched to translations of 'political fiction'. Inspired mainly by the Japanese example (the preface served as introduction to the Chinese translation of Shiba Shiro's *Kajin-no-kigu* or 'Strange adventures of a beauty'), Liang gave a fanciful, yet forceful, account of the genesis and prestige of political novels in foreign countries:[6]

Formerly, at the start of reform or revolution in European countries, their leading scholars and men of great learning, their men of compassion and patriotism, would frequently record their personal experiences and their cherished views and ideas concerning politics in the form of fiction. Thus, among the population, teachers would read these works in their spare time, and even soldiers, businessmen, farmers, artisans, cabmen and grooms, and schoolchildren would all read them. It often happened that upon the appearance of a book a whole nation would change its views on current affairs. The political novel has been most instrumental in making the governments of America, England, Germany, France, Austria, Italy, and Japan daily more progressive or enlightened.

The *locus classicus* of the argument for political fiction in the late Ch'ing was Liang's most celebrated essay, 'On the relationship between fiction and people's rule', published in *Hsin hsiao-shuo* in 1902. Drawing again upon foreign examples, Liang asserted that renovating fiction was crucial to renovating the people of a nation. Creating a new fiction could exert a decisive influence in all spheres of a nation's life – morality, religion,

6 This and the preceding quotes are translated by C. T. Hsia in his 'Yen Fu and Liang Ch'i-ch'ao as advocates of new fiction', in Adele A. Rickett, ed. *Chinese approaches to literature from Confucius to Liang Ch'i-ch'ao*, 230–2.

manners, mores, learning and the arts, even the character of its people. Besides listing the wide-ranging impact of fiction on society, Liang also attempted in this essay to pinpoint the four basic emotive powers of fiction: the power to 'incense' (*hsun*), to 'immerse' (*ch'in*), to 'prick' (*tz'u*) and to 'uplift' (*t'i*) the reader. Liang attached the greatest importance to the last virtue – its power to lift the reader to the level of the fictional hero and to imitate him. But the heroes worthy of Chinese emulation were to be drawn from Western, rather than Chinese, history: the real paragons of national virtue for Chinese were Washington, Napoleon, Mazzini, Garibaldi, and many other modern patriots, revolutionaries, and statesmen whose biographies Liang had described in his other works.

Strictly speaking, neither Yen Fu nor Liang Ch'i-ch'ao can be regarded as literary men. For them literature – especially fiction – served an ulterior purpose: the enlightenment of the Chinese people. Liang dabbled in fiction but never completed any of the several novels he had started. Their views on the function of fiction should not be seen as literary criticism, for which they were obviously unqualified, but rather as documents of social and intellectual history.

While both Yen and Liang were deeply steeped in the 'great tradition', they were also reacting against the recent degeneration of that tradition: eight-legged essays, the formalized but meaningless exercises of much of mid- and late-Ch'ing prose writing, resounding phrases of 'statecraft' which on closer scrutiny were but shallow clichés. With the ossification of the 'high' forms of culture, an effort to revitalize a 'lower' popular genre was highly opportune. But in this area of popularization Yen Fu's contribution was more limited than Liang's. Yen's translations of Spencer, Huxley and J. S. Mill were rendered still in elegant, often erudite, classical prose. He refused to compromise with 'popular tastes' in spite of his advocacy of fiction. Liang, on the other hand, proved far more receptive to both popular and foreign expressions. His essays were written definitely

---

7 Liang still used a *wen-yen* (classical style) syntax but suffused it with vernacular expressions. Many of his followers went a step further by experimenting boldly with the spoken vernacular – including both the Mandarin and the various local dialects (especially of the Kiangsu and Chekiang regions). One of the earliest newspapers written entirely in the vernacular was *Yen-i pai-hua pao* (Paraphrased news in vernacular), first published in 1897, which aimed to bring news – especially concerning foreign powers – to the general public in a more easily comprehensible form and to 'paraphrase various useful books, newspapers, and journals into vernacular with the expectation that they may prove beneficial to read' (A Ying, *Wan-Ch'ing wen-i pao-k'an shu-lueh*, 64) The resulting effect on literary journalism was a gradual blurring of the demarcation between *wen-yen* and *pai-hua* and the increasing importance of *pai-hua*. At the turn of the century, the vernacular was used not only in journalism and literature but also increasingly in works on history, geography, education, industry, and science. See Milena Doleželová-Velingerová, 'The origins of modern Chinese literature', in Merle Goldman, ed. *Modern Chinese literature in the May Fourth era*, 13.

to reach a wide audience.[7] Thus in a way Liang Ch'i-ch'ao's works managed to bridge the gap between the reformist elite – men like K'ang Yu-wei, T'an Ssu-t'ung and Yen Fu – and the urban populace. Without Liang's pioneering achievements in popular journalism, the impact of Yen Fu's translations and reformist thought in general would not have been so far-reaching.

Liang's championship of new fiction also represented a significant shift in political perspective. After the failure of the Hundred Days reform, Liang had turned his attention almost entirely to Chinese society; he tried to construct the blueprint of a new communal group (ch'ün) which would then constitute the modern Chinese nation. In spite of its many elitist implications, Liang's celebrated concept of Hsin-min (New People) was popular in intent and aimed at renovating the entire Chinese people. With this new orientation, Liang's advocacy of the power of fiction was both natural and inevitable, with or without his knowledge of the Meiji experience. And given his manifest socio-political purpose, Liang was not interested, as Hu Shih was later, in the problems of language per se, but in audience impact. His four characteristics of fiction were concerned not with the writer, nor with the intrinsic 'world' of literature, but solely with the reader.

While Liang took the credit for making fiction an important medium, he had little to do with the literary qualities of late Ch'ing fiction. In this respect, credit must go to the less well-educated but more literarily gifted treaty-port journalist-littérateurs.

The practice of new fiction

Two prevalent forms of fiction writing can easily be discerned on the late Ch'ing literary scene: the social novel (or, to use Lu Hsun's term, 'fiction of social criticism', ch'ien-tse hsiao-shuo) and the sentimental novel (hsieh-ch'ing hsiao-shuo), in which the central focus is on human emotions.

In Hu Shih's opinion, the majority of late Ch'ing social fiction was modelled on one seminal work, the eighteenth-century novel, Ju-lin wai-shih (The scholars).[8] Given the socio-political orientation of 'new fiction', as advocated with great impact by Liang Ch'i-ch'ao and Yen Fu, it was natural for the practitioners to find in The scholars a glorious precedent for social fiction. But Chinese society of the late nineteenth century was more crisis-ridden than the eighteenth-century world depicted in Wu Ching-tzu's celebrated novel. Thus, besides the obvious similarities of

8 Hu Shih, 'Wu-shih-nien-lai Chung-kuo chih wen-hsueh' (Chinese literature of the past fifty years), in Hu Shih wen-ts'un (Collected works of Hu Shih), 2. 233–4.

form and content, late Ch'ing fiction evinced a more strident tone of urgency and a more sombre mood of catastrophe. Often this sense of urgency is conveyed by heavy caricature: Wu Ching-tzu's gentle satire is carried to excess. In Wu Wo-yao's novel, *Erh-shih-nien mu-tu chih kuai-hsien-chuang* (Bizarre phenomena witnessed in the past twenty years),[9] light-hearted humour is so intertwined with revelations of the horrible and the ludicrous that the effect becomes more pathetic than funny. Li Pao-chia's *Kuan-ch'ang hsien-hsing chi* (Exposés of officialdom) is more morbid. One detects almost a conscious desire on Li's part to magnify the dark, grim aspects of life (perhaps an unintentional effect of the author's own suffering from tuberculosis). The abundance of burlesque and distortion in *Kuan-ch'ang hsien-hsing chi* seems to indicate the author's utter disgust with what took place around him. The novel is peopled with negative characters – all greedy, amorally ambitious, addicted to office-seeking and money-grabbing, and eager to bribe and to be bribed. Even reform programmes and the reform-minded of the officials were not spared Li's scathing satire, as can be noted in another novel by Li, *Wen-ming hsiao-shih* (A short history of civilization). What Professor Průšek calls the 'tragic' outlook of these authors is essentially a manifestation of personal exasperation: it was difficult to see hope for a country so permeated with ineptitude and hopelessness.[10]

In order to dramatize this feeling of near-despair, Li and Wu often resorted to striking epithets. The narrator of *Erh-shih-nien mu-tu chih kuai-hsien-chuang* called himself 'a lone survivor after nine deaths' (*chiu-ssu i-sheng*) who managed to escape from three types of 'creatures': snakes, wolves and tigers, and demons. Tseng P'u, author of the famous novel, *Nieh-hai hua* (A flower in a sea of retribution), adopted the pen-name of 'the sick man of East Asia' (*Tung-Ya ping-fu*). Two other authors wrote under the pseudonyms respectively of 'the foremost man of sorrow under Heaven' (T'ien-hsia ti-i shang-hsin jen) and 'the misanthrope of a Han country' (Han-kuo yen-shih che). Liu E (T'ieh-yun), the author of perhaps the best novel of the late Ch'ing period, *Lao Ts'an yu-chi* (Travels of Lao Ts'an), imparted in his chosen *nom de plume* the saddened metaphor of an 'old derelict' making the last few moves on a beleaguered chess-board. Novels bearing such titles as *T'ung shih* (Painful history), *Hen hai* (Sea of sorrow), *Chieh-yu hui* (Ashes after calamity), *K'u she-hui* (Miserable society) have given late Ch'ing fiction a dimension of uprecedented gloom

9 An abridged translation in English appeared under the title of *Vignettes from the late Ch'ing: bizarre happenings eyewitnessed over two decades*, trans. by Shih Shun Liu.
10 Some of this discussion is based on notes taken from Professor Průšek's lectures at Harvard in 1967. For a comprehensive analysis of late Ch'ing fiction, see the collection of scholarly articles in Milena Doleželová-Velingerová, ed. *The Chinese novel at the turn of the century*.

and a pervasive feeling of sad exasperation. Their accumulated depth of disturbed emotion is unmatched by the relatively more serene *The scholars*.

The overall debt of late Ch'ing social fiction to *The scholars* should not blind us to some of its more original features: foreign terms and ideas are freely mixed with native scenes and indigenous characters. *Kuan-ch'ang hsien-hsing chi* contains references to Rousseau's *Social Contract* and Montesquieu's *Esprit des lois*. In *Nieh-hai hua* even foreign characters – John Fryer, Thomas Wade, a Russian nihilist, and a German general (Waldersee) – make their appearance. Moreover, part of the action takes place in Europe. Discussions of 'foreign affairs' (*yang-wu*) and the influx of foreign fashions can also be found in many late Ch'ing novels. While most writers were eager to incorporate foreign ideas, they were notably uninterested in emulating Western literary technique, in spite of the increasing availablity of Western translations.[11] Rather, the extent of their literary borrowing was confined to some Western fictional heroes and heroines. Conan Doyle's Sherlock Holmes became an immensely popular figure and helped trigger a series of imitative Chinese detective heroes. The popularity of detective fiction was both a vulgarized extension of social fiction and the result of Western influence.

Political fantasies were another new feature of late Ch'ing fiction. The inspiration may have come from Liang Ch'i-ch'ao's uncompleted novel, *Hsin Chung-kuo wei-lai chi* (The future of new China) which begins fifty years after the founding of a utopian Chinese republic. Another popular novel, *Ch'ih-jen shuo-meng chi* (An idiot's dream tale) by Lü-sheng, ends with a dream of future Shanghai in which there are no more foreigners, foreign policemen, foreign signs on buildings or foreign debts but, instead, an abundance of railways and schools built by Chinese. In Ch'en T'ien-hua's novel, *Shih-tzu hou* (The lion's roar), the story takes place on the island of Chusan, which is turned by the offspring of some Ming loyalists into a political paradise. On the island there is a 'people's rights village' complete with 'assembly hall, hospital, post office, park, library, gymnasium', three factories, a steamship company and many modern schools – all run in an orderly fashion for the benefit of some three thousand families of the village.[12] Obviously, these novels owe much to the conventions of fantasy used in traditional Chinese literature. But their future-orientation and modern content are further indication of the general social temper for accelerated change. The utopias of new China

---

11 Hu Shih argues, however, that Wu Wo-yao's novel, *Chiu-ming ch'i yuan* (The scandalous murder case of nine lives), was influenced by Western fiction in its use of the flashback technique and in its structural unity. See Hu Shih, 'Wu-shih-nien-lai Chung-kuo chih wen-hsueh', 239.

12 A Ying, *Wan-Ch'ing hsiao-shuo shih* (A history of late Ch'ing fiction), 97.

offered to writers and readers alike both an ebullient political vision – the wish-fulfilment of their shared obsession with the fate of China – and a romantic escape from the problems of the contemporary scene.

While these utopian variations on the fate of China all pointed to the urgency for reform, by the turn of the century reformism itself had become a hackneyed style shorn of intellectual substance and political gravity. As depicted in the works of Li Pao-chia, Wu Wo-yao and Tseng P'u the reform ideology had degenerated into a set of clichés, parroted by a string of 'foreign affairs (*yang-wu*) experts' – products of the regional efforts at 'self-strengthening' – who were no more than clever dandies roaming in the glitter of the compradorial 'foreign mall' (*yang-ch'ang*) in such treaty-port cities as Shanghai, Canton and Tientsin. The landscape of late Ch'ing fiction is dotted with such figures who, moving in the twilight zone between East and West, mixed with greedy merchants, status-hungry *nouveaux riches*, and decadent scions of rural landlords who migrated into the cities for fun and pleasure. Reading through these satirical vignettes – the lighter side of an otherwise grim picture – we cannot fail to perceive the authors' self-mockery and ambivalence. As saddened commentators on the contemporary scene, these journalist-littérateurs nevertheless realized that their own livelihood depended on the very people they satirized; they, too, could be taken as indirect descendants of *yang-wu* and *wei-hsin* (reformism). The modish trend of reformism which they abhorred also served to make their works popular. Thus, in spite of their parasitical existence few were in favour of outright revolution which might destroy the very world in which they felt both at war and at ease.

While the major theme of late Ch'ing fiction is social satire, the critical perception of society and politics also involves a subjective awareness of the author's own sentiments. Often, the social and sentimental strains are combined to attain an emotional height and to justify the author's seriousness of purpose. In an essay published in *Hsin hsiao-shuo* under the title of 'The relationship between society and fiction of sentiment', Wu Wo-yao, who supposedly launched the 'novel of sentiment' with *Hen hai* (Sea of sorrow), made the following declaration:

I commonly hold the opinion that human beings are born with sentiment. . . . The common notion of sentiment refers not merely to the private emotions between man and woman. Sentiment, which is born in the human heart, can be applied everywhere as a human being grows up. . . . When applied to the emperor and the country, it is loyalty; when applied to parents, it is filial piety; when applied to children, it is kindness; when applied to friends, it is righteousness. Thus the cardinal virtues of loyalty and righteousness are all derived from sentiment. As for the kind of sentiment between man and woman, it can only be called idiotic madness [*ch'ih*]. And in cases where sentiments need not or should not be applied but are nevertheless squandered, we can only call it bewitchedness [*mo*]. . . . Many novels that pretend to describe sentiment describe in fact this bewitched fascination. . . .'[13]

In this lofty justification Wu wished to give subjective sentiments a broad social and ethical basis, much in the same way that Lin Shu (Ch'in-nan), the translator, sought to justify his emotions in moral terms. However, the Confucian contours of this manifesto do not prescribe the real content of late Ch'ing sentimental fiction. Most of it deals in fact with the 'idiotic madness' between man and woman and the 'bedevilled' excesses of sentimentality. As Lin Shu gradually came to realize, personal sentiments, if genuinely expressed, could be the central *weltanschauung* of a man, whether or not they reflected the established ethical norms.[14] The popular writers of sentimental fiction further diluted this ethical seriousness when they became aware that the portrait of sentiment, especially in its *ch'ih* or *mo* forms, fell on enthusiastic ears among their urban audience. Thus, this sentimental genre has been regarded by Chinese literary historians as representing a more trivial strain of late Ch'ing fiction.[15] While the model was clearly the great *Dream of the red chamber*, much of it had more in common with the mid nineteenth century 'talent-beauty' (*ts'ai-tzu chia-jen*) novels such as *Liu ts'ai-tzu* (Six talented men), and *Hua-yueh hen* (Vestiges of flowers and moonlight). The most popular ones catered, in fact, to prurient interests and came to be known as 'guides to brothels', since the 'beauties' in these works with whom the talented dandies become infatuated are invariably courtesans. Hu Shih has singled out two notable titles – *Hai-shang fan-hua meng* (Dream of the splendour at the seaside) and *Chiu-wei kuei* (Nine-tailed turtle) – for special reproach for their lack of intellectual insight and literary value. Consequently, the underside of the 'fiction of sentiment' seems to be an adulteration of sentiment – a practice which, according to the literary historian, A Ying, soon ushered in the more debased fiction of the 'Mandarin Duck and Butterfly' variety.[16]

BUTTERFLY FICTION AND THE TRANSITION
TO MAY FOURTH, 1911-17

The term, 'Mandarin Duck and Butterfly School' (*Yuan-yang hu-tieh p'ai*) has been traced to one of the best sellers of this type, Hsu Chen-ya's

13 *Ibid.* 173-4.
14 See Lee, *The romantic generation*, ch. 3. Lin's translation work is discussed in the second part of this chapter.
15 See A Ying, *Wan-Ch'ing hsiao-shuo shih*, ch. 13.
16 *Ibid.* 169, 176.

Yü-li hun (Jade pear spirit), first published in 1912 – a sentimental novel padded with poems comparing lovers to pairs of butterflies and mandarin ducks.[17] The label, initially pejorative, was applied in the era from about 1910 to about 1930 to an increasing crop of some 2,215 novels, 113 magazines and 49 newspapers. The label is also interchangeable with the title of the best-known magazine, *Li-pai-liu* (Saturday), which explicitly declared its purpose to 'help pass the time'.

The immense popularity of Butterfly fiction is one of the supreme ironies in modern China's literary history. It seems that the reformist thrust and serious intent of late Ch'ing fiction had gradually been dissipated as the dynasty came to an end. Just as sentimental fiction degenerated into 'courtesan' and Butterfly literature, the mainstream of social fiction also changed its basic orientation from conscientious criticism and exposé of socio-political ills to sensationalism for its own sake: the few respected masterpieces of 'social criticism' were replaced by a host of the so-called 'black screen' (*hei-mu*) novels of social scandal and crime. By the first decade of the republic, both types of mass literature – vulgarized modes of social and sentimental fiction – reached their hey-day of popularity. They commanded a readership and a sales record unsurpassed by works of either earlier or later periods.[18] In Perry Link's pioneering study of the Butterfly School, one confronts the striking conclusion that the genuine 'popular literature' before the 1930s – in the sense that it appealed to middle and lower class tastes and reflected their value system – is neither the 'new fiction' as advocated by Liang Ch'i-ch'ao nor the New Literature of the May Fourth era but these works of 'idle amusement'.

In Link's analysis, the rise of this type of urban popular fiction mirrored the psychological *angst* of urban dwellers as they experienced rapid change in a 'modernizing environment'. As the new urban life – especially in Shanghai – became burdensome, 'the reader's desire to keep up with the world gave way to the desire to forget that he could not keep up.'[19] Aside from fulfilling a need for escape from the realities of an urban world in transition, Link also implies that the successive waves of popular themes in Butterfly fiction can be correlated with specific socio-political developments. The first wave of love stories in the early part of

17 E. Perry Link, 'Traditional-style popular urban fiction in the teens and twenties', in Goldman, ed. *Modern Chinese literature*, 327–8. See also his Ph.D. dissertation, 'The rise of modern popular fiction in Shanghai' (Harvard University, 1976).
18 According to Link, the most popular works of this genre 'must have reached between four hundred thousand to a million people in Shanghai.' See Link, 'Traditional-style popular urban fiction', 338. The sales record of Butterfly fiction remained unsurpassed until the late 1930s, when it gradually declined. Circulation figures of communist fiction in the period after 1949 are, of course, much larger.
19 *Ibid.* 330.

the first decade of the 1900s took freedom of marriage as their common theme, as the issues of women's emancipation and women's education drew much attention within the ferment of late Ch'ing reforms. The subsequent waves of detective stories, scandal fiction and 'knight-errant' novels of the latter part of the 1910 decade and the early 1920s coincided with the political chaos created by Yuan Shih-k'ai and the warlord governments. In each of these waves, the keynote underlying all fictional escapism was one of reactionism and disillusionment. Writers had lost the faith in reform, modernization and progress towards new China which most of their predecessors – the late Ch'ing journalist-littérateurs – had espoused. Instead, they evinced a 'conservative attitude towards popular Chinese values'.[20] They considered the Westernization trend to be out of all proportion and reacted to native Chinese problems, not in the spirit of radical protest that favoured an alternative social order, but in the traditional manner of 'remedial protest' – against certain abuses and excesses of the Confucian value system.

Link's findings throw considerable light, by contrast, on the nature of popular literature during the period which immediately preceded Butterfly fiction and on the 'literary revolution' that was to follow. It seems apparent that late Ch'ing literature underwent a paradoxical process of popularization. It began as a conscious effort by members of the intellectual elite to enlighten the lower-class masses in Chinese society about China's precarious state and the urgency of reform. Thus, 'new fiction' emerged more as an ideological imperative than as a purely literary concern. But the seriousness of this ideological purpose became diluted by the commercial necessity of 'audience appeal' as the practice of fiction writing became lucrative. Popularization set the late Ch'ing writer the dual task to educate and entertain his reader. As it developed from an elitist design to a popular product, 'new fiction' also gradually lost the enlightened ethos with which it had been infused and which, in some cases, had given it its enduring literary worth. From a commercial viewpoint late Ch'ing popular fiction achieved unprecedented success; from an intellectual and artistic perspective, however, its development ended in failure, despite its initial promise. The reformist, progressive outlook in the fictional output of 1900–1910 was replaced in the next decade by conservatism and escapism. In *Lao Ts'an yu-chi*, written between 1904 and 1907, the reader could be moved by that memorable scene of distilled emotional intensity and lyrical beauty as the solitary hero, pondering the sad fate of his country and his life against the wintry landscape of the Yellow

20 *Ibid.* 339.

River in frozen grandeur, suddenly realizes that the tears on his face are also frozen. But the average urban reader in 1913 would only shed his tears on the fate of a pair of love-torn 'mandarin ducks' in Hsu Chen-ya's bestseller, *Yü-li hun.*

The phenomenon of Butterfly fiction's popularity therefore testified to the strongly felt need, on the part of a new and even more radical generation, to begin anew, to create a different type of popular literature as part of an overall intellectual revolution. From the 'new' perspective of the May Fourth writers, the 'new fiction' of the late Ch'ing, together with its Butterfly vulgarization, already looked 'old' and had to be relegated to the corrupt world of 'tradition', despite the considerable advances made by their late Ch'ing predecessors in establishing a vernacular style, a popular readership and a viable profession.

THE MAY FOURTH ERA, 1917-27

The early years of the republic have been perceived by most Chinese literary historians as a 'low' period in modern Chinese literature. A decade of dynamic creativity, which produced, among many others, the four great novelists of late Ch'ing literature – Wu Wo-yao, Li Pao-chia, Tseng P'u, and Liu E – had suddenly come to an end. Of these four gifted writers, Li Pao-chia died in 1906, having completed less than half of his projected 120-chapter masterpiece. The prolific Wu Wo-yao (15 novels) also died in 1910. Liu E, perhaps the most literary of the four, wrote only one novel, which did not receive its full popularity until it was reissued in the 1930s. Tseng P'u, the most revolutionary in his political convictions, was too busy with his many other activities to complete his novel which, like *Lao Ts'an yu-chi*, was not fully appreciated until the 1920s.[21]

The unexpected victory of the 1911 Revolution did not bring about an immediate literary renaissance. Rather, chaos on the political scene made the escapist Butterfly fiction the most popular type of reading. The only rival school of note was the *Nan she* (Southern Society), a loose grouping of revolutionary politicians and journalists who dabbled in literature. The Society, founded in 1903 by three journalists and members of the T'ung-meng hui (Revolutionary Alliance) – Liu Ya-tzu, Kao T'ien-mei, and Ch'en Ch'ao-nan – published periodically collections of poetry

21 For two recent scholarly studies of these two authors, see Peter Li, *Tseng P'u* and C. T. Hsia, 'The travels of Lao Ts'an: an exploration of its art and meaning', *Tsing Hua Journal of Chinese Studies*, 7. 2 (Aug. 1969) 40–66. See also Harold Shadick's masterful translation, with annotations, of *The travels of Lao Ts'an.*

and prose by its members, often the product of their social gatherings. Revolutionaries and young men in the early years of the republic are said to have received these works with enthusiasm. But as one reads samples of the Society's poetry half a century later, the mood and imagery seem generally traditional. Hu Shih went so far as to brand it 'debauched and extravagant'.[22] It seems that, in retrospect, the function of the Southern Society was not so much to echo the revolution as to provide an arena for the revolutionaries to display their literary talents.

Like the treaty-port journalist-littérateurs, most members of the Southern Society were men steeped in classical learning. But their style and diction proved even more elegantly classical than those of their late Ch'ing counterparts. If treaty-port literary journalism can be regarded as the literary side of late Ch'ing reformism, it was surely more radical in its thematic and stylistic aspects than the poetry of the Southern Society, in which 'rich and elegant diction' tended to overshadow its alleged 'emotions of patriotism, of grieved concern for the people, and of national regeneration.'[23] The Society, which at one time boasted a membership of more than 1,000, declined gradually after its last 'revolutionary' act against Yuan Shih-k'ai. Most of the prominent members plunged into the cauldron of warlord politics; others, like Liu Ya-tzu, after brief terms of governmental service, returned to journalism.

The Southern Society episode had been half forgotten when the May Fourth movement ushered in a changed socio-intellectual mood. Although an ideological gap was clearly visible, we can also find some institutional links between the May Fourth leaders and members of the two transitional groups. When Ch'en Tu-hsiu persuaded a Shanghai publisher to fund his new journal, *Ch'ing-nien* (soon retitled *Hsin ch'ing-nien*, or 'New youth') in 1915, members of the Southern Society and some powerful treaty-port journalist-littérateurs were still in control of the major newspapers. The literary supplements of the three major newspapers in Shanghai – *Shen-pao* (Shanghai times), *Hsin-wen pao* (News tribune), and *Shih-pao* – were under the editorship of such master craftsmen of Butterfly fiction as Chou Shou-chüan, Chang Hen-shui, Yen Tu-ho, Hsu Chen-ya, and Pao T'ien-hsiao, who was also an active member of the Southern Society. The May Fourth intellectuals were fortunate in being able to publicize their cause in some of the newspapers controlled by the Southern Society, and also in winning the support of other re-

22 Ts'ao Chü-jen, *Wen-t'an san i* (Three reminiscences of the literary scene), 150–1. For a general account of the Southern Society, see Liu Ya-tzu, *Nan-she chi lueh* (A brief account of the Southern Society).

23 Wang P'ing-ling, *San-shih-nien wen-t'an ts'ang-sang lu* (Changes on the literary scene in thirty years), 5.

volutionary journalists and followers of Liang Ch'i-ch'ao. Gradually, they also managed to wrest editorship of newspaper supplements and magazines away from the Butterfly writers. The most celebrated case was the change-over of format and content of the *Hsiao-shuo yueh-pao* (Short story monthly), published by the august Commercial Press, which had been a bastion of Butterfly literature until Mao Tun assumed the editorship in 1921 and turned it into a major organ for New Literature.

The literary revolution

As the *New Youth* gained increasing attention in journalistic and academic circles, a climate of intellectual revolution had already been fostered before the literary revolution was formally launched in February 1917. From 1915 to 1917 Ch'en Tu-hsiu's magazine published an increasing number of articles, by Wu Yü, I Pai-sha, Kao I-han, and Ch'en himself, which assailed Confucianism and extolled Western thought. The idea of a literary revolution, first conceived by Hu Shih in America, was welcomed enthusiastically by Ch'en Tu-hsiu as part of the movement of iconoclastic anti-traditionalism. This well-known story has been told with zest by Hu Shih himself, who also inadvertently perpetuated his 'version' of this important event.[24] The ensuing analysis may not agree entirely with Hu Shih's recapitulation, though it inevitably draws upon it.

When Hu Shih first used the term 'literary revolution' (*wen-hsueh ko-ming*) in a poem he wrote at Cornell University in 1915, his intention was initially confined to largely academic discussions with his friends on the Chinese language. He was eager to argue and to demonstrate the feasibility of *pai-hua* (vernacular language) as a viable literary tool. The significance of the vernacular had been recognized long before him; its function of popular enlightenment had been advocated and practised by a host of late Ch'ing thinkers and journalist-littérateurs. Aware of these precedents Hu Shih nevertheless made a truly 'revolutionary' observation – something his predecessors had failed either to notice or to argue with conviction. While the late Ch'ing advocates of *pai-hua* recognized it as a medium of popularization and political education, they

24 See Hu Shih's celebrated essay, 'Pi-shang Liang-shan' (Forced to the Liang mountain), appended to his *Ssu-shih tzu-shu* (Autobiography at forty), 91–122. See also his lectures in English at the University of Chicago, *The Chinese renaissance* and his 1958 speech in Taiwan, 'Chung-kuo wen-i fu-hsing yun-tung' (The Chinese renaissance movement), included in Liu Hsin-huang, *Hsien-tai Chung-kuo wen-hsueh shih-hua* (Discourse on the history of modern Chinese literature), 1–15. For secondary sources, see Jerome B. Grieder, *Hu Shih and the Chinese renaissance*, ch. 3; Yü-sheng Lin, *The crisis of Chinese consciousness: radical anti-traditionalism in the May Fourth era*, chap. on Hu Shih. Most of Hu's articles written during the period of the Literary Revolution are included in *Hu Shih wen-ts'un*, vol. 1.

stopped short of accepting it as *the* major form of literary expression. Hu Shih went much further than Yen Fu and Liang Ch'i-ch'ao by stating categorically that in the past millennium the mainstream of Chinese literature was to be found, not in poetry and prose written in the classical style, but in vernacular literature. In Hu's view, *wen-yen* had been a 'half dead' language which contributed to much ornamentation of form and ossification of substance in traditional Chinese literature, poetry in particular. *Pai-hua*, on the other hand, had been the natural result of literary revolution; its vitality as a living language had been demonstrated by the *yü-lu* (records of conversations) of Sung Neo-Confucianists and by drama and fiction in the Yuan and Ming periods. According to Hu Shih, the trend towards identification between the written and spoken language reached a peak during the Yuan. Had this tendency not been checked by the regressive practices of the 'eight-legged' essay and the restoration of the ancient style since the Ming, Chinese literature would have developed into a vernacular literature of the spoken language – a phenomenon which Hu Shih compared to Italian literature since Dante, English literature since Chaucer, and German literature since Luther. (Accordingly, in his subsequent lectures at the University of Chicago, Hu Shih considered the literary revolution to be a 'Chinese renaissance'.) He was therefore convinced that a living language was the prerequisite to modern intellectual movements, and the primary task for a literary revolution in China was to 'replace the classical style with the vernacular' – to restore, in other words, the natural sequence of literary evolution since the Sung dynasty.

Hu Shih was aware that vernacular literature did not itself constitute a new literature; 'a new literature must have new ideas and new spirit.' But he insisted on the priority of linguistic tools:

A dead language can never produce a living literature; if a living literature is to be produced, there must be a living tool. . . . We must first of all elevate this [vernacular] tool and make it the acknowledged tool of Chinese literature that totally replaces that half-dead or fully dead old tool. Only with a new tool can we talk about such other aspects as new ideas and new spirit.[25]

This preoccupation with what he later conceded to be purely a 'stylistic revolution' (*wen-t'i ko-ming*) was clearly evidenced in his letter to Ch'en Tu-hsiu in October 1916 in which he listed eight principles for the new literature:

(1) Avoid the use of classical allusions.
(2) Discard stale, time-worn literary phrases.

25 Hu Shih, 'Pi-shang Liang-shan', 112.

(3) Discard the parallel construction of sentences.
(4) Do not avoid using vernacular words and speech.
(5) Follow literary grammar.
(The above are suggestions for a revolution in literary form.)
(6) Do not write that you are sick or sad when you do not feel sick or sad.
(7) Do not imitate the writings of the ancients; what you write should reflect your own personality.
(8) What you write should have meaning or real substance.
(The above are suggestions for a revolution in content.)

In this initial formulation, Hu Shih's suggestions for literary form are obviously more detailed and concrete than his suggestions for content. Ch'en Tu-hsiu, while supporting Hu Shih with enthusiasm, was nevertheless wary that Hu's eighth principle might lend itself to a traditional interpretation of 'wen i tsai-tao' (literature to convey the Confucian way). Thus in Hu's subsequent article, 'Some Tentative Suggestions for the reform of Chinese Literature', published in New Youth in January 1917 (and The Chinese Students Quarterly in March) he had seen fit to change the order of his eight principles (the new sequence became 8, 7, 5, 6, 2, 1, 3, 4) and attempted to pay more attention to the 'substance' of new literature. Hu differentiated the new 'substance' from the Confucian 'way' by insisting on two basic components – 'feeling' and 'thinking' – which nevertheless remained vague generalities. He was considerably more at pains to explain the importance of three other principles: (2) do not imitate the ancients (he argued for an evolutionary view of literature and concluded with high praise for late Ch'ing fiction); (6) avoid the use of classical allusions (he tried to distinguish a broader category of allusions which still carried contemporary meaning and a narrow category of outmoded allusions whose use he rejected); and (8) do not avoid vernacular words and speech. The last point was obviously most central to his concerns and represented the crux of his earlier debates with friends.

Still, the tentative tone and scholastic approach in Hu Shih's article proved too moderate for the radical temper of the New Youth editors. Ch'ien Hsuan-t'ung took issue with Hu Shih's liberal view on classical allusions and argued for the rejection of all allusions. For Ch'en Tu-hsiu the need to substitute the vernacular for the classical language was self-evident; he had no patience for free academic discussions. Thus in the very next issue of New Youth, published on 1 February 1917, Ch'en simply brushed aside Hu Shih's modest reform intentions and proclaimed the coming of the literary revolution:

I am willing to brave the enmity of all the pedantic scholars of the country, and hoist the great banner of the 'Army of the Literary Revolution' in support of my friend [Hu Shih]. On this banner shall be written in big, clear characters my three great principles of the Revolutionary Army:

(1) To overthrow the painted, powdered and obsequious literature of the aristocratic few, and to create the plain, simple, and expressive literature of the people;

(2) To overthrow the stereotyped and over-ornamental literature of classicism, and to create the fresh and sincere literature of realism;

(3) To overthrow the pedantic, unintelligible, and obscurantist literature of the hermit and recluse, and to create the plain-speaking and popular literature of society in general.[26]

As Professor Chow Tse-tsung has pointed out, the targets of Ch'en's attack were the prevalent trends dominated by three literary schools – the T'ung-ch'eng and Wen-hsuan schools of prose, and the Kiangsi school of poetry.[27] But the constructive part of Ch'en's three principles, though it incorporated Hu Shih's plans for the *pai-hua* style, was more oriented towards matters of literary content. Ch'en had argued in earlier articles for the introduction of realism in China, because he was convinced that modern European literature had progressed from classicism and romanticism to realism and naturalism, and realism was more suitable for China than naturalism.[28] His other two principles seem to have transformed Hu Shih's stylistic concern for the vernacular language into a more politicized demand for the creation of a new literature which should be more 'popular' and 'social' in content.

But in spite of Ch'en's distaste for the elitism of traditional literature, his populist sympathies remained vague. The kind of new literature he might have conceived could at best be called 'social realism', but not necessarily socialist or proletarian literature. He would probably welcome new literary works that depicted, realistically and honestly, different aspects of the lives of all kinds of people so long as they did not belong to the 'aristocratic few'. A more class-conscious orientation towards the workers and peasants was not his exclusive concern at this early stage. While he envisaged a more expanded scope for the new literature, Ch'en offered no concrete proposals as to how to create such a literature. The task was taken up by Hu Shih in a long article published in the spring of 1918 entitled, more aggressively than before, 'On a constructive literary revolution'.

Hu's article carried a resounding slogan; 'a literature in the national

26 Chow Tse-tsung, *The May Fourth movement*, 275–6.
27 *Ibid.* 266–70.
28 *Ibid.* 272.

language, a literary national language (*Kuo-yü ti wen-hsueh, wen-hsueh ti kuo-yü*)'. The constructive goal of the literary revolution, he stated, was to create a new national literature in the vernacular language. But how could such a literature be created when there was no standard 'national language' to speak of? Hu Shih's response was characteristically experimental: new writers should try to write by employing all available vernacular possibilities. They could use the language of traditional popular fiction, supplemented by present-day spoken expressions and, if need be, even a few *wen-yen* words. They should practise using only the vernacular in all types of writing – poetry, letters, notes, translations, journalistic articles and even tombstone inscriptions. With constant practice, writing in the vernacular would gradually become easy. Concerning the 'methods' of literary creation, Hu Shih argued that the subject matter of New Literature should be broadened to include people in all walks of life, and that on-the-spot observation and personal experience, reinforced by vivid imagination, should be the prerequisites for writing.

Although Hu Shih went to great lengths to expound on linguistic tools and literary techniques, he was silent on what should have been the most crucial component of his constructive proposal: the intellectual substance of New Literature. Unlike Ch'en Tu-hsiu, Hu Shih was rather reluctant to specify the type of new literature (however vaguely defined) which he deemed most desirable for modern Chinese readers. It may have been that Hu Shih was more open-minded and less dogmatic than Ch'en Tu-hsiu.[29] More likely, however, he was simply not interested, since the literary revolution was for him essentially a revolution in language. But the intellectual revolution which had already begun dictated nothing less than a total change in the *content* of Chinese culture, of which literature formed an integral part. Ch'en Tu-hsiu had grasped this crucial link between the two revolutions – intellectual and literary – and effected its success. Hu Shih, on the other hand, had never been as committed as the other *New Youth* leaders to the cause of anti-traditionalism. His academic preoccupation with language, therefore, made him curiously unaware of its ideological implications.

Insofar as Hu Shih's personal objective was concerned, the literary revolution was a resounding success. The vernacular language came to be used in all the new literary journals which mushroomed. And by 1921 the Ministry of Education decreed that *pai-hua* would henceforth be used exclusively in primary school texts. The opposition was weak and belated, and easily crushed by the 'army of the literary revolution'. Lin Shu's

29 Hou Chien, *Ts'ung wen-hsueh ko-ming tao ko-ming wen-hsueh* (From literary revolution to revolutionary literature), 32.

famous long letter to Ts'ai Yuan-p'ei was written almost two years after the launching of the literary revolution in 1917. The magazine *Hsueh-heng* (Critical review), edited by Hu Shih's old friends and foes Mei Kuang-ti, Wu Mi and Hu Hsien-su, was not published until 1921 when the vernacular had already become a 'national language'. When Chang Shih-chao, then minister of education under the warlord government, fired a last shot in his *Chia-yin chou-k'an* (Tiger magazine) in 1925, Hu Shih and Wu Chih-hui in their rejoinder did not even take him seriously; the New Literature had advanced to such a point that they could afford to mourn facetiously the 'demise' of Old Chang and of old literature.

Aside from personal attacks, the arguments of the opposition groups centred around a few related themes. The *Critical Review* group took issue with Hu Shih's evolutionary justification by maintaining that the types of literature which emerged at the end of the evolutionary scale – such as realism, symbolism and futurism – were not necessarily better than earlier literature, nor would they take the place of earlier literature.[30] In a related sense, the classical heritage of every culture, they argued, had to be treasured, for it provided the foundation on which changes and reforms could be made. As the major vehicle of China's classical heritage, *wen-yen* could not be replaced entirely by *pai-hua*. Moreover, as Lin Shu argued, without comprehensive knowledge of *wen-yen* writings, writers could never create a vernacular literature.

These arguments clearly betray a classical bent and, in the case of the *Critical Review* group, the intellectual imprint of their teacher, Irving Babbitt, who had urged his Chinese disciples to 'retain the soul of truth that is contained in its great traditions'.[31] But in this new era of effusive iconoclasm, this rational defence of tradition, however well thought out, was doomed to failure, for it ran counter to the radical thrust for revolutionary change. The concept of literary evolutionism, which characterized not only Hu Shih but many members of this radical generation, was a direct expression of their future and Western orientation – that new ideas from the West had to replace old tradition in order to transform China into a modern nation. Even the opposition groups were not against change; they were only against certain excesses. The weakest link in their cultural conservatism was their condescending distrust of the vernacular language. They were worried that since spoken language changed too often, it was inadequate as a language of the 'classics', of literary masterpieces which could last to eternity or at least be comprehensible to posterity. Neither the advocates nor the opponents of vernacular literature

---

30 Hou Chien gives a sympathetic analysis of their views, see *ibid.* 57–95.
31 Chow Tse-tsung, *The May Fourth movement*, 282.

seem to have realized that the kind of 'national language' which finally emerged in May Fourth literature contained a mixture of spoken idioms, Europeanized phrases and classical allusions. The elitist worries of the conservative critics were misplaced, for the use of the vernacular in literature did not necessarily degrade quality; and premature, for the *pai-hua* literature of the May Fourth period itself was to come under attack in the 1930s by leftist critics like Ch'ü Ch'iu-pai for its aristocratic elitism under a modern garb.

The emergence of new writers

While the destructive task of the literary revolution was easily accomplished despite scattered rear-guard actions by a none-too-formidable enemy, the constructive phase proved to be more difficult.

The immediate and enthusiastic response of the 'new youth' of China went perhaps beyond the wildest expectations of the leaders of the literary revolution. In a few years, new literary magazines mushroomed, and more than a hundred literary societies were formed in the major cities.[32] All these spontaneous developments testified to the effusive mood generated by the May Fourth movement, particularly the student demonstrations in 1919.

The leadership of this emergent literary scene rested, initially, with the professors in the Peking area: Ch'en Tu-hsiu, Hu Shih, Ch'ien Hsuan-t'ung, Li Ta-chao, Shen Yin-mo, Lu Hsun (pen name of Chou Shu-jen), and Chou Tso-jen. Some of their students – Fu Ssu-nien, Lo Chia-lun, Chu Tzu-ch'ing, and Yeh Shao-chün – established the Hsin-ch'ao (New Tide) society and published a journal under the same name. A learned and enterprising editor, Sun Fu-yuan, took over the literary supplements of first the *Ch'en-pao* (Morning news) of Peking and then the *Ching pao* (Capital news) of Tientsin and turned them into prominent showcases of New Literature which featured the works of many new talents. These scholars, students, editors and contributors constituted a very loose grouping centred in Peking. Most of them evinced an urbane, scholarly outlook which contrasted with the Bohemian abandon of the literary upstarts in Shanghai. The older members of this 'Peking aggregate' – the Chou brothers, Sun Fu-yuan, Ch'ien Hsuan-t'ung and the publisher Li Hsiao-feng – subsequently founded the *Yü-ssu* (Threads of talk) weekly (1924–30) in which they further practised the celebrated *Yü-ssu* style of cultured criticism while shunning excessively radical stances. With the

32 Lee, *The romantic generation*, 9.

split of the New Youth leadership in 1921, Hu Shih soon branched off and joined hands with a group of mainly Anglo-American educated scholars – notably Ch'en Yuan and Hsu Chih-mo. Ch'en founded the *Hsien-tai p'ing-lun* (Contemporary review), and Hsu was the prime mover behind the Hsin-yueh (Crescent Moon) society, which later published the *Hsin-yueh* magazine (1928–33) and played a prominent role in literary polemics by defending its basically liberal outlook in literature and politics against the assaults from the left and Lu Hsun. But in the early 1920s, after the *New Youth* changed into a political magazine, thus forfeiting its leadership in New Literature, and before the *Yü-ssu* and *Hsin-yueh* journals were able to exert any impact, the literary scene was dominated by two major organizations: The Association for Literary Studies (Wen-hsueh yen-chiu hui) and the Creation Society (Ch'uang-tsao she).

The Association for Literary Studies was officially founded in January 1921 in Peking, with an initial membership of 21 drawn mostly from the 'Peking aggregate', such as Chou Tso-jen, Cheng Chen-to, Sun Fu-yuan, Yeh Shao-chün, Hsu Ti-shan, Wang T'ung-chao, and Kuo Shao-yü. Its formation was made possible by Mao Tun, one of the few non-Peking-related founders, who had just been appointed editor of the influential *Short Story Monthly*, thereby offering them a golden opportunity to renovate this established journal of Butterfly fiction for purposes of New Literature. The first issue of this refashioned magazine (volume 12, number 1) published the Association's manifesto which stipulated three fundamental principles: (1) 'To unite in fellowship' the practitioners of New Literature for 'mutual understanding' and to form 'a unified organization of writers'; (2) 'To advance knowledge', especially in foreign literature; (3) 'To establish a foundation' for a professional union of writers so as to promote the literary endeavour not as a form of amusement or diversion but as 'a life-time occupation'.[33]

This manifesto, issued in January 1921, marked a milestone in the history of modern Chinese literature, for it was the first proclamation by the new writers as a professional group dedicated to the practice of literature as an independent and honourable vocation. It legitimized two decades of efforts by their late Ch'ing predecessors towards literary professionalism, but invested it with a new aura of social prestige and self-esteem. By expanding its membership, establishing branch offices in many other cities, and publishing several new journals – besides *Hsiao-shuo yueh-pao*, notably *Wen-hsueh hsun-k'an* (Literature thrice-monthly), *Wen-hsueh chou-pao* (Literature weekly), and *Shih* (Poetry) – the Association was

33 *Ibid.* 12.

able to solidify and broaden the literary arena so that more and more young novices could develop their potential and build up their reputation as professional writers. In addition to Yeh Shao-chün, Mao Tun, Wang T'ung-chao, and Hsu Ti-shan, the Association also nurtured such diverse talents as Hsieh Ping-hsin, Hsu Ch'in-wen, Huang Lu-yin, and Ting Ling. The Association also sponsored massive translations of European literature. Special issues of the *Hsiao-shuo yueh-pao* were devoted to Tolstoy, Tagore, Byron, Hans Christian Andersen, Romain Rolland, the literature of 'oppressed nations', 'anti-war literature', French literature and Russian literature. The Association reached its peak of activity by 1925 and thereafter declined until its quiet demise in 1930.

The second major literary group, the Creation Society, emerged almost concurrently with the Association for Literary Studies. It first grew out of a small circle of close friends consisting initially of Kuo Mo-jo, Yü Ta-fu, Ch'eng Fang-wu, and Chang Tzu-p'ing – all of whom had been students at the Tokyo Imperial University. After a series of informal discussions they decided to publish a magazine for New Literature. When they returned to China, the manager of a small Shanghai publishing firm, T'ai-tung, was the first to capitalize on their talents. In July 1921 the Society was formally established in Shanghai with an initial membership of eight. At the suggestion of Kuo Mo-jo, they decided to publish a journal, *Ch'uang-tsao chi-k'an* (Creation quarterly, 1922–4). Two other periodicals followed: *Ch'uang-tsao chou-pao* (Creation weekly, May 1923–May 1924), and *Ch'uang-tsao jih* (Creation day, one hundred issues, 21 July–31 October 1923, attached to the newspaper *Chung-hua jih-pao* or *China Daily*). A group of younger writers joined the Society in 1924 and began to publish a new fortnightly newspaper, *Hung-shui* (Deluge). In 1926, when most of the veteran members of the Society went to Canton, Chou Ch'üan-p'ing was put in charge of the publications department and brought in his more radical friends. A widening chasm began to extend between the old and the new Creationists. The old members founded another new journal in 1926, *Ch'uang-tsao yueh-k'an* (Creation monthly) which lásted until January 1929. But the 'junior partners' who gained firm control in Shanghai, evicted Yü Ta-fu from membership and persuaded Ch'eng Fang-wu and Kuo Mo-jo to use the society publications as an 'ideological stronghold' of Marxism. Thus the Society is said to have undergone two phases: an early 'romantic period' from 1921 to 1925 and, after Kuo Mo-jo's conversion to Marxism in 1924, a gradual shift to the left – in their own well-known phrase, 'from literary revolution to revolutionary literature'.

Most literary historians have approached the differences between these two organizations in terms of a dichotomy between two slogans: 'art for life' versus 'art for art'.[34] The former stance was supposedly advocated by the Association, whose members favoured 'realism', while the latter position was assumed by the Creationists, who practised 'romanticism'. But on closer examination, this theoretical antagonsim is more apparent than real. The two groups represent, in fact, two related facets of a prevailing ethos which characterized most new writers of the May Fourth period. It is an ethos anchored in a humanistic matrix of self and society but often expressed in strong emotionalism. In the writings of the Associationists, this humanistic ethos was couched in more social and humanitarian terms than can be found in the early works of the Creation leaders, who tended to centre on the individual self. But the two types of propensities are not mutually exclusive. Thus, in Chou Tso-jen's two important articles – 'Humane literature' and 'The demands of literature' – he argued that literature should have close 'contact with life' through the writer's *own* feelings and thoughts. The expression of self, in other words, was invariably bound up with humanity, since Chou defined the individual as a 'rational' being and 'a member of humanity'.[35] In giving New Literature a more social focus, Mao Tun also reminded his readers that the genuine kind of self-assertion was not incompatible with 'social sympathies'.[36] In the Creationists' more 'romantic' formulations, glorifications of 'beauty', 'perfection' and the creative act were frequent. But their so-called 'art for art' slogan had little in common with what the phrase implied in European literature, which opposed an artistic world of deeper reality to the philistinism of external life and reality. Rather, the function of artistic 'beauty', in Ch'eng Fang-wu's view, was to 'nourish' and 'cleanse' life: 'Literature is the food for our spiritual life. How much joy of life, how much vibration of life can we feel!'[37] Kuo Mo-jo

---

34 Almost all standard Chinese secondary sources adopt this bifurcation. See, for instance, Li Ho-lin, *Chin-erh-shih-nien Chung-kuo wen-i ssu-ch'ao lun* (Chinese literary trends in the recent twenty years), ch. 4; Wang Yao, *Chung-kuo hsin-wen-hsueh shih-kao* (A draft history of China's new literature), 40–53; Liu Shou-sung, *Chung-kuo hsin wen-hsueh shih ch'u-kao* (A preliminary draft history of China's new literature), ch. 3.

35 Quoted in Lee, *The romantic generation*, 20. Chou Tso-jen's article, 'Jen ti wen-hsueh' (A humane literature), first appeared in *Hsin ch'ing-nien*, 5. 6 (Dec. 1918) 575–84, before the Association was founded and was, strictly speaking, not intended as a position piece for the Association.

36 Mao Tun, 'Shen-mo shih wen-hsueh?' (What is literature?), in Chang Jo-ying, ed. *Hsin wen-hsueh yun-tung shih tzu-liao* (Materials concerning the new literary movement), 312–3.

37 Quoted in Lee, *The romantic generation*, 21. For a balanced summary of literary polemics, see Cheng Chen-to, 'Wu-ssu i-lai wen-hsueh shang ti lun-cheng' (Literary controversies since the May Fourth period), which serves as an introduction to vol. 2 of Chao Chia-pi, ed. *Chung-kuo hsin-wen-hsueh ta-hsi* (Comprehensive compendium of China's new literature). The eight introductory essays of this compendium have been collected in Cheng Chen-to *et al. Chung-kuo hsin wen-hsueh ta-hsi tao-lun hsuan-chi* (Selected introductory essays to *Comprehensive compendium of China's new literature*; hereafter *Ta-hsi tao-lun hsuan-chi*).

had further turned this 'vibration of life' into a rebellious act of social discontent.

The Creationists in their pre-Marxist phase were more ecstatic about their 'life' than the more sedate Associationists. The differences between the two groups are, therefore, more of emphasis and predilection than of basic aesthetic theory. In varying degrees writers of both schools had lent strong support to one of Hu Shih's principles of literary reform: 'What you write should reflect your own personality.' But within this humanistic spectrum of self and society, the majority of modern Chinese writers in the early 1920s were more preoccupied with the former.

Romanticism and emancipation

Yü Ta-fu once wrote that 'the greatest success of the May Fourth movement lay, first of all, in the discovery of individual personality.'[38] In the first few years following the literary revolution, the literary market was congested with diaries, letters and heavily autobiographical works – all filled with youthful self-pity and self-glorification and written with an ebullient flair of youthful abandon. The literary revolution had ushered into prominence men and women who were still in their twenties. Their emotional effusions were partly a manifestation of their youth. In many ways, they truly embodied the qualities which Ch'en Tu-hsiu called for in his New Youth manifesto: they were progressive, adventurous, scientific and individualistic. Their lives and works brought, in Ch'en's metaphor, fresh and vital cells to the stale, decaying body of Chinese culture.

What characterized the May Fourth intellectuals in general and the writers in particular was a marked degree of dynamism which gave the May Fourth man of letters (*wen-jen*) a more positive stature and distinguished him from his frail and effete traditional counterpart. Much of this youthful energy was, of course, directed towards the destruction of tradition. As the theme of Kuo Mo-jo's long poem, 'The resurrection of the phoenixes', puts it most vividly: the fire of individual and collective passion would burn up all the remnants of the past and, out of their ashes, the phoenix of New China would be reborn. In this respect, as C. T. Hsia remarks, 'the optimism and enthusiasm with which the young Chinese greeted the May Fourth Movement are essentially of the kind that enkindled a generation of Romantic poets after the French Revolution.'[39]

But the vision of a rejuvenated China took much longer to realize than the May Fourth iconoclasts had expected. Having dislocated all

38 See *Ta-hsi tao-lun hsuan-chi*, 150.   39 Hsia, *A history*, 19.

traditional ways and values, destroyed all faith and proper orientation, the May Fourth writers found themselves in a cultural vacuum of a transitional period before a new system – the Thought of Mao Tse-tung – was evolved. The political chaos of warlordism further exacerbated the situation by enhancing their sense of alienation. Cut off from political power and lacking an organic contact with any social classes, the May Fourth writer was compelled to fall back upon himself and to impose the values of his own ego on the rest of society – all in the name of intellectual and literary revolution.

For almost a decade, the keynote of this youthful emotional outburst was summarized in the amorphous word, love. For the May Fourth youths 'riding on the tempestuous storm of romanticism',[40] love had become the central focus of their lives. The writers themselves were leaders of this trend. It was considered *de rigueur* to produce some confessional love pieces and to evolve a 'modern' (or *mo-teng*, in its chic Chinese transliteration) lifestyle based on love. Thus the popular image of the May Fourth writers was often that of a couple or even triangle bound and complicated by love. The importance of the individual personality was given wide recognition by the amorous acts and styles of such love-torn figures as Yü Ta-fu and Wang Ying-hsia, Hsu Chih-mo and Lu Hsiao-man, Ting Ling and Hu Yeh-p'in. Love had become an overall symbol of new morality, an easy substitute for the traditional ethos of propriety which was now equated with conformist restraint. In the general wave of emancipation, love was identified with freedom, in the sense that by loving and by releasing one's passions and energies the individual could become truly a full and free man – or woman. To love was also considered an act of defiance and sincerity, of renouncing all the artificial restraints of hypocritical society so as to find one's true self and expose it to one's beloved. In this sense, the romantic mood of the 1920s was completely secular and, in C. T. Hsia's criticism, 'philosophically unambitious and psychologically crude': it failed 'to explore the deeper reaches of the mind and to give allegiance to a higher transcendental or immanent reality.'[41]

But as an activistic ethos, romantic love had a particular bearing on social movements. This was especially true of the movement for women's liberation, which began at the turn of the century and reached a peak in the 1920s. Again, new writers played a crucial role. The 'godfather' of this movement was Hu Shih (who in his personal life was perhaps one of

40 This is the Creationist Cheng Po-ch'i's observation about the early May Fourth period. See *Ta-hsi tao-lun hsuan-chi*, 94.
41 Hsia *A history*, 18.

the least liberated of men). Introducing Ibsenism to China by translating *A doll's house* in 1918, Hu Shih had unwittingly propelled the play's heroine, Nora, to unsurpassed popularity as the symbol of women's liberation on the May Fourth scene. Countless young women who began to break away from the confines of their families and their childhood milieu justified their action with the example of Nora, whose final act of slamming the door on a family and a society that bred selfishness, slavishness, hypocrisy and cowardice (the four evils in Hu Shih's analysis) was, for them, the crux of her significance as a liberated woman. And they quoted with approval Nora's assertion, in response to her husband's accusation: 'My sacred duty is to myself.'[42] In the prevalent interpretation of the time, a Chinese Nora's primary duty to herself was her ability to love. In the name of love, traditional marriages were broken and new relationships were formed. *Lien-ai tzu-yu*, freedom to love, became the reigning slogan which was almost coterminous with women's liberation.

But this romantic credo for individual emancipation is also fraught with problems which, especially for modern Chinese women writers, served to accentuate in a poignant way the limitations of this all-embracing value. For the many Noras of the May Fourth generation, the crucial point of Ibsenism was the initial act of 'going away' (*ch'u-tsou*). As Nora slammed the door to 'a doll's house', her emancipation was considered complete. Very few of them gave serious thought to the question, first raised by Lu Hsun in 1923, 'What happens after Nora goes away?' As Yi-tsi Feuerwerker observes in her perceptive essay on women as writers in the 1920s and 1930s, the modern Chinese woman writer, 'having broken so drastically with authority, both literary and social, and with the old order and values that would have regulated her life, ... was suddenly on her own, with nothing to fall back on but her feelings or uncertain new relationships, which were also dependent on tenuous feelings. The right to self-affirmation when finally won proved to be but a precarious thing, and the reliance on love and sensitivity for the management of her life only made a woman all the more vulnerable to other kinds of suffering.'[43]

The works of some notable women writers of the period – Huang Lu-yin, Feng Yuan-chün and Ting Ling – gave moving testimony to this mixed feeling of courage and vulnerability, defiance and disillusionment. In her celebrated story, 'Separation' (*Ke-chueh*), Feng Yuan-chün depicted the trials and tribulations of an inexperienced romantic couple as they journeyed away from home following a 'break-up' with their families. In

42 Hu Shih, 'I-pu-sheng chu-i' (Ibsenism), in *Hu Shih wen-ts'un*, 1. 643.
43 Yi-tsi Feuerwerker, 'Women as writers in the 1920s and 1930s', in Margery Wolf and Roxanne Witke, eds. *Women in Chinese society*, 161–2.

the works of Huang Lu-yin, a member of the Association, one finds a persistent theme of deceit and victimization: her emancipated heroines, with their images of love nourished by the traditional sentimental novels they had read at home, are singularly unprepared for a society still dominated by men. Their initial rebellion soon leads to their 'fall', as the Nora-figures become debutantes in the world of 'debauchery' led by the fashion-conscious dandies who, with their smooth speech and self-proclaimed literary gifts, play adeptly the game of 'free love' and exploit the naive idealism of their inexperienced victims.

The early stories of Ting Ling, perhaps the foremost modern Chinese woman writer, provide the most daring case of this emotional confusion. 'The diary of Miss Sophie' (*Sa-fei nü-shih jih-chi*) her most celebrated story, portrays a 'modern girl' involved with two men: she is not satisfied with the weak and sentimental youth but finds herself attracted to a rich playboy from Singapore. Unlike Lu-yin's 'play with life' heroines, Miss Sophie manages to conquer both men, but her desire for conquest, which on the surface seems to demonstrate her strong personality, veils a complex inner agony of yearning and guilt. The story of Miss Sophie can be read as a story of a modern girl in conflict and confusion over the differences between physical and spiritual love; in her turbulent psyche, she fails to integrate them.[44]

For both Huang Lu-yin and Ting Ling the enduring quality of love was primarily spiritual. In reaction against the traditional practice of eroticism as a man's hobby, the May Fourth followers of Ibsenism, who sought to restore love to marriage, objected to China's customary polygamy on the grounds that its active element was carnal, not spiritual. Since love was regarded as a new morality, and the moral implications of love tended to more spiritual, the emotional experience of the Chinese Noras often engendered a new irony. Although they could easily reject the traditional marriage system in the name of love, they found it difficult to form new relationships or marriages based on their conception of love. With their 'spiritual' propensities they were at a loss to 'clarify and interpret to themselves the rush of impetuous, unsettling experiences they were living through.' Thus, they wrote with excessive self-absorption, in order to justify their existence as emancipated women, and at the same time 'to discover what they were through self-expression.'[45]

The intensely subjective quality of women's writings brings a new

44 For a different interpretation of Ting Ling, see Yi-tsi Feuerwerker, 'The changing relationship between literature and life: aspects of the writer's role in Ding Ling', in Goldman, ed. *Modern Chinese literature*, 281–308.
45 Feuerwerker, 'Women as writers', 108.

depth, and a new range of psychological complexity, to May Fourth literature. But it also betrays the limited nature of their art. As Yi-tsi Feuerwerker remarks, 'Whereas many male writers managed to move beyond self-indulgent, confessional writing, no women of the post-May Fourth period painted the broad social canvases of Mao Tun or achieved the ironic perspective of Lu Hsun or the satiric force of Chang T'ien-i.' The reason may be that 'the creative phase in the lives of most women writers was mainly coterminous with, and often did not outlast, the period following emergence from adolescence.'[46] Once they outlived this phase and their youthful search for self-definition and self-affirmation was over, their impetus to write also seems to have been lost. With the exception of Ting Ling most women writers settled down to more conventional lives after a period of wild indulgence in love. The euphoria of the 1920s was dissipated in the 1930s and most of the romantic Noras gave up their writing careers by becoming teachers, scholars or, as in the case of Ling Shu-hua and Ping Hsin, housewives. It seems that Lu Hsun's answer to his own question – 'What happens after Nora goes away?' – proved quite prophetic: Nora would either 'fall into debauchery' or 'return home'.[47] The implication of Lu Hsun's question and answer seems to be that without economic independence from and equal status with men Nora's emancipation can be at best a fashionable style, a romantic outlook and ultimately an illusion. Without a fundamental transformation of all segments of the Chinese people, the Chinese Noras will never attain complete emancipation.

In spite of his strong reservations about the feasibility of women's liberation in early twentieth-century China, the middle-aged Lu Hsun was sympathetic and even solicitous towards young women writers. For some of their male colleagues, however, he had nothing but cynical disdain. The term 'dilettantes plus rogues' was his pithy epithet, levelled especially against the Creationists. But he would have gladly extended it to a host of literary upstarts, each flaunting a story or a poem which had just been published in one of the new magazines and clamouring for immediate recognition. Their reputation was measured not so much by the quality of their works as by the style of their romantic behaviour. For many May Fourth writers, life was art and art, life. This exaltation of the writer's personality and life experience – the excessive preoccupation with self – had a crucial impact on the nature and quality of literary creativity during the May Fourth period.

46 *Ibid.* 108.
47 Lu Hsun, 'No-la ch'u-tsou hou tsen-yang' (What happens after Nora goes away), in his *Fen* (Graves), 141–50.

Lu Hsun and the modern short story

The most noteworthy feature of May Fourth literature is its intense subjectivism. The emergent strain in late Ch'ing fiction, in which the author's personal perception was given increasing prominence in his works, reached a full flowering in the May Fourth period. Whereas a few late Ch'ing writers still experimented with thinly disguised authorial protagonists (Liu E) or with the first-person narrator as conventional story-teller (Wu Wo-yao), the May Fourth writers dropped the story-telling pose altogether, 'and the narrator became one with the implied author and often with the author himself.'[48] In many cases, the author, undisguised, figured also as the 'fictional' protagonist. This 'emergence of a new authorial persona' is evidenced most frequently in the short story, which was undoubtedly the predominant literary form in the first decade after the literary revolution. It seems as if the May Fourth writers were too involved in the rush of their own impetuous, unsettling experiences to devote much time to writing long novels.[49]

According to Professor Průšek, this choice of the short story is also related to the dual impact of Western literature and China's literary tradition. In reacting against the dominant classical forms of Chinese literature, the May Fourth writers were naturally attracted to genres least bound by traditional conventions. Since the short story and the novel were 'forms which with certain exceptions were traditionally excluded from classical literature', they became the favourites of the new authors.[50] Poetry, which had an exalted position in classical literature, was demoted to a subordinate place. Of the two forms of prose narrative, the novel did not become prevalent until the late 1920s and early 1930s. The reason may be, as pointed out by Průšek, that the nineteenth-century European novel, which the May Fourth writers tried to imitate, is more unified in thematic plan, less loosely structured than the classic Chinese novel, and therefore more difficult for the modern Chinese writers to master. And in spite of its considerable artistic advances, the late Ch'ing novel was still too 'traditional' to be a feasible vehicle for the fervently iconoclastic new writers.

In the short-story genre, one of the most famous practitioners in the

48 Cyril Birch, 'Change and continuity in Chinese fiction', in Goldman, ed. *Modern Chinese literature*, 390.
49 For a few less emotional writers, the most coveted short literary form was the personal essay, a traditional genre developed to new heights by Chou Tso-jen and Lu Hsun. For an insightful discussion of Chou Tso-jen's art of essay-writing, see David E. Pollard, *A Chinese look at literature: the literary values of Chou Tso-jen in relation to the tradition*.
50 Jaroslav Průšek, 'A confrontation of traditional oriental literature with modern European literature in the context of the Chinese literary revolution', *Archiv Orientalni*, 32 (1964) 370.

early 1920s was Yü Ta-fu. The stories in his first collection – 'Sinking', 'Moving south', and 'Silver-grey death' – created a sensation by their unprecedentedly frank portrayal of 'sexual depravity'. But a more significant feature of Yü's early stories is his quest for emotional fulfilment, of which sexual frustration becomes a 'hypochondriac' expression. Life for this self-styled 'superfluous' loner is a sentimental journey in which the solitary hero wanders aimlessly in search of its meaning. Consequently Yü's stories are marked by a spontaneous flow of feelings, observations, and incidents which are not, however, compressed into a coherent structure. Layers of past and present are woven impressionistically, almost at the mental caprice of the autobiographical hero. Invocations of mood and memory are made not to forward the progression of the plot but to achieve a certain emotional intensity. At his best Yü imparts both an intensity and an authenticity of feeling; at his worst he leaves the reader with an impression of carelessness, fragmentation and incompleteness.[51]

In spite of his considerable talent Yü Ta-fu must be regarded as a novice writer who gropes, through imitation and experimentation, towards a novelist's technique. Some of his stories read, in fact, more like lyrical essays than well-wrought fiction. Compared with Yü Ta-fu's works the fictional output of other members of the Creation Society is crude (Ch'eng Fang-wu), unabashedly maudlin (Wang Tu-ch'ing), or downright exploitative (Chang Tzu-p'ing). The only exception may be Kuo Mo-jo, but his creativity is manifested, however, more in poetry than in fiction. The works of the Association writers, on the other hand, seem to fare slightly better. While a strongly autobiographical impulse likewise informs their fiction, the Association writers are, in general, less exaggeratedly self-glorifying than their colleagues in the Creation Society. The theme of emotional search for life's meaning is depicted with less self-indulgence and more humanitarianism. In Huang Lu-yin's works, as analysed earlier, this search takes the form of the heroine's progression from idealism to disillusionment. In Ping Hsin, the treatment of 'the dilemmas of the younger generation in a period of agonizing transition'[52] is more idealistic and 'philosophical'. Celebrated especially for her *Chi hsiao-tu-che* (Letters to my little readers), Ping Hsin, contrary to Huang Lu-yin, tends to sentimentalize mother love and idealize the world in the image of the author's own childhood happiness. The best specimens of creative writings from the Association are provided by Yeh Shao-chün.

51 For analyses of Yü Ta-fu's art, see Lee, *The romantic generation*, ch. 6; Anna Doleželová, *Yü Ta-fu: specific traits of literary creation*; Michael Egan, 'Yü Dafu and the transition to modern Chinese literature', in Goldman, ed. *Modern Chinese literature*, 309–24.
52 Hsia, *A history*, 73.

In the opinion of C. T. Hsia, of all the early writers who published articles in *Hsiao-shuo yueh-pao*, Yeh Shao-chün 'has best stood the test of time'. In his voluminous output of short stories he has maintained a 'standard of competence' and 'a civilized sensibility' rivalled by few of his contemporaries.[33] Most of Yeh's early stories deal with the theme of education, which reflects his own experience as a dedicated teacher. The pathos of these stories is derived not so much from the hero's personal suffering (as in Yü Ta-fu) as from a passionate concern with the social environment in which the hero attempts to realize his objectives. In story after story Yeh delineates a pattern of thwarted idealism: the zealous and idealistic teachers meet only with difficulty and frustration. In his novel entitled *Ni Huan-chih*, Yeh Shao-chün gives a summary portrait of the May Fourth intellectual as educational reformer. Largely autobiographical, the novel – one of the first of considerable merit to appear (1927) – depicts the experience of an elementary-school teacher whose rosy visions for educational and social reform, first nourished by his school principal and the love of his girlfriend, are crushed by the sombre realities of the political environment. The protagonist finally dies of typhoid fever.

Ni Huan-chih was hailed by Mao Tun as a notable achievement for the freshness of its realism, though Mao Tun also pointed out that despite the final tone of disillusionment Yeh Shao-chün was still something of an immature idealist. While he depicted the 'greyness' of urban intellectual life, he was not averse to giving a few touches of 'brightness'. For him, 'beauty' and 'love' were the essence of life's meaning and 'the essential requirements which transform a grey life into a bright one'.[34] For all his honesty, his sure craftsmanship, and his civilized sensibility, Yeh-Shao-chün is still no match for Lu Hsun, the most mature and profound writer in the May Fourth period. Although Lu Hsun has written only two collections of stories (as compared to Yeh Shao-chün's half a dozen), he has left behind a fictional legacy which gives both intellectual and artistic depth to an otherwise shallow corpus of early May Fourth literature. Accordingly, it deserves a more careful analysis.

Lu Hsun's genius as a creative writer was unique among his contemporaries; his first short story, 'Recollections of the past' (*Huai chiu*), which predated the literary revolution, already demonstrated an original sensibility and a masterful technique, although it was written in the *wen-yen* style.[35] Lu Hsun's subsequent stories, which were mostly cast in

33 *Ibid.* 57–8.
34 Quoted in Wang Yao, *Chung-kuo hsin-wen-hsueh shih-kao*, 89.
35 For an analysis of the story's importance, see Jaroslav Průšek, 'Lu Hsun's "Huai-chiu": a precursor of modern Chinese literature', *Harvard Journal of Asiatic Studies*, 29 (1969) 169–76.

the traditional milieu of his native place, Shao-hsing, were infused with a subjective lyricism which revealed his complex and ambiguous reactions to the problem of self and society. Although they were well received as anti-traditional literature, Lu Hsun's stories were rather atypical of the early crop of creative writing as represented by the two major literary groups.

Lu Hsun himself acknowledged at different times that two significant impulses lay behind his fictional writing. He declared that its purpose was to enlighten his people and to reform society: 'My themes were usually the unfortunates in this abnormal society. My aim was to expose the disease so as to draw attention to its cure.'[56] But he also admitted that his stories were products of personal memory: he wrote because he had been unable to erase from memory certain aspects of his past which continued to haunt him. Thus, in his fictional output he endeavoured to combine artistically a private act of remembrance of things past with a public concern for intellectual enlightenment. He attempted to rearrange recollections of personal experience in such a way as to fit them into a larger picture of China's national experience, thereby making it less ego-centred, as in most early May Fourth literature, and more significant to his readers. To some extent, Lu Hsun succeeded in blending expertly these two impulses into an artistic whole. But this creative interaction between the public and personal sides does not always result in harmony.

When Lu Hsun was first asked by Ch'ien Hsuan-t'ung to contribute to the *New Youth* magazine, he countered with a laden metaphor.

Imagine an iron house without windows, absolutely indestructible, with many people fast asleep inside who will soon die of suffocation. But you know since they will die in their sleep, they will not feel any of the pain of death. Now if you cry aloud to wake a few of the lighter sleepers, making those unfortunate few suffer the agony of irrevocable death, do you think you are doing them a good turn?[57]

To conceive such a gloomy image in an era of unbridled enthusiasm and optimism bespeaks the uniqueness of Lu Hsun's frame of mind. An iron house with no windows to usher in the light – certainly a dark image of enclosure – was what he considered to be a fitting symbol of Chinese culture and society. The obvious message, of course, calls for intellectual enlightenment. But implicit in this paradoxical metaphor is also an ominous inkling of tragedy: the 'lighter sleepers', when awakened, would

56 Lu Hsun, *Lu Hsun ch'üan-chi* (The complete works of Lu Hsun), 3. 230. See also, William Lyell, *Lu Hsun's vision of reality.*
57 Lu Hsun, 'Na-han tzu-hsu' (Preface to *A call to arms*), in *Na-han*, 10; English translation in Yang Hsien-yi and Gladys Yang *Selected stories of Lu Hsun*, 24.

eventually come to the same end as the 'sound sleepers', and Lu Hsun offered no clue for the destruction of the iron house. As his stories unfolded the 'iron house' theme was developed in a series of tragic confrontations between a few awakened or half-awakened individuals and the slumbering majority whose singular lack of consciousness is often exacerbated by acts of senseless cruelty. This central image of the loner versus the crowd thus discloses a profound sense of ambivalence in Lu Hsun's 'nationalism' and an unresolved mental paradox between what he called 'individualism' and 'humanitarianism': he was torn, in other words, between his public ideological commitment to enlightenment and a private pessimism he could not overcome.

Lu Hsun depicted the 'crowd' in several of his stories: the customers at the Prosperity Tavern in 'K'ung I-chi', the neighbours in 'A madman's diary' and 'Tomorrow', the villagers in 'New Year's sacrifice' and 'Storm in a teacup' and, the most graphic of all, in the relatively unappreciated piece, 'Peking street scene' ('*Shih chung*'). He is at his satirical best in castigating some of the crowd's older members in such stories as 'Master Kao', 'Soap', and 'Divorce'. Through these individual or collective sketches, Lu Hsun has pieced together a composite portrait of his countrymen – a people living in a world of 'sloth, superstition, cruelty, and hypocrisy.'[58] He has laid bare, in all its gloomy reality, a 'diseased' society in dire need of a cure. The essential cause of this 'disease', in Lu Hsun's view, was not physical or even environmental, but spiritual. His conception of the crowd was guided by a persistent effort, ever since he made the decision to forsake medicine for literature in 1906, to investigate its 'spiritual' content and to explore the depths of the Chinese 'national character' by means of literature. The result of his findings, which can be found in his many writings, was presented conclusively in the longest story Lu Hsun ever wrote, 'The true story of Ah Q'.

In this his most famous work Lu Hsun has not brought forth a powerful individual hero; instead, he has created, most impressively, a mediocrity – Ah Q, the most common of commoners, a face in the crowd. The biography of Ah Q can therefore be read as a summary portrait of the Chinese crowd. Ah Q's many flaws, which are also those of the Chinese as a people, can be grouped under two overriding negative qualities: his attitude of 'spiritual victory', a self-deluding way of rationalization to turn setbacks into apparent victories; and his 'slave mentality', which renders him a willing victim of oppression. These two traits, in turn, lie at the root of China's illness – the legacies of past history. Lu Hsun

58 Hsia, *A history*, 32. Hsia also gives a perceptive analysis of 'Soap' and 'Divorce' in 42–6.

implies that the historical experience of repeated humiliations, especially in the recent past, by stronger groups of barbarians has instilled in the Chinese mentality a passive, unreflective attitude of resignation. Thus the spirit of Ah Q is, ironically, a total lack of spirit.

Although Ah Q stands as the mirror image of the crowd, he is also alienated by the crowd – a labourer turned social outcast. In the last three chapters of the story Ah Q finds himself becoming first a 'revolutionary', then a robber, and finally an alleged criminal. In the 'grand finale' he is paraded in front of the crowd and executed. This final experience of his life thus offers a sad comment on the futility of the 1911 Revolution.[59] In his last moments, Ah Q does attain, albeit belatedly, a certain awareness – not of his own nature or of the meaning of revolution, but of the true character of the Chinese crowd: he realizes that the crowd of spectators – who seem eager to devour his flesh and blood and 'bite into his soul' – have been persecuting him: he has unknowingly allowed himself to become their victim and sacrificial lamb.

As a 'sound sleeper' Ah Q has not suffered the pain of death, in spite of his partial awakening by the end of his life. But when it comes to the 'lighter sleepers' – those unfortunate individuals, mostly intellectuals, who, unlike Ah Q, cry out in their alienated existence amidst the slumbering crowd – Lu Hsun's public didacticism is often tempered by a more personal feeling of sympathy and embittered hopelessness. These figures seem to emerge from a nightmare of memory, the result of Lu Hsun's painful *recherche du temps perdu*; they embody Lu Hsun's own confrontations with his inner psyche. Above all, they represent a central philosophical dilemma which Lu Hsun attributes to all the 'lighter sleepers', particularly himself: having awakened with a gift of sensitivity and perception, how do these unfortunate few find any meaning in suffering the 'agony of irrevocable death'?

The protagonist of 'A madman's diary' (the first modern Chinese short story) is the earliest and most dramatic of Lu Hsun's awakened intellectuals. He can be seen, to some extent, as a 'psychotic' descendant of the 'Mara poet' whom Lu Hsun so admired in his Japan years – a rebel and an originator of new ideas with which all political, religious and moral reforms begin. But this heroic stance is significantly modified by his total alienation, which makes his impact on society almost nil. His ex-

59 In Lin Yü-sheng's insightful analysis of this story, the 1911 Revolution not only failed to accomplish anything positive but, on the contrary, unleashed the evil forces of Chinese society from its conventional restraints. Ah Q's death as an unthinking 'revolutionary' points to the inevitable lesson that an intellectual revolution must be the precondition of change in China; see the chapter on Lu Hsun in his *The Crisis of Chinese Consciousness*.

cessively keen and probing consciousness is the hallmark of his madness and the curse of his existence. Because of it, he stands alone, victimized and alienated by the crowd of 'sound sleepers' around him.

Although his warnings about the cannibalistic nature of Chinese society are taken as the ravings of a madman, Lu Hsun's intellectual hero nevertheless utters a sober message at the end of his diary: 'Save the children.' In some of Lu Hsun's subsequent portraits of modern intellectuals, however, this didactic thrust gradually gives way to a more melancholy bent; the angry rebel is replaced by the pensive loner, the embittered sentimentalist, and the suicidal misanthrope. In three typical stories with strong autobiographical overtones, Lu Hsun's depiction of the 'light sleepers' also becomes progressively pessimistic, even verging on total despair.

In 'My old home', the intellectual narrator, Lu Hsun's fictional *alter ego*, encounters his childhood companion, Jun-tu, who has changed from a lively rustic youth into a weather-beaten man burdened with children. The narrator feels a profound sense of alienation, caused not only by the gap of social status between him and Jun-tu, but also by the ironies of time which transform the pleasures of his past into present miseries. He sees clearly Jun-tu's entrapment in a world which he can no longer re-enter and from which he has no way to extricate his former friend. His loneliness is, therefore, the result of a feeling of empathy stifled in hopelessness. Again it is the intellectual's power of perception that makes this confrontation between past and present all the more unbearable.

The narrator in 'In the wine shop' similarly interacts with an old friend he encounters in the wine shop. The two friends share a past of radical idealism and a more recent experience of deflated ambitions. Thus when the narrator listens to his friend's account of his recent visits to his little brother's grave and to his neighbour's family, their mutual understanding is akin to identification: the narrator and protagonist in the story can be seen, in fact, as two artistic representations of Lu Hsun himself. By cleverly manipulating the conversations of the two characters, Lu Hsun is adroitly conducting a kind of inner dialogue in fiction.

Lu Hsun's inner conflict in this story is not resolved positively. The central theme of both 'In the wine shop' and 'My old home' is, as Professor Patrick Hanan has suggested, the 'failure to live up to the ideals of social service and morality which Lu Hsun's generation espoused'; it involves 'matters of personal conscience and even guilt.'[60]

60 Patrick Hanan, 'The technique of Lu Hsun's fiction', *Harvard Journal of Asiatic Studies*, 34 (1975) 92-3.

In the most maudlin of Lu Hsun's stories, 'The misanthrope', guilt and disillusionment further deteriorate into utter self-disgust and self-defeatism. Having suffered a series of setbacks and having attended the funeral of his grandmother, the last kindred spirit in his life, Wei Lien-shu, the story's protagonist, is confronted with the central problem that afflicts all misanthropes: what is left in life that is worth living? Wei Lien-shu's answer, as evidenced in his final farewell letter, is revealing:

I have failed, I thought I had failed before, but I was wrong then; now, however, I am really a failure. Formerly there was someone who wanted me to live a little longer, and I wished it too, but found it difficult. Now, there is no need, yet I must go on living. . . .

I am now doing what I formerly detested and opposed. I am now giving up all I formerly believed in and upheld. I have really failed – but I have won.

Do you think I am mad? Do you think I have become a hero or a great man? No, it is not that. It is very simple: I have become adviser to General Tu. . . .[61]

The final ironical note thus brings Lu Hsun's image of the awakened loner facing a bitter end. He has lost the air of gifted madness, of lone heroism, and even of eccentricity and cynical arrogance. His disgust with himself, with a life of alienation and unappreciation, leads to a pessimistic end: by a suicidal act of compromise – the 'irrevocable death' – he has joined the mundane crowd.

'The misanthrope' was written in October 1925, at a time when Lu Hsun had reached the nadir of his depression. But he did not follow the example of his protagonist; rather, he was to bring himself gradually out of it in the next few years and embark upon a path of political commitment to 'leftist' literature. This phase in his life has come to be known as his Shanghai years (1928–36). The two collections of his short stories, which represent his initial 'outcry' in the May Fourth movement and his ensuing 'wandering' after its 'high tide' was over, provide a most profound testimony to his mental state as a May Fourth intellectual, which is qualitatively different from that of his younger contemporaries. With his mature perspective – the seasoned insight of a middle-aged man – he was able to see through the romantic glitter of May Fourth iconoclasm and locate the problems and conflicts which lurked behind it. He offered no solutions to the problems; in fact, his didactic intent of exposing the disease did not result in any definite prescription. The destruction of the 'iron house' was nowhere in sight. But, more than any other writer, Lu Hsun succeeded in subjecting some 'sound sleepers' inside it to scathing satire. He also succeeded in showing, in all its pathos and intensity, the tragic fate of the awakened intellectual in an era of turbulent transition. For

61 Lu Hsun, *P'ang-huang* (Wandering), 134.

this alone, Lu Hsun's importance in the history of modern Chinese literature is assured.

Impact of foreign literature

Aside from being the foremost short-story writer, Lu Hsun was also one of the most indefatigable translators of foreign literature. Together with his brother, Chou Tso-jen, he pioneered the first translations of some Russian and East European stories which were published in two volumes in 1909 under the title of *Yü-wai hsiao-shuo chi* (Stories from abroad). But the work proved a dismal commercial failure: the two volumes sold only about 20 copies each.[62]

A far more successful translator than the Chou brothers was Lin Shu, a late Ch'ing scholar who had never been abroad and knew no foreign languages. But by the time the Chou brothers' translation appeared, Lin had already published 54 titles. In an impressive career spanning more than 20 years, Lin had translated some 180 titles of which more than a third were completed in the last 13 years of the Ch'ing period and the rest during the first 24 years of the republic.[63] It is an unprecedented as well as unsurpassed record in modern China's literary history.

Lin Shu's popularity had to do first of all with his native literary sensibility and his command of an elegant classical style: aided by oral assistants, he was able to capture the mood and tone of a foreign novel with apparent ease. He once stated that he had acquired the ability to differentiate the nuances of one novel from another in the same way he grew accustomed to listening to the footsteps of his family members.[64] As an accomplished classical scholar steeped in the tradition of T'ang and Sung prose, Lin developed an uncanny sense of judging Western literature: he considered Charles Dickens to be a much better writer than Rider Haggard, and compared the various techniques of this English master to those of Ssu-ma Ch'ien, the great historian, and Han Yü, the 'ancient prose' master of the T'ang. His learned prefaces (which may have been no more than intellectual rationalizations of his translation efforts) must have

---

62 For Lu Hsun's early literary endeavour during his Japanese years, see Leo Ou-fan Lee, 'Genesis of a writer: notes on Lu Xun's educational experience, 1881–1909', in Goldman, ed. *Modern Chinese literature*, 179–86.

63 Chu Hsi-chou, Lin's disciple, gives the total figure of Lin's translations as 206. See Chu Hsi-chou, ed. *Lin Ch'in-nan hsien-sheng hsueh-hsing p'u-chi ssu-chung* (The life and works of Mr Lin Shu, four records), 'Ch'un-chueh chai chu-shu chi' (Works from the Ch'un-chueh study), 1.17. The number of 180 is based on Chow Tse-tsung, *The May Fourth movement,* 65. For a thematic account of Lin Shu's life and work, see Lee, *The romantic generation,* ch. 3.

64 See Lin's preface to his translation of Charles Dickens' *The old curiosity shop* in Ch'un-chueh chai chu-shu chi, 3.5.

appealed to readers of both elite and non-elite backgrounds. But Lin's commercial success may be more closely connected with his ability, and good fortune, to capitalize on the prosperous business of literary journalism and fit his translations into the prevailing modes of late Ch'ing fiction. For the largest number of his translations fell into the two popular categories of social and sentimental fiction; in addition, a sizeable number were detective stories and novels of adventure. (Haggard's works alone constituted 25 titles.)

It was Lin Shu, master of *wen-yen* and opponent of the literary revolution, who provided the essential nourishment that fed the imaginations of a younger generation: there was hardly any May Fourth writer who did not first come into contact with Western literature through Lin's translations. His renditions of the novels of Dickens, Walter Scott, Washington Irving, Rider Haggard, and, in particular, *La dame aux camélias* (*Ch'a-hua nü*) by Dumas *fils* have been perennial favourites. While Lin Shu made Western literature accessible to modern Chinese writers and readers, it remained for Lin's contemporary, Su Man-shu, to transform Western authors into glamorous legends.[65] With the publication of his *Selected poems of Byron* (1909) – especially his translation of Byron's 'Isles of Greece' – Su Man-shu made this English romantic poet a hero *par excellence* and perhaps the most glorified Western writer in modern Chinese literature. Su's idolization of and identification with Byron also set an interesting precedent for the Chinese reception of Western literature: just as Byron was worshipped by Su in the glittering image of the Byronic hero, the stature of a foreign author in China was henceforth measured by the legend of his life and personality; the literary worth of his work hardly mattered.

By the May Fourth period Su Man-shu's legacy, as perpetuated by Hsu Chih-mo and Yü Ta-fu and other Creationists, had become a new convention: foreign literature was used to bolster the new Chinese writer's own image and lifestyle. With their own inflated egos and mania for hero-worship, these leading men of letters established a fetish of personal identification: Yü Ta-fu with Ernest Dowson, Kuo Mo-jo with Shelley and Goethe, Chiang Kuang-tz'u with Byron, Hsu Chih-mo with Hardy and Tagore (two figures whom he met and became friends with); T'ien Han as a 'budding Ibsen', and Wang Tu-ch'ing as a second Hugo. To be '*à la mode*' on the literary scene required that a literary man display not only his new poem or story but also his pantheon of foreign masters: Byron, Shelley, Keats, Goethe, Romain Rolland, Tolstoy, Ibsen, Hugo

65 Lee, *The romantic generation*, ch. 4.

and Rousseau were among the favourites on almost everyone's list. Most of these 'heroes' are, of course, outstanding figures of European romanticism; even those who do not summarily fit into the romantic category – Tolstoy, Nietzsche, Hardy, Maupassant, Turgenev, to mention a few – were worshipped by their adulators in a romantic perspective as towering figures of 'crusading idealism' with superhuman vitality.

This emotional idolization of Western writers also led to a related tendency to regard foreign literature as a source of ideology. Terms like romanticism, realism, naturalism and neo-romanticism were bandied about in the same fervent spirit as were socialism, anarchism, Marxism, humanism, science and democracy. A superficial knowledge of these big '-isms', as with the big 'names' of foreign authors, served to bestow immediate status. For a historian of modern Chinese literature, one of the most thorny problems is to clarify, compare and evaluate the various literary '-isms' that originated from other countries and to gauge the true nature of this 'foreign impact'.

The sheer volume of translations presents the first Sisyphean task of classification and analysis. The section on translations in *Chung-kuo hsin wen-hsueh ta-hsi* (A comprehensive compendium of China's new literature), volume 10, lists a grand total of 451 titles of individual works and collections published in the period from 1917 to 1927. Another list, included in *Chung-kuo hsien-tai ch'u-pan shih-liao* (Historical materials on contemporary Chinese publications) and updated to 1929, gives the figure as 577.[66] Of these, translations from French literature led with 128 titles, followed by Russian (120), English (102), German (45) and Japanese (38). Multi-author and multi-nation collections (31) are not counted. And translated poems, stories, plays and articles which appeared in literary journals were too numerous to tabulate. Aided by a thriving publishing industry, translations of foreign literary works had reached immense proportions by the end of the decade following the literary revolution.

The popularity of a foreign author is hard to gauge, for it rested on a combination of his translations and his personal appeal. The more glamorous writers – Byron, Shelley, Keats, Dumas *fils*, and other romantics – became household names, however, in spite of the limited amount of their translated work. Other writers who were represented by extensive translations – Haggard, Andreev, Galsworthy, Hauptmann – nevertheless failed to achieve much popularity. Instances of a good balance between volume and popularity – Dickens, Maupassant – are rare.

---

66 *Chung-kuo hsin-wen-hsueh ta-hsi*, 355–79; Chang Ching-lu, ed. *Chung-kuo hsien-tai ch'u-pan shih-liao* (Historical materials on contemporary Chinese publications), *chia-pien*, 1st Series, 272–323.

The lists of translations encompassed authors from more than 20 countries and different historical periods. In general, however, the overwhelming majority of the works introduced belong to nineteenth-century European literature, of which two major trends held sway in China: realism and romanticism.

From the viewpoint of literary history it can be said that the mania in China for things Western represented a zestful effort to squeeze the entire nineteenth century into one decade. Almost all the May Fourth writers were scornful of Western classicism, because in their iconoclastic fervour they equated classicism with tradition. Only Chou Tso-jen professed an interest in the Hellenistic heritage. And only a handful of Chinese critics – most of them disciples of Irving Babbitt – seemed to share the views of Matthew Arnold. Of the pre-nineteenth-century authors, only Aristotle, Dante, Shakespeare and Goethe enjoyed some degree of recognition.[67] And what came to be known as 'modernism', which emerged in Europe following the First World War, did not interest the Chinese men of letters until the 1930s and 1940s – and then only a small coterie of writers and critics.

The main reason for this phenomenon may be traced to a prevalent conception of literary evolution. As Bonnie McDougall has shown in her valuable study of the introduction of Western literary theories into China, the Chinese writers, influenced by a host of textbooks in English and Japanese, apparently believed that European literature developed organically through the stages of classicism, romanticism, realism, naturalism and neo-romanticism.[68] While this scheme is not a gross misrepresentation of European literary history, the Chinese cast it as a *progressive* sequence of literary evolution: new forms were believed to be a definite improvement on the old. This conviction of the forward progress of literature led many Chinese followers not only to a general lack of interest in the classical, medieval and neo-classical literatures of the West but also to an over-eagerness to compress modern Chinese literature into these deterministic categories. Convinced that traditional Chinese literature stopped somewhere between the stages of classicism and romanticism, they decided that modern Chinese literature had to go through the stages of realism and naturalism, whether or not they might be personally attracted to them.

This evolutionary commitment to realism, in spite of a romantic temper,

---

67 Bonnie S. McDougall, *The introduction of Western literary theories into modern China, 1919–1925*, 256. For a study of Chou Tso-jen's interest in ancient Greek culture, see C. H. Wang, 'Chou Tso-jen's Hellenism', *Renditions* 7 (Spring 1977) 5–28.
68 McDougall, 254–5.

gave rise to a great deal of interpretive confusion. As mentioned earlier, Western realistic authors were often received 'romantically' in China. The anti-romantic stance of French masters of realism – Flaubert and Maupassant – was given an ideological twist as exposing bourgeois decadence. Tolstoy was admired for his moralism and humanism, in addition to his titanic stature as a 'superhuman' hero. Conversely, romantically-inclined Chinese writers tended to focus on the 'realistic' aspects of European romanticism: the mystical and transcendent dimensions of the romantic aesthetic were largely ignored in favour of a humanistic, socio-political interpretion. Emphasis was placed on self-expression, individual emancipation, and anti-establishment rebellion. T'ien Han even went so far as to equate romanticism with freedom, democracy, revolution and socialism.[69]

A typical May Fourth man of letters may be characterized, therefore, as a composite of three elements: romantic in temperament, 'realistic' in professed literary doctrine, and humanistic in general outlook. This peculiar synthesis was the product of two interrelated factors: the native predispositions of the May Fourth writers and the historical circumstance in which New Literature was created. Few of the modern Chinese 'theorists' and practitioners were interested in literary theory *qua* theory: in a heady decade of restless activism, they were in no mood to sort out the theoretical intricacies of an amorphous body of foreign doctrine – be it romanticism or realism. Rather, literary theories were employed for argument in order to attack or defend an extra-literary cause. The new-style intellectuals had nevertheless inherited their fundamental mode of thinking from the scholar-officials; the concern with contemporary society was deeply ingrained in their consciousness, even at a time when the majority of them felt politically powerless and alienated.

Beginning with Ch'en Tu-hsiu, the concept of 'realism' contained a strong dose of this socio-political obsession. As implied in his manifesto on the literary revolution, realism meant basically the combination of a humanistic concern for society with a simple, lively, vernacular style. It was used primarily as an ideological weapon to break the hold of past conventions in Chinese literature and to redefine the nature and task of New Literature. The new demand, as exemplified in the slogan of 'art for life', was for creative writing to reflect immediate social reality – to deal with the actual life experience without the artificial mediation of literary or cultural conventions. Given this utilitarian purpose, the principle of realism was, therefore, never intended by its May Fourth advocates as a

69 McDougall, 97.

pure canon of artistic theory which decrees a particular approach to literary creation or analysis. The 'realistic' literature produced in the early 1920s was a far cry from Balzac or Flaubert; it yielded not so much an objective representation of reality as 'reality refracted through a very subjective consciousness.'[70]

Subjectivism likewise seemed to characterize the Chinese reception of naturalism (it was often used interchangeably for realism). In this case, the May Fourth writers may have inherited a more immediate legacy from Japan where naturalism was particularly popular at the turn of the century. But the Zolaesque emphasis on social determinism and scientific objectivity proved too brutal for the Japanese writers to handle. Thus, by a clever twist in the implication of the word 'nature' (*shizen*), naturalism 'was given a new dimension of meaning: the principle of inward reflection and the subjective expression of human "nature" in isolation from objective realities.'[71] As the concept was introduced, with much intellectual sophistication, by Mao Tun in his famous 1922 article, 'Naturalism and modern Chinese fiction', this subjective 'bias' was preserved; between the 'absolute objectivity' of Zola and the 'partly subjective naturalism' of the Goncourts, Mao Tun favoured the latter.[72]

Mao Tun's original target for writing this article (published in the newly refurbished *Hsiao-shuo yueh-pao*) was the Butterfly School of fiction, whose mawkish sentimentality he detested; naturalism would therefore provide a necessary antidote. Mao Tun was fully aware that naturalism had a 'bad' tendency to exaggerate evils and to connote fatalism and despair. Nevertheless he argued on the basis of literary evolutionism that 'Chinese writers must first undergo the baptism of naturalism', at least for a brief period.[73]

Mao Tun did not practise what he preached until a decade later, when he finally wrote a long naturalistic novel, *Tzu-yeh* (Midnight), in which he paid the utmost attention to such 'objective' details as the Shanghai stock market and industrial management (the result of his painstaking research). But by the early 1930s realism and naturalism had also undergone a notable transformation. The overtly subjective trend of self-centred confessionalism in the early 1920s gradually gave way to a broader societal orientation. As Cyril Birch has pointed out, the good works were written by those writers who 'largely eschewed the autobiographical':[74] Lao She, Chang T'ien-i, Wu Tsu-hsiang, Shen Ts'ung-wen and Mao

70 Feuerwerker, 'Women writers', 159.
71 Cheng Ch'ing-mao, 'The impact of Japanese literary trends on modern Chinese writers', in Goldman, ed. *Modern Chinese literature*, 78.
72 McDougall, *Introduction of Western literary theories*, 177.
73 *Ibid.* 1895.
74 Birch, 'Change and continuity', 391.

Tun. In their fiction, which contained an artistic vision no less individual than that of the early May Fourth writers, we find a descriptive mode which embraced the larger reality: realism in the early 1930s was no longer 'romantic', but 'social' and 'critical' in its unadorned revelation of the dark side of urban and rural life. It was but one more radical step for Mao Tse-tung to politicize totally this new tradition of 'social realism' into 'socialist realism'.

According to the evolutionary scheme, the next stage after realism and naturalism should be symbolism or 'neo-romanticism'. Curiously, despite certain personal preferences, the two terms never seemed to catch on in the Chinese literary scene. This was due, partly, to changed socio-political circumstances: by the early 1930s the majority of modern Chinese writers had already leaned towards the left and begun to embrace such political slogans as 'revolutionary literature' and 'proletarian literature'. Symbolism was advocated and practised only by a few individual poets, most of them apolitical and associated with the *Hsien-tai* (Contemporary) magazine. But aside from political considerations, the issues involved had as much to do with definition as with application.

From the documentary evidence marshalled by Bonnie McDougall it is apparent that when the terms 'symbolism' and 'neo-romanticism' were discussed, they were treated in a tentative and perplexed manner, perhaps due to the lack of adequate information and perspective. Symbolism, as normally understood today, refers to a poetic movement that originated in France at the end of the nineteenth century and comprised such figures as Baudelaire, Verlaine, Rimbaud, Mallarmé and Valéry. 'Neo-romanticism', on the other hand, is a much more amorphous term which, for those who still prefer to use it, refers to the briefly resurgent literature of new idealism as represented by Romain Rolland, Henri Barbusse, Anatole France and Vincente Blasco Ibanez, among others.[75] The names of all these Western authors were known to the Chinese: some, like Romain Rolland, Baudelaire and Verlaine, were worshipped as romantic heroes. But the literary significance of French symbolist poetry was not appreciated by these early hero-worshippers until the 1930s, when Tai Wang-shu and Shao Hsun-mei began to translate Baudelaire's *Les fleurs du mal* into Chinese and to adapt his poetic imagery in their own works.[76]

75 The term 'neo-romanticism' has been used by Průšek and McDougall, but it is not found in such standard works as René Wellek, *Concepts of criticism*, or M. H. Abrams, *A glossary of literary terms*.
76 For a study of Baudelaire's influence in China, see the papers by Gloria Bien, 'Baudelaire and the Han Garden' (read at the Chinese Language Teachers Association panel at the Modern Languages Association annual meeting, New York, Dec., 1976); and 'Shao Hsun-mei and the Flowers of Evil' (read at the Association for Asian Studies annual meeting, Chicago, April, 1978).

The reigning theoretician of symbolism in China in the 1920s was Kuriyagawa Hakuson, whose book, *The symbol of suffering* (*Kumon no shōchō*) was translated three times into Chinese. But Kuriyagawa's theory is fraught with contradictions and inconsistencies which resulted from his own undigested borrowings from European sources. Following him, Chinese writers added more confusion. The otherwise astute Mao Tun at one point lumped together symbolism and neo-romanticism but, at another, considered neo-romanticism to be a brand-new wave which would replace symbolism. Yü Ta-fu divided neo-romanticism into two categories: the positive kind of neo-heroic and neo-idealistic literature (represented by Rolland, Barbusse, and Anatole France); and the negative type of symbolist poets who followed the decadent nihilism and moral anarchism of Baudelaire and Verlaine.[77] Although Yü professed public enthusiasm for the former, it is apparent that in his creative writing he was probably more sympathetic to the latter.

Despite their impressive knowledge of European literature, Yü Ta-fu and Mao Tun seemed as inclined to ideological posturing as their less well-informed colleagues. (This early tendency soon led to a series of literary polemics, to be discussed in a later chapter.) It is remarkable that very few May Fourth writers were able to apply the considerable corpus of Western literary theory to their own creative writing. The prevalent mode of realistic fiction of this period was singularly unconcerned with technique. The early crop of new-style poetry (Hu Shih, K'ang Pai-ch'ing, Liu Ta-pai *et al.*) shared a crudity of form, not to mention the shallowness of content. The most gifted poet of the early 1920s was Kuo Mo-jo, whose works were influenced by the Imagist School and Walt Whitman.[78] The uninhibited vitality of Kuo's poetry was, however, expressed in an intentionally crude form, and it was not until Hsu Chih-mo returned from England and inaugurated his *Poetry Journal* (*Shih-k'an*) in 1926 that serious efforts of reform – especially in matters of poetic metre – were underway, mainly under the influence of English Romantic poetry.[79] Several *avant-garde* schools of the early twentieth century – expressionism, futurism, Dadaism, and so forth – were likewise known and discussed in the 1920s, but few made much use of their new artistic offerings. The literary situation of this first decade thus had a certain historical irony: although the literary revolution, which had abolished old

---

77 McDougall, *Introduction of Western literary theories*, 202–3.
78 See Achilles Fang, 'From imagism to Whitmanism in recent Chinese poetry: a search for poetics that failed', in Horst Frenz and G. A. Anderson, eds. *Indiana University conference on Oriental-Western literary relations.*
79 See Cyril Birch, 'English and Chinese Meters in Hsu Chih-mo', *Asia major*, N.S. 8. 2 (1961) 258–93.

forms, compelled *all* modern Chinese writers to be formal experimentalists and borrowers from abroad, their actual literary practice showed an amazing lack of technical adaptation. The major exception in this regard was Lu Hsun and, to a lesser extent, Yü Ta-fu.

In his early stories Yü Ta-fu himself acknowledged his heavy debt to foreign literature. The setting in 'Silver-grey death' was taken from Robert Louis Stevenson's 'A lodging for the night', and the theme of a young man in love with a waitress from the life of Ernest Dowson. Though he did not mention it, the pastoral landscape in 'Sinking' was imitative of the Japanese romantic writer, Satō Haruo.[80] But as literary imitations these stories are definite failures, for their 'exotic' setting, laden with numerous quotations of European romantic poetry, presents a fictional landscape rather incongruous with the autobiographical content of the stories.

The case of Lu Hsun was truly exceptional on two accounts. First, as Patrick Hanan has demonstrated, he was uncommonly concerned with literary technique. His early stories showed a conscientious effort to incorporate some of the themes and conventions of Russian and East European fiction. Second, more intriguing than his technical adaptations was the fact that, unlike his fellow Chinese novelists, Lu Hsun was simply not interested in the theory and technique of realism.[81] He had no interest in French realists or naturalists, or Japanese naturalists. His early literary tastes tended rather to favour either 'pre-realists' like Gogol, Lermontov, Sienkiewicz, and Petofi, or 'post-realists' like Andreev, Artzybashev and Garshin. The title of his first story, 'The diary of a madman', is taken from Gogol, but the symbolic conception and the atmosphere of 'metaphysical horror' in this work and in 'Medicine' are indebted to Andreev (especially to such stories as 'Silence' and 'Red Laugh', as demonstrated convincingly by Professor Hanan).[82] Moreover, as Professor D. W. Fokkema has indicated, Lu Hsun's penchant for the outcast and underdog as well as the madman and the alienated intellectual, who speak the truth in a perpetual state of humiliation and oppression, may have been inspired by the Russian romanticist convention. As Fokkema concludes: 'Lu Hsun was attracted by romanticist and symbolist values. Of realist values, only the didacticism and the typicalness of characters attracted him.'[83] One might add that even his typical characters are impregnated with symbolic layers of meaning.

80 Lee, *The romantic generation*, 112-3.
81 Hanan, 'Lu Hsun's fiction', 61.
82 *Ibid.* 61-8.
83 Douwe W. Fokkema, 'Lu Xun: the impact of Russian literature', in Goldman, ed. *Modern Chinese literature*, 98.

The intriguing implication of this foreign literary impact on Lu Hsun is that almost alone in modern Chinese fiction, Lu Hsun had 'progressed' to the symbolist stage, though none of his contemporaries (with the exception of his brother, Chou Tso-jen) acknowledged it. This symbolist tendency is particularly noteworthy in his collection of prose poetry, *Yeh-ts'ao* (Wild grass), written between 1924 and 1926. Compared by Prŭšek to Baudelaire's *Petits poëmes en prose* in mood and tone, these 23 pieces evoke a nightmarish world suffused with such darkly glowing and oddly lyrical images as dilapidated tombstones, frozen flames of fire, ghost-infested 'hells', a beggar-like traveller journeying to the grave, a tormented Jesus in the last throes of the crucifixion, and a javelin-throwing fighter combating, single-handed, the throng of 'nothingness'.[84] As a symbolic representation of Lu Hsun's private psyche and a metaphorical record of his search for meaning, the collection is the most difficult of all his works and is, consequently, the least understood among Chinese readers. It seems as if in his prose poetry Lu Hsun had gone beyond the familiar sensibilities of his generation to the threshold of Western modernistic literature.

However, references to Nietzsche, Kierkegaard and Christian martyrdom notwithstanding, the basic ethos which informs this collection is nevertheless qualitatively different from that in Western modernistic literature. Rather than revealing the 'universal' human condition of absurdity – of the individual man trapped in the impasse of meaninglessness – this most 'surrealistic' of Lu Hsun's works still carries a humanistic compulsion to find meaning. While burdened with many paradoxes – of life and death, past and future, hope and despair – Lu Hsun's wandering spirit is not entirely lost in nihilism. On the contrary, several pieces of the collection seem to suggest that there is, indeed, a way out of the impasse: the frozen 'dead fire' finally opts to fling itself out of the icy valley, and the weary traveller, pausing on the road of life, finally decides to walk on. Although Lu Hsun never specifies it clearly, the message at the end seems to point to the possibility that an ethical act of human will can still impose a certain meaning on this existential condition of meaninglessness. Accordingly, Lu Hsun's artistic and 'metaphysical' flirtation with Western symbolism and modernism in this collection has not led him to Eliot's 'wasteland' or to the absurd world of Beckett or Ionesco. Instead, it compels him to return to humanity. At the end of a piece describing the last moments of Christ's crucifixion, Lu Hsun enters the closing comment: 'God has forsaken him, and so he is the son of man after all.'

84 Lu Hsun, *Yeh-ts'ao* (Wild grass).

After 1927 Lu Hsun himself had put an end to his inner torment and chose to confront the concrete realities of Chinese society by taking up his essay-writing on behalf of the 'leftist' cause. From a purely aesthetic point of view, this apparent volte-face spelled the end of Lu Hsun's career as a creative artist,[85] but from an ideological standpoint it was simply a case of political commitment overriding artistic interest. However, these two extremes of interpretation tend to obscure some of the more profound implications not only of Lu Hsun's relationship to Western literature but also of the true nature of modern Chinese literature when viewed in the comparative perspective of 'modernity'.

The quest for modernity

From the foregoing analysis of Lu Hsun it can be concluded that the Chinese preoccupation with the predominant trends of nineteenth-century European literature and their hesitant dallying with early twentieth-century developments reveal not merely the problem of 'natural time-lag' in any situation of inter-cultural contact but the inherent ambiguities of the term 'modernity'.

Viewed in a Western perspective the term 'modern' – defined as a temporal consciousness of the present in reaction against the past – had by the nineteenth century acquired two different kinds of connotations. According to Professor Matei Calinescu, since the first half of the nineteenth century, 'an irreversible split occurred between modernity as a stage in the history of Western civilization – a product of scientific and technological progress, of the industrial revolution, of the sweeping economic and social changes brought about by capitalism – and modernity as an aesthetic concept.'[86] This latter concept, which brought into being such new trends as symbolism and *avant-gardism*, represented a strong and radical reaction against the former modernity, which was characterized by the new rebels as the modernity of the middle class and of the philistine – 'with its terre-à-terre outlook, utilitarian preconceptions, mediocre conformity, and debasement of taste.'[87] The beginnings of this reaction can, in fact, be traced to certain strains of the Romantic movement which were opposed both to the classic notions of permanence and perfection

---

85 This is the view adopted by William Schultz and the late Tsi-an Hsia. See Schultz, 'Lu Hsun: the creative years' (University of Washington, Ph.D. dissertation, 1955); Tsi-an Hsia, 'Aspects of the power of darkness in Lu Hsun', in his *The gate of darkness: studies on the leftist literary movement in China*, 146–62. This article presents a brilliant study of Lu Hsun's literary mentality as exemplified mainly by his 'Wild Grass' collection.
86 Matei Calinescu, *Faces of modernity: avant-garde, decadence, kitsch*, 41.
87 *Ibid.* 45.

and to the hypocrisy and vulgarity embodied in the increasingly materialistic civilization of the nineteenth century. By the turn of the century,
however, this new modernism had taken on some definite polemical
positions. It was anti-traditional, anti-utilitarian and 'anti-humanist' in
the sense of seeking artistic 'dehumanization' (in Ortega y Gasset's famous
phrase). The new artistic rebels had become weary of empty romantic
humanitarianism; the human content of nineteenth-century life, with its
'bourgeois mercantilism and vulgar utilitarianism' had generated in them
'a real loathing of living forms or forms of living beings' and led to a
progressive elimination of the human elements which had been predominant in romantic and realistic art.[88] The new modernism was also
anti-rationalistic and anti-historical: as Georg Lukacs has charged,
'modernism despairs of human history, abandons the idea of linear historical development.'[89] This sense of despair, the result of a disillusionment
with the positivist notion of progress and the Enlightenment idea of
rationality, had caused the modernist writers and artists to lose their
interest in the outside world, by now seen as hopelessly recalcitrant and
alienating; rather, they took upon themselves, in an extreme gesture of
subjectivism and iconoclasm, to reinvent the terms of reality through
their own artistic creativity.

Viewed against this perspective, the Chinese concept of modernity
shows some striking differences. Since the late Ch'ing, the increasingly
'present-oriented' ideologies (as opposed to the general past orientation
of classic Confucianism) were filled, both literally and figuratively, with
a 'new' content: from the 'reform anew' (*wei-hsin*) movement of 1898 to
Liang Ch'i-ch'ao's concept of the New People (*Hsin-min*), to the May
Fourth manifestations of New Youth, New Culture and New Literature,
the epithet *hsin* ('new') had accompanied almost all the social and intellectual movements to free China from the shackles of the past so as to
become a 'modern' nation. 'Modernity' in China thus connotes not only
a preoccupation with the present but a forward-looking search for 'newness', for the 'novelties' from the West.[90] Accordingly, this new concept
of modernity in China seems to have inherited, in varying degrees, several
familiar notions of Western 'bourgeois' modernity: the idea of evolutionism and progress, the positivist belief in the forward movement of history, the confidence in the beneficial possibilities of science and tech-

---

88 José Ortega y Gasset, 'The dehumanization of art', in Irving Howe, ed. *The idea of the
modern in literature and the arts*, 85, 92.
89 Howe, *The idea of the modern*, 17.
90 One literary historian considers this quest for 'newness', rather than the use of vernacular
language, to be the central hallmark of modern Chinese literature. See Wang Che-fu, *Chung-
kuo hsin wen-hsueh yun-tung shih* (A history of the new literary movement in China), 1–13.

nology, and the ideal of freedom and democracy defined within the framework of a broad humanism. As Professor Benjamin Schwartz has noted, some of these liberal values received a very 'Chinese' reinterpretation in the works of Yen Fu and his contemporaries: the faith in the individual was combined with a fervent nationalism in an envisioned effort to achieve the goals of national wealth and power.[91] Thus, this Chinese view foresaw no necessary split between the individual and the collective.

When the May Fourth iconoclasts launched a totalistic attack on tradition, their emotive ethos brought about a romantic assertion of the self which was opposed to the 'philistine' society of early twentieth-century China. While sharing, to some degree, the sense of artistic revolt of Western aesthetic modernism, the May Fourth writers did not give up their faith in science, rationality and progress. In literature, the demand for 'realism', in fact, echoed Ortega y Gasset's summation of nineteenth-century European artists as a whole – that they 'reduced the strictly aesthetic elements to a minimum and let the work consist almost entirely in a fiction of human realities. In this sense all normal art of the last century must be called realistic.'[92]

In his otherwise perceptive assessment of the Chinese literary revolution, Průšek acknowledges this nineteenth-century impact but then goes on to state that the subjectivism and lyricism of May Fourth literature 'was certainly in essence closer to modern European literature after the First World War than to the literature of the nineteenth century' – the result, according to Průšek, of a 'convergence of the old Chinese tradition with contemporary European moods.'[93] In basic agreement with Průšek, McDougall likewise stresses the Chinese interest in *avant-gardist* trends. But as we examine closely McDougall's own evidence, the Chinese writers' sense of the '*avant-garde*', although springing from an artistic revolt against tradition, was still confined to the realm of 'life': in other words, their feelings of anger, frustration and loathing of contemporary reality propelled them to a stance of rebellion which, however, was rooted in a socio-political nexus. The Creationists' slogan of 'Art for art's sake' neither followed Gautier's idea of the gratuitousness of art nor echoed the Symbolists' polemical assertion of the superiority of a transcendental reality – not to mention the characteristic modernist claim of creating a new aesthetic world more 'authentic' than the shallow external world of contemporary life and society. Even the mood of flux and impermanence

91 See Benjamin Schwartz, *In search of wealth and power: Yen Fu and the West*.
92 José Ortega y Gasset, 'The dehumanization of art', 85.
93 Cited in McDougall, *Introduction of Western literary theories*, 262.

found in such works as Yü Ta-fu's early stories is connected with China's historical situation and not with the more abstract and ahistorical notions of 'the transitory, the fugitive, the contingent' (in Baudelaire's phrase). Finally, nowhere in May Fourth literature can we find any evidence of modernism mocking and turning against itself (as in 'decadence' and 'kitsch'). Yü Ta-fu's 'decadence' remained essentially a glamorous style that barely veiled his frustrations as a 'superfluous' intellectual afflicted with a sense of socio-political impotence.[94]

The most salient feature of the 'modernism' of May Fourth literature is that, instead of turning within himself and the realm of art, the modern Chinese writer displays his individuality most prominently and imposes it on external reality. In this sense, May Fourth literature resembles to some extent the first phase of Western modernism, according to Irving Howe, when modernism, not disguising its romantic origins, 'declares itself as an inflation of the self, a transcendental and orgiastic aggrandize-ment of matter and even in behalf of personal vitality.'[95] The epitome of this first stage is Whitman, an idol of the early Kuo Mo-jo. But modern Chinese literature has largely eschewed (until the 1960s in Taiwan) the middle and late stages of Western modernism: 'In the middle stages, the self begins to recoil from externality and devotes itself, almost as if it were the world's body, to a minute examination of its own inner dynamic: freedom, compulsion, caprice. In the late stages, there occurs an empty-ing-out of self, a revulsion from the weariness of individuality and psy-chological gain.' The exemplars of these stages are, respectively, Virginia Woolf and Beckett. As argued above, only Lu Hsun brought himself fortuitously into a Beckett-like landscape in his prose poetry; and the Virginia Woolf legacy was known only to two later women writers: Ling Shu-hua and Chang Ai-ling (Eileen Chang).[96]

Lu Hsun's 'return' from the frontiers of a Western type of modernism to Chinese reality is, therefore, indicative of the 'modernizing process' of his contemporaries. To be 'modern' in the May Fourth period means, on the superficial level, to be 'chic' (*mo-teng*), *à la mode*, to be abreast with the latest fashions from the West – from styles of clothing and hair to trends in literature. But on a deeper level, as represented by Lu Hsun, it implies a subjectivism in profound tension with the forward journey

94 Lee, *The romantic generation*, 250.
95 Howe, *The idea of the modern*, 14.
96 In an interview in London in 1968, Ling Shu-hua stated that her favourite Western author was Virginia Woolf. But nowhere in modern Chinese literature can we find better examples of the self recoiling from external reality and entering into a 'minute examination of its own inner dynamic' than in Eileen Chang's stories. For an analysis of Chang's works, see Hsia, *A history*, ch. 15.

towards a national modernity – to build a new China in a new and better world of the future. C. T. Hsia's judgment is therefore precisely on target:

He [the modern Chinese writer] shares with the modern Western writer a vision of disgust if not despair, but since his vision does not extend beyond China, at the same time he leaves the door open for hope, for the importation of modern Western or Soviet systems that would transform his country from its present state of decadence. If he had the courage or insight to equate the Chinese scene with the condition of modern man, he would have been in the mainstream of modern literature. But he dared not do so, since to do so would have blotted out hope for the betterment of life, for the restoration of human dignity.[97]

It seems that even the most profound modern Chinese writer – Lu Hsun – has been unable to transcend this obsession with China.

Lu Hsun's own journey to the left also typified the trend of literary politicization which began in the late 1920s. This further 'outward' drift eventually led to an end of subjectivism and individualism. Thus in historical hindsight, it can be said that the May Fourth era marked an unparalleled height in the development of these two varieties of the modern temper. At its best, May Fourth literature conveys a mode of mental conflict and agony perhaps even sharper than its Western counterparts, in the sense that the threat of outside reality did not retreat from the writer's consciousness but remained: the problem posed by a stagnant, philistine society intruded upon the writer's conscience with aggravating force. The modern Chinese writer, unlike his Western contemporary, could not afford to dismiss 'reality'; the price he paid for his 'patriotic provinciality' was, therefore, a deepened sense of spiritual torment which carries the 'realistic' force of imminent crisis. From a less aesthetic point of view, the quest for modernity in Chinese literature yielded a tragically human meaning. It never became 'inverted' to the *cul-de-sac* of 'pure aestheticism'. Nor was it confronted with the self-defeatist dilemma in which Western modernism defines itself: obsessed with the impermanence of time, modernism can never succeed, for if it does, it, too, becomes 'old', thereby ceasing to be modern. In Irving Howe's subtle summation, 'modernism must always struggle but never quite triumph, and then, after a time, must struggle in order not to triumph.'[98]

In his search for the 'betterment of life' and the 'restoration of human dignity' to himself and his country, the modern Chinese·writer kept on hoping for a bright future as he agonized over the gloomy reality of worsening social crisis. This conflict between ideal and reality provided

---

97 Hsia, *A history*, 536.   98 Howe, *The idea of the modern*, 13.

the source for some of the most mature works in the early 1930s. But modernity never really triumphed in the history of Chinese literature. After the outbreak of the Sino-Japanese war, the artistic side of this modern quest was overshadowed by political exigency. The value of creative literature was reduced to a position subservient to politics, in spite of its constant socio-political dimension. And with the canonization of Mao Tse-tung's Yenan 'Talks on literature and art', the very concept of artistic reality has been prescribed by political ideology; modernity, whether in its Western or Chinese connotations, thus ceased to be a central hallmark of Chinese Communist literature, as modern Chinese literature entered into its contemporary phase.

CHAPTER 4

LITERARY TRENDS: THE ROAD TO REVOLUTION 1927–1949

In its broadest connotation, the term 'May Fourth literature' (*Wu-ssu wen-hsueh*) encompasses at least two decades – the 1920s and 1930s. Most Western scholars have adopted this vague definition and equated, in fact, the May Fourth era with the modern phase of Chinese literature, to be followed by the Yenan (1942–9) and Communist (since 1949) phases. This facile division, while clearly juxtaposing the basic differences between the individualistic thrust of May Fourth literature and the collective orientation of Communist literature, seems to gloss over other areas. Most Chinese and Japanese scholars agree that the literary euphoria of the May Fourth period had gradually dissipated itself by the late 1920s, to be replaced by a more 'mature' phase of literary creativity in the early 1930s. The term 'literature of the thirties' (*san-shih nien-tai wen-hsueh*) thus refers essentially to works produced in the decade from 1927 to 1937.

In this perspective, the thirties represented a crucial phase in the history of modern Chinese literature. Inheriting the May Fourth legacy, writers of the thirties were able to attain a depth of vision and a sophisticated technique which the early May Fourth practitioners of New Literature failed to achieve (the major exception being, of course, Lu Hsun). This artistic depth was accompanied by a sharpened consciousness of the deepening social and political crisis as the spectre of Japanese invasion loomed large in the north and the Communist Revolution gathered new momentum in its rural headquarters in Kiangsi. It was in this momentous decade, therefore, that art became inextricably enmeshed with politics and the romantic temper of the early twenties gave way to some sombre reassessments of the writer's social conscience. By the early 1930s, a new leftist orientation was already taking shape in the literary scene.

From literary revolution to revolutionary literature

The impact of the May Thirtieth incident on the political sensibilities of modern Chinese writers was immense.[1] It triggered a shock of recognition among many of them and opened their eyes to the 'imperialistic' presence of the Western powers and to the plight of workers who lived with it, side by side, in the commercial metropolis of Shanghai. A process of politicization was set in motion as most writers' sympathies gradually drifted toward the left. Most literary historians agree that the May Thirtieth incident marked a crucial turning point: modern Chinese literature moved, in the memorable phrase of Ch'eng Fang-wu, from 'literary revolution' to 'revolutionary literature'.

For years before the incident occurred, a few groping attempts to relate literature to politics and revolution had been made. In 1923, some members of the newly founded Chinese Communist Party, notably Teng Chung-hsia and Yun Tai-ying in their journal *Chung-kuo ch'ing-nien* (Chinese youth), argued that literature should be used as a weapon to arouse people's revolutionary consciousness.[2] In 1924 and 1925, Chiang Kuang-tz'u, a young Communist writer who had just returned from Russia, published two articles: 'Proletarian revolution and culture' and 'Contemporary Chinese society and revolutionary literature'. Both Kuo Mo-jo and Yü Ta-fu used terms such as 'proletarian spirit' and 'class struggle' in their articles published in 1923. In 1925 Lu Hsun sponsored the publication of a translated text called *Literary debates in Soviet Russia* (*Su-e wen-i lun-chan*) by the Unnamed Society (Wei-ming she) in Peking, and thereafter avidly followed the rapid shifts of Soviet literary policy.

These isolated efforts, however, did not create much stir until the impact of the May Thirtieth incident brought the issue of literature and revolution to the fore. The leftist trend was again set by members of the Creation Society, particularly Kuo Mo-jo. Kuo claimed to have been converted to Marxism in 1924 after having read a book by the Japanese Marxist Kawakami Hajime. In 1926, he wrote what is now regarded as the manifesto of the revolutionary literature movement: a tendentious, badly argued, emotional essay titled, 'Revolution and literature' (*Ko-ming yü wen-hsueh*). Kuo broadly defined revolution as the revolt of the oppressed classes against the oppressors in different historical eras. He came to the presumptuous conclusion that: 'Everything that is new is

[1] On the incident see *CHOC* 12.548–9.

[2] Chang Pi-lai, 'I-chiu-erh-san nien "Chung-kuo ch'ing-nien" chi-ko tso-che ti wen-hsueh chu-chang' (The literary views of some authors from *Chinese Youth* in 1923), in Li Ho-lin *et al. Chung-kuo hsin wen-hsueh shih yen-chiu* (Studies of the history of new Chinese literature), 36–49.

good, everything that is revolutionary fulfils the need of mankind and constitutes the keynote of social organization.' Thus, he argued that good literature ought to be revolutionary, that genuine literature consisted only of revolutionary literature, and that 'the content of literature follows the changes of revolution'. Kuo believed that revolution brought out the strongest human emotions and that its failure resulted in noble tragedies, both on the individual and on the collective level. Therefore, a revolutionary period was bound to be 'a golden age of literature'. Literature and revolution never stood in opposition; rather, they always converged. Literature could, in fact, be 'the vanguard of revolution'.[3]

Kuo wrote his essay in Canton, the 'revolutionary' headquarters of the KMT-CCP united front, where the Northern Expedition was about to be launched. Kuo was to be a participant, marking the first involvement of a literary man in political action. The hyperbolic language of the article was a clear indication of Kuo's effusive mood. Instead of referring to Marxist theory, Kuo seemed eager to justify his new role as a literary intellectual turned revolutionary. Kuo's ebullience was shared by his fellow Creationists. Ch'eng Fang-wu, for instance, in his celebrated article, 'From literary revolution to revolutionary literature', echoed Kuo's emotionalism and further argued, with a flourish of his newly acquired jargon, that even the early romanticism of the Creationists represented the temper of this 'revolutionary intelligentsia' of the petty-bourgeois against the 'bourgeois class'. But times had changed, Ch'eng hastened to add, and their class was about to be '*aufheben*' (*ao-fu-he-pien*), their 'ideology' (*i-te-wo-lo-chi*) no longer useful. Ch'eng concluded: 'If we wish to shoulder the responsibilities of revolutionary "intelligentsia", we must negate ourselves once more (negating the negation). We must strive to acquire class consciousness. We must make our [literary] medium close to the idiom of the masses. We must treat the masses of peasants and workers as our subjects.'[4] Ch'eng's showy slogans were probably utterly incomprehensible to his colleagues, not to mention other writers and the masses. But in his laboriously pretentious way, Ch'eng managed to hit upon some of the central issues of the leftist polemics which would soon ensue.

In 1927, this type of slogan-shouting could only enrage Lu Hsun, whose realistic assessment of the situation in Canton convinced him that the revolutionary optimism of these former romantics was premature. Compared to Russia, China was not in the throes of a revolution, Lu Hsun

³ *Chung-kuo hsien-tai wen-hsueh shih ts'an-k'ao tzu-liao* (Research materials on the history of modern Chinese literature), hereafter *Ts'an-k'ao tzu-liao*, 1.214–16.
⁴ *Ibid.* 222–4.

commented; moreover, borrowing from Trotsky, he argued that there would be no literature in a truly revolutionary period. What was urgently needed was 'revolutionary men' rather than 'revolutionary literature' – the power of the gun rather than the impotence of the pen. But in April 1927 Lu Hsun was disillusioned by the 'revolutionary men' of the Kuomintang, whose massacre of Communists and other sympathizers in Shanghai and Canton shattered whatever residual hope he might have entertained for a possible 'revolution'.

From 1928 to 1930, Lu Hsun was embroiled in several heated debates with a younger group of revolutionary writers of the Creation and Sun Societies, who had replaced the veteran Creationists as leading theoreticians on the left. He first defended the intrinsic value of literature against the mere propaganda of his opponents: 'Great works of literature,' he remarked in 1927, 'have never obeyed any orders or concerned themselves with utilitarian motives. They must naturally spring from the heart. If a topic is hoisted in advance for writers to write on, how does it differ from composing eight-legged essays?'[5] Upon arriving in Shanghai, he remarked cynically on the empty 'advertisements' of his leftist opponents in the 'revolutionary coffee houses'. His charge of amorphous terminology – that they were so drunk with their own revolutionary slogans as to have 'blurred vision' – was matched by a counter-charge from his opponents that his criticism was itself 'blurred', that he was like an aged Don Quixote awkwardly fighting a windmill. His young opponents thus labelled him 'Don Lu Hsun' in addition to calling him an old man of 'leisure, leisure and leisure' (a reference to the title of one of his essay collections).

This welter of nasty metaphors and name-calling created sound and fury in debates which also touched on more substantive issues. The basic tenets of the revolutionary writers may be summarized as follows: (1) all literature is based on and determined by class; (2) all literature is a weapon for propaganda (an aphorism quoted *ad nauseam* from Upton Sinclair); (3) literary criticism must be derived from materialism (it must be interpreted from the point of view of Marxist economics); (4) revolutionary literature should be proletarian literature; that is, it should be written for and by the working class. For the time being, however, it could only be written by the petty-bourgeois intellectuals. The crucial determinant was the 'standpoint' or 'outlook': if a writer adopted the class standpoint and outlook of the proletariat, he could, in fact, still produce proletarian literature.[6]

[5] Lu Hsun, *Lu Hsun ch'üan-chi* (Complete works of Lu Hsun), 3.403.
[6] Lu Ho-lin, *Chung-kuo hsin wen-hsueh shih yen-chiu*, 61–2; Amitendranath Tagore, *Literary debates in Modern China, 1918–1937*, 86–94.

These injunctions, as Chinese Communist historians later admitted, were no more than doctrinaire formulas. In spite of their crudity and simplicity, these tenets represented the impetuous radicalism of a younger generation of self-styled Marxists such as Ch'ien Hsing-ts'un (A Ying), Li Ch'u-li and Chu Ching-wo, and their desire to edge out the domination of older writers on the literary scene. In their attempts to set a new literary trend they also wanted to give a political reorientation to May Fourth literature and to provide a theoretical framework which would henceforth guide and shape literary creation. This imposition of a radical orthodoxy was understandably unbearable to Lu Hsun, a man of indomitable spirit and himself a leader of youth.

Lu Hsun's rebuttals revolved around the recurring theme of his opponent's self-delusion: instead of boldly attacking the realities of the KMT reaction after 1927, he argued, these revolutionary writers were still complacently enveloped in their hollow 'revolutionary' theories. Their pose of self-righteousness presented merely a 'fierce and ugly appearance of extreme leftism' which veiled their ignorance of Chinese society. Lu Hsun first criticized the simplicity of their formulas. Turning Sinclair's phrase around, he argued in 1928 that although all literature is propaganda, not all propaganda, and certainly not the works of these revolutionary writers, is literature. Lu Hsun did not deny the class nature of literature, but he strongly doubted his opponent's claim to act as spokesman for the proletariat. The 'proletarian literature' created by a few armchair philosophers sitting in a café in Shanghai, he held, certainly did not reflect working-class demands. Lu Hsun indulged in a bit of satire:

This year, the literary ranks of Shanghai are supposed to welcome the representatives of the proletariat. Their arrival is announced in all pomp and circumstance. But one asks the rickshaw driver, and he says that he never pulls any representatives... So one searches for them inside the big mansions, the restaurants, the houses of foreigners, in bookstores and coffee houses...[7]

Lu Hsun's views are clear: the urban intellectual in his sheltered bourgeois existence had no contact with working-class life and it would be ridiculous for him to try to adopt the standpoint of the proletariat.

This view was shared by Mao Tun, whose trilogy, *Eclipse*, was criticized by the radical leftists for presenting a 'sick' portrait of the wrong class from the wrong standpoint. Mao Tun described the petty-bourgeois intellectuals' quest for idealism, their consequent vacillation and their final disillusionment during 'revolutionary' experiences on the Northern Expedition. In his essay, 'On Reading *Ni Huan-chih*', Mao Tun defended this realistic novel by Yeh Shao-chun and his own fictional work, arguing that a literary work reflecting the darker aspects in the lives of the 'backward' elements of the petty-bourgeoisie could still render a positive contribution to the leftist cause. 'In terms of moving or educating [the readers], this kind of dark portraiture,' Mao Tun added, 'may be more profound than those unrealistic, utopian, and optimistic descriptions!'[8]

The issue implicit in Lu Hsun's arguments but explicitly stated by Mao Tun was the crucial one of audience: who were the readers of New Literature? In his long essay written in 1928, 'From Kuling to Tokyo', Mao Tun acknowledged that modern Chinese literature in the past six or seven years had provided reading material only for educated youth, and noted that the readership of the recent 'revolutionary literature' was even narrower. As for the labouring masses, they would never understand it, nor would they be willing to listen even if it were fed to them. Rather than championing the proletariat, Mao Tun wanted to enlarge the scope of the petty-bourgeoisie both as readers and as subject matter:

Now for the future of 'New Literature' – or even more boldly, the future of 'revolutionary literature' – the first task is to move it out of youth and students and into the petty-bourgeois masses, where it will then take root. In order to achieve this, we must first of all redirect our subject-matter to the lives of such people as small merchants, middle and small peasants. We should not use too many new terms or Europeanized sentence structures. We should not merely do didactic propaganda of new ideas but should faithfully and forcefully depict the essence of petty-bourgeois life.[9]

Mao Tun did in fact carry out this injunction in the early thirties in his novel *Midnight* and his trilogy of stories – 'Spring silkworms', 'Autumn harvest', and 'Winter ruin'. His fictional canvas was peopled by a variety of petty-bourgeois characters in cities and the countryside. The revolutionary writers, on the contrary, offered only a meagre and slipshod corpus of 'proletarian literature', mainly by Chiang Kuang-tz'u.

Mao Tun and Lu Hsun succeeded in exposing the superficiality of the young radicals' arguments. Mao Tun's fiction and Lu Hsun's *tsa-wen* demonstrated the vitality of critical realism. But they did not offer an alternative theory that was diametrically opposed to the radicals' canon of revolutionary literature. Mao Tun was already a party member who differed with his fellow Communists only in his more sombre assessment of the revolution's prospects. Lu Hsun's experiences in Canton had made him disillusioned with the revolutionary potential of the Kuomintang. Circumstances under the new Nanking government further solidified his

[8] Li Ho-lin, *Chung-kuo wen-i lun-chan* (Literary debates in China), 412.
[9] *Ibid.* 379. An English translation by Yu-shih Ch'en of this article appeared in John Berninghausen and Ted Huters, eds. *Revolutionary literature in China: an anthology*, 37–44. The editors have also supplied a perceptive introductory essay.

opposition, especially after five young leftist writers, including his disciple
Jou Shih, were executed as part of a group of 22 CCP leaders shot at Lung
Hua outside Shanghai on 7 February 1931 (see above, p. 174). Lu Hsun
was so stricken by the tragedy that, more than ever, he felt persecuted
under the 'white terror'. Political urgency thus thrust him on to a common
ground with his leftist rivals.

Moreover, in order to pinpoint the weaknesses of the radicals' arguments,
Lu Hsun was compelled to delve into the foundations of Marxist
aesthetics. From 1928 to 1930, he began to read and translate the works
of Plekhanov and Lunacharsky. His self-education resulted in a gradual
reversal of his previous notion of literature's essential irrelevance to
politics. A literature of discontent against the status quo, he now believed,
could serve to undermine the existing political authority and could,
indeed, be termed 'revolutionary'.[10]

By 1930 Lu Hsun had virtually accepted the basic tenets of the young
radicals, albeit in his own refined formulation. He concluded that
revolutionary literature had to be produced precisely because of the
setbacks of the revolution; the writers and the workers were united in
their common 'passion' of suffering. This shared experience under
oppression forged a common bond which made this literature 'belong
to the broad masses of revolutionary toilers' and hence, proletarian.[11] Lu
Hsun's reconciliation with his radical critics did not necessarily signify
that he was won over in argument, for a man with his intractable
character and seasoned insight would never have bowed to anyone.
Rather, he must have sensed that for all their trendiness, the revolutionary
writers had captured the changed mood of the urban intelligentsia.

After a brief spell of political optimism in 1926–7 when the Northern
Expedition offered the prospect of genuine revolution, most of the young
Chinese intellectuals became alienated again from the state. Rather than
make an appeal to these literary intellectuals through accommodation or
persuasion, the new Nanking government under Chiang Kai-shek
demonstrated only distrust, followed in the early thirties by censorship
and oppression. As Chiang Monlin, a liberal sympathetic with the KMT,
later observed, the government had 'lost touch with the broad masses;
it had no deep or clear understanding of the mood of societal discontent'.[12]
The CCP, on the other hand, capitalized on this increasingly pervasive

[10] For an analysis of Lu Hsun's changing conceptions of literature and revolution, see Leo Ou-fan
Lee, 'Literature on the eve of revolution: reflections on Lu Xun's leftist years, 1927–1936', *Modern
China*, 2.3 (July 1976) 277–91.
[11] Gladys Yang, ed. *Silent China: selected writings of Lu Xun*, 176.
[12] Liu Hsin-huang, *Hsien-tai Chung-kuo wen-hsueh shih-hua* (Discourse on the history of modern
Chinese literature), 485.

sentiment and, with organizational acumen, made a concerted effort to rally the restless urban writers to its objectives. The stage was set for a leftist united front that was to dominate the literary scene in the 1930s.

THE LEAGUE OF LEFT-WING WRITERS AND THE POLEMICS ON LITERATURE

On 2 March 1930, about forty writers (out of an initial membership of more than fifty) gathered in Shanghai to found the League of Left-wing Writers. On 16 February, two weeks before this momentous gathering, preliminary discussions had been held at the invitation of Lu Hsun and Hsia Yen (Shen Tuan-hsien) to form a planning committee for the founding of the league. While Lu Hsun has been credited with a leading role, the real initiative came probably from the Chinese Communist Party through its agent Hsia Yen, who was specifically assigned to this task.[13] Under the Li Li-san leadership, the CCP had embarked upon a general programme in late 1929 and early 1930 to create in urban centres a series of cultural 'front organizations' in order to attract sympathetic fellow travellers like Lu Hsun.[14] Aside from the League of Left-wing Writers, several similar organizations – ranging from fields of drama, film, art and poetry to social science, education, journalism and Esperanto – were created. These front organizations fell under the general umbrella of the 'Left-wing Cultural Coalition' (Tso-i wen-hua tsung t'ung-meng), although the centre of activities was the League of Left-wing Writers.[15]

The leadership of the league consisted nominally of an executive committee of seven standing members: Hsia Yen, Hung Ling-fei (both party members in charge of cultural work), Feng Nai-ch'ao, Ch'ien Hsing-ts'un (Lu Hsun's former critic from the Sun Society), T'ien Han (a leading dramatist), Cheng Po-ch'i (one of the founding members of the Creation Society) and Lu Hsun. While Lu Hsun had the honour of giving the inaugural address, he was clearly isolated in the league's power structure both by his erstwhile opponents and by party activists. The position of the league's secretary was held by three party members

---

[13] According to an official source, as early as late 1928 the Kiangsu party committee of the CCP had dispatched Hsia Yen, Li Ch'u-li and Feng Nai-ch'ao to contact Lu Hsun to plan a united front. See *Tso-lien shih-ch'i wu-ch'an chieh-chi ko-ming wen-hsueh* (Proletarian revolutionary literature in the period of the Left-wing League), 353. A list of the inaugural membership is included in *Chung-kuo hsien-tai wen-i tzu-liao ts'ung-k'an ti-i chi* (Sources of modern Chinese literature, first series), 155–7.

[14] Harriet C. Mills, 'Lu Hsun: 1927–1936, the years on the left', 139.

[15] Ting I, 'Chung-kuo tso-i tso-chia lien-meng ti ch'eng-li chi ch'i ho fan-tung cheng-chih ti tou-cheng'(The founding of the League of Left-wing Writers and its struggle against reactionary political forces), in Chang Ching-lu, ed. *Chung-kuo hsien-tai ch'u-pan shih-liao* (Historical materials on contemporary Chinese publications), 2.42.

consecutively: Feng Nai-ch'ao, Yang Han-sheng and Chou Yang. (The last two, together with Hsia Yen and T'ien Han, later became the vicious gang of 'four heavies', whom Lu Hsun singled out for special attack in the battle of 'two slogans' in 1936.) It can be surmised that after an initial period of euphoria, Lu Hsun served merely as a figurehead who enjoyed neither power nor friendly relations with the party activists.

The league's two official documents – the 'Theoretical guideline of literature' adopted in the inaugural meeting, and a lengthier position paper drafted by the league's executive committee titled 'The new mission of the revolutionary literature of the Chinese proletariat' – were, like Lu Hsun's vague inaugural speech, unfocused. The 'Guideline' called upon league members to 'stand on the battle line of the proletariat's struggle for emancipation' and to 'assist and engage in the birth of proletarian art'. But it failed to define either the meaning or scope of proletarian literature. Three injunctions on writing were given in the position paper: first, the league writers must 'pay attention to the large number of subjects from the realities of Chinese social life', especially those related directly to revolutionary objectives; second, the league writers must 'observe and describe from the proletarian standpoint and outlook'; and third, the form of their literature 'must be simple and understandable to the workers and peasants. When necessary, dialects can be used.'[16] Again, except for the third injunction, the document did not define proletarian or revolutionary literature exclusively in the framework of workers, peasants and soldiers, as Mao later did in his Yenan talks. It called for the 'popularization' of literature – a reflection probably of Ch'ü Ch'iu-p'ai's ideas – but the issues were confined to language. As the Communist scholar Liu Shou-sung has pointed out, the two documents failed to give a genuine proletarian thrust to leftist literature.[17] The documents defined the league's standpoint, organization and mission as primarily a literary vanguard and a propaganda machine. The promotion of a genuine kind of proletarian literature was secondary in importance. Thus in the league's numerous publications, banned repeatedly by the government, there appeared a plethora of doctrinal criticism, but a paucity of good creative writing.

In its emphasis on ideological correctness, organizational discipline, but not literary creativity, the league resembled the RAPP organization in Soviet Russia: it attempted to define a 'we' group that was pitted against the 'they' of all other ideological persuasions.[18] And like RAPP, to which

---

[16] *Ts'an-k'ao tzu-liao*, 1.290–1.

[17] Liu Shou-sung, *Chung-kuo hsin wen-hsueh shih ch'u-kao* (A preliminary draft history of modern Chinese literature) 1.214–15.

[18] For the exclusivist position of RAPP (Russian Association of Proletarian Writers), see Edward J. Brown, *Russian literature since the revolution*, 112–13.

some of the league members owed a direct intellectual debt, the league was most active, not so much in promoting new proletarian talents, but in provoking ideological polemics. The seven-year record of the league was one of continuous debates against all kinds of 'enemies': beginning with Lu Hsun's polemic with the liberal Crescent Moon Society, the league combated successively the conservative proponents of 'nationalist literature', the left-leaning 'third category' writers, and finally some of its own members in the debate on 'mass language' and in the famous battle of the 'two slogans' connected with the league's sudden dissolution in 1936.

Prelude: Lu Hsun vs. the Crescent Moon

The most formidable enemies of the Left-wing League did not come initially from the right – the KMT government had never concentrated its efforts in the field of literature – but from the centre. Even before the league was formed, the Japanese-educated men of letters who comprised the majority in the Creation and Sun Societies could never get along with the Anglo-American group around the Crescent Moon (Hsin yueh). Since some of the Crescent Moon members had close associations with Ch'en Yuan and the *Contemporary Review* group who clashed with Lu Hsun in the early twenties, these 'gentlemen' scholars and writers were viewed with animosity even before Liang Shih-ch'iu, the theoretician of the Crescent Moon group, fired his first shot against proletarian literature. Personalities and personal backgrounds thus added the necessary fuel to the burning fire of crucial ideological differences.

When the *Crescent Moon* magazine was first published in March 1928, it featured an eight-page manifesto, supposedly written by Hsu Chih-mo, which set forth two guiding principles of the journal: 'health' and 'dignity'. With these two amorphous slogans, Hsu in his ebullient style declared war on all the 'bacteria' on the literary scene, which he divided into no less than 13 categories: sentimentalism, decadentism, aestheticism, utilitarianism, didacticism, detracticism, extremism, fragilism, eroticism, fanaticism, venalism, sloganism and 'ism-ism'. Apparently some of these 'isms' were aimed, explicitly or implicitly, at the revolutionary writers of the Creation and Sun Societies, who immediately rose to the occasion by calling Hsu Chih-mo a 'clown', Hu Shih a 'compromising idealist' and the Crescent Moon group a hypocritical bunch of compradorial 'gentlemen' in the service of the capitalist class.[19]

The substantive issue which divided the two camps lay deeper than mere name-calling. From its inception, the *Crescent Moon* posed the threat of

[19] The various polemical articles are included in *Ts'an-k'ao tzu-liao*, 1.359–412.

an alternative theory of literature. As voiced by its chief spokesman, Liang Shih-ch'iu (though Liang later claimed that he had no backing from his colleagues),[20] this theory offered the familiar Anglo-American notion of the autonomy of literature – that literature depicts 'eternal and universal human nature', that creative writing has always been the product of individuals (the 'aristocratic elite', in Liang's words), and that it must be judged by its own intrinsic values without considerations of historical age, environment or class. Moreover, Liang Shih-ch'iu clearly modelled himself after his most admired 'teacher' of Western literature – Irving Babbitt, with whom Liang had studied at Harvard. From Babbitt he had learned to distrust Rousseau, and to disdain chaos in favour of reason and discipline, an idea which Liang traced to Matthew Arnold. In a period in which the Chinese literary scene was fraught with chaos, what was most urgently needed, in Liang's view, was a commitment to catholic tastes and high standards. It is clear from Liang's various articles published at this time that his own ambition was to become a Chinese Dr Samuel Johnson – an arbiter of literary taste and a critic in the Arnoldian sense. The practice of literary criticism as a scholarly discipline was, of course, non-existent in modern China, and any attempts to emulate the likes of F. R. Leavis or Edmund Wilson (roughly Liang's contemporaries) were doomed to failure.

Liang Shih-ch'iu also proved to be an especially prickly thorn in the eyes of Lu Hsun, possibly because this doyen of the Shanghai literary scene felt the challenge of Liang's ambition and, to some extent, a certain envy of Liang's knowledge of Western literature. Before the league was formed, Lu Hsun was already involved in a few skirmishes in print with Liang. The incentive had been provided by two timely articles Liang published in *Crescent Moon* in 1929: 'Is literature conditioned by class?' and 'On Mr Lu Hsun's hard translation'. In these Liang elaborated on his ideas presented in a previous article, 'Literature and revolution' (1928), and maintained that neither revolution nor class – both extrinsic to literature – could serve as a criterion for literary criticism. Concerning the problem of proletarian literature, Liang asserted that since literature had always been the creation of a minority of talented minds, the term 'literature of the masses' was itself a contradiction. True literature, Liang argued, was above class; its right domain was the 'fundamental human nature' – love, hate, pity, terror, death – that could not be confined to any class. Liang Shih-ch'iu further found fault with Lu Hsun's translations of Plekhanov and Lunacharsky. Lu Hsun translated the 'hard' way, being conscientiously

---

[20] Hou Chien, *Ts'ung wen-hsueh ko-ming tao ko-ming wen-hsueh* (From literary revolution to revolutionary literature), 162.

literal and following the Japanese re-translation, and Liang found it difficult to understand. Finally, Liang opined that whatever effort Lu Hsun put into his translations, literary ideologies were still secondary to the quality of creative work: 'we do not want advertisements, we want goods'.[21]

Lu Hsun's rebuttal, titled 'Hard translation and the class nature of literature', was one of the longest essays he ever wrote. Obviously, Liang had hit where it hurt most, for to be affronted for his painstaking introduction of the Soviet canons of Marxist aesthetics was something Lu Hsun could hardly swallow. The tone of this long article was generally quite reasonable and, in several passages, touched with humane passion. He disagreed with Liang's classless view of literature not only on the basis of his recently acquired theory from Plekhanov, but also out of a sense of empathy for the lower classes. Liang was not aware, Lu Hsun argued, that his very position of literary autonomy was itself a reflection of his bourgeois background. As regards 'human nature' depicted in literature, would a poor starving peasant have enough leisure time to plant flowers simply for their beauty? 'How could an oil magnate understand the sorrow and suffering of an old Peking woman who picked charcoal for a living?' To appreciate literature was a privilege, but the physical conditions and the illiteracy of the poor made it impossible for them to enjoy such a privilege. Lu Hsun also conceded that, regrettably, thus far there had not been many 'goods' of quality in proletarian literature. But it was an act of 'bourgeois maliciousness' to demand immediate products from the proletariat.

While Lu Hsun may have revealed an unsure grasp of Marxist aesthetics (his defence of class remained elementary – an act of faith rather than erudite argument), he more than made up for this weakness by his honesty and humanity. This is especially true of his apologia for translation. He explained that he did it the 'hard' way because of his own language deficiencies, and because he had to be honest with himself and his readers. Moreover, since the task of translating Plekhanov and Lunacharsky served as a test for his leftist critics and himself to see whether or not they had erred in theory, Lu Hsun was compelled to remain faithful to the texts. 'When it hit upon the wounds of those critics I did not admire, I smiled; when it hit upon my own wounds, I bore with it but never wanted to alter [the text]. This was a reason for my persistent effort at "hard translation".'[22]

Lu Hsun's essay was written in early 1930 (probably shortly before the formation of the league) when he was well on his way to closing ranks

[21] Ibid. 167–8.   [22] Ts'an-k'ao tzu-liao, 1.394.

with his leftist opponents. The essay showed Lu Hsun in a spirit that was less caustic than either before or after its composition. It was also considerably less dogmatic than his writings in 1931 and 1932, for he agreed with Liang that propaganda was not literature and that leftist slogans in the past did not constitute true proletarian literature. But the essay nevertheless revealed the emotional commitment of a true convert to the leftist cause. His debate with Liang Shih-ch'iu and the Crescent Moon group did not represent an undisputed triumph of Marxist over liberal theories of literature. He did, however, win on other accounts. In a period of crisis and commitment, clarion-calls for the neutrality of literature could be seen, especially in leftist eyes, as both untimely and 'ivory-towerish'. In Communist literary history, therefore, the Crescent Moon group are viewed as arch-villains, whose 'defeat' by Lu Hsun is considered a major victory of the league.

The case of 'nationalist literature'

Compared to the liberal critics of the Crescent Moon Society, the proponents of the so-called 'nationalist literature' (min-tsu chu-i wen-hsueh), which emerged in June 1930, only three months after the founding of the Left-wing League, were weaker in ideological and organizational strength. Obviously, this was designed as a counter-league measure by a group of literary men – Wang P'ing-ling, Huang Chen-hsia and others – who had close associations with the Kuomintang. But their slogan, which smacked of Taine's theory of 'nationality, environment and time', was very vague, since it called for a literature that reflected a 'nationalistic spirit and consciousness' to replace the leftist view of class. As scholars from Taiwan have admitted, the group's criticism of the left consisted mainly of personal attacks, and none of its members commanded prestige or respect within the literary scene.[23] Their creative output was even less than that of the leftists. But the group's major liability lay in the fact that their pro-Kuomintang stance ran counter to the critical temper of the literary intelligentsia. It was almost unimaginable to the early thirties for a conscientious man of letters to be a mouthpiece of the government. The advocates of 'nationalist literature' were thus doomed to failure from its very inception. But this minor debate served, coincidentally, as a catalyst for a most intriguing polemical episode in modern Chinese literary history – the controversy over the 'free men' (tzu-yu jen) or 'the third category of men' (ti-san-chung jen) in literature.

---

[23] Liu Hsin-huang, 513–15. See also Li Mu, San-shih nien-tai wen-i lun (On the literature and arts of the 1930s), 61.

The case of 'free men' and the 'third category' of writers

In September 1931, Hu Ch'iu-yuan, a young scholar, published an essay attacking 'nationalist literature'. One of his central arguments was that literature should never be denigrated as a 'gramophone' of politics. Hu's assertion touched the very core of the leftist stance and was immediately taken as an attack on the league. A series of debates ensued between Hu and the league's major theoreticians.

Hu Ch'iu-yuan had been educated in Japan, where he acquired considerable knowledge of Marxism and wrote a lengthy book on Plekhanov and his theory of art, which was published in 1932. The league writers were probably unaware of Hu's background and treated his views as another variation of Crescent Moon liberalism. To their surprise, Hu proved himself to be a liberal Marxist whose command of Marxist scholarship was superior to that of his league critics. From his reading of Plekhanov, Trotsky, Voronsky and other Soviet theoreticians, Hu argued that although literature has a class basis, literary creation should not be subjected to the same laws as can be found in Marxist economic or political treatises. Literature, in Hu's view, reflected life aesthetically by showing its complexities and ambiguities. Reacting strongly against the mechanistic views of his leftist opponents, particularly Ch'ien Hsing-ts'un and other members of the Sun Society, Hu Ch'iu-yuan cited a battery of sources from the Marxist canon to show that the function of literary criticism was to understand literature 'objectively' rather than to dictate its creation. Literature, in other words, had its own values which could be beneficial to revolution, especially in the case of good literature. (Thus Hu admitted the possibility of good proletarian literature.) But he felt that literary creation should never be treated as something 'below' politics. In Hu's sense, being a 'free man' did not necessarily mean being anti-Marxist or apolitical as Liang Shih-ch'iu believed; it merely referred to 'an attitude' of a somewhat pedantic scholar who embraced Marxist theory with all seriousness but who opposed the tendency 'to judge everything in accordance with the current practical policies or urgent needs of the party leadership'.[24]

Hu's challenge to the league's monopoly of leftist literature was echoed in 1932 by Su Wen (Tai K'e-ch'ung) who, by no means unsympathetic to the leftist cause, voiced a similar concern over the excessive 'invasion' of literature by political necessities. The 'third category' of men, in Su's original meaning, referred to those writers who were caught between, or

[24] Su Wen, ed. *Wen-i tzu-yu lun-pien chi* (Debate on the freedom of literature and art), 20. For Hu's own recapitulation of the debate, see Liu Hsin-huang, 539–64.

left behind, the two types of Marxist advocates – Hu Ch'iu-yuan's 'free man' and the 'unfree, party-dominated' league. However sympathetic, a good writer simply could not write according to the dictates of the league's theoreticians. Literature, in Su's view, was more than a political weapon, although he admitted a need for such. 'I am not opposed to the political purpose of literature,' Su Wen stated, 'but I am against sacrificing reality because of this political purpose.' A writer had to be honest in depicting life as he saw it. 'We demand a truthful literature more than a utilitarian literature that serves a certain current political purpose.'[25] Thus, between the Kuomintang's oppression and the league's dictation of literature, the majority of writers, Su Wen argued, fell almost involuntarily into the 'third category'.

In the league's rebuttals, the most cogent argument was put forth by Ch'ü Ch'iu-pai. In a long essay, Ch'ü (using the pseudonym I-chia) criticized Hu and Su for their failure to recognize the fundamental Marxist tenet of the class basis of literature. In Ch'ü's judgment, Hu Ch'iu-yuan had overemphasized the function of literature as an aesthetic exploration of images and as a passive reflection of life. He attributed Hu's weaknesses to Plekhanov, who had himself been criticized in the Soviet Union for his 'idealistic' tendencies. Literary creation, in Ch'ü's view, could never be divorced from the socio-economic background of its author and had to serve its political function. For the Chinese proletariat who were engaged in a life-and-death struggle, literature had to be a weapon against the oppressors. 'When the proletariat demands openly that literature be a weapon of struggle,' Ch'ü asserted, 'whoever cries out against the "invasion of literature" is unconsciously becoming the "gramophone" of the bourgeois hypocrites and their theory of art above everything.'[26] In the period of class struggle, there could be no 'middle ground'.

While affirming class determinism and the need for commitment, neither Lu Hsun nor Ch'ü Ch'iu-pai was prepared to defend the league's infallibility. They freely acknowledged the folly of infantile leftism and mechanistic interpretations among a few of its members, particularly Ch'ien Hsing-ts'un. But Ch'ü argued that despite their weaknesses, these eager members were sincerely groping toward a revolutionary theory and practice, whereas Hu and Su, on the contrary, ignored political reality and did mere fence-sitting.

When compared with the vehement counter-attacks directed against other enemies, this was a mild response. How does one account for this 'soft' stance? The clue may be found behind the often verbose exchanges of theoretical differences. The arguments of Hu Ch'iu-yuan and Su

[25] Su Wen, 189–91.   [26] Su Wen, 85.

Wen – two individuals who were apparently not affiliated with any literary or political group – raised two important issues unprecedented in leftist literature in China (though Hu was clearly familiar with their Soviet precedents): the principle of *partiinost* ('party spirit') or party direction of literature, and the problem of the 'fellow travellers', those writers who were sympathetic to the leftist cause but did not choose to join the league or the party. The two problems were compounded by the league's own definition of its functions.

On the one hand, the formation of the league was meant to provide a unified direction to revolutionary literature. Since its leadership consisted mainly of party members, the way was paved for party domination and control of literature. However, the CCP in the early thirties was organizationally weak and beset with factional strife; it was in no position to enforce a consistent *partiinost*. The league was created, on the other hand, to provide a broad front for leftist writers as well as their sympathizers. Thus, from the party's operational standpoint, the league was a front organization to attract 'fellow travellers', those 'third category' writers who were followers of neither KMT nor CCP but who nevertheless harboured more sympathies for 'proletarian literature' than for 'nationalist literature'. Both Hu Ch'iu-yuan and Su Wen, like Lu Hsun before them, could be enlisted as fellow travellers. And according to Hu, some attempts to lure him into the leftist camp were actually made.[27]

It is interesting to see how the two issues were resolved by Ch'ü Chiu-pai and Feng Hsueh-feng (under the pen names Lo Yang and Ho Tan-lin) in their summary articles of the debate, which apparently represented the majority opinion of the league. In Ch'ü's article, the principle of *partiinost* was mentioned as being first laid down by Lenin in 'Party organization and party literature'. Lenin wrote that *partiinost* 'should naturally be applied to the creation of revolutionary and proletarian literature, particularly to criticism'. But Ch'ü made an important qualification: he felt that the issue lay in whether *partiinost* could be applied 'correctly or incorrectly'. Ch'ü added that even when it was applied to league writers, it was not to be 'coerced, but rather to be discussed, studied, and learned'. As for non-league writers, they were asked merely to 'recognize' the principle. Ch'ü further defended creative freedom within the league by explaining that its 'Guidelines' provided only some 'general directions' and did not constitute 'orders'.[28] In fact, throughout the league's history, the correct form and content of proletarian literature was repeatedly discussed and debated, but never enforced.

27 Liu Hsin-huang, 550.
28 Li Ho-lin, *Chin erh-shih-nien Chung-kuo wen-i ssu-ch'ao lun* (Chinese literary trends in the recent twenty years), 333–4.

With regard to the policy toward fellow travellers, Ch'ü dismissed the radical view ('if you don't follow us, you are an anti-revolutionary') as dogmatic and sensationalist – an indirect reference perhaps to radical young leftists and Chou Yang. But it was Feng Hsueh-feng who made the final conciliatory statement. At the end of his long article Feng made the following redefinition, couched in highly tendentious language, of the 'third category':

> If the third category of literature is 'opposed to the old ages and old society', it is certainly not anti-revolutionary literature, although it does not take a proletarian point of view. In that case, this type of literature is already beneficial to revolution, it is no longer neutral, and therefore it does not need the title of third category literature.[29]

Feng Hsueh-feng's conciliatory statement, at the end of a polite polemical rebuttal, apparently satisfied the two challengers, who later considered their battle a success, in the sense that the league was forced to admit certain errors and subdue its strident ideological tone.[30] But the 'third category' men were clearly no match for the league in terms of power and influence: neither Hu nor Su was a creative writer, and they faded from the literary scene shortly afterwards.

After 1932, there was no major challenge to the league's ideological domination. A considerable number of literary men revolved around Lin Yutang's three popular magazines – *Lun-yü* (Analects), *Jen-chien-shih* (Human world) and *Yü-chou feng* (Cosmic wind) – and remained purposefully 'apolitical' in their emphasis on humour and gentle satire, but they certainly posed no threat to the league's ideological authority. Lu Hsun's attacks against them were subdued, perhaps due to some soft spots in his heart for Chou Tso-jen, his 'separated brother', and even for Lin Yutang, his former friend and erstwhile employer. Other non-league writers, such as the *Hsien-tai* (Contemporary) magazine group, maintained a neutral stance, though still open to contributions or overtures from the left. The debates which ensued on 'mass language' and 'national defence' literature sprang essentially from within the leftist front and, in the latter case, all but terminated its ideological unity.

The debate on 'mass language' and 'Latinization'

The issue of 'mass language' (*ta-chung hua* or *ta-chung yü*) was first raised in 1932 by Ch'ü Ch'iu-pai, the most brilliant leftist theoretician of the 1930s.[31] Ch'ü's concern with language was inseparable from his Marxist

---

[29] Su Wen, 287.
[30] Liu Hsin-huang, 549.
[31] For a detailed study of this issue, see Paul Pickowicz, 'Ch'ü Ch'iu-pai and the Chinese Marxist

literary convictions: since proletarian literature was a literature for the masses, Ch'ü logically argued that it must be understood by the masses. The May Fourth *pai-hua*, as used in New Literature, had become in Ch'ü's opinion a new elitist idiom characterized by saturation with foreign terms, Europeanized syntax, Japanese phrases, and *wen-yen* remnants. It was, in short, a language monopolized by a small minority of urban intellectuals who were alienated from the masses. Ch'ü therefore called for a new 'literary revolution', this time led by the rising proletarian class against three targets: the residual *wen-yen*, the May Fourth *pai-hua* (which Ch'ü termed a new *wen-yen*), as well as the old *pai-hua* of the traditional vernacular novels. What emerged from this second revolution was to be a new mass language that reflected the living tongues of the populace. With his Marxist predilections, Ch'ü naturally envisioned the prototype of this new popular language to be a collection of 'common idioms' (*p'u-t'ung-hua*), much like the language spoken by the metropolitan workers who came from all over China and managed to communicate with one another in modern factories.[32]

In a critical article in response to Ch'ü's ideas, Mao Tun showed that the language of the urban workers was by no means uniform: in Shanghai, for instance, the popular tongues were naturally based on the Shanghai dialect, while in other cities the 'common idioms' varied greatly from region to region. There was no such thing, in Mao Tun's view, as a national 'common idiom'. Mao Tun further defended the May Fourth *pai-hua* as still viable, though needing to be simplified and de-Europeanized. The urgent task for Mao Tun was to reform the modern *pai-hua* and to enrich it with local dialects.[33] Thus, between Mao Tun's realistic defence of modern *pai-hua* and Ch'ü Ch'iu-pai's radical vision of *p'u-t'ung hua*, the leftist camp was divided, as the debate was renewed in 1934, into two different, but not mutually exclusive, positions on the basis of Ch'ü's general premise. Some argued that in order to establish a new common language of the masses, the elitist *pai-hua* had to be rejected in toto; others favoured the popular language but still wished to salvage *pai-hua*. After reaching a compromise solution to reject the bad and assimilate the good elements in *pai-hua*, the debate soon shifted to a discussion of the need for Latinization.

Conceding that the common idiom he had envisioned was still in the process of formation, Ch'ü Ch'iu-pai nevertheless maintained that it was definitely not to be encased in a written form. Chinese characters were

conception of revolutionary popular literature and art', *CQ* 70 (June 1977) 296–314. See also his book *Marxist literary thought in China: the influence of Ch'ü Ch'iu-pai*, ch. 9.
[32] Li Ho-lin, *Chung-kuo wen-i ssu-ch'ao lun*, 360–1.
[33] *Ibid.* 362–3.

too complicated to learn and also inadequate to register the living vitality of the popular language with its variegated spoken expressions. Other critics pointed out that the written *pai-hua* was a vehicle of the Peking dialect, as were the previous systems of romanization (the so-called *Kuo-yü lo-ma tzu*). The new phonetic scheme, according to Lu Hsun and others, should be simpler and without the four tonal indicators. This new system of Latinized Chinese ('Latinxua'), which presumably had been tried out by two Russian Sinologist-linguists on the Chinese residents in the Far Eastern Maritime province of the Soviet Union, would be the alphabetic script of the *p'u-t'ung hua* which would replace entirely the centuries-old written ideographs.[34] While allowing for regional variations, both Ch'ü and Lu Hsun were confident that the phonetic system would still be much easier to master than the written characters.

This naive utopian theory of language was clearly impracticable in the 1930s, and was never put into successful practice. The Latinized script has become, at best, a phonetic aid to reading Chinese characters, not their replacement. But the other parts of this language debate proved to be most useful to Mao Tse-tung. In his radical critique of May Fourth literature, Ch'ü Ch'iu-pai had laid the groundwork for Mao's Yenan Talks. Both Ch'ü and Mao agreed that the language of proletarian literature must be close to the idiom of the masses. The 'popularization' of literature was thus to become a hallmark of Mao's policy in 1942, and the second 'literary revolution', begun by Ch'ü with little success, was launched again in Yenan with spectacular results.

The battle of the 'two slogans'

With the departure from Shanghai in late 1933 of Ch'ü Ch'iu-pai and Feng Hsueh-feng for Juichin, the league lost two of its most influential leaders and entered a phase of uncertainty. From 1934 to 1936, the league's ties with the central organs of the CCP were tenuous at best, and the party's underground headquarters were decimated by arrests and executions. An internal split developed between the league's new organizational leadership, particularly Chou Yang, and Lu Hsun, his disciples and other veteran writers.[35] In 1934, Hu Feng arrived in Shanghai from Japan and in 1935, with Lu Hsun's support, twice challenged Chou Yang's ideological authority on matters of interpretation concerning models and typical characters in literature. But the crowning event, which brought

---

[34] Tagore, 160.
[35] For a brilliant analysis of this entire episode, see Tsi-an Hsia, 'Lu Hsun and the dissolution of the League of Leftist Writers', in his *The gate of darkness: studies on the leftist literary movement in China*, 101–45.

these internecine bickerings into the open, was the sudden dissolution of the league in the spring of 1936 in response to the CCP's declaration for a national united front against Japanese invasion. On this important move Lu Hsun was not even consulted.

It remains unclear, for lack of adequate documentation, how the decision to dissolve the league was made. But it can be surmised that the decision was carried out by the Chou Yang group, who wished to replace the league by forming a broader coalition: the Association of Chinese Writers and Artists (Chung-kuo wen-i chia hsieh-hui). This group was formally inaugurated on 7 June 1936, at least two or three months after the league was dissolved. This apparent delay, in a time in which patriotic organizations were springing up spontaneously and rapidly, indicated that factors other than simple confusion among leftist writers were involved. Lu Hsun, Pa Chin, Hu Feng, Huang Yuan and others were invited to join the new association, but the invitation was either refused or ignored. Shortly afterwards, on 1 July, Lu Hsun and others signed a 'Declaration of Chinese literary workers' (Chung-kuo wen-i kung-tso che hsuan-yen) without forming a formal organization. The rivalry between the two camps on the left was thus further demarcated.

Toward the end of 1935, articles had begun to appear in which slogans reflecting the new political situation were bandied about. The term, 'national defence literature' (kuo-fang wen-hsueh), was mentioned together with other terms like 'national self-defence literature' (min-tsu tzu-wei wen-hsueh) and 'national revolutionary literary movement' (min-tsu ko-ming wen-hsueh yun-tung). The decision to adopt 'national defence literature' as the formal literary slogan of the United Front policy and the guiding principle of the association was probably made by the Chou Yang group (with or without the tacit consent of the CCP leadership).[36] Its appropriateness was presumably justified by its Soviet origins and by the fact that Mao Tse-tung had called for the establishment of a 'national defence' government. But the vague implications of the term received instant criticism from the various writers of the left.

Recognizing the need to clarify definitions and to silence the 'Trotskyite' opposition, Chou Yang made his first public statement on behalf of 'national defence literature' in June 1936, after preparations for founding the association were completed. He berated his ultra-leftist opponents for their narrow-minded abstractionism and their refusal to recognize the new political situation created by the Japanese invasion. While still considering urban revolutionary literature to be the main force since 1927, he nevertheless argued that a vast readership of 'middle

[36] Liu Hsin-huang, 463.

ground' writers did exist and should be attracted to the common cause. This was essentially a faithful parroting of the CCP's new stance and a far cry from his earlier position against the 'third category' of writers. But in his eagerness to champion his slogan as 'literature', Chou Yang had probably gone beyond the primarily political purpose of the party: 'to crystallize a strong body of united intellectual opinion which would force the Nationalist Government to come to some sort of coalition with the Communists and thus fight the Japanese'.[37] For he proceeded to dictate the theme and method of 'national defence literature': he asserted that national defence should become the central theme in the works of *all* writers except traitors, and that since 'questions of theme are inseparable from questions of method, the creation of national defence literature must adopt the creative method of progressive realism'. In a subsequent article, he even argued (presaging his 1958 statements on 'revolutionary romanticism') that national defence literature 'should not only depict the present state of national revolutionary struggles but at the same time sketch out the future vistas of national progress ... national defence literature, therefore, should concurrently use romanticism as part of its creative method.'[38]

Chou Yang's 'dictatorial' tendencies met with immediate opposition from veteran writers including Lu Hsun. Writing from Japan and sensing the political connection of the slogan, Kuo Mo-jo tried to defend it while modifying Chou's literary pretensions. 'National defence literature,' he stated, 'ought to be a standard of relations among writers and not a principle of creative writing.' Mao Tun agreed with this understanding but further warned that to apply the slogan to creative writing faced the dangers of 'closed-door sectarianism' – a direct reference to Chou Yang's injunction. Against Chou Yang's desire to control literature and 'to regulate others through the use of a slogan', Mao Tun insisted on the writer's prerogative of creative freedom within the context of his political commitment.[39]

Mao Tun's resentment of Chou Yang was shared, even more intensely, by Lu Hsun. As the late T. A. Hsia has pointed out in his vivid recapitulation of Lu Hsun's last years, the dissolution of the league had 'triggered a crisis, the last one, alas, in his life. Not only had he to redefine his own position, but Marxism, the sustenance of his spiritual life for so many years, was at stake.'[40] The league's demise put a sudden end to seven years of hard struggle against forces of the right and the

[37] Tagore, 114.
[38] Chou Yang, 'Kuan-yü kuo-fang wen-hsueh' (Concerning national defence literature), in Lin Ts'ung, ed. *Hsien chieh-tuan ti wen-hsueh lun-chan* (Current literary debates), 36–7, 81.
[39] Lin Ts'ung, 311–12.   [40] T. A. Hsia, 129.

centre: Lu Hsun was now forced to ally himself with his erstwhile enemies. Moreover, the slogan of 'national defence literature', which was thrust upon him with all its compromise and authoritarian weight, represented both a rebuff of his Marxist convictions and an affront to his personal stature. Simmering in silence, he would not give in but worked on a new counter slogan 'which would not suggest the termination of leftist literature but rather an extension of it, and which would incorporate the new policy of the Communist Party into the tradition of the proletariat'.[41] The slogan finally decided upon, after he consulted Mao Tun and others, was 'mass literature of national revolutionary war' (*min-tsu ko-ming chan-cheng ti ta-chung wen-hsueh*).

In May 1936 the new slogan was used by Hu Feng, obviously under Lu Hsun's direction, in an article titled: 'What do the masses demand of literature?' The battle of the 'two slogans' was thus launched. For Hu Feng and Lu Hsun the slogan 'mass literature of national revolutionary war' clearly defined the 'common interest' which linked the proletarian revolutionary movement with the national struggle against Japan. In both, the common denominator was anti-imperialism. The slogan also served notice that the masses were the major force in the anti-Japanese war. For Chou Yang and Hsu Mou-yung, however, Hu Feng's article had pointedly ignored 'national defence literature' in favour of a long-winded, hard-to-remember phrase, whose intended function was to limit and de-emphasize the importance of the united front. The revolutionary writers, according to Chou Yang, should 'not only create pointed revolutionary works, but at the same time unite with those who originally stood at some distance from us in thought and art ... and extend the influence of the national united front to those readers exposed to revolutionary literature'.[42]

These statements from both sides seemed to give the impression that, in matters of literary policy, the dictatorial Chou Yang argued for more liberality whereas the anti-authoritarian opposition opted for more rigidity. But in matters of literary practice the situation was just the reverse: Lu Hsun and Mao Tun insisted on creative freedom for the revolutionary writer while Chou Yang considered it 'a dangerous illusion'. Veiled in their conflicting slogans was therefore a basic difference in outlook between the literary commissar and the creative writer. For Chou Yang, the literary commissar *par excellence*, the party policy of the united front took precedence over everything else, including artistic creation. As writers, Lu Hsun and Mao Tun placed more value on creative writing for the goals of the revolution: they were obstinate in their belief

[41] *Ibid.*   [42] Lin Ts'ung, 74.

that conscientious artists should never compromise their personal integrity or lose their creative prerogatives. They strongly resented the imposition of this new *partiinost* by a self-appointed party spokesman. For Lu Hsun, Chou Yang's action was especially distasteful because, instead of further consolidating the league, Chou Yang dissolved it and ordered the committed leftist writers to turn to the right!

Lu Hsun was finally angered to action by a letter from Hsu Mou-yung in which Hsu politely reminded Lu Hsun of the 'treachery' and 'flattery' of his two disciples, Hu Feng and Huang Yuan. Hsu also flatly dismissed Lu Hsun's painstaking effort to introduce a left-wing slogan into the united front as 'a mistake and harmful to the cause'. To be reprimanded by a young writer and former disciple who questioned the soundness of his judgment on human character and the current political situation was too great an insult to Lu Hsun's ego. In his long reply, written almost immediately after he received Hsu Mou-yung's letter, Lu Hsun vented his pent-up feelings in a passionate outpouring of unmitigated and undisguised wrath. He frankly exposed the 'treachery' of his opponents: the sectarianism of the Association of Chinese Writers and Artists, the slyness of Hsu Mou-yung, and above all the machinations of Chou Yang, T'ien Han, Hsia Yen, and Yang Han-sheng – the sinister gang of 'four heavies' (*ssu-t'iao han-tzu*) who were really behind Hsu Mou-yung's accusatory letter.[43]

Obviously Lu Hsun's anger was directed against Chou Yang's 'monopoly' in literature and his 'gang style' behaviour. The slogan 'national defence literature' was criticized more for its 'sectarian' implications (especially in Chou Yang's authoritarian interpretation) than for its theoretical errors. Lu Hsun acknowledged that he never regarded the two slogans as in opposition to each other; rather he considered the term 'mass literature of national revolutionary war' to be 'clearer and deeper in meaning and more substantive in content'. It could supplement and correct the obscurities of the 'national defence literature' slogan. In an interview he announced that 'mass literature of national revolutionary war' could serve as a 'general slogan' under which other strategic slogans such as 'national defence literature' could also be allowed to exist. Paraphrasing Lu Hsun's statement but giving it a more balanced focus, Mao Tun explained that 'mass literature of national revolutionary war' should be the slogan for creative writing among left-wing writers, whereas 'national defence literature' could be a banner to characterize relations among all writers.[44]

Lu Hsun's new slogan was certainly not what the party leaders had

[43] *Ibid.* 334–49.   [44] *Ibid.* 315, 342.

anticipated. But the sheer eloquence of such an eminent 'fellow traveller' had to be respected, for otherwise more denunciation would have been tantamount to an open admission of the failure of the united front. This was apparently the conclusion which party leaders other than Chou Yang had reached. Earlier in April 1936, Feng Hsueh-feng had come back to Shanghai as the party's liaison man from Yenan. Instead of joining up with Chou Yang, Feng became persuaded by the arguments of his old master and chose Lu Hsun's side. Shortly after Lu Hsun published his long rejoinder to Hsu Mou-yung, Feng wrote a most devastating critique of Chou Yang, in which he reiterated the charge, first raised by Mao Tun and Lu Hsun, that Chou Yang's high-handed monopolistic tendencies had led to a harmful sectarianism which 'closed the door' on other writers. Chou had made a gross error, Feng charged, by imposing a pre-emptive dichotomy between 'national defence literature' and 'traitor literature', in the same way that he had mechanically dismissed all 'non-proletarian literature' as 'capitalist literature' in the debate on 'third category men' three years before. Chou's most serious fault, in Feng's judgment, was his refusal to heed the demands for 'creative freedom'. 'Three years ago ... we did not positively unite all groups to fight for creative freedom; we did not acknowledge with maximum flexibility the principle of creative freedom in our criticism. This was certainly a mistake, which we must admit even three years later.' At a time when the mobilization of all writers was urgently needed for the anti-Japanese struggle, Feng concluded, Chou Yang's imposition of regulatory 'conditions' had 'greatly narrowed the anti-Japanese front' and his insensitivity to the issue of creative freedom was a clear indicator that he had accustomed himself to the role of a 'local emperor'.[45]

Feng Hsueh-feng's personal animosity revealed in this most blatant charge against Chou Yang did not, however, reflect well on his discretion as a party representative. According to T. A. Hsia, Feng's mismanagement in Shanghai caused him to be censured by the party. (He was eventually purged in 1957 by his old rival Chou Yang.) But one of the party leaders, Ch'en Po-ta, had seen fit to call a ceasefire on the battle of the two slogans. While still affirming the validity of 'national defence literature', Ch'en acknowledged that 'the attitudes toward this slogan need not be unified' (thus imparting a slight rebuff to Chou Yang). Out of respect for Lu Hsun's stance, Ch'en paid an equal tribute to the other slogan. 'Mass literature of national revolutionary war', Ch'en stated in a tactical synthesis, should belong to 'the left wing' of national defence literature because it constituted 'an essential part as well as a major force of national defence literature'.[46]

45 Ts'an-k'ao tzu-liao, 1.567–75.   46 Ibid. 1.561–4. T. A. Hsia, 125.

The battle of the two slogans can be said to have formally come to an
end in early October (shortly before Lu Hsun's death on 19 October 1936)
when twenty writers, including Mao Tun, Lu Hsun, Kuo Mo-jo, Pa Chin
and Lin Yutang (with Chou Yang's group conspicuously absent), signed
a joint declaration calling for a unified front of all writers – old and new,
left and right – for 'purposes of national salvation'. Neither slogan was
mentioned, but the principle of creative freedom, which had been
advocated forcefully by Lu Hsun, Mao Tun, Hu Feng and Feng
Hsueh-feng, was finally affirmed.

LITERARY CREATIVITY AND SOCIAL CRISIS

The series of ideological debates brought much sound and fury to the
literary scene of the early thirties, but they failed to stimulate much literary
creativity. It seems that the most ideologically vociferous writers were
often the least creative: Ch'ü Ch'iu-pai, Chou Yang, Feng Hsueh-feng,
Liang Shih-ch'iu, Hu Ch'iu-yuan and other theoreticians had no creative
output to their credit. Other ideological writers produced meagre work
of low quality. Chiang Kuang-tz'u, for instance, achieved popular status
by virtue of a best-selling novel, *Ch'ung-ch'u yun-wei ti yueh-liang* (The moon
forces its way through the clouds), which must be counted as artistically
one of the worst works of the period.[47] Even the energetic Lu Hsun
sometimes expressed personal regret for not being able to write more
lyrical pieces in the vein of his earlier stories and prose poetry.[48]

While the ideologues on the left often monopolized the spotlight, less
ideological, but by no means uncommitted writers made far more
significant contributions to the new literary legacy. Some of the best
creative writers in the 1930s – Mao Tun, Lao She, Wu Tsu-hsiang, Chang
T'ien-i, Pa Chin, Ts'ao Yü and Wen I-to – all had leftist leanings. But
their leftism was mainly the expression of personal conscience and of an
artistic sensitivity which was increasingly affected by their socio-political
environment. A small minority of others – Li Chin-fa, Tai Wang-shu,
Feng Chih – were mostly poets and not very political. Their works are
often artistically more inventive than the leftist writers, though their
impact remained marginal. It was mainly due to the efforts of these creative
writers that the thirties witnessed the flowering of fiction (mainly the
novel), poetry and drama. By the eve of the Japanese invasion, modern
Chinese literature was on the verge of a true literary 'renaissance' as
writers gradually established their mature identities as committed artists.

[47] The novel enjoyed six printings in the five-month period after it was published. See Tagore, 71–2.
For an analysis of Chiang's life and works, see T. A. Hsia, 'The phenomenon of Chiang
Kuang-tz'u', in his *Gate of darkness*, 55–100.
[48] Feng Hsueh-feng, *Hui-i Lu Hsun* (Reminiscence of Lu Hsun), 23.

But this surging creative potential was not fully realized: the war put a sudden end to the fertile experiments in modernistic poetry; it rechannelled the energies of novelists from their major literary projects. Only drama prospered as a means of wartime propaganda and, in Chungking and Japanese-occupied Shanghai, as escapist entertainment. In terms of artistic creativity, the true culprit in this period was not the Kuomintang (whose suppressive measures nurtured a writer's critical spirit quite conducive to creativity) nor the CCP (whose literary control policies under Chou Yang had little visible impact on creative writers) but the Japanese: almost overnight the literary milieu was destroyed by the invaders' bombs and cannon-fire in 1937.

The trauma of war experience in literature will be discussed in a moment, but first we must note the four burgeoning modes of literary creation: the essay, the novel, modern verse and spoken drama.

The essay (tsa-wen)

The immediate impact of ideological polemics on literature was the popularity of the *tsa-wen* – the 'miscellaneous essay' or, in Ch'ü Ch'iu-pai's foreign term, 'feuilleton'. For purposes of doctrinal debate as well as social criticism and cultural commentary, the *tsa-wen* proved to be a most effective form. In this genre, Lu Hsun was the undisputed master.

Lu Hsun began experimenting with the short essay form at the same time he started writing short stories. Published first in *New Youth* and later in *Yü-ssu*, his 'random thought' pieces combined a free-flowing prose (written in the vernacular but interlaced with classical terms and phrases) with flexibility of content. While most of his essays were social in thrust and satirical in tone, as most Lu Hsun scholars have noted,[49] his approach was by no means narrowly utilitarian. Especially in his essays written before 1930, the critical intelligence of a social commentator was often combined with the lyrical sensitivity of a personal essayist. Behind his didactic assault on the evils of Chinese culture and society lurked a highly subjective quest for the shadows of China's collective psyche. The interplay of prose and poetry, didacticism and lyricism, of a sharp cynical intellect and a tense emotional psyche, characterizes the best of Lu Hsun's creative work, including his *tsa-wen*. The formal differences of genres – essay, prose, poetry and short story – were not so clearly marked in Lu Hsun's mind as Western scholars might expect. The common denominator of Lu Hsun's work (except his translations) is the brevity of each piece

---

[49] For a detailed analysis of Lu Hsun's *tsa-wen* art, see David E. Pollard, 'Lu Xun's *Zawen*'.

in a lifetime's voluminous output. Perhaps his mind was cluttered with a chaotic array of thoughts and feelings which never took on a coherent, systematic form. Thus the *tsa-wen* served as both a communicative vehicle and a literary by-product of Lu Hsun's mode of creativity.

As Lu Hsun became more politicized in the early 1930s, the inner personal dimension of his essay writing also became submerged under public layers of polemical outcry. For Lu Hsun himself, this shift from lyricism to polemicism was necessitated by the demands of political commitment. But his followers and enemies had embraced the Lu Hsun *tsa-wen* style as a major canon, and a mass of imitations flooded the publishing scene. These lesser *tsa-wen* writers totally ignored the inner depth of Lu Hsun's prose in their efforts to emulate only the surface brilliance of his satire. The result was a corpus of crude, shrill and shallow essays devoid of lasting literary value. Thus Lu Hsun's inimitable *tsa-wen* left an ironic legacy: it procreated in later periods of modern Chinese literary history an over-cynical and unnecessarily satirical style of essay writing without, however, the kernel of intellectual sophistication.

If *tsa-wen* was defined by leftists as an essentially ideological weapon in the 1930s, some non-leftist writers rallied around the personal essay (*hsiao-p'in wen*) as an alternative form of prose writing. The major spokesmen were Lu Hsun's brother, Chou Tso-jen, and the group of writers published in Lin Yutang's three magazines. Chou's essay style owes a clear debt to the classical tradition, particularly the works of the Kung-an and Ching-ling schools in the seventeenth century, which emphasized essay writing as personal expression.[50] Chou cultivated this 'personal style' almost to perfection: his prose is terse yet unhurried, elegant yet not flowery, reflecting a balanced and temperate mentality at great odds with Lu Hsun's. Writing in a similar vein, Chu Tzu-ch'ing and Yü P'ing-po produced essays with a personal touch sometimes verging on sentimentality, as in Chu's famous essay about his father, 'Shadow' (*Pei-ying*). Both Chou Tso-jen and Yü P'ing-po were the major contributors to Lin Yutang's publications which, following the tradition of the personal essay, advocated apolitical humour written in an urbane leisurely tone. Lin argued for a purposefully apolitical stance perhaps as a gesture of protest against the over-politicization of literature. And as gems of stylized writing, some of the best specimens of the *hsiao-p'in wen* are much more flavourful than the crudely combative *tsa-wen*. But in spite of its popularity in the mid-1930s (in publishing circles the year 1934 was designated as the year of the 'personal essay'), the cause Chou Tso-jen

---

50 For an analysis of Chou Tso-jen's essays, see David E. Pollard, *A Chinese look at literature: The literary values of Chou Tso-jen in relation to the tradition.*

and Lin Yutang championed became increasingly out of date. It was against the prevalent impact of the 'personal essay' that Lu Hsun wrote his famous article, 'The crisis of the personal essay', in 1933. He attacked the 'leisure' and 'humour' of his brother and former friend as petty 'window dressing', 'elegant toys' and 'decorations for the rich and the powerful'. In an age of crisis, in which not only the writer's own survival but the survival of his art were at stake, Lu Hsun saw the essay form also reaching a point of crisis: 'The living essay must be a dagger and a spear with which it, together with the readers, can battle through a bloody path towards life.'[51]

Between the shoddiness of the *tsa-wen* and the frivolity of the *hsiao-p'in-wen*, the essay in the 1930s all but forfeited its creative potential. The most vital form of prose writing which combined a mature style with social meaning was fiction, particularly the novel.

Fiction

The period from 1928 to 1937 was clearly a decade of growth for modern Chinese fiction. In his masterful survey, *A history of modern Chinese fiction*, Professor Hsia devotes a chapter to each of the six outstanding authors of this period – Mao Tun, Lao She, Shen Ts'ung-wen, Chang T'ien-i, Pa Chin and Wu Tsu-hsiang – as compared to only one (Lu Hsun) in the preceding period (1917–27). The attention given here clearly indicates that modern Chinese fiction reached maturity in the 1930s. While Lu Hsun towered over May Fourth literature with his short stories, five of the six fiction writers in the second decade published novels, and all continued to produce short stories.

Of these six writers, Mao Tun played an instrumental role in shaping the novel into a major genre. By the time Mao Tun singled out Yeh Shao-chun's *School-teacher Ni Huan-chih* (1928) for praise as one of the few good novels of the May Fourth period, he had himself completed a trilogy of novels, *Shih* (Eclipse). As C. T. Hsia comments: 'this work was of such scope and honesty that it cast into utter insignificance the few novels of the first period'.[52] Following *Eclipse*, Mao Tun published another outstanding novel, *Hung* (Rainbow) and in 1933 his *chef-d'oeuvre*, *Tzu-yeh* (Midnight), which established him as one of the two or three foremost novelists in modern Chinese literature. In these pioneering works, Mao Tun succeeded in painting a social fresco of epic proportions by

[51] *Lu Hsun ch'üan-chi*, 5.173.
[52] C. T. Hsia, *A history of modern Chinese fiction*, 2nd. ed., 141.

modernizing the late Ch'ing social novel with the techniques of European naturalism.[53]

Mao Tun was a most learned and conscientious practitioner of 'naturalism' in his meticulous gathering and deployment of material, his adoption of a macroscopic objective point of view, and his portrait of characters as victims of socio-economic forces. But he was not a master of its technique. Rather, naturalism served as an artistic means to realize his truly monumental vision of modern Chinese society. Despite his early membership in the Chinese Communist Party, Mao Tun's fictional vision is essentially tragic, for it is concerned mainly with the futility of life in a class society doomed to decline and extinction. *Eclipse* drew upon Mao Tun's personal experience and depicted petty-bourgeois intellectuals disillusioned with 'making revolution' yet searching for personal fulfilment. In *Rainbow* Mao Tun continued his portraiture of urban intellectuals through his consummate portrait of the heroine. The story of her life is 'by design an allegory of recent Chinese intellectual history' as it captures the initial phase of the May Fourth cultural revolution through 'the bankruptcy of individualism in the early twenties, and its degeneration into libertinism and irresponsibility' to a leftist rejection of romantic idealism in favour of Marxist materialism.[54] However, the last part of this novel is inferior to the first two parts, precisely because Mao Tun failed to blend an ideological belief with a sense of artistic truth. As Mao Tun mentioned many times in his polemical essays, he felt more at home with the bourgeoisie than with the proletariat and he was prepared to defend his realistic and tragic view of this decadent class as in some way meaningful to 'revolutionary literature'. Nowhere is this vision more powerfully presented than in *Midnight*. In this long novel of more than 500 pages, Mao Tun erected a massive edifice of urban bourgeois society in Shanghai, dissected its many components – bankers, landlords, stockbrokers, students, socialites – and depicted in detail the process of its inevitable crumbling. The workers were not prominently represented.

It seems that from *Eclipse* to *Midnight* Mao Tun had delineated the urban milieu in the process of a 'long night before a dawn' with all its ambiguous anguish. When he turned his attention to the Chinese countryside of the 1930s, as in his famous rural trilogy of short stories ('Spring silkworms', 'Autumn harvest' and 'Winter ruin'), he was likewise torn by a dilemma in which he attempted to see more hope in

---

[53] For analysis of Mao Tun's early fiction, see the articles by Yu-shih Ch'en, John Berninghausen, and Cyril Birch in Merle Goldman, ed. *Modern Chinese Literature in the May Fourth era*, 233–80, 385–406.

[54] C. T. Hsia, *A history*, 153.

a landscape of despair. As one might expect, the first story of the trilogy, 'Spring silkworms', is an artistic masterpiece which is not matched in excellence by its two sequels, in which political messages intrude rather visibly into a naturalistic depiction of rural misery.

Like Mao Tun, Shen Ts'ung-wen and Lao She also evinced a strong sense of urban pessimism in their works. Shen Ts'ung-wen satirized the urban hypocrisy in a pointed fantasy, *A-li-ssu Chung-kuo yu-chi* (Alice's travels in China), while Lao She wrote a less successful satire entitled *Mao-ch'eng chi* (The city of cats). Clearly, the sympathies of both novelists lay with their rural characters, whether in an urban or rural setting. Shen Ts'ung-wen's approach was more pastoral: he saw in his beloved fellow provincials of the southern countryside a robust, earthy, almost 'noble savage' quality and a 'life-giving stream of emotional integrity and instinctive honesty.'[55] This pastoralism takes on a special moral nobility when contrasted with the malaise and decay of the cities. Unlike the sombre depiction in Lu Hsun's and Mao Tun's stories, Shen Ts'ung-wen's works are always informed with a glowing lyricism. In spite of the suffering and misery contained in their subject matter, Shen's rural portraits – in such memorable works as the short stories 'Ching' (Quiet) and 'Hsiao Hsiao', and the novelettes *Pien-ch'eng* (Border town) and *Ch'ang-ho* (Long river) – impart an endearing love of life which sprang from his personal experience. His autobiography, *Ts'ung-wen tzu-chuan*, recounting his colourful and many-faceted early life prior to becoming a writer, reads in fact like a vivid picaresque novel.

Like Shen Ts'ung-wen, Lao She had a profound sense of personal commitment to the rural values of 'old China' – simplicity, decency, honesty, and the high regard for manual labour. In Lao She's life and art, the city of Peking occupied a central place as a self-contained world which comprised the very best elements of traditional China. But as conveyed in his most famous novel, *Lo-t'o Hsiang-tzu* (Camel Hsiang-tzu),[56] even this cherished world was in a sorry process of deterioration. The tragedy of Camel Hsiang-tzu, a basically rural character whose dream to own his own rickshaw is gradually shattered by the corruptive influences around him, signifies also, in a larger scale, the tragedy of old Peking as it was caught in the currents of rapid social change. The sights and sounds of Lao She's beloved city provide a source of needed sustenance for Hsiang-tzu, but the reader is also made aware that it, too, has been

55 *Ibid.* 191.
56 An English translation by Evan King (Robert Ward) was published under the title *Rickshaw boy* and became a bestseller in the United States. But Mr King supplied his own 'happy ending' to the novel. For two recent translations with the original tragic ending, see *Rickshaw*, tr. Jean M. James; *Camel Xiangzi*, tr. Shi Xiaoqing.

contaminated by the evils of the 'modernizing' forces. The process of the brutalization of life was regarded by Lao She, not without a sense of pained resignation, as inevitable: the 'small men' like Hsiang-tzu, who should be the true 'souls' of Peking, were victimized and corrupted by an increasingly intolerable environment caused not only by socio-economic changes but by the slackened moral fibre of the middle and upper classes. This is a theme which recurred in several of Lao She's early works: *Chao Tzu-yueh*, *Niu T'ien-tz'u chuan* (Biography of Niu T'ien-tz'u), and *Li-hun* (Divorce).

A sensitive and refined man with broad humanitarian sympathies (Hsiang-tzu's onetime employer, a professor who treats him kindly and who embraces the ideals of Robert Owen, is probably Lao She's capsule self-portrait), Lao She is not a narrowly political writer. His leftist leanings were confined to a saddened comment on the futility of individual effort which made collective action more and more urgent. But as Lao She's own sad fate testifies, the socialist reality after liberation proved also too much for him: he committed suicide or was killed in 1966, at the beginning of the chaotic Cultural Revolution. Lao She once wrote that he was 'a good teller of stories but not a first-rate novelist': 'my sentimentalism exceeds my desire for positive struggle; and my humour dilutes my sense of justice.'[57] Yet precisely because of his gentle humanity and a tragic vision touched, however, with wit and humour, Lao She has been warmly received by Chinese readers of all political persuasions. In spite of his Manchu background and his brief sojourn in London, Lao She has always been remembered as one of the most popular 'native' writers.[58]

The most popular novelist of the 1930s, particularly among young readers, was undoubtedly Pa Chin, whose *Chia* (Family) has been called the 'Bible of modern Chinese youth'.[59] The popularity of *Family*, and of Pa Chin, is a phenomenon that can be analysed only from a historical perspective, for Pa Chin is not an accomplished writer despite his voluminous output. What he lacks in artistic craftsmanship he more than makes up for by an effusive display of passion. The story of *Family*, a largely autobiographical account, is basically the story of 'new youth': the three Kao brothers clearly represent three dominant types of the young

---

[57] Quoted in Wang Yao, *Chung-kuo hsin wen-hsueh shih-kao* (A draft history of modern Chinese literature), 1.232–3.

[58] For studies of Lao She, see Cyril Birch, 'Lao She: the humourist in his humor', *CO* 8 (Oct.–Dec. 1961) 45–62; Zbigniew Slupski, *The evolution of a modern Chinese writer*; Ranbir Vohra, *Lao She and the Chinese revolution*; and Hu Chin-ch'uan, *Lao She ho t'a-ti tso-p'in* (Lao She and his works).

[59] For a study of Pa Chin, see Olga Lang, *Pa Chin and his writings: Chinese youth between the two revolutions*. *Chia* has enjoyed 23 printings since its publication (Li Mu, 202). See also its English version, *Family*, tr. Sidney Shapiro.

May Fourth intelligentsia in rebellion against the 'feudal' society. Published in 1933, after a decade of heady activism on behalf of the causes of the May Fourth movement, the novel's instant popularity was almost guaranteed. In a way, Pa Chin celebrated in words the agony and ecstasy of a whole generation that lived through the May Fourth euphoria. Basking in its afterglow, most of Pa Chin's novels of this period – the *Love* trilogy and the trilogy *Torrent*, of which *Family* formed the first part – became, in a sense, outmoded in spite of their popularity: the battles of anti-traditionalism and personal emancipation were already won and the leftism of the early thirties called for a different set of political convictions. While variations on love and revolution among urban intellectuals continued to be written (by Pa Chin, Chiang Kuang-tz'u, and many lesser writers), the focus of creative attention gradually shifted by the mid-1930s to subjects other than urban radical youth. Placed side by side with the major works of his contemporaries, Pa Chin's fiction of unbridled passion reads as rather embarrassingly jejune, deficient in both ideological and artistic sophistication. By the time Pa Chin was able to demonstrate his full maturity as a novelist with the publication of *Han-yeh* (Cold nights) in 1947, the whole tradition of individual creativity – the legacy of the 1920s and the 1930s – had all but come to an end.

Of the numerous short-story writers of the period, the two most brilliant are Chang T'ien-i and Wu Tsu-hsiang. Both of them were committed to the Communist cause without, however, yielding to the temptation to be ideological.

C. T. Hsia considers Chang as possessing 'a breadth of human truth uncommon in an age of humanitarian didacticism'. 'Few of his contemporaries,' Hsia adds, 'have grasped so clearheadedly and dispassionately his satiric and tragic view of man's fundamental perversity and his disposition for evil.'[60] To convey this human truth with 'taut realism', Chang is adroit in the use of earthy colloquial expressions and in the subtle manipulation of conflict as an artistic means of depicting class inequality. In his story, 'Twenty-one', for instance, Chang pinpoints the conflict between the soldiers and their officers. In 'Spring breeze',[61] his famous long story, Chang depicts an elementary school as a microcosm of class oppression. The irony is all the more compelling because this segment of Chinese society – the educational institutions – should have been the least corrupt. Yet in Chang's story, the teachers are cruel and narrow-minded and pupils from well-to-do families become the teachers' accomplices in their oppression of poor pupils.

[60] C. T. Hsia, 223.
[61] This story, together with Wu Tsu-hsiang's 'Fan village' and others, is included in C. T. Hsia, ed. *Twentieth-century Chinese stories.*

Chang's effortless portrait of snobbery and tension in this and other stories thus reveals an insight into human perversity which is ultimately attributed to the larger social environment. In this regard, he is joined by Wu Tsu-hsiang, another committed leftist writer. Wu's approach has little of Chang's comic or satirical touch, but it carries the darker weight of 'bold symbolism' and 'savage irony.'[62] In 'Kuan-kuan's tonic', for example, the weakling son of a landlord literally supports his life on the blood and milk of peasants. In 'The Fan village', the glaring disparity between wealth and poverty, snobbery and misery, is presented in a daring way as a fatal conflict between mother and daughter.[63] By depicting the mother as a penny-pinching miser who through long habituation to city life has assimilated her urban employer's exploitative ideology, Wu Tsu-hsiang makes the strongest dramatic statement that class antagonism exists even among blood relations. To accentuate his Marxist perspective, Wu builds up to the tragic climax of matricide and leaves the reader to make his own judgment: is the peasant woman's murder of her own mother justifiable? By forcing the reader to arrive at a positive verdict, Wu thus points to the crucial issue of dire economic need.

Wu Tsu-hsiang certainly did not resort to sensationalism for its own sake. The tragic intensity in the works of this 'foremost practitioner of peasant fiction among leftist writers'[64] underlines his strong sense of political commitment to the revolutionary cause. However, like Mao Tun and Chang T'ien-i, Wu Tsu-hsiang was not so much enthused with the revolutionary future as he was anguished by the pre-revolutionary reality of pain and suffering, especially among the rural masses. Wu Tsu-hsiang's works were representative of a new trend in fiction. The more conscientious leftist writers could no longer afford to pose as arm-chair philosophers of Marxist theory in Shanghai cafés. Although most of them still lived in the cities, their attention was turned increasingly to the countryside; more and more writers began to depict rural subjects. According to the tabulations of a Kuomintang scholar from Taiwan, of the three major themes of thirties fiction – the rural situation, the intellectuals, and anti-Japanese patriotism – the rural theme dominated the majority of works.[65] These findings clearly indicate that the immediate May Fourth legacy of subjective individualism – of concentrating on the personal feelings and thoughts of the urban intellectual – was given a social

[62] C. T. Hsia, *A history*, 282–3.
[63] For English translations of Wu Tsu-hsiang's stories and many other works published from 1919 to 1949, see Joseph S. M. Lau, C. T. Hsia and Leo Ou-fan Lee, eds. *Modern Chinese stories and novellas, 1919–1949.*
[64] C. T. Hsia, *A history*, 286.   [65] Li Mu, 201.

reorientation, as the scope of fiction was extended to the countryside and 'realism' attained an authentically rustic ring.

A new literary sub-genre was gradually emerging – 'regional literature', in which the author attempted to capture the earthy flavour and local colour (*hsiang-t'u*) of a particular rural region, often the author's native place. A large volume of creative output can be included in this category. In addition to Wu Tsu-hsiang's fiction, some of Chang T'ien-i's works, and the rural trilogy of Mao Tun (all of which used the Lower Yangtze countryside as their setting), we find such leading samples as Shen Ts'ung-wen's writings on south and south-western China (*Border Town* and his stories of the Miao people), Lao She's novels set in Peking (an urban milieu depicted in rural terms), and the short stories of Sha Ting (about north-western Szechwan), Ai Wu (about Yunnan), Yeh Tzu (the villages of south-western Hunan) and many others. In all of them, an intense love of the 'good earth' is combined with an acute awareness of socio-economic crisis. Since most writers actually came from the rural areas which they depicted in their fiction, rural hardship and suffering are made all the more poignant by their deep-seated devotion to their original milieu. In some cases, such as Shen Ts'ung-wen's, a nostalgia for the rural scene is evoked by the author's bitter discomfort and alienation in his urban dwelling.[66] In others, such as Mao Tun and Wu Tsu-hsiang, the countryside is almost purposefully depicted as the victim of urban evils; the rape of rural China by the economic forces of Western imperialism from the coastal cities provides a painful reminder of the need for revolutionary action. But whatever their motivations, the glaring gap between rural and urban China – this fundamental source of the socio-economic crisis in the 1930s – was painfully perceived and vividly portrayed by these literary intellectuals who were totally alienated from the KMT government. Whether satiric, idyllic, realistic or agitational, their literature of the countryside thus became almost ipso facto a literature of protest and dissent against a regime which did so little to ameliorate the people's livelihood.

The political significance of this new type of regional literature was given a dynamic thrust by the arrival in Shanghai of a group of refugee writers from the North-eastern provinces (Manchuria), which the Japanese had invaded in 1931. In the vortex of patriotism that soon devoured the entire nation, these young writers, who were the first witnesses of Japanese aggression, became famous almost overnight. Their works depicting the Manchurian countryside, ravaged by the alien overlords,

---

[66] For a detailed study of Shen Ts'ung-wen's view of western Hunan, see Jeffrey C. Kinkley, 'Shen Ts'ung-wen's vision of Republican China' (Harvard University, Ph.D. dissertation, 1977).

brought freshness and vitality to regional literature and all but replaced the urban-style 'proletarian literature' in popularity and distinction.

The leader of this group of Manchurian writers was Hsiao Chün, whose novel, *Pa-yueh ti hsiang-ts'un* (Village in August), had the distinction of being the first contemporary Chinese novel to be translated into English, in addition to being the first specimen of war fiction.[67] Published in 1934 under Lu Hsun's aegis, the novel owed its scanty artistic structure to Fadeyev's *The rout*. But as Lu Hsun commented in the preface: 'It is serious and tense. The emotions of the author, the lost skies, earth, the suffering people, and even the deserted grass, *kao-liang*, frogs, and mosquitos – all are muddled together, spreading in gory-red colour before the very eyes of the reader.'[68] The authenticity of feeling – the emotions of Hsiao Chün from his immediate experience – accounted for the work's instant popularity. But at the age of 26, Hsiao Chün was still a novice craftsman whose art was better developed in later works, such as his short story, 'Yang' (Goats), and his long novel, *Ti-san tai* (The third generation).

A much more talented writer than Hsiao Chün in the Manchurian group was his wife, Hsiao Hung. Her debut piece, a novelette entitled *Sheng-ssu-ch'ang* (The field of life and death), was also published in 1934 but was not as popular.[69] With her expert use of the dialects and idioms of the Manchurian region, Hsiao Hung succeeded in giving a loving portrait of peasant life as it revolved around seasonal changes and the major stages of the human life-cycle – birth, age, sickness and death. But this natural rhythm was interrupted by the Japanese soldiers, whose presence became an inhuman violation of this harmonious world of nature and man. In Hsiao Hung's other stories and sketches (particularly *Hulan-ho chuan* or Tales of Hulan River), the peasant life-cycle is personified by a gallery of memorable characters – school children, hunters, bandits, old peasant women, newly-married young girls, even Russians – who also embodied for her the primitive vitality of the Manchurian people. With a sensitivity to the smells and sounds of her land, this most talented but short-lived woman writer brought to her readers a lively sense of Manchuria, the loss of which was both a personal blow and a national tragedy.

Another Manchurian writer, a friend of the Hsiaos and potentially a

---

[67] T'ien Chun (Hsiao Chün), *Village in August*, tr. Evan King, with an introduction by Edgar Snow. For a study of Hsiao Chün, see Leo Ou-fan Lee, *The romantic generation of modern Chinese writers*, ch. 11.

[68] Quoted in Lee, *The romantic generation*, 228.

[69] For English translation see Hsiao Hung, *Two novels of Northeastern China: The field of life and death and Tales of the Hulan River*, tr. Howard Goldblatt and Ellen Yeung. For a study, see Howard Goldblatt, *Hsiao Hung*.

more ambitious novelist, is Tuan-mu Hung-liang, whose works have received neither commercial popularity nor scholarly attention until very recently.[70] Tuan-mu wrote his first novel, *K'o-erh-ch'in ch'i ts'ao-yuan* (The steppe of the Khorchin banner), in 1933 at the precocious age of twenty-one. But unlike the Hsiaos' works which received Lu Hsun's immediate sponsorship, the novel was not published until 1939. If Hsiao Hung painted the Manchurian landscape with the subtlety of a sketch artist, Tuan-mu Hung-liang approached his native region even more ambitiously by imbuing it with epic grandeur. The long novel is a chronicle of a landlord family from its earliest Chinese settlement to its patriotic awakening on the eve of the Japanese invasion. Written in majestic prose and borrowing from film techniques, this sprawling novel, with its archetypal characterization, could have achieved the stature of a national epic. But Tuan-mu was perhaps too impetuous and ambitious a young writer to cultivate the narrative skills of telling a good story. This manifest defect mars an otherwise magnificent novel – a grand masterpiece *manqué* that could have been a milestone in the development of the modern Chinese novel.

After *The steppe of the Khorchin banner*, Tuan-mu produced two other major novels, *Ta-ti ti hai* (The sea of earth) and *Ta-chiang* (The great river), as well as several short stories. In these works, he further demonstrated his versatility as a 'descriptive lyricist' – an 'ability to define landscape and physical sensation with lyrical exactitude'. Two chapters from *The great river* are praised by C. T. Hsia as 'showpieces of modern Chinese prose'.[71] Had it not been for the eight long years of the Sino-Japanese War, which consumed the energies of the entire nation and deprived modern Chinese writers of a stable milieu to develop their art, the talents of Tuan-mu and others would have advanced modern Chinese fiction to a new height.

Poetry

The early phase of modern Chinese poetry was characterized by a persistent effort to break away from the shackles of the traditional poetic mode. In their eagerness to experiment with new forms and to have free expression, the new poets often disregarded matters of poetic meaning. Hu Shih, K'ang Pai-ch'ing, Ping Hsin and other early May Fourth poets

[70] Professor C. T. Hsia is at work on a full-scale study of war fiction, of which two papers on Tuan-mu Hung-liang have been completed.
[71] C. T. Hsia, 'The Fiction of Tuan-mu Hung-liang', 56–61.

shared a common weakness: a simplicity of conception and a paucity of imagery.[72]

It was not until Hsu Chih-mo returned from England in 1922 that experimentation with Western – mainly English – poetic forms began in earnest.[73] Hsu's early poems, as collected in his *Chih-mo ti shih* (Chih-mo's poetry, 1925), were outbursts of 'effusive, unbridled emotions' encased in stilted imitative forms borrowed from English Romantic poetry. His poetic techniques became more refined in his subsequent collections – *Fei-leng-ts'ui ti i-yeh* (A night in Florence, 1927) and *Meng-hu chi* (Fierce tiger, 1928). While he achieved more freedom and inventiveness in poetic metre and rhyme, the predominantly 'foreign' sentiments inspired by Wordsworth, Shelley and Keats read as curiously unoriginal, especially for students of Western poetry. Hsu was at his best when conveying a pleasant exoticism in such heavily foreign-flavoured poems as 'Second farewell to Cambridge' and 'A night in Florence', or when the auditory elements were blended with the visual to achieve an eerie state, as in 'Sea rhymes' (a work inspired by Keats's 'La belle dame sans merci', which was later set to music by Chao Yuan-ren). But when in his later poems Hsu attempted to be more philosophical or to adapt foreign imagery to a Chinese milieu, the result was not as successful. Even in his longest 'philosophic' statement, 'Love's inspiration' (1930), one senses an ebullient poetic mind struggling, yet unable, to reach full maturity. Had Hsu not met sudden death in a plane crash in 1931, his achievements would no doubt have been greater.

Hsu's friend and colleague at the Crescent Moon Society, Wen I-to, was more visually inclined, perhaps due to his training in painting. Like Hsu, Wen was interested in formalistic experimentation: his early works were sometimes designed to startle his readers with striking metaphors and allusions. But Wen's progress from the self-indulgent romanticism of his first collection, *Hung-chu* (Red candles, 1923), to the mature artistry in his second collection *Ssu-shui* (Dead water, 1929) is more impressive than Hsu Chih-mo, though Wen's total poetic output was far less than Hsu's. The appearance of Wen's poem, 'Dead water', was something of a landmark because of its original and poetic vision of Chinese society:

> Here is a ditch of hopelessly dead water.
> No breeze can raise a single ripple on it.
> Might as well throw in rusty metal scraps
> or even pour left-over food and soup in it.

---

[72] See Julia C. Lin, *Modern Chinese poetry: an introduction*, ch. 1.
[73] For an analysis of Hsu's borrowing from English poetry, see Cyril Birch, 'English and Chinese metres in Hsu Chih-mo', *Asia Major*, N.S., 8.2. (1961) 258–93.

Perhaps the green on copper will become emeralds.
Perhaps on tin cans peach blossoms will bloom.
Then, let grease weave a layer of silky gauze,
and germs brew patches of colorful spume.

Let the dead water ferment into jade wine
covered with floating pearls of white scum.
Small pearls chuckle and become big pearls,
only to burst as gnats come to steal this rum.

And so this ditch of hopelessly dead water
may still claim a touch of something bright.
And if the frogs cannot bear the silence—
the dead water will croak its song of delight.

Here is a ditch of hopelessly dead water—
a region where beauty can never reside.
Might as well let the devil cultivate it—
and see what sort of world it can provide.[74]

Julia Lin has commented on the 'compact stanzaic pattern' of this poem with its neat metrical sequence and end-stopped lines, which offers 'the structural integrity Wen strives for'.[75] But more important than poetic form is Wen's ability to compress immediate reality into a metaphorical vision. The sombre imagery of this poem is a far cry from Hsu Chih-mo's rosy idylls and Kuo Mo-jo's apocalyptic incantations. The symbolism of decay and rebirth is vaguely reminiscent of Kuo's 'Nirva of the phoenixes', but Wen's vision of China – as a ditch of dead water which may ferment to splendour – has an intellectual depth which is lacking in Kuo's fertile imagination. 'Dead water' is also more daringly 'modernistic' in its use of visual metaphors laden with considerable ambiguity.[76]

This attempt to create an imagistic world which may not show a clear correspondence with reality, to evoke and intimate rather than to state directly, is a familiar trait of Western Symbolist poetry which, to some extent, can also be found in traditional Chinese poetry. It is nevertheless a far cry from early May Fourth poetry which aims, as Hu Shih argued, to be simple, free, and easily understood. Whether or not modern Chinese poetry made a corresponding 'progress' from romanticism to symbolism as in Europe may be debatable,[77] but by the late twenties and early thirties a more 'symbolist' tendency was clearly visible in the works of a small number of poets.

[74] Translated by Kai-yu Hsu in his *Twentieth-century Chinese poetry: an anthology*, 65–6.
[75] Julia Lin, 82.
[76] For a study of the life and poetry of Wen I-to, see Kai-yu Hsu, *Wen I-to* and in Chinese *Hsin-shih ti k'ai-lu jen – Wen I-to* (A pioneer of modern poetry – Wen I-to).
[77] For a detailed analysis of this issue, see the section on 'Impact of Foreign literature' in Leo Ou-fan Lee, 'Literary trends 1: the quest for modernity, 1895–1927', CHOC 12.489–99.

One of the chief contributors to this trend was Li Chin-fa. While studying in France as a member of the Work-Study Programme in the early 1920s, Li began to write poetry. Chou Tso-jen noticed his originality and arranged to have two volumes of Li's poetry published in 1925 and 1927. Upon his return to China in 1925, Li was called a 'poet eccentric', his poetry curiously 'incomprehensible'. Criticized by many leftist and non-leftist writers but appreciated by a few (among them, Chou Tso-jen and Chu Tzu-ch'ing), Li naturally thought of himself as an 'avant-gardist' ahead of his time.[78]

Li's poetry does not claim to have any 'meaning' except as a series of fragmentary images and symbols which he makes no attempt to elucidate. Apparently indebted to Baudelaire, Verlaine and Mallarmé, whose works he read with avidity and introduced into China, Li Chin-fa seems enamoured of 'exotic' elements. In the opinion of Communist literary historians, these boldly sensual and sometimes grotesque images are but empty devices which veil Li's decadent, reactionary mentality.[79] But a modern Western scholar considers Li's poetry to be 'the most defiant departure from tradition, and at the same time the most daring innovation, in the course of modern Chinese poetry'.[80] A more balanced perspective might place Li as one of the few 'new rebels' who reacted strongly against the superficial romanticism or realism of early May Fourth poetry; he performed a second 'emancipation' which freed modern Chinese poetry, at least temporarily, from its obsessive concern with nature and society and pointed to the possibility of a surrealistic world of artistic symbols. He came close to creating an aesthetic vision so daringly new that, as in European surrealistic art, it could serve as an artistic statement of protest against the philistine status quo.

Li Chin-fa's pioneer efforts were taken up in the pages of a new journal, *Hsien-tai* (Contemporary, 1932–5) edited by Shih Chih-ts'un. The reigning poet of the *Hsien-tai* group, who professed to be politically neutral, was Tai Wang-shu. Likewise interested in French symbolism, Tai had inherited Li's penchant for impressionism and mysticism; he claimed that the purpose of poetry was to express that 'poetic mood', which he defined as an evocation of 'something between the self and the hidden self.'[81] But Tai's poems did not achieve the jarring effect of Li's dark, bizarre imagery. Instead, he seemed to carry on the aural values of Hsu Chih-mo's poetry; he shared with the Crescent Moon poets – particularly Ch'en Meng-chia

[78] See the fascinating interview of Li Chin-fa by the poet Ya Hsien in *Ch'uang shih-chi* (The epoch poetry quarterly), 30 (Jan. 1975) 5. See also Liu Hsin-huang, 687–8.
[79] Wang Yao, 1.201.
[80] Julia Lin, 153.
[81] Quoted in Wang Yao, 1.200.

and Fang Wei-te, after the untimely deaths of Hsu and Chu Hsiang – the emphasis on musicality, texture, and suggestive nuance. An example of Tai's 'softer' symbolism can be found in 'The alley in the rain' (1927), the poem which earned him the sobriquet, 'the poet of the rainy alley':

> She seems to be in this lonely alley,
> Holding an oilpaper umbrella
> Like me,
> Just like me,
> Silently walking back and forth,
> Cold, lonely, and melancholy.
>
> Silently she moves close;
> Moving close, she casts
> A glance like a sigh,
> She floats by
> Like a dream,
> Sad lingering, and faint.
>
> Drifting by in a dream,
> Like a spray of clove,
> She passes by my side:
> Farther, farther away she goes,
> To the broken hedge walls,
> To the end of the rainy valley.
>
> Holding an oilpaper umbrella, alone,
> Wandering in the long, long,
> Desolate alley in the rain,
> I hope to encounter
> The girl who holds her grief
> Like cloves.[82]

The effect of 'synesthesia' created in the poem, according to Julia Lin's analysis, produces 'an atmosphere permeated with effeminate charm, languorous grace, and mellifluous music that is worthy of his poetic guide, Paul Verlaine'.[83]

In the leftist scholarship of modern Chinese literature, the works of Li and Tai are viewed as an 'adverse current'; for they were against the mainstream of the thirties literature which continued to be preoccupied with the reality of life and society.[84] But new talents continued to emerge. Three students of Peking University – Pien Chih-lin, Li Kuang-t'ien and Ho Ch'i-fang – published a joint collection titled *Han-yuan chi* (The Han

---

[82] Quoted and translated in Julia Lin, 165–6. For a collection of Tai's poetry, see Ya Hsien, ed. *Tai Wang-shu chüan* (Collected works of Tai Wang-shu).   [83] Julia Lin, 166.

[84] Wang Yao, 1.201. However, since 1981, Tai's stature has been reassessed and his works republished in China.

garden) which contained some of the most original work of the period. Of the three, the most learned was probably Pien Chih-lin. A translator of Baudelaire, Mallarmé, and later an admirer of Yeats, Auden and T. S. Eliot, Pien Chih-lin has informed his own works with a meditative, sometimes metaphysical quality which is rare among modern Chinese poets. For this 'beauty of intelligence'[85] Pien's works are not easily understood by most Chinese critics who tend to prefer the more flamboyant and more proletarian Ho Ch'i-fang.

Ho Ch'i-fang's early poems were even more ornately romantic than Pien Chih-lin's. Likewise influenced by French symbolism, Ho believed that in poetry 'beauty is achieved primarily through the use of imagery or symbols' and that the ultimate goal of poetry is 'to release the imagination, to escape from reality into dreams and fantasy'.[86] But as Bonnie McDougall has shown, 'the political crisis which forced Ho Ch'i-fang home in the summer of 1933 brought an abrupt change in his work. The luxuriant imagery of his verse was toned down.'[87] In a group of poems written in 1936–7, Ho bade farewell to Western romantic works which had failed to sustain him. Instead, he discovered a new reality – the impoverished and dislocated peasants:

> 'I love those clouds, those drifting clouds...'
> I am the stranger in Baudelaire's prose poem,
> Mournfully craning his neck
> To look at the sky.
>
> I went to the countryside.
> The peasants were too honest and lost their land.
> Their households shrank to a bundle of tools.
> By day they seek casual work in the fields,
> At night they sleep on dry stone bridges.
>
> In the future I'll insist on expressing my opinions:
> I want a thatched roof,
> I do not love the clouds, I do not love the moon,
> I do not even love the many stars.[88]

'I have always recalled with gratitude,' Ho wrote, 'that small district in the Shantung peninsula where my thoughts of resistance ripened like a fruit. At least I clearly realized that a true individual had only two choices: either to commit suicide, or abandon his isolation and indifference and go to the masses, to join in the struggle ... from now on I will use my

[85] The phrase, made in English, is by Liu Hsi-wei, as quoted in Chang Man-i *et al. Hsien-tai Chung-kuo shih-hsuan, 1917–1949* (Modern Chinese poetry: an anthology, 1917–1949), 1.709.
[86] Bonnie S. McDougall, ed. and tr. *Paths in dreams: selected prose and poetry of Ho Ch'i-fang*, 223–4.
[87] *Ibid.* 228.   [88] *Ibid.* 126.

writing as a weapon in the struggle, as Lermontov once said, "Let my song become a whip".'[89]

In poetry, the modernist experiments came to a sudden halt in the mid-thirties, to be replaced by a simple, proletarian style. The young poet who embodied this new trend was Tsang K'o-chia, whose first collection of poetry, *Lo-yin* (Branded imprint), was hailed in 1934 as a major event by Wen I-to, Mao Tun and other writers. In their view, Tsang's poetry achieved more force by its very simplicity, its 'refusal to paint and decorate reality' through 'beautiful words'. Tsang explained the title of his first collection in two lines: 'The pain brands my heart / Reminding me, every minute, that this is life.'[90] Tsang K'o-chia was one of the harbingers of rural proletarian poetry – a trend which prospered during the war years in the works of Ho Ch'i-fang, Ai Ch'ing, T'ien Chien, and the later Kuo Mo-jo. A positive outlook on life through suffering, a poetic focus on the 'flesh-and-bone' figures of the Chinese countryside, and a more adroit use of the colloquial idiom for poetic effect, became their common hallmarks. By the beginning of the Sino-Japanese War, both poetry and fiction had converged on themes of immediate reality. And the urban tradition of symbolism and modernism disappeared from the Chinese mainland.[91]

Drama

The development of modern Chinese drama shows many parallels to that of modern Chinese poetry. Both began as Western-inspired new forms in conscious reaction against tradition. From its inception in 1907, when a small group of Chinese students organized the Spring Willow Society (Ch'un-liu she) in Japan and performed such translated plays as *La dame aux camélias* (*Ch'a-hua nü* or Lady of the camellias) by Dumas *fils* and Mrs Stowe's *Uncle Tom's cabin* (*Hei-nu yü-t'ien lu*) with an all-male cast, the amateur practitioners of this new genre called it 'new theatre', 'new drama' and later 'civilized drama' or 'modern drama' to distinguish it from traditional theatre. In 1927, T'ien Han, one of the early playwrights, adopted the term 'spoken drama' (*hua-chü*), to demarcate its important departure from the traditional-style Peking opera which is essentially a 'singing drama'.[92]

Like new poetry, the new drama formed an integral part of the Literary Revolution and, in fact, played a more prominent role as a medium of

---

[89] *Ibid.* 169.
[90] Wang Yao, 1.208–9; Kai-yu Hsu, *Chinese poetry*, 277.
[91] This modernistic tradition, however, has been revived and is now thriving in Taiwan and in urban China as 'obscure poetry'.
[92] John Y. H. Hu, *Ts'ao Yü*, 16.

propagating new ideas. Hu Shih's introduction of Ibsen in *New Youth*, followed by the Chinese translation of *A doll's house* and Hu Shih's Ibsenesque play, *Chung-shen ta-shih* (The great event in life), turned the new dramatic medium toward social reform. But in artistic quality, the new drama developed in the 1920s was even more crude than poetry, despite the considerable number of foreign plays translated into Chinese. The few plays then written were no more than literary exercises on the themes of social rebellion or personal frustration: Hu Shih's *Chung-shen ta-shih*, Kuo Mo-jo's trilogy, *San-ko p'an-ni ti nü-hsing* (Three rebellious women), Hung Shen's *Chao yen-wang* (Chao the King of Hell), and T'ien Han's *Hu-shang ti pei-chü* (Tragedy on the lake), *K'a-fei tien chih i-yeh* (A night at the café), and *Ming-yu chih ssu* (The death of a famous actor).

As a performing art, the new drama met with more difficulties than the written genres of poetry and fiction. Although a number of dramatic clubs or societies were organized in the 1920s, particularly the Popular Drama Society (Min-chung chü she, 1921) and South China Society (Nan-kuo she, 1922), they were 'amateurish' in both senses of the term, merely groups of writers and students who 'loved' the theatre (*ai-mei*) and had little or no professional knowledge of stagecraft. In spite of the efforts of T'ien Han, Ou-yang Yü-ch'ien, and especially Hung Shen (who had received practical training with Professor Baker's 47 Workshop at Harvard), there was no professional 'theatre' to speak of in the 1920s. A play seldom received more than one or two performances, often given in high school auditoriums or at other public functions as part of the festivities. The non-professional troupes lacked money and resources; sometimes their performances were stopped by school or local authorities as a source of bad influence on student morals. As late as 1930, according to an interesting account by Hsia Yen, the amateur group he belonged to gave a 'grand performance' of Remarque's *All quiet on the Western Front* in a rented Japanese-owned theatre in Shanghai with a movable stage, but the few 'actors' and 'actresses' had to perform several roles each besides serving, together with the director, as stage hands to change the sets and move the stage between acts.[93]

Not until the early 1930s did modern Chinese drama finally come of age in both writing and performance, due in large measure to the efforts of a single man.

Ts'ao Yü wrote his first play, *Lei-yü* (Thunderstorm), while a student at Tsing-hua university: published in 1934, it was performed in 1935 by

---

[93] T'ien Han, Ou-yang Yü-ch'ien *et al. Chung-kuo hua-chü yun-tung wu-shih-nien shih-liao chi, 1907–1957* (Historical materials on the modern Chinese drama movement of the last fifty years, 1907–1957), first collection, 151.

students at Futan University under the direction of Hung Shen and Ou-yang Yü-ch'ien. In 1936, it was taken on tour by the Travelling Dramatic Troupe and achieved unprecedented success.[94] Ts'ao Yü's next play, *Jih-ch'u* (Sunrise, 1936), received a literary prize from the Shanghai newspaper *Ta-kung-pao*. More plays followed as Ts'ao Yü gradually developed his art in the wake of wide popularity – *Yuan-yeh* (The wilderness, 1937), *Shui-pien* (Metamorphosis, 1940), *Pei-ching jen* (Peking man, 1940), and *Ch'iao* (The bridge, 1945) – which established Ts'ao Yü as the foremost playwright in modern China.

Of all his plays, *Thunderstorm* and *Sunrise* remain the most popular, although *Peking man* may be artistically his best work. The popular success of *Thunderstorm* is easily understandable, for its subject involves the crucial May Fourth issue: the assertion of 'personal freedom and happiness under the crippling weight of the traditional patriarchal society'.[95] Added to this reigning theme of emancipation is a nascent socialist concern for the plight of the workers under capitalist exploitation. But Ts'ao Yü was not content to cast his first work in the simplistic mould of the early May Fourth 'social problem' play. Rather, the message is conveyed in a complex plot of passion and fate in the tradition of Greek tragedy, through which Ts'ao Yü showed himself to be a most resourceful playwright, far more talented than all his predecessors. The protagonist of the play, Chou Fan-yi, is a woman, a possessed figure who has an incestuous passion for her stepson. The sources of Ts'ao Yü's characterization, as Joseph Lau has convincingly demonstrated, can be traced to Racine (*Phaedre*), Eugene O'Neill (Abbie Putnam in *Desire under the elms*) and Ibsen (Mrs Alving in *Ghosts*).[96] It is possible that Ts'ao Yü conceived of the play as a Chinese variation on *A doll's house* (similar to the way in which Ibsen wrote *Ghosts* in order to convince the audience that what befalls Mrs Alving in the end could have been the fate of Nora if she had chosen to stay with her husband). But Ts'ao Yü's attempt to explore the theme of incestuous passion as a tragic protest against traditional family ethics was even more daring. Ts'ao Yü deserved the popularity he received for this creative use of Western dramatic sources.

In *Sunrise*, Ts'ao Yü's intention is more sociological. Like Mao Tun's *Midnight*, Ts'ao Yü's play is designed as a scathing portrait of the passing of the capitalist order. To heighten this theme, Ts'ao Yü took another bold step. 'When I wrote *Sunrise*,' he recalled, 'I decided to abandon the structure of *Thunderstorm* and not to concentrate on a few characters. I

wanted to use the fragmentary method for *Sunrise*, in which a certain
conception is expounded through slices of human life.'⁹⁷ The play presents
a cluster of characters without any central protagonist. And to show the
contrasting slices of life, Ts'ao Yü encompasses in four acts both the upper
and lower classes. Act 3, which takes place in a brothel, invokes a poignant
mood of debauchery and suffering, perhaps the most daringly conceived
dramatic act in modern Chinese theatre.⁹⁸

One of the crucial factors in Ts'ao Yü's success was his acute sense
of drama. He was one of the two modern Chinese playwrights (the other
being Hung Shen) who conceived of drama not only as literature but also
as performance. His stage directions were elaborately prepared in order
to achieve maximum tension. The brothel scene in *Sunrise* is presented
on a split stage with two sets of action proceeding simultaneously. In *The
wilderness*, tom-tom drums and mute visions are employed in the manner
of O'Neill's *Emperor Jones* to create an atmosphere of psychological horror.
And the conscious use of Greek tragedy conventions in *Thunderstorm* is
another example of Ts'ao Yü's zealous endeavour to master stagecraft.

While clearly imitative of Western models in technique, Ts'ao Yü's
plays are distinctly Chinese in content. His works dramatized the shared
feelings and concerns of his generation. The themes of his plays,
exemplified in *Thunderstorm* and *Sunrise*, are quite familiar: the tragedy of
the old marriage system, the feudal family structure, the oppression of
the lower classes, the corruption of urban capitalists, and the frustrations
of young intellectuals. But Ts'ao Yü was able to bring to these themes
the shattering force of emotional expression. In this he resembled Pa Chin,
whose novel *Family* he adapted into a play. Like Pa Chin, Ts'ao Yü was
very much at the mercy of his emotions. When writing *Thunderstorm*, he
wrote: 'I was seized with a sudden passion so overwhelming that I could
not but seek to release it.' He was likewise dominated, when writing
Sunrise, by 'strong emotion from beginning to end'.⁹⁹ In fact, most of
Ts'ao Yü's plays can be seen as enactments of his own emotions. They
also betray the same defects one finds in Pa Chin's novels: undisciplined
style, over-zealous use of hyperbolic language, and a tendency toward
melodrama and sensationalism. But as a dramatist, Ts'ao Yü had an
obvious advantage over Pa Chin in being able to convey his emotional
truth through a live medium.

For all his sympathies with the downtrodden, Ts'ao Yü was not
narrowly political. He was not interested in using the medium which he

⁹⁷ Quoted and translated in John Hu, 54.
⁹⁸ Because of its bold content, this act was often omitted in performance, much to Ts'ao Yü's
   chagrin.   ⁹⁹ Joseph Lau, 6; John Hu, 24.

had so painstakingly developed merely as a propaganda vehicle. As an artist and social critic he was concerned only with his vision of the pervading gloom before 'sunrise' – the evils of gruesome reality on the eve of war and revolution. Like Lu Hsun and Mao Tun, he could offer neither positive remedies nor concrete vistas of the future. At the end of *Sunrise*, the heroine quotes from her dead poet-husband's novel: 'The sun is risen, and darkness is left behind. But the sun is not for us, and we shall be asleep.'[100]

These celebrated lines were prophetic. In 1936 China was indeed on the eve of a national cataclysm but the new 'dawn' did not bring much light to the lives of Ts'ao Yü's compatriots; rather, it ushered in a period of prolonged warfare and protracted revolution.

WAR AND REVOLUTION 1937–1949

The saga of 'national resistance'

When the Marco Polo Bridge incident on 7 July 1937 set off full-scale war between China and Japan, it also unleashed a crescendo of literary activities. An unprecedented unity among literary intellectuals replaced the factionalism of the early thirties. The debate over the 'two slogans', which had so divided the leftist literary ranks, disappeared almost overnight. All slogans were submerged under the resounding call to 'the war of resistance' (*k'ang-chan*). Organizations were formed spontaneously and anti-Japanese manifestos issued. Finally, in March 1938, shortly after the Japanese invasion of Shanghai in January, an overall All-China Resistance Association of Writers and Artists (Chung-kuo ch'üan-kuo wen-i chieh k'ang-ti hsieh-hui) was established in Hankow with Lao She as president and with branches soon springing up in a score of major cities.

This association initiated a series of activities to further the war effort. It organized writers into 'battlefront visiting teams', who made trips to military defence positions, fraternized with the troops, and wrote emotion-tinged reports. The association also set up a network of 'literary reporters' (*wen-i t'ung-hsun yuan*): inexperienced young writers, some in rural areas, were organized into local groups under the direction of the branch offices of the association. They met frequently to discuss themes assigned by the association and wrote reports on local literary activities

---

[100] Ts'ao Yü, *Jih ch'u* (Sunrise), 236. For an English translation of Ts'ao Yü's plays, see *Thunderstorm* and *Sunrise*, both translated by A. C. Barnes; *The wilderness*, tr. Christopher C. Rand and Joseph S. M. Lau.

which, together with samples of their creative writing, were forwarded to their superiors in the association for comments and corrections. In Kwangtung province, more than three hundred initial literary reports were organized in a matter of days; the Shanghai area boasted an equal number. Even in the rural regions of North China, membership supposedly reached five to six hundred. Most of these reporters were students, but some were shop clerks, workers, or minor functionaries in local governments.[101]

Aside from the writers' visiting teams and the literary reporters programme, the association also organized initially five propaganda teams (each consisting of sixteen members) and ten dramatic troupes (with thirty members each). Popular dramatic groups sprang up with such speed that by 1939, according to one account, there were 130,000 people engaged in dramatic performances.[102]

These organizations gave clear evidence that as a result of the war modern Chinese literature was losing its urban elitist character. Joining in the nationwide movement to resist aggression, the urban writers forsook their sheltered existence, whether willingly or not, and reached out to their compatriots in the countryside and on the battlefront. Two reigning slogans indicated the mood of patriotic commitment: 'Literature must go to the countryside! Literature must join the army!' 'Propaganda first, art second!' Some zealous writers even championed 'going to the front' and giving up literature altogether.

In 1938, Kuo Mo-jo was appointed to head the Third Section of the National Military Council's newly created Political Department in charge of propaganda. Thus, the writers' propaganda activities became formally sanctioned by the government and more of them were drawn into official ranks. But in spite of this initial gesture the Kuomintang was obviously preoccupied with military and administrative matters, thus leaving the field of propaganda almost entirely to Communists and their sympathizers.[103] The various propaganda units staffed mainly by writers and artists came to be, in fact, front organizations of the CCP, which deftly capitalized on the energies and emotions of this broadening mass of intelligentsia.

The Japanese occupation of the major coastal cities forced Chinese writers into the hinterland. From 1937 to 1939, Wuhan and Canton replaced Shanghai and Peking as new centres of literary activity. While some of the major journals in Shanghai folded, new ones, often hastily

[101] Lan Hai, *Chung-kuo k'ang-chan wen-i shih* (A history of Chinese literature during the war of resistance), 51–2.
[102] *Ibid.* 47. See also Liu Hsin-huang, 748.   [103] Liu Hsin-huang, 756.

and sloppily printed on primitive paper, mushroomed in smaller cities. The total volume of book production and sales in the war period actually increased. According to one widely cited source, sales of new books doubled from one or two thousand copies per printing in the prewar period to three or four thousand, sometimes even ten thousand.[104]

With the loss of Wuhan and Canton in 1939, literature penetrated further inland; Chungking, the wartime capital, 'hummed with literary activity almost as Peking did during the Literary Revolution twenty years ago'.[105] But the momentum of the first years of war did not persist. As the second United Front fell apart, the Nationalist government in Chungking returned to its repressive policies against leftist writers through censorship and arrests. Some of them made the exodus to Yenan; others, like Mao Tun, withdrew to Hong Kong, which prospered briefly as a centre of literary activity. On Christmas day, 1941, Hong Kong was captured by the Japanese, and Kweilin took its place for the congregation of writers. After Kweilin fell to the Japanese in 1944, Chungking became the last bastion of the 'great interior'.

The protracted war exacted a heavy toll – both physical and spiritual. Writers' living conditions deteriorated. Under rampant inflation, Chungking newspapers could offer their contributors one to two dollars (local currency) per thousand characters – roughly the same fee a printer received for typesetting the same number of characters.[106] Several young writers died of poverty and illness. Men as famous as Tsang K'o-chia and Lao She had to live on coarse rice, and meat was hard to come by even for Ting Ling. Wang Chi-chen notes that 'newspapers of the time carried frequent appeals on behalf of sick and undernourished writers'.[107] With no victory in sight, low morale, decay and paralysis set in. The militancy of early war literature subsided. Of about thirty plays produced in Chungking in 1942–3, only one third dealt directly with war themes; the rest were historical dramas and translations. Reprints of older works and translations of long Western novels became increasingly popular, as did erotic and pornographic works for those seeking escape from the grim realities of their lives.[108]

For the conscientious writer who had not migrated to Yenan, it was, as Shao Ch'üan-lin put it, like 'living in an endlessly long night, not knowing when the day would break'.[109] During the early years, the nation

---

[104] Lan Hai, 40.   [105] Chi-chen Wang, ed. *Stories of China at war*, v.

[106] Liu I-ch'ang, 'Ts'ung k'ang-chan shih-ch'i tso-chia sheng-huo chih k'un-k'u k'an she-hui tui tso-chia ti tse-jen' (The responsibility of society toward writers: a view based on the writers' impoverished lives during the war years), *Ming-pao yüeh-k'an* (Ming-pao monthly), 13.6 (June 1978) 58–61.   [107] Chi-chen Wang, vi.

[108] Lan Hai, 60–1.   [109] *Ts'an-k'ao tzu-liao*, 2.279.

had been united to fight the invader from without. Now the enemy was mainly within, as this hilly city became a world of frustration and lethargy – a claustrophobic world hemmed in by the almost daily Japanese air raids, when thousands died of suffocation in poorly ventilated shelters. War-profiteering ran rampant, and deep-seated animosities between the native Szechwanese and the outsiders from 'down river' flared up time and again. It was also increasingly a world of Tai Li's secret police, of government arrests and assassinations in an effort to clamp down on dissent.

The fall of Kweilin in late 1944 finally roused some intellectuals to action. On 22 February 1945, a manifesto of Chungking cultural circles appeared in newspapers demanding an end to censorship, secret police activities, military infighting and war profiteering, and asking for guarantees of personal safety, freedom of speech, congregation, research, publication, and cultural activity generally. On 4 May, the Resistance Association at its seventh anniversary celebration declared May Fourth each year to be 'the day of art and literature' in order to resuscitate the May Fourth legacy of science and democracy.[110] But the government retaliated with some arrests and assassinations. In 1946, one of the most prominent spokesmen of this rising 'tide of democracy', the poet and scholar Wen I-to, was assassinated in Kunming. Wen's death, attributed to KMT agents, heightened the anti-government sentiments of the intelligentsia, which the CCP utilized again to its great advantage. The Sino-Japanese War had politicized the intellectuals and the CCP again became their champion.

The literature of 'patriotic gore'

War focused the attention of all writers on the exigencies of the national situation. Artistic experimentation for its own sake was immediately irrelevant. Literature was entirely oriented towards the realities of life – no longer fragments of individual experience but the collective experience of a whole nation. In the first years of the war, different forms of short reportage – reports, sketches, posters, speeches, poems and stories designed to be read aloud, and one-act plays to be performed in street corners and market places – all but replaced the longer forms of fiction as the most popular modes of literature.[111] These numerous pieces of journalistic or proto-journalistic literature, steeped as they were in what Edmund Wilson called 'patriotic gore', were written 'with more

110 Lan Hai, 62.   111 Ibid. 68–73.

sentiment than artistry; their topical interest and emotional appeal are quickly lost when read out of context.'[112]

While they lacked artistic qualities, they gained immeasurably in popularity. Reportage, in Chou Yang's view, was the 'major form of national resistance literature', because it served most effectively the immediate goal of 'educating the masses' to the realities of this 'national self-defensive struggle'.[113] The war had accelerated the process of popularization by bringing literature, however sloppy in quality, away from the urban ivory tower in Shanghai to the small towns and villages. This period witnessed the first large-scale effort of writers 'going to the people'. In order to appeal to the tastes of the rural populace, the erstwhile urban writers eagerly resorted to the use of folk themes, idioms, tunes, as well as such traditional popular forms as village operas, oral story-telling, and *ta-ku* (beating the drum while telling a story). Suddenly, the use of 'old forms' with 'new content' became a fad; Lao She was one of the most avid practitioners.

Some writers went in for collective authorship. A few days after the Marco Polo Bridge incident, some sixteen dramatists in Shanghai organized themselves to write a three-act play, *Pao-wei Lu-kou-ch'iao* (Defend the Marco Polo Bridge), which several theatrical troupes competed to have the rights to perform even before it was finished.[114] Reports of writers' teams visiting the battlefront were sometimes also written collectively.

In an article of 1939, Hu Feng detected five major weaknesses of war literature: (1) it gave merely neat propaganda formulas; (2) it tended to present all the trivial details without, however, attaining any depth of vision, thus losing rather than gaining a sense of reality; (3) in some cases it gave fantastic twists to real stories; (4) due to these defects, war literature had not produced either great heroic epics or works of vivid realism; (5) 'intellectual poverty' in turn begot artistic poverty, and the task of popularizing literature was yet to achieve success.[115] Hu Feng's criticism obviously showed his dissatisfaction with the lowering of artistic standards. Together with Mao Tun, he was opposed to the excessively politicized view that wartime literature should only depict the 'healthy' and 'bright' side of life. A critic of integrity should call upon writers, as Mao Tun put it, not only to portray 'the new brightness' but also to expose aspects of 'new darkness'.[116] Some critics in Chungking, however, opposed the erosion of literary quality by propaganda and argued, on the

---

[112] Julia Lin, 171.   [113] *Ts'an-k'ao tzu-liao*, 1.631, 638.

[114] Lan Hai, 43.

[115] Hu Feng, *Min-tsu chan-cheng yü wen-i hsing-ko* (The national war and the character of literature), 53–5.   [116] *Ts'an-k'ao tzu-liao*, 1.670–1.

contrary, that the two should be totally separated. Chu Kuang-ch'ien stressed the importance of 'dispassionate observation' and the autonomy of art. Shen Ts'ung-wen saw a clear distinction between writers, who should be artists, and cultural workers, who were propagandists. Writers, Shen argued, should not be mixed up with political tasks. Liang Shih-ch'iu, the erstwhile foe of the leftists, went one step further by promoting the cause of 'irrelevant' literature: 'There are many subjects in human life that we can write about; we should not restrict our works to those related to the war.'[117]

These pleas for literary quality went unanswered. C. T. Hsia has concluded that the fiction produced in the 'great interior' generally lacked 'excitement and distinction'; the number of good works was much smaller than that of the prewar decade. 'The stereotypes of guerrilla warfare and student romance and the ubiquitous note of patriotic propaganda mar most of the wartime novels.'[118]

Of the established writers, only Mao Tun and Pa Chin produced significant works. Mao Tun's two novels written before 1942 – *Fu-shih* (Putrefaction) and *Shuang-yeh hung ssu erh-yueh hua* (Maple leaves as red as February flowers) – were not overtly concerned with wartime. *Maple leaves* deals with a small-town situation in 1926. *Putrefaction*, on the other hand, is a strictly political novel which depicts the evils of Kuomintang secret police. A fictional interpretation of the infamous 'New Fourth Army' incident of 1941, the novel has been acclaimed by Communist critics as on a par with *Midnight*.[119]

Compared to Mao Tun, Pa Chin made steady progress during the war years. His two sequels to *Family* are better written: *Ch'iu* (Autumn), in particular, represents Pa Chin's emotional maturity. But his best work is surely *Han-yeh* (Cold nights), written near the end of the war and published in 1947, which established Pa Chin as 'a psychological realist of great distinction'. In his depiction of three ordinary characters – a man, his mother and his wife – living under the same roof in wartime Chungking and caught in the familial web of love and jealousy, Pa Chin succeeds in presenting 'not only a parable of China in her darkest hour of defeat and despair but a morality play about the insuperable difficulties facing Everyman walking the path of charity'.[120]

Another veteran, Lao She, wrote many propaganda plays and poems in the folk idiom, but could produce only one mediocre novel, *Huo tsang*

---

[117] *Ibid.* 691–5; Liu Shou-sung, 2.63–4.

[118] C. T. Hsia, *A history*, 317.

[119] Wang Yao, 2.87. The Japanese scholar Osaka Tokushi also gives it high praise for its inventive technique; see his *Chūgoku shin bungaku undō shi*, 2.245–7.

[120] C. T. Hsia, *A history*, 386.

(Cremation), which he hastily published in order to get money for food. His ambitious undertaking, a three-part novel entitled *Ssu-shih t'ung-t'ang* (Four generations under one roof), begun immediately after the war, was never fully completed and the first two parts, published in 1946, 'must be rated as a major disappointment'.[121]

Like reportage, poetry of the war period was written to serve only one purpose – to arouse patriotic sentiments against the enemy. It was often meant to be recited aloud or sung to a large audience. Thus, simple, prose-like language, folk idioms, realistic descriptions, and slogan-shouting became the common features characterizing a host of 'patriotic poets'. Two of the most avid practitioners were Tsang K'o-chia and T'ien Chien. Tsang spent five years in the front lines and wrote more than a dozen collections of poetry. 'I love peasants,' he once confessed. 'I feel close even to the scars on their bodies.'[122] Praised with equal fervour by Wen I-to as the 'drummer of our age', T'ien Chien had dropped his early idol, Mayakovsky, and began writing 'drumbeat verse' with short lines and quick vigorous rhythm deemed more suitable to the tempo of war. The following shoddy example of T'ien's drumbeat verse was seen by Wen as 'exploding with life's heat and energy':

> This Asian
> Soil
> Is dyed in
> Anger and
> Shame.
>
> O tillers of my fatherland!
> Leave those dirty ditches
> And run-down
> Villages!
> To the war,
> Drive away the imperialist
> Armies.
> With our stubborn will
> Let's start sowing
> Mankind's new birth![123]

The literary genre which proved more enduringly popular than poetry and reportage was spoken drama. The profusion of one-act plays in the early years of the war had established a new tradition of living theatre, of which audience response and participation was an integral part. Moreover, the Shanghai film industry in the early thirties had nurtured a first crop of

[121] *Ibid.* 369.
[122] *Hsien-tai Chung-kuo shih hsuan*, 2.912.
[123] Quoted and translated in Julia Lin, 191–2.

actors and actresses who now entered the theatrical profession. Numerous amateur troupes in various regions – composed mainly of teachers and students – also stood ready to perform new works from Chungking and Kweilin, the two centres of wartime drama in the great interior. Wu-chi Liu says, 'at one time ninety dramatic troupes from five south-western provinces assembled for a dramatic festival in Kweilin', and 'during two seasons of fog in Chungking, when the city was comparatively safe from air raids, more than thirty full-length plays were presented to capacity audiences'.[124]

As patriotic idealism waned after the initial years of the war, the theatre assumed the function of escapist entertainment. But it also allowed the playwrights and actors of the Communist-dominated theatre world 'to sidestep censorship regulations and still make oblique comments on contemporary events'.[125]

Sung Chih-ti's *Wu Ch'ung-ch'ing* (Foggy Chungking), which focused on war-profiteering businessmen and intellectual opportunists, Ch'en Pai-ch'en's *Sheng-kuan t'u* (A chart for official promotion) which satirized official corruption, and above all Ts'ao Yü's *Shui-pien* (Metamorphosis) which depicted the primitive conditions of a poorly managed military hospital, were all successful.[126] In these works of negative exposure the authors had returned to the familiar mentality of the thirties.

The flowering of modern drama during wartime was also a phenomenon in Japanese-occupied Shanghai. The ban on American films and Japanese control of the Chinese film industry led to a commercial boom in the new drama, which competed successfully with traditional theatre. Historical plays, comedies, and romantic 'soap operas' enjoyed unparalleled popularity partly because they were safe subjects for innocuous entertainment. Yao K'o wrote a well-structured historical play about the late Ch'ing empress dowager and the Kuang-hsu Emperor, *Ch'ing-kung yüan* (translated into English as *The malice of empire*)[127] which has been hailed as a landmark. A Ying (Ch'ien Hsing-ts'un), an erstwhile leftist turned literary historian, wrote a dozen plays, of which *Ming-mo yi-hen* (Sorrows of the fall of the Ming) was his *chef-d'oeuvre*. Yang Chiang, wife of Ch'ien Chung-shu and perhaps the most polished comedy writer, established her reputation with *Ch'eng-hsin ju-i* (As you desire) and *Nung-chen ch'eng-chia* (Truth into jest).

As Edward Gunn has argued, most of these plays bespeak a traditional trend which was also a subtle gesture to preserve notions of Chinese

[124] Wu-chi Liu, 'The modern period', in Herbert A. Giles, *A history of Chinese literature*, 479–80.
[125] C. T. Hsia, *A history*, 320.
[126] Wu-chi Liu, 481.
[127] See Yao Hsin-nung, tr. Jeremy Ingalls, *The malice of empire*.

culture against Japanese domination.[128] Chou Tso-jen, living in Peking in the style of a traditional recluse, suggested subtly in his essays that it was still the Chinese people, and not their Japanese rulers, who could best appreciate the humanity of their own tradition. Chang Ai-ling (Eileen Chang), whom C. T. Hsia regards as modern China's finest writer, used the family system as a central focus in stories like 'The golden cangue' to explore the impact of tradition on the modern psyche.[129] And finally, Ch'ien Chung-shu, in *Wei-ch'eng* (Fortress besieged), in a picaresque fashion dissected with learned wit and scathing satire a host of characters that 'in absurd postures of vanity and fraud' show an intelligentsia failing to grasp the essence of both traditional and modern cultures.[130] Thus some of the finest works of both drama and fiction were created in 'occupied' China.

Few committed writers in the 1930s foresaw any possible discrepancy between their creative vision and the socio-political goals they espoused. During the war period, however, several prominent writers, Lao She in particular, voluntarily gave up their individual visions in their patriotic zeal to serve their country. The result was an increasing emphasis on the significance of one's audience and so drama naturally became the most powerful literary medium. The issue of individual creativity became a serious political problem when such a vision came to be at odds with a prescribed collective vision which the individual author *also* fervently supported; when the modern Chinese writer could no longer claim, as he had done ever since the May Fourth period, that he was endowed with more sensitivity and compassion toward his fellow countrymen, which enabled him to achieve more profound insight into his society. The challenge to individual creativity in this sense never existed in occupied China, nor was it perceived by writers in the great interior. It was not until Mao Tse-tung delivered his Talks on Art and Literature at Yenan in 1942 that this challenge was brought forth, with all the intellectual force and political power at Mao's command, for the specific purpose of rectifying the thinking of the literary intellectuals and altering the very definition of literature.

---

[128] This information on wartime drama in Japanese-occupied Shanghai is entirely drawn from the pioneering research of Edward Gunn. See his *Unwelcome muse: Chinese literature in Shanghai and Peking, 1937–1945*, and his research paper, 'Chinese writers under Japanese occupation (1937–45)'.

[129] The novelette is included in C. T. Hsia, ed. *Chinese stories*, 138–91, and in Lau, Hsia and Lee, eds., 530–59.

[130] C. T. Hsia, *A history*, 445.

Mao's convening of the famous Yenan Forum on Literature and Art in May 1942 was part of the newly initiated rectification campaign directed at all Communist cadres. Mao's ideological intent – to remould the minds of Yenan intellectuals – was evident. But as an intellectual himself, Mao was also interested in new literary trends since the May Fourth period. As his Talks revealed, he was well informed about literary debates in the early thirties and he may have kept up with some of the creative writings, particularly the works of Lu Hsun, produced in leftist literary circles. Thus the Yenan Talks can be read as Mao's own reassessment, following the footsteps of Ch'ü Ch'iu-pai, of modern Chinese literature from May Fourth to 1942. But at the same time, Mao was certainly aware of certain recent issues on the literary scene which required clarification and solution.

Earlier in 1938, in a speech at the CCP sixth plenum, entitled 'The position of the Chinese Communist Party in the national struggle', Mao called upon his fellow party members to 'make Marxism concretely Chinese', to abolish 'foreign-slanted pedantry and obscurantism', and to replace it with a 'fresh and vivid Chinese style and manner, of which the Chinese masses are fond'. Mao concluded by asserting that 'to separate international content from national forms is to betray one's ignorance of internationalism; we must weld the two closely together'.[131]

Mao's directive did not specifically touch on literature, but its relevance to the literary field was soon picked up by the Yenan cultural commissars – notably Ch'en Po-ta, Ai Ssu-ch'i and Chou Yang. The ensuing debate on 'national forms' in 1939–40 was extended to Chungking. Articles arising from the debate were filled with confusing arguments, because no one was exactly clear what Mao meant by 'national forms' and 'international content'; the heated diatribes therefore were really groping attempts by the authors concerned to find the true source of 'national forms'. One group, represented chiefly by Lin Ping, considered 'national forms' to be the same as traditional popular art forms enjoyed by the people. Following Ch'ü Ch'iu-pai, they attacked the May Fourth brand of new literature as 'foreign-slanted pedantry' and products of the urban bourgeoisie which must be rejected. Writers in the opposite camp, however, rallied to the defence of the 'May Fourth revolutionary tradition' by maintaining that the mainstream of the New Literature represented, in fact, the 'national form' or was moving in this direction. In the words of Hu Feng, its most articulate spokesman, 'national forms

---

[131] Quoted in *ibid.* 301–2.

represent in essence the direction of the May Fourth tradition of realism
in its active development under new conditions'.[132] Moreover, Hu Feng
considered this new tradition as a complete break with the old tradition,
which was feudal and regressive. Arguing in a convoluted Marxist vein,
Hu Feng admitted that foreign borrowings were, in fact, viable. To this
extent Hu Feng directly challenged Mao's implicit denigration of Western
influence. A third group, mainly of party commissars and Kuo Mo-jo,
attempted to reconcile the two sides. Chou Yang argued that one should
assimilate the 'superior elements' of traditional art forms, while the 'new
forms' arising from New Literature should also be retained and further
developed. On balance, however, Chou Yang's argument was closer to
Hu Feng's than to Lin Ping's, for he concluded that 'the establishment
of new national forms cannot depend merely on old forms but rather on
a serious understanding of all aspects of the present life of our nation'[133] – in
other words, realism.

Chou Yang's implicit agreement with Hu Feng behind his fence-sitting
posture testifies to Hu Feng's prestige as a disciple of Lu Hsun and the
leading leftist critic in Chungking, with whom Chou Yang could not afford
to clash again (as he had done in the debate on the 'two slogans'). It is
also likely that the issues raised by Mao's terms were barely comprehensible
even to the commissars themselves. Himself a fairly informed student of
Soviet literary theory, Chou Yang may have interpreted Mao's dictum
as a call for further popularization and not an all-out critique of May
Fourth literature. It was time for Mao himself to resolve all ambiguities.

The tentative tone in Chou Yang's pronouncements seems also to
indicate that party bureaucrats like him were not in a commanding
position over writers. Before the launching of the rectification campaign,
the heroic self-image of Yenan intellectuals had not been challenged. For
several writers who had migrated to this primitive mecca of revolution,
the reality of life there fell far short of their preconceived ideas. In early
1942, Wang Shih-wei led the attack with a series of articles, in the style
of Lu Hsun's essays and published in the *Liberation Daily* under the title
of 'Wild lilies'. Ting Ling deplored the fate of women in Yenan in an
article commemorating 8 March, Women's Day, and in a story, 'In the
hospital'. Hsiao Chün soon followed suit with a scathing critique of
higher-echelon party cadres.[134] Thus the confusion and discontent among
many literary intellectuals in Yenan presented a potentially explosive

[132] Wang Yao, 2.26.
[133] *Ibid.* 2.23. See also Li Mu, 104.
[134] For an analysis of the dissenting writers in Yenan, see Merle Goldman, *Literary dissent in Communist
China*, ch. 2.

situation which Mao had to deal with in a decisive fashion. Hence the convening of the Yenan Forum on 2 May 1942.

Mao gave two speeches at the forum: an introduction (on 2 May) and a long conclusion (23 May). In his introductory remarks, Mao confronted his audience of some two hundred writers and artists and unequivocally defined the objectives of the forum in the following way:

> It is very good that since the outbreak of the war of resistance against Japan, more and more revolutionary writers and artists have been coming to Yenan and our other anti-Japanese base areas. But it does not necessarily follow that, having come to the base areas, they have already integrated themselves completely with the masses of the people here. The two must be completely integrated if we are to push ahead with our revolutionary work. The purpose of our meeting today is precisely to ensure that literature and art fit well into the whole revolutionary machine as a component part, that they operate as powerful weapons for uniting and educating the people and for attacking and destroying the enemy, and that they help the people fight the enemy with one heart and one mind.[135]

With this clearly articulated political purpose, Mao then proceeded to attack some erroneous tendencies in the behaviour of Yenan writers. He raised four problems, all intended for these recalcitrant writers: 'class stand', 'attitude', 'audience' and 'study'. The general theme is quite clear. Some of the Yenan 'comrades' had failed to adopt the class stand of the proletariat. They were unaware of the radically different situation in the base areas when they continued in their zeal to 'expose', rather than to 'praise' the new revolutionary reality. They persisted in this erroneous path because they failed to realize that their audience had changed; in the 1930s in Shanghai 'the audience for works of revolutionary literature and art consisted mainly of a section of the students, office workers, and shop assistants' – in other words, the petty-bourgeoisie – but the new audience in the base areas was composed of 'workers, peasants, soldiers, and revolutionary cadres'. In order to change their mistaken perceptions and behaviour, the writers and artists had to plunge seriously into 'the study of Marxism-Leninism and of society' – and, of course, the theories of Mao Tse-tung.

In his conclusion, Mao returned to these problems, elaborated upon their ramifications and, in some cases, provided specific solutions. In expounding his views, Mao also subjected the two vital legacies of modern Chinese literature – the May Fourth tradition and its extension in the 1930s – to a veiled, but nonetheless devastating critique.

In the rectification campaign, the two hallmarks of May Fourth

[135] Mao Tse-tung, 'Talks at the Yenan Forum on literature and art', in *Mao Tse-tung on literature and art*, 2. For a more scholarly translation, see Bonnie S. McDougall, *Mao Zedong's 'Talks at the Yan'an conference on literature and art': a translation of the 1943 text with commentary.*

literature – individualism and subjectivism – were transformed from positive to negative values, because these romantic traits had led, from a Maoist point of view, to their worst excesses: self-aggrandizement, elitism, and total disregard for the masses. The concepts of love and humanitarianism, so central to the romantic ethos of the 1920s, were singled out by Mao for specific disparagement: 'As for love, in a class society there can be only class love; but these comrades are seeking a love transcending classes, love in the abstract.... This shows that they have been very deeply influenced by the bourgeoisie. They should thoroughly rid themselves of this influence and modestly study Marxism-Leninism.' 'As for the so-called love of humanity, there has been no such all-inclusive love since humanity was divided into classes.... There will be love of all humanity when classes are eliminated, but not now. We cannot love enemies, we cannot love social evils, our aim is to destroy them. This is common sense; can it be that some of our writers and artists still do not understand this?'[136]

This kind of class analysis of love and humanitarianism had already been advanced by Lu Hsun and other leftist writers in their critique of Liang Shih-ch'iu. Mao incorporated it in his Talks and turned this Marxist 'common sense' into official canon. While he commended the leftist stance against 'bourgeois' and 'reactionary' writers in the 1930s, he was not generous in his assessment of its achievement. In Mao's view, even at its best (as in Lu Hsun's satirical *tsa-wen* and the fiction of social realism) the literature of the 1930s had expressed a sense of moral outrage on the part of the individual leftist writer. It had performed a 'critical' function in exposing the evils of the old society. In his glowing tribute to Lu Hsun, who symbolized this critical spirit, Mao also argued, albeit implicitly, that writers like Lu Hsün had already served their purpose, living as they did 'under the rule of the dark forces'. In the new revolutionary environment of Yenan, however, 'where democracy and freedom are granted in full to the revolutionary writers and artists and withheld only from the counter-revolutionaries, the style of the essay should not simply be like Lu Hsun's'.[137]

This is tantamount, in fact, to a censure of all Lu Hsun imitators, whether in spirit or in style, and a virtual announcement that the era of Lu Hsun – and of critical realism – was over. A new era had begun and a new kind of literature had to be created which would represent a radical break, both in content and form, from that of the 1920s and 1930s. Essentially, this literature should be a positive literature of the people and for the people; it should have, in other words, a clear peasant-

[136] Mao Tse-tung, 'Talks', 8.　　　　[137] *Ibid.* 33–4.

worker-soldier focus in its content and it must fulfil the needs of the masses before it could educate them. The order of priorities since the May Fourth period was now reversed: instead of the personality and imagination of the author being reflected in his literary work and imparted to an adulatory audience, it was now the audience of peasants, workers and soldiers that provided the subject-matter of revolutionary literature and guided the creativity of the author.

Mao chose to formulate this audience-oriented view of literature and art in a pragmatic question – the 'crux of the matter' at the Yenan Forum: how could literature and art serve the masses? Mao enjoined Yenan writers to 'take the class stand of the proletariat' and to 'fuse their thoughts and feelings with those of the masses of workers, peasants, and soldiers' by living with them and learning from them. In addition to giving this pragmatic piece of advice, which applied to all cadres, Mao also tried to enter the realm of Marxist literary theory. His 'theoretical' arguments were presented dialectically as a series of interrelated contradictions: popularization vs. raising standards, motive vs. effect, political criterion vs. artistic criterion, political content vs. artistic form. While demanding 'the unity of politics and art, the unity of content and form, the unity of revolutionary political content and the highest possible perfection of artistic form[138] – a goal all Marxist theoreticians would heartily agree to – Mao spelled out only the political side in these dialectical polarities but left the aesthetic side unspecified, presumably for writers and artists themselves to solve.

As a new theory of Marxist aesthetics, the Yenan Talks left more lacunae than the works of Marx and Engels. As might be expected, there was considerable divergence of opinion on how to interpret this new orthodox canon and how to fill its gaps. The role of arbiters was assumed, however, by the party literary bureaucrats, whose views and criticism were resented by the creative writers. It was these literary bureaucrats – Ch'en Po-ta, Ai Ssu-ch'i, and especially Chou Yang – who in the name of implementing Mao's theoretical injunctions instituted 'literary control' and imposed the 'party line' on creative writers. The dissension between these two groups grew into large-scale ideological campaigns and purges in which a number of writers – Wang Shih-wei, Ting Ling, Hsiao Chün, Hu Feng, Feng Hsueh-feng – became victims to party discipline.[139]

The literary bureaucrats emphasized correctly the political thrust of Mao's Talks, for Mao did decide that of his dialectical polarities the political factors ultimately held sway over artistic factors. For instance,

---

[138] *Ibid.* 30.
[139] This is the theme of Merle Goldman's *Literary dissent*; see especially chs. 1–8.

on the important issue of popularization vs. raising standards, Mao concluded that 'in present conditions' the former was 'the more pressing task'. He also affirmed that 'all classes in all class societies invariably put the political criterion first and artistic criterion second' and that the socio-political effect of a piece of literary work was more important than the author's original 'motive'. But the exact issues of aesthetics were hardly touched upon. For instance, Mao chose to sidestep the problem, which had been debated heatedly during the 'national form' controversy, as to whether the existing traditional folk arts contained too many 'feudal' elements. Presumably new content had to be instilled, but in what 'popular forms'? The widely practised approach of 'putting new wine in old bottles' was also problematic, especially when applied to such forms as the Peking opera. On a more sophisticated level, the issues of literary technique and literary quality, which distinguish a piece of revolutionary literature from revolutionary propaganda, were barely analysed in the Yenan Talks. Mao intimated, perhaps in reaction against the exposure-oriented realistic literature of the 1930s, that new works of literature and art 'ought to be on a higher plane, more intense, more concentrated, more typical, nearer the ideal, and therefore more universal than actual everyday life'.[140] This vague generalization smacks of a rudimentary reformulation of Soviet 'socialist realism'. Mao in fact called his new literature 'socialist realism', which further revealed his indebtedness to the Soviet example.

In this regard, Mao's emphasis was certainly placed, as in the Soviet case, more on 'socialism' than on 'realism' – to extol the typical and the ideal, and to portray reality on a higher ideological plane. But Mao seems to have contradicted his earlier injunction to abolish 'foreign-slanted pedantry and obscurantism'. Although he was clearly influenced by the familiar Soviet concepts of *partiinost* (party spirit), *ideinost* (ideology) and *narodnost* (national character),[141] he did not openly acknowledge this borrowing, nor did he confront the more relevant and pressing question: whether the Soviet models could be effectively transplanted on to Chinese soil.

It is evident that Mao had made a strong case for the political nature of literature, but his venture into more strictly literary matters – especially his attempt to evolve a Marxist view of literary criticism – betrayed the shallowness of a layman. The most fundamental issue in Marxist aesthetics – the problem of the integral relationship between form and content – was never explored in depth. Bypassing any discussion of the social origins of various literary forms, Mao concentrated on matters of

---

[140] Mao Tse-tung, 'Talks', 19.
[141] T. A. Hsia, 'Twenty years after the Yenan Forum', in his *Gate of darkness*, 255.

content. In so doing, he also imposed certain limitations on the themes and subject-matter of socialist realism. The peasant-worker-soldier nexus dictated a confining scope of such themes as land reform, struggles against landlordism, guerrilla warfare, and industrial construction. And the rigid manner in which the Maoist literary bureaucrats later carried out such specifications, leaving little room for writers to reinterpret the canon or to fill in its gaps, served only further to cripple creative efforts even to produce good socialist literature.

Yenan literature

The most pronounced feature of Yenan literary practice immediately after the Talks was its experimentation with native folk forms and idioms. According to Lu Ting-i, Mao's Talks prompted the emergence, in the order of popularity, of the following new types of literature and art: (1) folk dance and folk drama; (2) woodcuts in the 'national' style; (3) novels and stories in the traditional style of story-telling; (4) poetry in imitation of the folk-song rhythm and idiom.[142] All of them involved folk elements and apparently appealed, directly or indirectly, to the 'audio-visual' senses of the mass audience.

The best example – and the most prevalent – of this new folk culture was the *yang-ko* ('rice-sprout song'), a local song-and-dance which became immensely popular in the 'liberated' areas. Originally a ritual dance performed by villagers during the lunar new year, it was spotted by Yenan cadres for its propaganda potential. A certain Liu Chih-jen is said to have been the first to modernize this folk form by instilling revolutionary content and by combining it with other forms of popular theatre. Aside from the *yang-ko* dance, the '*yang-ko* opera' was invented, which fused *yang-ko* dance steps with local folk songs, modern costumes, and dramatic gestures and expressions borrowed from Peking opera. Both forms provided opportunities for mass participation, and reportedly everyone in Yenan was soon dancing the *yang-ko*. In 1943, a new *yang-ko* campaign was launched which resulted in the production of fifty-six new *yang-ko* operas.[143] The most famous of these was *Pai-mao nü* (The white-haired girl), a collaborative effort by the staff members of the Lu Hsun Academy of Arts and Literature in Yenan, who turned an apparently real story into a 'first-rate melodrama' about a servant girl who, exploited

---

[142] *Ibid.* 246. For a detailed analysis of the various forms of Yenan literature, see Kikuchi Saburō, *Chūgoku gendai bungaku shi* (History of contemporary Chinese literature), vol.2, chs. 2–5. See also Ting Miao, *P'ing Chung-kung wen-i tai-piao tso* (On representative works of Chinese Communist literature).

[143] Lan Hai, 77–8; Liu Shou-sung, 2.24.

and oppressed by a landlord family, escaped into the wilderness and became a ghost-like white-haired goddess.[144] At the end of the play, the heroine, rescued by the Red Army, took her revenge on the landlord in a climactic mass meeting. From its first performance in 1944, *The white-haired girl* reaped such public acclaim that it was later adapted into a Peking opera, a film and a revolutionary ballet.

The popularity of *The white-haired girl* and other *yang-ko* operas also led to the revamping of another popular form, the Peking opera. The successful experiment was an opera called *Pi shang Liang-shan* (Driven to join the Liangshan rebels). First performed in 1943, the work was taken from Mao's own favourite novel, *The water margin*, and told the story of Lin Ch'ung, a military officer who, pursued by government agents, finally abandoned his career and family and joined the rebels of Liangshan. The current relevance of this new opera – as it obviously referred to the many intellectuals who joined the Communist forces in Yenan – and its attention to the 'people' in history won high praise from no less an authority than Chairman Mao himself.[145]

But experiments of putting new content in old forms also encountered unsurmountable obstacles. The plots of Peking operas abound in emperors, kings, generals and ministers; it was often impossible to inject revolutionary content into such 'feudal' structures short of writing totally new plays. The coupling of new plots with old music and performance conventions created an utterly incongruous effect which in turn might lose audience interest.[146] The problem was further compounded when the oral traditions of folk culture were adopted in a written medium, as in the case of novels and stories written in the style of traditional story-telling. Lao She's experiments in the initial period of the war were artistically disastrous. In Yenan, Chao Shu-li, perhaps the most celebrated folk novelist to emerge in this period, made a similar attempt in his short stories, such as 'The rhymes of Li Yu-ts'ai' and 'Hsiao Erh-hei's marriage'. The former uses the oral tradition as an integral part of the story, as the hero effortlessly makes up rhymes satirizing local events, exposing corruption and praising land reform. The latter story incorporates an abundance of folk idioms, phrases and aphorisms in dialogue and narration. In both cases, the liveliness of the oral elements is ill-matched with the dry prose narrative. The earthy humour and healthy fun exhibited

---

[144] The play is included in Walter and Ruth Meserve, eds. *Modern drama from Communist China*, 105–80.

[145] Yih-jian Tai, 'The contemporary Chinese theater and Soviet influence' (Southern Illinois University, Ph.D. dissertation, 1974), 96–7.

[146] In the 1960s, the Peking opera – in whatever form or content – was rejected entirely in favour of Chiang Ch'ing's 'revolutionary operas'. After the Cultural Revolution, however, old folk forms, including the Peking opera, were revived.

in the oral parts would certainly provide good entertainment for the audience, if they could be rendered 'live' or performed on stage. Yet imprisoned in a written story, they serve rather to deflate the tension and suspense which could have been effected through a well-constructed plot or carefully written descriptive passages. Chao seemed to waver between the oral and written elements in his stories, but eventually he returned to the latter.[147]

Chao Shu-li's works were hailed by Chou Yang as 'a triumph of Mao Tse-tung's thoughts in the practice of creative writing'. Aside from them there was little fiction of note published immediately following the Yenan Talks, in sharp contrast to the profusion of *yang-ko* operas and folk ballads.[148] If this phenomenon could be taken as an accurate reflection of Mao's intentions, it seems that the new path opened by the Yenan Talks would lead modern Chinese literature away from the confines of its written conventions and re-establish direct 'audio-visual' contact with the mass audience. This drastic measure may have been Mao's response to the series of leftist debates to popularize and Latinize the Chinese language in the early thirties. In a culture in which the written word had always been sacrosanct as the only enduring medium of literature (even the oral traditions in classical China were subsequently transcribed in writing), this Maoist trend would indeed have constituted a second literary revolution. Judged from this perspective, the emergence of revolutionary operas under Chiang Ch'ing during the Cultural Revolution was definitely a logical extension of Mao's literary radicalism.

But Mao did not entirely succeed in dispensing with the written forms; the momentum of fictional writing, which began as a major leftist mode of literary expression in the early thirties, was carried forward in the period 1945–9 in a more proletarian direction by creative writers, notably Ting Ling, Chou Li-po and Ou-yang Shan, who seem to have turned for guidance to Soviet novels of socialist realism available in Chinese translations. As C. T. Hsia observes, 'they celebrated the transformation of land and people under Communism in the standard socialist-realist manner rather than in a manner suggestive of a return to "national forms".'[149] But the impact of the Yenan Talks is also noticeable. The result,

---

[147] In Chao's short novel, *Li-Chia-chuang ti pien-ch'ien* (Changes in the Li village), published in 1945, the oral elements were largely dispensed with. Yet in the opinion of C. T. Hsia, it remained 'the most readable of his works'. See Hsia, *A history*, 483.

[148] Wang Yao, 2.123. For a sample collection of stories and reportage written during the Yenan period (both before and after the Talks), see Ting Ling, *et al. Chieh-fang ch'ü tuan-p'ien ch'uang-tso hsuan* (Selected short works from the liberated areas). In poetry, aside from folk ballads, the volume of creation was even slimmer. Ho Ch'i-fang stopped writing poetry altogether in favour of prose reportage. See McDougall, *Paths*, 173.

[149] C. T. Hsia, *A history*, 472–3.

therefore, was at best a mixed blessing. The case of Ting Ling is a most illuminating example.

Ting Ling was probably the best example of the romantic writer turned leftist; she was also the most prestigious writer in Yenan. Some of her better stories, such as 'New convictions' (1939) and 'When I was in Hsia village' (1940), were written before the Yenan Forum.[150] Both stories deal with peasant resistance to Japanese aggression, and Ting Ling imbues her rural characters, especially the heroine of the latter story, with a mature nobility and humanism in the best tradition of leftist fiction of the 1930s. After the Yenan Forum, which was convened partly to criticize writers like Ting Ling, she was reportedly 'caught up in the high tide of learning from the rectification movement'.[151] Instead of fiction, she wrote only journalistic pieces – records of her field work in the midst of the rural masses. Finally in 1949 her long novel, *T'ai-yang chao-tsai Sang-kan ho shang* (The sun shines over the Sangkan River), was published and won the Stalin Second Prize for Literature in 1951.

Ting Ling had conceived of portraying the process of land reform in a fictional trilogy, of which *The Sangkan River* dealt only with the initial phase of 'struggle'. The second and third parts – on redivision of land and militarization of the peasantry – were never written. This grand design might have been Ting Ling's ultimate statement of her devotion to the Chinese Communist Party and to the cause of social revolution. Ironically, the very success of the first volume brought about her eventual purge for being, among other charges, a 'one-book' author.

As a novel, *The Sangkan River* stands as an ambitious experiment. It presents a series of vignettes and a mosaic of character portraits, all loosely connected, which bring a vivid sense of life to the rural locale which Ting Ling had come to know so well. At the mid-point of the novel, Ting Ling introduces her 'positive hero', the model Communist cadre Chang P'in, who crosses over from the other side of the river and gradually, but masterfully, sets in motion the mechanism of peasant organization which finally culminates in a mass struggle meeting. Apparently Ting Ling intended her new novel to be documentary fiction, a new literary genre that had become popular during the early war years. It was also meant to be 'socialist realism', in the Soviet manner, which encompasses reality 'collectively' and 'positively' so that the intended effect would be, as Mao stated, 'more typical, more ideal, and therefore more universal than actual everyday life'. Yet the weaknesses of the novel stem also from this

---

[150] A translation of the latter story can be found in Lau, Hsia and Lee, eds., 268–78.

[151] Wang Yao, 2.123. On Ting Ling's writing overall, see Yi-tsi Feuerwerker, *Ding Ling's fiction – ideology and narrative in modern Chinese literature.*

very observation of the Maoist formula. Her treatment of party cadres is flat, as compared to her depiction of peasant characters with whom she evinced a certain emotional affinity. And the message-ridden mass meeting near the end is curiously lacking in cathartic power. Again it is the more 'realistic' aspects of the novel, rather than the socialist aspects, which hold the reader's attention.

The relative merits and demerits of Ting Ling's novel reflect a fundamental change, as a result of the Yenan Talks, in the very definition of creative writing in China. The familiar Western yardsticks – 'imagination, aesthetic experience, and the workings of the creative mind' which T. A. Hsia valued so highly in his devastating summation of the Yenan legacy[152] – are no longer so crucial in the Maoist perspective. For the function of the writer is no longer that of a creator or originator but that of a human medium through whom experiences of the mass audience are recorded and then transmitted back to them. Since audience participation is encouraged in the very process of creating a literary work, the written text is no longer authentic: constant revisions become the rule rather than the exception. Above all, the demands of ideology and popularization render an individual point of view, either as an extension of the author's personality or as an artistic device, all but impossible. The 'literary' quality of a work is judged by the degree of its appeal to the audience, in addition to its correct political content. Unlike wartime drama, the combination of politics and popularization had a crippling effect on writers, for, in order to find the correct 'political content', they had to follow every shift and turn of the party's policies. In linking a literary work with specific political issues or movements, Mao had also divested it of any enduring worth, artistic or political: the very elements that made a piece of literature topical at one time diminished its validity once the historical situation had changed. From hindsight, Ting Ling's fate after 1949 seems rather 'typical' and inevitable. As Berninghausen and Huters have pointed out, 'if revolutionary literature is required merely to follow the development of the political dialectic, it loses its capacity for independent criticism[153] – and, one might add, its very source of creativity.

However, the stultifying impact of Mao's Yenan canon was not immediately apparent in the brief postwar period of 1945–9, when the CCP leadership was too preoccupied with the military conquest of the KMT regime to enforce strictly its literary policy. It was in this period that literary creativity in both Communist-dominated areas and in the newly recovered urban centres reached another height.

152 T. A. Hsia, *Gate of darkness*, 168.   153 Berninghausen and Huters, 10.

ON THE EVE OF REVOLUTION 1945-1949

When the eight-year war of resistance finally came to an end in 1945, the mood of euphoria and relief proved short-lived. For millions of Chinese who returned to their home provinces, the new reality confronting them was even more chaotic. The Nationalist government was caught unprepared by the sudden victory over the Japanese. Instead of reconstruction, corruption and inflation became more acute, which generated growing unrest. The familiar Chungking syndrome – demoralization on top and disillusionment below – was now extended to the entire country. The poet and essayist Chu Tzu-ch'ing summed up a pervasive mood in 1946:

As victory arrived, we took an easy breath, and we couldn't help but envision an era of peace and prosperity which might be realized in three or five years ... But the cheers for victory soon passed away like lightning to be replaced by volleys of muffled thunder. The change has been too swift, and the disillusionment has come too fast.[154]

As warfare was resumed between Nationalist and Communist troops, the nationwide desire for peace was expressed most articulately in demonstrations and 'hunger strikes' by students and teachers from universities and middle schools. Again this hope for peace was cleverly exploited by the CCP to focus on the Kuomintang, which procrastinated in a belated process of constitution making. Anti-government sentiment, nurtured during the last years of the war, became stronger. A growing majority of Chinese intellectuals looked to the CCP as the only party which could bring them freedom, democracy and a new China. Thus on the eve of the CCP's military victory in 1949, its ideological hold on the Chinese intelligentsia was virtually assured.

In this uneasy atmosphere of chaos and unrest the literary scene fell increasingly under Communist influence. As hordes of writers and artists returned from the interior or re-emerged from semi-seclusion under Japanese occupation, the eastern cities resumed their role as centres of literary activity. Magazines published in Chungking moved to Shanghai or Peking. New journals were founded, old ones revived. Books were reprinted on better quality paper. The All-China Resistance Association, renamed the National Association of Chinese Writers and Artists, sponsored a flurry of activities, including an elaborate commemoration of Lu Hsun's death at its tenth anniversary (1946) and the republication of his complete works.

[154] Quoted in Liu Hsin-huang, 767.

The reorganized association, though maintaining a semblance of the united front, was clearly dominated by Communists or Communist sympathizers. Leftist writers also dominated the literary supplements of major newspapers: some were established as exclusive forums for leftist authors (such as the supplement to *Wen-hui pao* in Shanghai); others were compelled to include a number of leftist works, because of their fame. The assassination of Wen I-to, the liberal voice of the 'Third Force', on 15 July 1946 further strengthened the Communist cause because it was widely believed to be the work of the Kuomintang secret police. And the appearance of a few significant non-Communist fictional works – Ch'ien Chung-shu's *Fortress besieged* (1947), Pa Chin's *Cold nights* (1947), and Shih T'o's *Marriage* (1947) – had no visible impact on the leftist literary scene; they served merely as 'isolated examples' of creative integrity, utterly impotent to oppose the rising tide of a new Communist literature.[155]

Even C. T. Hsia, an avowed anti-Communist, notes that the period 1945–9 witnessed heightened productivity among Communist-area authors, especially novelists.[156] Aside from Ting Ling's *The Sangkan River* (1949), such works appeared as Chou Li-po's *Pao-feng tsou-yü* (The hurricane, 1949), Chao Shu-li's *Li-chia chuang ti pien-ch'ien* (Changes in Li village, 1949) and Ou-yang Shan's *Kao Ch'ien-ta* (1946). In poetry, Li Chi's long poem, 'Wang Kuei and Li Hsiang-hsiang' (1945) successfully adopted the folk ballad form of northern Shensi to tell a familiar story of landlord tyranny and chequered romance. Following the triumph of *The white-haired girl*, another folk opera, *Liu Hu-lan*, reaped critical acclaim.[157]

Against the burst of creativity in Communist-controlled areas, the urban literary scene of this period was relatively arid. Most of the works published were reissues or reprints of popular fiction and poetry. In the area of translations, an impressive array of Western authors – Flaubert, Zola, Balzac, Tolstoy, Dostoevsky, Gorky, Chekhov, Ibsen, Romain Rolland, Dickens and Shakespeare, among many others – were represented in multi-volume series. According to one account, the most popular Western novel of this period was Margaret Mitchell's *Gone with the wind*, translated by the versatile Fu Tung-hua under the succinctly appropriate title of *P'iao*.[158]

[155] C. T. Hsia, *A history*, 501.
[156] *Ibid.* 472. Kikuchi Saburō discusses the flow and ebb of Communist and non-Communist literature in the framework of a north-south polarity. The postwar years thus witnessed the triumph of the 'literature of the north' (Yenan) and the collapse of 'southern literature' (Chungking and Shanghai). See his *Chūgoku gendai bungaku shi*, vol. 2, pts. 3–4.
[157] Liu Shou-sung, 2.262–4.
[158] Ts'ao Chü-jen, *Wen-t'an wu-shih nien hsu-chi* (Sequel to Fifty years on the literary scene), 126.

The major creative medium in the cities was the cinema, which replaced drama in popularity. The two genres had had a close relationship of cross-fertilization. From its very beginning, the Chinese film industry had drawn upon talent from the world of drama. During the war years, film personnel enlisted in the numerous theatrical troupes in the service of the nation. With the end of the war, drama had outlived its propaganda purpose; most of the amateur troupes were disbanded. The influx of American movies (banned during the Japanese occupation) gave added stimulus to the film industry. The postwar years were a golden age of modern Chinese cinema.[159]

The reasons for the artistic success of this new genre are not hard to find. First-rate talent from literary circles was employed by the film industry: Eileen Chang, Yang Han-sheng, T'ien Han, Ou-yang Yü-ch'ien and Ts'ao Yü wrote original screen plays; other dramatists (such as K'o Ling) became expert adaptors of literature into film. Some of the best plays written during the war years – particularly *Cheng-ch'i ko* (The song of righteousness, about the famous Ming loyalist, Wen T'ien-hsiang), and *Ch'ing-kung yüan* (The malice of empire) – were made into excellent films. Fictional works became another rich source for adaptation: in some cases, such as Lao She's novelette, *Wo che i pei-tzu* (This life of mine), the film version even surpassed the original. To promote the cause of this new art form, T'ien Han and Hung Shen assumed the editorship of special film supplements to two major Shanghai newspapers, *Ta-kung-pao* and *Hsin-wen pao*. Finally, the acting skills of Liu Ch'iung, Shih Hui, Pai Yang and Hu Tieh (most of whom had their first training in dramatic troupes) also reached a height of subtlety and sophistication.

The literary and dramatic aspects of this new genre outshone the purely cinematic. The quality of a film was often due more to its script and acting than to its visual technique (camera work, lighting, cutting, montage, etc.). Cinema could be viewed, therefore, as a creative extension of dramatic literature. The film medium appropriated from literature not only some of its personnel but also its typical 'obsessions'. One was the postwar chaos. The high-handed, irregular practices of the so-called 'confiscation tycoons' (*chieh-shou ta-yuan*) from Chungking, who made personal fortunes in the name of the Nationalist government by confiscating property owned by former collaborators with the Japanese, were bitterly criticized in

---

[159] Serious research on modern Chinese cinema as art and as social history has not been done. There has been only one study in English, Jay Leyda, *Dianying, an account of films and the film audience in China*; see particularly ch. 6. For Chinese sources, see Ch'eng Chi-hua, *et al. Chung-kuo tien ying fa-chan-shih* (A history of the development of Chinese cinema), 2.213–14. This two-volume book remains the most comprehensive on Chinese cinema to date. A preliminary catalogue of Chinese films from 1908 to 1949 has been completed by Steve Horowitz for the Chinese Cinema Project sponsored by the Chinese Culture Foundation of San Francisco.

Huan-hsiang jih-chi (Diary of returning home), directed by Yuan Chün (Chang Chün-hsiang). Many film-makers were obsessed with the inequalities of wealth and poverty in China's cities. In a light, satirical vein, *Chia-feng hsü-huang* (The make-believe couple), one of the most popular films of the period, tells the story of how a poor barber, camouflaged as a rich dandy, courts an equally poor woman pretending to be wealthy. Another renowned film, *Yeh tien* (Night lodging) was based on Gorky's 'The lower depths', but the setting was changed to the Shanghai slums. The films of this period were infused with an overpowering humanism which not only deeply moved the viewer but compelled him to draw political messages; invariably it was the lower classes that represented the residual core of humanity in a society torn with inequalities and devoid of justice.

What was to be done? The more moderate films advocated education (as in *Ai-lo chung-nien* or The sorrows and joys of middle age). But the radical ones blatantly called for collective action: at the end of one such film, the rickshaw pullers of the entire city rise to save the victimized hero. If films can truthfully indicate the social mood, the solutions seemed to revolve around reform or revolution – gradual reform through education and other humanitarian means or total revolution so that the oppressed would 'turn over' (*fan-shen*) and become their own masters. Out of sheer desperation, more and more film-makers – and presumably much of their audience – opted for the latter. In short, the better films of this period may have done more to propagate the need for revolution than any other artistic genre. As the popular medium that reached the largest urban audience, the film proved its effectiveness. It combined the best elements of modern Chinese fiction and drama: in some ways, it was more 'live' than fiction and more flexible than drama. That Mao Tse-tung never paid much attention to the political potential of this new medium is obviously due to its urban, rather than rural, origin. But as the most recent urban art form it yields some historical lessons.

The urban-rural dichotomy has been a dominant feature in the history of modern Chinese literature. From its late Ch'ing beginnings, modern Chinese literature was nurtured in the urban setting. As it grew into 'New Literature' during the May Fourth period, it also became the exalted mouthpiece of the urban intelligentsia. But the urban writer's aggravated feelings of social discontent led him to look beyond the city walls into the countryside. Rural and regional literature, the artistic product of the conscience-stricken urban writer, thus became the major form of creativity in the 1930s. But the best poetry written in this period remained urban-oriented, and it inevitably became a symbol of urban decadence in the eyes of the committed leftist writers.

However, the leftist writers were themselves urban products. The advocates of proletarian revolutionary literature in the late twenties and early thirties, echoing perhaps the urban-based Chinese Communist Party, focused their sympathies mainly on the urban proletariat, only to be exposed by Lu Hsun for the hypocrisy of their ideological stance. As Lu Hsun was politicized to join the left in the League of Left-wing Writers the urban orientation of their activities and pronouncements continued to be evident. But Lu Hsun regarded the urban milieu as the very bastion of the dark forces – depravity, corruption, and the oppressive atmosphere produced by the Kuomintang's 'White terror'. Living in their midst, he took upon himself the role of a revolutionary 'rear-guard' by engaging those dark forces in mortal combat while harbouring no illusions of victory for himself.

Lu Hsun never claimed to understand the Chinese countryside. Despite his enthusiasm for the Long March, he refused to write a novel about it for reasons of ignorance of the rural scene.[160] Even his early stories reveal not so much an affinity with his rural characters (as most of his worshippers have argued) but a sense of alienated compassion on the part of an urban intellectual. Besides, the Shao-hsing countryside for Lu Hsun was part of a traditional world – an 'iron house' of cultural backwardness which ought to be destroyed (though he could not foresee such a possibility).

With Lu Hsun's death in 1936 and the outbreak of war in 1937, modern Chinese literature entered its rural phase. The 'great interior' centred in Chungking had a certain rural ambience, and the patriotic ethos led most writers to embrace the rural population. This populism, plus repeated demands for popularization of literature, provided the logical setting for Mao Tse-tung's theory of art and literature in Yenan. Of the three central subjects in this new canon the peasants, rather than the workers or soldiers, received the major share of creative attention from Yenan authors, just as the peasantry formed the backbone of Mao's own revolutionary strategy.

After the Yenan Forum in 1942, and even during the height of Soviet influence in the 1950s, peasant literature far outshone stories about industrial workers. Such urban masterpieces as Eileen Chang's stories, Ch'ien Chung-shu's *Fortress besieged*, or Yang Chiang's sophisticated comedies remained isolated cases.

Thus the urban film ran counter to the rural orientation of Communist literature. As a popularized version of the literature of the 1930s it expressed discontent, the compulsion to expose, rather than to extol, social

160 Feng Hsueh-feng, 93–4.

reality. Literary creativity in modern China has thrived in the worst of times: the last decade of the Ch'ing, the chaotic period of warlordism, the years of impending war with Japan, and the eve of the final victory of the Communist Revolution. As Lu Hsun once remarked, literature is never content with the status quo, while politics always seeks to preserve it.[161] But Mao's redefinition of politics (as the revolutionary ideology for change) and literature (as a revolutionary weapon) meant that in a post-revolutionary situation there could be only laudatory works, and discontent would cease to be a motive for literary creation. Instead of the essential divergence between literature and politics, the Maoist canon posited their convergence.

In the Maoist version of the new China, moreover, the discrepancy between urban and rural – either as fact or as idea – never existed. The success of the Communist Revolution stripped modern Chinese literature of its urban component. With the loss of the urban 'mentality', modern Chinese literature also lost its subjective *élan*, its individualistic vision, its creative *angst*, and its critical spirit, even though it gained through the rural mainstream a genuinely popular scope and a more 'positive' character. 'Obsession with China' was superseded by adulation of the motherland and its people. In the collective moralism of the socialist society, what C. T. Hsia perceived to be the 'moral burden'[162] of modern Chinese literature was missing.

[161] *Lu Hsun ch'üan-chi*, 7.470–1. See also Lee, 'Literature on the eve of revolution', 278–86.
[162] C. T. Hsia, 'Obsession with China: the moral burden of modern Chinese literature', in his *A history*, 533–61.

CHAPTER 5

MAO TSE-TUNG'S THOUGHT
TO 1949

Mao Tse-tung's thought, as it had found expression prior to the establishment of the Chinese People's Republic, was at once the synthesis of his experience down to 1949, and the matrix out of which many of his later policies were to grow. This chapter seeks to document and interpret the development of Mao's thought during the first three decades of his active political life. It also tries to prepare the reader better to understand what came after the conquest of power. While stressing those concerns which were uppermost in Mao's own mind in the earlier years, it also devotes attention to ideas of which the implications were fully spelled out only in the 1950s and 1960s.

As will be abundantly clear from earlier chapters, the period from 1912 (when Mao, at the age of 18½, returned to his studies after half a year as a soldier in the revolutionary army) to 1949 (when he became the titular and effective ruler of a united China) was one of ceaseless and far-reaching political, social and cultural change. Mao lived, in effect, through several distinct eras in the history of his country during the first half-century of his life, and the experience which shaped his perception of China's problems, and his ideas of what to do about them, therefore varied radically not only from decade to decade, but in many cases from year to year. The present effort to bring some order and clarity to the very complex record of Mao's thought and action adopts an approach partly chronological and partly thematic. It begins by looking at the development of Mao Tse-tung's political conceptions from early manhood down to 1927, when he first embarked on a revolutionary struggle of a distinctive stamp in the countryside.

FROM THE STUDENT MOVEMENT TO THE PEASANT MOVEMENT
1917-1927

In terms both of age and of experience, Mao Tse-tung was a member of the May Fourth generation. An avid reader of *New Youth* (*Hsin ch'ing-nien*) from the time of its first appearance in 1915, he served his apprenticeship in political organization and in the study of politics under the influence of the 'new thought' tide, and his career as a revolutionary effectively began in the wake of the May Fourth demonstrations.

Although he had many strongly marked individual traits, Mao shared certain attributes characteristic of this group as a whole. One of the most important was that it was a transitional generation. Of course all generations are 'transitional', since the world is constantly changing, but Mao's life and that of his contemporaries spanned not merely different phases but different eras in China's development. The process of adaptation to the Western impact had begun in the mid-nineteenth century and was to continue into the mid-twentieth century and beyond, but the May Fourth period marked a great climacteric after which nothing would ever be the same again. In a word, the members of the May Fourth generation were aware of the certainties regarding the enduring superiority of the Chinese Way which had comforted their elders, but they were never able to share this simple faith. Some of them, including Mao, soon espoused Westernizing ideologies to which they remained committed for the rest of their lives, but most remained deeply marked both by faith in the intrinsic capacities of the Chinese people, and by the traditional modes of thought which they had repudiated. Thus they were fated to live in circumstances of permanent political and cultural ambiguity and instability.

Mao Tse-tung's political views prior to his early twenties are known only from odd fragments of contemporary documentation, and from his own recollections and those of others many years afterwards.[1] He first emerges clearly into our field of vision with an article written when he was approximately 23, and published in the April 1917 issue of *New Youth*.

Although this, Mao's first article, was written long before he was exposed to any significant Marxist influences, it reveals many personality traits, and many strands of thought, which can be followed through subsequently. The overriding concern – one might almost say obsession – which penetrates the whole article is anxiety lest the Chinese people should suffer the catastrophe of *wang-kuo*, that is, of losing their state and

---

[1] The fullest account of Mao's life and thought in the early years is to be found in the biography of the young Mao by Li Jui, first published in 1957 under the title *Mao Tse-tung t'ung-chih ti ch'u-ch'i ko-ming huo-tung*. This version has been translated into English by Anthony W. Sariti as *The early revolutionary activities of Comrade Mao Tse-tung*, ed. James C. Hsiung, with introduction by Stuart R. Schram. Li Jui has now published a very substantially revised and expanded second edition, *Mao Tse-tung ti tsao-ch'i ko-ming huo-tung*. This version incorporates a considerable amount of new material, including a whole chapter on Mao's thought before and after the May Fourth period, originally published in *Li-shih yen-chiu*, hereafter *LSYC*, 1 (1979) 33–51. It should henceforth be regarded as the standard. In some cases, for the convenience of non-Sinologist readers, I also cite the translation.

becoming 'slaves without a country'. This theme, so widespread in China in the late nineteenth and early twentieth centuries, is vigorously stated in the opening sentences:

Our nation is wanting in strength. The military spirit has not been encouraged. The physical condition of the population deteriorates daily. This is an extremely disturbing phenomenon....If this state continues, our weakness will increase further....If our bodies are not strong, we will be afraid as soon as we see enemy soldiers, and then how can we attain our goals and make ourselves respected?[2]

Mao thus evoked at one stroke two basic themes of his thought and action throughout the whole of his subsequent career: nationalism, or patriotism, and admiration for the martial spirit. But if he is clearly preoccupied here with what might loosely be called nationalist goals, was his nationalism at this time conservative or revolutionary? An obvious touchstone for deciding this point is whether or not he saw the aim of *fu-ch'iang* (increasing the wealth and power of the state) as in any way tied to a social and cultural revolution perceived as a necessary precondition for strengthening the nation. In fact, the article shows us a Mao concerned with China's fate, but almost totally uninterested in reform, let alone revolution.

Of the twenty-odd textual quotations, or explicit allusions to particular passages from classical writings contained in the article, there are a dozen to the Confucian canon; one to the Confucian 'realist' Hsun-tzu, a precursor of the Legalists, and two to the Sung idealist interpreter of Confucianism, Chu Hsi, as well as one to his late Ming critic, Yen Yuan. There are also three references to Mao's favourite Taoist classic, the *Chuang-tzu*. The range of his knowledge at this time was clearly very wide, for he refers in passing to obscure biographical details regarding a number of minor writers of various periods. (It is all the more noteworthy that eleven out of twelve references to the Confucian classics should be to the basic core of the *Four books*).

And yet, though there are no explicit references to social change, nor even any suggestion that it is necessary, the article does contain many traces of modern and non-conformist thinking, of both Chinese and

---

[2] 'Erh-shih-pa hua sheng' (Mao Tse-tung), 'T'i-yü chih yen-chiu' (A study of physical education), *New Youth*, 3.2 (April 1917) (separately paginated) 1; translated in S. Schram, *The political thought of Mao Tse-tung*, hereafter *PTMT*, 153. This book contains only extracts from Mao's 1917 article. I have also published a complete translation in my monograph *Mao Ze-dong. Une étude de l'éducation physique*. In 1975, M. Henri Day translated the whole text into English in his Stockholm thesis *Máo Zédōng 1917–1927: documents*, 21–31. This very valuable work, which contains translations of all of Mao's writings included in volume 1 of the Tokyo edition of the Chinese text (Takeuchi Minoru, ed. *Mao Tse-tung chi*, hereafter *MTTC*), together with provocative and original, though occasionally unconvincing commentaries, is an important contribution to our knowledge of the young Mao and his thought.

Western origin. To begin with, there is the emphasis on the value of the martial spirit, expressed in the opening sentences quoted above, and summed up in the statement: 'The principal aim of physical education is military heroism.'[3] To justify this view, Mao hails the example of many heroes of ancient times, and quotes from Yen Yuan, who had denounced Chu Hsi for 'emphasizing civil affairs and neglecting military affairs' (*chung-wen ch'ing wu*), thus creating a harmful tradition contrary to the teachings of Confucius.[4]

The dual matrix out of which Mao's thinking at this time had evolved is explicitly evoked in a letter he wrote in 1916, at about the time when he was working on the article for *New Youth*:

In ancient times, what were called the three great virtues of knowledge, benevolence, and courage were promoted simultaneously. Today's educationalists are of the view that we should combine virtue, knowledge, and [a sound] body. But in reality, virtue and knowledge depend on nothing outside the body, and knowledge, benevolence, and [a sound] body are of no use without courage.[5]

Thus Mao not only underscored at the outset the crucial importance of the body, i.e., of material reality, but also exalted the ancient Chinese virtue of courage (*yung*). Mao did not of course derive this strain in his thought primarily from books. Like many other Chinese in the early twentieth century, he developed his ideas in response to circumstances similar to those which prevailed at the end of the Ming, when the unity and integrity of the Chinese nation was threatened as a result of military weakness.

If this enthusiasm for things military remained a permanent trait of Mao's thinking, an even more basic theme of the 1917 article, and one which revealed more unmistakably modern influences, was that of the importance of self-awareness (*tzu-chueh*) and individual initiative (*tzu-tung*). He put the point forcefully in the opening paragraph of his article: 'Strength depends on drill, and drill depends on self-awareness.…If we wish to make physical education effective we must influence people's subjective attitudes and stimulate them to become conscious of physical education.'[6]

The source for the idea that the key to effective action lies in first transforming the hearts of men lies, of course, partly in the Confucian tradition. But the main inspiration for passages such as this is to be found

[3] *Ibid.* 5; *PTMT* 157.
[4] Yen Yuan, 'Ts'un hsueh', book 2 in Yen Yuan, *Ssu ts'un pien*, 63.
[5] 'Kei Li Chin-hsi ti hsin' (Letter to Li Chin-hsi), *MTTC, pu chüan*, 1, 17–18. Li Chin-hsi was a former teacher at the Normal School in Changsha who had moved to Peking. (See Li Jui, 28 for a brief biography.) The contemporary 'educationalists' referred to by Mao who spoke of virtue, knowledge and a sound body included in particular, as Benjamin Schwartz has pointed out, Herbert Spencer, whom Mao had certainly read in Yen Fu's translation.
[6] Mao Tse-tung, 'T'i-yü', 1; *PTMT* 153.

no doubt in the eclectic, and yet basically Westernizing ideas Mao had absorbed from his reading of *New Youth* and from the lessons of his ethics teacher and future father-in-law, Yang Ch'ang-chi.

Yang, who was a disciple of Chu Hsi as well as of Kant and Samuel Smiles, taught a moral philosophy which combined the emphasis of Western liberalism on self-reliance and individual responsibility with a strong sense of man's duty to society.[7] To this end, he had compiled a volume of extracts from the Confucian *Analects*, with accompanying commentaries, to illustrate his own interpretation of 'self-cultivation'. The first chapter of this book took its title from the concept of 'establishing the will' (*li chih*), and contains the statement: 'If one has an unbreakable will, there is nothing that cannot be accomplished.'[8]

Like Yang Ch'ang-chi, Mao laid particular stress on the role of the will. 'Physical education,' he wrote in his 1917 article, 'strengthens the will....*The will is the antecedent of a man's career.*'[9] This belief in the importance of the will and of subjective forces was a central and characteristic element of his outlook. In a letter he wrote to Miyazaki Toten in March 1917, with the aim of inviting him to give a speech at the First Normal School in memory of Huang Hsing, Mao described himself as a student who had 'to some extent established [his] will (*p'o li chih-ch'i*)'.[10]

But at the same time, in very Chinese fashion, he regarded an authentic will as impossible without understanding or enlightenment. In a letter of 23 August 1917 he wrote: 'truly to establish the will is not so easy; one must first study philosophy and ethics, in order to establish a standard for one's own words and actions, and set this up as a goal for the future'. But it was not merely a matter of subjective attitudes; action and commitment were required:

Then one must choose a cause compatible with this goal, and devote all one's efforts to pursuing it; only if one achieves this goal, is it possible to speak of having [a firm] will. Only such a will is a true will, not the will which consists in blind obedience....A simple inclination to seek the good, the true or the beautiful is nothing but an impulse of passion, and not an authentic will....If, for a decade, one does not obtain the truth, then for a decade, one will be without a will...[11]

[7] Edgar Snow, *Red star over China*, 143.
[8] Li Jui, *Mao Tse-tung tsao-ch'i*, 30; translation, 18.
[9] Mao Tse-tung, 'T'i-yü', 5–6; *PTMT* 157–8.
[10] Or, as Jerome Ch'en translates, 'disciplined [his] aspirations' (*Mao papers*, 3). Text in *MTTC* 1.33. For the circumstances in which this letter was written, see Day, *Máo Zédōng*, 18–20.
[11] In one Cultural Revolution collection (*Tzu-liao hsüan-pien*, 10–11) this is identified as having been written to Yang Huai-chung (Yang Ch'ang-chi) himself, but it was in fact addressed to Li Chin-hsi. For the full text, see *MTTC*, *pu chüan*, 1, 19–23; the passage quoted here is on pp. 20–1.

Some idea of Mao's overall political position at this time is furnished by the fact that he says only three people in China have had, in recent years, ideas about how to rule the country as a whole (*chih t'ien-hsia*): Yuan Shih-k'ai, Sun Yat-sen and K'ang Yu-wei. Of these, only K'ang really had something like basic principles (*pen-yuan*), and even his ideas were mainly rhetoric. The sole figure of the modern age he truly admired, wrote Mao, was Tseng Kuo-fan, whom he called (as in the *New Youth* article) by his posthumous title, Tseng Wen-cheng.[12]

Despite this, the pattern of Mao's thinking of 1917 was by no means purely traditional. The goal he wished to pursue was, of course, the strengthening and renewal of China. The realm (*t'ien-hsia*), he wrote, was vast, the organization of society complicated, and the knowledge of the people limited. In order to get things moving, it was necessary to move people's hearts. The first requirement for this was to have some great basic principles (*ta pen-yüan*). At present the reformers were beginning with details, such as assemblies, constitutions, presidents, cabinets, military affairs, industry, education and so on. The value of all this should not be under-estimated, but all these partial measures would be ineffectual if they were not founded in principle. Such principles should embrace the truth about the universe, and about man as a part of the universe. And, Mao went on:

Today, if we appeal (*hao-chao*) to the hearts of all under heaven on the basis of great principles can any of them fail to be moved? And if all the hearts in the realm are moved, is there anything which cannot be achieved? And...how, then, can the state fail to be rich, powerful, and happy?

In Mao's view, the place to start was with philosophy and ethics, and with changing the thinking (*ssu-hsiang*) of the whole country. China's thinking, he wrote, was extremely old, and her morals extremely bad. Thought ruled men's hearts, and morals ruled their actions; thus both must be changed.[13]

But though Mao saw China's ancient and rigid thought-patterns as an obstacle to progress, he did not propose wholesale Westernization as a remedy. Commenting on the view, attributed by Yang Ch'ang-chi to 'a certain Japanese', that Eastern thought entirely failed to 'correspond to real life', Mao observed: 'In my opinion, Western thought is not necessarily all correct either; very many parts of it should be transformed at the same time as Oriental thought.'[14]

[12] *Ibid.* 19–20.   [13] *Ibid.* 20.

[14] *Ibid.* 20–1. In his view that China, too, had something to contribute to the world, Mao was following the basic orientation of his teacher, Yang Ch'ang-chi, who had taken the style 'Huai-chung' (literally, 'yearning for China') during his long period of study abroad, to express his patriotic sentiments. On this, see Li Rui, 'Hsueh-sheng shih-tai ti Mao Tse-tung' (Mao Tse-tung during his student years), *Shih-tai ti pao-kao* 12 (December 1983); reprinted in *Hsin-hua wen-chai* 1984 1.178.

Having said this, however, Mao embarks on a notably untraditional discussion of the importance, in the enterprise of uniting the hearts of the people on the basis of thought and morals, of the little people (*hsiao-jen*), as compared to the 'superior men' (*chün-tzu*). To be sure, it is the latter who have a high level of knowledge and virtue, but they exist only on the basis of political institutions and economic activities mainly established by ordinary people, the mass of whom constitute the source of the 'superior men' (*hsiao-jen lei chün-tzu*). Thus, the 'superior men' must not only be benevolent toward the little people, but must educate and transform them in order to attain the goal of 'great harmony' (*ta-t'ung*). Already at this time Mao proposed to set up a private school (*ssu-shu*), combining traditional and modern methods, to prepare people for study abroad.[15]

As for the theme of practice, which was to play so large a part in Mao's subsequent thinking, he asserted in his 1917 article that hitherto there had been all too much talk about physical education: 'The important thing is not words, but putting them into practice.'[16] Mao's stress on linking theory and practice has often been traced back to Wang Yang-ming, but this is mere speculation; there is not the slightest mention of Wang in any of Mao's known writings, and no evidence that he was influenced by him. More relevant, in any case, to Mao's development during the May Fourth period are the Westernizing ideas he assimilated in 1917-18.

Mao's thinking evolved very rapidly during his last two years at the First Normal School in Changsha. Perhaps the most important single element which makes its appearance at this time is an explicit and strongly-marked individualism. For example, in marginal annotations to a textbook on ethics by the German neo-Kantian, Friedrich Paulsen, Mao wrote:

The goal of the human race lies in the realization of the self, and that is all. What I mean by the realization of the self consists in developing our physical and mental capacities to the highest degree....Wherever there is repression of the individual, wherever there is a violation of individuality, there can be no greater crime. That is why our country's 'three bonds' must go, and why they constitute, with the churches, capitalists, and autocracy, the four evil demons of the realm....[17]

Like older and more eminent intellectuals of the time, such as Ch'en Tu-hsiu, Li Ta-chao or Lu Hsun, Mao had seized on the notion of the absolute value of the individual as a weapon to 'break out of the nets' of the old culture and the old society. He was by no means unaware of the social framework necessary to the realization of the individual,

[15] *MTTC, pu chüan*, 1, 22-3.
[16] Mao Tse-tung, 'T'i-yü', 7; translated in *Mao Ze-dong. Une étude de l'education physique*, 52; and Day, 27.
[17] Quoted by Li Jui, 110. The full text of Mao's annotations on Paulsen has been reproduced in *MTTC, pu chüan*, 9, 19-47.

describing how groups were formed from individuals, societies were formed from groups, and states were formed from societies. In this complex interrelationship between the individual and the state, or civil society (*kuo-min*), Mao stressed that the individual was primary; Paulsen's contrary emphasis reflected, he said, the influence of 'statism' in Germany.[18]

A dialectical approach to the relations between opposites is, indeed, one of the hallmarks of Mao's thought from this time forward. Among the pairs which he treated as in some sense identical were concept and reality, finite and infinite, high and low, *yin* and *yang*, as well as two which would be criticized by the Soviets decades later: life and death, and male and female. Man he saw as the unity of matter and spirit, and morality as arising from the interaction of conscience and desire. (The view that moral law had been laid down by a command of the spirits he stigmatized as a 'slave mentality'.) Moreover, because matter was indestructible, man and society were likewise indestructible, though constantly changing and renewing themselves through reform and revolution. For this reason, he no longer feared, as he had done, that China would perish; she would survive by reform of the political system, and transformation of the nature of the people. Such reform was possible only under the guidance of new knowledge, and knowledge would be effective if it was first built into belief, and then applied. 'Knowledge, belief, and action,' he wrote, 'are the three steps in our intellectual activity.' The medium of action could only be 'various social and political organizations'.[19]

Thus the stress of the April 1917 article on practice was strongly reasserted, and a new theme, that of organizing for reform, emerged. Both of these were to be central to the very important essay entitled 'The great union of the popular masses', which Mao published in July and August 1919.

The most startling passage of Mao's 1919 article[20] is no doubt that contrasting Marx and Kropotkin:

As to the actions which should be undertaken once we have united, there is one extremely violent party, which uses the method 'Do unto others as they do unto you' to struggle desperately to the end with the aristocrats and capitalists. The leader of this party is a man named Marx who was born in Germany. There is another party more moderate than that of Marx. It does not expect rapid results,

---

[18] *MTTC*, *pu-chüan*, 9, 21, 40–1.

[19] *Ibid.*, 28–34, 37–9, 42, 45–6. Most but not all of these passages are included in Li Jui, 114–16; translation, 40.

[20] I have published a full translation in *The China Quarterly*, hereafter *CQ*, together with an analysis. Mao Tse-tung, 'The great union of the popular masses', followed by S. Schram, 'From the "Great union of the popular masses" to the "Great alliance"', *CQ* 49 (Jan.–March 1972) 76–105. See also Day, 85–100. The Chinese text is available in *MTTC* 1.57–69.

but begins by understanding the common people. Men should all have a morality of mutual aid, and work voluntarily....The ideas of this party are broader and more far-reaching. They want to unite the whole globe into a single country, unite the human race into a single family.... The leader of this party is a man called Kropotkin, who was born in Russia.[21]

Quoting this passage verbatim, Li Jui comments that, although at this time Mao could not clearly distinguish between Marxism and anarchism, 'The great union of the popular masses' and other articles he wrote for the journal he edited in Hunan, the *Hsiang River Review* (*Hsiang-chiang p'ing-lun*), already displayed glimmerings of class analysis, and constituted the earliest building blocks of the future great edifice of Mao Tse-tung's Thought.[22] But while Mao was unquestionably, in the summer of 1919, learning rapidly about the theory and practice of revolution, it is very difficult to find in his writings of the period serious elements of Marxist analysis. Concepts such as class struggle, dialectics, or the materialist view of history are not even mentioned, and the very term 'class' is used only once, and then in a totally un-Marxist sense (the 'classes' of the wise and the ignorant, the rich and the poor, and the strong and the weak).[23] If the article has a discernible philosophical bias, this is to be found neither in Marx nor in Kropotkin, but in the ideas of Western liberals as transmitted – and transmuted – by certain Chinese writers of the late nineteenth and early twentieth century. Among these were Yen Fu and Liang Ch'i-ch'ao, the Hunanese revolutionary thinker and martyr T'an Ssu-t'ung, as well as Mao's teacher Yang Ch'ang-chi, all of whom developed in one way or another the view that spontaneous action by members of society, unfettered by the old hierarchical bonds, would maximize the energy of society as a whole.

Another important influence on Mao's thought during the May Fourth period was that of Hu Shih. It has often been pointed out that Mao's articles of 1919 were enthusiastically hailed following their publication by the Peking journal *Weekly Review* (*Mei-chou p'ing-lun*). Summarizing the contents of the first few issues of Mao's *Hsiang River Review* one commentator said: 'The strong point of *Hsiang River Review* lies in discussion. The long article "The great union of the popular masses" published in the second, third and fourth issues...exhibits exceedingly

[21] *CQ* 49. 78–9. Understandably, this paragraph was not included in the extracts from this article reproduced in 1957 by Li Jui, since it would hardly have supported the view he put forward there to the effect that 'The great union of the popular masses' was 'one of the most important writings' in which Mao 'began to combine a Marxist-Leninist viewpoint with the reality of the Chinese revolution'. (*Ibid.* 1st ed., 106; translation, 115.) As noted below, his approach in the revised edition of 1980 is radically different.

[22] *Ibid.* 213.   [23] *CQ* 49. 77–8.

far-reaching vision, and exceedingly well-chosen and effective arguments. Truly it is one of the important articles which have appeared recently.'[24] The author of these words was in fact none other than Hu Shih himself.

This appears less surprising when we note that, in his editorial for the first issue of the *Hsiang River Review*, Mao said, after enumerating the progress in various domains which had been achieved by humanity since the Renaissance (for example, from a dead classical literature for the aristocracy to a modern, living literature for the common people, and from the politics of dictatorship to the politics of parliamentarianism), that in the field of thought or philosophy (*ssu-hsiang*) 'we have moved forward to pragmatism'.[25] I do not mean to suggest, in noting this point, that Mao was a disciple of Hu Shih or John Dewey. His favourable evaluation of pragmatism in 1919 did reflect, however, an attitude he was to maintain *almost* until the end of his life, to the effect that one should not spin theories without linking them to concrete experience.

If Mao's ideas in 1919, like those of older and more learned men at the time, were a mosaic of many influences, his article 'The great union of the popular masses' had one remarkable peculiarity: it represented one of the few attempts to put forward a general programme on the basis of concrete experience of the revolutionary mass movements of the May Fourth period. It is true that Mao's hierarchy of social categories in the total picture as he saw it was quite un-Marxist: he attributed maximum importance to the student movement, and relatively little to the peasants, not to mention the workers. He also, characteristically, devotes considerable attention to women, and to school teachers. Looked at as a whole, his vision of the revolutionary alliance he is striving to create is not unlike that of the 'New Left' in the United States and elsewhere in the 1960s. The central theme of the articles is that China's renewal will come above all from the rebellion of young people, and especially of students, against the old order. The instrument and motive force of change lies in democratic organizations spontaneously building up from the grass roots. The goal of the whole process will be, in Mao's view (and here he

---

[24] *Mei-chou p'ing-lun*, 36 (24 August 1919), 4.

[25] *MTTC* 1.53–4, translated in Day, 81. (For the reasons for translating *shih-yen chu-i* as 'pragmatism' see Day, 83, n. 2.) Hu Shih's influence on Mao at this time (which had earlier been acknowledged by Mao himself in his autobiography as told to Edgar Snow) was, of course, unmentionable in China until recently. (For some brief but pithy observations on the subject by a Western scholar, see Day, 47–8.) It is a reflection of the remarkable revolution which has taken place since 1978 in the climate of intellectual enquiry in China that an article published in 1980 should not only call attention to Hu's praise of Mao and to Mao's regard for pragmatism as the 'leading ideology' (*chih-tao ssu-hsiang*) of the time, but should explicitly state that in 1919 differences of principle had not yet emerged between them. See Wang Shu-pai and Chang Shen-heng, 'Ch'ing-nien Mao Tse-tung shih-chieh-kuan ti chuan-pien' (The transformation in the world view of the young Mao Tse-tung), *LSYC* 5 (1980) 83.

reveals himself as a true disciple of Yen Fu), not merely the liberation of the individual from the shackles of the old society, but also, and by that very fact, the strengthening and renewal of the Chinese nation as a whole. In a supremely eloquent peroration, Mao addressed his compatriots thus:

in every domain we demand liberation. Ideological liberation, political liberation, economic liberation, liberation [in the relations between] men and women, educational liberation, are all going to burst from the deep inferno where they have been confined, and demand to look at the blue sky. Our Chinese people possesses great inherent capacities! The more profound the oppression, the greater its resistance; since [this] has been accumulating for a long time, it will surely burst forth quickly. I venture to make a singular assertion: one day, the reform of the Chinese people will be more profound than that of any other people, and the society of the Chinese people will be more radiant than that of any other people. The great union of the Chinese people will be achieved earlier than that of any other place or people. Gentlemen! Gentlemen! We must all exert ourselves! We must all advance with the utmost strength! Our golden age, our age of glory and splendour, lies before us![26]

There is more than one echo here of Mao's 1917 article, in the emphasis on persistent efforts and a firm resolve as the keys to national resurgence. In the intervening two years, he had learned much, both from books and from experience, about the way to tap and mobilize the energies which he perceived to be latent in the Chinese people. He had, however, a great deal still to learn before he could even begin to devise a complete and effective strategy for making revolution in a country such as China.

Although Mao showed little understanding of Marxism at this time, his imagination had been caught by the victory of the Russian Revolution. He listed the establishment of a soviet government of workers and peasants first among the worldwide exploits of what he called the 'army of the red flag', and went on to mention the Hungarian Revolution, and the wave of strikes in America and in various European countries.[27] Other articles by Mao in the *Hsiang River Review* evoke themes which were later to become classic in his thought, such as the need of politicians to 'wash their brains' and 'go to the factories to work and the countryside to cultivate the land, together with the common people' (*p'ing min*), or the idea that 'the true liberation of humanity' would come on the day when thousands and tens of thousands of people in America shouted together in the face of injustice and the despotism of the trusts, 'This must not be!' (*pu-hsu*). But Mao also expressed very strong support for the Germans, who are presented as an oppressed people dictated to by the Entente.[28]

[26] *CQ* 49.87.   [27] *CQ* 49.84.
[28] On going to the factories, see [Mao] Tse-tung, 'Cha-tan pao-chü' (A brutal bomb attack), *Hsiang River Review*, 1 (14 July 1919), 3. On shouting in unison, Tse-tung, 'Pu-hsu shih-yeh chuan-chih'

The idea of China as a proletarian nation, which should show solidarity with other oppressed peoples, was of course commonly put forward in the years immediately after the May Fourth period by Li Ta-chao, Ts'ai Ho-sen and others. Mao, too, was naturally drawn in this direction.

A phase in Mao's subsequent apprenticeship, which provides a highly suggestive complement to his analysis, in 1919, of the role of grass-roots organizations in social change, was his participation in the Hunanese autonomy movement in the following year. This hitherto obscure episode has only recently been illuminated by the publication of important documents.[29] The record of this episode throws a revealing light not only on Mao's intense Hunanese patriotism, but on his attitude to political work generally. In an article published on 26 September 1920, Mao wrote:

In any matter whatsoever, if there is a 'theory', but no 'movement' to carry it through, the aim of this theory cannot be realized....I believe that there are two kinds of real movements: one involves getting inside of things (*ju yü ch'i chung*) to engage in concrete construction; the other is set up outside, in order to promote [the cause].

Both types of movement, he added, were and would remain important and necessary. At the same time, he stressed that an effective movement must have its origin in the 'people' (*min*). 'If this present Hunanese autonomist movement were to be successfully established, but if its source were to reside not in the "people", but outside the "people", then I venture to assert that such a movement could not last long.'[30]

As for the broader context in which these statements were made, Mao and the co-authors of the proposal of 7 October 1920 for a constitutional convention summed up their views about the relation between political developments at the provincial and national levels as follows:

The self-government law the Hunanese need now is like that of an American state constitution....China is now divided into many pieces, and we do not know when a national constitution will be produced; in fact, we are afraid that first

(No to the despotism of industry and commerce), *ibid.* 1.3. On the oppression of Germany see (among many articles, some by other authors) Tse-tung, 'Wei Te ju hu ti Fa-lan' (France fears Germany as if it were a tiger), *ibid.* 3 (28 July 1919), 2. Giorgio Mantici has published a complete Italian translation of the available issues of the *Hsiang River Review* under the title *Pensieri del fiume Xiang*. The articles just mentioned appear on 76–8 and 164–5. I wish to thank Mr Mantici for kindly giving me a copy of the Chinese text of these materials. All of these texts have now been published in *MTTC, pu chüan*, 1.

[29] These materials – four articles by Mao, and a proposal for a constitutional convention drafted jointly with two others, were discovered by Angus McDonald in the course of research on his doctoral dissertation 'The urban origins of rural revolution' (University of California, Berkeley, 1974), also published in book form under the same title. McDonald has published the Chinese texts in *Hōgaku kenkyū*, 46.2 (1972) 99–107, with a commentary in Japanese, and has also discussed them in English in *Rōnin* (Tokyo), 14 (December 1973), 37–47, and in *CQ* 68 (December 1976), 751–77. [30] *MTTC, pu chüan*, 1.229–30.

every province will have to produce its own constitution, and only later will we have a national constitution. This is just like the route from separation to unification followed by America and [Bismarckian] Germany.[31]

This dimension of Mao's 1920 writings reflects the circumstances of the times, and by no means corresponds to his long-term view, which consistently stressed, from 1917 to the end of his life, the importance of national unity and a strong state. In other respects, however, the ideas put forward in the passages quoted above are altogether typical of Mao Tse-tung's political approach throughout his subsequent career as a revolutionary. On the one hand he called for 'getting inside things' to engage in concrete construction, by which he meant obviously that revolutionaries, or reformers, should immerse themselves in social reality. But at the same time, he perceived the need for a movement set up outside, in order to promote the cause. In other words, although political activists should respond to the objective demands of the 'people', and should immerse themselves in the people, in order to mobilize them, another organization, standing outside the people, was also required. It could be said that the Leninist-type Communist Party which Mao joined in the following year was precisely such an organization which did not allow itself to be confounded with the masses but stood outside them. But at the same time Mao never hesitated, throughout his political career, to enter boldly into things, and to participate in concrete organizational work.

The other question raised by Mao's writings during the Hunanese autonomist movement concerns the 'people' on whose behalf these activities were to be carried out, and from whom the initial impulse and inspiration for the movement were to come. By putting the term in quotation marks, Mao himself underscored its ambiguity. Were these the 'popular masses' (*min-chung*) of his 1919 article? Or were they the 'Chinese people' or 'Chinese nation' (*Chung-hua min-tsu*), who were never far from the centre of his concerns? It is perhaps a characteristic trait of Mao's thought that these two entities are indissolubly linked. He was never, at any time after 1918 or 1919, a nationalist solely, or primarily, interested in China's 'wealth and power'. But neither was he a 'proletarian' revolutionary like M. N. Roy, who never thought in terms of the nation.

In the course of the year 1920, Mao Tse-tung's attitude toward the problem of learning from the West how to transform Chinese society underwent a significant change. This shift is symbolized by the changing views regarding the narrower problem of study abroad expressed by Mao Tse-tung in a letter of 14 March 1920 to Chou Shih-chao, and another of 25 November 1920 to Hsiang Ching-yü. In the first, he declared that,

[31] *Ibid.* 242.

although a lot of people had a kind of superstitious reverence for the benefits of foreign study, in fact only a very few of the tens or hundreds of thousands of Chinese who had gone abroad had really learned anything of value. In any case, he wrote, the two currents of Eastern and Western culture each occupied half the world, and Eastern culture 'could be said to be Chinese culture' (*k'o-i shuo chiu shih Chung-kuo wen-ming*); he would master that first, before proceeding abroad, though he was not opposed in principle to all study abroad.[32]

Half a year later, Mao wrote, on the contrary, to Hsiang Ching-yü in France complaining that there was very little progressive education for women (or for men either) in Hunan, and urging her to lure as many women comrades as possible abroad, adding: 'One more person lured [abroad] is one more person saved (*yin i jen, chi to chiu i jen*).'[33]

The shift in Mao's basic attitude toward ideologies of Western origin was not so dramatic as suggested by these contrasting passages. One of his reasons, in March, for preferring to remain in China was, according to his letter to Chou Shih-chao, that a person could absorb foreign knowledge more rapidly by reading translations. His ideological orientation remained unsettled, however, as he said himself: 'To be frank, among all the ideologies and doctrines, I have at present still not found any relatively clear concept.' Mao's aim was to put together such a 'clear concept' (*ming-liao kai-nien*) from the essence of culture Chinese and Western, ancient and modern. In his plans for creating a 'new life' in Changsha within three years or so, Mao said that the individual was primary, and the group secondary. He went out of his way to stress his links with Hu Shih, and even noted that Hu had coined the name 'Self-Study University' (*tzu-hsiu ta-hsueh*) for an institution Mao proposed to set up in Changsha. But in this university, said Mao, 'we will live a communist life' (*kung-ch'an ti sheng-huo*), and he also declared that 'Russia is the number one civilized country in the world'.[34]

By the end of November 1920, Mao still advocated, in his letter to Hsiang Ching-yü, that Hunan should set itself up as an independent country (*tzu li wei kuo*), in order to detach itself from the backward northern provinces, and 'join hands directly with the nations of the world endowed with consciousness'. But at the same time he expressed great disillusionment with the absence of ideals and of far-sighted plans even among the educated elite of Hunan, and with the corruption of political

---

[32] *Hsin-min hsueh-hui tzu-liao*, hereafter HMHHTL (*Materials on the New People's Study Society*), 62–5. (*Chung-kuo hsien-tai ko-ming-shih tzu-liao ts'ung-k'an*). Reprinted in *MTTC, pu chüan*, 1.191–4.
[33] HMHHTL 75–6. *MTTC, pu chüan*, 1.261–2.
[34] HMHHTL 63–5. *MTTC, pu chüan*, 1.192–4.

circles, which made reform wholly illusory. It was necessary, he said, to 'open a new road'.[35]

An important influence in Mao's search for such a road was the group of Hunanese students, members of the New People's Study Society, then studying in France, and above all his intimate friend (who was also Hsiang Ching-yü's lover), Ts'ai Ho-sen. This was, incidentally, the case not only in the explicitly political realm, but in the attitude of iconoclasm and rebellion against established customs which was so prominent a feature of the May Fourth era and its aftermath. Having learned, in a letter of May 1920 from Ts'ai, that he and Ching-yü had established 'a kind of union based on love', Mao responded with enthusiasm, denouncing all those who lived under the institution of marriage as the 'rape brigade' (*ch'iang-chien t'uan*), and swearing that he would never be one of them.[36]

A year earlier, in the context of his campaign against arranged marriages, following the suicide of a young girl in Changsha forced by her father to marry against her will,[37] Mao had called rather for the reform (*kai-ko*) of the marriage system, to replace 'capitalist' marriages by love matches. Already in 1919 he had concluded that among the various human desires, for food, sex, amusement, fame, and power, hunger and sexual desire were the most important. Then he had written that members of the older generation were interested only in food, and hence in exploiting their daughters-in-law as slaves, and not, like the young, in love and sexual desire, which involved 'not only the satisfaction of the biological urge of fleshly desire, but the satisfaction of spiritual desires, and desires for social intercourse of a high order'. Thus they were the natural allies of capitalism against the fulfilment of the desires of young people.[38] Now he decided that marriage as such was the 'foundation of capitalism', because it involved the prohibition of 'that most reasonable thing, free love' (*chin-chih tsui ho-li ti tzu-yu lien-ai*).[39]

Just as the strongly patriotic Li Ta-chao went in 1920 through an internationalist phase, in which he proclaimed that all the members of humanity were brothers,[40] Mao Tse-tung, as he embraced Ts'ai Ho-sen's

[35] *HMHHTL* 75–6. *MTTC, pu chüan*, 1.261.

[36] *HMHHTL* 127 (Ts'ai's letter of 28 May 1920) and 121 (Mao's letter of 25 November 1920 to Lo Hsueh-tsan). The latter is also in *MTTC, pu chüan*, 1.275–7.

[37] Mao wrote in all nine articles on this theme. For a brief summary, see Li Jui, translation, 119–21. Extracts are translated in *PTMT* 334–7. For the full texts of all nine articles, published in the Changsha *Ta-kung-pao* between 16 and 28 November 1919, see *MTTC, pu chüan*, 1.143–72.

[38] See, especially, 'Lien-ai wen-t'i – shao-nien-jen yü lao-nien-jen' (The question of love – young people and old people), *ibid.* 161–3. Also 'Kai-ko hun-chih wen-t'i' (The problem of the reform of the marriage system), *ibid.* 149.   [39] *Ibid.* 276.

[40] Li Ta-chao, 'Ya-hsi-ya ch'ing-nien ti kuan-ming yun-tung' (The luminous Asiatic youth movement), *Li Ta-chao hsuan-chi*, 327–9; extracts in H. Carrère d'Encausse and S. Schram, *Marxism and Asia*, 208–10.

vision of a revolution like that of the Russians, also accepted Ts'ai's view that all socialism must necessarily be internationalist, and should not have a 'patriotic colouration'. Those born in China should work primarily (though not exclusively) in 'this place, China', because that was where they could work most effectively, and because China, being both 'more puerile and more corrupt' than other places in the world, was most in need of change, but this did not mean that they should love only China and not other places. But in the same letter of 1 December to Ts'ai Ho-sen, and in discussions at a meeting of the New People's Study Society in Changsha on 1–3 January 1921, Mao insisted that the goal of the society should be formulated as 'transforming China and the world'. Others argued that, since China was part of the world, it was not necessary to mention it separately. For Mao it was important.[41]

As for the goals of political change, and the methods to be used in pursuing them, Mao replied on 1 December to several communications he had received from Ts'ai Ho-sen, Hsiao Hsü-tung (Siao Yü) and others detailing their own views and the debates among members of the society in France about these matters. Ts'ai and Hsiao had formed, with Mao, during their years at the Normal School in Hunan, a trio who called themselves the 'three worthies' (san-ko hao-chieh), but following their exposure to Western influences they had moved in opposite directions, Ts'ai toward Bolshevism and Hsiao toward a more moderate vision of revolution vaguely anarchist in character. Mao agreed unequivocally with Ts'ai's view that China's road must be the Russian road. But at the same time, in the process of refuting the arguments of Hsiao, and of Bertrand Russell, who had just been lecturing in Changsha along similar lines, in favour of non-violent revolution, without dictatorship, he showed only the vaguest understanding of Marxist categories. Thus he divided the world's total population of one and a half billion into 500 million 'capitalists' (tzu pen chia) and a billion 'proletarians' (wu-ch'an chieh-chi).[42]

Plainly, Mao's usage here reflects an understanding of the term wu-ch'an chieh-chi closer to its literal meaning of 'propertyless class' than to the Marxist concept of the urban, or even of the urban and rural proletariat. In the course of the next few years he came to know better intellectually, though it is a moot point whether, in terms of instinctive reactions, the Chinese expression did not continue to signify for him something more like 'the wretched of the earth'.

[41] HMHHTL 146, and 15–41, especially 20–3.

[42] HMHHTL 144–52; MTTC, pu chüan, 1, 289–96; extracts translated in PTMT 196–8 (there misdated, following the then available source, November 1920). For the letters of August 1920 from Ts'ai and Hsiao, see HMHHTL 128–43. The problem of Ts'ai's influence on Mao at this time is discussed by R. Scalapino in 'The evolution of a young revolutionary – Mao Zedong in 1919–1921', JAS 42.1 (Nov. 1982) 29–61.

Nevertheless, although his understanding of Marxist categories was as yet somewhat uncertain, Mao was definitely moving, during the winter of 1920–1, toward an interpretation of politics more in harmony with that of Lenin. Above all, he had grasped a Leninist axiom which was to remain at the centre of his thinking for the rest of his life, namely the decisive importance of political power. Replying on 21 January 1921 to a letter of 16 September 1920 from Ts'ai, declaring that the only method for China was 'that of the proletarian dictatorship as applied now in Russia',[43] Mao wrote:

The materialist view of history is our party's philosophical basis....In the past, I had not studied the problem, but at present I do not believe that the principles of anarchism can be substantiated.

The political organization of a factory (the management of production, distribution etc. in the factory) differs from the political organization of a country or of the world only in size, and not in nature [chih yu ta-hsiao pu t'ung, mei yu hsing-chih pu-t'ung]. The view of syndicalism [kung-t'uan chu-i] according to which the political organization of a country and the political organization of a factory are different in nature, and the claim that these are two different matters which should be in the hands of different kinds of people...only proves that they are confused and do not understand the principles of things. Moreover, if we do not obtain political power, we cannot promote [fa-tung] revolution, we cannot maintain the revolution, and we cannot carry the revolution to completion....What you say in your letter [to the effect that China needs a proletarian dictatorship exactly like that in Russia] is extremely correct, there is not a single word with which I disagree.[44]

Mao Tse-tung's experience during the six years after the First Congress of the Chinese Communist Party in July 1921 falls neatly into three segments. During the first two years he was engaged in organizing the labour movement in Hunan, and this could be called his workers' period. Thereafter, in 1923 and 1924, he served as a member of the Chinese Communist Party's Central Committee, and of the Shanghai Executive Bureau of the Kuomintang, in Canton and Shanghai, and this could be called his period as an 'organization man'. Finally, as everyone knows, he devoted himself in 1925–7 largely to organizing the peasant movement, and this could be called his peasant period.

The most striking thing about the first of these periods is that it appears, on the basis of all the available primary and secondary sources, to have been, in comparison with what came before and after, intellectually sterile. In any case, Mao's writings from this workers' period are few in number,

43 HMHHTL 153–62.
44 HMHHTL 162–3. This and the previous letter, as well as Ts'ai's letters of 28 May and 13 August, and Mao's letter of 1 December 1920 to Ts'ai and Hsiao, are reproduced in a more widely available openly published source: Ts'ai Ho-sen wen-chi (Collected writings of Ts'ai Ho-sen), 37–40, 49–73. Mao's letters of December 1920 and January 1921 to Ts'ai are the first two items in Mao Tse-tung shu-hsin hsuan-chi (Selected letters of Mao Tse-tung), 1–16.

and largely lacking in the fire and eloquence which, on other occasions, he showed himself so capable of manifesting. To be sure, Mao, like everyone else in the party, was overwhelmingly busy with organizational tasks during these first two years. The main explanation lies, however, in the fact that Mao himself had never really lived the life of a worker, as he had lived both the life of a peasant and the life of a student and city-based intellectual. He had, to be sure, organized a night-school for workers when he was a student at the Normal School in Changsha, and befriended individual workers on many occasions. His instinctive understanding of their problems was not, however, quite the same. Thus, although Mao's work in organizing strikes in a variety of industries undoubtedly influenced his intellectual and political development in the long run, at the time the harvest was meagre.

It is suggestive that the only item by Mao dating from the period mid-1921 to mid-1923 available in complete form outside China until very recently (thanks to the fortuitous circumstance that a widely-circulated magazine reprinted it in 1923) belongs in fact rather to the tail end of Mao's May Fourth period activities. It is the 'Declaration on the inauguration of the Hunan Self-Study University' which Mao wrote in August 1921 when he finally set up that intriguing institution.[45]

This text places, as Mao had done since 1917, the emphasis on individual initiative and self-expression in the learning process; it also echoes the articles Mao had written a year earlier on the mission of the Hunanese. But though Mao denounces vigorously the fact that 'learning is monopolized by a small "scholar clique" and becomes widely separated from the society of the ordinary man, thus giving rise to that strange phenomenon of the intellectual class enslaving the class of ordinary people', he shows as vague an understanding of what is meant by the 'so-called proletariat' as he had in his letter to Ts'ai of the previous December.

The writings of Mao's 'workers' period' relating specifically to the workers' movement are few and far between. Li Jui, whose biography of the young Mao is the principal source for texts of this period, is able to find only one item worthy of quoting at any length. This dates from December 1922, a time when Mao was engaged in leading the strike of the Changsha printing workers, and constitutes his reply to an attack by the editor of the Changsha Ta-kung-pao on the workers for getting involved in politics and lending themselves to other people's experiments. In a few characteristic sentences, Mao wrote:

What we workers need is knowledge; that is entirely correct. We workers are more than willing that people with knowledge should come forward and be our

[45] MTTC, 1.81–4; Day, Máo Zédōng, 140–3. This appeared in Tung-fang tsa-chih, 20.6 (1 March 1923).

real friends....Sir, you must never again stand on the sidelines....We acknowledge as good friends only those who are capable of sacrificing their own positions, and of enduring hunger and hardship in order to work on behalf of the interests of us workers, who constitute the great majority [of society]....Please, take off your long robe in a hurry![46]

We find here once again the recurrent theme that those who seek to reform society (as the *Ta-kung-pao* editor claimed he also wanted to do) should 'enter into the midst of things', and not remain on the sidelines as observers, or believe themselves superior to ordinary people. There is nothing here, however, about the role of the working class in the revolution, not to mention working-class hegemony. The *Ta-kung-pao* was not, perhaps, the place to put forward such ideas, but Li Jui is not able to cite anything at all from Mao's period as a labour organizer on this theme.

The explanation may well lie in the line of the Chinese Communist Party at the time. In 1922 the Comintern envoy Maring (Sneevliet) had pushed his Chinese comrades into the singular organizational form for a united front with the Nationalists known as the 'bloc within', under which the Chinese Communists joined the Kuomintang as individuals. This idea was originally put forward in March 1922 by Maring on the basis of his experience in the Dutch East Indies, where left-wing socialists had cooperated in a similar way with Sarekat Islam, a nationalist organization with (as the name implies) a pronounced religious colouration. Ch'en Tu-hsiu and a majority of the other leading members of the Chinese Communist Party having rejected this idea out of hand, Maring travelled to Moscow, put his case to the Executive Committee of the International, and obtained a formal mandate from the Comintern endorsing his policy. Armed with this, he was able, following his return to China in August 1922, to ram the 'bloc within' down the throats of his reluctant Chinese comrades.[47]

This pattern of collaboration has been the object of intense controversy

---

[46] Li Jui, 428–30; translation, 251–2. The editors of the supplement to the Tokyo edition of Mao's works, who have cast their net very widely indeed, have also come up with only two or three very brief texts, in addition to this one, relating to the workers' movement. See *MTTC, pu-chüan*, 2.89–107.

[47] He lied, therefore, when he told Harold Isaacs that he had persuaded the Chinese to accept the proposal simply on the basis of his personal authority, and had 'no document in his hand' from Moscow to back him up. (*CQ* 45 (January–March 1971) 106.) The essential facts are conveniently outlined by Dov Bing, 'Sneevliet and the early years of the CCP', in *CQ* 48 (Oct.–Dec. 1971) 677–97; see also his reply, in *CQ* 54, to criticisms published in *CQ* 53. His view, which I have summarized in the text, is shared by both Soviet and Chinese scholars. See, on the one hand, V. I. Glunin, 'The Comintern and the rise of the communist movement in China (1920–1927)', in R. A. Ulyanovsky, ed. *The Comintern and the East*, 280–344, esp. 289–93. For a recent Chinese account, see Hsiao Sheng and Chiang Hua-hsuan, 'Ti-i-tz'u Kuo-Kung ho-tso t'ung-i chan-hsien ti hsing-ch'eng' (The formation of the first Kuomintang-Communist United Front), *LSYC*, 2 (1981), 51–68, esp. 58.

ever since its inception. So far as is known, Mao Tse-tung played no significant part either in devising it, or in securing its adoption. He was, however, one of the first to participate actively in implementing it. In the summer of 1922, Mao was involved in the organization of the Socialist Youth League in Hunan, and wrote to the Central Committee of the league in his capacity as secretary of the Changsha branch. Fifteen months later, in September 1923, he was already active in establishing Kuomintang organizations in the same localities, and wrote to the Central Office of the Kuomintang asking that he be formally appointed a member of the Preparatory Committee for this purpose, in order to facilitate contacts on all sides.[48]

From that time onwards, Mao Tse-tung was to play an important role in 'united front work'. Broadly speaking, once Ch'en Tu-hsiu and the other Chinese Communist leaders had accepted the 'bloc within', there was a tendency on their part to conclude that this implied accepting the leadership of the Nationalists, as the 'party of the bourgeoisie', at least for the time being. Such was Ch'en's position in 1923, and Mao for his part went very far in that direction during his period as an 'organization man'.

This is clearly apparent in the article entitled 'The foreign powers, the militarists, and the revolution' which Mao published in April 1923, on the eve of the crucial Third Congress, which formally adopted the 'bloc within'. Within China, he declared, only three factions (*p'ai*) were to be found: the revolutionary democratic faction, the non-revolutionary democratic faction (*fei ko-ming ti min-chu p'ai*), and the reactionary faction. Regarding the first of these, he wrote: 'The main body (*chu-t'i*) of the revolutionary faction is, of course, the Kuomintang; the newly-arisen (*hsin-hsing*) Communist faction (*kung-ch'an p'ai*) is cooperating with the Kuomintang.'.

The non-revolutionary democratic faction included on the one hand the Research Clique and the 'faction of the newly-arisen intellectual class' (*hsin-hsing ti chih-shih chieh-chi p'ai*) of Hu Shih, Huang Yen-p'ei and others; and on the other hand the newly-arisen merchant faction. The reactionaries were, of course, the three main cliques of militarists.

The division of the totality of social forces into three was, and would remain, highly characteristic of Mao's approach to politics and to revolution. Another trait very much in evidence here is what might be called the dialectics of disorder and oppression, on which Mao had laid

---

[48] See his letter of 20 June 1922, 'Chih Shih Fu-liang ping She-hui-chu-i ch'ing-nien-t'uan chung-yang' (To Shih Fu-liang and the Central Committee of the Socialist Youth League), and his letter of 28 September 1923, 'Chih Lin Po-ch'ü, P'eng Su-min' (To Lin Po-chü and P'eng Su-min), *Selected letters*, 21–4.

great stress in his 1919 article 'The great union of the popular masses'. Because of the power of the militarists, and because the union of China under a democratic government would be contrary to the interests of the imperialists, there can be, Mao argues, neither peace nor unity for another eight or ten years. But the more reactionary and confused the political situation, the more this will stimulate the revolutionary sentiments and organizational capacity of the people of the whole country, so that in the end democracy and national independence will triumph over the militarists.[49]

The merchants, who were to have a share in the victory of the democratic forces, revolutionary and non-revolutionary, were featured more prominently in an article of July 1923 entitled 'The Peking coup d'état and the merchants', which has been the subject of considerable controversy. In this text, Mao stated in part:

The present political problem in China is none other than the problem of a national revolution [*kuo-min ko-ming*]. To use the strength of the citizens [*kuo-min*, literally the people of the country] to overthrow the militarists, and also to overthrow the foreign imperialists with whom the militarists are in collusion to accomplish their treasonable acts, is the historic mission of the Chinese people. This revolution is the task of the people as a whole, and the merchants, workers, peasants, students and teachers should all come forward to take on the responsibility for a portion of the revolutionary work. Both historical necessity and present realities prescribe, however, that the work for which the merchants must take responsibility in the national revolution is both more urgent and more important than the work that the rest of the people should take upon themselves....

The broader the organization of merchants, the greater will be their...ability to lead the people of the whole country, and the more rapid the success of the revolution![50]

It has been suggested that Mao's July 1923 article is not about the role of the merchants in the Chinese revolution at all, but rather about the nature of the tasks in the present 'bourgeois-democratic' stage of the revolution.[51] This view not only flies in the face of the evidence, but completely fails to note the epoch-making shift in Mao's outlook between 1923 and 1925–6, from an urban-oriented perspective to one turned toward the countryside. In another passage of his July 1923 article, Mao wrote:

---

[49] 'Wai li, chün-fa yü ko-ming' (The foreign powers, the militarists, and the revolution), *MTCC*, *pu-chüan*, 2.109–111.
[50] *The Guide Weekly*, 31/32 (11 July 1923), 233–4; translated in *PTMT* 106–9.
[51] Lynda Shaffer, 'Mao Ze-dong and the October 1922 Changsha construction workers' strike', *Modern China*, 4 (Oct. 1978) 380, 416–71. The same argument is repeated in L. Shaffer, *Mao and the workers: the Hunan labor movement, 1920–1923*, 1–2, 222–3.

We know that the politics of semi-colonial China is characterized by the fact that the militarists and foreign powers have banded together to impose a twofold oppression on the people of the whole country. The people of the whole country obviously suffer profoundly under this kind of twofold oppression. Nevertheless, it must be acknowledged that the merchants are the ones who feel these sufferings most acutely and most urgently.

In other words, Mao regarded the merchants, and more broadly the city-dwellers directly exposed to imperialist oppression, as most capable of playing a leading role in the national revolution because they suffered the most. This whole sociological analysis was turned right around three years later, after Mao had discovered the revolutionary potential inherent in the peasantry. Before we consider these developments, another persistent trait in Mao's July 1923 article deserves to be noted. The conclusion reads as follows:

Everyone must believe that the only way to save both himself and the nation [*kuo-chia*] is through the national revolution [*kuo-min ko-ming*]....Circumstances call upon us to perform an historic task....To open a new era by revolutionary methods, and to build a new nation – such is the historic mission of the Chinese people [*Chung-hua min-tsu*]. We must never forget it!

Here once again, we can see how clearly people in the political sense (*kuo-min* or citizens) and people in the biological sense (*min-tsu* or nation) were linked in Mao Tse-tung's thought.

Few substantial texts by Mao are available outside China for the period of nearly two and a half years from the appearance of this and two briefer articles in the Chinese Communist Party organ *Hsiang-tao* (The guide) until Mao took up the editorship of the Kuomintang organ *Cheng-chih chou-pao* (The political weekly) in December 1925. He spoke briefly at the First KMT Congress in January 1924, and drafted some resolutions for submission to the KMT Central Executive Committee (of which he was a member) in February 1924. Even in this formal context, some of Mao's utterances illustrate the persistent traits of his work style and political strategy. Thus, at the first KMT Congress, he opposed a proposal for setting up a 'research department' on the grounds that this would have as its consequence 'the separation of research from application – something which our party, as a revolutionary party, cannot do'.[52]

Following his sojourn in Shanghai as a member of the Shanghai Executive Bureau of the KMT, Mao returned in early 1925 to Hunan for a rest, and began his practical apprenticeship in organizing the peasants. He came back to Canton in the autumn of 1925 to take de facto charge

---

[52] *Chung-kuo Kuo-min-tang ch'üan-kuo tai-piao ta-hui hui-i-lu* (Minutes of the National Congress of the Kuomintang of China), 47.

of the Kuomintang Propaganda Department, edit *Cheng-chih chou-pao*, begin lecturing at the Peasant Movement Training Institute (which he was to head from May to October 1926), and participate in the Second Congress of the KMT. By this time he had come to hold the view, from which he was never afterwards to waver, that the centre of gravity of China's revolution lay with the peasants in the countryside.

Enumerating the weak points of Kuomintang propaganda in his report on the subject to the Second Congress in January 1926, Mao noted: 'We have concentrated too much on the cities and ignored the peasants.'[53] To some extent, this shift in Mao's outlook merely reflected the changing pattern of the revolution itself: the increasing militancy of the peasantry, and the activity of P'eng P'ai and many others, as well as of Mao, in mobilizing the peasants. Only by tapping this potential, Mao had concluded, would the revolutionary party (or parties) be able to create the force necessary to the achievement of their anti-imperialist goals – which Mao continued to proclaim in all his writings of the 'peasant period', 1925–7. But though the Chinese Communist Party, or a substantial fraction of it, turned its attention to the peasantry in the mid-1920s, the case of Mao Tse-tung is unique, not only in the obvious sense that he subsequently assumed the leadership of a revolution which effectively encircled the cities from the countryside, but because he formulated as early as 1926 theoretical propositions foreshadowing the future course of the Chinese revolution.

The emergence of Mao's ideas regarding a peasant-based revolution has probably been the subject of more discussion than any other single topic in the history of the Chinese Communist movement. Many historical and theoretical questions have been clarified in the course of this scholarly debate, but some points have until very recently remained obscure for lack of adequate documentation. In his interviews of 1936 with Edgar Snow, Mao declared that he had become aware of the revolutionary potential to be found in the Chinese peasantry only after the May Thirtieth incident of 1925 and the subsequent upsurge of patriotic sentiment in the countryside as well as in the city. The available evidence tends to confirm Mao's statement, and indeed suggests that he truly shifted his attention to the problem of rural revolution only toward the end of 1925. In order to bring out the over-arching continuity in Mao's thinking, despite such shifts of focus, however, it is appropriate to say a few words about his attitude toward the peasantry on the eve of the foundation of the Chinese Communist Party, before analysing the ideas he put forward in 1926–7.

In the latter part of 1919, Mao had drawn up an extensive plan for

[53] Day, 232; *MTTC* 1.151.

promoting 'new villages' along the lines earlier advocated in Japan, and a chapter from this was published in Changsha in December. Apart from the 'new village' slogan itself, this article called for young Chinese to follow the example of Russian youth in entering the villages to preach socialism.[54] In both these respects, the ideas advocated by Mao on this occasion reflected Li Ta-chao's influence.[55] Other elements, however, such as the discussion of the concept of 'work and study' in the United States, of which 'our Chinese students in America have taken advantage' seem to come rather from Dewey and Hu Shih.

More important, however, than these intellectual influences was Mao's own experience of peasant life, upon which he drew in developing his ideas in the early 1920s. In a lecture of September 1922, at the Self-Study University, Mao expounded views on the class structure of the Chinese countryside contained in an article published in a party organ in December 1920. Although Mao most probably had not written this article, he implicitly endorsed the analysis put forward there by taking it as his text. Refuting those who said that the life of the Chinese peasants was not so very hard, and the distribution of land not so very unequal, Mao divided the 'classes making up the peasantry' into four categories:

1. Those who own a lot of land but do not till it themselves (either employing people to till it, or renting it out for cultivation) and sit at home collecting rent. Such people do not really count as peasants, and where I come from we call them local moneybags [*t'u ts'ai-chu*].
2. Those who till their own land and are able to keep their whole family on the produce. They may also rent other people's land and till it, in addition to their own. These are the middle peasants.
3. Those who do have a bit of land, but are quite unable to keep their whole family on what it produces, and who thus have no alternative but to rely on tilling other people's land and being allotted a measure of what is produced in order to support themselves. These can be called lower [*hsia-chi*] peasants.
4. There are the paupers [*ch'iung kuang-tan*], who have not even a piece of land big enough to stick a needle into it, and rely exclusively on other people's land to keep body and soul together. These are the poorest of all the peasants.

The third and fourth categories, said Mao, made up the overwhelming majority of the peasantry, and moreover those in the third category were constantly being obliged by debt to sell their land to the 'rural money-bags' or the middle peasants, and descend into the fourth category.[56]

54 Mao Tse-tung, 'Hsüeh-sheng chih kung-tso' (The work of the students), *Hunan chiao-yü* (Hunan education), 1.2 (Dec. 1919), quoted in Wang Shu-pai and Chang Shen-heng, *LSYC* 5 (1980) 59–60.
55 See Maurice Meisner, *Li Ta-chao and the origins of Chinese Marxism*, esp. 55–6 and 80–9.
56 'Kao Chung-kuo ti nung-min' (Address to China's peasants) was originally published in *Kung-ch'an-tang* 3 (23 December 1920); it is reproduced in *I-ta ch'ien-hou* (Before and after the First Congress), 207–14. The fact that Mao gave a lecture using this text is noted in Li Jui, 455. The attribution of authorship to Mao in *Tzu-liao hsuan-pien*, 24, appears to be wrong.

Although the analysis is far more rudimentary, one can detect a faint resemblance between the text I have just summarized and Mao's two articles of January and February 1926, analysing respectively the class structure of the Chinese countryside and of Chinese society as a whole.[57] When, after analysing class relations in the countryside, and discussing the exploitation of the tenants by extortionate rents, and the tendency toward the concentration of land ownership, Mao went on to draw the political consequences, he adopted a categorically egalitarian position. 'We members of the human race,' he declares, 'are all equal as we come from our mother's womb; all of us should, in the same way, have food to eat and clothes to wear, and we should all work in the same way.' Formerly, everyone had used the land in common; the private property which allowed a minority to live in idleness, eating meat and wearing satin, was based on nothing else but the theft of what should rightfully belong to the peasants, and the peasants should arise and take it back. As soon as they arose, communism (which meant food and work for all) would come to their aid.[58] No doubt this rhetoric was designed to appeal to the peasants' mentality, but it also reflected the fact that, even in 1922, neither Mao nor the Chinese Communist Party as a whole had a coherent and realistic strategy for rural revolution. Four years later Mao had gone a long way toward the elaboration of such a strategy.

The general level of Mao's understanding of Marxist theory in 1925–6 was by no means high. Toward the beginning of his article of February 1926, he declared: 'In any country, wherever it be under the heavens, there are three categories of people; upper, middle, and lower.'[59] In this general framework, he classified the big landlords as part of the big bourgeoisie, and the small landlords as part of the bourgeoisie, and defined sub-groups in classes, both urban and rural, as much by their levels of wealth or poverty as by their relation to the means of production. In thus stressing whether or not peasant households could 'make ends meet', rather than the more orthodox Marxist criteria of land ownership or the hiring of labourers as the standard for defining strata in Chinese rural society, Mao adopted a framework quite different from that employed in 1923 by Ch'en Tu-hsiu.[60]

---

[57] 'Analysis of the various classes of the Chinese peasantry and their attitudes toward revolution' (January 1926) and 'Analysis of all the classes in Chinese society' (February 1926), in *MTTC* 1.153–73; extracts from the article on the peasantry analogous to the passages quoted above are translated in *PTMT* 241–6. [58] *I-ta ch'ien-hou*, 212–14.

[59] Mao Tse-tung, 'Chung-kuo she-hui ko chieh-chi ti fen-hsi' (Analysis of all the classes in Chinese society), *MTTC* 1, 161–74. The sentence quoted is translated in *PTMT* 211.

[60] I have compared Mao's analysis of class relations in the countryside and that of Ch'en Tu-hsiu in my article 'Mao Zedong and the role of the various classes in the Chinese revolution 1923–1927', in *Chūgoku no seiji to keizai* (The polity and economy of China – The late Professor Yuji Muramatsu commemoration volume), 227–39.

It is therefore entirely wrong to argue[61] that Mao's categories and those of Ch'en were basically the same. But it is true that the main difference between the two men, and Mao's essential originality, lay elsewhere, namely in his resolve to make rural revolution on the basis of his own experience, and in his propensity to interpret, or even mould analysis to fit tactical goals.

Mao's analysis of social forces in China in their attitudes toward revolution in fact took shape in late 1925. One of five articles he contributed to the first five issues of *Cheng-chih chou-pao* under the pseudonym 'Tzu Jen' outlined essentially the same scheme he was to use in early 1926, minus the division of the peasant proprietors and other 'petty bourgeois' elements into those with a surplus, those who could just make ends meet, and those who did not have enough to live on.[62] In this piece, published in January, but corresponding probably to the substance of a speech he delivered in October 1925 to the First Kwangtung Provincial Congress of the KMT, Mao discussed, basically in the same terms he was to use in his famous article 'Analysis of all the classes in Chinese society' of February 1926, the implications of social divisions for political behaviour, and more particularly for factionalism within the Kuomintang. Here the apparently unorthodox division of society into 'upper', 'middle' and 'lower' came into its own, for having put the upper classes (big bourgeoisie and big landlords) firmly in the camp of the counter-revolution, and the lower classes (petty-bourgeoisie, semi-proletariat, urban and rural, and proletariat) in the camp of revolution, Mao proceeded to consider how the 'bourgeoisie' (national bourgeois and small landlords) would be pulled asunder and forced to choose, in the wake of the polarization which had developed following the emergence of the 'Western Hills' faction. As he did in 1926, and was consistently to do thereafter, Mao placed the overwhelming majority of the Chinese people (395 out of 400 million) on the side of revolution, leaving only one million hard-core reactionaries,

---

[61] As Philip Huang has done in his article 'Mao Tse-tung and the middle peasants, 1925–1928', *Modern China*, 1.3 (July 1975), 279–80.

[62] These articles were first attributed to Mao Tse-tung by John Fitzgerald in his article 'Mao in mufti: newly identified works by Mao Zedong', *The Australian Journal of Chinese Affairs*, 9 (January 1983) 1–16. Fitzgerald's arguments are altogether convincing in themselves, but the fact of Mao's authorship was also confirmed by Hu Hua, head of the Department of Party History of People's University, in a conversation with me on 10 September 1982. For a complete translation of Mao's article entitled 'The reasons underlying the secession of the GMD rightist faction and its ramifications for the future of the revolution', *Cheng-chih chou-pao*, 4 (10 January 1926) 10–12, see Fitzgerald, 9–15. Mao had, in fact, taken the name Tzu-jen as an alternative style as early as 1910, when he was a student at the Tungshan Higher Primary School. He did so out of respect for Liang Ch'i-ch'ao, whose influence on Mao at that time has already been noted. Liang's honorific name being Liang Jen-kung, 'Tzu-jen' had the meaning 'son of Jen'. See Li Jui, 'Hsueh-sheng shih-tai ti Mao Tse-tung', 176.

corresponding to the 'upper' category, and four million of those wavering people in the middle, who were torn both ways.[63]

As for the problem of leadership, Mao, in early 1926, while stressing the numerical importance of the peasantry and the degree of privation – and therefore of sympathy for the revolution – prevailing in the countryside, also characterized the urban proletariat as the 'main force' in the revolution.[64] Thus, even though the concept of 'proletarian hegemony' was inserted in this text only in 1951, he did recognize in early 1926 the Marxist axiom that the workers would play the central role in the revolutionary process. In September 1926 he allowed himself to be carried away by enthusiasm for the revolutionary forces which had been unleashed in the countryside to such a point that he turned the axiom of working-class leadership explicitly on its head.[65]

Mao's article, 'The national revolution and the peasant movement', published at this time, begins with the statement: 'The peasant question is the central [chung-hsin] question in the national revolution.' This in itself was not at all remarkable, for the upsurge of revolutionary activity in the country, since the middle of 1925, had forced itself on the attention even of the most urban-oriented, to such an extent that a bow in the direction of the peasant movement had become a cliché automatically included in almost every utterance of a Communist and/or Kuomintang spokesman. Mao's argument demonstrating the importance of the peasantry in terms of the structure of Chinese society was, on the other hand, very remarkable indeed. 'The greatest adversary of revolution in an economically backward semi-colony,' he wrote, 'is the feudal-patriarchal class [the landlord class] in the villages.' It was on this 'feudal landlord class' that the foreign imperialists relied to support their exploitation of the peasantry; the warlords were merely the chieftains of this class. Thus, as the example of Hai-feng showed, the domination of the imperialists and the warlords could be overthrown only by mobilizing the peasantry to destroy the foundations of their rule. 'The Chinese revolution,' he wrote, 'has only this form, and no other.'[66]

Not only did Mao Tse-tung assert the importance of the rural forces

---

[63] For the argument to the effect that the article by Tzu Jen corresponded to Mao's speech of 1 October see Fitzgerald, 5 and 9. The identical figures used in this article and in that of February 1926 for various categories of the population are clearly presented in the table in Fitzgerald, 4. The parallel passages in the two articles stressing that 395 millions support the revolution are translated in Fitzgerald, 14–15, and PTMT 213–14.

[64] Mao Tse-tung, 'Analysis of all the classes', MTTC 1.170; PTMT 247.

[65] Mao Tse-tung, 'Kuo-min ko-ming yü nung-min yun-tung' (The national revolution and the peasant movement), MTTC 1.175–9; for a more detailed discussion, with extracts in translation, see my article 'Mao Zedong and the role of the various classes'.

[66] MTTC 1.175–6.

of reaction in the old society, and of the rural revolutionary forces in overthrowing them – he went on to argue against the importance of the cities:

There are those who say that the rampant savagery exercised by the compradors in the cities is altogether comparable to the rampant savagery of the landlord class in the countryside, and that the two should be put on the same plane. It is true that there is rampant savagery, but it is not true that it is of the same order. In the whole country, the areas where the compradors are concentrated include only a certain number of places such as Hong Kong, Canton, Shanghai, Hankow, Tientsin, Dairen, etc., on the sea coast and the rivers. It is not comparable to the domain of the landlord class, which extends to every province, every *hsien*, and every village of the whole country. In political terms, the various warlords, big and small, are all the chieftains chosen by the landlord class. . . . This gang of feudal landlord chieftains. . .use the comprador class in the cities in order to dally with the imperialists; both in name and in fact the warlords are the hosts, and the comprador class are their followers. Financially, 90 per cent of the hundreds of millions of dollars the warlord governments spend each year is taken directly, or indirectly, from the peasants who live under the domination of the landlord class...Hence, although we are aware that the workers, students, and big and small merchants in the cities should arise and strike fiercely at the comprador class, and directly resist imperialism, and although we know that the progressive working class, especially, is the leader of all the revolutionary classes, yet if the peasants do not arise and fight in the villages, to overthrow the privileges of the feudal-patriarchal landlord class, the power of the warlords and of imperialism can never be hurled down root and branch.

Despite the ritual reference to the 'leading role' of the working class, the implication of this passage is clearly that the real centre of power of the old society is to be found in the countryside, and the real blows must therefore be struck in the countryside. This is spelled out explicitly, in startlingly bald terms, in the concluding paragraph of the article:

The peasant movement in China is a movement of class struggle which combines political and economic struggle. Its peculiarities are manifested especially in the political aspect. In this respect it is somewhat different in nature from the workers' movement in the cities. At present, the political objectives of the urban working class are merely to seek complete freedom of assembly and of association; this class does not yet seek to destroy immediately the political position of the bourgeoisie. As for the peasants in the countryside, on the other hand, as soon as they arise they run into the political power of those village bullies, bad gentry, and landlords who have been crushing the peasants for several thousand years...and if they do not overthrow this political power which is crushing them, there can be no status for the peasants. This is a very important peculiarity of the peasant movement in China today.[67]

In other words, the workers ('at present' – but for how long?) are merely

[67] *Ibid.* 176–7.

reformists, pursuing limited benefits for themselves; they are animated, it could be said, by 'trade union consciousness'. The peasants, on the other hand, not only occupy a decisive position in society, so that they cannot achieve their aims without overthrowing the whole edifice of the old order; they are aware of the situation, and are deliberately waging a broad struggle, political as well as economic.

Never afterwards was Mao to go so far in explicitly putting the peasants in the place of the workers as the conscious vanguard of the revolution. His Hunan peasant report of February 1927 attributed to the poor peasants the leading role in the struggle in the countryside; it did not downgrade the importance of the cities, and of the classes based in the cities, in the same graphic terms, though there are indications suggesting that he had not abandoned his position of the previous September. The famous phrase attributing 70 per cent of the achievements of the revolution to date to the peasants[68] might be interpreted as relating to force rather than to leadership, and as merely describing a temporary condition. Another passage summarizes in capsule form the analysis developed in the September article to the effect that the 'patriarchal feudal class of local tyrants, evil gentry and lawless landlords has formed the basis of autocratic government for thousands of years and is the cornerstone of imperialism, warlordism, and corrupt officialdom', and adds: 'To overthrow these feudal forces is the real objective of the national revolution.'[69]

That the peasantry, though it is an important revolutionary force, must follow the leadership either of the workers or of the bourgeoisie, and cannot play an autonomous political role, is one of the most basic political axioms of Marxism, going back to Marx himself. Mao's theoretical contribution, during the ensuing half century, consisted not in replacing this axiom by its opposite, but in weaving together the principle of working-class leadership and his conviction that the fate of the Chinese revolution ultimately depended on what happened in the countryside.

In September 1926 Mao said, in effect, that the peasants could not emancipate themselves without emancipating the whole of Chinese society. He seemed to be investing them with a mission not unlike that which Marx attributed to the urban proletariat in the capitalist societies of the West. At the same time, as we have seen, he recognized that the workers were the 'leaders of all the revolutionary classes'. These two statements can be reconciled if we take the one as relating to the form of the revolutionary struggle in the immediate future, and the other as defining the long-term pattern of events, though the synthesis implied by such an interpretation would attribute to the peasants a degree of initiative scarcely

---

[68] *MTTC* 1.211–12; *PTMT* 252.   [69] Mao, *SW* 1.27.

compatible with Marxist orthodoxy. In any case, if this was Mao's understanding of the matter, the second half of his approach to the peasant problem would come into play only after the conquest of power, in fixing the pattern for the revolutionary transformation of society. And before that moment arrived, both Mao and the Chinese Communist movement had a long road to travel.

PARTY, ARMY AND MASSES 1927–1937

As noted in the previous section of this chapter, Mao Tse-tung, though he played no part in devising the singular organizational framework of the 'bloc within', worked forcefully to implement it from 1923 onwards. Manifestly, he was able to work effectively in such a context because he attached primary importance to national unification and China's struggle to throw off the domination of the imperialists, and accepted that, for the moment, the Kuomintang and its army were the best instrument for achieving this.

Mao therefore did his utmost, in particular during the eight-month period from October 1925 to May 1926, when he effectively ran the Propaganda Department of the Kuomintang Central Executive Committee, to consolidate the overwhelming majority of the Nationalist Party and its supporters on positions which were radical, but in no sense Communist or Marxist. Indeed, he devoted a large part of his introductory editorial for the Kuomintang organ *The Political Weekly* (*Cheng-chih chou-pao*) to refuting the accusations that Kwangtung was being 'communized'. The true goals of the revolution, he wrote, were 'to liberate the Chinese nation...to bring about the rule of the people...to see that the people attain economic prosperity'.[70] In other words, the goal was to implement the 'Three People's Principles'.

In his article of January 1926, 'The reasons underlying the secession of the KMT rightist faction and its ramifications for the future of the revolution', Mao argued that the emergence of a new rightist faction was not the result of the machinations of the KMT left, but the natural outcome of the interaction between the development of the revolution and the class basis of the KMT. 'The real force for revolution,' he wrote, was the alliance of petty-bourgeoisie, semi-proletariat, and proletariat. Landlord and big-bourgeois elements who had supported the anti-Manchu Revolution of 1911 could not accept the demand for 'people's rights' and 'people's livelihood'. 'Hence, as the revolution has developed and the

---

[70] *MTTC* 1.109–11; translated in Day, 205–6.

KMT has progressed, the old and the new rightist factions have split off one by one like bamboo shoots from their stem.'[71]

At this time, in early 1926, as I noted above in discussing Mao's approach to peasant revolution, he still believed that 395 million of China's 400 million people were on the side of the revolution. Thus he was able to accept Stalin's view that the Kuomintang was the only vehicle for reaching the vast masses, particularly in the countryside.

Following his investigation of the peasant movement in Hunan in early 1927, Mao's views on this and other matters changed fundamentally. He expressed his new insights more forthrightly in a separate report, dated 16 February 1927, to the Central Committee of the Chinese Communist Party than he did in the well-known document openly published at the time. Dividing the course of events in the countryside into three periods – that of organizing the peasant associations, that of the rural revolution, and that of setting up a united front – he stressed very strongly that a genuine revolutionary catharsis was indispensable between the first and third stages. The united front would not produce the desired results unless it was preceded by a period of 'fierce struggle to overthrow the power and prestige of the feudal landlords'. To be sure, he said that conflicts which arose in the countryside should, insofar as possible, be dealt with through the KMT apparatus rather than directly by the Communist Party under its own banner, but Mao clearly saw this as a temporary tactic. The masses, he said, were moving toward the left, and were eager for another revolution; the Communist Party must not shrink back from leading them in that direction.[72] Later in 1927, in any case, having lost all hope that Chiang Kai-shek or even the so-called 'Left Kuomintang' would support action by the peasants which went dead against their own class interests, Mao Tse-tung was one of the very first to call for a radical break with these former allies, and for the raising of the red flag in the countryside.

The twenty-two years from the Autumn Harvest uprising to the proclamation of the Chinese People's Republic were spent by Mao Tse-tung almost wholly in a rural environment, and witnessed the emergence and triumph of a strategy of 'surrounding the cities from the countryside'. In this sense, they marked the continuation and fulfilment of his earlier ideas regarding the role of the peasants in the revolution. But they were also years of unremitting military struggle, and to that extent constituted a fundamental rupture with the past. Mao Tse-tung had, of course, known

---

[71] *MTTC, pu chüan,* 2; translated in Fitzgerald, 9–15.

[72] 'Shih-ch'a Hunan nung-yun kei chung-yang ti pao-kao' (Report to the Central Committee on an inspection of the peasant movement in Hunan), *MTTC, pu-chüan,* 2.255–7.

intermittent fighting throughout the greater part of his life, and had been a soldier at the age of 18. He had also shown a keen insight, in 1925–7, into the political opportunities offered by the civil war between the Kuomintang and the northern warlords. It was, however, quite another matter for the Communists to organize their own independent armed forces, and to rely on these as a primary instrument in the revolutionary struggle.

The imprint of this dimension of Mao's experience on his theoretical contributions, beginning in 1927, was many-faceted. To begin with, he developed progressively more elaborate conceptions of the strategy and tactics of guerrilla warfare, which must be regarded as an integral part of his thought as a whole. The matrix of guerrilla warfare which shaped the Chinese Communist movement in Ching-kang-shan, Kiangsi and Yenan days did not, however, merely incite Mao to write about military problems; it also influenced deeply both his ideas as to how revolutionary leadership should be organized, and the spirit which pervaded his outlook. The last point, though very important, should not be exaggerated. Mao's stress on the role of armed force in the Chinese revolution did not make of him, as Wittfogel and others have argued, a thug or fascist who delighted in naked military force for its own sake. It did, however, unquestionably strengthen the emphasis on courage, firmness of heart, and the martial spirit which is visible in his first published article, and never left him until the end of his life.

Of more lasting significance were the patterns of organization and political work adopted by the Chinese Communists at the time, and to some extent conserved by them later, even when circumstances had changed. In a word, a guerrilla army mobilizing peasant masses is a thing quite different from a Communist Party mobilizing the urban workers, and neither the relation between the revolutionary elite and its supporters, nor the ideology which defines and justifies the nature of the whole enterprise, can be entirely the same.

The contrast between the Chinese revolution and its Russian and European predecessors was not, of course, so stark as the preceding one-sentence summary suggests. Even in Kiangsi, if not on the Ching-kang-shan, there was some small-scale industry and therefore some workers; and throughout the whole period 1927–49, there existed a Chinese Communist Party to which the Red Army was theoretically subordinate. Therefore, it was not a question of the army leading the peasants, but of party and army leading 'masses', rural and urban. The fact remains that, throughout the greater part of these twenty-two years, the party existed in significant measure as a soul or parasite in the body of the army. Even to the extent that the Chinese Communist Party appeared on the stage as an actor in its own right, it owed its very survival to the protecting shield of the Red Army, rather than to the solidity of its working-class basis. And though neither party nor army could have endured without the support of a large proportion of the population, the relation of such a Communist movement to the people was different from any which had been known before.

As Mao himself pointed out in later years, the differences between the patterns of the Chinese and Soviet revolutions lay not merely in the fact that the Chinese Communists had engaged in armed struggle, and armed struggle in the countryside. They also flowed from the exercise, by Mao and his comrades, of effective political control over varying but often considerable areas and populations, long before the actual conquest of power. Because of this the Chinese Communist movement stood in a threefold relationship to the people: that of a revolutionary army, seeking to draw from the 'ocean' of the masses the sustenance necessary to the conduct of its operations; that of the 'vanguard party', seeking to guide the proletariat in the accomplishment of its historical mission; and that of government, or state within a state, in which capacity it established with the population under its control a complex network of interactions on many levels.

Mao Tse-tung was one of those most closely attuned to the singular realities of the Chinese revolution, and these various dimensions of the relationship between leaders and masses all find expression in his thought. The over-arching concept which, in principle, infused all of these relationships was that of the 'mass line'.

The mass-line approach to leadership represents a very important element in the political and ideological heritage of the Chinese Communist Party, which sets off Chinese communism from that of the Soviet Union. Although it was fully elaborated by Mao in theoretical terms only in the early 1940s, the key concepts and methods emerged progressively during the previous decade and a half, when the sheer necessity of survival required that the Chinese Communists establish the closest kind of relationship with the populations among whom they worked.

To work with the people did not, however, mean for Mao to lose oneself in them, in some great orgy of populist spontaneity. Nor should the Yenan heritage be romanticized, or sentimentalized, to make of Mao a believer in some kind of 'extended democracy' with overtones of anarchism. The classic directive of 1 June 1943 itself, in which Mao first formulated systematically his ideas on the mass line, reflected, to be sure, his concern that policy-makers should listen to those below and learn from experience at the grass roots. His injunction to 'link the nucleus of leadership closely with the broad masses', and to 'sum up the experience of mass struggles' was seriously meant. But in the end the aim was to take the 'scattered and unsystematic ideas of the masses', turn them into 'concentrated and systematic ideas', and then 'go to the masses and propagate and explain these ideas *until the masses embrace them as their own* (*hua wei ch'ün-chung ti i-chien*)...'[73]

In other words, the people were to be made to interiorize ideas which they were quite incapable of elaborating for themselves. There is a remarkable parallel between this last phrase and Lenin's view that class consciousness could only be imported into the proletariat from outside. And yet there were significant differences between Mao's approach to leadership and that of Lenin, as well as in the revolutions they led. Let us now look at the development of Mao's ideas regarding these matters, from 1927 onwards, beginning first with the role of the army.

In August 1927, when the Central Committee criticized his strategy for the Autumn Harvest uprising, accusing him of attaching undue importance to military force, lacking faith in the strength of the masses, and turning this action into a 'mere military adventure', he replied bluntly that the Central Committee was practising 'a contradictory policy consisting in neglecting military affairs and at the same time desiring an armed insurrection of the popular masses'.[74] In fact, Mao had already answered such criticisms in his remarks at the 7 August emergency conference, where he said:

In the past, we criticized Sun Yat-sen for running a purely military movement, and we did just the opposite, not engaging in any military movement but concentrating on the mass movement....Now we have begun to pay attention to this, but we have not grasped the issue resolutely. For example, the Autumn Harvest uprising will be impossible without attention to military matters, and the present meeting must attach due importance to this question....We must be aware that political power grows out of the barrel of a gun.

This appears to be the first occasion on which Mao used this famous aphorism. He repeated it ten days later at a meeting of the Hunan Provincial Party Committee, adding that in the existing circumstances 60 per cent of the party's energies should be devoted to the military movement.[75] Only armies, Mao was persuaded, or in any case organized

---

[73] *PTMT* 316–17. (Italics added.)

[74] For the text of letters dated 20 and 30 August 1927, and presumed to have been written by Mao, see *MTTC* 2.11–14. Extracts from this correspondence are translated and its implications analysed in my article, 'On the nature of Mao Tse-tung's "deviation" in 1927', *CQ* 27 (April–June 1964), 55–66.

[75] *MTTC*, *pu-chüan*, 2.297–8, 299–300.

and disciplined guerrilla units, could fight armies; the masses could not fight the white armies bare-handed.

For a moment, in the autumn of 1927, the Central Committee, in the context of the chiliastic vision of uninterrupted revolution which had seized the Ch'ü Ch'iu-pai leadership, was persuaded that they could, but these hopes and illusions soon evaporated. For his part, Mao never wavered, after the Autumn Harvest uprising, from the conviction that a Red Army was indispensable to the survival of the revolution.

Until the collapse of the Li Li-san line in the late summer of 1930, Mao Tse-tung was inclined to believe that the central role of the army was merely a temporary phenomenon; thereafter, he came to see the encirclement of the cities from the countryside as the long-term pattern of the Chinese revolution. (I shall return subsequently to the strategic aspect of Mao's thinking.) But despite these changes in his ideas regarding the time-scale of the revolution, his view of the relations between the army and the masses, so long as the form of the struggle was primarily military, remained constant. In essence, they were summed up in the metaphor of the fish and the ocean, which he put forward in the 1930s. Clearly, this formulation does not underestimate the importance of the population, for without the 'ocean' of mass sympathy and support, the 'fish' of the revolutionary army would die helplessly. The Communists must therefore cultivate carefully the sources of popular support, so that the ocean which sustains them does not dry up. But, at the same time, Mao's metaphor makes perfectly clear that the military struggle will be waged by the Red Army on behalf of the masses, and not by the masses themselves.

A detailed analysis of the evolution of Mao Tse-tung's thought in all its aspects from the 1920s to the 1940s would overlap to a great extent with the chronological accounts of chapters 3 and 10. What follows is a succinct summary of the main traits of Mao's ideas regarding the aims and tactics of the revolution, by broad periods.

As early as 1920, in the Ching-kang-shan, Mao discovered the importance not only (as already noted) of regularly constituted guerrilla units, but of base areas, in which the Red Army could rest and recuperate, and where it could develop the contacts with the population without which its campaigns would become mere military adventures. Mao did not, however, at that stage, have a clear idea of the relation between the actions in which he was engaging in a remote mountainous area, and the nationwide 'revolutionary high tide' which not only Li Li-san, but Mao himself, was confidently expecting. In his report of 25 November 1928 on the struggles in the Ching-kang-shan, Mao declared that the activities of his forces did not amount to an insurrection, but merely to 'contending for the country' (*ta chiang-shan*), and would remain so as long as there was no revolutionary high tide in the country as a whole. But very rapidly the idea began to germinate in his mind that the rapid expansion of the territory held by the Red Army could significantly contribute to the rising of the tide. Thus, replying on 5 April 1929 to a letter from the Central Committee advising him and Chu Te to scale down their efforts to small-scale guerrilla activities aimed at arousing the masses, Mao replied that the assessment of the situation on which this advice was founded was excessively pessimistic. It was perfectly feasible, taking advantage of the conflict between Chiang Kai-shek and the Kwangsi clique, to conquer all of Kiangsi, as well as western Fukien and western Chekiang, within one year. At the same time, bases for proletarian struggle could be created in Shanghai, Wusih, Hangchow, Foochow and other places, to lead the struggle in these three provinces.[76]

For its part, the Comintern, though it frequently could not make up its mind as to how fast the high tide was approaching, and consequently whether it should tell the Chinese Communists to advance or consolidate their positions, had a perfectly clear and coherent theoretical position on these matters. In essence, Moscow's view was that the activities of the Red Army and the establishment of base areas in the countryside were important, but could lead to the victory of the revolution only if these activities were carried out side by side with effective work in the cities, to make the urban proletariat once more a force to be reckoned with. Thus, in February 1928, the Executive Committee of the International declared in a Resolution:

In leading spontaneous [*sic*] demonstrations by peasant partisans in the different provinces, the party must bear in mind that these demonstrations can become a starting point for a victorious national uprising only on condition that they are linked with the new upsurge of the tide of revolution in the proletarian centres. Here too, the party must see its main task as the organization of general and coordinated demonstrations in the country and in the *towns, in a number of neighbouring provinces*, and of other uprisings on a *wide* scale.[77]

A Comintern letter of December 1929 gave a decisive impetus to Li Li-san's plans for immediate revolutionary action, by telling the Chinese Communist Party that a new upsurge was beginning, and steps must therefore be taken to set up a peasants' and workers' dictatorship as soon as the tide had risen high enough. The Comintern further explained: 'One distinctive characteristic of the national crisis and the revolutionary upsurge in China is the peasant war.' But although the movement in the

---

[76] For the relevant passage from the report of November 1928, see *MTTC* 2.59. Mao's letter of 5 April 1929 is now available in *MTTC, pu-chüan*, 3.37–45.

[77] Translated in Carrère d'Encausse and Schram, 243. (Italics in Russian original.)

countryside (in which the Comintern lumped together the soviets under Mao's leadership and the activities of traditionalistic organizations such as the 'Red Spears') was 'in the process of becoming one of the courses along which the mighty upsurge of the all-Chinese revolution will continue to develop', the 'truest and most substantial indication of the swelling upsurge' was 'the animation of the workers' movement, which has emerged from its depressed state following the heavy defeat of 1927'.[78]

In other words, guerrilla warfare in the countryside was a legitimate and valuable part of the revolutionary effort, under Chinese conditions, but the more conventional and less exotic activities of the workers in the cities were not only more fundamental, but in the last instance would be more decisive. For his part, Li Li-san was initially far more sceptical than the Comintern regarding the significance of anything which took place in the countryside. In early 1930, however, as he began to lay his plans for a great offensive the following summer, it struck him that the Red Army could provide an extremely useful auxiliary force to distract the attention of the Kuomintang from the workers' movement, and ultimately to permit victory through a two-pronged attack from the cities and from the countryside.

On the issue of the relative weight of the cities and the countryside in the Chinese revolution, Mao Tse-tung and Li Li-san stood at opposite extremes, with Moscow occupying a centrist position. On the two other points, of the time-scale of the revolution and of the central role of China in the world revolution, Mao and Li stood in many respects close to one another, and in opposition to Moscow.

The divergences between Li Li-san and Moscow about the immanence of the revolutionary high tide are somewhat obscured by the fact that communications between China and the Soviet Union were poor, so that letters often took several months to reach their destination. As a result, the two protagonists were often responding to positions which had long since been abandoned. To take only one example, the Comintern letter of June 1930 (commonly dated 23 July in Chinese sources because that is when it was received in Shanghai) was drafted in Moscow in May in response to what was known there of decisions adopted by the Chinese Communist Party in February.[79] Even if the sequence of argument and

[78] *Ibid.* 243–4.
[79] These matters have been clarified by recent Soviet publications, which, though strongly biased in their interpretations, are probably accurate regarding many such factual details, drawn from the Comintern archives. Perhaps the most conveniently available of these is A. M. Grigoriev, 'The Comintern and the revolutionary movement in China under the slogan of the soviets (1927–1931)', in Ulyanovsky, ed., 345–88. The correct date of the June 1930 directive was given in Soviet publications of the 1930s, and there is no excuse whatsoever for continuing to refer to it as the '23 July directive'.

counter-argument is thus obscured, however, this does not prevent us from grasping the broad differences in perspective between Stalin and Li Li-san, though it does complicate the historian's task of assigning responsibility for specific decisions, and in particular for costly blunders, during the first half of 1930. (For these matters see above, chapter 3.)

Thus in June 1930, the Comintern, while noting that there was still not an objective revolutionary situation in the whole country, because the 'waves of the workers' movement and the peasants' movement' had still not merged into one, predicted that the revolutionary situation would shortly encompass 'if not the whole of Chinese territory, then at least the territory of a number of key provinces'.[80] None the less, though the Comintern expected the decisive battles in China to take place in the near future, they did not agree with Li Li-san that the time for an offensive had already come. Moscow therefore explicitly refused to sanction Li's decision to order an attack on Wuhan, Changsha, etc. and for co-ordinated uprisings in those cities, arguing that both the Red Army and the workers' movement should first be further strengthened.[81]

For his part, Mao Tse-tung was initially reluctant to throw his forces against such Kuomintang strongpoints, thus risking both the future of the revolution and the foundations of his own power. To this extent he was in agreement with Moscow. But by early 1930, he had in fact become extremely sanguine regarding the prospects for rapid victory. In a letter of January 1930 to Lin Piao, he criticized Lin for his undue pessimism about the coming of the high tide, and declared that though the time limit of one year he himself had set in April 1929 for the conquest of all of Kiangsi had been 'mechanical', such an achievement was not far off.[82]

Mao Tse-tung's attitude toward the Li Li-san line in 1930 has recently been the subject of a wide-ranging debate among Chinese scholars, enjoying access to the relevant sources. Although some of these authors still adhere to the view laid down in the resolution of 1945 on party history according to which Mao never agreed with Li's plan to attack the cities, and only implemented it because discipline required obedience to orders, others argue that Mao Tse-tung was won over to this strategy by the spring of 1930, and some even go so far as to suggest that from early 1930 he followed it spontaneously and enthusiastically. In any case, there is clear evidence that as late as October 1930 Mao Tse-tung continued to profess a radical line. A resolution adopted in Chi-an on 7 October, when Mao's forces were holding the town, noted the existence of 'a revolutionary situation in the whole world, in the whole country, in all

[80] Carrère d'Encausse and Schram, 244.   [81] Grigoriev, 369–73.
[82] MTTC 2.139.

provinces', and concluded: 'In the course of this revolutionary "high tide"...soviet power must undoubtedly burst upon the scene in the whole country and in the whole world.' And a letter by Mao dated 19 October called for the rejection of pessimism, and for an immediate attack on Nanchang and Chiu-chiang to annihilate the enemy, in the context of the existing 'high tide'.[83]

If there is still room for some disagreement as to the extent of Mao's chiliastic expectation of an immediate and all-encompassing revolutionary tide in the autumn of 1930, since some of the above statements might be interpreted as telling the Central Committee what he thought it wanted to hear, there can be no argument at all about Mao's conviction that the Chinese revolution was a central and decisive factor in the world revolution. And in this respect, he was altogether in agreement with Li Li-san, and aligned with Li against Moscow.[84]

On one point in particular Mao's agreement with Li was complete: they both held that foreigners did not, and could not, understand the Chinese revolution. At the 'trial' to which he was summoned in Moscow in the winter of 1930–1, Li Li-san was quoted by a Comintern inquisitor as saying: 'The Chinese revolution has so many peculiarities that the International has great difficulty in understanding it, and hardly understands it at all, and hence cannot in reality lead the Chinese Communist Party.' In consequence, he was denounced by Manuilsky as an 'extreme localist'. For his part, Mao declared, three decades afterwards:

Speaking generally, it is we Chinese who have achieved understanding of the objective world of China, not the comrades concerned with Chinese questions in the Communist International. These comrades of the Communist International simply did not understand...Chinese society, the Chinese nation, or the Chinese revolution. For a long time even we did not have a clear understanding of the objective world of China, still less the foreign comrades![85]

On another and crucial aspect of this matter, however, Mao Tse-tung did

[83] For articles illustrating a range of views on this issue, see the contributions to the authoritative inner-party journal *Tang-shih yen-chiu* (Research on party history) by Lin Yun-hui, 'Lueh lun Mao Tse-tung t'ung-chih tui Li-san lu-hsien ti jen-shih ho ti-chih' (A brief account of Comrade Mao Tse-tung's understanding of and resistance to the Li-san line), *TSYC* 4 (1980) 51–9; T'ien Yuan, 'Tsai lun Mao Tse-tung t'ung-chih tui Li-san lu-hsien ti jen-shih ho ti-chih' (More on Comrade Mao Tse-tung's understanding of and resistance to the Li-san line), *TSYC* 1 (1981) 65–71; and Ling Yü, 'Mao Tse-tang t'ung-chih ho Li-san lu-hsien ti kuan-hsi t'ao-lun tsung-shu' (A summary of the discussion regarding Comrade Mao Tse-tung's relationship to the Li-san line), *TSYC* 3 (1982) 78–80. The resolution of 7 October 1930 is quoted in an article by Ch'ü Ch'iu-pai in *Shih-hua* (True words) (Shanghai) 2 (9 December 1930), 3–4. For Mao's letter of 19 October, see 'Kei Hsiang tung t'e-wei hsin' (Letter to the East Hunan Special Committee), *MTTC*, *pu-chüan*, 3.157–8.

[84] For a brief summary of some of Li's statements about China's role in the world revolution, see S. Schram, *Mao Tse-tung*, 148–9.

[85] Talk of 30 January 1962, in S. Schram, *Mao Tse-tung unrehearsed*, 172. (See also the official version, translated in *Peking Review* 27 (1978) 14.)

not take the same line as Li Li-san. Li set out quite explicitly to provoke Japanese and other imperialist intervention in North-east China, and thereby to unleash a 'world revolutionary war' into which the Soviet Union would be drawn whether she liked it or not.[86] With such a strategic vision Mao could not possibly agree, for it implied that the fate of the Chinese revolution would ultimately be decided outside China, and not in the first instance by the Chinese themselves. He was, of course, acutely conscious of the weight of the foreign imperialist presence in China, and of the importance of the international factor in the Chinese revolution. It was, however, a corollary of the shift in his sociological perspective, between 1923 and 1926, analysed above, that since the main foundations of the old reactionary order were to be found in landlord domination in the countryside, and not in the influence of the imperialists and their urban allies, victory in the Chinese revolution could only be achieved by mobilizing the workers, peasants and other exploited classes throughout the length and breadth of the land to destroy this 'feudal power' of the landlords and their political agents.

Whatever Mao's position in the summer of 1930, there is no doubt that the retreat from Changsha in September 1930 marked a crucial turning point in his thinking toward a relatively long-term strategy of encircling the cities from the countryside. In such a context, the military tactics he had been developing since he had ascended the Ching-kang-shan and joined forces there with Chu Te, in 1928, became an explicit and integral part of Mao's political thought.

According to Mao's own statement, it was in 1931, by the time Chiang Kai-shek's third 'encirclement and annihilation' campaign had been defeated, that 'a complete set of operational principles for the Red Army' took shape.[87] The earliest known text by Mao himself in which these principles were expounded is a short book entitled *Guerrilla war*, dated 1934.[88] This may well have been his first systematic formulation of the strategic ideas he was to put forward in debates at the Tsun-yi Conference, which marked a decisive stage both in the emergence of a new military line, and in opening the road to Mao's rise to supreme power in the party eight years later.[89] In December 1936, Mao delivered a series of lectures entitled *Problems of strategy in China's revolutionary war*, reviewing in detail

---

[86] Li's 'plot' to involve the Soviet Union in a war for the sake of the Chinese revolution naturally excites great indignation on the part of the Soviet authors; see, for example, Grigoriev, 365–7.

[87] Mao, *SW* 1.213.

[88] For a summary of a portion of this work, see Ch'en Po-chün, 'Lun k'ang-Jih yu-chi chan-cheng ti chi-pen chan-shu: hsi-chi' (On the basic tactic of the anti-Japanese guerrilla war: the surprise attack), *Chieh-fang*, 28 (11 Jan. 1938) 14–19.

[89] The Tsun-yi Conference is dealt with in chapter 4. For the latest and most authoritative collection of sources, see *Tsun-yi hui-i wen-hsien* (Documents on the Tsun-yi Conference).

the lessons of the five encirclement campaigns, and restating his case against his critics. Finally, in 1938, he wrote two works regarding the application of guerrilla tactics in the special circumstances of the Anti-Japanese War: *Questions of strategy in the Anti-Japanese guerrilla war*, and *On protracted war*. A third book, *Basic tactics*, was attributed to him in some editions.[90]

Military tactics is a specialized domain, which cannot be dealt with here at length. What follows therefore tries to view the matter from the interface between war and politics. Mao himself summed up the whole question when he wrote: 'Our strategy is "pit one against ten", and our tactics are "pit ten against one"; these contrary and yet complementary propositions constitute one of our principles for gaining mastery over the enemy.'[91]

The meaning of this aphorism is, of course, as Mao explained at length in the remainder of the passage, that while the Red Army at that time was greatly inferior in numbers and equipment to the Kuomintang and other white forces in the country as a whole, and even in each separate theatre of operations, it should fight only when it enjoyed overwhelming superiority on the battlefield. Such a tactical advantage should be obtained by concentrating the greater part of one's own forces against isolated white units, and thus 'destroying the enemy one by one'. And this, in turn, while it depended partly on skill in using troops, was very largely the result of superior intelligence, obtained by the Red Army thanks to its intimate links with the population.

The methods of the Communists for mobilizing the peasantry and thereby obtaining not only information regarding the adversary's movements but other advantages, such as voluntary service by the masses as porters or auxiliary troops, were different from anything envisaged by China's ancient military strategist Sun Tzu, yet Mao's strictly tactical principles were strikingly similar to those of Sun Tzu, who wrote:

By discovering the enemy's dispositions and remaining invisible ourselves, we can keep our forces concentrated while...the enemy must be split up into fractions. Hence there will be a whole pitted against separate parts of the whole, which means that we shall be many in collected mass to the enemy's separate few [literally, 'ten against one']....And if we are thus able to attack an inferior force with a superior one, our opponents will be in dire straits.[92]

[90] Some of the editions of this book have Mao's name on the title page, others do not, and his authorship is doubtful. Although it appears in a bibliography of Mao's works published by the PLA (Chung-kuo jen-min chieh-fang chün cheng-chih hsueh-yuan hsun-lien pu t'u-shu tzu-liao kuan, *Mao Tse-tung chu-tso, yen-lun, wen-tien mu-lu* (Peking), Feb. 1961, 28), the weight of the evidence at present is against attributing it to Mao. In the introduction to my English translation (*Basic tactics*), I have sketched an interpretation of the stages in the elaboration of Mao's military tactics.   [91] Mao, *SW* 1.237.

[92] Sun Tzu, *The art of war*, Giles' trans., Ch. VI, par. 13.

Mao himself, questioned in his later years about what he had learned from the Chinese classics, was generally whimsical and frequently contradictory in his replies. In one of his most balanced statements, he said in 1968 that he had read the *Romance of the three kingdoms* before he began to fight in 1927, and that he had taken a look at Sun Tzu before writing his own works on military tactics in 1936–8.[93] There is no doubt, in any case, that he very frequently quoted, in these writings, both from Sun Tzu and from historical works, as well as from novels such as the *Romance of the three kingdoms* and *Water margin*.

How did Mao Tse-tung contrive to justify in theoretical terms the view that a Communist Party of uncertain composition, operating primarily through the instrumentality of the army, in a highly ambiguous social context, could yet constitute the vanguard of the proletariat? A crucial issue here is the role of the subjective factors in defining man's class nature, and the possibility of modifying a person's objective essence by changing his thinking. We have seen that Mao's emphasis on the importance of subjective attitudes goes back to 1917. One of the most striking formulations of the period under consideration here is to be found in his report of 28 November 1928 on the struggle on the Ching-kang-shan. Discussing the problem raised by the fact that the greater part of his small Red Army was made up not of workers, or even of proper peasants, but of rural vagabonds or *éléments déclassés*, Mao said:

The contingent of *éléments déclassés* should be replaced by peasants and workers, but these are not available now. On the one hand, when fighting is going on every day, the *éléments déclassés* are after all especially good fighters. Moreover, casualties are mounting high. Consequently, not only can we not diminish the *éléments déclassés* now in our ranks, but it is even difficult to find more for reinforcements. In these circumstances, the only method is to intensify political training, so as to effect a qualitative change in these elements.[94]

In his letter of January 1930 to Lin Piao, Mao criticized Lin for 'over-estimating the importance of objective forces and underestimating the importance of subjective forces'.[95] By 'objective forces' Mao meant in particular the white armies, which were outside the Communists' direct control, whereas 'subjective forces' referred to the Red Army, which they perceived from inside, and whose motivation and strategy they therefore understood. But it is plain that he was also talking about objective factors in the broader sense of objective historical circumstances, and subjective factors in the sense of the human capacity to influence those circumstances by 'conscious action'.

[93] Dialogue with Red Guards, 28 July 1968, in *Miscellany of Mao Tse-tung thought*, 476 (JPRS no. 61269). Chinese in *Mao Tse-tung ssu-hsiang wan-sui* (1969), 694.
[94] *MTTC* 2.36–7; *PTMT* 268–9.   [95] *MTTC* 2.130.

This element in Mao's thinking had been, as I suggested earlier, reinforced by the context of military struggle in which he developed his ideas and undertook to make revolution from 1927 onwards. Mao saw war as the highest manifestation of 'conscious action' and the supreme test of the human spirit. He put the point in a passage which he liked so much that he repeated it in almost identical words in 1936 and in 1938:

Conscious activity is a distinctive characteristic of man, especially of man at war. This characteristic is manifested in all of man's acts, but nowhere more strongly than in war. Victory or defeat in a war is decided on the one hand by the military, political, economic, and geographical conditions, by the character of the war, and by international support on both sides. But it is not decided by these alone; these alone constitute only the possibility of victory or defeat; they do not in themselves decide the issue. To decide the issue, subjective efforts must be added, efforts in directing and waging the war, i.e. conscious activity in war.

People who direct a war cannot strive for victories beyond the limit allowed by the objective conditions, but within that limit they can and must strive actively for victory. The stage of action for these directors of war must be built upon objective conditions, but on this stage, they can direct the performance of many living dramas, full of sound and colour, of power and grandeur...[96]

This passage eloquently expresses what I have called Mao Tse-tung's 'military romanticism', born out of the experience of many years of bitter struggle for survival. It would, however, be a gross over-simplification to interpret Mao's faith in the limitless capacities of man, and especially of the Chinese people, solely in terms of his romantic temperament, or of his life of combat. His emphasis on subject factors corresponded also, as I have already suggested, to the necessities of revolution in a transitional society made up of many disparate elements.

It is this aspect of Chinese reality which provides the link between the military and political dimensions of Mao's thought and experience. Just as the outcome of a battle can rarely be predicted with certainty, but depends in part, as Mao stressed in the passage just quoted, on subjective factors such as the courage of the soldiers and the tactical skill of the commanders, so the terms of the political combat appeared less clearly defined in China than in Western Europe or even in the former Russian empire. Although the Chinese Communist Party and the Kuomintang might be regarded loosely as the representatives respectively of the workers and of the capitalists, the socio-economic weight of the peasants in the former, and of the landlords in the latter, was in fact greater. Moreover, the picture was significantly modified by the impact of the foreign presence. Marx and Engels, with reference to the Polish question, and Lenin, with reference to the colonies in the twentieth century, had

[96] *MTTC* 6.98–9, 284–5.

already established the principle that the behaviour of classes within a
given society might be modified by a reaction of solidarity against the
foreign oppressor. Mao Tse-tung, for his part, did not merely accept this
as a theoretical possibility; he was persuaded, from the early 1930s onward,
that an alliance for the pursuit of national goals could be effectively
realized, and that its establishment depended in large part on the success
of the Communists in modifying the subjective attitudes of other strata
of Chinese society, apart from the workers and their immediate allies
the peasantry.

This concern with national unity as the condition of national salvation,
though it marked Mao's thought and policies to a greater or lesser degree
from beginning to end, by no means signified that he had become a mere
nationalist. Even in the late 1930s, as he concluded and implemented a
new alliance with Chiang Kai-shek, Mao made crystal clear that the
Chinese Communist Party had no intention of abandoning its maximum
programme. And in the late 1920s and early 1930s, social revolution was
the main focus of his thought and action. Nor did he approach it solely
in terms of moral values and psychological transformation. Though he
believed that objective social realities could be modified by changes in
consciousness, he also saw participation in revolutionary action as one
of the most effective means for changing men's thinking. Indeed, an acute
awareness of the interaction between the subjective and the objective, and
the deliberate manipulation of this dialectic was one of the hallmarks of
Mao Tse-tung's thought, and one of the secrets of his political success.

The concept of revolutionary struggle as an instrument for promoting
cultural revolution was formulated by Mao as early as 1927, in his Hunan
peasant report, where he wrote: 'The abolition of the clan system, of
superstitions, and of one-sided notions of chastity will follow as a natural
consequence of victory in the political and economic struggles. ... The
idols should be removed by the peasants themselves...'[97]

Throughout the ensuing two decades, the countryside remained the
main theatre of Mao's experiments both in social and in cultural revolution.
The heart of his activity in this domain was, of course, land reform. That
topic is not discussed here, because agrarian policy has been dealt with
at length in chapter 5. One episode, which offers particularly striking
illustration of Mao's faith in the technique of changing attitudes through
revolutionary struggle, was the 'land verification movement' of 1933-4.
Mao may not have launched this, but he did place his stamp on it in 1933.
The ostensible economic goal of this campaign, which was to determine
whether or not land reform had been properly carried out, in fact merely

[97] MTTC 1.237-8; PTMT 259.

provided the framework within which to pursue essentially political aims. Given the inherited prestige of the landlords and rich peasants, and the fact that they had the advantage of literacy and facility in speech, Mao was convinced that whatever changes were made in the formal property structure, these formerly privileged elements would succeed in one way or another in worming their way back into positions of authority in the peasant associations. The only way to prevent such a disguised return to the old order of things was constantly to stir up the peasantry at the grass roots and encourage poor peasants to engage in struggle against their former exploiters, in order to develop their self-confidence and allow the conviction to take root that henceforth they were the masters of society.

Exactly similar aims were pursued during the land reforms which accompanied and followed the civil war and the conquest of power in the late 1940s. The mass meetings, at which the peasants were encouraged to 'speak their bitterness' against the landlords for their previous oppression, followed in some cases by the execution of the worst offenders, were designed not only to break the spirit of the gentry, but above all to allow the peasants to rid themselves of their inferiority complex and stand up as men at last. Thus Mao undertook to carry out a cultural revolution in the sense of a change in attitudes toward authority, and used revolutionary struggle as an instrument toward this end. But while this method of work was prominent in his line from the 1920s to the 1940s and after, the political context within which he applied these techniques changed significantly over the years.

A crucial aspect of the tactical situation during the period of the Kiangsi Soviet Republic was the contradiction between military and political imperatives. In order to obtain maximum support from the population, Mao Tse-tung and Chu Te had practised in earlier years the principle of 'luring the enemy deep' into the heart of the base area, where land reform had been carried out and the sympathy for the Red Army was therefore warmest. These tactics meant, however, that the faithful supporters of the Communist forces were frequently exposed to the perils and losses of war, and this undermined the credibility of the Chinese Soviet Republic to constitute a veritable state within a state, since it could not protect its own citizens. In a sense, the 'forward and offensive strategy' constituted a response to this dilemma – a response which consisted in putting the political imperative of defending the prestige and integrity of the soviet republic ahead of realistic evaluation of the military possibilities. It ended in disaster, but that does not necessarily mean that Mao's earlier tactics would have worked in 1934. In any case, it was only the rapidly accelerating Japanese advance into China, and the consequent threat to China's very survival as an independent nation, which effectively allowed the Communists to break out of the dilemma in which they found themselves. Moreover, it was only in the new circumstances which took shape in 1935–7 that Mao, who had had little of any theoretical interest to say for several years, once more began to speak out in confident tones. No doubt the fact that he was again in a strong position in the party, whereas in 1933–4 he had been reduced to little more than a figurehead, had something to do with his new eloquence. But the phenomenon also resulted, unquestionably, from the fact that a war for national liberation was something about which he had a great deal to say. Even in the early 1930s, Mao's statements about the relation between the internal and external enemies of the revolution were suggestive of what was to come.

The evolution which brought Communists and Kuomintang, and the old enemies Mao Tse-tung and Chiang Kai-shek, once more into an alliance was very much against the grain of both parties. What was the theoretical justification which Mao put forward for the second united front?

In September 1931, when the Japanese action in Manchuria first brought to the fore the issue of resistance to foreign aggression, the position of the Chinese Communist Party regarding collaboration with the bourgeoisie was basically similar to that of the Comintern, summed up in the slogan of 'class against class'. Nevertheless, although this was understood to mean in principle the struggle for hegemony between the proletariat and the bourgeoisie, Mao's sociological vision of the concrete struggle remained that which he had entertained in 1926. A letter of 25 September 1931, signed by Mao and others, to 'our brothers the soldiers of the White Army', after calling on them to kill their reactionary superior officers and unite with the workers, peasants, and toiling masses to overthrow the 'fucking Kuomintang government', continued:

confiscate the land of the landlord class and distribute it among the poor peasants; confiscate the food and the houses of the wealthy and distribute them among the poor; let the workers do only eight hours of work a day; then, organize yourselves to run your own affairs. In this way, you will have created a government of workers, peasants, and soldiers, that is, a soviet government.[98]

Clearly, for Mao the countryside was where the Chinese revolution principally was at. In this text, the 'Kuomintang militarists' were treated as the 'running dogs of imperialism', as well as the creatures of the landlord class, just as in Mao's writings of the 1920s, but the domestic reactionary role of the Kuomintang in 'exploiting and butchering the

98 *MTTC* 3.14; *PTMT* 219.

masses' was still given the greatest prominence. To the extent that Mao's attack focused on the problem of resistance to Japanese aggression, his position was the mirror image of Chiang Kai-shek's 'unify before resisting'. Since 'only the Red Army' could 'overthrow imperialism and really defend the people', it was necessary first to deal with the domestic enemy, in order to make possible effective action against the foreign invader.

In April 1932, in the wake of the Japanese aggression against Shanghai in January of that year, the Chinese Soviet government declared war on Japan, thus bringing questions of foreign affairs closer to the centre of its political strategy. A change in Mao's outlook regarding collaboration with other political forces was signalled by a declaration of 17 January 1933, which offered, on certain conditions (cessation of attacks on the soviet regions, granting of democratic rights, and arming of the masses against Japan), to conclude an agreement with 'any armed force', that is, with any dissident commander prepared to deal with the Communists.[99] Although this position still remained within the framework of the 'united front from below' laid down in the line of the Comintern, that is to say, an alliance with the supporters of other political movements rather than with their leaders, the willingness to deal with high-ranking officers of the Kuomintang (though not with Chiang Kai-shek himself) marked a significant step toward the 'united front from above' which was to be set up in 1937.

In the proclamation on the northward march of the Red Army to fight Japan, which he signed on 15 July 1934 together with Chu Te, Mao called once again for a 'national revolutionary war', and an alliance with those willing to wage such a war, while striving to overthrow the 'band of traitors of the Kuomintang'.[100] Nevertheless, while Mao Tse-tung gave high place to nationalism as an idea and a political force, he was markedly more reticent than the Soviet leaders about going all the way to a second united front, and the declaration of 1 August 1935 calling for such a front was in fact issued from Moscow on behalf of the Chinese Communist Party by Wang Ming, in the context of the Seventh Comintern Congress.

For their part, Mao and his comrades found it far more distasteful than did Stalin to embrace once again Chiang Kai-shek, whom they knew as the butcher of their friends and perceived as a traitor to the revolution. By the end of 1935, as his forces regrouped in December in Wayaobao, Mao was prepared to cooperate not only with the 'national bourgeoisie' but with those sectors of the capitalist class who were linked to European

<hr>

[99] *Su-wei-ai Chung-kuo*, 91–4; *MTTC* 3.183–5.   [100] *MTTC* 4.363–7; *PTMT* 220–2.

and American imperialism, and were therefore inclined to oppose
'Japanese imperialism and its running dogs'. With their support, the
'workers' and peasants' republic' would be changed into a 'government
of national defence'. But Chiang Kai-shek, as the 'chieftain' of the 'camp
of traitors to the nation', and the representative of the evil gentry,
warlords and compradors, was specifically excluded from the proposed
united front.[101]

By April 1936, however, Chang Hsueh-liang had met with Chou En-lai,
and had urged the Communists to stop fighting Chiang and concentrate
on the Japanese, promising to use his influence with Chiang to persuade
him to accept such a truce. On 5 May 1936, a telegram was accordingly
addressed directly to the Military Affairs Council in Nanking, and this
was subsequently characterized by Mao as marking the 'abandonment of
the anti-Chiang Kai-shek slogan'.[102] Henceforth, Mao was in regular
contact with Chang Hsueh-liang, Yang Hu-ch'eng and other political and
military leaders about the possibility of cooperation against Japan,[103]
writing in particular to Chang on 5 October 1936 expressing his desire
for an 'agreement between the Kuomintang and the Communist Party
to resist Japan and save the country'. On 1 December 1936, Mao signed,
together with eighteen other senior Communist political and military
leaders, a letter to Chiang himself, expressing the hope that he would
change his ways, so posterity would remember him not as the man
responsible for China's ruin, but as 'the hero who saved the country and
the people'.[104]

All of these gestures, which were based on political realism, did not
mean that the feelings of the Communists toward Chiang had changed
fundamentally. When he was taken prisoner by Chang Hsueh-liang and
Yang Hu-ch'eng in Sian on 12 December, there was an instinctive
reaction on the part of Communist cadres, high and low, that it would
be very agreeable to put him on trial for his crimes against the revolution,
but there is no evidence that such a policy was seriously considered by
Mao and others at the top level. On the contrary, Mao Tse-tung wrote
to Yen Hsi-shan on 22 December 1936 assuring him that 'we do not in
the least wish to take revenge on Nanking'.[105] Mao's frequently reported
rage on receipt of a peremptory telegram from Moscow ordering him not
to kill Chiang was therefore provoked not by frustration at being deprived

[101] Report of 27 December 1935, Mao, *SW* 1.153–78. The term used in the *Selected works* is 'people's government'; I am assuming that Mao originally spoke in 1935, like the Central Committee resolution of two days earlier (*MTTC* 5.26–8), of a government of national defence.
[102] Mao, *SW* 1.264, 279–80.
[103] See the numerous letters from the second half of 1936 in *Selected letters*, 30–97.
[104] *Ibid.* 78–9, 87–90.   [105] *Ibid.* 95–7.

of his victim, but by Stalin's doubts about his loyalty, or his common sense.[106]

In any case, once embarked on a policy of cooperation with the Kuomintang, the Chinese Communists, and Mao in particular, showed themselves inclined to throw themselves into it with a will. The reason was, manifestly, that for them the salvation of the Chinese nation was not merely, as for Lenin, the basis for tactical manoeuvres; it was a value in itself.

Mao could not, of course, call for a change of such importance without justifying it, both for himself and for his followers, in terms of the stage currently reached by the Chinese revolution, and the tasks which could accordingly be pursued at that time. He began to sketch out his ideas on this theme in his speech of 27 December 1935 just mentioned; they were fully elaborated and given their definitive formulation only in 1939–40. But before continuing this discussion of Mao's political thought, which reached a notably higher level of maturity and complexity during the Yenan period, it is necessary to give some account of the emergence, in 1937, of philosophical ideas which were to occupy an increasingly central place in his thinking as a whole.

NATIONAL CONTRADICTIONS AND SOCIAL CONTRADICTIONS 1937–1940

While Mao Tse-tung had occasionally touched on philosophical questions in his writings of the 1920s and 1930s, it was in the winter of 1936–7 that he first undertook the serious study of Marxist philosophy. Edgar Snow has recorded how Mao interrupted the interviews, which were to form the basis for his autobiography, in order to devour a pile of Soviet works on philosophy in Chinese translation which had just reached the Communist capital of Pao-an. Having read these, Mao proceeded almost immediately to deliver a series of lectures on dialectical materialism, of which the works now known as 'On practice' and 'On contradiction' were originally the concluding sections.[107]

Only 'On practice' and 'On contradiction' have, of course, been

---

[106] For details regarding the sequence of events, and further references, see above, ch. 12 by Lyman Van Slyke. The above interpretation is based on interviews with Hu Hua and Li Hsin, respectively on 10 and 23 September 1982 in Peking.

[107] 'Pien-cheng-fa wei-wu-lun (chiang-shou t'i-kang)' (Dialectical materialism – lecture notes) in *K'ang-chan ta-hsueh*, 6 to 8 (April to June 1938). This portion of the text includes chapter 1, and the first six sections of chapter 2. It is not known whether or not the remainder of the work was serialized in *K'ang-chan ta-hsueh*. Sections 7 to 10 of chapter 2 were included in a version circulated during the Cultural Revolution (*Mao Chu-hsi wen-hsuan*), and the whole of the first two chapters, less section 11 of chapter 2 (corresponding to 'On practice'), was reproduced in *MTTC* 6.265–305. Subsequently, two editions of the work containing the original version of

officially published in China since 1949, respectively in 1950 and 1952. The contemporary evidence that Mao did in fact deliver a course of lectures on dialectical materialism in 1937 is, however, conclusive and irrefutable.[108] It is therefore of some moment that, when asked about the matter by Edgar Snow in 1965, Mao denied authorship of *On dialectical materialism*.[109] It is true that he generally preferred people to read his works only in editions revised and approved by himself, but he did not always go to the trouble of explicitly repudiating items no longer thought suitable.

The reasons for Mao's sensitivity in this case are not far to seek. A reputation as a Marxist theoretician and philosopher has been regarded, since Lenin's day, as one of the indispensable qualifications for leadership within the Communist movement. It was no doubt with the aim of establishing his credentials in this respect (as Stalin had sought to do before him) that Mao had originally delivered these lectures. His rivals in the party, with whom he was to have an ongoing trial of strength during the next five or six years, were all schooled in Moscow, and he thus felt himself vulnerable to the charge that he was nothing but a leader of peasant guerrillas, with no grasp of Marxist theory and no capacity for dealing with abstract categories. It soon became apparent, however, that Mao's lectures on dialectical materialism did not effectively serve their purpose. In very large part, they amounted (especially in the early sections) to unashamed plagiarism of his Soviet sources, and where Mao had expressed himself in his own words, the result was often very crude.[110]

'On practice' have come to light, and one of these also contains chapter 3, corresponding to 'On contradiction'. The complete text appears in *MTTC*, *pu-chüan*, 5.187–280. For a translation of selected passages and a detailed analysis both of the form and of the content of the original version of 'On contradiction', see Nick Knight, 'Mao Zedong's *On contradiction* and *On practice*: pre-liberation texts', *CQ* 84 (December 1980), 641–68. Mr Knight has also published a complete translation: *Mao Zedong's 'On contradiction'. An annotated translation of the pre-liberation text*.

108 It suffices to mention three points, any of which would be sufficient in itself. The first is that, as already indicated, a considerable portion of the text was published at the time in *K'ang-chan ta-hsüeh*. The second is the reference to this work by Chang Ju-hsin, then (with Ch'en Po-ta) one of those most actively engaged in building up Mao as a theoretician, in an article published in *Chieh-fang jih-pao* (18 and 19 February 1942), where he characterized it as the most important source on Mao's methodology and dialectics. Finally, almost the whole text of the work, broken up into fragments by theme, is reproduced in an authorized compilation on Mao's philosophical thought: 'Pei-ching ta-hsüeh che-hsüeh hsi', *Mao Tse-tung che-hsüeh ssu-hsiang (chai-lu)*, 11–14, 19–21, 49–51, 53–5, 64–9, 97–9 and *passim*.

109 As originally published in *The New Republic*, this disclaimer was strong, but Mao carefully edged away from a flat statement that he had never given any such lectures; when the interview was re-published as an appendix to *The long revolution*, it was 'improved' to make of it a categorical denial of authorship. A comment by Snow (*The long revolution*, 194–5) suggests that this may have been done at the request of the Chinese authorities, or of Mao himself.

110 On Mao's plagiarism, see the note in my article 'Mao Tse-tung and the theory of the permanent revolution, 1958–1969', *CQ* 46 (April–June 1971), 223–4; also K. A. Wittfogel, 'Some remarks

In the context of the view (explicitly stated in 1981, but implicit since 1978 or 1979) that Mao Tse-tung was a man subject to human error, and that 'Mao Tse-tung thought' was not his creation alone, both the fact that Mao did indeed lecture on dialectical materialism in 1937, and his debt to other authors, especially to Ai Ssu-ch'i, have now been officially placed on record in China.[111]

I shall not analyse here Mao's lectures as a whole, but this episode does provide valuable background for evaluating the two essays that did become an integral part of 'Mao Tse-tung thought'. The first point to be made is that the portions of the lectures corresponding to 'On practice' and 'On contradiction' are notably more original and more interesting than the earlier part of the work. Moreover, while epistemology was often dealt with at some length in writings and translations from Soviet works to which Mao was exposed in 1936–7, and often came (like 'On practice') relatively near the end of one-volume surveys of Marxist philosophy, the prominence given by Mao to the subject of contradictions was without parallel in any of his potential sources. Most of these had a section on the unity and struggle of opposites, the negation of the negation and related topics, but it was generally short, and in no case was it placed, as in Mao's lectures, at the end, thus making it the culmination and synthesis of the whole course.

Many reasons could no doubt be given for the prominence Mao attached to contradictions. Two of them flow naturally from the interpretation of his thought already sketched in this chapter. On the one hand, his understanding of dialectics was strongly marked by Taoism and other currents in traditional Chinese thought. On the other, he was, as I have stressed throughout, acutely aware of the complex and ambiguous character of Chinese society (in other words, of the contradictions within it), and sought to incorporate these insights into his revolutionary tactics. The first of these characteristics might be seen by some as a flaw in his understanding of dialectics; the second might well be construed as an

on Mao's handling of concepts and problems of dialectics', *Studies in Soviet thought*, 3.4 (Dec. 1963), 251–77.
[111] See the materials in *Chung-kuo che-hsueh*, 1.1–44, including Mao's extensive reading notes on Ai's *Che-hsueh yü sheng-huo* (Philosophy and life) dated September 1937, a letter of early 1938 from Mao to Ai about a point in this work, and an article (Kuo Hua-jo, 'Mao chu-hsi k'ang-chan ch'u-ch'i kuang-hui ti che-hsueh huo-tung' (Chairman Mao's brilliant philosophical activity during the early period of the anti-Japanese war)) discussing the variants between the original versions of 'On practice' and 'On contradiction' and those in Mao, *SW*. Other writings by Ai which Mao certainly read included his translation of an article by Mitin from the Great Soviet Encyclopedia, *Hsin che-hsueh ta-kang* (Outline of the new philosophy) (Tu-shu sheng-huo ch'u-pan-she, 1936), from which he cribbed many passages, and *Ta-chung che-hsueh* (Philosophy for the masses), which a reader of *K'ang-chan ta-hsueh* (8, 187) showed an embarrassing tendency to confuse with Mao's lectures.

advantage. The ensuing brief discussion of Mao's 'On contradiction' deals first with the one and then with the other of these two points.

Some idea of the importance attached by Mao to contradictions can be gained from the fact that chapter 3 ('Materialist dialectics') of his lecture notes runs to 53 out of a total of 110 pages of the Dairen edition of *Dialectical materialism*. The portion of this chapter (beginning on p. 64) which corresponds fairly closely to 'On contradiction' runs to approximately 25,000 characters, as compared to about 22,000 for the *Selected works* version. While there are significant differences between the two texts, the correspondence is sufficiently close to dispose once and for all of the theory, put forward by Arthur Cohen and others, according to which Mao could not possibly have written such a substantial work in 1937.[112] There remains, however, the problem of why this portion of the lectures was so much superior to the earlier sections. In essence, the answer lies, I think, in the fact that Mao was dealing not only with notions which appealed to him, but with their concrete application to the circumstances of the Chinese revolution. The first chapter of *Dialectical materialism* was, on the other hand, in large part simply a summary of the history of philosophy in Greece and the West, as perceived by Soviet authors. Here Mao could only copy his sources, and was in no position to add anything of himself.

As for the substance of 'On contradiction', the problem of the unorthodox character of Mao's dialectics became acute only after 1949, partly as a result of polemics with the Soviets, and to this extent does not fall within our scope here. In a word, it is commonly held that Soviet journals (which had praised 'On practice' in 1950) took no notice of 'On contradiction' two years later because they objected to the implied challenge to Stalin's theoretical primacy. There is no doubt whatever that this was indeed a factor, but it is altogether possible that the Soviets also found Mao's understanding of dialectics strange and heretical.

On many occasions in the 1950s Mao complained that the *Concise*

---

[112] It is true, of course, that this text was published nearly a decade later. On the other hand, editions of Mao's writings which appeared in 1946–7 do not commonly show extensive rewriting. Moreover, this version has been placed in circulation by the Soviets, who would surely not wish to contribute to any misunderstanding which might enhance Mao Tse-tung's reputation for theoretical maturity during the Yenan period. In other words, if it had been rewritten, as Cohen argues, to take account of Stalin's works of the late 1930s, Soviet specialists would certainly have pointed this out. For Cohen's argument (now invalidated), see A. Cohen, *The communism of Mao Tse-tung*, 14–28.

Confirmation both of Mao's authorship of the lecture notes on dialectical materialism, and of the fact that the 1946 Ta-lien edition was simply a reprint of what had been reproduced in mimeographed form in Yenan in 1937, without editorial changes, has been provided recently from an extremely authoritative source. See the article by Kung Yü-chih, Deputy Director of the Research Centre on Party Literature under the Central Committee, '"Shih-chieh lun" san t'i' (Three points regarding 'On practice'), in *Lun Mao Tse-tung che-hsüeh ssu-hsiang* (On Mao Tse-tung's philosophical thought), 66–86, especially 66–72.

philosophical dictionary made a speciality of criticizing his view of contradictions, and on one occasion he noted that he was speaking of the fourth edition of this work (published in Moscow in 1953) which reflected, he said, Stalin's views. The Soviet complaint was that the transformation of birth into death was 'metaphysical', and that the transformation of war into peace was wrong.[113] A case can be made regarding the para-traditional character of Mao's dialectics in his old age, when (in 1964) he abandoned two of the three basic axioms of Marxist and Hegelian dialectics, including the negation of the negation.[114] And while his outlook in 1937 was more derivative, and therefore on the whole more orthodox in Marxist terms, it could be argued that he was already leaning in the direction he was to follow a quarter of a century later. Perhaps the clearest pointer is to be found in the statement that 'the law of the unity of opposites' is 'the fundamental law of thought',[115] which seems to place this axiom in a higher category than the other two principles (the negation of the negation, and the transformation of quantity into quality) Mao subsequently rejected.[116]

The original version of Mao's lecture notes contains an allusion to the fact that Lenin regarded the unity of opposites as the 'kernel of dialectics',[117] and in 1957 Mao cited the relevant fragment explicitly: 'In brief, dialectics can be defined as the doctrine of the unity of opposites. This grasps the kernel of dialectics, but it requires explanations and development.'[118] This remark of Lenin's occurs, however, in rough reading notes on Hegel's *Logic*, and the passage summarizing Hegel's ideas to which it refers mentions both the negation of the negation, and the transformation of quantity into quality.[119]

To pursue this problem further would not only require detailed discussion of developments in Mao's thought after 1949, but would take us too far from the mainly political concerns of this chapter toward the consideration of strictly philosophical issues. Mao's analysis of Chinese society, and the theoretical conclusions he drew from it, lie on the other

[113] Mao, *SW* 5.368; Schram, *Mao unrehearsed*, 109 (speech of 20 March 1958).
[114] I have examined this problem in my essay 'The Marxist' in Dick Wilson, ed. *Mao Tse-tung in the scales of history*, 60–4. See also F. Wakeman, *History and will*, 297–9, 310, 323–6, etc.
[115] Mao, *SW* 1.345.
[116] This point was noted by Wang Jo-shui in a conversation of 7 May 1982 in Peking, though Mr Wang did not agree that Mao's emphasis on the unity and struggle of opposites reflected traditional influences. Steve Chin has interpreted Mao's stress on the unity of opposites as a new theoretical development going well beyond Marx and Engels. (Steve S. K. Chin, *The thought of Mao Tse-tung*, 60–4.) The preface to a 1946 edition of the lectures points out that the sections on the other two laws are 'missing'. *MTTC, pu-chüan*, 5.279. Note also Mao's disagreement with Ai Ssu-ch'i's view that mere differences (such as between pen, ink and table) do not necessarily constitute contradictions: *Chung-kuo che-hsueh*, 1.29.
[117] Knight, trans., 39.   [118] Mao, *SW* 5.366.
[119] V. I. Lenin, 'Conspectus of Hegel's *Science of logic*', *Collected works* 38, 222–3.

hand at the centre of our concerns, and can serve as a convenient transition from philosophy to other aspects of Mao's thought. It has often been argued, and up to a point the claim is accepted even by Cohen, that Mao's most notable contribution to the science of dialectics lay in his elaboration of the concepts 'principal contradiction' and 'principal aspect of the principal contradiction'. I should like to suggest, to begin with, that Mao's use of these categories can be linked directly to his subtle understanding of Chinese reality. A Marxist revolutionary in a society of the type observed by Marx himself, which was perceived as increasingly polarized into capitalists and proletarians, should have been in no doubt as to which were the basic contradictions between classes, or between the productive forces and the mode of production. In broad terms, this pattern was expected to remain more or less the same until the conflict was resolved by revolution. In China, on the other hand, where neither the internal situation nor relations with foreign powers were stable or predictable, it was not merely an intriguing intellectual problem, but a pressing tactical necessity, to determine which factor, or contradiction, was crucial or dominant at a given time.

It is interesting to note that one of the earliest Soviet writings translated in China, a volume published in Shanghai in 1933, devoted a section to the 'leading' (*chu-tao*) aspect of contradictions, but stated that this was in general always *the same*: for example, in the contradictions between base and superstructure, the base was always dominant.[120] This is one of the points in Mao's essay which Cohen finds most significant; he draws attention to the passage which reads:

Some people think that...in the contradiction between the productive forces and the relations of production, the productive forces are the leading aspect; in the contradiction between theory and practice, practice is the leading aspect; in the contradiction between the economic foundation and its superstructure, the economic foundation is the leading aspect, and that there is no change in their respective positions.... True, the productive forces, practice, and the economic foundation generally manifest themselves as the leading and decisive factors...But there are times (*yu shih*) when such aspects as the relations of production, theory and the superstructure in turn manifest themselves as the leading or decisive factors; this must also be admitted. When the productive forces cannot be developed unless the relations of production are changed, the change in the relations of production plays the leading and decisive role.... When the superstructure – politics, culture, and so on – hinders the development of the economic foundation, political and cultural reforms become the leading and decisive factors...[121]

---

[120] Li Ta and others (translators), *Pien-cheng-fa wei-wu-lun chiao-ch'eng* (by Hsi-lo-k'e-fu (Shirokov), and others), 295.

[121] *Pien-cheng wei-wu-lun*, 93; *MTTC, pu-chüan*, 5.264. There are some variants in this passage, but with

Cohen makes of this passage one of the key links in his argument that Mao did not write 'On contradiction' in 1937; Mao could not possibly, he says, have gone against Marxist 'determinism' in this fashion until Stalin had shown him the way, with his writings of 1938 and 1950. The facts speak otherwise. It would seem that Mao derived his 'voluntarism' directly from the study of Lenin (to whom the term was, after all, first applied), and also from his own personality, and the experience of the Chinese revolution. Indeed, it could be argued that the original text of 'On contradiction' puts even more emphasis on subjective factors.

The most important variant here is the replacement of the expression 'there are times' by 'in certain circumstances'. The implication of this formulation, inserted in the *Selected works*, would appear to be that such circumstances, or the totality of the necessary preconditions, will be present only for limited periods, at times of crisis or revolution. The looser 'at times' might be taken, on the other hand, to suggest that this reversal of roles between basis and superstructure might last for a significant period. This conclusion is reinforced by the sentence which follows immediately the passage just quoted (in both versions, original and rewritten): 'The creation and advocacy of revolutionary theory plays the principal and decisive role in those times of which Lenin said, "Without revolutionary theory there can be no revolutionary movement".'[122] Since Lenin saw this axiom as applicable to the whole historical period in which the proletarian revolution was to be planned, organized and carried out, Mao's use of it here can well be interpreted to mean that, while generally speaking the superstructure does not play the leading and decisive role in historical change, one of those 'times' when it does will occur, in fact, in China during a large part of the twentieth century.

One final point about Mao as a philosopher concerns his debt to Stalin. The current version of 'On contradiction' has a long and fulsome passage about Stalin's analysis of the peculiarities of the Russian Revolution as a 'model in understanding the particularity and universality of contradiction'.[123] This turns out to have been completely absent from the original version, where Mao illustrates his point rather by the exegesis of a quotation from Su Tung-p'o, who is said to have thoroughly understood the relation between the universal and the relative.[124]

the exception of the replacement of *chu-tao* (leading) by *chu-yao* (principal), Mao made no fundamental changes in 1952 in those portions which I have actually quoted here. (The translation is from *PTMT* 199; see also Nick Knight, trans., 28 and notes.) Mao's criticism may have been directed against the work cited in the previous note, though in 1941 he recommended Shirokov's book for study by cadres (*Selected letters*, 189).

[122] Knight, trans., 28.
[123] Mao, *SW* 1.229–30.
[124] *Pien-cheng wei-wu-lun*, 86; *MTTC*, *pu-chüan*, 5.258; Knight, trans., 24, and 146. The passage in

Chapter 2 of *Dialectical materialism* contains the statement that, because the 'dialectical materialist currents developing in China today do not result from taking over and reforming our own philosophical heritage, but from the study of Marxism-Leninism', we must 'liquidate the philosophical heritage of ancient China', which reflected the 'backwardness of China's social development'.[125] Plainly, this statement was the product of a momentary feeling of intimidation on Mao's first exposure to Marxist dialectics. It was entirely superseded by his call, in October 1938, for the 'sinification of Marxism', and did not represent a consistent position even in 1937.

If we look now concretely at Mao Tse-tung's analysis of strategic and tactical problems in the late 1930s, a fundamental issue is that of the relation between the Chinese Communist Party and the 'general staff of the world proletariat' in Moscow. Mao's view of this matter was absolutely clear. He summed it up in 1936 when, replying to a question from Edgar Snow as to whether, in the event of a Communist victory, there would be 'some kind of actual merger of governments' between Soviet China and Soviet Russia, he declared: 'We are certainly not fighting for an emancipated China in order to turn the country over to Moscow!' And he continued, spelling out the basis for this rejoinder:

The Chinese Communist Party is only one party in China, and in its victory it will have to speak for the whole nation. It cannot speak for the Russian people, or rule for the Third International, but only in the interests of the Chinese masses. Only where the interests of the Chinese masses coincide with the interests of the Russian masses can it be said to be 'obeying the will' of Moscow. But of course this basis of common benefit will be tremendously broadened once the masses of China are in democratic power and socially and economically emancipated, like their brothers in Russia.[126]

This passage shows that Mao, in 1936, felt the bond of solidarity uniting all the world's Communist Parties. But it also makes plain that for him solidarity did not mean subservience. Other things being equal, an 'emancipated China' – that is, a China ruled by the Communist Party – would have more intimate ties with the Soviet Union than with other countries. But if things were *not* equal – if Moscow did not show the respect for China's interests which Mao regarded as normal and

question is from Su's famous poem 'The red cliff', and reads as follows: 'If we regard this question as one of impermanence, then the universe cannot last for the twinkling of an eye. If, on the other hand, we consider it from the aspect of permanence, then you and I, together with all matter, are imperishable' (Cyril Drummond Le Gros Clark, *The prose-poetry of Su Tung-p'o*, 128).

[125] *MTTC* 6.275; *PTMT* 186.
[126] Originally published in the *Shanghai Evening Post and Mercury*, 3–5 Feb. 1936; reproduced from Edgar Snow's manuscript in *PTMT* 419.

appropriate – China's policy, under his guidance, might take a different direction.

There were those in the Chinese Communist Party in the 1930s who did not adopt the same independent attitude, just as there were those in later years who were prepared to be more flexible than Mao in dealings with Moscow. The history of the struggle between Mao Tse-tung and the so-called 'internationalist' (i.e. pro-Soviet) faction in the Chinese Communist Party from 1935 to 1945 is a long and complicated story, which has been told elsewhere in this volume. Here our concern is not with power relations between Moscow and the Chinese Communist Party, or its various factions, but rather with the nature and significance of the theories by which Mao asserted his independence from Soviet tutelage. And among the concepts Mao put forward in the late 1930s, the boldest and most unequivocal symbol of his belief in the uniqueness of the Chinese revolution, and the need for the Chinese to solve their own problems in their own way, was that of the 'sinification of Marxism'.

This slogan was in fact used by the Chinese Communists only for a relatively short period, which began in 1938, when Mao first made the term his own, and reached its culmination in 1945 when, at the Seventh Congress of the Chinese Communist Party, Liu Shao-ch'i hailed Mao's gigantic achievements in creating theories which were 'thoroughly Marxist, and at the same time thoroughly Chinese'. But if the term itself was relatively ephemeral, the concerns it expresses were present before 1938, and have not only survived but grown in importance since the establishment of the Chinese People's Republic.

Mao Tse-tung's reasons for putting forward this idea are not difficult to understand. The concept of sinification symbolized the affirmation of China's national dignity in the face of the patronizing and domineering attitude of the Comintern; it was therefore valuable not only as a weapon in the inner-party struggle, but as a slogan for appealing to non-Communist opinion at a time of national crisis. But it also reflected a genuine conviction on Mao's part that in the last analysis an ideology of Western origin would not work in the Chinese context, unless it were adapted to the mentality and conditions of the Chinese people.

Exactly what sinification meant to Mao in 1938 is a more complex question. To call for the 'nationalization' of Marxism (as Liu Shao-ch'i put it in 1945),[127] not only in China but in other non-European countries, implies the adaptation of Marxist theories to national reality at many different levels, from language and culture to the economic and social structure of largely pre-capitalist agrarian societies. Moreover, the

[127] Carrère d'Encausse and Schram, 260.

question also arises as to which 'Marxism', or what elements of Marxism, are to be sinified.

The intermingling of the various dimensions of the problem is evoked in Mao Tse-tung's classic statement regarding sinification, in October 1938, when he said in part:

Today's China is an outgrowth of historic China. We are Marxist historicists; we must not mutilate history. From Confucius to Sun Yat-sen we must sum it up critically, and we must constitute ourselves the heirs to this precious legacy. Conversely, the assimilation of this legacy itself becomes a method that aids considerably in guiding the present great movement. A Communist is a Marxist internationalist, but Marxism must take on a national form before it can be of any practical effect. There is no such thing as abstract Marxism, but only concrete Marxism. What we call concrete Marxism is Marxism that has taken on a national form, that is, Marxism applied to the concrete struggle in the concrete conditions prevailing in China, and not Marxism abstractly used. If a Chinese Communist, who is a part of the great Chinese people, bound to his people by his very flesh and blood, talks of Marxism apart from Chinese peculiarities, this Marxism is merely an empty abstraction. Consequently, the sinification of Marxism – that is to say, making certain that in all of its manifestations it is imbued with Chinese characteristics, using it according to Chinese peculiarities – becomes a problem that must be understood and solved by the whole party without delay. We must put an end to writing eight-legged essays on foreign models; there must be less repeating of empty and abstract refrains; we must discard our dogmatism and replace it by a new and vital Chinese style and manner, pleasing to the eye and to the ear of the Chinese common people.[128]

The simplest and least controversial aspect of Mao's conception of sinification is that dealt with in the last sentence of this quotation. Obviously, if Marxism is to have any impact in a non-European country, it must be presented to the people of that country in language which is not only intelligible to them but vivid and meaningful in the light of their mentality and traditions, rather than in jargon literally translated from another language and another culture. But such sinification of the form of Marxism, though indispensable in Mao's view, was only the outward manifestation of a more fundamental enterprise, aiming to transform the very substance of Marxism in order to adapt it to Chinese conditions.

In seeking to clarify the issues involved here, let us look first of all at the meaning of Mao Tse-tung's statement: 'There is no such thing as abstract Marxism, but only concrete Marxism.' In the light of his other writings in Yenan days, and of his words and actions in later years, the ideas underlying this assertion could be spelled out roughly as follows. The theory of scientific socialism was first expounded by Marx. Certain aspects of his writings – for example, his analysis of capitalism, and of

[128] MTTC 6.260–1; PTMT 172–3.

the transition from capitalism to socialism, and the basic axioms of dialectics – are of universal validity, but the theory as a whole reflects both its origins in the nineteenth century, and Marx's specifically European mentality and experience. When we talk, therefore (like Stalin and everyone else from Lenin on down), about applying the universally valid principles of Marxism to Chinese conditions, it is the timeless kernel of these theories which we should seek to grasp and adapt to our needs.

And what is that timeless kernel? Mao himself, in the report of October 1938 already quoted, declared: 'We must not study the letter of Marxism and Leninism, but the standpoint and methodology of its creators, with which they observed and solved problems.'[129] In February 1942 he called upon his comrades of the Chinese Communist Party to 'take the standpoint, viewpoint and methods of Marxism-Leninism, apply them to China, and create a theory from the conscientious study of the realities of the Chinese revolution and Chinese history'.[130]

These formulations raise two problems. What did Mao mean by 'standpoint', 'viewpoint', and 'methods'? And what was the relation between such attitudes or principles derived from Marxism, and the 'method' which, he said, could emerge from the assimilation of the precious legacy of China's past?

As for the first point, the current Chinese interpretation is that Mao was talking about adopting the standpoint of the proletariat, the viewpoint of historical materialism, and the method of dialectics. But if Mao was indeed referring to aspects of Marxism as broadly defined as these, does it not follow that, in his view, the theories of Marx himself constituted in fact 'German Marxism', just as the ideas of Lenin were characterized by his critics in the early twentieth century as 'Russian Marxism'? In other words, by 'abstract Marxism' Mao meant 'absolute Marxism', or Marxist theory unconditionally valid in all countries and at all times. And when he said that such Marxism 'did not exist', he meant that Marx's own writings did not have the status of a higher-level general theory, but were merely one concrete incarnation of the standpoint, viewpoint and methods which he had devised, in no way superior to the application of the same principles by Stalin, or by Mao himself.

For Mao it was not, however, merely a question of applying Marxism to China; he also proposed, as we have seen, to enrich it with elements drawn from China's experience. Nor were the 'Chinese peculiarities' with which Mao proposed to imbue his Marxism merely the economic traits China shared with other Asian countries. They were also the 'precious qualities' which, as he put it in 1938, had been exhibited 'in the history

<hr/>

[129] *PTMT* 171.   [130] *MTTC* 8.75; *PTMT* 179–80.

of our great people over several millennia', and had been shaped both
by historical experience and by the genius of the Chinese people.[131]

The view that China today bears the imprint of the past is in no way
remarkable. Marxists, at least those of the Leninist persuasion, have long
agreed that social customs and forms of political organization, though
they change in the wake of modifications in the economic infrastructure
of society and as a result of the class struggles these engender, are
themselves a variable in the historical equation. But the question must
be raised whether, in Mao's view, cultural realities were basically
determined by levels of technology and 'modes of production', or whether
the 'national peculiarities' he stressed constituted for him an independent,
or partially independent, variable.

In my opinion, there is very little doubt that for Mao Tse-tung culture,
both in the narrow and in the broad sense, constituted a partially
autonomous dimension of human experience. One may applaud or
deplore this attitude on his part, and there are those who do both, often
with considerable heat. We cannot, however, ignore this aspect of his
thought without distorting our perception of the man and his ideas.

Precisely how central this theme was to Mao Tse-tung's whole vision
of revolution in China is indicated by the extraordinary statement, in the
passage quoted earlier from his report of October 1938, that the assimilation
of the Chinese heritage 'itself becomes a method that aids considerably
in guiding the present great movement'. The preceding injunction to 'sum
up critically' the experience of the past does not carry the same
implications, for in it the active and guiding role appears to rest with the
'viewpoint and methodology' of Marx and Lenin, which is to be used
to sort out the wheat from the chaff in the record of Chinese history. The
suggestion that a deeper knowledge of the past will not merely widen
the revolutionaries' understanding of their own society, but will actually
provide an instrument for leading the revolution is something else again,
and opens vistas without precedent in the history of Marxism down to
1938.

What was the nature of this method, which Mao said could be distilled
from the experience of 'historic China', and what elements in the past
were to be drawn upon in producing it? He did not spell this out explicitly,
but there are hints in his writings of the Yenan period that he was thinking
about a domain which could be loosely defined as that of the art of

---

[131] *MTTC* 6.260; *PTMT* 172. Ray Wylie has discussed the problem of the 'sinification of Marxism'
and its significance from a parallel but somewhat different perspective, placing greater emphasis
on the philosophical issue of the relation between the universal and the particular and its
implications for the originality of 'Mao Tse-tung thought': Ray Wylie, *The emergence of Maoism:
Mao Tse-tung, Ch'en Po-ta, and the search for Chinese theory, 1935–1945*, 55–8, 88–95 and *passim*.

statecraft.[132] Thus, in another section of the report of October 1938 in which he first put forward the idea of sinification, Mao dealt with the problem of making proper use of cadres – which, he said, had been referred to in the past as 'employing people in the administration' (*yung-jen hsing-cheng*). He went on to discuss the continuity between the present and the past in the following terms:

Throughout our national history there have been two sharply contrasting lines on the subject of the use of cadres, reflecting the opposition between the depraved and the upright, one being to 'appoint people on their merit', and the other being 'to appoint people by favouritism'. The former was the policy of sagacious rulers and worthy ministers in making appointments; the latter was that of despots and traitors. Today, when we talk about making use of cadres, it is from a revolutionary standpoint, fundamentally different from that of ancient times, and yet there is no getting away from this standard of 'appointing people on their merit'. It was utterly wrong in the past, and is still utterly wrong today, to be guided by personal likes and dislikes, to reward fawning flatterers and to punish the honest and forthright.[133]

Here Mao was clearly indicating that in his view there were standards of political conduct which remained valid for Communist revolutionaries in the present, even though they were originally evolved in the context of a pre-capitalist and bureaucratic society.

Rather more surprisingly, Mao Tse-tung also found positive elements in Confucian philosophy. Commenting in 1939 on an article by Ch'en Po-ta on this theme, Mao indicated that he was basically in agreement, but that, in criticizing Confucius' doctrine of the rectification of names as 'idealist', Ch'en had failed to note that, from the epistemological standpoint, it contained important elements of truth, because of its emphasis on the link between theory and practice. He also saw Chu Hsi's interpretation of Confucius' theory of the mean as parallel to the Communists' principle of struggle on two fronts, against left and right deviations. Not going far enough (*pu chi*), he said, stood for rightism; going too far (*kuo*) stood for leftism.[134]

Appeals of this kind to the national past were, of course, singularly appropriate at a time when Mao Tse-tung was concerned to address himself to the widest possible spectrum of opinion, in order to promote the establishment of a new united front. They must also be taken seriously, however, as an expression of the substance of his thinking. Before turning to the analysis of Mao's ideas specifically about the alliance with bourgeois nationalists against Japanese aggression, let us explore further his

---

[132] On this tradition, see *CHOC* 11, 145–7.
[133] Mao, *SW* 2.202, supplemented by *MTCC* 6.250–1.
[134] 'Chih Chang Wen-t'ien' (To Chang Wen-t'ien), 20 Feb. 1939, *Selected letters*, 144–8.

interpretation of Chinese history, especially in the nineteenth and twentieth centuries, for it is this context which served to define the current stage of the Chinese revolution as he saw it, and accordingly the tactics appropriate at such a time.

The most systematic statement of Mao's views regarding Chinese history in general dating from the Yenan period is to be found in the first chapter of *The Chinese Revolution and the Chinese Communist Party*. (Strictly speaking, this text was not drafted by Mao himself, who wrote only the second chapter of the work, but Mao did choose to include it in his *Selected works*, and thereby took responsibility for the contents.) The details of this wide-ranging discussion fall for the most part outside the scope of this chapter, but certain points should be noted.

To begin with, Mao here places the transition from slave-holding society to feudalism at the beginning of the Chou dynasty, or roughly in the eleventh century BC. The relevant passage reads as follows:

[China's] feudal society, beginning with the Chou and Ch'in dynasties, lasted about 3,000 years...
It was the feudal landlord state which protected this system of feudal exploitation. While the feudal state was torn apart into rival principalities under the Chou, it became an autocratic and centralized feudal state after Ch'in Shih-huang unified China, though a degree of feudal separatism remained...[135]

Thus the Ch'in dynasty was seen as marked simply by a change in the form of the state, and not by a transition from one mode of production to another.[136]

The notion of an 'autocratic and centralized feudal state', which may appear to Western readers to be a contradiction in terms, was the formula arrived at by Mao and his comrades, after the debates of the 1920s and 1930s about the nature of traditional society, in order to assert simultaneously the 'feudal' (and hence universal) character of Chinese society and its uniqueness. At the same time, there remained in the original version of this text of 1939 traces of the notion of China as an 'Asiatic' society, which had in principle been repudiated. Thus, Mao asserted that Chinese society prior to the Opium War had been completely stagnant for centuries, and was only prodded into motion by the impact of the West.[137]

---

[135] Mao, *SW* 2.307–8; *MTTC* 7.100–1.
[136] Although there was ongoing scholarly controversy on this point, it did not become a burning political issue until the *p'i-Lin p'i-K'ung* campaign of 1973–4. The views put forward at that time were in flat contradiction with those Mao had espoused in 1939.
[137] In 1952, he would insert into *SW* the thesis, more agreeable to national pride, that changes were already at work which would have led to the birth of capitalism in China even without foreign intervention (Mao, *SW* 2.307–9; *MTTC* 7.100–3).

Two other points in Mao's survey of Chinese history are worthy of special emphasis. We have seen that, in 1919, Mao Tse-tung had boldly made what he called a 'singular assertion': 'one day, the reform of the Chinese people will be more profound than that of any other people, and the society of the Chinese people will be more radiant than that of any other people'. Twenty years later, the same faith in the exceptional capacities of his compatriots found expression in passages such as this:

In the many-thousand-year history of the Chinese people, many national heroes and revolutionary leaders have emerged. China has also given birth to many revolutionary strategists, statesmen, men of letters and thinkers. So the Chinese people [min-tsu] is also a people with a glorious revolutionary tradition and a splendid historical heritage.[138]

Secondly, Mao continued, as he had done since 1926, to give particular emphasis to the role of the peasantry. Not only were the 'hundreds of peasant revolts' throughout Chinese history characterized as the decisive cause of each and every dynastic change, but these 'peasant revolts and peasant wars', on a 'gigantic scale…without parallel in world history' were said to form the only 'real motive force of China's historical evolution'. At the same time, however, Mao stressed the limitations on such actions by the peasants alone, in a 'feudal' society, as far as their capacity to promote the development of the productive forces or change the mode of production was concerned. On this point, he wrote:

each peasant revolt and peasant war dealt a blow to the existing feudal regime; thus to some extent it changed the productive relations of society and to some extent furthered the development of the productive forces of society. However, since neither new productive forces nor new modes of production nor a new class force nor an advanced political party existed in those days, and the peasant wars and revolts consequently lacked the leadership of an advanced class and an advanced political party, such as the correct leadership given by the proletariat and the Communist Party today, the peasant revolutions invariably failed, and the peasants were utilized…by the landlords and the nobility as a tool for bringing about dynastic changes. Thus, although some social progress was made after each peasant revolutionary struggle, the feudal economic relations and feudal political system remained basically unchanged.[139]

When and how, in Mao's view, did a situation arise in which the proletariat and the Communist Party could exercise 'correct leadership' over the Chinese revolution? As he saw it, this process took place in two stages. First, the 'feudal' relations of production which had existed until the

[138] Mao, *SW* 2.306; *MTTC* 7.99.
[139] Mao, *SW* 2.308–9; *MTTC* 7.102. Here, and elsewhere in *SW*, Mao replaced the term he had originally used for peasant uprisings, *pao-tung* (revolt, armed rebellion), with *ch'i-i* (righteous uprising). The nuance lies, of course, in the fact that *pao-tung* suggests something more sporadic and less directly linked as a precursor to the rural revolution led by the Communists.

nineteenth century were partly broken down, and the position of the old ruling class undermined by the impact of the West and the ensuing development of capitalism, and of an embryonic bourgeoisie. At this stage, the landlord class, backed by the imperialists, still constituted the ruling class of Chinese society, but the bourgeois elements were the natural leaders of the revolutionary challenge to the existing order. Then, in a second stage, conditions became ripe for the proletariat to assert its hegemony over the revolution.

In Mao's interpretation, this transition took place roughly at the time of the May Fourth movement; the periods of bourgeois and proletarian hegemony he referred to respectively as the 'democratic' or 'old democratic' revolution and the 'New Democratic' revolution. Before discussing his periodization of modern Chinese history, let us consider what precisely he meant by 'New Democracy', for this concept was not only important in its day, but has continuing relevance to China's later problems.

Since 'New Democracy' was intended to be a category of Marxist-Leninist analysis, it is necessary to remind ourselves briefly of the doctrinal background. Marx had considered that, as a matter of course, the capitalist stage in the development of society would be characterized by the domination of the bourgeoisie, just as the feudal stage had been marked by the domination of the nobility. The bourgeois-democratic revolution which constituted the decisive phase in the transition from feudalism to capitalism would likewise be the task of the bourgeoisie. As for the proletariat, it would support the bourgeoisie in the democratic revolution, meanwhile prodding it forward to satisfy in so far as possible the immediate demands of the workers, until the time came to put an end to the capitalist system by a socialist revolution led by the proletariat.

The writings of Marx and Engels regarding revolution in pre-capitalist societies, especially those which had felt the impact of Western colonialism, are fascinating and suggestive, but at the same time fragmentary and contradictory. In any case, it is impossible (whatever attempts may have been made) to extract from them a clear tactical line for the guidance of Asian revolutionaries. At the time of the 1905 Revolution, first Trotsky and then Lenin put forward the view that, in such backward lands, the 'bourgeois-democratic revolution' could take place under the hegemony of the proletariat, that is, in a political context dominated by the Communist Party. This idea, subsequently elaborated by Stalin, Mao and many others, has been an axiom of Marxism, as interpreted by the Soviets and their disciples, ever since.

Thus, the class nature of a given historical stage was effectively dissociated from the class character of the actors in such a stage. The proletarian dictatorship, or some precursor or variant of it, can, it has been postulated for three-quarters of a century, preside over a 'bourgeois' revolution which will constitute the functional equivalent of the capitalist stage in the development of Western societies.

To return now to the nature and significance of Mao Tse-tung's ideas regarding this stage, which he baptized 'New Democratic', it is of interest to note not only how he defined its content, but when he postulated that it had begun. For it was in this context that Mao undertook to justify the new alliance with the Nationalists, in terms of the evolving balance of forces, and the aims of the revolution at that time.

In some passages Mao dated the transition from 'old' to 'new' democracy in 1919 precisely, and for purposes of convenience the dividing-line between 'modern' and 'contemporary' Chinese history has been fixed since Yenan days at the time of the May Fourth movement. Mao was, however, naturally aware that decisive changes such as this do not occur overnight, and for the most part he situated the emergence of 'New Democracy' more loosely in the period from the outbreak of the First World War to the foundation of the Chinese Communist Party (that is, in the 'May Fourth period' as commonly and broadly defined). In *On new democracy*, Mao wrote in January 1940: 'A change...occurred in China's bourgeois-democratic revolution after the outbreak of the first imperialist world war in 1914 and the founding of a socialist state on one-sixth of the globe as a result of the Russian October Revolution of 1917.'[140]

The reasons here given or suggested for the change in the nature of China's revolution include the weakening and discrediting of Western 'bourgeois' democracy, the emergency of an alternative model in the new Soviet republic, and also the possibility of material and moral assistance from the Soviets. It was partly for this last reason that Mao, following Stalin (who himself was following Lenin), declared China's New-Democratic revolution to be an integral part of the proletarian-socialist world revolution. On this theme, he wrote:

In an era in which the world capitalist front has collapsed in one corner of the globe... and has fully revealed its decadence everywhere else, in an era in which the remaining capitalist portions cannot survive without relying more than ever on the colonies and semi-colonies... in such an era, a revolution in any colony or semi-colony that is directed against imperialism... no longer comes within the old category of the bourgeois-democratic world revolution, but within the new category...

[140] Mao, *SW* 2.343; *MTTC* 7.153.

Although during its first stage or first step, such a revolution in a colonial and semi-colonial country is still fundamentally bourgeois-democratic in its social character, and although its objective demand is still fundamentally to clear the path for the development of capitalism, it is no longer a revolution of the old type, led *entirely* by the bourgeoisie, with the aim of establishing a capitalist society and a state under bourgeois dictatorship. It is rather a revolution of the new type, *with the participation of the proletariat in the leadership*, or led by the proletariat, and having as its aim, in the first stage, the establishment of a new-democratic society and a state under the joint dictatorship of all the revolutionary classes...[141]

This passage speaks of a 'joint dictatorship', and the words in italics (which Mao removed in 1952) imply that the proletariat might not even enjoy primacy among the various dictators. Indeed, in the original version of *On new democracy* Mao went so far as to state explicitly that, if the Chinese bourgeoisie should prove itself capable of leading the people in 'driving out Japanese imperialism and introducing democratic government', they (i.e., the Kuomintang) would continue to enjoy the people's confidence.[142] It was plain, however, that this was merely a rhetorical gesture to Chiang Kai-shek, and that Mao fully intended his own party to exercise hegemony on behalf of the proletariat within the 'joint dictatorship of all the revolutionary classes'. In *The Chinese Revolution and the Chinese Communist Party*, addressed directly to party members rather than to a non-party audience of intellectuals (as was *On new democracy*), Mao said bluntly, 'Unless the proletariat participates in it and leads it, the Chinese revolution cannot... succeed.'[143] And on the eve of victory in June 1949, he put the same view more categorically still: 'Why did forty years of revolution under Sun Yat-sen end in failure? Because in the epoch of imperialism the bourgeoisie cannot lead any genuine revolution to victory.'[144]

In sum, though he expressed it with varying degrees of frankness, Mao's view from the time he first began to use the term 'New Democracy' in 1939 was that in China, after 1919 or thereabouts, leadership of the revolution rightfully belonged to the proletariat. How could he claim such a role for a class which, in the second decade of the twentieth century, was only beginning to develop, and for a party which counted, until the alliance with the Nationalists in 1923–7, only a handful of members? Apart from the fact that the Communists, as already noted, enjoyed external support and sympathy from the Soviet Union, Mao argued as follows:

As distinct social classes, the Chinese bourgeoisie and proletariat are new-born and never existed before in Chinese history.... They are twins born of China's

---

[141] Carrère d'Encausse and Schram, 252; *MTTC* 7.153–4. (The words in italics have been removed in Mao, *SW*.)   [142] Carrère d'Encausse and Schram, 254; *MTTC* 7.162.
[143] Mao, *SW* 2.325; *MTTC* 7.126.   [144] Mao, *SW* 4.422; *MTTC* 10.305.

old (feudal) society, at once linked to each other and antagonistic to each other. However, the Chinese proletariat emerged and grew simultaneously not only with the Chinese national bourgeoisie but also with the enterprises directly operated by the imperialists in China. Hence, a very large section of the Chinese proletariat is older and more experienced than the Chinese bourgeoisie, and is therefore a greater and more broadly-based social force'.[145]

This is an ingenious argument, and not without substance. Nevertheless, Mao's assertion of proletarian hegemony from 1917–21 onwards must be read not as a statement of fact about the strength of the opposing political forces, but as an assertion that, from this time forward, it was appropriate, and not wholly unrealistic, for the Communists to *strive* for leadership over the national revolution.

If such was indeed Mao's intimate conviction, even though he did not always state this openly, was it not meaningless or hypocritical to talk about a 'united front' at all? Or, to put it differently, would not such an alliance necessarily assume the character of a 'united front from below', that is, of an attempt to mobilize the rank and file of the Kuomintang against its leadership? Not necessarily, especially if we interpret Mao's periodization, as I have done above, in the sense that, in the late 1930s, it had long been legitimate for the Communists to seek to assert their hegemony. For what was legitimate might not, at any given time, be expedient, or politically 'correct'. If the external threat from Japan to China's very existence as an independent state, and therefore to the possibility of political change within the country, became so grave that the struggle against Japan replaced the struggle against Chiang Kai-shek as the Communists' number one policy goal, and if the Kuomintang was not only militarily and politically stronger than the Communists but willing to fight Japan, then it might be appropriate to accept, for a time, Kuomintang predominance in such a struggle.

As noted above, Mao had accepted by December 1935 the need for a new united front, and he had agreed, by late 1936, that Chiang Kai-shek must be the titular leader of such an alliance. It was in October 1938, in his report to the sixth plenum of the Central Committee, that Mao went farthest in recognizing the leading role of the Kuomintang, not only during the Anti-Japanese War, but in the phase of national reconstruction which would follow it. In a paragraph entitled 'The Kuomintang has a brilliant future' he declared:

The Kuomintang and the Communist Party are the foundation of the Anti-Japanese United Front, but of these two it is the Kuomintang that occupies first place....In the course of its glorious history, the Kuomintang has been responsible for the

[145] Mao, *SW* 2.310; *MTTC* 7.104–5.

overthrow of the Ch'ing, the establishment of the Republic, opposition to Yuan Shih-k'ai...and the great revolution of 1926–7. Today it is once more leading the great anti-Japanese war. It enjoys the historic heritage of the Three People's Principles; it has had two great leaders in succession – Mr Sun Yat-sen and Mr Chiang Kai-shek....All this should not be underestimated by our compatriots and constitutes the result of China's historical development.

In carrying out the anti-Japanese war, and in organizing the Anti-Japanese United Front, the Kuomintang occupies the position of leader and backbone [*chi-kan*]...Under the single great condition that it support to the end the war of resistance and the United Front, one can foresee a brilliant future for the Kuomintang...[146]

Although this report expressed the softest line ever taken by Mao Tse-tung toward Chiang Kai-shek and the Kuomintang, it was by no means the blank cheque it might at first glance appear. The 'single great condition' alone, stated in the last sentence of the preceding quotation, limited severely the scope of Mao's concessions to Chiang. To the extent that he regarded Chiang and the Kuomintang as, in the long run, congenitally incapable of supporting unflinchingly the united front and the war against Japan, Mao looked forward to the time when his acceptance of Chiang's leadership would necessarily lapse. Moreover, though the original 1938 text of this report did not speak, as do the rewritten extracts in the *Selected works*, of leadership by the Communists, it did refer to 'the way in which the Communists should become conscious of their own role and strengthen themselves, in order to be in a position to assume their great responsibilities in the national war'. And these responsibilities he defined succinctly by saying that the Communists 'should exercise the role of vanguard and model in every domain'.[147] Quite obviously, if the Kuomintang should falter in its leadership, its place would be taken by those who had already established themselves as 'vanguard and model'.

Finally, Mao's proposal, in his report of October 1938, that the 'bloc within' should be resuscitated, and that Communists should once more join the Kuomintang as individuals, was a two-edged and ambiguous one. For though he offered in advance to give Chiang Kai-shek a complete list of all such Communists with dual party membership, thus satisfying one of the conditions which Chiang had laid down following the 'reorganization' of May 1926, he also sought to persuade Chiang to turn the Kuomintang into a 'national league'. The aim of this second proposal was all too obviously to weaken the Leninist stranglehold which had made it impossible, in 1926–7, for the Communists to manipulate the

[146] *MTTC* 6.198; *PTMT* 228–9.
[147] *MTTC* 6.243–4; *PTMT* 229.

Kuomintang from within. It is therefore not surprising that Chiang saw this as a 'Trojan horse' manoeuvre, and rejected it.[148]

In a little over a year, Mao's position evolved, as we have already seen, from recognition that the Kuomintang must take 'first place' in the united front to the assertion of Communist leadership as an accomplished fact. In *On new democracy* (January 1940) this bald claim was covered with a rhetorical fig leaf; in *The Chinese Revolution and the Chinese Communist Party* (December 1939) it was quite unambiguous.[149] *The Chinese Revolution and the Chinese Communist Party*, though written chiefly for a Communist audience, was openly sold. In his Introduction to the inner-party periodical *The Communist* (October 1939), Mao did not even raise the question of who should exercise hegemony; he simply assumed that leadership belonged to the Communists, and proceeded to discuss how they should go about exercising it.

Apart from the question of leadership, two directly related points merit discussion here: Mao's views regarding the role of various classes in the revolution, and about the nature of the political movement or regime which should represent the revolutionary forces.

In essence, Mao's view regarding the class forces supporting the revolution at the time of the Anti-Japanese War was simple and consistent. He saw them as composed of Stalin's four-class bloc of the 1920s, with the addition of a certain portion of the 'comprador bourgeoisie' tied to powers whose interests were in conflict with those of Japan. Understandably, the line enclosing possible allies was drawn most tightly in the Introduction to *The Communist*, and most loosely in *On new democracy*. In the former, the peasantry is characterized as a 'firm' ally of the proletariat, and the urban petty-bourgeoisie as a 'reliable' ally. As for the national bourgeoisie, it will take part in the struggle 'against imperialism and the feudal warlords' at 'certain times and to a certain extent', because it suffers from foreign oppression, but it will also 'vacillate and defect' on occasion 'because of its economic and political flabbiness'. The bourgeoisie or big bourgeoisie, even when it joins the united front against the enemy, 'continues to be most reactionary', opposes the development of the proletarian party, and ultimately plans to capitulate to the enemy and split the united front.[150]

The original version of *On new democracy* exhibits one curious anomaly:

---

[148] On this episode, see chapter above by Lyman Van Slyke, as well as S. Schram, *Mao Tse-tung*, 202–3. For the text of Mao's proposal, see *MTTC* 6.228–9.

[149] *MTTC* 7.129; *PTMT* 230–1.

[150] Mao, *SW* 2.228–89; *MTTC* 7.228–9. The passage (paragraph 3) putting a slightly more optimistic view of the (comprador) bourgeoisie was added in *SW* and does not appear at all in the 1939 text.

it refers throughout to a three-class, rather than a four-class bloc. The difference is one of form rather than substance, but it is not without interest. It results from lumping together the peasantry (which has always been regarded by Marxists as petty-bourgeois in nature) with the urban petty-bourgeoisie, and calling the resulting category '*the*' petty-bourgeoisie, instead of counting the peasants as a separate class. Thus we read, for example, that in 1927–36, as a result of the 'going over of the Chinese bourgeoisie to the counter-revolutionary camp...only two of the three classes originally composing the revolutionary camp remained...': the proletariat and the petty-bourgeoisie (including the peasantry, the revolutionary intellectuals, and other sections of the petty-bourgeoisie).[151]

With the coming of the Anti-Japanese War, continued Mao, the Chinese revolution, 'pursuing its zig-zag course', had again arrived at a united front of three classes. But this time, he added,

the scope is much broader. Among the upper classes, it includes all the rulers; among the middle classes, it includes the petty-bourgeoisie in its totality; among the lower classes, it includes the totality of the proletarians. All classes and strata of the country have become allies, and are resolutely resisting Japanese imperialism.[152]

It is quite clear that the swallowing-up of the peasantry in the catch-all category of the 'petty-bourgeoisie' served to attenuate the emphasis on the unique character of China's revolution, and especially on one of its original traits: guerrilla warfare in the countryside. In his Introduction to *The Communist*, Mao made of these aspects of China's experience one of the main themes of his analysis:

since China is a semi-colonial and semi-feudal country, since her political, economic and cultural development is uneven, since her economy is predominantly semi-feudal and since her territory is vast, it follows that the character of the Chinese revolution in its present stage is bourgeois-democratic, that its principal targets are imperialism and the feudal forces, and that its basic motive forces are the proletariat, the peasantry, and the urban petty-bourgeoisie, with the national bourgeoisie etc. taking part at certain times and to a certain extent; it also follows [*sic*] that the principal form of struggle in the Chinese revolution is armed struggle.

It is not quite clear why the last conclusion should follow from the facts enumerated by Mao Tse-tung in this sentence, but it is obviously a valid

[151] *MTTC* 7.196; Carrère d'Encausse and Schram, 256–7. There is an intriguing prefiguration of this three-class analysis in Mao's reply of November 1925 to a survey by the Young China Association (*MTTC*, *pu-chüan*, 2.127), in which he declared that though he was a Communist and a partisan of a 'proletarian social revolution', a single class was not in a position in China, to overthrow the internal and external forces of reaction, so the 'national revolution' must be carried out by the proletariat, the petty-bourgeoisie, and the left wing of the middle class (*chung-ch'an chieh-chi*).   [152] *MTTC* 7.197–8; Carrère d'Encausse and Schram, 257.

one. 'Indeed,' Mao goes on, 'the history of our party may be called a history of armed struggle. Comrade Stalin has said, "In China the armed people are fighting armed counter-revolution. That is one of the specific features of the Chinese revolution." This is perfectly true.' The quotation from Stalin represents a particularly cynical instance of citing out of context; when Stalin made this statement in December 1926 the 'armed people' he was talking about were represented by Chiang Kai-shek, in whose fidelity to the cause he still had full confidence, and Mao knew this very well. Still, once again, the point was well taken: 'armed struggle in China', added Mao, 'is, in essence, peasant war and the party's relations with the peasantry and its close relation with the peasant war are one and the same thing'.[153]

In this text, Mao Tse-tung characterizes the united front, armed struggle, and party-building as the Chinese Communist Party's three 'magic weapons'. We have already spoken in this chapter of the place of armed struggle in Mao's strategy. As for the united front, his essential message in the Introduction to *The Communist* is that it should be marked by both unity and struggle. The precise form such unity should take is not discussed, but as we have already seen Mao laid down in the other two basic texts of this same period that the vehicle for cooperation should be the 'joint dictatorship of all the revolutionary classes'. In *The Chinese Revolution and the Chinese Communist Party* he also referred to it as the 'joint revolutionary-democratic dictatorship of several revolutionary classes over the imperialists and reactionary traitors'.[154] The term 'revolutionary-democratic dictatorship' was obviously modelled on Lenin's 'revolutionary-democratic dictatorship of the workers and peasants', a slogan first coined at the time of the 1905 Revolution and often reiterated thereafter. Mao's dictators were, of course, more numerous than Lenin's; the difference he explained, as we have already seen, by the special conditions of a country under foreign domination.

The third of Mao's 'magic weapons', party-building, meant in fact something far more sweeping and significant than would at first glance appear. It implied defining a correct doctrine, and unifying and rectifying the party on the basis of that doctrine. A passage somewhat modified in the *Selected works* noted that, if in the past the Chinese Communist Party had been unsuccessful in its pursuit of consolidation and 'bolshevization', this was because its members had not adequately linked Marxism to the concrete practice of the Chinese revolution, and did not have an adequate knowledge of Chinese history and of Chinese society.[155]

[153] Mao, *SW* 2.286–7; *MTTC* 7.72. [154] *MTTC* 7.129; *PTMT* 230.
[155] Mao, *SW* 2.292–3; *MTTC* 7.79–80.

This meant, quite plainly, that they did not yet have the benefit of the 'sinified Marxism' which Mao Tse-tung was then engaged in elaborating, precisely in the works we have been discussing. In other words, the 'party-building' for which Mao called in October 1939 was destined to take the form of the great rectification or *cheng-feng* campaign which, in 1942–3, definitively established his ideological predominance in the party.

THE TRIUMPH OF MAO TSE-TUNG'S THOUGHT 1941–1949

When Mao had first put forward the slogan of adapting Marxism to Chinese conditions, his main concern, as I have already suggested, was to shape the approach of the Chinese Communist Party to fit the political and cultural circumstances of the time. The next main phase in the development of his ideas on this theme, in 1941–3, was much more directly linked to Mao's struggle with his rivals in the party, and the views he propagated were explicitly designed to serve his interests in that struggle.

The same was true of other aspects of Mao's thought. If the philosophical core of his thinking had taken shape as early as 1937 with the theory of contradictions, in a wide range of other domains, from economic work to literature and from administrative principles to the interpretation of the Marxist heritage, the definitive formulation of Mao's ideas prior to 1949 dates from the early 1940s. And in all of these areas the links between ideology and political in-fighting are palpable and direct.

This chapter focuses, of course, primarily on ideas rather than on historical fact. The following succinct chronology brings out clearly, however, the concrete significance of certain theoretical statements:

5 May 1941. Mao makes a speech to a cadre meeting in Yenan criticizing 'scholars of Marxism-Leninism' who 'can only repeat quotes from Marx, Engels, Lenin and Stalin from memory, but about their own ancestors...have to apologize and say they've forgotten'.

1 July 1941. Adoption of Central Committee resolution on 'strengthening the party spirit', stressing the importance of discipline and of absolute subordination of cadres at all levels to higher authority.

13 July 1941. Sun Yeh-fang writes a letter to Liu Shao-ch'i (using the pen name Sung Liang), referring to the two opposing deviations of slighting theoretical study and scholasticism, and asking for some 'Chinese examples' of the correct relation between theory and practice. Liu replies the same day stressing the difficulties of sinifying Marxism, and blaming the lack of progress thus far partly on the fact that few Chinese Communist Party members can read Marx in the original.

23 January 1942. Mao orders army cadres to study his Ku-t'ien Resolution of December 1929 until they are thoroughly familiar with it.

1 February and 8 February 1942. Mao delivers his two keynote speeches on rectification. In the second of these, he complains that his 1938 call for 'sinification' has not been heeded.

May 1942. Mao delivers two talks to the Yenan Forum on Literature and Art, but these are not published for nearly a year and a half.

December 1942. Mao delivers a report *On economic and financial problems.*

20 March 1943. Mao elected chairman of the Politburo of the Chinese Communist Party, and chairman of the three-man Secretariat, with the right to outvote the two other members.

April 1943. Movement to investigate cadres pressed forward vigorously in Yenan – in fact, a harsh purge of dissident or anti-Maoist elements in the party, under the control of K'ang Sheng.

26 May 1943. Mao, commenting on the dissolution of the Comintern, declares that, although Moscow has not intervened in the affairs of the Chinese Communist Party since the Seventh Comintern Congress of August 1935, the Chinese Communists have done their work very well.

1 June 1943. Resolution, drafted by Mao, on methods of leadership puts forward the classic formulation of the 'mass line'.

6 July 1943. Liu Shao-ch'i publishes the article 'Liquidate Menshevik thought in the party', hailing Mao as a true Bolshevik and denouncing the 'International faction' as Mensheviks in disguise.

19 October 1943. Mao's 'Yenan Talks' finally published in *Chieh-fang jih-pao.*

April 1945. Apotheosis – Mao's thought written into the party constitution as the guide to all the party's work, and Mao hailed by Liu Shao-ch'i for his earth-shaking contributions in 'sinifying' or 'nationalizing' Marxism.[156]

These facts have, of course, been selected and arranged to suggest that the establishment of Mao Tse-tung's absolute predominance in the party was, from the outset, a primary goal of the rectification campaign of 1942–3. Though they may sharpen and oversimplify the picture to some extent, I do not believe that they distort the broad outline.

---

[156] Most of these events are well known, and since the main stuff of this chapter is ideas rather than facts, I shall not footnote them all in detail. Liu Shao-ch'i's article 'Liquidate Menshevik thought', and the Central Committee resolution of 1 July 1941 are translated by Boyd Compton, *Mao's China: party reform documents, 1942–44.* The 1 June 1943 resolution and Mao's speeches (except *Economic and financial problems*) are to be found in Mao, *SW* and many other sources, including the Compton volume. Liu's letter to 'Comrade Sung Liang' has long been known to exist. See my discussion of it in 'The party in Chinese Communist ideology', in J. W. Lewis, ed. *Party leadership and revolutionary power in China,* 177.

It has now been reprinted, and Sung Liang identified as Sun Yeh-fang (*Hung-ch'i* 7 (1980) 2–4), but Sun's original letter is not included in this version. For the latter, see Liu Shao-ch'i, *Lun tang* (On the party), 345–6. For key passages from Liu's report of April 1945 (which has recently been reprinted in China), see Carrère d'Encausse and Schram, 259–61. Regarding Mao's formal position in the party from March 1943, see *Tang-shih yen-chiu,* 2 (1980), 77–8.

To be sure, Mao wrote, with real or feigned modesty, in April 1943, when the rectification campaign had basically achieved its objectives, that his thought, which was a form of Marxism-Leninism, was not in his own opinion fully mature and thought out, and did not constitute a system. It was, he said, still not in the stage where it should be preached or advocated (*ku-ch'ui*), except perhaps for a few pieces contained in the documents studied during the campaign.[157] The fact remains, however, that it was quite clearly regarded, from 1943 onwards, and especially from 1945, as the definitive exemplar of the adaptation of Marxism-Leninism to Chinese conditions, and the summing-up and culmination both of Marxism and of Chinese culture.[158]

If we accept that Mao, after his humiliation at the hands of the '28 Bolsheviks' in 1932–4, and a long hard struggle, from 1935 to 1943, to establish his own political and ideological authority, at length achieved this goal in the course of the rectification campaign, what sort of political and economic system did he establish at that time in the Yenan base area, and what were the principles underlying it? It has been repeatedly argued that the essence of the Yenan heritage lies in an intimate relationship between the party and the masses. There is much truth in this, but the matter should not be looked at too one-sidedly.

In the second section of this chapter, I evoked the classic directive of 1 June 1943 on the 'mass line', and argued that this was an ambiguous concept, which pointed in two directions: toward Leninist elitism, and toward the genuine involvement of people in their own affairs.

To suggest that ordinary people may be a source of ideas from which correct policies are elaborated, and that they can in turn understand these policies, rather than blindly applying them, marked a very great rupture with one of the central themes of traditional Chinese thought. According to the *Analects*: 'The people may be made to follow a path of action, but they may not be made to understand it.'[159] This is one of the Confucian prejudices that Mao strove for half a century to break down. As already emphasized, he did not, however, cast doubt in so doing on the Leninist axiom that class consciousness can only be imported into the working class from outside, and more broadly that the Communist Party must provide ideological guidance to society as a whole.

[157] 'Chih Ho K'ai-feng' (To Ho K'ai-feng), 22 April 1943, *Selected letters*, 212–13.
[158] On this point, Ray Wylie (273–4) is, in my opinion, right, and Franz Schurmann wrong, about the interpretation of Liu Shao-ch'i's report to the Seventh Congress, and of the party statutes adopted on that occasion. Whether or not, in the early 1950s, the Chinese adopted a distinction between 'pure' and 'practical' ideology is quite another question, which I shall not take up here.
[159] *Confucian analects*, 8, ch. 9, in James Legge, *The Chinese classics*, 1.211.

Within the broad limits defined by Mao's insistence both on a measure of initiative and involvement from below, and on firm centralized guidance from above, there is room for an infinite variety of formulations and shades of emphasis. From Yenan days onwards, Mao Tse-tung rang the changes on these themes. Consistently, however, at least until the Cultural Revolution, he regarded centralized leadership as in the last analysis even more important than democracy.

Mao's ideas about methods of work and patterns of organization had taken shape progressively during a decade and a half of military and political struggle in the countryside, from the Autumn Harvest uprising to the rectification campaign. Now, in the early 1940s, the lessons of this experience were summed up, systematized, and applied to economic work as well as to guerrilla tactics.

A key slogan of this time was 'centralized leadership and dispersed operation' (*chi-chung ling-tao, fen-san ching-ying*). Such an approach was particularly appropriate in circumstances where only a relatively small proportion of the total area controlled by the Communists was located in the main Yenan base area, and the technical level of the economy was so low that rigorously centralized planning of inputs and outputs was neither possible nor desirable. Even in these circumstances, however, the accent was by no means on continued and unmitigated dispersion of responsibility and effort. Mao Tse-tung made this point quite unequivocally in his report of December 1942, *Economic and financial problems*.[160] Asking the rhetorical question why the self-sufficient industry of the Border Region should be run in such a dispersed fashion, Mao replied:

The main reason is that the labour force is divided among the various branches of the party, government and army. If it were centralized, we would destroy their activism. For example, we encouraged 359 Brigade to set up the Ta-kuang Textile Mill and did not order it to combine with a government mill because most of the several hundred employees at the mill were selected from the officers and men of 359 Brigade. They work to produce the bedding and clothing requirements of the Brigade and their enthusiasm is high. If we centralized, we would destroy this enthusiasm.... Adopting the policy of 'dispersed operation' is correct and ideas aimed at centralizing everything are wrong. However, enterprises of the same kind carried out within the same area should be centralized as much as possible. Unlimited dispersal is not profitable. At present we are already carrying out...centralization of this kind....Perhaps this process of dispersal at first and centralization later cannot be avoided...[161]

---

[160] Only the first part of this very long work appears in the current canon of Mao, *SW*. The passages quoted below are from part 7, 'On developing a self-sufficient industry', *MTTC* 8.263–4.
[161] The translation is that of Andrew Watson, *Mao Zedong and the political economy of the border region*, 149–50.

Later in the same section, listing the economic measures which should be
pursued in 1943, Mao placed second (immediately after increased capital
investment) that of 'establishing a unified leadership for the whole of
self-supporting industry, overcoming the serious anarchy which exists
now'.[162] In order to achieve this result, he called for the establishment
of a 'unified plan', drawn up under the 'unified leadership' of the Finance
and Economy Office (*Ts'ai-ching pan-shih-ch'u*), but at the same time he
specified that agriculture, industry and commerce should not be 'put
entirely in the hands of one single official organization for the whole
Border Region'. Instead, the unified plan should be 'handed over to the
party, government and army systems for separate implementation'.
Nevertheless, Mao's final conclusion was that the problem of unified
leadership was 'the central problem in advancing self-supporting industry
during 1943'.[163]

The sentence just quoted poses explicitly the problem of the relation
between party, state and army, which remained a central and often
controversial issue after 1949. A key concept, introduced in Yenan,
conveys the essence of the party's unifying and guiding role as conceived
at that time. The term is *i-yuan-hua* – literally 'to make one', 'to make
monolithic'. It has sometimes been translated 'to coordinate', but that is
probably too weak a rendering; 'to unify', which has also been used, is
unsatisfactory because it seems best to reserve this English term as the
equivalent for *t'ung-i*, just as 'centralized' is best kept for translating
chi-chung. The English equivalent which I propose to use is 'integrate',
but this question of translation is less important than the concerns which
underlay the adoption of the Chinese expression in the early 1940s.
Because this concept has hitherto received far less attention than
democratic centralism or the mass line, I shall give a number of
illustrations of its use, before summing up my understanding of its
significance.

The *locus classicus* of this term seems to be found in the Resolution of
the Politburo dated 1 September 1942, 'On the unification of party
leadership in the anti-Japanese bases, and adjusting the relations between
various organizations'.[164]

This resolution asserts explicitly and forcefully the link between
party-government and party-army relations on the one hand, and the

---

[162] Watson, *Mao Zedong*, 160.

[163] *MTTC* 8.265, 273; Watson, *Mao Zedong*, 151, 160–1.

[164] This is one of the documents studied in the course of the rectification campaign, and an English
translation can be found in Boyd Compton, *Mao's China*, 161–75. Authorship of the resolution
has not been officially attributed to Mao, but the Chinese text is included in the Tokyo *MTTC*,
8.155–63.

hierarchical structure of each individual organization on the other. Paragraph 8 of the resolution begins as follows:

The integration [*i-yuan-hua*] of party leadership is [to be] expressed on the one hand in the mutual relations between party, governmental, and mass organizations at the same level; on the other hand, it is [to be] expressed in the relations between upper and lower levels. In this [latter respect], strict adherence to the principle of obedience of lower to higher echelons and obedience of the entire party to the central committee is of decisive significance in unifying party leadership...[165]

A somewhat clearer definition and explanation of the meaning of the elusive term *i-yuan-hua* is to be found in the decision of 1 June 1943, drafted by Mao Tse-tung, from which I quoted earlier the well-known paragraph on the 'mass line'. In an immediately following passage (paragraph 7) of this directive, Mao declares:

In relaying to subordinate units any task... a higher organization should in all cases go through the leader of the lower organization concerned, so that he may assume responsibility, thus achieving the goal of combining division of labour with unified leadership [*i-yuan-hua*]. A department at a higher level should not go solely to its counterpart at the lower level (for instance, a higher department concerned with organization, propaganda or counter-espionage should not go solely to the corresponding department at the lower level), leaving the person in overall charge of the lower organization (such as the secretary, the chairman, the director or the school principal) in ignorance or without responsibility. Both the person in overall charge and the person with specific responsibility should be informed and given responsibility. This *i-yuan-hua* method, combining division of labour with unified leadership, makes it possible, through the person with overall responsibility, to mobilize a large number of cadres...to carry out a particular task, and thus to overcome shortages of cadres in individual departments and turn a good number of people into cadres for one's own work. This, too, is a way of combining the leadership with the masses...[166]

It will have been seen (as well as such things can be seen in translation) that *i-yuan-hua* is twice used as an appositive for 'combining division of labour with unified leadership'. The sense, plainly, is that the necessary division of labour between various organs can exist without posing a threat to the unity of the movement only on condition that the whole system be penetrated and controlled by a unifying force in the shape of the party. To convey this function, the English equivalent 'to integrate' seems most appropriate.

The use of the term *i-yuan-hua*, with its strong verbal force, reflects the perception, on the part of the Chinese Communist leadership, of the situation that prevailed in the early 1940s in the base areas, which were

---

[165] Compton, 171–2; translation modified on the basis of the Chinese text in *MTTC* 8.161.

[166] *SW* 3.120–1; revised on the basis of *MTTC* 9.29, to take account of changes (which are not particularly extensive) in the official Chinese text as compared to the 1943 version.

fragmented, often isolated, and exposed to enemy attack. In such circumstances, the various agencies of political, economic, and administrative control could scarcely be effectively integrated. They stressed, therefore, the necessity of *making* things monolithic (*i-yuan-hua*), because excessive dispersal in fact prevailed.

One might assume that, once the Chinese Communists had established their authority throughout the whole of the country and set up the People's Republic of China, dispersionism would no longer be a threat. In fact, for many complex historical and practical reasons, the problems of fragmentation and of divided authority by no means evaporated in 1949, and the concept of 'integrated leadership' therefore did not become irrelevant, even though the whole context did, of course, change radically with the conquest of power.

CONCLUSION: TOWARD A PEOPLE'S DEMOCRATIC MODERNIZING AUTOCRACY?

As indicated in the third section of this chapter, Mao had already in 1939–40 characterized the regime to be established after the war as a 'joint dictatorship of several revolutionary classes', and had made it fairly clear that this dictatorship was to be under the effective control of the proletariat, or of its 'vanguard', the Chinese Communist Party. When the prospect of a 'coalition government' with the Kuomintang, which Mao had envisaged as a useful tactical expedient in 1944–5, finally evaporated in 1946, and was replaced by open civil war, there was no longer any reason for maintaining the slightest ambiguity about the party's immediate political goals. Mao therefore spelled out, on 30 June 1949, in an article written to commemorate the 28th anniversary of the foundation of the Chinese Communist Party, the precise nature of the 'people's democratic dictatorship' which he proposed to establish three months later.

As for the class nature of the new state, Mao defined the locus of authority in terms of what has often been called a concentric-circle metaphor. The 'people' who were to exercise the dictatorship would be composed of the working class, the peasantry, the urban petty-bourgeoisie and the 'national bourgeoisie'. Of these four classes, the workers would enjoy hegemony, and the peasants constituted their most reliable allies. The petty-bourgeoisie were to be largely followers, while the national bourgeoisie had a dual nature: they were part of the people, but at the same time exploiters. Consequently, those elements among them who behaved badly could be re-classified as not of 'the people', and find themselves on the receiving end of the dictatorship, the objects rather than the subjects of revolutionary change.

Mao made no mystery at all of the form of the state which was to represent these four classes. Replying to imaginary critics who complained that the Communists were 'autocrats', he declared:

My dear sirs, you are right, that is just what we are. All the experience the Chinese people have accumulated through several decades teaches us to enforce the people's democratic dictatorship – which one could also call people's democratic autocracy [*tu-ts'ai*], the two terms mean the same thing – that is, to deprive the reactionaries of the right to speak and let the people alone have that right...

Don't you want to abolish state power? Yes, we do, but not right now; we cannot do it yet. Why? Because imperialism still exists, because domestic reaction still exists, because classes still exist in our country. Our present task is to strengthen the people's state apparatus – mainly the people's army, the people's police, and the people's courts – in order to consolidate the national defence and protect the people's interests. Given this condition, China can develop steadily, under the leadership of the working class and the Communist Party, from an agricultural into an industrial country, and from a new-democratic into a socialist and communist society, abolish classes and realize the Great Harmony [*ta-t'ung*].

In this task of guiding the development of China 'from an agricultural into an industrial country', Mao said that 'the education of the peasantry' was 'the serious problem'. For, he added: 'The peasant economy is scattered, and the socialization of agriculture, judging by the Soviet Union's experience, will require a long time and painstaking work.'[167]

These brief quotations evoke several crucial dimensions of the problem of carrying out a Marxist revolution in China after 1949. On the one hand, Mao's theory of the 'people's democratic dictatorship' was the lineal descendant of Lenin's 'revolutionary-democratic dictatorship of the workers and peasants', and of Stalin's 'four-class bloc', and Mao himself freely acknowledged this ideological debt, and went out of his way to stress the relevance of Soviet experience. Indeed, however unorthodox his road to power, as soon as victory was plainly within his grasp Mao had announced his intention of doing things henceforth in the orthodox way. 'From 1927 to the present,' he declared in March 1949, 'the centre of gravity of our work has been in the villages – gathering strength in the village in order to surround the cities, and then taking the cities. The period for this method of work has now ended. The period of "from the city to the villages" and of the city leading the village has now begun. The centre of gravity of the party's work has shifted from the village to the city.'[168] Hence Mao's statement: 'the serious problem is the education of the peasantry', in other words, the bringing of modern knowledge, and the resources of the modern industrial sector, from the cities to the countryside. Hence the stress, in 1949, on working-class leadership of the

---

[167] Mao, *SW* 4.418–19. [168] Mao, *SW* 4.363.

'people's dictatorship'. Hence the attempt, which was to be made in the early 1950s, to draw large numbers of real flesh-and-blood workers into the Chinese Communist Party, in order to 'improve' its class composition.

And yet, despite all this, and despite Mao's explicit statement, in 1962, that during these early years there had been no alternative to 'copying from the Soviets',[169] his article of 30 June 1949 itself contained, as already suggested, elements that point in a significantly different direction. Thus the old-fashioned term 'autocracy' (*tu-ts'ai*) was used as a synonym for dictatorship (*chuan-cheng*), *ta-t'ung* or 'Great Harmony' was used as an equivalent for communism, and the unique character of China's revolutionary experience was repeatedly underscored.

The question of whether or not the Chinese revolution after 1949 followed a course which could be characterized as 'orthodox' in Marxist terms, and of when, how, and why it diverged from the Soviet model is not a proper topic for discussion here, since it will be taken up in two further volumes of the *Cambridge History of China*. What does seem appropriate, in summing up the record of Mao's development as a theorist of revolution during the period ending in 1949, is to consider which of the trends that were to emerge during the first three decades of the People's Republic were already implicit in his thinking prior to the conquest of power, if people had only had the wit to read the signs of the times.

One domain where, in my opinion, this is not the case is that of the political economy of development. There are, of course, those who argue that 'Maoist economics' was born in Yenan, if not before. While it is certainly true that there are significant hints of Mao's future economic thinking to be found in the experience of the Yenan base areas (as summed up in 'Economic and financial problems'), these beginnings were too one-sided to justify the conclusion that the ideas of the Great Leap Forward of 1958 were in any sense implicit in them. They involved only peasant self-help and not the complex multi-faceted organization which characterized the communes; only a stress on indigenous methods, and not large-scale inputs or modern technology. In a word, there was no 'walking on two legs' combining the large and the small, the modern and the traditional in Yenan, and no idea of 'walking on two legs' in Mao's writings of the period. As already noted, Mao proposed in 1949 to transform China 'from an agricultural into an industrial country' through a process of modernization and economic development. And the rural population, though it would participate actively in this process, was to have no say as to the ultimate destination: it would have to accept 're-education', and the resulting change in its mentality and way of life.

[169] Schram, *Mao unrehearsed*, 178 (speech of 30 January 1962).

Thus, if one can distinguish a certain existential continuity between the self-sufficient economy of Yenan and the new policies adopted under the slogan of self-reliance (*tzu-li keng-sheng*) a decade and a half later, there was no intellectual continuity in terms of detailed policy formulations, and certainly no unbroken chain of development in Mao's own thinking, since he explicitly repudiated in 1949 many of the rudimentary ideas he had put forward in the early 1940s. There was, to be sure, as already noted, substantial continuity in the philosophical core of Mao Tse-tung's thought, from 1937 to the early 1960s at least. But if Mao's theory of contradictions was ultimately incompatible with the logic of the Soviet model of economic development, Mao himself did not discover this until the period of the Great Leap.

The one domain in which there was almost total continuity in Mao's approach from the 1930s to the 1970s was that of patterns and methods for the exercise of political authority. Moreover, in this case it should have been possible, I would argue, to discern in Mao's speeches and writings prior to 1949 the signs of many things to come.

Mao said in 1949 that the new regime he was about to set up could be called a 'people's democratic autocracy' just as well as a 'people's democratic dictatorship'. Too much should not be made of this terminological difference, for *tu-ts'ai* was sometimes used in years past, when Marxist expressions did not yet all have standard equivalents in Chinese, as a translation for 'dictatorship'. None the less, to the extent that it carries an aura of old-fashioned Chinese-style autocracy, this term in fact sums up rather well the essence of Mao's approach to political leadership.

On the one hand, he promoted grass-roots participatory democracy on a larger scale than any other revolutionary leader of modern times. In this respect he served the Chinese people well, and helped to prepare them for the next stage in their political development. But at the same time he regarded the promotion of democracy as feasible only within the framework of a 'strong state'. In this he was, in my opinion, correct. Unfortunately, his idea of a strong state was something very like an autocracy, in which he, as the historic leader of the Chinese revolution, remained in the last analysis the arbiter as to what political tendencies were legitimate, and which were not.

As stressed in the third section of this chapter, Mao sought to promote, in the period from 1939 onwards, a 'new democratic' revolution in China which would be a kind of functional equivalent of the capitalist stage in the development of European society. On the one hand, this meant, of course, modernization and industrialization, in order to create the economic foundation on which socialism could ultimately be established. But he was also bent on completing the work of China's abortive capitalist stage in another sense, by continuing the attack on the old Confucian values launched at the time of the May Fourth movement. Indeed, he actually wrote, in August 1944, in a letter calling for emancipation from the old family system: 'There are those who say we neglect or repress individuality [*ko-hsing*]; this is wrong. If the individuality which has been fettered is not liberated, there will be no democracy, and no socialism'.[170] One must none the less ask whether this goal was compatible with Mao's outlook as a whole.

  ˙ Behind this, and the other questions I have just posed, lurk the fundamental issues raised by the process of cross-cultural borrowing which has been under way in China since the beginning of this century, and has still not led to any clear-cut result. The violent rejection of traditional Chinese values in favour of ideas of Western origin which had characterized, on the whole, the May Fourth period, had been succeeded in the 1930s, in the context of the Anti-Japanese War, by a reaffirmation of the dignity of Chinese culture. In the case of Chiang-Kai-shek and the Kuomintang, this swing of the pendulum had led virtually to the negation of the whole May Fourth spirit, and the assertion that Confucianism provided the answer to all the world's problems. Mao Tse-tung, as an adherent of that most radical of Westernizing philosophies, Marxism-Leninism, could not go to such an extreme, but there is none the less a certain parallelism between the trends in Kuomintang ideology which led to the writing of *China's destiny*, and Mao's call for 'sinification'.

  In the late 1940s, as nationwide victory approached, Mao Tse-tung began to emphasize more strongly, as noted above, explicitly Marxist concerns such as the need for leadership by the cities and by the working class, and the central role of industrialization in transforming both Chinese society and Chinese culture. But could 'feudal' culture truly be abolished, and could a party truly undergo reform and acquire a more democratic work style, under the guidance of an 'autocrat', albeit a benevolent one? Could a 'people's democratic autocracy', such as Mao Tse-tung set up in 1949, truly carry out modernization, if this included by implication profound changes in the traditional political culture? Or would the form of such a regime ultimately vitiate or distort the content? That is the question which can be clearly seen to hang over Mao's political creed, at his moment of triumph in 1949.

[170] 'Chih Ch'in Pang-hsien' (To Ch'in Pang-hsien), 31 August 1944, *Selected letters*, 239.

CHAPTER 6

THE PARTY AND THE INTELLECTUALS: PHASE TWO

THE DENIGRATION OF INTELLECTUAL ENDEAVOR IN THE GREAT LEAP FORWARD

The suppression of specific intellectuals in the Anti-Rightist campaign turned into anti-intellectualism in general in the Great Leap Forward (GLF). The leadership's hope of using the intellectuals as key figures in China's modernization had been dashed when both intellectuals and students criticized the Party in the Hundred Flowers. After a decade of indoctrination and ideological remolding campaigns, intellectuals still questioned Party policies. The leadership's disillusion with the intellectuals was reflected in Propaganda Director Lu Ting-i's statements in the GLF period. Whereas in the Hundred Flowers he had used Mao's slogan to encourage intellectuals with Western learning to participate actively in the nation-building, effort, in a *Kuang-ming Daily* article of 13 March 1958 he rejected Western learning as "poisonous weeds": "There is bankruptcy in bourgeois philosophy, science, social sciences, literature and arts. The only value in studying them is that we can learn to recognize them as 'poisonous weeds' and by weeding, use them as fertilizer."

Even though the intellectuals in the GLF were less direct objects of attack than in the Anti-Rightist Campaign, their relative position in Chinese society deteriorated further. In contrast to the Hundred Flowers period, the GLF emphasized political reliability rather than professional skill. A new slogan was advanced, calling on people in all walks of life, including intellectuals, to be "Red and expert," with the emphasis on "Red." As the movement gained momentum, the emphasis shifted almost wholly to redness. Intelligence was equated with political commitment and was no longer regarded as the monopoly of the few, and this change presaged the Cultural Revolution. Party cadres armed with the ideological weapons of Marxism-Leninism and Mao Tse-tung Thought were praised as superior to intellectuals and professionals trained in Western methods and ideas. Moreover, to a much greater extent than ever before, the creativity and intellectual capacities of the masses were idealized and accepted as articles of almost mystical faith. Peasants and workers, just emerging from illiteracy, were praised as scientists, philosophers, and poets, capable of virtually any achievement because of their "proletarian" consciousness. By contrast, intellectuals were denigrated because they were imbued with the bourgeois concepts of individualism, liberalism, and anarchism.

Scholarship was treated as purely functional and coordinated with industrial and agricultural production. The importance of science and engineering increased still more in relation to the social sciences and humanities, but even scientists and engineers were ordered to learn from the achievements of ordinary peasants and workers. Academic standards were watered down. The study of math and scientific theory, crucial to modernization, was slighted in favor of mastery of technical skills.

Almost all the older urban intellectuals and students were sent to the countryside and smaller towns for a period of labor reform, where they were to be reeducated by doing manual labor and mixing with the masses. Their positions in universities and research centers were filled by younger, more politically indoctrinated Party cadres who were able to insert themselves into the intellectual establishment at this time. Older intellectuals who managed to remain at their institutions were relegated to subservient or even menial positions. The old textbooks were dispensed with and new ones were written as collective works by Party cadres and younger scholars and graduate students. Like the rest of the population, intellectuals were ordered to produce whatever they did in great quantities for the sake of the revolution. Quantity was exalted at the expense of quality.

The harnessing of literature for the GLF exemplified what happened in other fields of intellectual and creative endeavor. Writers were given grandiose plans that had to be completed in 1958. The eminent writer Pa Chin, who had produced little since the Party's accession to power, pledged to write one long novel, three medium-length novels, and several translations within the course of a year. The Writers Union announced that China's professional writers would produce seven hundred stories, plays, and poems, all of which would be easy to understand and conducive to the emergence of new heroes and new phenomena. Despite the extraordinary demands placed on professional writers, more emphasis was given to unskilled, politically committed writers. As in other fields, the distinction between the professional and amateur was blurred. The number of "writers" jumped from fewer than a thousand in 1957 to more than two hundred thousand in 1958. Thousands of loyal amateurs even became members of the elite Writers Union.

The anti-intellectual and collectivist spirit of the GLF was expressed in the creative activity of anonymous groups of amateurs. They produced the most distinctive cultural products of the GLF – poems and songs of workers and peasants created at large meetings. Party cadres suggested themes and ideas and wrote down the lines as the masses spoke them out. The Party manipulated these poetry-writing sessions into expressing the Party's will and then used the poems to stimulate mass enthusiasm for rapid economic advances.

The CCP had used such methods of indoctrination and mobilization since the late 1930s, but never on such an intensive, widespread scale as in the GLF, when poems and songs were incessantly broadcast over loudspeakers and ubiquitously pasted on walls. China's foremost literary journal, *Jen-min wen-hsueh* (People's literature) gave itself over entirely to publishing the writings of workers and peasants.

China's cultural czar, Chou Yang, provided a theoretical framework for the literature and art of the GLF – the combination of revolutionary realism and revolutionary romanticism. Although this theory was introduced as an original concept of Mao Tse-tung, it was a restatement of the Soviet concept of socialist realism. In fact, as early as 1934 the Soviet cultural chief, Zhdanov, had advocated revolutionary romanticism, defined as the description of characters and events as they will be in the ideal state of communism. At a time of worsening relations with the Soviet Union, the CCP, in the GLF, tried to dissociate its cultural policies from their Soviet derivation, and from the Soviet emphasis in the post-Stalin era on realism rather than socialism, by presenting the Soviet literary theory under another name. Yet, just as before the GLF, at a time when relations with the Soviet Union were better, literary works were to capture in ordinary life a vision of the future and arouse enthusiasm for Party policies.

THE INTELLECTUAL RELAXATION IN THE AFTERMATH OF THE GREAT LEAP FORWARD

As a result of economic chaos in the late 1950s and early 1960s, the Party modified the commune system, allowed private plots, sanctioned private service trades, and permitted material incentives in order to repair the economic damage of the GLF. It also relaxed its grip on the intellectuals in order to win their cooperation in this endeavor. The period of relative relaxation that began in 1961 and extended through the autumn of 1962 was similar to, and yet different from, the Hundred Flowers. Both interludes of a more moderate, more tolerant approach toward intellectuals were in part a by-product of prior periods of intellectual repression.

The Anti-Rightist Campaign and GLF had silenced and demoralized a larger number of intellectuals than the Hu Feng campaign of 1955. A substantial number had become increasingly passive in the face of intensive criticism and enforced labor reform. Scholars in the social sciences, humanities, arts, and even the more general sciences were reluctant to innovate and participate. In addition to this dialectical process, the shift from repression to relative relaxation was governed by political and economic considerations. Confronted with an economy in shambles and the withdrawal of Soviet scientific and technical experts due to the Sino-Soviet split of 1960, the Party was in desperate need of the services of the intellectuals. Thus, it offered them intellectual and material incentives in the expectation of reactivating them.

The moving force behind the 1961-62 relaxation was Liu Shao-ch'i and the Party bureaucracy rather than Mao, who had been so instrumental in initiating the Hundred Flowers. Whereas Liu and most of the bureaucracy had gone along reluctantly with the Hundred Flowers, they now led the effort to rejuvenate the intellectual community. Like Mao, they had no interest in liberalizing China's intellectual life or making it more pluralistic. But they were willing to encourage a degree of intellectual ferment and criticism if it created a more favorable climate for scientific, technical, and economic development and did not weaken political control.

Superficially, the relaxation of 1961-62 had many of the same trappings and slogans as the Hundred Flowers. It was heralded by several high officials. Vice-Premier Ch'en I, in a speech given in August 1961, reminiscent of the one Chou En-lai had given in January 1956 to usher in the Hundred Flowers, sought to invigorate the intellectual community by urging that greater respect be shown to the scholar and higher regard be given to his contribution to the nation. Ch'en explained, as Mao had during the Hundred Flowers period, that years of Party indoctrination had rendered the intellectuals politically trustworthy. In fact, Ch'en had so much confidence in the transformation of the intellectuals that he believed they need no longer spend time in political sessions and manual labor to the neglect of their own work. He declared, "As long as experts show results in their profession and contribute to the construction of socialism, there should be no objection to their taking only a small part in political activity." Furthermore, he announced that an intellectual need not be thoroughly versed in Marxism-Leninism and completely committed to the Party ideology. In Maoist jargon, that meant that one could be more expert than Red.

Ch'en redefined communism in terms closer to Khrushchev's pragmatic interpretation than to the Chinese Communist Party's more ideological approach. The intellectual demonstrated his political spirit, Ch'en declared, not by constantly professing his devotion to the regime or to its political system, but by contributing to the development of modern industry, agriculture, science, and culture. In Ch'en's view, such activity was "a manifestation of the politics of socialism." He feared that unless there were these changes in attitudes toward intellectuals, "Our country's science and culture will lag behind for ever."[1]

Chou En-lai also encouraged greater freedom of speech, particularly in a talk on 19 June 1961 that was not published until 1979 but whose ideas must have been known in the intellectual community. He went so far as to sanction criticism of decisions that had already been accepted by Party leaders. "Even things officially approved and passed by the working conference, convened by the Party's Central Committee, can be discussed and even revised."[2] Although Chou did not call for legal guarantees of the right to speak, he advocated an approach more in tune with Western attitudes than previous Party treatment of intellectuals. As long as one's work was not against the Party and against socialism, it should be permitted. There should also be a separation between intellectual activities and political activities. He discarded as well the emphasis on political reliability, characteristic of the GLF, in favor of expertise.

Chou's view of the early 1960s was that one who was skilled in his work was much more valuable to the development of socialism than one who was versed in politics but unskilled. Even Mao expressed the general feeling at this time that intellectuals should be allowed to

---

1 *KMJP*, 3 September 1961, 2.
2 Chou En-lai, "On literature and art," *Wen-i pao* (Literary gazette), February 1979, *Peking review* (30 March 1979), 9.

work relatively unhindered by political considerations. On 30 January 1962, at the Seven Thousand Cadres Conference, Mao pointed out that intellectuals need not be revolutionary: "As long as they are patriotic, we shall unite with them and let them get on with their work."[3] In apparent support of the relaxation, he urged people to present their views without fear of punishment so long as they did not violate Party discipline and engage in secret activities.

The Party made a special effort to win the cooperation of the scientists. To remedy the lowering of scientific standards during the GLF, in January 1961 the Ninth Plenum of the Eighth Central Committee called for improvement in the quality of scientific work. Scientists were assured sufficient time for their own research and given added material incentives. They were also given more responsibility in directing their work. Administrators at all levels were directed to heed the advice of scientific and technical personnel on technical matters. A scientist was to be judged by his expertise, not by his ideology. The *Kuang-ming jih-pao* stated on 5 November 1961; "We should not judge a scientist's achievement in natural science by the standard that he is a materialist or an idealist in his philosophical thinking. A scientist who is philosophically an idealist may attain great achievements in natural science."

As during the Hundred Flowers, courses were given in Morgan genetics, and such formerly deprecated scientists as Newton, Copernicus, and Einstein were spoken of favorably. More attention was also given to providing students with a broader theoretical scientific education rather than just specialized technical training. With scientists and technicians given wider discretion in meeting their obligations to the state, the Party had created the conditions for the emergence of a new class of specialists whose decisions would be based on more apolitical standards and whose activities might represent a potential challenge to Party control.

Even in the social sciences, intellectuals were given more latitude. Social scientists were encouraged to explore different methods of research, conduct various experiments, and raise different assumptions. Several articles in the authoritative journal *Hung-ch'i* (Red flag) advised social scientists that they need not concentrate on subjects directly related to the political and class struggle. With such urging, some unprecedented discussions occurred, particularly in the field of economics. Several economists offered suggestions that paralleled the

3 Stuart Schram, ed., *Mao Tse-tung unrehearsed*, 169.

ones being made by reformist economists in the Soviet Union. They, like their Soviet counterparts, called for a pragmatic rather than an ideological approach to economic problems. They urged that profitability and efficiency instead of political criteria be made the basis of investments and that the marketplace rather than administrative decisions determine prices. In addition to the profit and price mechanisms, some economists also recommended the use of mathematical methods, differentiated rent, economic accounting, and interest on capital as means for promoting China's modernization.

The latitude granted to writers in 1961–62 was similar in scope to that granted them in previous periods of relaxation. Writers, as in earlier interludes, were urged to use a variety of styles and methods of expression. Socialist realism and revolutionary romanticism were no longer prescribed, as they had been in the GLF, as the only literary forms. In addition, there was emphasis on more professional literary standards and on the intrinsic value of art. This more creative approach was not merely tolerated but was actively promoted by Party leaders. As in the Hundred Flowers, writers were allowed diversification not only of style but also of subject matter and theme. An editorial in *Wen-i pao* declared, "A writer, according to his different circumstances, [should] freely select and arrange the material with which he is most familiar and which he enjoys."[4] No longer did writers have to depict construction projects or even the class struggle; they were now allowed to describe family life, love affairs, nature, and the small details of everyday living.

Yet unlike the Hundred Flowers, the few intellectuals who did speak out in 1961–62 limited their statements to a parroting of the official line. Though the debate by the economists certainly had political implications, the regime refrained from counterattack at this time. The anxiety of Party leaders during this period of economic crisis was evident from their willingness to explore, or at least permit, the publication of comparatively radical economic suggestions that might lead to more efficient use of scarce resources.

Even an apparently bold article by the novelist Pa Chin, "The writer's courage and responsibility," written in commemoration of the twentieth anniversary of Mao's Yenan "Talks on literature and art," conformed to the Party line. Although his arguments were strongly stated, they coincided with the regime's attack on the bureaucracy's suffocation of China's cultural life. His essay began on

4 *Wen-i pao*, 3 (1961), 3.

a note of sadness as he expressed anxiety over growing old without having created anything he considered worth while. This anxiety must have been shared by most May Fourth writers who had produced few literary works after 1949. Instead of fulfilling his responsibility as a writer, he lamented, "I have spent myself on all kinds of things. I have advanced much politically, but I have written little and moreover have written it badly." What prevented him from carrying out his duty as a writer, Pa Chin asserted, was the literary bureaucracy, which dictated what he could write.

He described these bureaucrats as "people with a hoop in one hand and a club in the other who go everywhere looking for persons who have gone astray.... They enjoy making simple hoops ... and wish to make everyone jump through them.... If there are people who do not wish to go through their hoops and if there are some who have several kinds of flowers blooming in their gardens ..., these people become angry, raise up their clubs, and strike out."[5] He did not draw the obvious conclusion that the existence of bureaucrats with hoops and clubs was due to the Party's policies. Speaking in more general terms, he stressed the need, as did the regime at this time, for greater unity between leaders and led. He proposed that this be done by the democratic method of expressing diverse viewpoints, rather than by the authoritarian method of frightening people with different opinions into submission.

Outwardly, therefore, this period of relaxation appeared to be in the spirit of the original Hundred Flowers campaign. In actual fact, it was not. Although many of the same techniques were employed and several of the same terms were used, from the very start its scope was restricted to scientific and academic subjects. The Party was unwilling to allow the wide-open discussions of spring 1957. As soon as the relaxation began, it called for a clear-cut distinction between contention in the academic sphere and contention in the political arena. Some intellectuals had previously demanded this separation so they could express themselves more freely in their own fields without the imposition of political criteria. The Party now demanded it so that the intellectuals would not interpret the Party's tolerance of freer discussion in academic subjects as a sanction to examine political issues as had happened in 1957.

The restricted nature of this relaxation is seen in the speech by Ch'en I that urged intellectuals to contend. Besides emphasizing

5 *Shang-hai wen-hsueh*, 5 (1962), 3.

intellectual merit and deemphasizing political reliability, he insisted on the need for continued ideological indoctrination. The concession was that thought reform was to be carried out in a different manner than in the more intense periods of regimentation. The Party sought to indoctrinate the intellectual by making acceptance of Marxism-Leninism a voluntary rather than an enforced act. This aim was clearly stated by Ch'en I when he declared, "Since thought reform relies chiefly on the individual's consciousness, the individual must come to conclusions himself. Therefore, it is not feasible to use forceful measures and exert popular pressure."[6]

Thought reform sessions were to be conducted in an atmosphere that was psychologically less threatening. The Party called these sessions of the early sixties "meetings of the immortals" to distinguish their more easygoing approach from the intense pressure applied during the criticism and self-criticism sessions of preceding campaigns. The meetings were to leave an ethereal feeling, as if one were immortal; instead of reforming the intellectual by coercion, they were to wash him with "gentle breezes and mild rain."

This phrase had also been used in the Hundred Flowers campaign, but for a different purpose. It was the method to be used by the intellectuals in criticizing the cadres, not the reverse. The meaning of this phrase in practice was described by Ch'en I when he stated that in reforming another individual, one must "not hurt his feelings or deal blows to his soul. One must be patient and understanding."[7] As before, the intellectuals were divided into small study groups, but the discussions in these groups were to be conducted as informal chats rather than as confessions extorted by the cadres. If ideological "mistakes" were made in the course of a chat, the individual was not to be ostracized but was to remain part of the group and be treated in a comradely fashion. The Party's aim, as stated in the People's Daily, was that "by exchanging thoughts and helping one another, all people will naturally ... acquire an identical, definite understanding of right and wrong."[8]

The Party's call for a clear division between debate in academic and in political spheres was meant to confine the intellectuals' discussions to the academic realm, but it was not meant to confine the Party to the political realm. The Party, as in the past, sought to exert its

6 KMJP, 3 September 1961, 2.
7 Ibid.
8 Lin Kuo-chün, "Meetings of Immortals drive the intellectuals forward in self-remolding," JMJP, 16 May 1961, SCMP, 2.513, 11.

control over scholarship, particularly in nonscientific fields. Only academic discussion useful to the Party was allowed. Contradictory goals continued to characterize the Party's policy toward the intellectuals. It sought to foster intellectual and scientific endeavor while at the same time it maintained ideological control. Scholars were urged to look for the truth, but the truth could not be contrary to Mao's teaching or to the Party's current program. The printing of unofficial journals and wall posters and the formation of independent groups engaging in a spontaneous exchange of ideas, as in the spring in 1957, were not permitted.

The uniqueness of the relaxation of 1961–1962

With a few exceptions, most intellectuals and non-Party people were reluctant to participate because of the undefined nature of the new freedom and because of their past experience. They feared that the movement was designed to investigate their minds rather than to enrich culture and science. Pointing to the ambiguity between the line dividing debate in the political and in the academic spheres, several refused to express their own opinions. They claimed their views on academic questions would be construed as opinions on political issues. Still others excused themselves from the debate with the plea of insufficient knowledge.

Unlike the Hundred Flowers, when criticism came principally from the intellectual community and students, the criticism that was heard in 1961–62 came from intellectual-officials high in the Party hierarchy, principally in the Propaganda Department and the Peking Party Committee, the very organizations instrumental in implementing the relaxation. They used the more indirect Confucian style of criticism through literary and historical allusions rather than the more forthright Western style of the Hundred Flowers. Moreover, whereas in the spring of 1957 the "democratic" leaders and students challenged the one-party rule of the CCP, in 1961–62 the intellectual-officials did not attack the Party in which they had prominent positions. Rather, they subtly criticized Mao and his policies of mass mobilization, economic leaps forward, and thought reform campaigns. They also defended former Defense Minister P'eng Te-huai, whom Mao dismissed for criticizing the GLF in July 1959.

Yet the easier atmosphere of the early 1960s, increasing disillusion with the GLF, and concern over the capabilities of China's aging leader still do not fully explain why these intellectual-officials, who were well aware of the consequences of dissent, chose to criticize publicly. There is little proof for the charges made in the Cultural Revolution that Liu Shao-ch'i and Teng Hsiao-p'ing were the behind-the-scenes manipulators. They were linked more directly to the head of the Peking Party Committee, P'eng Chen, who had special jurisdication over intellectuals and the director and deputy director of the Party's Propaganda Department, Lu Ting-i and Chou Yang. Yet it is unlikely that these politically astute officials would have allowed the attack on Mao and his policies unless they had support from Liu and Teng, who could not explicitly criticize Mao themselves without shattering the façade of a coherent, unified leadership. Liu had, in fact, gone along with the GLF and had seconded Mao in implementing it. However, in his report in January 1962 at the Seven Thousand Cadres Conference, he expressed disillusion with the GLF's methods of revolutionary exhortation and episodic upheaval. Such methods had been appropriate to the guerrilla days, but now he condemned them as detrimental to building a modern, industrialized society. This view gave implicit sanction to the criticism of the intellectual-officials.

The Peking Party Committee intellectuals

In May 1961, P'eng Chen instructed his closest deputies in the Peking Party Committee to evaluate the GLF. Under the direction of Teng T'o, head of the Peking Party Committee Secretariat, about a dozen members of the committee gathered to study the Central Committee directives of the GLF. As a result of their deliberations, they not only presented P'eng Chen with a critique of the GLF but also burst forth with criticism, albeit oblique, of Mao, and a defense, similarly veiled, of P'eng Te-huai in the theater, newspapers, journals, films, lectures, and discussions in Peking. Whether P'eng Chen specifically called for such attacks is not clear, but it is obvious that they could not appear in his domain without his sanction or at least his tolerance. Given his past political orthodoxy, it is unlikely that he identified entirely with the intellectual-officials ideologically. Yet when P'eng read some of their articles, he was quoted as saying, "They are rich and colorful" in content and "highly welcome."[9]

---

9 Wu Tung-hui, "Destroy the black backstage manager of 'The three-family village,'" KMJP, 18 June 1967, SCMP, 3977, 14.

Teng T'o was the leader of the intellectual-officials associated with the Peking Party Committee. A journalist, historian, poet, and classicist, he set the intellectual standard of the group with his Marxist critique of the GLF, combined with the reassertion of Western liberal values of the May Fourth era and some of the traditional values of Confucianism, particularly a concern for the plight of the peasant. Between 1952 and 1957 he was editor-in-chief of the *People's Daily*, and from 1954 to 1960, president of the All-China Journalists Association. In 1957 he was dismissed as editor-in-chief of the *People's Daily*, perhaps because he, along with his patron P'eng Chen, had reluctantly gone along with Mao's Hundred Flowers and supposedly had refused to publicize Mao's ideas on the correct handling of internal contradictions. His old associate P'eng Chen then appointed him to the Peking Party Committee, where he established a theoretical journal called *Ch'ien-hsien* (Front line).

He worked closely with a vice-mayor of Peking, Wu Han, a major historian of the Ming dynasty, who represented a different intellectual strand. In the 1930s and 1940s, he was active in the democratic parties and had associated with Westernized academics such as Hu Shih and Feng Yu-lan. Another collaborator was the writer Liao Mo-sha, one of the luminaries of the Shanghai literary world of the 1930s, who was the director of the United Front Work Department of the Peking Party Committee and also in the Propaganda Department. These men came from different backgrounds but had a long personal association and had agreed on certain principles.

Their sharpest weapon was the *tsa-wen*, the short, subtle, satirical essay form that Lu Hsun had used so effectively against the Kuomintang and his ideological enemies in the 1930s and his followers had used in Yenan. Teng T'o, Wu Han, and Liao Mo-sha were masters of this form. Under the pen name Wu Nan-hsing, they published sixty-seven *tsa-wen*, called "Notes from a three-family village" in *Front Line*. Teng T'o also published his own series, "Evening talks at Yen-shan," in the *Peking Evening News* (*Pei-ching wan-pao*) and the *Peking Daily* (*Pei-ching jih-pao*).

What the bureaucratic leaders supposedly said behind closed doors they expressed allegorically, yet vividly, in the public arena. Because of their subtlety and sophistication, it is unlikely that they were fully appreciated by a wide audience. But it is likely that their indirect messages were understood by the political and intellectual elite cognizant of Party concerns. Using ancient characters and historical incidents, Teng T'o in particular obliquely criticized contemporary people and events. On the surface his essays appeared to be mild social and historical commentaries, but in reality they were devastating, though subtle, criticisms of Mao's leadership and policies. Like Lu Hsun's *tsa-wen*, the essays were written in an Aesopian language intended to be understood by a limited circle of like-minded intellectuals and leaders.

Several of the *tsa-wen* appeared to denounce the personality cult of Mao. They pointed out that it was impossible for one man or even a small group to understand everything and command everything. In one of their essays, "A special treatment for amnesia," they implied that Mao suffered from a form of mental disorder that led him to irrational behavior and decisions. "People suffering from this disease ... often go back on their word and do not keep their promises.... It will not only bring forgetfulness, but will gradually lead to abnormal pleasure or anger ... easiness to lose one's temper and finally insanity." The advice, obviously directed to Mao, was that under such conditions "a person must promptly take a complete rest. ... If he insists on talking or doing anything, he will get into a lot of trouble."[10]

Perhaps Teng T'o's most daring criticism of Mao was in "The royal way and the tyrant's way." He contrasted the ancient historian Liu Hsiang's definition of the royal way, which was "combining human sentiments with law and morality," with the tyrant's way, which "relied on authority and power, used violence and coercion, ordered others about and robbed people by force or by tricks." In terms of the present, he said, the royal way would be called following the mass line, whereas the tyrant's way would be called "arrogant, subjective, dogmatic, and arbitrary."[11]

As sharply as Teng questioned Mao's ability to rule, he attacked his policy of the GLF. In "The theory of treasuring labor power," he protested against the forced use of peasant labor for large-scale construction projects. Once again he used the example of ancient rulers to criticize the present one. He wrote, "Even as early as the Spring and Autumn period and the Warring States, our great politicians already understood the meaning of caring for human labor. The *Book of rites* states that the labor power of the people can be requisitioned no more than three days a year." He concluded, "We should draw new enlightenment from the experience of the ancients

10 Wu Nan-hsing, "Notes from a three-family village: A special treatment of amnesia," *Ch'ien-hsien* (Front line), 14, 1962, *CB*, 792, 4.
11 Ma Nan-ts'un (Teng T'o), "The royal way and the tyrant's way," *Yen-shan yeh-hua*, 4. 13–16.

and take care to do more in every way to treasure our labor power."[12]

In another essay, on the German philosopher Ernst Mach, he allusively criticized Mao's voluntarist view of development by lamenting the belief of Mach and his followers that they could accomplish whatever they wished. The result was that they ran up against the limitations of reality and in the end destroyed themselves. In an essay entitled "This year's spring festival," he directly referred to the food shortages caused by the GLF by pointing out that whereas traditional governments had guarded against these shortages, the present one had not fulfilled its responsibility to the people.

While attacking Mao and the GLF, he defended P'eng Te-huai. In obvious allusions to P'eng, several of his *tsa-wen* described courageous, incorruptible officials who had been accused unjustly of crimes for protesting against injustice. He described one, Li San-ts'ai, a high official of the Ming who, because he boldly exposed the crimes of the eunuchs at court, was dismissed from office. Li submitted memorial after memorial requesting a personal hearing from the emperor, but he was refused. Li then reportedly said, "Unable to contain myself, I take up 100 pieces of silk to point out my misery in all its detail,"[13] perhaps an allusion to Peng's own 80,000-word defense of himself, which it was rumored he was writing at the time. Teng published this essay on 29 March 1962 in the *Peking Evening News*. P'eng's defense was finally presented to the Party's Central Committee in June 1962.

However critical these *tsa-wen* were of Mao and the GLF, they generally conformed to the view of the bureaucratic leadership. Other *tsa-wen*, however, were not necessarily in conformity with the leadership. They asked for a degree of autonomy and a voice for scholars in political decision making that was not sanctioned by the leadership. They described Sung, Ming, and Ch'ing scholars, poets, artists, and advisors who were courageous and honest in criticizing harsh rulers no matter what the cost. Teng also praised traditional rulers who "welcome miscellaneous scholars," by whom he meant intellectuals with unorthodox approaches. "It would be a great loss to us if we now failed to acknowledge the general significance of the wide range of knowledge of 'miscellaneous scholars' for all kinds of leadership as well as for scientific research."[14]

Teng often cited the Tung-lin scholars in the late Ming dynasty as

12 Teng T'o, "Treasuring labor power," ibid., 1, 58.
13 Teng T'o, "In defense of Li San-ts'ai, ibid., 3, 150.
14 Teng T'o, "Is wisdom reliable?" ibid., 4, 17–19.

the paradigm of a group of intellectuals engaged in politics. In direct contradiction to Mao's disdain for learning in officials or for scholars advising on politics, Teng declared: "To be learned without being interested in politics is just as wrong as being politically inclined without being learned."[15] He concluded by asking why, if one's ancestors understood these truths, those who lived now could not understand and try to emulate them. He also admired the Tung-lin because they risked death to right the wrongs they saw in society. He printed a verse that depicted their courage:

> Do not think of them as mere intellectuals indulging in
>   empty talk
> Fresh were the bloodstains when the heads rolled
> Fighting the wicked men in power with abiding will
> The Tung-lin scholars were a stout-hearted generation.[16]

This was an epitaph that could also have been written later for Teng T'o and his associates.

Despite a relative silence after the establishment of the PRC in 1949 and an active role in attacking rightists in 1957, Wu Han suddenly began to write articles in 1959 about the upright Ming official Hai Jui. At Party meetings in April–May 1959, Mao had urged emulation of Hai Jui's criticism of bureaucratic misdeeds. The Chairman's secretary Hu Ch'iao-mu asked Wu Han as a Ming historian to write about him. But one of Wu Han's writings, a play which dealt with the dismissal of this famous magistrate from office, was later attacked as an indirect criticism of Mao's policies, the GLF, and the dismissal of P'eng Te-huai.

It focused on the plight of the Soochow peasants who complained to Hai Jui that their lands had been confiscated by local officials. Despite threats and bribes from local officials, Hai Jui demanded that illegally confiscated land be returned, that grievances be redressed, and that arbitrary acts be stopped in an effort to restore prosperity and stability to the area. He also ordered the death of a landlord's son because he had killed an elderly peasant. The local landlords and officials appealed to the emperor to spare the landlord's son and dismiss Hai Jui, which the emperor did. Though presented in a historical context, this play denounced policies that impoverished and disregarded the wishes of the peasants and could be interpreted as defending P'eng Te-huai's efforts to help the peasants. Although

15 Teng T'o, "A concern for all things," ibid., 2, 60–62.
16 Teng T'o, "Sing the praise of Lake T'ai," KMJP, 7 September 1960.

the play, staged in February 1961, received good reviews, it was suspended after a few performances.

The May Fourth writers associated with the Party's Propaganda Department

Views similar to those of the intellectual-officials in the Peking Party Committee were expressed by a group of writers, playwrights, literary critics, poets, and journalists who held high positions in the Party's propaganda bureaucracy. These groups had been closely associated since the 1930s in the long struggle to bring the Party to power. They had worked together in the leftist cultural and journalist community at different times in Japan, Shanghai, Yenan, Chungking, and Hong Kong. Within the group associated with the Propaganda Department were some of China's most famous May Fourth writers such as T'ien Han, Hsia Yen, Yang Han-sheng, Pa Chin, and Mao Tun. The Party leaders of this group were Chou Yang and a coterie of close associates formed in Yenan in the 1940s.

Although Chou Yang's main function since Mao's 1942 Yenan "Talks on literature and art" was to ensure ideological orthodoxy and carry out a series of relentless campaigns and purges, in the early 1960s he was a member of the group that questioned Mao's infallibility in directing China's development. He was a leader of the retreat from the GLF's educational revolution and the revival of intellectual and cultural endeavor. In his public statements, he sanctioned more creative, more diversified styles and less ideological subject matter. In talks before small meetings and to his associates, he encouraged a more Westernized approach to culture. In the Cultural Revolution, it was charged that he had expounded a liberal, bourgeois view all along, but in reality up until the early 1960s he had been unswerving in his implementation of Mao's cultural policies.

It could be that as the bureaucracy and Mao diverged after the GLF, Chou Yang, the quintessential Party organization man, went along with the bureaucracy and unquestioningly carried out its policies as previously he had carried out Mao's. But his diversion from Mao was more than factional or organizational. In addition to his disillusion with Mao's policies, he also diverged from the anti-intellectual, antiprofessional approach exhibited during the GLF. Though a cultural bureaucrat par excellence, he was also an urban, Westernized intellectual steeped in a tradition that included the great writers of nineteenth-century Europe. Although he was a leader in the GLF movement to promote collectivized amateur writing inspired by native folk tales, he retained a conventional Westernized view of literature and scholarship.

He and his colleagues in the early 1960s sought to lessen the effects of the GLF on culture and reinvigorate China's intellectual life. At a literary forum in 1961, Chou recommended a deliberate depoliticization of culture as a way to lessen the strains caused by the GLF. To advocate apolitical creativity in such a highly politicized society was a significant political act, but one in conformity with the Party's efforts to lessen the political zeal of the previous period.

Chou also downplayed class orientation as a criterion for judging literature. With the exception of the reactionaries, literature should appeal to all classes, not just to workers and peasants. A *People's Daily* editorial "Serve the broadest masses of people," in celebration of the twentieth anniversary of Mao's Yenan talks, explained that because the times had changed since Yenan, it was also necessary to change the culture so that it could serve a more sophisticated audience.[17]

Although intellectuals were allowed to turn away from Marxism-Leninism, they could not look outward as they had in the Hundred Flowers because of the break with the Soviet Union and alienation from the West. Thus, they revived plays and films written in the relatively free Shanghai of the 1920s and 1930s. One play that was revived was "The death of Taiping general Li Hsiu-ch'eng," by Yang Han-sheng, a vice-chairman and Party secretary of the All-China Federation of Literary and Art Circles. It had first been performed in 1937 as a product of national defense literature, the cultural policy of the united front, and had been officially endorsed by the Party at that time. It was revived in 1956 and restaged in February 1963. In the 1930s the play advocated class collaboration against the common enemy, but in the context of the early 1960s it appeared to symbolize the conflict between P'eng Te-huai and Mao. Li was depicted as a courageous figure who dared to risk his own life to challenge the leader of the Taipings, Hung Hsiu-ch'üan, who was portrayed as unwilling to listen to the advice of this associates, adhering stubbornly to a policy which led to the defeat of the Taipings.

The characters in the novels and stories of the 1930s re-created on the screen and in the theater in the early 1960s were questioning, agonized, ambivalent people caught in the midst of revolution and

17 JMJP, 13 May 1962.

uncertain which way to turn. It was as if they were presented in opposition to the idealized heroes and villains of the GLF literature which, like traditional Chinese literature, taught values and norms through the models of fictitious heroes and villains.

A variation of these 1930s characters was the "middle character" depicted in stories in the late 1950s and early 1960s. These also were ambiguous protagonists caught between the old society and the new, whose contradictions were more within themselves than between them and other classes. They were the topic of a conference held in Dairen in August 1962, presided over by Chou Yang and discussed by Chou's chief lieutenant, Shao Ch'üan-lin. Though originally a short story writer, Shao was known primarily as a powerful literary bureaucrat. After 1949 he rapidly made a name for himself as a leader of the thought reform campaigns. Yet at the Dairen Conference he asserted that the "middle character" represented the ordinary Chinese peasant, who was not the perfect hero the Party portrayed but a person in an intermediate stage between "backward" and "advanced" thinking, and with both positive and negative elements within himself. Instead of depicting heroic and villainous extremes, he urged writers to portray the vast majority of people, who were as yet uncommitted to the revolution.

Shao's approach struck directly at the Party's basic political and ideological teachings. He exposed the differences between the official view of reality and what actually existed, and implied that millions of Chinese workers and peasants, supposedly the bulwark of the revolution, were not the exemplary revolutionaries officially pictured. In reality, those who wavered between the "progressive" and "backward" paths were not just a small number of bourgeois and intellectuals, as the Party claimed, but the vast majority of the population.

Because writers had been forced to use ideological stereotypes rather than write with tough-minded realism, Shao lamented that model people had been "described to an inordinate degree in the GLF," which meant that "we lose touch with reality."[18] The peasants' latent communist motivation had not emerged in the GLF as Mao and the Party had anticipated. The overestimation of the ideological readiness of the peasants for revolution, Shao believed, had contributed to the failure of the GLF.

Critics of Mao's policies had thus gone beyond the criticism sanctioned by their political backers. Liu and the bureaucracy may

18 *Wen-i pao*, 8/9 (1964), 15–18.

have wanted criticism of the GLF, mass mobilization, and economic irrationalities. They even desired more intellectual and cultural "blooming" and a loosening of ideological restraints on scholarship and creative work to help resolve some of the problems brought on by the GLF. But in the charges later hurled against the Party's bureaucratic leaders in the Cultural Revolution, there is no evidence that they were willing to give up political and ideological control over scholarship – particularly humanistic scholarship of the type Teng T'o and Wu Han were requesting. Furthermore, Liu and the bureaucracy were as unwilling as Mao to allow intellectuals a voice in policy-making or public criticism of their policies through regular procedures. Nor were they willing to allow questioning about the basic commitment of peasants and workers to the revolution. That the leadership encouraged specific criticisms and a relative relaxation of control did not mean it would tolerate pluralism, diffusion of its power, or doubts about its mass support.

RESISTANCE TO MAO'S IDEOLOGICAL CLASS STRUGGLE

At the Tenth Plenum, held in September 1962, Mao announced a shift from the relative relaxation of the early 1960s to increased control over intellectual activity. He called for ideological class struggle, which was an implicit summons for an attack on his critics. He expressed concern that public opinion, greatly influenced by ideas and even by works of fiction, could overthrow political power, a reflection of his increasing obsession with ideological consciousness. The Tenth Plenum marked the beginning of Mao's effort to stop criticism of his policies, halt the slowing down of revolutionary momentum, and implement a cultural revolution. He sought to do this first through the Party bureaucracy.

In academic circles, however, Mao's call for ideological class struggle activated a new form of dissidence. Party as well as non-Party intellectuals engaged in debates over class struggle in which the underlying ideological basis of Mao's thought was questioned. Although the dissidence took different forms, a unifying theme was the desire for less rather than more polarization – a diminution rather than intensification of class struggle and a reconciliation rather than accentuation of the differences in Chinese society.

A number of eminent scholars spoke of the need to unite the country to strive toward goals shared by all classes of society. They sought to find in Chinese tradition ethical and aesthetic values relevant not merely to certain times and certain classes but to all times and all classes. By looking for the middle ground in their respective fields – history, philosophy, and aesthetics – their debates implicitly subverted Mao's call for ideological class struggle. The Socialist Education movement launched in the countryside in 1963 to halt the spontaneous trend toward individual farming did not spread into the intellectual community.

How then could divergent ideas be expressed in the period when Mao called for ideological struggle and tighter control over the intellectual community? Those with responsibility for tightening up, the Propaganda Department and the Peking Party Committee, were the very organizations that had presided over the relaxation of the 1960s. Verbally they went along with Mao's demand for renewed ideological class struggle, but actually they were reluctant to embark on a new campaign for fear it would lead to disruptions like those of the GLF. Disillusion with Mao's previous policy left the leadership less responsive to his new demands. Furthermore, since their baili-wicks were the centers of dissidence, they were not anxious to pursue a campaign that would ultimately redound on them.

Also, as Mao later charged, a growing process of bureaucratization had occured in the various cultural hierarchies, as is inevitable in any totalitarian organization after the end of the revolutionary phase. The cultural officials were entrenched, held together by close personal ties developed in the freer atmosphere of Shanghai in the 1930s and the civil war of the 1940s. They also were concerned with the erosion of revolutionary spirit, but exhausted and embittered by previous campaigns, they were reluctant to launch again the nationwide, inten-sive thought reform campaigns they had engineered in the past. Hence, though their rhetoric called for class struggle, their tone was moderate. They may not have agreed with some of the intellectuals whose views were as opposed to theirs and Liu Shao-ch'i's as to Mao's, but they permitted some genuine ideological debates to take place. The result was a watering down of Mao's demand for a class struggle. In the aftermath of the GLF, cultural officials as well as intellectuals shared a desire for a period of unity rather than of conflict.

These officials played a major role in the return of China's univer-sities to conventional educational practices after the GLF. The Party Secretariat put Chou Yang in charge of selecting materials for the liberal arts courses in the universities. He sought to reverse the GLF stress on politics, Mao Tse-tung Thought, and mass research and to reintroduce professional and academically oriented education to help in China's modernization. He pointed out: "If we train all students to be political activists, then we will have too many political activists. These will become empty-headed politicians without professional knowledge."[19] As part of the move to raise academic standards, the salaries of the older Western-trained professors were increased considerably over the younger teachers spawned in the GLF. Chou Yang also appointed a number of outstanding Western-trained scholars to head the committees that would select the liberal arts texts to replace the materials prepared by the younger teachers and students in the GLF. These intellectuals also dominated the major academic journals as the May Fourth writers dominated the literary journals. In their pages raged intellectual debates that ultimately touched on the fundamental ideological questions facing China's leadership.

Another aspect of the retreat from the revolutionary practices and severe disruption of the GLF was a more positive view of Confucianism because it embodied universal and enduring moral values. This effort to reassess Confucianism in universal terms had begun during the Hundred Flowers. Resurrected in the aftermath of the GLF, it had gained a certain momentum by 1963. Scholars couched their reevaluation in Marxist terminology, much as the nineteenth-century Chinese literati couched their introduction of Western thought in orthodox Confucian doctrine. The philosopher Feng Yu-lan, for example, pointed to a small portion of early Marxism, *The German ideology*, as the authority for his view of the universality of Confucianism. Although Feng presented Confucius as representing the emerging new landlord class as China moved from a slaveholding to a feudal society, Confucianism, Feng believed, had meaning for all nonruling classes – peasants, artisans, merchants – as well as for the landlords. In the struggle with the slave masters and the nobility, it was necessary for the landlords to endow their ideology with a "universal pattern."[20] Feng claimed that the Confucian concept of *jen*, benevolence or human kindness, has a class character, but also embodies a universal ethic for all classes because the landlords used it to gain broad support.

19 "A Collection of Chou Yang's counter-revolutionary revisionist speeches," SCMM, 648, 11, 15.
20 Feng Yu-lan, "Criticism and self-criticism in discussion about Confucianism," Che-hsueh yen-chiu (Philosophical research), 1963. 6 in IASP, Chinese Studies in History and Philosophy 1. 4 (Summer 1968), 84.

Another impetus to a more positive evaluation of Confucianism was a conference convened in November 1962, just a month after Mao's Tenth Plenum speech. Attended by noted scholars from all over China, it became a platform for a variety of non-Marxist interpretations of Chinese history. Among the most controversial was the view of Liu Chieh of Chungshan University in Canton that China's history had a different pattern than that of the West. Whereas class struggle may have governed Western historical development and may explain contemporary events, it had not governed China's development. Because the theory of class struggle was formulated in modern times by Marx and Engels, Liu insisted that the thinkers of ancient times could not have understood this concept. "We must not improperly impose on the ancients the problems of our times."[21]

In addition to challenging the Marxist class view of history, a number of historians questioned the Maoist view that peasant rebellions were revolutionary movements in Chinese history. Some argued in strictly Marxist terms that the peasantry was a conservative force and did not desire a new order but wanted only wealth and power like those of the upper classes. Although their arguments were couched in historical terms and were filled with Marxist jargon, they, like those who upheld the concept of the "middle character," contested the Maoist glorification of the peasant as a revolutionary and presented another form of criticism of the GLF. They argued that political elites as well as peasants made history and warned against exaggerating the role of peasant rebellion. Though their criticism was supported in part by the official Marxist denigration of the peasant's revolutionary potential, it was also influenced by the Confucian tradition of concern for the peasants and by the Western academic tradition of letting historical facts determine analysis. These facts had shown, they said, that peasant rebellions against the ruling class were spontaneous, improvised actions against repression, not an organized revolutionary movement.

For a number of years and in discussions in 1963, the chairman of the Peking University history department, Chien Po-tsan, presented the concept that came to be called the concession theory. It implicitly questioned revolution as the impetus for improving the lot of the Chinese peasant. After a dynasty was overthrown, the new unifying dynasty temporarily relaxed its suppression of the peasants. It offered concessions to them, such as reducing taxes, parceling out small plots

---

21 IASP, *Chinese Studies in Philosophy* (Fall–Winter 1972–73), 18.

of land, and opening up new land. These actions were not revolutionary; on the contrary, they prevented revolution by contributing to the peasant's welfare. Therefore, it was class reconciliation rather than class struggle that improved the peasants' lives.

Feng Yu-lan, in line with his view of the common interest between classes, also pointed out: "Ruling class thinkers, for the sake of the long-range interest of their own class, often advocated that some concessions be made to the interests of the ruled classes in order to diminish the latter's opposition."[22] Peasant discontent with the threat of insurrection gave an impulse to the working together of opposing classes of society, which in turn advanced society. The amelioration, not the intensification, of class struggle was regarded as the motivating force of history and as the impetus to the peasants' betterment.

A number of economists in the Economics Institute of the Chinese Academy of Sciences also questioned Mao's effort to intensify class struggle in the economic sphere in the Socialist Education movement. The most prominent of these was Sun Yeh-fang, director of the Economics Institute. A Party member since the 1920s, he had studied in the Soviet Union and had visited Moscow again in the early 1960s, at the time the Liberman economic reforms were being dicussed. Upon his return, he suggested similar reforms such as giving more autonomy to the operation of an enterprise and allowing a portion of the profit to remain with the enterprise to be used as a bonus to stimulate increased production and better management. As scientific knowhow was to replace mass movements, profit rather than political consciousness was to be the determinant for investment and development. Sun saw profit as the most sensitive indicator of technological feasibility and competent management. In the rural economy, he favored restoration of the individual family economy and prescribed output targets to each peasant household. He and his colleagues did not question the principle of socialist planning or the regulatory role of the state, but they pointed out that disregard of material incentives was economically irrational and harmful.

More directly critical of Mao's policies was Sun's characterization of the commune as a "mistake of rash and reckless advance." In a talk to a cadre training class, he noted: "We want to reach heaven in one step and so think the bigger [the project] the better, and as a result we have encouraged blind direction. . . . We have forgotten productivity

22 Feng Yu-lan, "Criticism and self-criticism," 86–87.

and over-exaggerated man's subjective initiative."[23] He restated the traditional Marxist view that revolution depends on the increase of production and technological progress. Only when productivity is developed to a high degree is it possible to put into effect the principle of distribution according to everyone's needs. Although Liu Shao-ch'i was accused in the Cultural Revolution of parroting Sun's ideas, Liu had not called for "profits in command" as charged, and his material incentives policies were relatively narrow in comparison with those of the 1st Five-Year Plan.

Nevertheless, the criticisms and suggestions made by Sun as well as by other academic and cultural figures played a role in creating the climate of opinion for the broad, far-reaching economic, educational, and cultural shift away from the policies of the GLF. They also provoked Mao to enlist another group of intellectuals to refute their criticisms and propose different solutions.

THE RADICAL INTELLECTUALS

As Mao's old comrades and the Party bureaucrats questioned his leadership after the GLF, Mao became increasingly suspicious of them and turned more and more to a handful of trusted intimates, particularly his wife, Chiang Ch'ing; his former secretary-ghostwriter Ch'en Po-ta; and K'ang Sheng, who had a long association with the Party's security apparatus. They, in turn, developed close contacts in the early 1960s with a group of young radical intellectuals who played a conspicuous role in condemning the views of the older, established intellectuals. Comprising two distinct but overlapping groups from the philosophy and social sciences department of the Chinese Academy of Sciences and the Shanghai Party Committee's Propaganda Department, they too were skilled in intellectual debate. Though academically trained, they differed from the senior intellectuals in that they had a more Marxist-oriented education and were lower in the academic hierarchy. They also had less experience in organization and administration. Their opposition to the senior intellectuals was generational, personal, and opportunistic, as well as ideological.

Chang Ch'un-ch'iao was the elder of this group. He was born in

23 Kung Wen-sheng, "Sun Yeh-fang's theory is a revisionist fallacy," *JMJP*, 8 August 1966, *SCMP*, 3766, 17.

1910 into an intellectual family. Like his intellectual rivals, he was active in left-wing literary circles in Shanghai in the 1930s and did propaganda work in the border areas in the 1940s. It was not until after 1949, however, that he began to achieve important positions. In the GLF, he was active in articulating Mao's policies, and shortly after he was made a member of the Shanghai Party Committee and of its standing committee. His contact with high Party officials came in 1963–64 when K'o Ch'ing-shih, a Politburo member, First Secretary of the Shanghai Party Committee and confidant of Mao, gave Mao's wife, Chiang Ch'ing, the opportunity she was denied in Peking by the Party Propaganda Committee and the Peking Party Committee: to reform the Peking-style opera. The Shanghai Propaganda Department, particularly Chang and his younger colleague Yao Wen-yuan, was mobilized to help her.

Yao had first made a name for himself by allying with the literary bureaucrats around Chou Yang in the Propaganda Department.[24] Although he was active in the campaigns against Hu Feng, Ai Ch'ing, Ting Ling, and Feng Hsueh-feng and the rightists, he was particularly conspicuous in the late 1950s for his attacks on the literary theorist Pa Jen for his view that there were elements of human nature common to all people, and Pa Chin, whom he labeled a "reactionary" shortly after his works had been reprinted in 1958. He came to be known as "the stick," one who suppressed writers by calling them names. His criticisms so infuriated the older May Fourth writers that Chou Yang and his assistant Lin Mo-han personally intervened to stop his attacks on them.

Having been rebuffed by the cultural bureaucracy, Yao, Chang, and Chiang Ch'ing joined together as natural allies. Their link with a group of young philosophers and historians associated with the philosophy and social sciences department of the Chinese Academy of Sciences – the leading ones being Kuan Feng, Ch'i Pen-yü, Lin Yü-shih, and Lin Chieh – added substantial intellectual substance to their challenge to the views of the senior intellectuals.

Chang had been associated with a few of them, at least as early as the GLF, when he and the philosopher Kuan Feng and another colleague Wu Ch'uan-chi wrote articles calling for restrictions on material incentives in the manner of war communism and the Paris Commune. In fact, Chang's article pushing Mao's GLF views supposedly caught Mao's attention. It was published in *People's Daily*

24 See Lars Ragvald, *Yao Wen-yuan as a literary critic and theorist.*

with an editorial note by Mao that did not fully endorse its ideas, but urged readers to use it as a starting point for discussion.[25]

The articles and speeches of the radical intellectuals in the early 1960s were on a variety of subjects, but a common denominator was that they drew more from the radical aspects of Mao's thought than from traditional Marxism. They continued to expound Mao's beliefs as articulated during the GLF, but now expressed in ideological and political rather than economic terms. Like their mentor, they insisted that socialist transformation of the economy did not automatically transform bourgeois ideology. It was necessary to wage ideological class struggle against the bourgeois superstructure that survived and exerted influence, even though its means of production had been eliminated. The subjective will that had been aroused to overcome the forces of nature and economic limitations in the GLF was now to be aroused against bourgeois and revisionist ideological forces. Equating the subjective will with revolutionary zeal, they sought to mobilize the subjective will of the masses against the prevailing bourgeois superstructure and particularly against the senior intellectuals.

The arguments, rhetoric, and symbols used in the 1963–64 debates with the senior intellectuals provided the ideological underpinnings for the Cultural Revolution. In their protest against the existing intellectual and bureaucratic establishment, they were China's New Left. Their arguments not only expressed their own ideological disagreements and personal rivalries, but also reflected genuine socioeconomic grievances of a segment of the population, particularly educated youth, against the lack of mobility in the hierarchy and the inequalities between the well-trained older and the less well-trained younger.

Their contention with famous intellectuals gave them some support among radical intellectuals and students and gained them prominence and notoriety that could be used by political leaders seeking to undermine the establishment. To what extent Mao instigated this group and to what extent they instigated him is not yet clear. In the pre-Cultural Revolution period, Mao and his confidants Chiang Ch'ing, Ch'en Po-ta, K'ang Sheng, and K'o Ch'ing-shih often suggested the general themes and symbols, but they did not directly supervise their writing until the start of the Cultural Revolution – and even then, the radical intellectuals could not be fully controlled.

25 *JMJP*, 13 October 1958. See also Parris Chang, *Radicals and radical ideology in China's Cultural Revolution*, 81.

In contrast to the senior intellectuals, the radicals took up Mao's call for ideological class struggle quickly and energetically after the Tenth Plenum speech. Though the senior intellectuals dominated the editorial boards of the scholarly journals, the radicals were able to publish in them. Their general criticism of the senior scholars was that they had spread the idea that classes had common interests, when in reality there was only class struggle. But their intellectual and ideological disagreements with the senior intellectuals in 1963–64 were not as polarized as they would become in the Cultural Revolution. Positions had not hardened enough to cause an irrevocable split between Mao and the Party bureaucracy, or between them and the senior intellectuals. Although the radicals echoed Mao's call for class struggle, their arguments in 1963–64 were not the simplified clichés that they were to become. They used a wide range of references and acknowledged the complexities of the questions. They engaged in lively exchanges and debated on an academic level and, for the most part, in a nonbelligerent, balanced manner. At this point they were not yet in opposition to the Propaganda Department, but constituted a faction within the cultural organization.

Among the younger intellectuals at the philosophy and social sciences department, the philosopher Kuan Feng was perhaps the best known. Since the early 1950s he had written a number of erudite articles on ancient Chinese philosophers such as Chuang-tzu, Hsun-tzu, and Confucius. Several were written in collaboration with two other colleagues, Lin Yü-shih and Lin Chieh. He became prominent in the late 1950s and early 1960s for his criticism of Feng Yu-lan for disregarding class characteristics and promoting supraclass interpretations of philosophical concepts. His attack on such a well-known philosopher may have been motivated partly by a desire for fame, but it was also consistent with his previous views that stressed in a scholarly fashion the class character of philosophical and social theory. Kuan and one associate asserted that class struggle and development were inseparable: "The history of objective civilized society is a history of class struggle."[26] In their rebuttal of Chien Po-tsan's view that peasant uprisings were spontaneous acts against oppressors, they asserted that to deny that uprisings against landlords were against feudalism was to deny the revolutionary character of the peasants. In an article published a bit later, the radical historians

26 Kuan Feng and Lin Yü-shih, "Some problems of class analysis in the study of the history of philosophy," *Che-hsueh yen-chiu* (Philosophical research), 6 (1963) in IASP, *Chinese Studies in History and Philosophy*, 1. 4 (Summer 1968), 66.

Ch'i Pen-yü and Lin Chieh insisted that it was not concessions to the peasants, as Chien claimed, but the peasants' "revolutionary struggles against the landlord class [that] have impelled historical development."[27]

With this view of history, the authors concluded, "It is necessary to adhere firmly to the theory of class struggle and to wage a tit-for-tat struggle against the class enemy."[28] They charged that scholars like Chien Po-tsan not only opposed using class struggle to interpret history, but opposed using historical research to serve present-day politics. This rebuttal presaged the Cultural Revolution and more specifically the attack on intellectuals who refused to obey Mao's summons to struggle, whether it be in the context of one's research or against one's colleagues.

The radical intellectuals also used historical figures as analogies to criticize current leaders. Ch'i Pen-yü used the character Li Hsiu-ch'eng, the last general of the Taipings, in a way diametrically opposed to his use by Yang Han-sheng in his play. Whereas Yang had depicted Li as a courageous figure challenging an arbitrary leader, Ch'i depicted him as one who had abandoned the revolutionary struggle and betrayed its leader. Given the current effort to rehabilitate P'eng Te-huai and criticize the GLF, Ch'i's portrayal could be analogous both to P'eng's criticism of Mao and to Liu's and the Party leaders' subsequent rejection of Maoist policies. Ch'i did not deny that Li had taken part in a revolutionary struggle, "but his participation and his position as a commander could not negate the facts about his surrender and desertion at the last minute." We must "despise those who deserted their revolutionary cause under adverse conditions." The desertion was not just a shortcoming or a mistake, but counterrevolutionary. Li therefore cannot be pardoned, because "the foremost question about revolution is to distinguish between friend and foe."[29] Ch'i argued against any tolerance of critics of revolutionary policies.

Although the radical intellectuals criticized prominent scholars such as Feng Yu-lan and Chien Po-tsan, they did not publicly attack those well connected to the Peking Party Committee or the Party Propaganda Department. Some of Wu Han's ideas on history were

27 Ch'i Pen-yü and Lin Chieh, "Comrade Chien Po-tsan's outlook on history should be criticized," *Hung-ch'i* (24 March 1966), 19–30, JPRS, 35, 137.
28 Ibid.
29 Ch'i Pen-yü, "Comment on Li Hsiu-ch'eng's autobiography," *LSYC*, reprinted as "How should we look at the surrender of Li Hsiu-ch'eng?" *JMJP* and *KMJP*, 23 August 1963; also in *Pei-ching ta-kung pao*, JPRS, 26, 631. 13–14, 15.

criticized, but no public mention was made of his *tsa-wen* or his use of the Hai Jui figure. In 1964, Ch'i Pen-yü, Kuan Feng, and Lin Chieh wrote criticisms of Wu Han's play, but their articles were blocked from publication by the Peking Party Committee and the Propaganda Department. It was only when the Peking intellectual-officials and their political backers were about to be overthrown that these criticisms were published in April 1966.

It was charged in the Cultural Revolution that there was a deliberate effort to keep these debates within a strict historical and philosophical context in order to prevent attacks on specific individuals and specific policies. Consequently, the debates had the appearance of academic discussions, rather than of the surrogate political and ideological struggles they were. Both sides, even the radicals, cited a range of Western as well as Chinese historical sources and acknowledged complexities and qualifications. Their arguments were to be turned into slogans in the Cultural Revolution, but in the period before, they were seemingly scholarly and knowledgeable.

The reform of Peking Opera

The other flank of the radical attack on the cultural establishment was the effort to reform Peking Opera. It is not surprising that Chiang Ch'ing should take the lead in this endeavor, because that was the area of her own experience.[30] Although she regarded herself as an intellectual, her formal education was not extensive. She graduated from junior high school and studied at the Shantung Experimental Drama Academy. In the early 1930s she went to Shanghai, where she played bit parts in low-grade films. At that time the May Fourth writers T'ien Han, Hsia Yen, and Yang Han-sheng, who were later to become the leaders of theater and screen in the PRC, were among the major screen writers and film directors in left-wing circles. Unappreciative of her dramatic talents, they refused to give her important parts, apparently instilling in her a hostility toward them that she was later to avenge during the Cultural Revolution.

When the Japanese bombed Shanghai in 1938, she, along with many Shanghai intellectuals and students, made her way to Yenan. There she was befriended by K'ang Sheng, who came from her county of Chu-ch'eng, in Shantung. He helped her get a position in the Lu Hsun Academy of Arts. She also married Mao after his

30 See Roxane Witke, *Comrade Chiang Ch'ing.*

divorce from his third wife. Because of the protests of some members of the Party hierarchy, she was made to promise that she would not engage in political activities in the early years of the PRC. Her old "enemies" from Shanghai moved into powerful positions in the cultural sphere, while her role and contacts were limited to membership in the Film Guidance Committee of the Ministry of Culture, which censored films.

She was relatively inactive until the early 1960s, when the indirect criticisms of Mao and the GLF activated her. She claimed she had brought these criticisms to Mao's attention. She has said of her role at this time, "In the field of education and culture, I was a roving sentinel. . . . My job is to go over some periodicals and newspapers and present to the Chairman . . . things . . . which are worthy of attention."[31] She also reviewed more than a hundred plays and had K'ang Sheng transmit to her old adversary Hsia Yen, the head of the theater in the PRC, her views that the bulk of recently performed plays were bad and that Wu Han's *Hai Jui dismissed from office* should be withdrawn. Hsia appears to have paid little heed. Although Wu Han's play was banned, traditional, historical, and ghost plays continued to be performed. Again in December 1962, she criticized the theatrical repertoire and called this time for the banning of ghost plays. But although ghost plays subsequently were banned, traditional and historical plays continued to be staged.

With such resistance from the propaganda bureaucracy, Chiang Ch'ing turned her attack on Peking Opera. This dominant form of the traditional Chinese theater is called opera because it combines singing, acting, mime, recitation, and acrobatics. Its stereotyped characters and plots, which dramatize the confrontation between good and evil, were an effective medium for communicating ideological teachings and moral values to the illiterate masses, as well as to the cultural elite. Chiang Ch'ing sought to transform the traditional relationships into class struggle confrontations between worker, peasant, and soldier heroes and landlord and bourgeois villains.

In contrast to stories portraying "middle characters," her operas projected a world of heroes and heroines with no doubts, weaknesses, sorrows, or disorders, thoroughly infused with ideological goals, carrying out superhuman feats for the revolution. Her effort to reform China's traditional opera dispensed with its content but used

---

31 Chiang Ch'ing, "Do new services for the people," *Tung fang hung* (The east is red), 3 June 1967, *SCMP-S*, 192, 7.

its formalized techniques and styles, combined with Chinese folk dances and revolutionary songs. She repudiated Western culture but injected the most banal, conventional Soviet-style dance, music, and song. These devices, together with the content of class struggle, military conflict, and heroic characters for emulation, presaged the official culture that would dominate the Cultural Revolution.

She had Mao's support in this effort. Since Yenan he had been concerned with transforming traditional opera, but it had proved resistant to change. Even during the GLF, when most of the creative arts depicted contemporary class struggle, Peking Opera troupes continued to perform the traditional repertoire. In the early 1960s, Peking Opera, as well as regional operas, was flourishing. In November 1963, Mao lashed out at traditional opera not only because it was resistant to change but also because it was being used to criticize him. He also attacked the cultural officials responsible for staging the operas: "The Ministry of Culture cares little about culture. Operas abound with feudal emperors, kings, generals, ministers, scholars, and beautiful women, but the Ministry of Culture doesn't care a bit."

In another speech at about the same time, he called for immediate action on this matter: "In the field of culture, particularly in the sphere of drama, feudal and backward things predominate while socialist things are negligible.... Since the Ministry of Culture is in charge of cultural matters, it should pay attention to problems arising from this respect, conduct investigations, and put things right in real earnest. If nothing is done, the Ministry of Culture should be changed into the Ministry of Emperors, Kings, Generals, Ministers, Scholars, and Beauties or the Ministry of Foreign Things and the Dead." Mao's words also signaled the rhetoric of the Cultural Revolution. Yet he still left open an opportunity for change by adding, "If things are righted, no change of name will be made."[32]

With Mao's imprimatur, Chiang Ch'ing embarked on her program to produce model revolutionary operas. The purposes of the program were stated at the East China Drama Festival from 25 December 1963 through 26 January 1964 under the auspices of the Shanghai Propaganda Department. K'o Ch'ing-shih opened the festival by restating publicly Mao's directive of the previous month and decrying the influence on the masses of "the unhealthy bourgeois atmosphere and reactionary, erratic, superstitious plays." By contrast, "socialist

32 "Chairman Mao's important instructions on literature and art since the publication of 'Talks at the Yenan Forum on Literature and Art' (1942–1967)," *Wen-i hung-ch'i* (Red flag of literature and art), 30 May 1967, *SCMP*, 4000, 23.

literature and art are ideological weapons to educate and rally the people and criticize and destroy the enemy."[33] New model revolutionary operas were to perform that function.

The cultural establishment responded sluggishly to Mao's pressure and Chiang Ch'ing's reform efforts. But to depict the controversy over this issue as a two-line ideological struggle, as it would be described in the Cultural Revolution, is not exactly accurate. The cultural establishment, like Chiang Ch'ing and her associates, also advocated reform, but it tried to reconcile reform with its own bureaucratic imperatives. Still, although this was not yet a direct confrontation between two explicitly opposed lines, it did not mean that there was no conflict between the two groups. The fact that Chiang Ch'ing was only listed as a speaker in the discussions on opera reform and that there was no record of her speeches in the press at this time suggests, as she later charged, that the bureaucracy refused to give her media coverage.

Although some cultural officials were somewhat reluctant to reform Peking Opera, conflict between her and the bureaucracy was not so much over the need to reform as over who would do the reforming. It was more a factional than an ideological struggle. The rebuffs given her by the cultural officials were not so much because they were unwilling to go along with Mao's demand for opera reform as because they resented her interference in their domain. Only when these officials were purged in the Cultural Revolution was she given a free hand to revolutionize the opera and turn it into China's main cultural fare.

PARTY RECTIFICATION, 1964–1965

Since Mao's call for ideological class struggle and suggestions for opera reform were being echoed in the media and at meetings but not being carried out in fact, in late 1963 and 1964 he went beyond criticism of specific art forms such as opera and fiction to attack the cultural bureaucracy itself. On 12 December 1963 he declared, "Problems abound in all forms of art.... In many departments very little has been achieved so far in socialist transformation. The 'dead' still dominate.... The social and economic base has changed, but the arts as part of the superstructure which serve this base, still remain a serious problem. Hence we should proceed with investigation and

33 Editorial, *CFJP*, 25 December 1963, 3.

study and attend to this matter in earnest. Isn't it absurd that many Communists are enthusiastic about promoting feudal and capitalist art, but not socialist art?"[34] The following day he expressed even harsher criticism in his 13 December instruction to the Central Committee, in which he charged some members with being "conservative, arrogant, and complacent."[35] He blamed this on the fact that they talked only of their achievements, but did not admit their shortcomings or dealt with them superficially.

The extreme anti-intellectualism of the Cultural Revolution was foreshadowed in his February 1964 speech at the Spring Festival on Education: "Throughout history, very few of those who came in first in the imperial examinations have achieved great fame." He pointed out that the only two emperors of the Ming who did well were barely literate. He disparaged the role of intellectuals in China's development. "In the Chia-ch'ing reign [1522–67], when the intellectuals had power, things were in a bad state, the country was in disorder. . . . It is evident that to read too many books is harmful."[36] He ordered that "actors, poets, dramatists, and writers" be "driven out of the cities" and government offices. They should periodically go down in groups to the villages and factories. He even threatened harsh sanctions. "Only when they go down will they be fed."[37]

The cultural officials either did not understand, misinterpreted, or chose to ignore Mao's statements. They may have felt sure enough of their bureaucratic patronage to pay lip service to Mao's views but not actually carry them out except in a perfunctory manner. They did, as Mao asked, send groups of intellectuals, cultural cadres, and students to the countryside and factories. However, they disregarded his instructions of December 1963 to implement an "ideological transformation" in their domain and investigate their own departments "in earnest."

Implicitly rejecting Mao's major criticism of them for obstructing the revolution, they accepted his lesser charge of not carrying out his policies energetically enough. Chou Yang, at a meeting convened in early January 1964, conceded "failure on some occasions to exercise a tight enough grip on work" and "failure to make enough effort in

34 Mao Tse-tung, "Comment on comrade K'o Ch'ing-shih's report," *Long live Mao Tse-tung Thought*, in *CB*, 901, 41.
35 Mao Tse-tung, "Instruction of the Central Committee on strengthening of learning from each other and overcoming conservatism, arrogance, and complacency," *Long Live Mao Tse-tung Thought*, in *CB*, 892, 15.
36 Schram, *Mao Tse-tung unrehearsed*, 204.
37 Ibid., 207.

cultivating . . . the new things of socialism."[38] But this criticism of his department and colleagues was halfhearted. His resistance to Mao's demand for ideological struggle may have been bolstered by the knowledge that Liu Shao-ch'i, shortly after Mao's 1963 announcements, enunciated a view of the superstructure diametrically opposed to Mao's. Whereas Mao believed the superstructure lagged behind changes in the economic base, Liu was reported to have said that "work in the superstructure corresponds to the economic base these days."[39] Chou had official justification for his weak response to Mao's summons to transform the cultural arena.

With the cultural bureaucracy sidestepping his orders, Mao on 27 June 1964 issued a more emphatic and accusatory directive. Again his anger was directed not so much at the intellectuals engaged in these debates as at the cultural officials who permitted the debates to take place. "In the last fifteen years, these associations, most of their publications (it is said a few are good), and by and large the people in them (that is not everybody) have not carried out the policies of the Party. They have acted as high and mighty bureaucrats, have not gone to the workers, peasants, and soldiers and have not reflected the socialist revolution and socialist construction. In recent years they have slid right down to the brink of revisionism. Unless they remold themselves in real earnest at some future date, they are bound to become groups like the Hungarian Petöfi Club."[40]

But the rectification they launched in the summer of 1964 was not due only to Mao's pressure; it also expressed their own concern with the deterioration of ideological discipline. While some of the senior intellectuals continued to press for relaxation, the bureaucracy sought to tighten controls. They had allowed the intellectuals to criticize for practical reasons, not because they were advocates of intellectual freedom. Since economic recovery was under way, they did not want too much criticism, which might be just as disruptive to orderly development as Chiang Ch'ing's effort to circumvent regular Party procedures. The divergence between the bureaucracy and Mao was not so much on the need to reimpose tighter controls as on how to do it. Whereas Mao was calling for a large-scale mass campaign that would reach the top levels of the cultural establishment, the

---

38 "The tempestuous combat on the literary and art front," *Shou-tu hung-wei-ping* (Capital Red Guards), 7 July 1967, *CB*, 842, 17.

39 "Hail the Victory of the Mao Tse-tung Line on Literature and Art," NCNA, 17 May 1967, *SCMP*, 3950, 13.

40 "Instructions concerning literature and art," *Long live Mao Tse-tung Thought*, in *CB*, 891, 41.

bureaucracy carried out a rectification limited to the literary and academic sphere. It touched only superficially on a very small number of "the high and mighty" cultural officials whom Mao had denounced.

It was carried out by the usual managers of thought reform campaigns – the officials in the Propaganda Department, Ministry of Culture, and Peking Party Committee. In the spring of 1964 the Party Secretariat had set up a high-level task force known as the Five-Man Group to coordinate the cultural reform. It was headed by P'eng Chen and had Lu Ting-i, K'ang Sheng, Yang Shang-k'un, director of the Central Committee's General Office, and Wu Leng-hsi, editor-in-chief of the *People's Daily* and director of the New China News Agency, as its members. The only one of the group close to Chiang Ch'ing and her associates was K'ang Sheng; the rest were identified with the cultural establishment. Mao's confidants and the radical intellectuals through K'ang Sheng were able to inject themselves into the rectification, but they played a minor role.

The army also played a minor role in the campaign. After Lin Piao replaced P'eng Te-huai as minister of defense in 1959, the PLA had become increasingly conspicuous in cultural activities. It set up opera, literary, and art groups in the PLA, but at this time they were to parallel – not to replace – the Party groups. Political officers of the PLA were inserted into the cultural, propaganda, and educational bureaus, as they were inserted into the economic and administrative bureaus, in an effort to revitalize the bureaucracy, with Mao's Thought. This network, however, was under the control not of the General Political Department of the PLA but of the Party Central Committee. The Party leadership was very much in charge of the rectification and determined to keep it from exploding into a mass movement that could be turned against itself. Actually, the Party's rectification, launched in the summer of 1964, was not one hard-hitting campaign, but a series of mini-campaigns against a number of famous intellectuals just below the top echelon of cultural officials.

As if in an effort to divert attention from itself, the bureaucracy chose as its foremost target an intellectual outside its inner circle. He was Central Committee member and leading Marxist theoretician Yang Hsien-chen. He had spent twenty years in the Soviet Union, where he had studied at the University of Toilers of the East in Moscow in the 1920s and was head of the Chinese department of the Soviet Foreign Languages Institute in the 1930s. Given the regime's increasingly anti-Soviet invective, Yang was a convenient target. He also had been in factional conflict with Ch'en Po-ta at the Higher Party School. Perhaps more important, he presented concepts that were in opposition to Mao's current stress on struggle.

As the campaign against him unfolded in the media, Party schools, universities, and research institutes focused on countering the desire for compromise, as expressed in a slogan associated with Yang that "two combine into one," in opposition to Mao's slogan "one divides into two," which stressed class struggle. Mao had also talked of the union of opposites in the concept of nonantagonistic contradictions in "On the correct handling of contradictions among the people" and in the interrelation of opposites in "On contradiction." But whereas Mao emphasized that the transformation of one force by another in endless struggle was more fundamental than union, Yang emphasized that the union did not dissolve the opposites but each remained separate, held together by mutual need. He advocated seeking common ground with opposing ideologies, but allowing differences to remain. The implication of this concept for the PRC was the toleration of a diversity of viewpoints and classes within a unified nation.

In addition to silencing the demand for compromise, criticism of Yang was also used to stifle criticism of the GLF, still echoing into 1964. In the GLF, Yang had initiated a debate in academic circles called "the question of thinking and being" that could be interpreted as implicit criticism of Mao's policies. He argued that no one, no matter how omniscient, could afford to disregard the inexorable laws of history or oppose his will to the built-in limitations of the objective situation. Implicit in Yang's argument was the Marxist orthodoxy that a society must go through economic stages of development and could not leap into communism. Since China was an economically backward country, radical changes were counterproductive because they were not in accord with China's reality.

As in the attack on the concept of "two into one," these ideas were attributed to Yang largely on the basis of unpublished articles. In 1958, after a visit to the countryside, he had written an article that questioned the revolutionary nature of Chinese society and denied the dynamic role of the masses in the GLF. He warned that "the abandonment of objective laws and one-sided discussion of subjective function means metaphysics and this can only be changed into the theory of sole obedience to the will."[41] As in the discussion of the

---

41 Ts'ung Wei, "Yang Hsien-chen and the 'Identity of thinking and existence,'" *KMJP*, 11 December 1964, *SCMP*, 3380, 5.

"middle character," Yang attributed the failure of the GLF to the discrepancy between Mao's revolutionary vision and the reality of nonrevolutionary peasants.

Yang's main critic was an old ideological opponent, Ai Szu-ch'i, who chastized Yang and people like him who were not fully committed to continuing struggle. His words already hinted at the imminent Cultural Revolution attack on Party colleagues who sought moderation. He pointed out that the line "one divides into two is not only between friend and foe but also among friends – distinguishing the closest friends from the vacillating ones." He warned that if the Party tolerated those who vacillate, then socialism will not be achieved. "Instead of distinguishing friend from foe, we mix them up and desist from waging struggle among friends, but 'only seek agreement and reserve differences.' [We] may lead the revolution astray and cause it to fail."[42] While concern with vacillating comrades and continuing struggle was only one among a number of strands of the 1964 rectification, it was to become a keynote of the Cultural Revolution.

The rectification also attacked Yang's traditional Marxist view that policy must conform to the unfolding stages of history in order to create the conditions for socialism. The discussion resembled a number of Western ideological and philosophical debates in the nineteenth and early twentieth centuries between those who believed in the existence of immutable laws of history and those such as Lenin who believed in man's ability to shape his own history. Mao's latest statement in the Leninist tradition was in May 1963 in "Where do correct ideas come from?" in which he wrote: "Once correct ideas . . . are grasped by the masses, these ideas turn into a material force which changes society and changes the world." The question whether one knows if he correctly reflects the laws of the objective world is not proved until "the stage leading from consciousness back to matter in which they are applied in practice."[43] Thus, Mao insisted that one must act in order to know if one accurately reflects the objective world.

In contrast to Mao's belief that ideas depended on action, Yang was charged with believing that ideas were only a passive reflection of material progress. He was criticized for rejecting subjective initiative

---

42 Ai Szu-ch'i, "Surreptitious substitution of the theory of the reconciliation of contradictions and class for revolutionary dialectics must not be permitted," *JMJP*, 20 May 1965, *SCMP*, 3475, 7.
43 Mao Tse-tung, "Where do correct ideas come from?" *Four essays on philosophy*, 134–35.

and revolutionary spirit. In actuality Yang did not reject the subjective and revolutionary spirit, but he maintained that it had to be combined with a sober respect for objective limitations. Undoubtedly, he and several members of the Party hierarchy who shared his views felt they were acting in good Leninist, as well as Marxist, tradition. Even Lenin's emphasis on the subjective factor and revolutionary will was accompanied by a genuine effort to comprehend "objective reality" accurately.

The discussion of Yang's ideas was primarily an ideological debate between the orthodox Marxist view of sequential stages of development and the Rousseauian-Jacobin voluntarist view transmitted through Marxism-Leninism to Mao. For the most part, the Party bureaucracy appears to have taken a middle course on this issue. Yang was removed from his position as vice-chairman of the Higher Party School to be replaced by his old rival, Ai Szu-ch'i. But Yang was not denounced with the fervor and epithets meted out to intellectual targets in previous campaigns. Most of the criticism was more academic than political, more balanced than polemical.

As Yang's views had criticized the regime for projecting future utopias rather than dealing with present realities, so did Shao Ch'üan-lin's view of the peasant as a "middle character" rather than as a revolutionary imply that the bureaucracy as well as Mao did not understand the real needs of the peasantry. Thus, another purpose of the rectification was to reject Shao's concept of the "middle character." Instead of confronting this issue, the regime threw Shao's criticisms back at him by charging that it was he and a number of fiction writers, such as Chao Shu-li, Chou Li-po, and Ma Feng, who showed themselves out of touch with the peasants by depicting them as vacillating and ambivalent.

But Shao was the main target of the campaign against the "middle character." Even though there was pressure from Mao and his associates, the choice of someone like Shao, directly connected to the cultural bureaucracy as head of the Party group in the Chinese Writers' Union, appears to have been made by the bureaucracy itself in order to hold onto its power. Narrowing the attack to one important official protected his colleagues, particularly Chou Yang. Thus Shao became the scapegoat for the "failings" of the cultural establishment.

Chou Yang personally supervised the campaign against Shao. He himself revised a number of the criticisms and sought to keep the discussion limited to literary matters and away from political matters.

Under Chou Yang's guidance, the drive quickly moved from the negative stage of denouncing Shao and the "middle character" to the positive stage of defining new behavior patterns, new values, and new beliefs for a new socialist man. In contrast to Shao's image of the peasant as suspicious of the revolution, riddled with conflicts and desirous of material benefits, the regime depicted the peasant as a hero of unqualified optimism, unstinting self-sacrifice, and abiding faith in the revolution.

Despite Chou Yang's efforts to control the campaign, the radical intellectuals, most prominently Yao Wen-yuan, injected themselves into this discussion. Their public views at this time were not too different from those of the cultural establishment. Even Yao admitted indirectly that the majority was still nonrevolutionary, but to write about the majority meant "a fundamental exclusion and suppression of new things which are germinating or developing, and an extension of protection to old things which superficially still exist extensively."[44] He therefore advised writers to depict not the majority but the few. "Mold energetically, richly and vividly the heroic characters ... thus enlightening and encouraging the people."[45]

Several heroic figures were molded in this period to contrast with the "middle character." The shift from a number of nonheroic literary characters of the late 1950s and early 1960s to heroic figures of the mid-1960s reflects the shift from recognition of human and economic limitations to the belief that self-sacrificing new men could overcome all obstacles. The main literary protagonists changed from ordinary peasants and workers whose commitments were ambiguous to "ordinary" heroes, usually from the PLA, such as Lei Feng, whose commitment to the Maoist virtues of sacrifice, selflessness, and devotion to Mao was unswerving.

Accompanying this shift was a move away from conventional literary forms of the novel and short story, written by individual writers, to the more controllable semi-fictional diary presented almost as myth, written by committees, such as *The diary of Lei Feng*. Less and less was published by the established writers still writing in the late 1950s and more and more by anonymous groups, attached primarily to the Propaganda Department of the PLA, an indication of the increasing intrusion of the PLA into the cultural realm.

44 Yao Wen-yuan, "A theory which causes socialist literature and art to degenerate," *KMJP*, 20 December 1964, *SCMP*, 3374, 9.
45 Ibid., 4.

There was a carryover of the campaign against the "middle character" into the cinema. Not only had the cinema portrayed nonheroic protagonists, particularly in the films based on the literary works of the 1930s, but it was directed by Hsia Yen and Yang Han-sheng, who had antagonized Chiang Ch'ing. She had tried to insert herself into films as into the opera. She pointed out to Lu Ting-i and Chou Yang a large number of films she claimed Mao wanted repudiated. But only a few were criticized. True, the films that were criticized were associated with her old enemies, but the criticism itself, under the supervision of the Propaganda Department, was generally mild. The film that received the most attention was *The Lin family shop*, based on a story by Mao Tun and adapted for the screen by Hsia Yen. Though well received when it was first shown, in 1959, it was criticized in 1964 because the principal protagonist's relationships were not based on sharp class conflict. It was acknowledged that the story had had a positive influence in the 1930s because it showed the difficulties of the petty bourgeoisie and gained their support for the revolution. But now it was regarded as inappropriate because it was no longer necessary to have cooperation between workers and bourgeoisie.

Generally, rectification of the cinema was relatively restrained. This film plus a few others were criticized, but there was no mass campaign or large-scale meetings to repudiate them. Instead, there were bland critiques by colleagues who were closely connected with the people who had written and produced these films. Yet a few criticisms gave hints of the kinds of attacks that would pour down on the May Fourth writers in the Cultural Revolution. One, for example, asserted that Hsia Yen represented the type of intellectuals who, though Party members, still had "a bourgeois realm hidden deep in their hearts."[46] Moreover, it was charged that their bourgeois ideas had a corrosive influence on the young.

The rectification was similar to other thought-reform campaigns in its use of the media, criticism and self-criticism sessions, and the selection of personalized targets. But its approach was different. Though for the most part the same group from the Propaganda Department that conducted the Hu Feng campaign of 1955 and the Anti-Rightist Campaign of 1957–58 were in charge, the rectification was less direct, less thorough, and more tolerant of its victims. Probably this group was just as anxious as they had been previously

---

46 Su Nan-yuan, "*The Lin family shop* is a picture for prettifying the bourgeoisie," *JMJP*, 29 May 1965, *CB*, 766, 9.

to stop what Mao called "a slide toward revisionism," but there were factors that held them back – increasing bureaucratization, the fear of another full-scale campaign reeling out of control, and the questioning of Mao's policies. Moreover, a rectification in which the masses were activated would not only be a threat to themselves personally, as it was in the Hundred Flowers, but a threat to the Party as a whole.

As a result, there appears to have been in some cases genuine, in other cases deliberate, misinterpretation of Mao's wishes. Mao's speech before the national propaganda work conference on 12 March 1957, in the midst of the Hundred Flowers Campaign, which had not previously been published, appeared in June 1964 just as the rectification was to be launched. Though some of the language appears to have been revised, this speech, given at a time when Mao was less disillusioned with the intellectuals and the Party, called for criticism with restraint and understanding. He cautioned that criticism of intellectuals must be "fully reasoned, analytical, and convincing and should not be brutal, bureaucratic, or dogmatic." Furthermore, he advocated a gradual approach toward dissenting intellectuals: "Such people will remain for a very long time to come, and we should tolerate their disapproval."[47] This speech, together with Mao's short directives, were ambiguous on how the rectification was to be implemented and, if anything, advocated persuasion rather than coercion.

Whether purposely or not, the propaganda bureaucracy chose to interpret Mao's words as an order for a limited rectification. As in the past, personalized targets served as vehicles for transmitting ideological messages. But this time, instead of one specific target as in the Hu Feng campaign of 1955 or one specific group like the Ting Ling clique or the China Democratic League in the Anti-Rightist Campaign, several different campaigns, launched simultaneously against several related but different targets, tended to diffuse the movement.

In addition to Yang Hsien-chen and Shao Ch'üan-lin, the rectification criticized the philosopher Feng Ting for emphasizing instincts common to all people, the writer Ou-yang Shan for describing love without class content, and the aesthetician Chou Ku-ch'eng for talking of a "unified" consciousness. It was a broad campaign, touching philosophy, history, literary theory, the arts, and ideology, but it was

47 Mao Tse-tung, "Talk at the national conference on propaganda work of the CCP," CB, 740, 10.

not thorough – there was a gap between the rhetoric and the reality, between the enunciation of policy and its implementation. Moreover, the revolutionary fervor of previous movements was missing; those affected were a small group of Party intellectuals in the large cities. As opposed to the Hu Feng campaign, which affected the masses as well as the intellectuals, there was little effort to involve ordinary workers and peasants. There were no big struggle meetings or large wall posters, features that characterized past and future campaigns.

Most of the rectification was carried out quietly behind closed doors, primarily in the Ministry of Culture and the All-China Federation of Literary and Art Circles. In contrast to the publication of Hu Feng's letters or the republication of Ting Ling's stories and essays in the Anti-Rightist Campaign, there was what appeared to be a deliberate paucity of material so that it was difficult to generate large-scale criticism. Except for disconnected quotations from Shao Ch'üan-lin's speech at Dairen, there was no real record of anyone else speaking there. Chou Yang supposedly stopped their publication. Except for the slogan "one into two, two into one," little effort was made to simplify the ideological themes to ensure that they could be understood by the uneducated. Most of the criticism had the character of an abstruse, intellectual exercise filled with Marxist abstractions, as if to distract from its political implications. Though the rectification was implicitly political, the substance was explicitly academic.

The personalized targets were treated leniently. They were referred to throughout as "comrade," an appellation that Hu Feng and Ting Ling had lost with the initial charges leveled against them. Unlike the past, the rectification ended without abject self-criticisms published throughout the land as a source of further indoctrination. No public confessions came forth from Yang Hsien-chen, Shao Ch'üan-lin, or the others. The people and journals that had not recognized their "mistakes" did not suffer to any extent. In contrast to the purge of Feng Hsueh-feng and his associates from the *Literary Gazette* in 1954 for rejecting student criticism of Yü P'ing-po, *Chinese Youth* issued a mild self-criticism for its turning down the initial attack on Feng Ting, and that was all.

Nevertheless, there were signs that Chou Yang and the cultural establishment were under pressure. Not only Shao Ch'üan-lin, but Chou Yang's close colleagues and Chiang Ch'ing's old enemies T'ien Han, Hsia Yen, and Yang Han-sheng were removed from office. Mao Tun stepped down as minister of culture. The journal with which Chou Yang and his associates were closely identified, *Literary Gazette*, published a number of articles criticizing itself for having praised writers like Chao Shu-li and Ou-yang Shan, who had portrayed "middle characters." One critic accused *Literary Gazette* of being revolutionary in words but revisionist in implementation. Another accused it of relying on a small group of professional writers without allowing input from the masses. These were the main charges to be leveled against the cultural bureaucrats in the Cultural Revolution.

The removal of some of his close colleagues and the challenge from Chiang Ch'ing appeared to mark the beginning of the end for the cultural bureaucracy that Chou Yang had built up for almost thirty years. Yet although the cultural bureaucracy had gone a long way to placate Mao by removing some of its most famous names and reshuffling its leadership, its operation continued intact. Although Mao had accused the majority of cultural officials of revisionism, as opposed to the earlier campaigns when all the disciples, as in the case of Hu Feng, and all the associates, as in the case of Ting Ling, suffered a fate similar to that of their leader, the criticism stopped with a small number of colleagues and the charges against them for the most part were limited to a few specific misdeeds. As later described in the Cultural Revolution, they were like "the castles" that were sacrificed to protect "the king" – Chou Yang. Chou's other close colleagues, Lin Mo-han, Yuan Shui-po, and Ho Ch'i-fang, were not even criticized at the time.

Chou's superior, Director of Propaganda Lu Ting-i, took over from Mao Tun as minister of culture. By the spring of 1965 criticism of Hsia Yen, Yang Han-sheng, and T'ien Han had waned. Chou was able to shelter most of his apparatus from attack. Furthermore, he appears to have protected it from the infiltration by the PLA that had affected other bureaucracies. Whereas by the end of 1964 the establishment of political departments on the model of the PLA commissar system had made some headway in the economic ministries, there was little evidence of this system in the Ministry of Culture.

Although those selected for criticism were not, as in the past, well-known intellectuals, but Party members with long careers in propaganda and ideology, they were not at the very top of the cultural hierarchy. Moreover, they were not the ones who had most sharply criticized Mao and the GLF. When one member of the Three Family Village group, Liao Mo-sha, had written a self-criticism, he had made no mention of his participation in the Three Family Village or of his criticism of Maoist programs. Most likely, P'eng Chen protected the Three Family Village as Chou Yang sought to ensure mild criticism of his cronies. A hard-hitting campaign against their underlings would have ricocheted onto them as their sponsors. Nothing was said, as in past campaigns, about the fact that the errors of the subordinates reflected those of their leaders.

Perhaps the most important difference from previous campaigns was that there was no unanimity of views in the negative appraisal of the scapegoats and in the imposition of one definitive line. This time there was a diversity of views, with some defense of the victims and some divergence from the line being imposed. The attackers dominated, but the defenders and modifiers did not vanish from the scene as they had in other campaigns. The themes that were to dominate the Cultural Revolution were all present in the 1964 rectification – class struggle, transformation of consciousness, concern over the deterioration of the revolutionary spirit among youth and Party leaders. But the discussion was contradictory, reflecting again the differing views of the cultural authorities, which in turn reflected division within the political leadership.

Another distinctive feature of this rectification was that as it was unfolding, there was open criticism of some of the critics, particularly the radical intellectuals. Yao Wen-yuan was censured in 1964 for his earlier comments on the aesthetician Chou Ku-ch'eng. A *People's Daily* article on 2 August 1964 termed Yao's criticism "self-contradictory" and "not in correspondence with the facts of history." In perhaps an indirect criticism of Mao, a few critics described Yao's approach as based on rigid formulas that distorted reality.[48] These countercriticisms reflected the still dominant position of the cultural bureaucrats. Yet they were not pushed too far, because Mao likewise protected the radical intellectuals.

By the beginning of 1965, Chou Yang quickly sought to bring the rectification to a formal close. He had suspended it earlier, in November 1964, in the various unions of the All-China Federation of Literary and Art Circles on the grounds that the cadres were needed elsewhere. At the end of February 1965, he called a meeting of editors and journalists where he denounced recent criticism in the rectification as dogmatic, simplistic, and exaggerated. Subsequently, the rectification faded away. As was his custom in previous campaigns,

48 Chin Wei-min and Lin Yun-ch'u, "Some queries on the spirit of the times," *JMJP*, 2 August 1964, *CB*, 747, 25.

on 15 and 16 April 1965 he summed up the results and announced its conclusion.

Chou admitted once again, in his final report, that he had been slow in criticizing revisionism and implementing rectification. But he did not admit to any serious shortcomings as Mao had demanded in his 13 December 1963 directive. In reference to some of his colleagues, Chou agreed that they did some things for which they should be criticized, but he insisted, "The Party does not regard them as rightists. Our contradictions with and our struggle against them remain to be a contradiction among the people and an inner-party struggle."[49] They might have deviated in the cultural sphere, but were not guilty of revisionism in the political sphere. Moreover, Chou Yang claimed they had already ceased holding some of these views and, therefore, should no longer be criticized.

In the sciences, as well as in the arts and humanities, Mao's directives were disregarded and in some cases resisted. In the Spring Festival in Education speech of 13 February 1964, Mao had praised Benjamin Franklin and James Watt as examples of scientists who made discoveries in the course of their everyday work. In contrast, a number of university science departments were merely gathering places where "bourgeois ideology exists in serious proportion."[50] Ai Szu-ch'i argued in a new section in *Red Flag*, "Natural science and dialectic materialism," that scientific achievement depended on the use of the Marxian dialectic and denounced those who refused to apply it to scientific research.

Yet in 1965 *China Youth News* published a set of articles urging youth to become "expert" without being "Red." It advised them to disregard the Marxian dialectic and work in research centers rather than in fields and factories. At a forum on "Red and expert," some even encouraged the use of bourgeois experts precisely because they were motivated by bourgeois values. "Some bourgeois technical experts whose world outlook has not been remolded can still serve socialism under proletarian leadership. Had they spent too much time on Marxism-Leninism, their expertness surely would have suffered."[51]

A *China Youth News* editorial held that a person's "Redness" is

49 "The tempestuous combat on the literary and art front," *Shou-tu hung-wei-ping*, 7 June 1967, CB, 842, 27.
50 Schram, *Chairman Mao talks to the people*, 208.
51 Tien Ho-shui, "When one cannot be both red and expert," *Chung-kuo ch'ing-nien pao*, 26 December 1964, CB, 757, 6.

not expressed by attendance at meetings and political study. For a scientist, it is expressed by devoting the greater part of one's time to professional activity. It warned, "Under no circumstances should we critically regard devotion to study and energetic effort to conduct intensive research and professional work as a manifestation of individualism."[52]

There was reason, therefore, for Mao to be dissatisfied with the 1964–65 rectification. Instead of swelling into a major mass movement, it had petered out, becoming a relatively low-key, inconclusive affair that became the medium for a variety of views, some diverging from his own. Whereas the PLA was infusing its ideological efforts with revolutionary fervor and action, the Party's rhetoric intensified but its actual implementation was superficial. The very organization Mao had empowered to carry out the ideological transformation he deemed so necessary resisted and even opposed his demands. By the fall of 1965 he had abandoned his reliance on the Party to carry out a cultural revolution and launched his own with his intimates Chiang Ch'ing and Ch'en Po-ta, the PLA, and the radical intellectuals. In contrast to the Party's rectification, Mao's Cultural Revolution would compel unanimity in ideology, activation of the masses, and a thorough purge of those who did not follow his orders.

The concerns expressed by the intellectuals since the early 1960s for a period of stability and reconciliation, for professional and intellectual standards, for concurrence between ideology and reality, and for recognition of the genuine demands of the peasants were pushed underground. Their advocates were purged, and some of them were killed in the Cultural Revolution. But in the post-Mao era, the Teng Hsiao-p'ing leadership as well as a small number of intellectuals and youth would seek to carry out reforms that addressed these same concerns.

---

52 "Redness and expertness is what the era demands of our youth," editorial, *Chung-kuo ch'ing-nien pao*, 24 July 1965, *SCMP*, 3517, 5.

CHAPTER 7

MAO TSE-TUNG'S THOUGHT
FROM 1949 TO 1976

Like Lenin, Mao Tse-tung, on coming to power, continued to develop his ideas in a context different from that within which he had operated while in opposition. In so doing, he modified, adapted, and elaborated positions he had adopted earlier. In many respects there was substantial continuity, but there were also startling ruptures and reversals, and in addition, Mao struck out in new directions he had never previously had the occasion to explore.

One important constant in the development of Mao Tse-tung's thought was his concern to adapt Marxism, or Marxism-Leninism, to the economic and social reality of a backward agrarian country, and to the heritage of the Chinese past, which for Mao was no less real. Before the conquest of power, the first aspect of this project involved devising theoretical justifications for attributing to the peasantry a political role greater than that implied by the model of the October Revolution, and more specifically for the strategy of surrounding the cities from the countryside. In this respect, it might have been assumed, and probably was assumed by Mao himself in 1949, that Chinese practice, and Chinese theory, would move closer to that of the Soviet Union. Having taken power in the cities as well as in the countryside, the Chinese Communist Party was effectively in a position to develop modern industry, and thus to create its own supposed class basis as the "vanguard of the proletariat," and to open a road to convergence with more advanced countries under communist rule.

During the first few years of the People's Republic, such a trend appeared to be emerging, but it was rapidly reversed, and a decade after 1949 China and the Soviet Union were moving farther apart than they had ever been before. In *The Cambridge History of China*, Volume 14, these events are chronicled, and their causes analyzed. What interests us in this chapter is, of course, the role played by Mao Tse-tung and his ideas in these changes of direction. It will be argued here that the explanation lies partly in the continuing weight of the peasantry in Chinese society, as well as the influence on Mao himself of ideas current among the peasantry. But that is by no means the whole answer. The influence of the Yenan matrix, both in terms of an ethos of struggle and sacrifice and in terms of decentralized and self-reliant methods of economic work, must also be taken into account. Yet another factor manifestly important but difficult to assess, is Mao's goal, already mentioned, of adapting Marxism to China. Although the term he had put forward in 1938 to evoke this process, "the Sinification of Marxism," had gone out of use by the early 1950s, largely because Stalin resented the suggestion that there might be other theoretical authorities in the world communist movement apart from himself, the impulse it expressed remained very much part of Mao's thinking.

Mao's conviction that Chinese culture was a great, perhaps a unique, historical achievement strengthened his sentiments of national pride. On the other hand, his explicit aim was to enrich Marxism with ideas and values drawn from the national past, and thereby render it more potent as an agent of revolutionary transformation, and ultimately of Westernization, not to replace it with some kind of neotraditionalism in Marxist dress. Nonetheless, it became increasingly hard, especially in his later years, to determine whether the basic structure of "Mao Tse-tung Thought" was Chinese or Western.

This is particularly true of his theory of contradictions, although it can legitimately be asked whether Mao, during his last decade and a half, was as interested in such intellectual issues as he had been in the past, or whether he was above all preoccupied with achieving his own goals, which he regarded as by definition revolutionary. Another ambiguous element in Mao's thought is the stress on the role of subjective forces, "conscious activity," and the superstructure that runs through the whole of his career, from beginning to end. To the extent that this reflects a Promethean impulse, which was not prominent in premodern Chinese culture, or in other non-European civilizations, it cannot be seen as a traditionalistic element in Mao's thought. On the other hand, to the extent that the display of virtue by the ruler came to be seen as the chief guarantee of happiness, and the emulation of virtue became a key instrument of social control, the parallels with imperial China are obvious.

In Mao's final years, he was, of course, explicitly likened to the first Ch'in emperor, presented as a great revolutionary precursor and a master in the use of revolutionary violence. And yet, at the very same time, the idea of mass participation, and of relying on the masses, which was a real (though often misunderstood) element in the Yenan heritage, was also trumpeted more loudly than ever.

Proletarian party and peasant constituency, the logic of modernization and the ethos of revolutionary war, Marxism and the Chinese tradition, determinism and voluntarism, salvation through virtue and salvation through technology, autocracy and mass democracy – these are some of the contradictions with which Mao wrestled during the years from 1949 to 1976.

In discussing the complex record of his efforts to deal with these and other issues, an approach partly thematic and partly chronological has been adopted. In many important respects, the second half of 1957 constituted a geat climacteric in Mao's life, marked by changes in outlook and personality that were to cast their shadow over the whole of his last nineteen years. The account of many aspects of Mao Tse-tung's thought will therefore be divided into two halves, before and after 1957. This pattern will not, however, be applied rigidly, especially as some key ideas of Mao's later years did not even emerge untill well after 1957.

FROM PEOPLE'S DEMOCRACY TO
CONTRADICTIONS AMONG THE PEOPLE

Patterns of rule

This first theme is one for which, precisely, 1957 does not appear to have seen a decisive change in Mao's thinking, but there was very great continuity from the Ching-kang-shan and Yenan to the early 1960s. Throughout this period, his thought was strongly marked by an insistence on the need for firm leadership by a political elite.

This trait is, in fact, an integral part of the "mass line" itself, so often romanticized, or sentimentalized, during the Cultural Revolution to signify a project for allowing the people to liberate themselves and to run things in their own spontaneous way. In fact, while Mao Tse-tung saw the process of government as in part an educative process, he had no Spockian notions to the effect that the "students" should be entirely free to decide what they should learn. On the contrary, the "mass line," correctly understood, must be seen not as the negation or polar opposite of Lenin's conception of "democratic centralism," but as a complementary idea, emphasizing a particular dimension of the relation between leaders and led.[1]

At the same time, it must be recognized that the concept of the "mass

---

1 For a discussion of the complex and ambiguous relation between "traditional" and "modern" elements in Mao's thought and behavior, see Stuart R. Schram, "Party leader or true ruler?: Foundations and significance of Mao Zedong's personal power" in S. Schram, ed., *Foundations and limits of state power in China*.

line" does evoke a real and significant aspect of the theory and leadership methods of the Chinese Communist Party, rooted in that Party's experience. The emphasis on close links with the masses emerged during the Kiangsi period, for the obvious reason that without such links the fragile bases could not possibly have survived.[2] The term "mass line" was not first used by Mao Tse-tung; it has been variously credited to Chou En-lai and to Ch'en I.[3] These ideas were, however, at the center of Mao's own thinking, as expressed in particular in the Ku-t'ien Resolution of December 1929, and it was Mao who gave the concept its definitive formulation.

His classic definition, put forward in Yenan in 1943 at a time when so many aspects of the experience of the Chinese Communist Party were being drawn together and systematically formulated for the first time, reads in part as follows:

... all correct leadership is necessarily from the masses, to the masses. This means: take the ideas of the masses (scattered and unsystematic ideas) and concentrate them (through study turn them into concentrated and systematic ideas), then go to the masses and propagate and explain these ideas *until the masses embrace them as their own*, hold fast to them and translate them into action.[4]

As the italicized words make plain, the people, though taken into the confidence of the leaders of the revolutionary movement, were in the end to be made to embrace, and to interiorize, ideas that, if left to themselves, they were quite incapable of elaborating in systematic form. There is an obvious parallel here with Lenin's thinking, and it is therefore not surprising that, about the same time as he put forward this formulation of the "mass line," Mao should have reaffirmed in its full Leninist rigor the principle of centralized guidance by a revolutionary elite. "Some comrades," he complained in his speech of 1 February 1942,

... do not understand the Party's system of democratic centralism; they do not know that the Communist Party not only needs democracy, but needs centralization even more. They forget the system of democratic centralism, in which the minority is subordinate to the majority, the lower level to the higher level, the part to the whole, and the entire membership to the Central Committee.[5]

Within the broad limits defined by Mao's insistence both on a measure of initiative and involvement from below and on firm centralized guid-

---

2 See Stuart R. Schram's chapter in *CHOC*, 13. 820-22 and 826-66.
3 See, for example, Ting Wei-chih and Shih Chung-ch'üan, "Ch'ün-chung lu-hsien shih wo-men tang ti li-shih ching-yen ti tsung-chieh" (The mass line is the summation of the historical experience of our Party), *Wen-hsien ho yen-chiu, 1983*, 420-28, esp. 421-22.
4 Mao, *SW*, 3.119.   5 Ibid., 3.43-44.

ance from above, there is room for an infinite variety of formulations and shades of emphasis. From Yenan days onward, Mao Tse-tung rang the changes on these themes. Consistently, however, at least until the Cultural Revolution, he regarded centralized leadership as in the last analysis even more important than democracy.

And yet, although Mao was in no sense a partisan of what Lenin stigmatized as "tailism" (more accurately translated "backsideism"), that is, of following the rank and file rather than leading them, he was prepared, to a greater degree than Lenin, not to mention Stalin, to listen to the people and take account of their views. Such was the case, at least, until the 1960s. Another dimension of the problem of the "mass line" must also be noted, however. At issue was not merely the relation between the leaders and the led, but the nature, and in particular the social composition, of the Party's members and supporters.

A Communist Party was, for Lenin as for Marx, the party of the proletariat, even though Lenin expanded the social basis of the movement to make a somewhat larger place for the peasants. Mao, however, while continuing to talk about proletarian hegemony, had recruited, from 1927 onward, among a much wider range of social categories: rural vagabonds or *éléments déclassés (yu-min)*, shopkeepers, office workers, minor civil servants, and intellectuals of all descriptions, as well as "national capitalists," "patriotic gentry," and others. Most of these categories were relatively low on the scale of social privilege, and in this sense belonged to the "people" rather than the "elite." All the same, whereas "masses" (or "toiling masses") was in the Soviet context essentially a synonym for the workers plus reliable elements among the peasantry, used instead of more precise class labels to stress the inchoate character of the followers, and therefore their need for leadership, for Mao it signified rather the overwhelming majority of the Chinese people who could, in the end, be made to rally to the revolution.[6]

The precise role of the various classes in Mao's pattern of socialist development will be considered in subsequent sections. The simple fact of the heterogeneity of the "masses" with which he had to deal carries, however, certain implications about the nature and function of leadership in the political order he sought to create.

When the prospect of a "coalition government" with the Kuomintang, which Mao had envisaged as a useful tactical expedient in 1944–45, finally evaporated and was replaced by open civil war, there was no longer any

---

6 For a discussion of these issues from a somewhat different methodological perspective, see Tang Tsou, "Marxism, the Leninist Party, the masses, and the citizens in the formation and the structure of the Communist Party-state in China," in Schram, *Foundations of state power*.

reason for maintaining the slightest ambiguity about the Party's immediate political goals. Mao therefore spelled out, on 30 June 1949, in an article written to commemorate the twenty-eighth anniversary of the foundation of the Chinese Communist Party, the precise nature of the "people's democratic dictatorship" that he proposed to establish three months later.

The term "people's democracy" had, in fact been introduced by Mao as early as May 1939, in his speech on the twentieth anniversary of the May Fourth Movement. "The present stage," he said then, "is not socialism, but destroying imperialism and the feudal forces, transforming this [present] semi-colonial and semi-feudal position, and establishing a people's democratic system (*jen-min min-chu chu-i ti chih-tu*)."[7] Now, in 1949, characterizing the new people's democratic regime, Mao made use of a distinction he had employed in "On New Democracy" between the "state system" (*kuo-t'i*) and the "system of government" (*cheng-t'i*).[8] Not surprisingly, since they viewed the matter in a Marxist framework, Mao and other writers in the early years of the Chinese People's Republic defined the state system primarily in class terms. Thus, one reference work for political study by basic-level cadres, first published in 1952, said in part:

The state system is the class essence of the state. The question of the state system is the question of the place of the various social classes in the state, i.e., it is the question of which class controls the political power of the state. For the most part, the state system of the various countries of the world at the present time can be divided into three types: (1) the capitalist state system, marked by the dictatorship of the reactionary bourgeoisie; (2) the socialist state system, marked by the dictatorship of the working class; and (3) the new-democratic state system, marked by the joint dictatorship of the various revolutionary classes, led by the working class and with the worker-peasant alliance as the foundation.[9]

This had been the classification laid down by Mao in 1939–40. The state established in 1949 was called a people's dictatorship rather than a proletarian dictatorship, because it was seen as a hybrid form adapted to the circumstances prevailing during the "period of transition" from postwar reconstruction to the building of socialism. Although it was an axiom of Marxism that power in a society where capitalism had begun to develop could be exercised only by the proletariat or by the bourgeoisie, and not by any intermediate class or combination of classes, Lenin had

7 Takeuchi Minoru, ed., *Mao Tse-tung chi*, 6.238. (Hereafter *MTTC*.) Apart from variations resulting from changes in the Chinese text, the translation in Mao, *SW*, 2.243 is so imprecise that "people's democratic system" becomes simply "people's democracy."
8 Mao, *SW*, 2.351–52.
9 Ch'en Pei-ou, *Jen-min hsueh-hsi tz'u-tien* (People's study dictionary). (2nd. ed.), 288–89.

put forward, in 1905, the formula of the "revolutionary-democratic dictatorship of the workers and the peasants" to characterize the political system under which certain reforms could be carried out in Russia before the establishment of a full-blooded proletarian dictatorship. Mao's "people's democratic dictatorship" was a lineal descendant of this Leninist concept, which had been applied to China and other Asian countries by the Comintern in the 1920s and 1930s.[10]

In 1949, Mao defined the locus of sovereignty in such a state in terms of concentric circles, or of an atom or onion metaphor. The hard or heavy center was made up of the working class, which was to exercise hegemony through the Party presumed to represent it. Next to the center were the peasants, said to constitute the most reliable allies of the proletariat. Then came the petty bourgeoisie, who were to be largely followers. As for the national bourgeoisie, they had a dual nature; they were patriotic, but they were also exploiters. They therefore dwelt on the outer fringes of the "people," perpetually in danger of flying off into the camp of the "non-people" hostile to the revolution.

These four classes (corresponding, of course, to Stalin's "four-class bloc" of the 1920s) were to exercise the "people's democratic dictatorship." Since the "state system" was thus made to include not only the class nature of the state but also the mode of rule (dictatorship), what realm of meaning was left to be covered by "system of government"? Most definitions of the *cheng-t'i* of the Chinese People's Republic in its earliest years[11] refer back to Mao's formulation in "On New Democracy," where he wrote in part:

As for the question of the "system of government,"[12] this is a matter of how political power is organized, the form in which one social class or another chooses to arrange its apparatus of political power to oppose its enemies and protect itself.... China may now adopt a system of people's congresses, from the national people's congress down to the provincial, county, district and township people's congresses, with all levels electing their respective governmental bodies. But if there is to be a proper representation for each revolutionary class according to its status in the state, a proper expression of the people's will.... then a system of really universal and equal suffrage, irrespective of sex, creed, property or education, must be introduced. Such is the system of democratic centralism....

10 On Mao's evolving ideas regarding the role of various classes in the Chinese revolution and the hegemony of the proletariat, see *CHOC*, 13.851–58.
11 See, for example, *Jen-min ta hsien-chang hsueh-hsi shou-ts'e* (Handbook for the study of the people's constitution), 135, and *Jen-min ta hsien-chang hsueh-hsi tzu-liao* (Materials for the study of the people's constitution), 31.
12 In the original version, this reads "political power" (*cheng-ch'üan*), rather than "system of government" (*cheng-t'i*), but the latter term is used in the first sentence of the ensuing paragraph, so the overall sense of the passage is not substantially affected. (See *MTTC*, 7.165–66.)

The state system, a joint dictatorship of all the revolutionary classes and the system of government, democratic centralism – these constitute the politics of New Democracy.[13]

This passage was, of course, written in 1940, when Mao was still operating within the context of the United Front with the Kuomintang and the position of the Chinese Communist Party was relatively weak. By 1949, his idea of a "republic of New Democracy" stressed rather the need for dictatorship over the "reactionary" classes than direct elections based on universal suffrage as the key to genuine democracy. The affirmation of "democratic centralism" as the basic organizational principle of the new state remained, on the other hand, intact.

But while he showed his debt to the Soviet example by maintaining key Leninist slogans such as democratic centralism, Mao also used, in his article of 30 June 1949, terms and concepts pointing in a different direction. Thus he employed the old-fashioned word *tu-ts'ai*, or "autocracy," as a synonym for dictatorship (*chuan-cheng*). To be sure, this compound had sometimes been employed in years past, when Marxist expressions did not all have standard equivalents in Chinese, as a translation for "dictatorship." Mao cannot, however, have been unaware of the traditional overtones *tu-ts'ai* would have for his readers, any more than he was unaware of the connotations of the ancient term *ta-t'ung*, or "Great Harmony," which had been refurbished half a century earlier by K'ang Yu-wei, and which he employed as a synonym for "communism."

In 1953, when a committee headed by Mao was engaged in drafting a constitution for the People's Republic of China, an eight-line rhyme was coined to sum up the criteria for the proper functioning of the political system:

> Great power is monopolized,
> Small power is dispersed.
> The Party committee takes decisions,
> All quarters carry them out.
> Implementation also involves decisions,
> But they must not depart from principles.
> Checking on the work
> Is the responsibility of the Party committee.[14]

In other words, there should be participation, by the citizens and by lower-level cadres, but it must be kept firmly under centralized control.

Mao's speech of 25 April 1956 to the Politburo, entitled "On the ten

---

13 Mao, *SW*, 2.352
14 "Sixty articles on work methods," *Wan-sui* (supplement), 34. (S. Schram's translation; see also the version in Jerome Ch'en, ed., *Mao papers: anthology and bibliography*, 68–69.)

great relationships," is unquestionably one of his half-dozen most important utterances after 1949, and one of the two or three most authoritative statements of his administrative philosophy. This remains true, in my view, even though the economic ideas Mao expounded on this occasion were in large part derived, as will be noted, from reports by the planners.

Section V of the speech, on the relationship between the Center and the localities, must be interpreted in the context of the speech as a whole, which tended above all to argue that the one-sided and doctrinaire pursuit of any policy goal was self-defeating. Thus, if you really want to develop heavy industry, you must not neglect light industry and agriculture; and in order to build up new industrial centers in the hinterland, you should make proper use of the existing industry in the coastal areas. Reasoning in similarly dialectical fashion, Mao said, on the question that concerns us here:

The relationship between the Centre and the localities is also ... a contradiction. In order to resolve this contradiction, what we now need to consider is how to arouse the enthusiasm of the localities by allowing them to run more projects under the unified plan of the Centre.

As things look now, I think that we need a further extension of local power. At present it is too limited, and this is not favourable to building socialism.[15]

In the last analysis, Mao continued to attach supreme importance to the cohesion and efficiency of the state as a whole, and he valued decentralization and grass-roots initiative within the limits thus set. Summing up his discussion in Section V of "On the ten great relationships," he declared:

There must be proper enthusiasm and proper independence.... Naturally we must at the same time tell the comrades at the lower levels that they should not act wildly, that they must exercise caution. Where they can conform, they ought to conform.... Where they cannot conform ... then conformity should not be sought at all costs. Two enthusiasms are much better than just one.... In short, the localities should have an appropriate degree of power. This would be beneficial to the building of a strong socialist state.[16]

The emphasis on centralism is even stronger in the official version than in the unofficial text from which I have been quoting. The new text adds, at this point: "In order to build a powerful socialist state, we must have strong and united leadership by the Centre, we must have unified plan-

15 This quotation is taken from the version of Mao's speech reproduced by the Red Guards in 1967–69, as translated in S. Schram, *Mao Tse-tung unrehearsed: talks and letters, 1956–71*, 71–72.
16 Schram, *Mao unrehearsed*, 73.

ning and discipline throughout the whole country; disruption of this necessary unity is impermissible."[17]

Although these differences of emphasis were clearly evident at the time when the official version of "On the ten great relationships" was published three months after Mao's death, it was impossible at that time to assess their significance for lack of information about the sources, and the course of editorial work on this key text. Indeed, some observers regarded the new passages added at that time as forgeries. Information subsequently published enables us to clarify these issues.

This talk, while it dealt at length with the problems of patterns of rule that concern us here, was in the first instance an attempt to define an overall strategy for economic development. For a month and a half, in February and March 1956, Mao Tse-tung had listened, in the company of some leading members of the Party and of the government, to reports from a large number of economic departments. On 25 April 1956, he summed up his own understanding of the conclusions that flowed from these discussions at an enlarged session of the Politburo; on 2 May, he repeated substantial portions of this talk, in revised form, before the Supreme State Conference. The official version is a marriage of the two.[18]

Despite his abiding emphasis on a strong centralized state, Mao's immediate concern in 1956 was with widening the scope of local authority, since he regarded the existing degree of centralization as self-

17 Mao, *SW*, 5.294.
18 The 25 April version was disseminated only to upper-level Party cadres at the time; in December 1965, "On the ten great relationships" was circulated down to the *hsien* and equivalent levels, but this text, though dated 25 April, was in fact an edited version of the 2 May 1956 talk. The latter, because it was delivered before a non-Party audience, was understandably less explicit and forceful in dealing with various issues such as relations with the Soviets. (On one point, the proclamation of the "Hundred Flowers" slogan, Mao had in fact gone well beyond his April position on 2 May, but that passage, discussed later in the chapter, was not included in the December 1965 text.) It was such a truncated version of Mao's 2 May talk that the Red Guards reproduced under the title "On the ten great relationships" and that was translated in the West in the 1970s. Only in July 1975 were the two speeches combined, at the suggestion of Teng Hsiao-p'ing, into what was to become the official version. The editorial work was done by Hu Ch'iao-mu, under Teng's authority. Approved by Mao at the time for inner-Party distribution, it was published only in December 1976. In the light of these facts, the title of an article written immediately after its appearance (Stuart Schram, "Chairman Hua edits Mao's literary heritage: 'On the ten great relationships,' " *CQ*, 69 [March 1977]) now appears slightly ironic.
   All of the information in the above note is taken from *Kuan-yü chien-kuo-i-lai tang-ti jo-kan li-shih wen-t'i ti chueh-i chu-shih pen (hsiu-ting)* (Revised annotated edition of the Resolution on certain questions in the history of our party since the founding of the PRC, 243-45.) (Hereafter, "1981 resolution, annotated edition.") This volume, compiled by the "Research Center on Party Literature under the Central Committee (Chung-kung chung-yang wen-hsien yen-chiu-shih), the organ responsible for the publication of all writings by Mao Tse-tung (as well as other leaders including Liu Shao-ch'i, Chou En-lai, and Teng Hsiao-p'ing) is unquestionably authoritative. The openly published, revised edition of this work is slightly fuller than the original *nei-pu* version that appeared in 1983, and is therefore to be preferred. In the case of "On the ten great relationships," the relevant passage is virtually identical.

defeating. In another talk at the same April 1956 Politburo meeting, he said: "The relationship between the lower echelons and the higher echelons is like that of a mouse when it sees a cat. It is as if their souls have been eaten away, and there are many things they dare not say."[19]

But how was effective centralization to be combined with an "appropriate degree" of local power? This problem, in Mao's view, was inextricably linked to the issue of dual versus vertical control (see CHOC, 14, ch. 2), which is explicitly raised in Section V of "On the ten great relationships":

At present dozens of hands are meddling in local affairs, making them difficult to manage.... Since the ministries don't think it proper to issue orders to the Party committees and people's councils at the provincial level, they establish direct contact with the relevant departments and bureaux in the provinces and municipalities and give them orders every day. These orders are all supposed to come from the central authorities, even though neither the Central Committee of the Party nor the State Council knows anything about them, and they put a great strain on the local authorities.... This state of affairs must be changed....

We hope that the ministries and departments under the central authorities will ... first confer with the localities on all matters concerning them and issue no order without full consultation.

The central departments fall into two categories. Those in the first category exercise leadership right down to the enterprises, but their administrative offices and enterprises in the localities are also subject to supervision by the local authorities. Those in the second have the task of laying down guiding principles and mapping out work plans, while the local authorities assume the responsibility for putting them into operation.[20]

The last paragraph of the above quotation refers to the policy, adopted in 1956–57, of keeping only large-scale or important enterprises, especially in the field of heavy industry, under the direct control of the central ministries, and handing other industrial and commercial enterprises over to the lower levels (see CHOC, 14, ch. 3). The complex pattern that resulted has been the subject of many studies. Two decades ago, Franz Schurmann drew a distinction that remains useful between what he called "decentralization I," involving the transfer of decision-making power to the production units themselves, and "decentralization II," signifying the transfer of power to some lower level of regional administration. He viewed Ch'en Yun as an advocate of the first plan, which would have led China in the direction of a Yugoslav-type economy, and

19 Wan-sui (1969), 35; Miscellany of Mao Tse-tung Thought (1949–1968), 30.
20 This version is based primarily on the official Chinese text, as translated in Mao, SW, 5.293, but the translation had been modified in places, sometimes making use of the phrasing employed in Schram, Mao unrehearsed, 72.

Mao Tse-tung and Liu Shao-ch'i as partisans of the second. He found, however, that Ch'en Yun's approach constituted a "contradictory" combination of centralization, decentralization I, and decentralization II.[21]

Harry Harding, who uses a sixfold set of criteria for approaching the problem, likewise concludes that the policy (in fact drafted by Ch'en Yun) adopted by the Third Plenum in the autumn of 1957 was an "eclectic" one, combining centralization and decentralization.[22] Such a contradictory or "eclectic" approach was, in reality, characteristic of everyone in the leadership at the time; the differences were matters of emphasis. During the Great Leap Forward, Schurmann added, this policy of combining centralism and democracy in a "unity of true opposites" consisted of "centralization of general policy impulses and decentralization of specific policy impulses."[23] Plainly, what he calls here "general policy impulses" are in essence what Mao's 1953 jingle referred to as *ta-ch'üan*, or "great power"; "specific policy impulses" (or the right to generate them) can be equated with *hsiao-ch'üan*, "small power."

On 31 January 1958, Mao revised the "Sixty articles on work methods," the directive constituting in effect the blueprint for the Great Leap Forward. In Article 28 of this directive, the 1953 jingle is first quoted and then explained in the following terms:

"Great power is monopolized" [*ta-ch'üan tu-lan*] is a cliché which is customarily used to refer to the arbitrary decisions of an individual [*ko-jen tu-tuan*]. We borrow this phrase to indicate that the main powers should be concentrated in collective bodies such as the Central Committee and local Party committees; we use it to oppose dispersionism. Can it possibly be argued that great power should be scattered? ... When we say, "All quarters carry them out," this does not mean that Party members do so directly. It is rather that there must first be a phase in which Party members enter into contact with those who are not Party members in government organs, enterprises, co-operatives, people's organizations, and cultural and educational organs, discuss and study things with them, and revise those parts [of higher-level directives] which are inappropriate [to the particular conditions]; only then, after they have been approved by everybody, are they applied.[24]

This text, it will be seen, deals both with relations between levels, and with the co-ordinating role of the Party. Mao's deliberate emphasis on the parallel between the current maxim *ta-ch'üan tu-lan* and the term *tu-tuan*,

---

21 Franz Schurmann, *Ideology and organization in Communist China*, 167–175, 196–98.
22 Harry Harding, *Organizing China: The problem of bureaucracy 1949–1976*, 107–15, 175–82. Both Schurmann and Harding rely to a great extent on secondary sources for Ch'en's views; Ch'en Yun's own words can now be read in Nicholas Lardy and Kenneth Lieberthal, eds. , *Chen Yun's strategy for China's development: a non-Maoist alternative.*
23 Schurmann, *Ideology and organization*, 86–87.
24 *Wan-sui* (supplement), 34–35 (translation by Stuart Schram).

which normally refers, as he says, to the arbitrary or dictatorial decisions of an individual, shows once again that he did not shrink from asserting the need for strong, centralized rule – or from implementing such ideas in practice.

How could such centralization be combined with the exercise of real and significant, though subordinate, "small power" at lower levels? Primarily through the coordinating role of the Party, to which the greater part of Mao's commentaries on the 1953 jingle are devoted. Although he did not here employ the term *i-yuan-hua*, meaning "to integrate," "to make monolithic," or "to make monistic," which had figured so largely in his administrative philosophy during the Yenan period,[25] it is clear that the impulse expressed in this concept was at the center of his thinking. In remarks of April 1956, he recalled that, in response to the emergence of excessive decentralization and local independence in the base areas of the Yenan period, the Central Committee had adopted a resolution on strengthening the "party spirit" (*tang-hsing*, a translation of the Russian *partiinost'*). "Integration [*i-yuan-hua*] was carried out," he continued, "but a great deal of autonomy was preserved."[26]

In comments of January 1958 on the 1953 jingle, Mao referred to the fact that the system of one-man management had been discredited. He included among the most basic organizational principles to be observed "the unity of collective leadership and individual role," which he equated with "the unity of the Party committee and the first secretary."[27] This can be taken as a reaffirmation of Mao's Yenan-style understanding of *i-yuan-hua* or integrated leadership, as opposed to Kao Kang's ideas on the subject. For Kao, *i-yuan-hua* had a sense very close to its literal meaning of "to make monolithic." A monolithic pattern of organization implied, in his view, that each entity such as a factory could be responsible to only one outside authority, which in practice meant the relevant ministry in Peking. The factory manager, as the agent or point of contact of this authority, must therefore have unchallenged authority within the factory. According to Mao's view, which was the prevailing view in the late

---

25 For a more detailed discussion of the emergence and significance of this concept, see Schram, "Decentralization in a unitary state: theory and practice 1940–1984," in Stuart Schram, ed., *The scope of state power in China*, 81–125, esp. 87–89. On *i-yuan-hua* as "integrate," see also Schram's chapter in *CHOC*, 13.864–66.

26 *Wan-sui* (1969), 36; *Miscellany*, 31. The "Resolution on strengthening the party spirit" adopted by the Politburo on 1 July 1941 (Boyd Compton, *Mao's China*, 156–60) did not in fact use the term *i-yuan-hua* but referred to the importance of centralization, and of "unified will, action and discipline." Manifestly, Mao regarded this decision as the first step in a process of establishing integrated Party control, which found further expression in 1942 and 1943.

27 Talk of 11 January 1958 at the Nan-ning Conference, *Wan-sui* (1969), 148; *Miscellany*, 79–80. *Wan-sui* (supplement), 34–35.

1950s, integration had to be carried out not merely at the national level, but in the localities. Otherwise, even "small power" could not be dispersed without leading to confusion. And the agent of integration could only be the Party committee at each level. Party control, whether at the Center or in the localities, involved, as Mao made clear, first taking decisions on matters of principle, and then subsequently checking on their implementation.

Further discussion of the leading role of the Party can best be deferred until we consider Mao's political and economic strategy at the time of the Great Leap Forward as a whole. Meanwhile, to round off this discussion of patterns of rule, it suffices to recall that in his speech of January 1962, after asserting that centralism and democracy must be combined "both within the Party and outside," and stressing once again, as he had in Yenan, that centralism was even more important than democracy, Mao went on to say that genuine centralization was possible only on a basis of democracy, for two main reasons. On the one hand, if people were not allowed to express themselves, they would be "angry" and frustrated, and therefore would not participate willingly and effectively in political and economic work. And on the other hand:

If there is no democracy, if ideas are not coming from the masses, it is impossible to establish a good line.... Our leading organs merely play the role of a processing plant in the establishment of a good line and good ... policies and methods. Everyone knows that if a factory has no raw material, it cannot do any processing.... Without democracy, you have no understanding of what is happening down below; the general situation will be unclear; ... and thus you will find it difficult to avoid being subjectivist; it will be impossible to achieve unity of understanding and unity of action, and impossible to achieve true centralism.[28]

Here the term "democratic centralism" is made to cover both the fundamental dilemma of combining effective "centralized unification" with active support and initiative from below, and the problem of the upward and downward flow of ideas evoked by the slogan of the "mass line." Mao's overall view of this cluster of issues is clearly reflected in the metaphor of the processing plant. To be sure, this plant is incapable of producing anything meaningful if it is not constantly fed with information and suggestions, but in the last analysis the correct line can only be elaborated by the brain at the center. The deprecatory adverb "merely" before "processing plant" does not change the fact that this is where the decisive action takes place.

28 Schram, *Mao unrehearsed*, 163–64.

Such was, broadly speaking, Mao's view of democracy and centralism, from Yenan days to the early 1960s. At the same time, although an overarching consistency marked, as noted at the beginning of this section, his line on these matters, there was undeniably a certain change of emphasis in 1957–58. This shift was closely linked to Mao's increasing radicalism, both in economic matters and in the domain of class struggle, which will be discussed in the following sections. It had, however, a direct impact on the questions of the structure of power we are considering here.

We have already seen that although Mao did seek, within the limitations imposed by his ultimate attachment to the ideal of a "strong socialist state," to foster the participation of the people in the country's affairs, the scope for political choice involved in such practices was slight. Above all, Mao gave little thought to the establishment of a political system democratic in its structure and mechanisms, and not merely in the sense that it was held to represent the "people."

That is, of course, one of the criticisms that has been made of him in China since 1978, and we shall return to it in the conclusion to the chapter. It is important to note, however, that from the time of the Great Leap, Mao Tse-tung attached even less importance to institutions than he had previously done. In a word, down to 1956 or 1957, while defining democracy in terms of the class character of the state, rather than in terms of political mechanisms, he nonetheless treated the state structure as something that had to be taken into account.

For example, in Mao's April 1956 discussion of centralization and decentralization, he declared:

According to our Constitution, the legislative powers are all vested in the central authorities. But, provided that the policies of the central authorities are not violated, the local authorities may work out rules, regulations and measures in the light of their specific conditions and the needs of their work, and this is in no way prohibited by the Constitution.[29]

In his speech of 27 February 1957 "On the correct handling of contradictions among the people," Mao emphasized that democracy was a means and not an end, and he poured scorn on Western ideas and practices such as parliamentary democracy and the two-party system.[30] China's own political system he treated whimsically and cavalierly, but he did at least take note of its existence. Discussing the problem of whether

29 Mao, *SW*, 5.294. This version is substantially identical in substance with the unofficial text (Schram, ed., *Mao unrehearsed*, 72), except that the latter contains an explicit reference to the National People's Congress as the sole legislative body.
30 Mao, *SW*, 5.398.

the not very numerous counterrevolutionaries still present in the country should be liberated in a big way (*ta fang*), even though under the constitution they were supposed to be objects of the dictatorship, Mao quoted an imaginary critic as saying: "This is laid down in the Constitution. You are the Chairman; aren't you supposed to observe the Constitution?" His very characteristic response to this dilemma was to suggest that most, though not all, of these people should be released, but that one should certainly not announce such a policy publicly.[31]

By the time of the Great Leap Forward, Mao had come to set very little store indeed by such institutional niceties. But because this evolution in Mao Tse-tung's thought was a direct consequence of the radical climate engendered by the ongoing revolution in the economy and in society, let us turn to those dimensions of the matter, before examining Mao's approach to political power in his later years.

Patterns of development

In approaching Mao's ideas regarding patterns of socialist development, it is perhaps worth emphasizing by way of introduction that his attitude toward modernization and industrialization was consistently positive. There has been a tendency in recent years to treat Mao as a believer in some kind of pastoral utopia, a partisan of a "steady-state" economy as an alternative to our so-called advanced industrial society. In reality, throughout the twenty-seven years during which he presided over the destinies of the People's Republic of China, Mao never ceased to call for rapid economic progress, and for progress defined in quantitative terms: tons of steel, tons of grain, and all the rest.

The very use of the term "modernization" was often taken, in the recent past, as a manifestation of Western cultural arrogance because it seemed to imply that in joining the "modern" world, the peoples of Asia and Africa would necessarily become like the Americans or the Europeans. In fact, Mao himself had no such scruples, and consistently defined China's economic aims in these terms, from the 1940s to the 1960s. Thus, for example, in his report of April 1945 to the Seventh Party Congress, he said China's agriculture must be made to progress from its "old-style, backward level" to a "modernized [*chin-tai-hua ti*] level," in order to pro-

---

31 This passage had been removed from the June 1957 edited text of Mao's speech (Mao, *SW*, 5.398-99). See the text as delivered in *Hsueh-hsi wen-hsuan* (Selected documents for study), 201-2. The content of Mao's February 1957 speech is discussed in detail later in this section.

vide markets for industry, and "make posssible the transformation of an agricultural country into an industrial country."[32]

Industry was, in Mao's view, of primary importance because of the role it played, or could play, in assuring the wealth and power of the Chinese state. Noting, in his article "On the people's democratic dictatorship," that "imperialism, a most ferocious enemy, is still standing alongside us," Mao added (in a comment removed from the *Selected works* text): "A very long time must elapse before China can achieve genuine economic independence. Only when China's industry has been developed, so that economically China is no longer dependent on foreign countries, will she enjoy genuine independence."[33]

The introduction to this chapter spoke of the continuing weight of the peasantry in Chinese society, and of the influence of this fact, and of peasant ideology, on Mao Tse-tung himself. This factor undeniably existed, and was of crucial importance, but it manifested itself very much more strongly from 1955, and especially from 1958, onward. On the eve of the conquest of power, in contrast, Mao repudiated, or in any case played down, the significance of the Party's rural experience. "From 1927 to the present," he declared in March 1949,

the centre of gravity of our work has been in the villages – gathering strength in the villages, using the villages in order to surround the cities, and then taking the cities. The period for this method of work has now ended. The period of "from the city to the village" and of the city leading the village has now begun. The centre of gravity of the Party's work has shifted from the village to the city.[34]

In other words, hitherto we have been doing it the unorthodox way, because that is the only way in which we could win victory, but henceforth we will do it in the orthodox Marxist, or Leninist, way, with guidance and enlightenment radiating outward from the urban industrial environment to the backward peasants in the countryside. Such a perspective was clearly in evidence in Mao's article of June 1949 "On the people's democratic dictatorship," in which, after declaring that state power could not be abolished yet because imperialism and domestic reaction still existed, and that the present task, on the contrary, was to strengthen the people's state apparatus, he went on to say, "Given this condition, China can develop steadily, under the leadership of the working class and the Communist Party, from an agricultural into an industrial country, and from a

---

32 *MTTC* 9.244. (The clause referring to agricultural modernization had been excised from the current official version of this speech in Mao, *SW*, 3.297.)
33 *MTTC* 10.304; see also Mao, *SW*, 4.421, where the last two sentences quoted are missing.
34 Mao, *SW*, 4.363.

new-democratic into a socialist and communist society, abolish classes and realize the Great Harmony [*ta-t'ung*]." In this task of guiding the development of China "from an agricultural into an industrial country," it would be relatively easy, in Mao's view, to reeducate and remold the national bourgeoisie. "The serious problem," he declared, "is the education of the peasantry." For, he added, "The peasant economy is scattered, and the socialization of agriculture, judging by the Soviet Union's experience, will require a long time and painstaking work."[35]

Mao's stress on educating the peasants, and on working-class leadership of the "people's dictatorship" that was to do the educating, appears to offer clear confirmation of the reversal of priorities between cities and countryside he had announced in March 1949.

Another intriguing indication to this effect may be found in Mao's decision of December 1951 to abandon a formulation, put forward the previous spring by Liu Shao-ch'i and used thereafter by the Central Committee, according to which the "semi-working class" (*pan kung-jen chieh-chi*) in the countryside was, like the urban working class, one of the classes leading the revolution. Although Mao himself had earlier characterized the "semi-proletariat (the poor peasants)" as a leading class in the new-democratic revolution, he now found it "erroneous" to attribute leadership to any class save the urban workers. This plainly marked a shift toward greater orthodoxy.[36]

Moreover, in the early 1950s, these ideological trends were translated into action by an energetic attempt to draw large numbers of real flesh-and-blood workers into the Chinese Communist Party, in order to "improve" its class composition (see Chapter 2).

And yet, despite Mao's statement, in 1962, that during these early years there had been no alternative to "copying from the Soviets,"[37] he did not, like the Soviets, confuse the industrial revolution with the socialist revolution. And although scientific and technical modernization was a central and crucial strand in Mao's conception of socialist development, one may legitimately ask whether his broader vision of the Chinese revolution, even as he entertained it in 1949, would ultimately prove compatible with such technical modernization.

At the outset, the economic policies explicitly formulated by Mao were prudent and gradualist ones. Thus, in June 1950, he called for "maintaining the rich peasant economy in order to facilitate the early rehabilitation of rural production," and summed up the overall goals as follows:

---

35 Ibid., 418-19.
36 "Chih Liu Shao-ch'i" (To Liu Shao-ch'i), 15 December 1951, *Mao Tse-tung shu-hsin hsuan-chi*, 427-28.
37 Schram, *Mao unrehearsed*, 178.

... existing industry and commerce should be properly readjusted, and relations between the state sector and the private sector and between labour and capital should be effectively and suitably improved; thus under the leadership of the socialist state sector all sectors of the economy will function satisfactorily with a due division of labour to promote the rehabilitation and development of the whole economy. The view held by certain people that it is possible to eliminate capitalism and realize socialism at an early date is wrong, it does not tally with our national conditions.[38]

Even after the beginning of the 1st Five-Year Plan (FYP), Mao's perspective on these matters remained essentially similar. In August 1953, he defined the "general line" for the period of transition as "basically to accomplish the country's industrialization and the socialist transformation of agriculture, handicrafts and capitalist industry and commerce over a fairly long period of time."[39]

In September 1954, he declared:

The people of our country should work hard, do their best to draw on advanced experience in the Soviet Union and other fraternal countries, be honest and industrious, encourage and help each other, guard against boastfulness and arrogance, and gird themselves to build our country, which is at present economically and culturally backward, into a great industrialized country with a high standard of modern culture in the course of several five-year plans.[40]

In November 1954, Mao Tse-tung called the attention of Liu Shao-ch'i and Chou En-lai to what he described as an "erroneous formulation" in the extracts from the Soviet textbook of political economy just published in *People's Daily*: "Until socialism has been built completely or to a very large extent, it is impossible that there should be socialist economic laws."[41] In repudiating this view, Mao was quite plainly concerned with the theoretical foundations for China's claim to be already in some degree socialist in nature.

Nevertheless, as late as March 1955, Mao recognized that the road to socialism would be a long one:

It is no easy job to build a socialist society in a large country such as ours with its complicated conditions and its formerly very backward economy. We may be able to build a socialist society over three five-year plans, but to build a strong, highly industrialized socialist country will require several decades of hard work, say fifty years, or the entire second half of the present century.[42]

38 Mao, *SW*, 5.29–30.   39 Ibid., 102.   40 Ibid., 148–49.
41 "Chih Liu Shao-ch'i, Chou En-lai teng" (To Liu Shao-ch'i, Chou En-lai and others), 18 November 1954, *Mao Tse-tung shu-hsin hsuan-chi*, 484–85.
42 Mao, *SW*, 5.155.

Then, suddenly, in the middle of 1955 Mao's attitude changed, and (as described in *CHOC*, 14, ch. 2) he launched a movement for more rapid cooperativization in the countryside that, almost overnight, transformed the whole atmosphere of Chinese society. Mao's new mood, as well as his new framework of analysis, is vividly evoked by his annotations in the volume *Socialist upsurge in China's countryside*, written at the end of 1955, when the acceleration of cooperativization for which he had called on 31 July was proceeding even faster than he himself had predicted.[43]

In these texts, we can see clearly foreshadowed certain basic themes of the Great Leap Forward, and even of the Cultural Revolution, such as Mao's belief in the omnipotence of the subjective efforts of the mobilized masses to transform themselves and their environment. For example, in a passage praising the Wang Kuo-fan cooperative, nicknamed "The Paupers' Co-op," which had accumulated "a large quantity of the means of production" in three years by their own efforts, Mao commented: "In a few decades, why can't 600 million paupers, by their own efforts, create a socialist country, rich and strong?" Noting, in another passage, that tens of millions of peasant households had swung into action during the second half of 1955, thus completely transforming the atmosphere in China, Mao commented: "It is as if a raging tidal wave has swept away all the demons and ghosts."[44]

In this context of enthusiasm for the zeal and fighting spirit of the peasants, Mao wrote in December 1955:

If you compare our country with the Soviet Union: (1) we had twenty years' experience in the base areas, and were trained in three revolutionary wars; our experience [on coming to power] was exceedingly rich.... Therefore, we were able to set up a state very quickly, and complete the tasks of the revolution. (The Soviet Union was a newly established state; at the time of the October Revolution, they had neither army nor government apparatus, and there were very few Party members.) (2) We enjoy the assistance of the Soviet Union and other democratic countries. (3) Our population is very numerous, and our position is excellent. [Our people] work industriously and bear much hardship, and there is no way out for the peasants without co-operativization. Chinese peasants are even better than English and American workers. Consequently, we can reach socialism more, better, and faster.[45]

Thus, Mao suggested as early as 1955 that because they came to power after twenty years' struggle in the countryside, instead of by suddenly seizing the reins of government in the capital city, the Chinese Com-

---

43 *Socialist upsurge in China's countryside*, passim: Mao's commentaries are also reproduced in Mao, *SW*, 5.235–76.
44 *Socialist upsurge*, 5–6.159–60.   45 *Wan-sui* (1969), 27; *Miscellany*, 29.

munists knew more in 1949 than Lenin and his comrades had known in 1917 about exercising authority over the population at the grass roots, and securing their support. Moreover, the Chinese peasantry, in his view, provided splendid human material for building a socialist society.

And yet, it was by no means a one-sided "rustic" revolution that Mao sought to promote at this time. Though a distinctive feature of his 31 July 1955 speech on cooperativization had been the demand that in China, collectivization should come before mechanization, it was not to come very *far* before it, and the provision of the necessary tractors, pumps, and other industrial products was therefore urgent. More broadly, Mao continued to subscribe to the view he had put forward in 1949, according to which "the serious problem" was "the education of the peasantry." The implication plainly was that these rural dwellers would have to be brought into the modern world by causing them to assimilate knowledge, and especially technical knowledge, originating in the cities. And in this process, scientists, technicians, and other intellectuals would have a key role to play. Indeed, Mao recognized this in January 1956 when he declared, in the context of his twelve-year program for agricultural development, that the Chinese people "must have a far-reaching comprehensive plan of work in accordance with which they could strive to wipe out China's economic, scientific and cultural backwardness within a few decades and rapidly get abreast of the most advanced nations in the world." And he added that "to achieve this great goal, the decisive factor was to have cadres, to have an adequate number of excellent scientists and technicians."[46]

Mao therefore called, in January 1956, for a conciliatory and understanding approach to the intellectuals inherited from the old society. At a conference on the problem of the intellectuals called by the Central Committee, Mao underscored the various respects in which China was industrially and technologically backward, and in a dependent position because it could not make key products for itself, and commented:

There are some comrades who say not very intelligent things, such as "We can get along without them [i.e., the intellectuals]!" "I'm a revolutionary" [*lao-tzu shih ko-ming ti*]! Such statements are wrong. Now we are calling for a technical revolution, a cultural revolution, a revolution to do away with stupidity and ignorance [*ko yü-chun wu-chih ti ming*], and we can't get along without them. We can't do it by relying only on uneducated people [*lao-ts'u*] like ourselves.[47]

---

46 Speech of 25 January 1956, *JMJP*, 26 January 1956; extracts translated in Hélène Carrère d'Encausse and Stuart R. Schram, comps., *Marxism and Asia: an introduction with readings*, 293.
47 *Wan-sui* (1969), 34.

Mao's overall approach to building socialism in the mid-1950s is most cogently summed up in his speech of 25 April 1956 to the Politburo, "On the ten great relationships." In every domain, the lesson of this well-known utterance was the same: Understand the interconnectedness of things, and do not seek to maximize one while neglecting the effects on others. Thus, as we have already seen, he called in the political domain for an increase in the power and initiative of the localities, in order to contribute to the building of a strong socialist state. In the economic field, he called for reducing (but not reversing, as is sometimes suggested) the overwhelming priority to heavy industry, at the expense of agriculture and light industry, which he held to be self-defeating. But at the same time (thus illustrating his balance and evenhandedness at the time), he urged that proper attention should be given to developing further the existing industrial base in Shanghai and other coastal cities, rather than putting all the available resources into spreading industry throughout the hinterland.[48]

In drafting this speech Mao Tse-tung had, as noted earlier, taken careful account of the views of Ch'en Yun and other experts in economic work, and "On the ten great relationships" as a whole undoubtedly represented an attempt on his part to lay down a compromise position that would command wide agreement within the Party. The fact that Mao thus adopted a moderate and conciliatory attitude on specific issues by no means implied, however, that he was prepared in all respects to bow to the will of the majority of his leading comrades.

Already, in his manner of launching an accelerated collectivization drive in 1955, Mao Tse-tung had shown his disposition to ride roughshod over all opposition on a matter close to his own heart.[49] In mid-1956, he revealed a similar intolerance once again, in a more veiled, but ominous, manner. In early 1956, Mao had been persuaded that, as a result of the success of the "high tide" of socialism in the countryside, all economic work could be accelerated. When, in the face of the resulting contradictions and disequilibrium, the important editorial of 20 June 1956 on "Opposing adventurism" was drafted under the supervision of Chou En-lai, Mao saw the text in advance but did not express himself one way or the other. His colleagues were left with the impression that he had endorsed this statement, but in fact he had reservations about it. While acknowledging that it was undesirable to go *too* fast in economic development, he was persuaded that China could go very fast. For a year and a

---

48 Schram, *Mao unrehearsed*, 61–83; official text in Mao, *SW*, 5.284–307.
49 See the discussion in *CHOC*, 14. 110–17, 167–69, and also the analysis by Schram in "Party leader or true ruler?," 214–16.

half, he harbored his resentment at this editorial in general and at Chou
En-lai in particular, before giving vent to his feelings on the eve of the
Great Leap Forward.[50]

Meanwhile, in the spring and summer of 1956, Mao not only launched
the slogan of a "Hundred Flowers" but also adopted a very soft approach
toward problems of classes and class struggle, the relation between the
Communist Party and other forces in society, and the relation between
right and wrong. These issues were dealt with in more detail in his speech
of 27 February 1957, "On the correct handling of contradictions among
the people," but Mao had frequently referred to them in earlier texts.
Because of the importance that "class struggle" was to assume from 1957
to 1976, this theme merits detailed discussion in a separate section.

People, classes, and contradictions

The theoretical framework in which Mao considered these matters before
February 1957 was essentially that laid down in 1937 in "On contradiction." In this article, Mao had argued that although contradiction "per-
meates each and every process from beginning to end," and although all
contradictions involved struggle, they were not necessarily antagonistic,
and contradictions different in nature should be resolved by different
methods. In the text of this essay as Mao originally wrote it, the realm
of "non-antagonistic contradictions" was defined very broadly, and the
scope of class struggle thereby restricted:

For instance, the contradictions between correct and incorrect ideas in the Communist Party, between the advanced and the backward in culture, between town
and country in economics, between the forces and relations of production,
between production and consumption, between exchange value and use value,
between the various technical divisons of labour, between workers and peasants
in class relations, between life and death in nature, between heredity and
mutation, between cold and hot, between day and night – none of these exist in
antagonistic form [*tou mei-yu tui-k'ang hsing-t'ai ti ts'un-tsai*].[51]

50 For Mao's continuing optimism and impatience, see his speech at the Second Plenum of 15
    November 1956, Mao, *SW*, 5.332–35. The importance of Mao's psychological reaction to the
    criticism of "adventurism" is widely stressed in recent Chinese accounts of this period. In a con-
    versation of 24 April 1986, Kung Yü-chih characterized it as perhaps the first step on the road to
    the Cultural Revolution. For a summary of evidence regarding Mao's anger at this editorial
    published during the Cultural Revolution, see Roderick MacFarquhar, *The origins of the Cultural
    Revolution, 1: contradictions among the people 1956–1957*, 86–91. Regarding Chou En-Lai's contri-
    bution to the writing of the article of 20 June 1956, see Hu Hua, *Chung-kuo she-hui-chu-i ko-ming ho
    chien-she shih chiang-i* (Teaching materials on the history of China's socialist revolution and con-
    struction), 146.;
51 Nick Knight, *Mao Zedong's "On contradiction": an annotated translation of the preliberation text*,
    38. (Translation slightly modified on the basis of the Chinese text.)

In the revised version of 1951, which constituted, of course, the standard of ideological orthodoxy during the period we are considering here, Mao drew the lines much more carefully, explaining that "as long as classes exist, contradictions between correct and incorrect ideas in the Communist Party are reflections within the Party of class contradictions," and that such contradictions *could* become antagonistic "if the comrades who had committed mistakes did not correct them." He also noted that, while the contradiction between town and country was nonantagonistic in the base areas, or in a socialist country, it was "extremely antagonistic" in capitalist society, and under the rule of the Kuomintang.[52]

These are important differences as far as the tone of the work is concerned, and reflected an emphasis on the need to wage class struggle that Mao Tse-tung was to exhibit to a greater or lesser degree throughout the 1950s, but as regarded the attitude adopted toward the only two classes that (as we have seen from our earlier consideration of "On the people's democratic dictatorship") constituted a serious problem for the new regime, the line laid down was not significantly altered in 1951. The contradiction between the proletariat and the bourgeoisie was still to be resolved "by the method of socialist revolution"; and that between the workers and peasants in socialist society, which in 1937 was supposed to be resolved by the "socialization of agriculture," now called for the method of "collectivization and mechanization in agriculture," which was really a more concrete way of saying the same thing.[53]

In June 1950, Mao Tse-tung confirmed the basic moderation of his approach at that time in a speech to the Third Plenum entitled, in the *Selected works*, "Don't hit out in all directions" – in other words, don't struggle with too many classes at the same time. Summing up the Party's current attitude toward that ambiguous class, the national bourgeoisie, he declared:

The whole Party should try earnestly and painstakingly to make a success of its united front work. We should rally the petty bourgeoisie under the leadership of the working class and on the basis of the worker–peasant alliance. The national bourgeoisie will eventually cease to exist, but at this stage we should rally them around us and not push them away. We should struggle against them on the one hand, and unite with them on the other.[54]

By June 1952, things had progressed to the point where, in Mao's view, the contradiction between the working class and the national bourgeoisie had become the "principal contradiction" in China; hence it was

52 Mao, *SW*, 1.344–45.   53 Knight, *Mao Zedong's "On contradiction."* Mao, *SW*, 1.321–22.
54 Mao, *SW*, 5.35.

no longer appropriate to define the national bourgeoisie as an "intermediate class."[55]

And yet, in September 1952 he wrote to Huang Yen-p'ei that it would be unreasonable, throughout the whole period of the 1st FYP (i.e., until 1957), to expect more than a small fraction of the bourgeoisie to accept socialist ideas. They must accept working-class leadership, but to ask them to accept working-class thought, and not to be concerned with making money, was "impossible, and should not be done."[56]

In the summer of 1955, Mao Tse-tung gave renewed impetus to class struggle in the countryside, in particular by adopting the distinction between "upper" and "lower" middle peasants, and treating the line between these two categories as the fundamental cleavage in Chinese rural society. Summing up the situation in his concluding speech at the Sixth Plenum of October 1955, which formally endorsed his rural policies, Mao repeated that the Communists had two alliances, one with the peasants and the other with the national bourgeoisie. Both of them were "indispensable," but of the two, the alliance with the peasants was "principal, basic and primary," whereas that with the bourgeoisie was "temporary and secondary." Stressing the interrelationship between these two alliances, he said:

At the Third Plenary Session in 1950, I spoke against hitting out in all directions. The agrarian reform had not yet been carried out in vast areas of the country, nor had the peasants come over entirely to our side. If we had opened fire on the bourgeoisie then, it would have been out of order. After the agrarian reform, when the peasants had entirely come over to our side, it was possible and necessary for us to start the movements against the "three evils" and the "five evils" [i.e., the Three Antis and the Five Antis]. Agricultural co-operation will enable us to consolidate our alliance with the peasants on the basis of proletarian socialism and not of bourgeois democracy. That will isolate the bourgeoisie once and for all and facilitate the final elimination of capitalism. On this matter we are quite heartless! On this matter Marxism is indeed cruel and has little mercy, for it is determined to exterminate imperialism, feudalism, capitalism, and small production to boot.

During the fifteen-year period of the first three five-year plans (of which three years had already elapsed), "the class struggle at home and abroad will be very tense," he noted.[57] In fact, the socialist transformation of agriculture and of capitalist industry and commerce, which Mao said in the speech just quoted would take about three five-year plans, was carried through on all fronts by the end of 1956 (see *CHOC*, 14, ch. 2). Already,

55 Ibid., 77.
56 "Chih Huang Yen-p'ei" (To Huang Yen-p'ei), 5 September 1952, *Mao Tse-tung shu-hsin hsuan-chi*, 441–43.
57 Mao, *SW*, 5.213–15.

by early 1956, sensing the favorable prospects and feeling himself in a position of strength, Mao Tse-tung took, as we have seen, a far softer and more conciliatory line on class struggle, and especially on the role of bourgeois intellectuals, and stressed the importance of scientists and technicians.

Another reflection of the same trend was the ending of the discrimination previously exercised against nonproletarian elements in recruiting new Party members. As already noted, strenuous efforts had been made in the early years of the Chinese People's Republic to recruit more workers into the Party, in order to improve its class composition. Then, in 1956, the more rigorous selection procedures formerly applied to nonworkers were abolished in the new Party constitution, on the grounds that, as Teng Hsiao-p'ing put it in his Report to the Eighth Congress, "the former classification of social status has lost or is losing its meaning." It is perhaps worth recalling the details of Teng's argument, for they provide the background against which Mao's views on class developed during the last two decades of his life:

The difference between workers and office employees is now only a matter of division of labour within the same class.... Poor and middle peasants have all become members of agricultural producers' co-operatives, and before long the distinction between them will become merely a thing of historical interest.... The vast majority of our intellectuals have now come over politically to the side of the working class, and a rapid change is taking place in their family background.... Every year large numbers of peasants and students become workers, large numbers of workers, peasants, and their sons and daughters join the ranks of the intellectuals and office workers, large numbers of peasants, students, workers and office workers join the army and become revolutionary soldiers.... What is the point, then, of classifying these social strata into two different categories?[58]

To the extent that Teng here attached more importance to subjective attitudes, and willingness to work for the revolution, than to family origins, his views are consonant with a continuing (though not a consistent) trend in Mao's thinking. But to the extent that he indicated that class struggle within Chinese society was rapidly dying away, his ideas obviously go completely against the tide that was later to rise, and to swamp the Party. That does not, of course, mean that Mao Tse-tung disagreed with him at the time. Even during the first upsurge of the Cultural Revolution, in 1966, when K'ang Sheng complained that the political report at the Eighth Congress had contained the theory of the disappearance of classes, Mao recognized that he had shared these views in 1956: "I read the report, and it was passed by the congress; we cannot make these two – Liu and Teng – solely responsible."[59]

How and why did Mao come to change his attitude toward classes and class struggle so dramatically that Liu became a decade later the "number one capitalist-roader"? The general context is well known. An aspect that merits emphasis is the crucial generational change in China's educated elite, which was inevitable in any case but was accelerated by the events of 1957. During the early years after 1949, both technical and managerial cadres were, of necessity, largely people inherited from the old society, "bourgeois" in their social origins or in that they had been trained in the West or in universities staffed by graduates of European, American, or Japanese schools. Mao believed that the loyalty of these people could be gained, and that being already expert, they could be made red as well. The "Hundred Flowers" policies Mao launched in the spring of 1956 were primarily designed to serve this aim of drawing the pre-1949 intellectuals into active participation in political and social life, improving their morale, and remolding them in the process.

In his speech "On the ten great relationships" as originally delivered to the Party on 25 April 1956, Mao Tse-tung, while reiterating that "inner-Party controversies over principle" were "a reflection inside the Party of the class struggle in society," stressed the importance of exchanging ideas, especially in the scientific domain, with people in and outside China.[60] The Hundred Flowers formula emerged in the course of the discussion of his report by the Politburo. In an intervention of 28 April, Mao declared that if one's views were true, more and more people could be expected to believe in them, adding that the Party's orientation (*fang-chen*) in literature should be "Let a Hundred Flowers bloom," and in scholarly matters, "Let a Hundred Schools contend."[61]

It was in the version of "On the ten great relationships" presented on 2 May 1956 to the Supreme State Conference that Mao gave, for the first time, a systematic account of his ideas on this topic. According to the fullest available summary, he declared that spring had now come, and that a hundred flowers, and not just a few kinds, should be allowed to bloom. The formula of a hundred schools of thought contending dated, he recalled, from the Spring and Autumn and Warring States periods, when there were a hundred schools of leading philosophers, with many different doctrines, all freely engaging in controversy. The same thing, he said, was necessary at present. Within the limits set by the constitution, the

59 Schram, *Mao unrehearsed*, 269. 60 Mao, *SW*, 5.301–6.
61 *1981 resolution, annotated edition*, 253–54.

partisans of every sort of scholarly theory should be able to argue about the truth or falsity of their ideas, without interference. We still haven't sorted out, he remarked, whether Lysenko's ideas are right or wrong, so let each school put forward its ideas in the newspapers and journals.[62]

Not only were Lysenko's ideas discussed in the newspapers, but in August 1956 at Tsingtao, a large-scale scholarly conference debated for a fortnight the opposing views of genetics, under the slogan "Let a hundred schools of thought contend!"[63] When one of the participants in this gathering subsequently expressed his enthusiasm in an article published in *Kuang-ming jih-pao*, Mao Tse-tung personally decided that it should be reprinted in the *People's Daily*, with a new subtitle supplied by Mao: "The way which the development of science must follow" (*fa-chan k'o-hsueh pi-yu chih lu*).[64]

The related but distinctive idea of contradictions among the people first emerged in the autumn of 1956, in the aftermath of de-Stalinization in the Soviet Union, and of the Polish and Hungarian events. In his speech of 15 November 1956 to the Second Plenum, Mao indicated that class contradictions within Chinese society had already basically been resolved, although he spoke out firmly in support of class struggle and the dictatorship of the proletariat in dealing with counterrevolutionaries, and against Khrushchev's ideas of peaceful transition by the parliamentary road.[65]

So far as is known, Mao first used the actual term "contradictions among the people" on 4 December 1956 in a letter to Huang Yen-p'ei, a leading representative of one of the minor parties. On this occasion, he stated that although class struggle within China (as opposed to conflicts with imperialism and its agents) had "already been *basically* resolved" (*i-ching chi-pen-shang chieh-chueh le*), problems among the people would, in future, "ceaselessly arise."[66] Plainly, the suggestion is that they would be more numerous.

The *People's Daily* editorial of 29 December 1956, entitled "More on

62 Ibid., 254.

63 The full record of the formal discussions at this conference was published nearly thirty years later. See *Pai-chia cheng-ming – fa-chan k'o-hsueh ti pi-yu chih lu. 1956 nien 8 yueh Ch'ing-tao i-ch'uan hsueh tso-t'an hui chi-shu* (Let a hundred schools of thought contend – the way which the development of science must follow. The record of the August 1956 Tsingtao Conference on Genetics).

64 Ibid., 10 (Introduction). For a fuller account, see Kung Yü-chih, "Fa-chan k'o-hsueh pi-yu chih lu – chieh-shao Mao Tse-tung t'ung-chih wei chuan-tai 'Ts'ung i-ch'uan-hsueh t'an pai-chia cheng-ming' i wen hsieh ti hsin ho an-yü" (The way which the development of science must follow – presenting Comrade Mao Tse-tung's letter and annotation relating to the republication of "Let a hundred schools of thought contend viewed from the perspective of genetics"), *KMJP*, 28 December 1983.

65 Mao, *SW*, 5.341–48 passim; *1981 resolution, annotated edition*, 51.3

66 "Chih Huang Yen-p'ei" (To Huang Yen-p'ei) 4 December 1956, *Mao Tse-tung shu-hsin hsuan-chi*, 514–15. (Mao himself underscored the adverb "basically.")

the historical experience of the dictatorship of the proletariat,"[67] constituted the first public exposition of Mao's ideas on this topic.[68] This text,
which aimed to combat excessive discrediting of Stalin and of Soviet
experience in the wake of the Polish events and the Hungarian revolt,
took a slightly harder position, stating that no one adopting the standpoint of the people should "place the contradictions among the people
above the contradictions between the enemy and ourselves," adding:
"Those who deny the class struggle and do not distinguish between the
enemy and ourselves are definitely not Communists or Marxist-Leninists."[69]

At a conference of provincial and municipal Party secretaries on 27
January 1957, Mao declared, "During the period of building [socialism],
our experience of class struggle (which is partial), and contradictions
among the people (which are primary) has been inadequate. This is a science, and we must study it very well."[70]

A month later, Mao devoted the greater part of his celebrated speech
"On the correct handling of contradictions among the people" precisely
to this science. In the original version of this talk, Mao expressed some
reservations about the December editorial (even though he had personally revised it),[71] saying that it had not dealt explicitly with the problem of
the national bourgeoisie, and had not made plain that the contradictions
with this class were definitely contradictions among the people. To be
sure, under certain circumstances, they could become antagonistic, but
one should not mistake well-intentioned criticisms for hostile attacks.
Lenin had not had time to analyze this problem properly, and Stalin did
not even try to make the distinction:

You could only speak favourably, and not unfavourably; you could only sing
praises to his successes and virtues, but were not allowed to criticize; if you
expressed any criticisms he suspected you of being an enemy, and you were in
danger of being sent to a camp or executed.

Leftists are left opportunists. The so-called "leftists" raise the banner of the
"left," but they are not really left, for they exaggerate the contradictions between
ourselves and the enemy. Stalin, for example, was such a person.

67 For a translation, see *The historical experience of the dictatorship of the proletariat*, 21–64.
68 The novelty of this formulation was widely noted at the time, and these ideas were commonly
   attributed to Mao. (This passage was included in Stuart R. Schram, *The political thought of Mao
   Tse-tung* in 1963.) The fact that Mao had not previously expressed the same ideas in any unpublished text is confirmed by Liao Kai-lung, "She-hui-chu-i she-hui chung ti chieh-chi tou-cheng ho
   jen-min nei-pu mao-tun wen-t'i" (The problem of class struggle and of contradictions among the
   people in socialist society), in Liao Kai-lung, *Ch'üan-mien chien-she she-hui chu-i ti tao-lu* (The road to
   building socialism in an all-round way), 245.
69 *The historical experience*, 25.   70 *1981 resolution, annotated edition*, 532.
71 *Wan-sui* (1969), 89; *Miscellany*, 61. This source indicates simply that the meeting took place in
   January 1957; the date of 27 January is given in the version published in Mao, *SW*, 5.359–83,
   which does not, however, include this passage.

China, too, said Mao, had suffered from such errors, especially during the campaign against counterrevolutionaries.[72]

The original text of Mao's 27 February speech contained extremely long and important passages both on the differences between China and the Soviet Union and on the related problem of war and peace, which will be discussed in a later section, on the Sino-Soviet split. It also dealt in passing with a variety of issues that cannot be taken up in this chapter, such as the "anarchism" prevailing in the realm of birth control,[73] or the inability of China at the present stage to provide secondary education for all.[74] Regarding the problem concerning us here, Mao declared that the "basic" (*chi-pen-ti*) contradiction in Chinese society was that between the relations of production and the productive forces, or between the basis and the superstructure.[75] At the same time, he made plain that, in his view, class struggles had basically come to an end in China.[76]

One can find a similar emphasis on the crucial role of contradictions among the people in the official text of Mao's February 1957 speech. For example, he declared: "It is precisely these contradictions [among the people] that are pushing our society forward"; since contradictions were, in Mao's view, the motor of change, the particular contradiction, or type of contradiction, that moves society forward ought logically to be the principal contradiction. Moreover, in the same passage, Mao went on to say:

Contradictions in socialist society are fundamentally different from those in the old societies, such as capitalist society. In capitalist society contradictions find expression in acute antagonisms and conflicts, in sharp class struggle; they cannot be resolved by the capitalist system itself and can only be resolved by socialist revolution. The case is quite different with contradictions in socialist society; on the contrary, they are not antagonistic and can be ceaselessly resolved by the socialist system itself.[77]

Such statements apper to support the view, put forward by some leading Chinese theoretical workers in recent years, to the effect that Mao's ideas of late 1956 and early 1957 implied the replacement of class struggle by contradictions among the people (which cannot, generally speaking,

---

72 *Hsueh-hsi wen-hsuan*, 193–95. For another version of this passage in the original February 1957 text, see *Mao Chu-hsi wen-hsien san-shih p'ien* (Thirty documents by Chairman Mao) (Peking: Special Steel Plant, 1967), 94–95.

73 *Hsueh-hsi wen-hsuan*, 209.   74 Ibid., 211.   75 Ibid., 212–13.

76 Ibid., passim, esp. 201. See also Su Shao-chih's assessment in *Tentative views on the class situation and class struggle in China at the present stage* ("Selected writings on studies of Marxism," No. 6), 35. (Chinese text, "Shih lun wo-kuo hsien chieh-tuan ti chieh-chi chuang-k'uang ho chieh-chi tou-cheng," in *Hsueh-shu yen-chiu-k'an*, 1 [October 1979].)

77 Mao, *SW*, 5.393.

be regarded as a form of class struggle) as the "principal contradiction" in Chinese society after the socialist transformation of 1955–56.[78]

An issue closely related to that of contradictions among the classes making up Chinese society is the problem of the role of the intellectuals. Mao's relatively tolerant and gradualist attitude toward the elimination of class differences in this domain was expressed in a statement of January 1957 noting that 80 percent of university students in China were still children of landlords, rich peasants, upper middle peasants, and the bourgeoisie. "This situation," he commented, "should change, but it will take time."[79] Nonetheless, he stressed forcefully, in the original version of his speech on "contradictions among the people," the importance of making the intellectuals reform themselves, so as to do away with their self-indulgent attitudes. All they wanted, he said, was two things: a high salary and "an old lady" or an "old man" (*t'ao lao p'o, t'ao lao kung*) – in other words, "to eat and to produce children."[80]

Mao's disdain for goals such as these (in both of which, it is hardly necessary to observe, he had himself freely indulged) was expressed in another passage of the 27 February 1957 speech on the corrupting effects of material well-being. The Chinese, he said, had two characteristics: Their standard of living was low, and their cultural level was low. Both of these traits, he said, were ambiguous:

If China becomes rich, with a standard of living like that in the Western world, it will no longer want revolution. The wealth of the Western World has its defects, and these defects are that they don't want revolution.... Their high standard of living is not so good as our illiteracy [*laughter*].[81]

This strain in Mao's thought was to come to the fore and find further expression during the Great Leap Forward, as we shall see. Meanwhile, however, Mao remained on the whole, in early 1957, relatively well disposed toward both the bourgeoisie and the intellectuals.

As late as 2 May 1957, an editorial in the *People's Daily*, which according to a well-informed Chinese specialist "reflected completely Comrade Mao Tse-tung's views at the time," argued: "Following the decisive victory in socialist transformation, the contradiction between the proletariat and the bourgeoisie in our country has already been basically resolved, and the previous several thousand years of history in a system of class exploitation has been basically concluded." As a result, the editorial

78 Liao Kai-lung, "She-hui-chu-i she-hui chung ti chieh-chi ...," 246–53; Su Shao-chih, *Tentative views on the class situation*, 22–26.
79 Mao, *SW*, 5.353. 80 *Hsueh-hsi wen-hsuan*, 207. 81 Ibid., 225–26.

MAO'S THOUGHT, 1949-76

stated, the principal contradiction in China was no longer that between hostile classes, but the contradiction between "the demand to build an advanced industrial country and the reality of a backward agrarian country," and others of a similar nature.[82]

But in mid-May, Mao's attitude changed radically as a result of continuing harsh criticism, and he perceived among the members of the Party "a number of" revisionists and right deviationists, whose thinking was a "reflection of bourgeois ideology inside the Party," and who were "tied in a hundred and one ways to bourgeois intellectuals outside the Party."[83]

Rewriting his February speech in June 1957, Mao qualified his original conclusion that class struggles were over by adding: "The large-scale, turbulent class struggles of the masses characteristic of times of revolution have basically come to an end, but class struggle is by no means entirely over."[84] This was still a relatively soft position, but Mao progressively hardened it. Thus, in July 1957, as the Hundred Flowers Campaign was being transformed into an Anti-Rightist Campaign, he asserted, "To build socialism, the working class must have its own army of technical cadres and of professors, teachers, scientists, journalists, writers, artists and Marxist theorists.... This is a task that should be basically accomplished in the next ten to fifteen years." To be sure, he added that his new army would include intellectuals from the old society "who would take a firm working-class stand after having been genuinely remoulded," but it was plain that most members of this army were to be young people of good class background. "The revolutionary cause of the working class," he added, "will not be fully consolidated until this vast new army of working-class intellectuals comes into being."[85]

As for the existing intellectuals, Mao warned them disdainfully:

Intellectuals are teachers employed by the working class and the labouring people to teach their children. If they go against the wishes of their masters and insist on teaching their own set of subjects, teaching stereotyped writing, Confucian classics or capitalist rubbish, and turn out a number of counter-revolutionaries, the working class will not tolerate it and will sack them and not renew their contract for the coming year.[86]

"Wei shih-mo yao cheng-feng?" ("Why do we want to carry out rectification?"), *JMJP*, 2 May 1957. For the judgment quoted above regarding Mao's approval for the article, see Liao Kai-lung, "Kuan-yü hsueh-hsi 'chueh-i' chung t'i-ch'u ti i-hsieh wen-t'i ti chieh-ta" (Answers and explanations regarding some questions which have been posed in connection with study of the "Resolution"), *Yun-nan she-hui k'o-hsueh*, 2 (March 1982), 104–5. (At a meeting of Party and state cadres in Yunnan on 8 October 1981.)

"Things are beginning to change," 15 May 1957. Mao, *SW*, 5.440.   84 Ibid., 395.

"The situation in the summer of 1957," July 1957, Mao, *SW*, 5.479–80.

"Beat back the attacks of the bourgeois rightists," 9 July 1957, Mao, *SW*, 5.469–70.

From this time forward, Mao increasingly saw "ghosts and monsters opposed to the Communist Party and the people" everywhere.[87]

MAO'S SEARCH FOR A "CHINESE ROAD"

As argued in the introduction to this chapter, the Anti-Rightist Campaign of autumn 1957 constituted a major turning point not only in Chinese politics generally, but in the development of Mao Tse-tung's thought. The changes that took place at this time made themselves felt across the whole range of Mao's intellectual interests and political concerns, from economics to philosophy, and from China's own internal problems to relations with the Soviet Union. In substantial measure, however, the central core of these new trends in Mao Tse-tung's thinking, and the impulse that led to their emergence, can be found in his ideas about "building socialism."

Determinism and utopian visions:
the theory of the "Great Leap Forward"

One aspect of the sea change in Mao's mind and thought that took place at this time was, as just noted, a sharp reversal of his attitude toward the intellectuals. By their harsh and, to his mind, negative and destructive criticisms, the scholars and writers participating in the "great blooming and contending" of early 1957 had cast doubt on Mao's own judgment in pressing ahead with these policies in the face of opposition from many of his senior comrades, and thereby, in Mao's view, undermined his prestige and authority. He therefore turned savagely against them. Henceforth, apart from training new, red intellectuals of good class origin, Mao Tse-tung would rely rather on the enthusiasm and creativity of the masses.

As for those wretched bookworms who had so betrayed his confidence during the Hundred Flowers period, who needed them? Mao therefore made repeated statements, and actively promoted policies, entirely at variance with his view of 1956 that scientists were the decisive factor, stressing that "all wisdom comes from the masses," and that "the intellectuals are most ignorant." In March 1958, he declared:

Ever since ancient times the people who founded new schools of thought were all young people without much learning. They had the ability to recognize new things at a glance and, having grasped them, opened fire on the old fogeys.... Franklin of America, who discovered electricity, began as a newspaper boy....

87 Ibid., 444.

Gorki only had two years of elementary schooling. Of course, some things can be learned at school; I don't propose to close all the schools. What I mean is that it is not absolutely necessary to attend school.[88]

However pithy and forceful we may find this, and Mao's many other anti-intellectual statements of the Great Leap period, it would be wrong to take any of them as a full and balanced expression of his view on these matters. At this time, he was still striving to hold together in creative tension, and to manipulate, polarities such as mass creativity and the scientific inputs necessary to economic development, or the rural and urban sectors in Chinese society.

In December 1958, Mao wrote to Lu Ting-i endorsing a report from the Tsing-hua University Party Committee about correcting the leftist errors committed in dealing with teachers in the Physics Department, and requesting that it be reproduced for general distribution. There was a widespread feeling, said this document, that "intellectuals are objects of the revolution during the period of the socialist revolution, and even more so during the transition to communism, because the overwhelming majority of them are bourgeois intellectuals and belong to the exploiting class. Even assistant professors who are members of the [Communist] Youth League are regarded as objects of the revolution." The only reason for having them around at all, in this prevalent view, was to set up an object of struggle; if the professors refused to reform, and to cut their salaries voluntarily, they should be sent to an old people's home.

This view Mao (like the Tsing-hua University Party Committee) entirely rejected, on the grounds that it was necessary to rally as many teachers and research workers as possible of all ranks to serve proletarian education, culture, and science.[89] But nevertheless, the weight of Mao's interest, and of his hopes, had unquestionably shifted toward the masses and the countryside.

Apart from Mao's exasperation with urban intellectuals, an important factor contributing to the turn of his thoughts, and also of the main thrust of Party policy, toward the countryside was the growing trend in the direction of creating larger rural organizations to cope with tasks such as mechanization and irrigation. Already in late 1955, in one of his editorial annotations to *Socialist upsurge in China's countryside*, Mao had proclaimed the superiority of big co-ops, adding: "Some places can have one co-op for every township. In a few places, one co-op can embrace

---

88 Schram, *Mao unrehearsed*, 119–20.
89 "Chih Lu Ting-i" (To Lu Ting-i), 22 December 1958, *Mao Tse-tung shu-hsin hsuan-chi*, 554–55. (For some reason, the name of the university is omitted here.) Both Mao's letter and the text of the relevant document are included in *Wan-sui* (1969), 267–69.

several townships. In many places, of course, one township will contain several co-ops."[90]

During the period from the spring of 1956 to the autumn of 1957, when the campaign against "adventurism" and other factors had led to the eclipse of some of Mao's more radical policy initiatives, this advice had, on the whole, not been put into effect. (See *CHOC*, 14, chs. 2 and 3, the discussion of political and economic developments in the run-up to the Great Leap.) During the winter of 1957–58, however, a movement for the amalgamation of the existing higher-stage cooperatives emerged. At the Chengtu Conference of March 1958, Mao threw his weight behind this development, and on 8 April 1958, the Central Committee issued a directive in the same sense, reading in part:

... if the agricultural producers' co-operatives are on too small a scale, there will be many disadvantages in future concerning both organization and development. In order to adapt to the needs of agricultural production and cultural revolution, small co-operatives must, in those localities where the conditions exist, be combined into large-scale co-operatives.[91]

By a coincidence far too striking to be accidental, this directive was issued the very day after Mao's visit to the "big co-op" at Hung-kuang in Szechwan had been announced in the press. (The visit had taken place in mid-March, while the Chengtu Conference was in session.)[92]

As already noted, the impulse toward larger-scale organization had emerged from the concern with creating a more effective infrastructure in the countryside, and above all with promoting the development of water-works. It is thus not surprising that during the very same Chengtu Conference of March 1958 at which he advocated larger cooperatives, and at the Nanning Conference that had led up to it, Mao Tse-tung should have devoted a considerable amount of time to listening to conflicting views regarding the "Three Gorges" plan for a giant dam to control the waters of the Yangtze, and chairing meetings to decide policy on this issue.[93]

At the early stage of the Chengtu Conference, the *ta-she*, or "big co-ops," were not yet formally invested with the administrative and military functions that were one of the distinctive aspects of the "people's communes" as endorsed in August 1958 at Peitaiho, and one cannot say,

90 *Socialist upsurge*, 460; Mao, *SW*, 5.273–74.
91 *1981 resolution, annotated edition*, 323–24. Mao's intervention at Chengtu in favor of *ta-she*, referred to here, does not appear in the texts of any of his three speeches at this meeting available outside China. (See Schram, *Mao unrehearsed*, 96–124.)
92 David S. G. Goodman, *Centre and province in the People's Republic of China: Sichuan and Guizhou, 1955–1965*, 144–45.
93 See Li Jui, *Lun San-hsia kung-ch'eng* (On the Three Gorges project), 8–10, 94–99, 171, 243, and passim.

therefore, that they were communes in all but name. They were, however, already beginning to take on some of these characteristics, and thus constituted a stage in a process of development that soon culminated in the communes.

The history of the emergence of the communes is not, of course, in itself our concern here, but the facts just presented are relevant to the theme of this chapter because they demonstrate that Mao's own thought and action contributed directly to the institutional revolution that burst on the scene in the summer of 1958 and was to shape Chinese rural society for a quarter of a century.

The inspiration for this trend can be found not simply in Mao's identification with the rural world, but in the millenarian visions that had gripped him during the collectivization drive of 1955. These ideas found expression in the thesis, repeatedly expounded by Mao between 1956 and 1958, according to which the Chinese people could draw positive advantages from the fact that they were "poor and blank." "Poor people," he wrote in April 1958, "want change, want to do things, want revolution. A clean sheet of paper has no blotches, and so the newest and most beautiful words can be written on it, the newest and most beautiful pictures can be painted on it."[94]

Mao was here making the same two linked points he had conveyed in different language in his speech of 27 February 1957 when he referred to the superiority of China's "illiteracy" over the wealth of the West. To the extent that the peasants were even blanker than the Chinese people as a whole, that is, even less corrupted by material well-being, and even more innocent of the wiles of the modern world, they were evidently superior in virtue, and in revolutionary capacities.

The roots of this strain in Mao's thinking go back deep into the past, to the twenty-two years of bitter struggle in the countryside that preceded his triumphal entry into Peking. I argued in the conclusion to my chapter on Mao's thought down to 1949 in Volume 13 of *The Cambridge History of China* that the economic policies of the late 1950s could not be characterized in terms of a "Yenan model," because the concrete circumstances were too different.[95] There was, however, an existential continuity with the *spirit* of Yenan, and of the Ching-kang-shan.

This continuity is revealed with extraordinary vividness in Mao Tse-tung's speeches at the Peitaiho meeting of August 1958, which officially endorsed the formation of the people's communes. Calling repeatedly for the abolition of the wage system, and the reintroduction of the free

94 *HC*, 1 June 1958, 3-4; *PR*, 15 (10 June 1958), 6.   95 *CHOC*, 13.868-69.

supply system followed during the war years, Mao declared that just feeding men was no different from feeding dogs. "If you don't aid others, and engage in a bit of communism, what's the point?" The wage system, he asserted, was "a concession to the bourgeoisie," and its result had been "the development of individualism." Some people, he remarked, argue that egalitarianism makes for laziness, but in fact that is the case of the grade system.[96]

This whole ethos of struggle and sacrifice Mao linked explicitly to the past of armed struggle. "Our communism," he declared, "was first implemented by the army. The Chinese Party is a very special Party, it fought for several decades, all the while applying communism." Now, in the twin struggle against imperialism and the forces of nature, the goals were equally clear, and the introduction of the free supply system would in no way reduce people's motivation or commitment.[97]

Arguing that the communes contained "sprouts of communism," Mao contrasted them with the cities, where people wanted "regularization" (*cheng-kuei-hua*), and which were full of big *yamens* divorced from the masses. Calling for desperate efforts (*p'in-ming kan*) to make steel, Mao noted that some criticized backyard steel production as "a rural work style" or "a guerrilla habit." In fact, he declared, such views were the expression of "bourgeois ideology," which had already eliminated many good things in the Party's heritage.[98]

Speaking to a reporter on 29 September 1958, Mao repeated publicly this denunciation of those who regarded mobilizing the masses for industrial production as "irregular" or a "rural work style."[99] Less than a year later, in July 1959, he was obliged to recognize that this had been a misguided undertaking that led to "chaos on a grand scale" and a substantial waste of resources.[100]

Mao Tse-tung was only dissuaded from going ahead with his plan for the introduction of a military-communist style of free supply system because Chou En-lai produced detailed estimates, based on materials from various ministries, to show that it would be ruinously expensive as compared to the wage system.[101] It constitutes, incidentally, remarkable

96 Speeches of 21 August 1958 (morning) and 30 August 1958 (morning), *Hsueh-hsi wen-hsuan*, 304, 306–7, 318. (This is a different collection from that cited in note 31.)
97 Speech of 30 August 1958, ibid., 318. (See also speech of 21 August, 306.)
98 Speeches of 17 August, 21 August (morning), and 30 August (morning) 1958, ibid., 302, 305–7 passim, 318.
99 Schram, *Political thought*, 353.   100 Schram, *Mao unrehearsed*, 144–46.
101 Liao Kai-lung, "Li-shih ti ching-yen ho wo-men ti fa-chan tao-lu" (The experience of history and the path of our development), *CKYC*, September 1981, 123. This report, delivered on 25

testimony both to Chou's steadiness of purpose and to his prestige that he was able to persuade Mao on this point even though he had been a primary butt of the fierce attack on those who had "opposed adventurism" in 1956, which Mao had launched at the Nanning Conference of January 1958 and pressed home at Chengtu in March.[102] But though Mao accepted that this idea was impracticable for the moment, he continued to dream such rural utopian dreams.

And yet, Mao recognized as early as the First Chengchow Conference of November 1958 that the peasants displayed a certain attachment to their own material interests, declaring: "The peasants after all remain peasants, throughout the period when the system of ownership by the whole people has not yet been implemented in the countryside, they after all retain a certain dual nature on the road to socialism." At the Second Chengchow Conference of February–March 1959, he reiterated this statement several times, adding that at the present stage the workers, not the peasants, still played the role of "elder brother" in the relationship between the two.[103]

Perhaps Mao never truly resolved, either in practice or in his own mind, the dilemma of a peasantry that was simultaneously the salt of the earth and the "younger brother" of the working class in building socialism.

A particularly suggestive symbol of the overall pattern of socialist development that Mao Tse-tung sought to promote at the time of the Great Leap Forward was the theory of the "permanent" or "uninterrupted" revolution, which he defined as follows in the "Sixty articles on work methods" of January 1958:

Our revolutions follow each other, one after another. Beginning with the seizure of power on a nation-wide scale in 1949, there followed first the anti-feudal land reform; as soon as land reform was completed, agricultural co-operativization was begun.... The three great socialist transformations, that is to say the socialist revolution in the ownership of the means of production, were basically completed in 1956. Following this, we carried out last year the socialist revolution on the political and ideological fronts [i.e., the Anti-Rightist Campaign].... But the problem is still not resolved, and for a fairly long period to come, the

October 1980 at a meeting for the academic discussion of the history of the Chinese Communist Party called by the Central Party School, has been officially published in China only in a revised version, but there is every reason to believe that the original text as reproduced in Taipei is authentic. It is translated in *Issues & Studies*, October, November, and December 1981; the passage cited here appears in the October issue, p. 84. For the new version, see Liao Kai-lung, *Tang-shih t'an-so* (Explorations in Party history), 308–65. The historical overview of the 1950s and 1960s has been significantly condensed in the official version, and does not contain details about Chou's role in persuading Mao to abandon the "free supply system."

102 See, in particular, the passage in his talk of 22 March 1958, Schram, *Mao unrehearsed*, 122.
103 *Wan-sui* (1969), 247; *Wan-sui* (1967), 12, 17, 49, etc.

method of airing of views and rectification must be used every year to solve the problems in this field. We must now have a technical revolution, in order to catch up with and overtake England in fifteen years or a bit longer.[104]

As this passage makes plain, it was characteristic of the Great Leap Forward, as of Mao's approach to revolution generally, that economic, social, political, and cultural transformation were to be carried out simultaneously. At the same time, a dramatic raising both of technical levels and of levels of material production was very much part of the Maoist vision in 1958. This concern found clear expression in Mao's call for a "technical revolution," as well as in the slogan "Overtake England in 15 years," which had been proclaimed in December 1957.

Twice, indeed, in the course of the radical phase of the Great Leap, Mao dated the beginnings of the process of modernization and change in China from the moment when, at the end of the nineteenth century, Chang Chih-tung embarked on his program of industrialization. In September 1958, Mao measured progress in terms of numbers of machine tools; in February 1959, his criterion was the growth of the Chinese working class. In both cases, he compared China's achievements before and after 1949 in catching up with the more advanced countries of the world.[105]

This does not mean, of course, that Mao regarded industrialization, or even economic development in general, as the whole essence of revolution. In a speech at the Second Session of the Eighth Party Congress in May 1958, at which the Great Leap Forward was officially proclaimed, he asserted his resolve to press ahead with rapid economic growth, but indicated that revolution would not result from development alone:

We do not put forward the slogans "Cadres decide everything" and "Technology decides everything," nor do we put forward the slogan, "Communism equals the Soviets plus electrification." Since we do not put forward this slogan, does this mean that we won't electrify? We will electrify just the same, and even a bit more fiercely. The first two slogans were formulated by Stalin, they are one-sided. [If you say] "Technology decides everything" – what about politics? [If you say] "Cadres decide everything" – what about the masses? This is not sufficiently dialectical.[106]

Thus, although China intended to "electrify," that is, to develop its economy (in Lenin's metaphor) just as fast as the Soviets, Mao saw this process as intimately linked to human change.

The Great Leap Forward thus involved the juxtaposition of many

104 *Wan-sui* (supplement), 32–33; translation from Schram, "Mao Tse-tung and the theory of the permanent revolution 1958–1969," *CQ*, 46 (April–June 1971), 226–27.
105 *Wan-sui* (1969), 245, and *Wan-sui* (1967), 15.   106 *Wan-sui* (1969), 204.

diverse inspirations and imperatives, the simultaneous insistence on technical revolution and political mobilization being only one instance of this. One of the most flagrant of such contradictions was that between the stress on unified Party leadership, expressed in the slogan "Politics in command," and the fragmentation of economic initiative and control to such an extent that, as Mao later recognized, effective planning largely ceased to exist. This problem arose in large part because the system of "dual rule," which had been reintroduced in 1956 (see *CHOC*, 14, ch. 3), was tilted so far in favor of the Party in 1958 that effective control at every level was vested in Party cadres who had no machinery at their disposal for checking, even if they had wanted to, on the wider consequences of economic decisions.

At the time, Mao suggested that this was nothing to worry about, since disequilibrium was a "universal objective law" that acted as a spur to progress.[107] Back of this ideological formulation lay the conviction that it was imperative to mobilize the population as a whole to play a dynamic role in economic development. This, in turn, implied not only stressing the creativity of the masses, as opposed to the experts, but attributing to the "revolutionary people" as a whole (experts, or at least "red" experts among them) virtually unlimited capacities to modify their own environment. Thus we find, in ideological writings of the Great Leap period manifestly reflecting Mao's viewpoint, quite extraordinary statements such as "There is no such thing as poor land, but only poor methods for cultivating the land," or even "The subjective creates the objective."[108]

It might be said that at the time of the Great Leap, a decade before the events of May 1968, Mao grasped and illustrated the slogan that the students of Paris were later to make famous: "L'imagination au pouvoir!" The difference was, of course, that he really *was* in power. In the summer of 1958, fantasy rather than sober observation came all too often to be the criterion for defining truth and reality generally.

Summing up the situation in September 1958, Mao declared that the national grain output had more or less doubled, and might be expected to double again in 1959, so that soon there would be too much even to feed to the animals, and there would be a problem in disposing of it.[109]

In his speech of 9 December 1958 at the Sixth Plenum of the Central Committee in Wuchang, Mao Tse-tung noted that, at the informal discussions which had taken place just before the plenum, the slogan "Seek

107 See Schram, "Mao Tse-tung and the theory of the permanent revolution," esp. 232–36.
108 Wu Chiang, article in *Che-hsueh yen-chiu* 8 (1958), 25–28; extracts in Schram, *Political thought*, 99, 135–36.
109 *Wan-sui* (1969), 228.

truth from facts" had been put forward once again. He interpreted this to mean that in planning work, it was necessary to be both hot and cold; to have lofty aspirations and yet at the same time to carry out considerable scientific analysis. Concretely, Mao said that, when he had forecast a production of 120 million tons of steel in 1962, he had been concerned only with the demand for steel in China, and "had not considered the problem of whether or not it was possible." In fact, he said, such a target was neither possible nor realistic. Nor should the Chinese confuse the transition to socialism with the transition to communism, or seek to enter communism ahead of the Soviet Union.[110]

In the early months of 1959, as the "wind of communism" blew across the land, Mao himself once again entertained unrealistic hopes. In March 1959, he told Anna Louise Strong that if steel production met the targets set for 1959, as it had done in 1958, 6 million tons a year could be allocated to the production of agricultural equipment, and mechanization would soon be completed.[111] By July, he had come to regard the backyard furnaces as an ill-advised adventure for which he was to blame.[112] Nevertheless, though the time scale for achieving a decisive economic breakthrough was soon revised in the direction of greater realism, the ultimate aim of rapid and decisive economic progress remained unchanged.

In order to achieve this goal, effective coordination of efforts on a national scale would be required. Mao, who in July 1959 took responsibility also for the dismantling of the planning system during the high tide of the Great Leap,[113] therefore endorsed the slogan, adopted in early 1959: "The whole country a single chessboard."

At the same time, while accepting the need for more effective centralized control of the industrial sector, Mao took the lead in decentralizing ownership and control in the communes. In March 1959, intervening to settle a sharp argument as to whether the basic level of accounting and distribution should be pushed down one level or two, Mao opted for the second and bolder solution.[114] (The unit in question was the *sheng-ch'an tui*; normally translated "production team," this meant, in the context of 1959, what is now called the brigade, that is, roughly the equivalent of the old higher-stage APC.) The intermediate solution, which Mao rejected, would have consisted in taking as the basic unit an entity equivalent to the administrative area, which was subsequently abolished. For further details, and an account of later developments, see *CHOC*, 14, ch. 8.

110 *Wan-sui* (1969), 262–62, 264–65; *Miscellany*, 141–42, 144–45.
111 Anna Louise Strong, "Three interviews with Chairman Mao Zedong," *CQ*, 103 (September 1985).
112 Schram, *Mao unrehearsed*, 143.   113 Ibid., 142.
114 *Wan-sui* (1967), 106–7. (Letter of 15 March 1959.)

Mao was persuaded that the system of people's communes was basically sound, and could easily be consolidated by the adjustments carried out in the spring and early summer of 1959.[115] Probably he thought that, by himself taking action to correct defects in the system he had devised, or in any case promoted, he would disarm potential critics in the Party. If this was indeed his expectation, he. was bitterly disappointed. At the Lushan Plenum of July–August 1959, P'eng Te-huai, Chang Wen-t'ien and others openly attacked the whole range of Great Leap policies.[116]

It would be hard to overestimate the impact of the confrontation on Lushan, not only on Mao's attitudes toward his comrades, but on the substance of his thought. As in 1957, he had committed errors of judgment, and the experience had not chastened him, but rather rendered him more sensitive regarding his own dignity. Psychologically, the consequence was that, from Lushan onward, Mao Tse-tung not only sought to punish everyone who disagreed with him, but came increasingly to regard any and every idea he put forward as the standard of orthodoxy. In other words, dissent from orthodoxy as defined by Mao became "revisionism," if not outright counterrevolution.[117]

Synthesis or eclecticism: Chinese and Marxist elements in Mao's thought

This evocation of Mao's image of himself as ruler necessarily raises the problem of another duality that became prominent in his thought from the late 1950s on: the relation between Marxism and the Chinese tradition. In May 1958, at the Second Session of the Eighth Party Congress, Mao declared that the new policies of the Great Leap Forward represented an attempt to vie with China's "teacher" in revolution, the Soviet Union. And he added, "We have two parents: Kuomintang society and the October Revolution."[118] This statement, he made plain, was intended to apply to politics as well as to economics.

Of the two "parents" acknowledged by Mao, the significance of the

---

115 Strong, "Three interviews," 496–97.
116 Chang Wen-t'ien's three-hour intervention was, in fact, more systematic, and couched in more rigorous theoretical terms, than P'eng Te-huai's "Letter of opinion." See the analysis of Li Jui, who was present at the time, in his article "Ch'ung tu Chang Wen-t'ien's ti 'Lushan ti fa-yen'" (On rereading Chang Wen-t'ien's intervention at Lushan), *Tu-shu*, 8 (1985), 28–38. The text of Chang's speech has now been published in *Chang Wen-t'ien hsuan-chi* (Selected works of Chang Wen-t'ien), 480–506.
117 The fullest and most accurate account in English of the events at Lu-shan and their significance is that of Roderick MacFarquhar, *The origins of the Cultural Revolution. 2. the Great Leap Forward 1958–1960*, 187–251.
118 *Wan-sui* (1969), 222; *Miscellany*, 121.

October Revolution requires little comment or explanation. China, he is saying, has learned about the theory and practice of making revolution, and in particular of establishing a socialist state, from Lenin, Stalin, and Soviet experience since 1917. The reference to "Kuomintang society," on the other hand, means far more than might at first be apparent. The Chinese People's Republic, he is saying, is the creation of the Chinese people as they existed in 1949, and therefore reflects the ideas, attitudes, and institutions that they have developed not only during the two decades of Kuomintang rule but throughout the whole of their long history.

To be sure, China needed a revolutionary transformation guided by Marxist theory, but this did not mean turning the country into a carbon copy of the Soviet Union. "There are some things," said Mao in March 1959, "which need not have any national style, such as trains, airplanes and big guns. Politics and art should have a national style."[119] Back of this statement, we can sense once again the conviction, expressed by Mao in 1938, that the assimilation of the past provides not only raw material but also a "method" for elaborating a correct line today.

By the time of the Great Leap, Mao was thus placing side by side, on the same level, the Marxist-Leninist and Soviet tradition, on the one hand, and the lessons of Chinese history, on the other, and even mentioning Kuomintang society first among the two "parents" of the current stage in the revolution. Six or seven years later, he had shifted the emphasis still further, remarking several times to comrades in the Party: "I am a native philosopher, you are foreign philosophers."[120]

Mao's claim, in 1964 and 1965, to be a "native" or "indigenous" thinker by no means signified that he had abandoned Marx for Confucius. It does, however, confirm beyond any question that the traditional roots of his thinking remained important to the end of his life. But how, precisely, were the Chinese and Western elements in Mao's thought combined in the late 1950s and early 1960s? Were they fused together or integrated into a new synthesis? If so, which of the two components defined the structure of his system as a whole? Did "Mao Tse-tung Thought" remain essentially a variant of Marxism, and hence in the last analysis a vehicle of Westernization? Or was, rather, the logic and pattern of his thought increasingly Chinese? Or was there no system, and no clear structure, but two skeletons working sometimes to reinforce each other, sometimes at cross purposes, in an unwieldy body composed of disparate elements?

---

119 *Wan-sui* (1967), 48.   120 Schram, *Mao unrehearsed*, 225, 239.

There can be little doubt that, as has already been suggested, both the nature of Mao's thought and his own perception of it changed as the years passed. In the early years of the People's Republic, he still saw a theory of Western origin – Marxism – as the warp, and Chinese culture as the woof, of the new social and political fabric he was bent on weaving. But by the late 1950s, his interpretation of Marxist theory was beginning to evolve in directions that reflected simultaneously the influence of the political climate of the Great Leap and a growing stress on modes of thought derived from the Chinese past.

In "On contradiction," Mao Tse-tung had accepted implicitly the "three basic laws" of Marxist and Hegelian dialectics (the unity and struggle of opposites, the transformation of quantity into quality, and the negation of the negation), but at the same time he had given a hint of a new approach to these problems by characterizing the "law of the unity of opposites" as the "fundamental law of thought," thus seemingly placing it in a higher category than the other two.[121] To be sure, Lenin had said, in a passage quoted by Mao in January 1957, "In brief, dialectics can be defined as the doctrine of the unity of opposites." But he had immediately added, "This grasps the kernel of dialectics, but it requires explanations and development."[122] Mao, on the other hand, was ultimately to move toward the view that the law of the unity of opposites in itself summed up the whole essence of dialectics.

In the section "On dialectical and historical materialism" that he contributed to the *History of the CPSU* in 1938, Stalin had enumerated four "principal features" of the Marxist dialectical method: that phenomena are all interconnected; that nature is in a state of continuous movement and change; that development takes the form of gradual quantitative change leading to qualitative changes or "leaps"; and that contradictions are inherent in all things, and the struggle between opposites "constitutes the internal content of the process of development."[123]

In his talk of January 1957 with Party secretaries, Mao explicitly took issue with Stalin's views on this topic, criticizing both the philosophical inadequacy of his fourfold classification and its political implications:

Stalin says Marxist dialectics has four principal features. As the first feature he talks of the interconnection of things, as if all things happened to be interconnected for no reason at all.... It is the two contradictory aspects of a thing that

---

121 Mao, *SW*, 1.345. See also Schram's chapter on Mao's thought to 1949 in *CHOC*, 13, and note 87 thereto. In "On dialectical materialism," Mao had explicitly confirmed that Marxist dialectics as developed by Lenin comprised the three laws. (See *MTTC*, 6.300.)
122 Mao, *SW*, 5.366. (Talk of 27 January 1957.)
123 *History of the Communist Party of the Soviet Union (Bolshevik). Short Course*, 106–10.

are interconnected.... As the fourth feature he talks of the internal contradiction in all things, but then he deals only with the struggle of opposites, without mentioning their unity.

Clearly the reference here is to Stalin's stress, from 1938 onward, on class struggle, which Mao, at this stage, did not wish to exacerbate to the same degree. But he then went on to discuss other differences between his conception of dialectics and that of Stalin:

Stalin's viewpoint is reflected in the entry on "identity" in the *Shorter Dictionary of Philosophy*, fourth edition, compiled in the Soviet Union. It is said there: "There can be no identity between war and peace, between the bourgeoisie and the proletariat, between life and death and other such phenomena, because they are fundamentally opposed to each other and mutually exclusive." ... This interpretation is utterly wrong.

In their view, war is war and peace is peace, the two are mutually exclusive and entirely unconnected.... War and peace are both mutually exclusive and interconnected, and can be transformed into each other under given conditions. If war is not brewing in peace-time, how can it possibly break out all of a sudden? ...

If life and death cannot be transformed into each other, then please tell me where living things come from. Originally there was only non-living matter on earth.... Life and death are engaged in constant struggle and are being transformed into each other all the time. If the bourgeoisie and the proletariat cannot transform themselves into each other, how come that through revolution the proletariat becomes the ruler and the bourgeoisie the ruled? ...

Stalin failed to see the connection between the struggle of opposites and the unity of opposites. Some people in the Soviet Union are so metaphysical and rigid in their thinking that they think a thing has to be either one or the other, refusing to recognize the unity of opposites. Hence, political mistakes are made. We adhere to the concept of the unity of opposites and adopt the policy of letting a hundred flowers blossom and a hundred schools of thought contend.[124]

The following month, in the original version of "On the correct handling of contradictions among the people," Mao repeated many of these criticisms of Stalin as a philosopher, in very similar terms. Stalin, he said, was relatively deficient (*hsiang-tang ch'ueh-fa*) in dialectics, though not completely without it. His dialectics was a "dialectics of hemming and hawing" (*t'un t'un t'u t'u pien-cheng-fa*). Mao's overall verdict was that Stalin had been 70 percent a Marxist, and 30 percent not a Marxist.[125]

The political lesson is clear enough, though as we have seen, Mao's view on class struggle shifted dramatically six months later. The philosophical implications are, however, somewhat more obscure, or at least ambiguous. The discussion of the interrelation between life and death evokes unmistakably the old Taoist dialectics of the ebb and flow of na-

124 Mao, *SW*, 5.367-96.   125 *Hsueh-hsi wen-hsuan*, 212-13, 220.

ture. And yet, in April 1957, Mao remarked: "Dialectics is not a cyclical theory."[126]

How was it possible to preserve the basic feeling for the essence of the dialectical process reflected in the passages of 1957 quoted above, and in many other statements by Mao, while remaining within a modern and Marxist system of categories? Mao's solution to this dilemma was of startling simplicity – so much so that, when confronted with it, I (and to my knowledge, all other foreign students of these problems) totally failed to grasp its significance.

In the "Sixty articles on work methods," to which he put his name in January 1958, when this directive was distributed in draft form, Mao included a sentence that, a decade ago, I translated as follows: "The law of the unity of opposites, the law of quantitative and qualitative change, the law of affirmation and negation, exist forever and universally."[127] What is rendered here as "law of affirmation and negation" (*k'en-ting fou-ting ti kuei-lü*) I took to be the kind of elliptical formula commonly used in Chinese political and philosophical language, "affirmation and negation" being intended to evoke the Hegelian and Marxist progression "affirmation, negation, and negation of the negation." On the basis of this assumption, I subsequently wrote that, in contrast to the views he was to put forward in the mid-1960s, Mao in 1958 had "reaffirmed" the classic formulation of the three laws by Engels.[128]

It turns out that the Chinese expression just cited should in fact be translated "the law of the affirmation of the negation," and that it was so understood, and treated as a major theoretical innovation by Chairman Mao, in China at the time.[129]

This may seem a very abstruse point, of little interest to anyone save hairsplitting expositors of Marxist doctrine. In fact, the implications, both political and intellectual, are of considerable moment. There is, first of all,

---

126 *Wan-sui* (1969), 104; *Miscellany*, 66.

127 Schram, "Mao Tse-tung and the theory of the permanent revolution," 228.

128 "The Schram, Marxist," in Dick Wilson, ed., *Mao Tse-tung in the scales of history: a preliminary assessment*, 63. As early as 1976, Steve Chin had grasped that this formulation involved a significant new departure, but unfortunately he got things backward, taking it to mean "the negation of the affirmation." See Chin, *The thought of Mao Tse-tung: form and content*, 60, 66–67, etc.

129 See two important compilations from Mao's writings produced in 1960 for internal use: *Mao Tse-tung che-hsueh ssu-hsiang (chai-lu)* (Mao Tse-tung's philosophical thought – [extracts]), 195–220; and *Mao tse-tung t'ung-chih lun Ma-k'o-ssu-chu-i che-hsueh (chai-lu)* (Comrade Mao Tse-tung on Marxist philosophy – [extracts]) (preface dated May 1960), 150 et seq. Both volumes contain extended sections bearing the title "The law of the affirmation of the negation," although the materials for these are drawn largely from writings of the Yenan period, and of the mid-1950s, about combining the old and the new, Chinese and foreign ideas, and so on. (It is perhaps worth noting that the first of these volumes contains, broken up into sections by theme, the whole of the lecture notes on dialectical materialism of which Mao denied authorship in his 1965 interview with Edgar Snow.)

the issue of Mao's personal authority in the philosophical domain. A recent work by a scholar who was, in Yenan days, a member of Mao's small philosophical study group, declares: "In the 'Sixty articles on work methods' Comrade Mao Tse-tung changed the name of what had used to be called the law of the negation of the negation to the law of the affirmation of the negation. This is an important question which he left to us, *without providing any sort of further demonstration [ping wei chin-hsing keng to ti lun-cheng]*, and which our philosophical circles must inquire into [*t'an-t'ao*] further."[130]

It is hardly necessary to elaborate on the significance of the words italicized in the preceding sentence. Thus, a phrase inserted by Mao Tse-tung into a directive, and never subsequently elaborated, became for two decades a new law, accepted without question by China's philosophers. The parallel with Stalin's "contributions of genius" in biology, linguistics, and other domains is unmistakable.

The trends of thought on Mao's part underlying this theoretical innovation are, however, also worthy of attention. In March 1983, Chou Yang went so far as to state explicitly that by failing to correct Stalin's "one-sided" view casting doubt on the "negation of the negation" because it smacked of Hegelianism, Mao ultimately opened the door to the destructive excesses of the Cultural Revolution. The core of Chou Yang's argument is that Mao's misgivings about the old concept reflected a tendency to exaggerate the absolutely antithetical and mutually exclusive nature of successive moments in the dialectical process, and to lose sight of the fact that "negation" meant the supersession of some elements of the thing negated, while retaining others and incorporating them into a new synthesis.[131] If that is what Mao meant, then the new theory did indeed point

---

130 Yang Ch'ao, *Wei-wu pien-cheng-fa ti jo-kan li-lun wen-t'i* (Some theoretical problems of materialist dialectics) (hereafter *Problems of dialectics*), 211. This was a revised version of a book originally devoted explicitly to Mao's thought: Yang Ch'ao, *Lun Mao Chu-hsi che-hsueh t'i-hsi* (On Chairman Mao's philosophical system), 2 vols. (hereafter *Mao's philosophical system*) (Nei-pu t'ao-lun kao [Draft for internal discussion]). Regarding Yang Ch'ao's participation in Mao's philosophical study group in 1939, see Wen Chi-tse, "Mao Tse-tung t'ung-chih tsai Yenan shih-ch'i shih tsen-yang chiao-tao wo-men hsueh che-hsueh ti?" (How did Comrade Mao Tse-tung teach us to study philosophy during the Yenan period?), in *Ch'üan-kuo Mao Tse-tung che-hsueh ssu-hsiang t'ao-lun hui lun-wen hsuan* (Selected essays from the national conference to discuss Mao tse-tung's philosophical thought), 69. The other members of the group, apart from Mao himself, were Ai Ssu-ch'i, Ho Ssu-ching, Ho P'ei-yuan, and Ch'en Po-ta.
131 Chou Yang, "Kuan-yü Ma-k'o-ssu-chu-i ti chi-ko li-lun wen-t'i ti t'an-t'ao" (An exploration of some theoretical questions of Marxism), *JMJP*, 16 March 1983, 4. This article, based on Chou Yang's speech on the occasion of the centenary of Marx's death, was criticized during the campaign of the winter of 1983–84 against "spiritual pollution" because of references to alienation under socialism, but there has never been any suggestion that Chou Yang's analysis of Mao's dialectics was erroneous. For the circumstances surrounding the publication and criticism of this speech, see Stuart Schram, *Ideology and policy in China since the Third Plenum, 1978–84*, 41–56.

straight toward Cultural Revolution notions of overthrowing everything and negating everything.

Yang Ch'ao, for his part, declares that in Mao's view most of the previous phase was eliminated at each negation. He also suggests that Mao had doubts about the old formulation, and replaced it by a new concept that "enriched its content," because he thought it implied that the end result of the whole process was a return to the *initial* affirmation, rather than a progression to a new and higher level. And he adds that Mao believed in the dialectical unity of the opposites "affirmation" and "negation," just as he believed in the unity of peace and war, life and death, proletariat and bourgeoisie, and so forth. All things, in Mao's view, were "contradictory entities made up of affirmation and negation."[132]

It is, perhaps, possible to combine these two perspectives, and thereby to arrive at a reasonably good understanding of what Mao was seeking to achieve by introducing this new concept. Plainly, the formulation "affirmation of the negation" stresses the fact that, in the historical process, new things are constantly emerging. It also suggests, however, that such new things do not arise simply as a reaction against what has come before ("negation of the negation"), but that they are affirmed or asserted by historical actors: classes, or those leaders and parties that claim to speak for classes. In other words, "affirmation of the negation" evokes both the ceaseless change that is the essence of "permanent revolution" (not surprisingly, since the two terms were used side by side in the "Sixty Articles" of January 1958), and the role of the will. Or to put it another way, it corresponded to a further shift in emphasis from the basis to the superstructure.

In terms of the concrete political significance of Mao's ideas, the concept of the affirmation of the negation can perhaps best be seen as the symbolic expression of the "poor and blank" hypothesis discussed above. In other words, it is a way of saying that the negative can be transformed into the positive, or that a situation comprising many negative factors can, in the course of a process of transformation baptized "affirmation" instead of "negation" (of the negation), be turned into a new situation, rich with promise for the future. To the extent that we accept Chou Yang's analysis, this "affirmation" would consist in the chiliastic hope of a rapid and total change, rather than a gradual and incrementalist strategy building on what has already been achieved.

Then, in the 1960s, Mao went beyond simply renaming and in some degree redefining the negation of the negation to repudiating this basic

---

132 *Problems of dialectics*, 199-217, esp. 212-13; *Mao's philosophical system*, 247-63.

Marxist concept altogether. On 18 August 1964, in the course of a conversation on philosophy with K'ang Sheng, Ch'en Po-ta, and others, K'ang asked the Chairman to "say something about the problem of the three categories." Obviously he knew that Mao had new ideas to put forward, as indeed the Chairman proceeded to do:

Engels talks about the three categories, but as for me I don't believe in two of those categories. (The unity of opposites is the most basic law, the transformation of quality and quantity into one another is the unity of the opposites quality and quantity, and the negation of the negation does not exist at all.) The juxtaposition, on the same level, of the transformation of quality and quantity into one another, the negation of the negation, and the law of the unity of opposites is "triplism," not monism.... Affirmation, negation, affirmation, negation ... in the development of things, every link in the chain of events is both affirmation and negation. Slave-holding society negated primitive society, but with reference to feudal society it constituted, in turn, the affirmation. Feudal society constituted the negation in relation to slave-holding society but it was in turn the affirmation with reference to capitalist society. Capitalist society was the negation in relation to feudal society, but it is, in turn, the affirmation in relation to socialist society.[133]

The following year, at the Hangchow Conference of December 1965, Mao summed up his view very succinctly once again, on the eve of the Cultural Revolution:

It used to be said that there were three great laws of dialectics, then Stalin said there were four. In my view there is only one basic law and that is the law of contradiction. Quality and quantity, positive and negative ... content and form, necessity and freedom, possibility and reality, etc., are all cases of the unity of opposites.[134]

In the past, some Western scholars, including Frederic Wakeman and Stuart Schram, have seen in this development a turn, or reversion, on Mao's part toward a more traditional approach to dialectics.[135] Whether or not one accepts such a view of this point, there can be no doubt that in the 1960s the influence of traditional Chinese thought across the board came increasingly into prominence in Mao's thought as a whole.

One important index of Mao's evolving attitude toward traditional Chinese culture was manifestly his evaluation of Confucius. Mao, who denounced teachers of Chinese literature during the May Fourth period as "obstinate pedants" who "forcibly impregnate our minds with a lot of stinking corpse-like dead writings full of classical allusions,"[136] had come

133 Schram, *Mao unrehearsed*, 226.   134 Ibid., 240.
135 Frederic Wakeman, *History and will*, 323–26; Schram, "The Marxist," 63–64.
136 "The great union of the popular masses"; Schram translation from *CQ*, 49 (January–March 1972), 80–81.

to take the view, as early as 1938, that the classical heritage had a positive as well as a negative aspect, and that it was therefore necessary to deal selectively with it. On the one hand, he had no more doubts than he had ever had since the May Fourth period about the reactionary and harmful character of Confucianism as an answer to the problems of the twentieth century. But at the same time, from the 1930s to the 1950s, he alluded with approval to various attitudes defined by tags from the Confucian classics, such as Confucius's practice of going about and "enquiring into everything,"[137] his attitude of "not feeling ashamed to ask and learn from people below,"[138] and the recommendation from the *Mencius*: "When speaking to the mighty, look on them with contempt."[139]

It was in 1964, however, that Mao's turn back to the Chinese classics for inspiration led him to a surprisingly favorable view of Confucius. While criticizing the Sage for his contempt for manual labor, and for his lack of interest in agriculture, Mao declared in February 1964, at the Spring Festival Forum on Education:

Confucius was from a poor peasant family; he herded sheep, and never attended middle school or university either.... In his youth, he came from the masses, and understood something of the suffering of the masses. Later, he became an official in the state of Lu, though not a terribly high official.[140]

The following August, in his philosophical conversations with K'ang Sheng and Ch'en Po-ta, Mao quoted with approval a passage from the *Shih-ching*, commenting: "This is a poem which accuses heaven and opposes the rulers. Confucius, too, was rather democratic."[141]

Perhaps the most distinctive expression of a "Chinese national style" in Mao's approach to politics is to be found in his emphasis on the political relevance of moral values and, more generally, on the educational function of the state. In January 1958, Mao included in the directive that constituted the blueprint for the Great Leap Forward a call to train new, communist intellectuals, in the following terms:

The various departments of the Centre, and the three levels of the province, the special area and the *hsien*, must all compete in training "*hsiu-ts'ai*." We can't do without intellectuals. The proletariat must definitely have its own *hsiu-ts'ai*. These people must understand relatively more of Marxism-Leninism, and they must also have a certain cultural level, a certain amount of scientific knowledge and of literary training.[142]

137 "Oppose book worship," in Mao, *Selected readings*, 34. (*Analects* VII.2; Legge, *The Chinese classics*, 1.195.)
138 Mao, *SW*, 4.378. (*Analects* V. 14; Legge, *The Chinese classics*, 1.178.)
139 Schram, *Mao unrehearsed*, 82. (*Mencius* 6.ii, 34; D. C. Lau, *Mencius*, 201.)
140 Schram, *Mao unrehearsed*, 208.   141 Ibid., 215.
142 *Wan-sui* (supplement), 37. (Article 47 of the "Sixty Articles.")

The deliberate use of the term *hsiu-ts'ai* or "cultivated talent," the popular name for the lowest-level graduates of the imperial examination system (*sheng-yuan*), with all of its traditional connotations, cannot be dismissed as a mere pleasantry. No doubt Mao intended the parallel to be taken with a pinch of salt, but there is also implicit in it the deep-seated conviction, which lay at the heart of the Confucian orthodoxy, that people are educated in order to assume political responsibilities, and that having been educated, it is their duty to take up the burdens of power.

Another echo of the past can be found in Mao's statement, in May 1958, at the Second Session of the Eighth Party Congress, that "for the layman to lead the expert" (*wai-hang ling-tao nei-hang*) is a universal law. To be sure, he noted that this question had been raised in the previous year by the rightists, who had created a tremendous disturbance, claiming that laymen could not lead experts.[143] In other words, his formula was a refutation of the view, which Mao had already dismissed in the "Sixty articles," that "we are petty intellectuals, incapable of leading the big intellectuals."[144] But apart from the resentment of the normal-school graduate against the "bourgeois academic authorities" who had criticized him in the spring of 1957, it is hard not to see, in the argument advanced by Mao in this same speech of May 1958 to the effect that "politicians handle the mutual relations among men," a reaffirmation of the moral basis of politics and society.

A few months later, at the Peitaiho meeting of August 1958, Mao declared, in discussing the question of rule by law (as advocated by Han Fei-tzu) and rule by men (as advocated by the Confucians):

You can't rely on law to rule the majority of the people; for the majority of the people you have to rely on cultivating [the right] habits ... I took part in establishing the Constitution, but I don't remember it.... Every one of our [Party] resolutions is a law; when we hold a meeting, that's law too. Public security regulations will only be respected if they rely on cultivating habits.... Our various systems of constitutional instruments [*hsien-chang chih-tu*] are concocted for the most part, to the extent of 90 per cent, by the bureaus. Basically, we do not rely on all that, we rely mainly on our resolutions ..., we do not rely on civil or criminal law to maintain order. The National People's Congress and the State Council have their stuff [*t'a-men na-i-t'ao*], while we have this stuff of ours.[145]

Apart from the implications of this passage regarding the relation between the Chinese Communist Party and the administrative machine,

143 *Wan-sui* (1969), 210–11; *Miscellany*, 110–11.
144 Schram translation, from "Mao Tse-tung and the theory of the permanent revolution," 227.
145 Speech of 21 August, *Hsüeh-hsi wen-hsuan*, 310.

Mao here conveys very forcefully his feeling for the traditional role of the state as supreme educator.

In April 1964, Mao discussed problems of reform through labor with the minister of public security, Hsieh Fu-chih. "In the last analysis," said Mao, "what is most important – transforming people, the production output of those engaged in reform through labor, or both of them equally? Should we attach importance to men, to things, or to both? Some comrades think only things, not men, are important. In reality, if we do our work with men well, we will have things too." To this, Hsieh replied, "I read out the 'Double Ten Articles' [also called the First or Former and the Later Ten Points, guidelines for the Socialist Education Campaign then under way, which has been discussed in *CHOC*, 14, ch. 7] to the prisoners of the Shou-shih production team of the First Prison of Chekiang Province.... Afterward, the overwhelming majority of the prisoners who had not confessed before now admitted their guilt, and many obstinate prisoners also underwent a conversion."[146]

I would not go so far as to suggest that reading a directive on the Socialist Education Campaign in the countryside to political prisoners was strictly equivalent to convoking the population in the old days to listen to the reading of the imperial edicts (*hsiang-yueh*), but surely there is a certain underlying continuity in the conviction that moral exhortation is an important dimension of political leadership. Perhaps it was implicit in Mao's view that intellectuals in the new society should be Marxist or "proletarian" in their political outlook, "bourgeois" in the sense that they must be the bearers of the modern knowledge developed under capitalism, and "feudal" to some extent in their conception of their own role.

As for the problems of the structure of power discussed in the first section of this chapter, the relation between Marxism-Leninism and the Chinese tradition was perhaps, in this domain, an even more ambiguous one. The blend of Confucianism and Legalism that defined, on the whole, the orthodox view of the state in late imperial times, was hierarchical and authoritarian, and so too was Leninism, to a very high degree. To this extent, there was convergence. Moreover, if Mao saw in politics the "leading thread" that always had priority over economics, and ultimately shaped the pattern of social change, he was following in this not only Lenin but also the monistic and state-centered vision of the social order that had prevailed in China for two thousand years.[147] At the same time,

146 *Wan-sui* (1969), 493; *Miscellany*, 347.
147 On this theme, see Schram, prefaces to *The scope of state power* and *The foundations of state power*, and the latter volume, passim, especially the contributions of Jacques Gernet and Benjamin Schwartz.

there were profound differences between Mao's ideas and those of the Chinese past, regarding both the persons and the institutions that were seen as the wielders of the transformative power of correct thought, and the goals of political action.

In view of the overriding emphasis on centralism in Mao's thinking about the state, which was, as we saw in a previous section, starkly consistent in all of his writings from the 1940s to the 1960s, it is not surprising that he should have spoken out repeatedly in praise not only of the first Ch'in emperor, but of other strong rulers in the Chinese past as well. "King Chou of the Yin dynasty [commonly known as the "Tyrant Chou"], who was well versed in both literature and military affairs, Ch'in Shih-huang and Ts'ao Ts'ao have all come to be regarded as evil men," he wrote in 1959. "This is incorrect."[148] And in a famous passage from one of his speeches to the Second Session of the Eighth Party Congress in May 1958, Mao had hailed Ch'in Shih-huang-ti as a "specialist in stressing the present and slighting the past," quoting with approval Li Ssu's proposal, endorsed by the emperor, that "those who make use of the past to disparage the present should be exterminated together with their whole families" (*i ku fei chin che tsu*). He had also boasted that the Chinese Communist Party had executed a hundred times as many counterrevolutionary intellectuals as Ch'in Shih-huang-ti, who had buried only "460 Confucian scholars."[149]

And what, if anything, did Mao Tse-tung take from that other tradition, often seen as the ideology of the failures and misfits of the imperial system, Taoism? As already noted, events in the Chinese People's Republic, under Mao's leadership, were marked by a succession of campaigns, interspersed with periods of repose, to make a pattern of what G. William Skinner and Edwin Winckler have called "compliance cycles," and which Mao himself characterized as alternating "hard fighting" and "rest and consolidation" in a "wavelike form of progress."[150]

Angus Graham has remarked that the *Lao-tzu* "advises Doing Nothing as a means of ruling, not as an abdication of ruling."[151] Some curious parallels can be observed between aspects of Mao's role as Chairman during the last two decades of his life, when he first retired to the "second line," and then, although reasserting his authority, remained in seclusion except for the first Red Guard rallies, and the principles asserted in the chapter of the *Chuang-tzu* entitled "The Way of Heaven":

148 Schram, *Mao unrehearsed*, 101.   149 *Wan-sui* (1969), 195.   150 Schram, *Mao unrehearsed*, 106–7.
151 Angus Graham, *The book of Lieh-tzu*, 10.

... those who of old reigned over the empire, though wise enough to encompass heaven and earth would not do their own thinking, though discriminating enough to comprehend the myriad things would not do their own explaining, though able enough for all the work within the four seas would not do their own enacting.... Emperors and kings do nothing, but the world's work is done.... This is the Way by which to have heaven and earth as your chariot, set the myriad things galloping, and employ the human flock.[152]

Looking at the pattern of Mao's thought and action throughout his career, and especially in the period after 1949, it seems evident that he was, in the last analysis, more strongly influenced by the "great" than by the "little" tradition.[153]

These paratraditional ideas regarding the role of the ruler were to grow still more in importance during Mao's last decade, and constitute, with the leftist attitudes he increasingly displayed in economic and political matters, one of the roots of the Cultural Revolution. A third, and in many respects crucial, dimension of the situation was, however, the unfolding of Sino-Soviet relations, and Mao's response to these developments.

CAUSES AND CONSEQUENCES OF THE SINO-SOVIET SPLIT

From the very inception of the Chinese Communist Party, Soviet influence on its development was, of course, many-sided and profound. Moscow was at once the locus of authority and the source of inspiration for the world communist movement from the 1920s to the 1940s and beyond. Mao's response to these two dimensions of the Soviet role was markedly different. The validity of the Soviet model he called into question only progressively, and relatively late. The notion that China was not merely a junior partner in the cause of communism but should subordinate itself entirely to a worldwide revolutionary organization, and lose its own identity in the process, he was, on the contrary, never at any time willing to accept.

In a sense, the whole of this dimension of the problem is summed up in Mao's reply to Edgar Snow when, in 1936, Snow asked him whether, in the event of a Communist victory, there would be "some kind of actual merger of governments" between Soviet China and Soviet Russia. "We are not fighting for an emancipated China in order to turn the country over to Moscow!" Mao shot back at him, adding: "The Chinese Commu-

---

152 Angus Graham, *Chuang-tzu: The seven inner chapters and other writings from the book "Chuang-tzu,"* 261.

153 For further discussion of this point, and a refutation of Wolfgang Bauer's ideas to the contrary, see Schram, "Party leader or true ruler?"

nist Party cannot speak for the Russian people, or rule for the Third International, but only in the interests of the Chinese masses."[154]

The evolution of relations between the Soviet and Chinese Communist Parties, and between Mao and Stalin, during the Yenan period falls outside the scope of this chapter. It does seem appropriate, however, to note, by way of introduction to what happened after 1949, Mao's own assessment of Stalin's behavior during the crucial years of civil war, beginning in 1945. Recalling, at a meeting of the Central Committee of the Chinese Communist Party in September 1962, that since 1960 the Chinese had been distracted from their internal tasks by the need to "oppose Khrushchev," he commented: "You see that among socialist countries and within Marxism-Leninism, a question like this could emerge." Then, turning back to earlier events, he continued:

In fact its roots lie deep in the past, in things which happened very long ago. They did not permit China to make revolution: that was in 1945. Stalin wanted to prevent China from making a revolution, saying that we should not have a civil war and should co-operate with Chiang Kai-shek, otherwise the Chinese nation would perish. But we did not do what he said. After the victory of the revolution he next suspected China of being a Yugoslavia, and that I would become a second Tito. Later when I went to Moscow to sign the Sino-Soviet Treaty of Alliance and Mutual Assistance, we had to go through another struggle. He was not willing to sign a treaty. After two months of negotiations he at last signed. When did Stalin begin to have confidence in us? It was the time of the Resist America, Aid Korea campaign, from the winter of 1950. He then came to believe that we were not Tito, not Yugoslavia.[155]

In June 1949, on the eve of victory in the civil war, Mao nonetheless proclaimed that solidarity with the Soviet Union would be the cornerstone of the new China's foreign policy, which he summed up as follows: "Unite in a common struggle with those nations of the world which treat us as equals and unite with the peoples of all countries. That is, ally ourselves with the Soviet Union, with the People's Democracies and with the broad masses of the people in all countries, and form an international united front."

Replying to an imaginary interlocutor to whom he attributed the comment "You are leaning to one side," he elaborated on the reasons for this policy:

Exactly. The forty years' experience of Sun Yat-sen and the twenty-eight years' experience of the Communist Party have taught us to lean to one side, and we are firmly convinced that in order to win victory and consolidate it we must lean to

154 Schram, *Political thought*, 419.   155 Schram, *Mao unrehearsed*, 191.

one side. In the light of the experiences accumulated in these forty years and these twenty-eight years, all Chinese without exception must lean either to the side of imperialism, or to the side of socialism. Sitting on the fence will not do, nor is there a third road.[156]

Although this was the clearly enunciated foreign policy line in 1949, Stalin's attitude did not always make it easy, or agreeable, for Mao to carry it out. When Mao went to Moscow in December 1949, it took him, as he himself later recalled, two months of negotiations, "amounting to a struggle," to get Stalin to offer China even that minimum of assistance and support which Mao regarded as essential. One dimension of the problem was, of course, the clash between the national interests of China and the Soviet Union, and the place of these two states in the larger unity known in the 1950s as the "Socialist camp." Mao explained his own approach to these matters during the Moscow negotiations of 1950 in a speech of March 1958:

In 1950 I argued with Stalin in Moscow for two months. On the questions of the Treaty of Mutual Assistance, the Chinese Eastern Railway, the joint-stock companies and the border we adopted two attitudes: one was to argue when the other side made proposals we did not agree with, and the other was to accept their proposal if they absolutely insisted. This was out of consideration for the interests of socialism.[157]

Back of these discords lay, of course, not merely Stalin's lack of enthusiasm for the emergence of another communist great power that might ultimately be a rival to the Soviet Union, or at least demand the right to have its say as to how the "interests of socialism" should be pursued on the world scene, but twenty years of conflict between Mao and Stalin as to the way in which the Chinese revolution should be carried out. Referring to the events of the 1920s and 1930s, Mao said, in his important speech of 30 January 1962:

Speaking generally, it is we Chinese who have achieved understanding of the objective world of China, not the comrades concerned with Chinese questions in the Communist International. These comrades in the Communist International simply did not understand, or we could say they utterly failed to understand, Chinese society, the Chinese nation, or the Chinese revolution. For a long time even we did not have a clear understanding of the objective world of China, let alone the foreign comrades![158]

156 Mao, *SW*, 4.415.   157 Schram, *Mao unrehearsed*, 101.
158 Ibid., 172. The officially published text does not underscore quite so strongly the point that the
   foreign comrades were even more incapable of understanding the Chinese revolution. (See
   PR, 27 [1978], 14.)

"Understanding the objective world of China" meant, of course, grasping the special circumstances of a revolution under communist leadership in a vast and overwhelmingly peasant country, and devising a pattern of struggle based on agrarian reform and guerrilla warfare from rural bases. But it also meant working out new methods for transforming society and developing the economy once the struggle for power had been carried to a victorious conclusion. The crucial years during which Chinese and Soviet perceptions of these realities gradually diverged to the point of sharp, if as yet undeclared, conflict extended from the beginning of the 1st Five-Year Plan in 1953 until the Great Leap Forward of 1958–60.

The problem of the relation between foreign and domestic developments during this period is a complex one, and there was undoubtedly action and reaction in both directions. The Chinese probably soon became aware, after the upheavals in Poland and Hungary in the autumn of 1956, that Moscow would henceforth be in a position to offer less economic assistance, because it was necessary to spend more on Eastern Europe in order to stabilize the situation there. To this extent, the emphasis on "self-help" in Chinese policy beginning especially in 1958 did not reflect a purely arbitrary decision on Mao's part, but also constituted a response to the realities of the international situation. There was also the behavior of the "ugly Russian," who was plainly no more appealing than the "ugly American" who served in certain other countries during the same period as adviser and technical specialist. But apart from these diplomatic and psychological aspects of Sino-Soviet economic and technical cooperation, reliance on foreign experts for leadership in China's program of economic development also raised more basic problems of the role of the Chinese people themselves in shaping their own future.

Mao's overall approach to the various interrelated aspects of the problem of a Chinese road to socialism is clearly and forcefully projected in a passage from his speech of 30 January 1962. In the first few years after 1949, he said,

the situation was such that, since we had no experience in economic construction, we had no alternative but to copy the Soviet Union. In the field of heavy industry especially, we copied almost everything from the Soviet Union, and we had very little creativity of our own. At that time it was absolutely necessary to act thus, but at the same time it was also a weakness – a lack of creativity and lack of ability to stand on our own feet. Naturally this could not be our long-term strategy. From 1958 we decided to make self-reliance our major policy, and striving for foreign aid a secondary aim.[159]

159 Schram, *Mao unrehearsed*, 140–41.

Mao's formulation here strongly emphasizes considerations of national dignity; wholesale imitation of foreign experience, he says, however necessary for a time, simply "could not be" the long-term strategy of the Chinese people. In 1958, when the economic and social experiments of the communes and the Great Leap Forward were first implemented, Mao stated bluntly that he was aware of the resentment that the Soviets might feel at China's refusal to follow them blindly – and could not care less. In a discussion of the need to smash "blind faith" in the Soviet example, specifically in the military field, he said: "Some people mentioned that when the Soviet comrade advisers saw that we were not copying their [combat regulations], they made adverse comments and were displeased. We might ask these Soviet comrades: do you copy Chinese regulations? If they say they don't, then we will say: if you don't copy ours, we won't copy yours."[160]

Mao's insistence on breaking with the Soviet model was not, however, motivated simply by considerations of pride; for several years before 1958, he had been having increasing doubts about the value of Russian methods in the Soviet Union itself, as well as about their applicability to China. In the speech of April 1956 "On the ten great relationships," which marked the beginning of his attempt to sketch out in systematic form the ideas underlying the Chinese road to socialism, Mao declared:

We have done better than the Soviet Union and a number of Eastern European countries. The prolonged failure of the Soviet Union to reach the highest pre-October Revolution level in grain output, the grave problems arising from the glaring disequilibrium between the development of heavy industry and that of light industry in some Eastern European countries – such problems do not exist in our country.... The Soviet Union has taken measures which squeeze the peasants very hard.... The method of capital accumulation has seriously damp-ened the peasants' enthusiasm for production. You want the hen to lay more eggs and yet you do not feed it, you want the horse to run fast and yet you don't let it graze. What kind of logic is this?[161]

Despite these misgivings about the Soviet experience of economic development, and despite his own criticism both of Stalin's obsession with class struggle, and of Stalin's weaknesses as a dialectician, Mao Tse-tung had serious reservations regarding both the manner and the substance of the enterprise of de-Stalinization launched by Khrushchev in 1956. It is time to consider more systematically his response to these events.

160 Ibid., 126–27.
161 Mao, *SW*, 5.185 and 291. For the reasons explained in the first section of this chapter, this official text of Mao's "On the ten great relationships" is more explicit in its criticism of the Soviets than that reproduced by the Red Guards and translated in Schram, *Mao unrehearsed.*

De-Stalinization and "modern revisionism"

The problem of the Chinese reaction to the Twentieth Soviet Party Congress, which was for so long the object of speculation and controversy on the basis of fragmentary texts released by one side or the other, can now be examined in the light of an abundant, though not altogether complete documentation, and it is dealt with in Volume 14, chapter 6, of *The Cambridge History of China.* As early as April 1956, the Central Committee of the Chinese Communist Party had decided on the assessment of 30 percent for mistakes and 70 percent for achievements in looking at Stalin's career as a whole. Mao declared in "On the ten great relationships" that the editorial of 5 April 1956 had been written "on the basis of this evaluation," although the figures do not actually appear there.[162] Despite Stalin's wrong guidance of the Chinese revolution, Mao thought the thirty–seventy assessment was "only fair."[163]

Half a year later, in the aftermath of the Hungarian and Polish events, Mao made his famous remarks, at the Second Plenum on 15 November 1956, regarding the "sword of Stalin" and the "sword of Lenin." In Mao's view, even the first of these should not simply be discarded, in the name of opposition to "so-called Stalinism." Although he criticized Stalin's mistakes, he felt the Soviet leader's reputation should be protected. As for the "sword of Lenin," that is, the insistence on the model of the October Revolution, as opposed to the "parliamentary road," Mao argued that it should under no circumstances be abandoned.[164]

This trend of thought was continued in the *People's Daily* editorial of 29 December 1956, "More on the historical experience of the dictatorship of the proletariat," which placed greater emphasis both on Stalin's merits and on the continuance of class struggle under socialism than that of the previous April. In his speech of 27 February 1957, on contradictions among the people, on the other hand, Mao Tse-tung spelled out his views about Stalin, and about related issues, both theoretical and concrete, in a somewhat different spirit.

The first section of this chapter quoted a passage about Stalin's propensity to exterminate his critics. Following on from this, Mao developed, under the heading of eliminating counterrevolutionaries, a comparison between China and the Soviet Union as regarded the use and abuse of revolutionary violence:

How has the work of eliminating counter-revolutionaries been carried out after all in our country? Very badly, or very well? In my opinion, there have been

162 *The historical experience*, 18–19.   163 Mao, *SW*, 5.304.   164 Ibid., 341–42.

shortcomings, but if we compare ourselves with other countries, we have done relatively well. We have done better than the Soviet Union, and better than Hungary. The Soviet Union has been too leftist, and Hungary too rightist.

China, too, he acknowledged, had at times committed leftist errors, but mostly in the base areas in the South, under Soviet influence; these had been rectified by the directive of 1942 against killings and excessive arrests. Even after that, there had been some shortcomings, but nothing like the Soviet Union when Stalin was in power: "He didn't deal with this matter well at all [*t'a na-ko tung-hsi kao-ti pu-hao*]. He had two aspects. On the one hand, he eliminated genuine counterrevolutionaries; this aspect was correct. On the other hand, he wrongly killed a large number of people [*hsu to jen*], important people, such as delegates to the Party Congress."

Here Mao alluded to the figures for percentages killed given by Khrushchev in his secret speech, before confirming that in 1950–52, 700,000 had been executed in China, a measure he characterized as "basically correct."[165]

Apart from criticizing Stalin's policy of sending to a camp or killing anyone who dared to say anything negative about the Party or the government, Mao also commented once again, as he had done in his talk of January 1957 to Party secretaries, on Stalin's deficiencies as a Marxist theoretician. This time, however, he went further, and claimed philosophical originality for himself as compared to Marx and Lenin, as well as to Stalin:

Contradictions among the people, and how to resolve this problem, is a new problem. Historically, Marx and Engels said very little about this problem, and though Lenin referred to it, he only just referred to it [*chien-tan t'an-tao*]. He said that in a socialist society, antagonisms died away, but contradictions continued to exist; in other words, ... the bourgeoisie had been overthrown, but there continued to be contradictions among the people. [Thus] Lenin said there were still contradictions among the people, [but] he didn't have time to analyze this problem systematically. As for antagonism, can contradictions among the people be transformed from non-antagonistic to antagonistic contradictions? It must be said that they can, but in Lenin's day there was as yet no possibility of investigating this problem in detail. There was so little time allotted to him. Of course, after the October Revolution, during the period when Stalin was in charge, for a long time he mixed up these two types of contradictions.[166]

165 *Hsueh-hsi wen-hsuan*, 197–98. The Soviet Union is not even mentioned in the corresponding section of the official revised text (Mao, *SW*, 5.396–99) – not surprisingly, since this was first published in June 1957, when any such negative comments would have been quite out of the question.

166 *Hsueh-hsi wen-hsuan*, 194. For a comparison of Mao's ideas regarding nonantagonistic contradictions with those of Lenin and Stalin, see Stuart Schram, *Documents sur la théorie de la "rév-*

Lenin's failure to develop the concept of contradictions among the people Mao excused by the lack of experience in those early days of the revolution.[167] Stalin's mistakes, on the other hand, Mao attributed to his inherently inadequate understanding of dialectics.[168]

Summing up regarding the criticism of Stalin at the Twentieth Congress, Mao declared that this business had a dual nature. On the one hand, to smash blind faith in Stalin, and to take the lid off, was a "liberation movement" (*i-ko chieh-fang yun-tung*). But on the other, Khrushchev's manner of doing it, without analysis, and without taking account of the consequences in the rest of the world, was wrong. We have, said Mao, complained of this in face-to-face discussions with the Soviets, saying that they were great-nation chauvinists.[169]

When he visited Moscow for the second time, in November 1957, to attend the conference of Communist and workers' parties, Mao remarked that he still had a "belly full of pent-up anger, mainly directed against Stalin," although he would not elaborate on the reasons, because it was all in the past. He then proceeded, in characteristic fashion, to do precisely that: "During the Stalin era, nobody dared to speak up. I have come to Moscow twice and the first time was depressing. Despite all the talk about 'Fraternal Parties' there was really no equality."

Now, he said, we "must admit that our Soviet comrades' style of work has changed a lot." Consequently, he expressed the opinion that "first of all, we must now acknowledge the Soviet Union as our head and the CPSU as the convenor of meetings, and that, secondly, there is now no harm in doing so."[170] Although the available record of the Moscow meetings suggests a reasonably cordial atmosphere between Mao and Khrushchev, a formulation such as this clearly does not indicate a degree of veneration for Soviet ideological or political authority that would make it in any way surprising that, within a year, signs of conflict were to emerge. A major factor in this deterioration of relations was, of course, Moscow's reaction to the new economic policies of the Great Leap Forward.

---

olution permanente" en Chine, xxxii–xxxviii. In the official text of the 27 February 1957 speech, Mao's judgment on his predecessors is turned into its opposite; Lenin, it reads, "gave a very clear exposition of this law." (Mao, *SW*, 5.392–93.)

167 *Hsueh-hsi wen-hsuan*, 211–21.   168 Ibid., 212–13.

169 Ibid., 223–24. (The text as printed in this collection actually says "our great nation-chauvinism," but I take *wo-men* to be a misprint for *t'a-men*. Alternatively, Mao might have indicated that when he criticized Khrushchev's handling of the problem of Stalin, the Soviets denounced *China's* great-nation chauvinism, that is, her insistence on having a voice in such matters.

170 Speech of 14 November 1957, translated by Michael Schoenhals in *The Journal of Communist Studies*, 2.2 (June 1986).

The Soviets, not surprisingly, saw only the heterodoxy of some of Mao's new methods, and not the basic consistency of many of his policies and aims with the logic of Leninism. They took a particularly dim view of the people's communes, set up in the summer of 1958, which Khrushchev ridiculed first privately, and soon afterward in public as well. (See *CHOC*, 14, ch. 11.)

Undoubtedly, the Soviets were also shocked and irritated by what they saw as the extravagant and boastful claims of the Chinese in the domain of industrial production. They must have been particularly taken aback when one of the most extreme of these, the call to overtake England in fifteen years in the output of steel and other major industrial products, was first put forward by Mao under their very noses, at the November 1957 meeting of Communist and workers' parties.[171]

Mao's new approach to internal problems, accompanied as it was by a greater reluctance to rely on Soviet assistance, implied in itself a loosening of the ties between China and the Soviet Union. As late as December 1956, Mao had reaffirmed unequivocally the policy of "leaning to one side" that he had first put forward in 1949:

The principal components of the socialist camp are the Soviet Union and China. China and the Soviet Union stand together. This policy line is correct. At present, there are still people who have doubts about this policy. They say, "Don't stand together." They think that China should take a middle course and be a bridge between the Soviet Union and the United States. This is the Yugoslav way, a way for getting money from both sides. Is this way of doing things good or not? I don't think it is good at all, it is not advantageous to our people. Because on one side is powerful imperialism, and this China of ours has suffered from imperialist oppression for a long time. If China stands between the Soviet Union and the United States, she appears to be in a favorable position, and to be independent, but actually she cannot be independent. The United States is not reliable, she would give you a little something, but not much. How could imperialism give you a full meal? It won't.[172]

In 1958, however, there took place a sharp deterioration in the relations between Mao and Khrushchev going far beyond what was implied by the logic of the Great Leap policies. This growing estrangement was not simply, or even primarily, the result of disagreement about de-Stalinization, although, as we have seen, Mao had strong reservations about the way in which Khrushchev had carried out that operation, with-

---

171 See Mao's speech of 18 November 1957, as translated by Schoenhals in ibid. These events are also discussed in Hu Hui-ch'iang, "Ta lien kang-t'ieh yun-tung chieh-k'uang" (A brief account of the campaign to make steel in a big way), *Tang-shih yen-chiu tzu-liao* (Materials for research on Party history), 4.726.
172 *Wan-sui* (1969), 62–63.

out consulting him. For at the same time, Mao nourished strong resentment against Stalin for his high-handed treatment of the Chinese, and he therefore approved – up to a point – Khrushchev's effort to cut him down to size. "Buddhas," he said in March 1958, "are made several times lifesize in order to frighten people.... Stalin was that kind of person. The Chinese people had got so used to being slaves that they seemed to want to go on. When Chinese artists painted pictures of me together with Stalin, they always made me a little bit shorter, thus blindly knuckling under to the moral pressure exerted by the Soviet Union." And in April 1958, he declared: "This Comrade Stalin of ours had something of the flavour of the mandarins of old.... In the past, the relations between us and the Soviet Union were those between father and son, cat and mouse."[173]

But nevertheless, he objected, he said in March 1958 at Chengtu, to Khrushchev's action in "demolishing Stalin at one blow." Stalin's errors should be criticized, but it was necessary to recognize that he also had a correct side, and that correct side "we ought to revere and continue to revere for ever."

Despite his reservations on this point, Mao still held up Khrushchev, at the same conference in Chengtu in March 1958, as an example of those excellent and vigorous revolutionaries who emerge from the local Party organizations: "Comrades working in the provinces will sooner or later come to the Centre. Comrades at the Centre will sooner or later either die or leave the scene. Khrushchev came from a local area. At the local level the class struggle is more acute, closer to natural struggle, closer to the masses. This gives the local comrades an advantage over those at the Centre."[174]

It is fair to say, I think, that never again, after the middle of 1958, would Mao have spoken of Khrushchev in such basically positive terms as these. A decisive episode in the deterioration of relations between the two men was, of course, the foreign policy crisis (or crises) of the summer of 1958. Khrushchev's attempt to solve the Middle Eastern conflict of July 1958 without the participation of Peking was clearly a major source of annoyance. Even more important, perhaps, was Mao's conviction that the Soviet leader was trying to dictate China's foreign policy.

On 29 July 1959, as the confrontation with P'eng Te-huai at the Lushan meeting of the Central Committee was approaching its climax, Mao wrote a brief annotation to three documents regarding foreign criticism of the communes, including press reports of Khrushchev's remarks on the subject in the United States. Three days later, he sent a copy of

173 Schram, *Mao unrehearsed*, 99; also *Wan-sui* (1969), 183.   174 Schram, *Mao unrehearsed*, 114–55.

these materials and of his accompanying comment to an old comrade, with a note saying in part:

The Khrushchevs oppose or are dubious about these three things: letting a hundred flowers bloom, the people's communes, and the Great Leap Forward. I think they are in a passive position, whereas we are in an extremely active position. What do you think? We must use these three things to fight the whole world, including a large number of opponents and skeptics within the Party.[175]

Obviously Mao was both angry and contemptuous at the suggestion that his methods for building socialism were not compatible with Marxist orthodoxy. At the same time, his resentment at slurs against the communes, and more broadly at Khrushchev's meddling in the internal affairs of the Chinese Communist Party (through his criticisms of the communes, his relations with P'eng Te-huai, etc.) was greatly exacerbated by the anxiety he felt because the Soviet reservations were shared in some degree within China.

There followed, in the autumn of 1959, the incident of the TASS communiqué, and then a series of other clashes with the Soviets, which Mao summarized briefly as follows in his speech at the Tenth Plenum:

... in September 1959 during the Sino-Indian border dispute, Khrushchev supported Nehru in attacking us and Tass issued a communiqué [in this sense]. Then Khrushchev came to China and at our Tenth Anniversary Celebration banquet in October, he attacked us on our own rostrum. At the Bucharest Conference in 1960 they tried to encircle and annihilate us. Then came the conference of the Two Communist Parties [of China and of the Soviet Union], the Twenty-Six-Country Drafting Committee, the Eighty-One-Country Moscow Conference, and there was also a Warsaw Conference, all of which were concerned with the dispute between Marxism-Leninism and revisionism.[176]

Mao's use in this context of the term "encircle and annihilate" (*wei chiao*), which was that employed by Chiang Kai-shek in the 1930s to characterize the campaigns of extermination launched by him against the Communists, vividly reflects the degree of hostility that Mao perceived in his erstwhile comrades. But although he reacted to this hostility with anger, he remained wholly imperturbable in the face of it. In a speech of March 1960, he expounded the reasons for his confidence:

After all, who are the people of the so-called great anti-China [movement or chorus]? How many are there? There are merely imperialist elements from certain Western countries, reactionaries and semi-reactionaries from other countries, and

175 Letter to Wang Chia-hsiang, in *Mao Chu-hsi tui P'eng, Huang, Chang, Chou fan-tang chi-t'uan ti p'i-p'an*, 14.
176 Schram, *Mao unrehearsed*, 190-91.

revisionists and semi-revisionists from the international communist movement. The above three categories of people can be estimated to constitute a small percentage, say 5 per cent of mankind. At the most, it cannot be more than 10 per cent.... So far as we are concerned, their anti-China activities are a good thing, and not a bad thing. They prove that we are true Marxist-Leninists, and that we are doing our work pretty well.... The hatred which has grown up between the United States and us is somewhat greater, but they do not engage in anti-China activities daily either. Not only is there now a brief pause between two waves of anti-China activities, but also there may be a pause of longer duration in the future.... [I]f the entire party, and the entire people really unite as one, and we can catch up with or overtake them in gross output and per capita output of our main items of production, then such pauses will be prolonged. This is to say that this will compel the Americans to establish diplomatic relations with us, and do business with us on an equal basis, or else they will be isolated.[177]

The improvement in Sino-American relations that Mao predicted in 1960 was not to materialize for another decade. Meanwhile, China's relations with the Soviet Union rapidly moved toward a climax. A month after Mao made the speech just quoted at length, the Chinese opened a massive ideological offensive with the publication of an editorial entitled "Long Live Leninsim!" and a series of other texts, ostensibly directed against the "revisionists" mentioned by Mao as members of the "great anti-China chorus," that is, against the Yugoslavs, but in fact aimed at the Soviet "semi-revisionists," who were soon to become openly the principal villains in Mao's book. A decisive turning point was reached in January 1962, when Mao Tse-tung, at the Seven Thousand Cadres Conference, called, in effect, for the overthrow of the existing Soviet regime.

In a passage from his remarks on this occasion (published as a "directive" in 1967) Mao said:

The Soviet Union was the first socialist country, and the Soviet Communist Party was the party created by Lenin. Although the Party and state leadership of the Soviet Union have now been usurped by the revisionists, I advise our comrades to believe firmly that the broad masses, the numerous Party members and cadres of the Soviet Union are good; that they want revolution, and that the rule of the revisionists won't last long.[178]

Although this speech was not publicly divulged at the time it was delivered, the Soviet leaders assuredly soon grasped the fact that Mao considered them beyond the pale. In any case, the rupture between Moscow and Peking was made abundantly manifest in the public polemics of 1963–64. The history of the Sino-Soviet dispute is dealt with in CHOC 14, ch. 11, and even though authorship of the nine Chinese replies to the

177 Wan-sui (1969), 316–18.   178 Schram, Mao unrehearsed, 181.

Soviets, from 6 September 1963 to 14 July 1964, has been attributed to Mao, I shall not review their contents here. What is relevant in this context is how rapidly Mao himself gave ideological and policy substance to the anti-Soviet rhetoric generated beginning in early September.

In late September 1963, the Politburo held an enlarged meeting. On 27 September, Mao put forward in this context a "Directive on opposing revisionism in Sinkiang." The first point, he said, was to do economic work well, so that the standard of living of the population was improved until it surpassed not only the level that had existed under the Kuomintang, but that "in the Soviet Union under revisionist domination" (*hsiu-cheng-chu-i t'ung-chih hsia ti Su-lien*). Less grain should be requisitioned, and in order to heighten the favorable contrast with the situation across the border, the supply of cotton cloth, tea, sugar, and so forth, should be "a bit more ample than in other areas."

Against this background, Mao then enunciated the second point:

2) We must put politics in command, and strengthen ideological and political education. We must carry out very well anti-revisionist education directed at the cadres and people of every nationality.... Cadres of the Han nationality should study the languages and literatures of the minority nationalities, they must pay attention to dealing well with relations among nationalities, and to strengthening solidarity among them. We must educate cadres and people of the Han nationality strictly to observe the Party's policy toward nationalities, to uphold a class viewpoint, and to implement a class line.... In the anti-revisionist struggle, we must have participation by units of the army and of the militia made up of national minorities, in order to guarantee the success of the anti-revisionist struggle.

The third point for attention was the education of the local Han population to respect the customs and habits of the local minorities. Some idea of what this signified is conveyed by the fact that under this heading Mao called for assistance to the Han workers sent to Sinkiang in resolving their "marriage and other difficulties." The fourth point was constant attention to the situation on the border, and intensifying the "anti-revisionist struggle on the border." The fifth point was vigilance against subversion and sabotage, as well as military incursions, by the "Soviet modern revisionists." The last point, finally, was "integrated leadership" (*i-yuan-hua ling-tao*) of the antirevisionist struggle.[179]

Mao Tse-tung was, in fact, convinced that China was rapidly catching

---

179 *Mao Chu-hsi kuan-yü kuo-nei min-tsu wen-t'i ti lun-shu hsuan-pien* (Selections from Chairman Mao's expositions regarding problems of nationalities within the country, October 1978), 40–41.

up with the Soviet Union in terms of standard of living, not only in Central Asia, but in the country as a whole. "Khrushchev," he told Anna Louise Strong in January 1964,

has said that we have one pair of trousers for every five people in China, and sit around eating out of the same bowl of watery cabbage soup. Actually, when he said that, his own economic situation was getting worse, and he said it for the Soviet people to show how well off they were. Now they are getting shorter on trousers and their soup is getting more watery. Actually, the livelihood of the people in the Soviet Union now is not much better than that of our own people.[180]

Whether or not Mao actually believed this, he was assuredly persuaded that the Soviet Union sought to use its primacy in the socialist camp to promote its own selfish economic interests. In his reading notes of 1960 on the Soviet textbook of political economy, Mao had attacked Moscow's policy of economic specialization within Comecon, the Soviet-dominated Eastern European economic organization – a policy designed to keep certain countries in the position of suppliers of agricultural raw materials to their more advanced neighbors, in particular to the Soviet Union.[181] This point continued to rankle, and in his January 1964 interview with Anna Louise Strong, Mao declared, "The problem with the socialist countries is that Khrushchev wants them to stick to a one-sided economy producing to meet the needs of the Soviet Union. It's hard to be the son of a patriarchal father."[182]

Thus, in the late 1950s and early 1960s, Mao Tse-tung voiced an increasingly assertive nationalism as a response not only to the boycott of China by the imperialists, but to Soviet great-power chauvinism. Linked to this trend, and to the evolution of Sino-Soviet relations generally, was a growing radicalism, manifesting itself above all in an emphasis on class struggle. This turn toward the left was, as noted in this chapter's first section a natural outgrowth of the Great Leap policies, but further impetus was given to it by Mao's revulsion at Khrushchev's "goulash communism." Moreover, having been struck by the emergence of revisionism within the Soviet Union, Mao Tse-tung began to discern the existence of similar phenomena within China itself. Thus yet another factor was injected into the complex process that ultimately culminated in the Cultural Revolution.

180 Strong, "Three interviews," 504.
181 *Wan-sui* (1967), 226–27; *Miscellany*, 296.   182 Strong, "Three interviews," 504.

The enemy within: Mao Tse-tung's growing obsession with class struggle

As noted at the end of the first section of this chapter, Mao drastically changed his position regarding the nature of the contradictions in Chinese society during the summer of 1957. The consequences of this shift for economic policy have already been explored, and some of its implications in the philosophic domain have also been evoked. Now, having reviewed the interaction between trends in Mao's thought after 1957 and the Sino-Soviet conflict, it is time to consider how Sino-centrism, a radical interpretation of Marxism, and leftist sentiments engendered by nostalgia for the heroic virtues of the past, came together to lead Mao toward unprecedented experiments.

A central element in the growing radicalization of Mao Tse-tung's thought and political stance in the early 1960s was, of course, his increasingly strident and persistent emphasis on the existence and importance of class struggle within Chinese society. Let us therefore begin by reviewing briefly the evolution of Mao's ideas regarding classes and class struggle from the Greap Leap to the eve of the Cultural Revolution.

The first systematic formulation of his new approach was contained in Mao's speech of 9 October 1957 at the Third Plenum. Abandoning the position that had been adopted a year earlier at the Eighth Congress, and that, as we have seen, he had himself reiterated in February 1957, to the effect that the basic contradiction in China at the present stage was between the productive forces and the relations of production, Mao asserted that

the contradiction between the proletariat and the bourgeoisie, between the socialist road and the capitalist road, is undoubtedly the principal contradiction in contemporary Chinese society.... Previously the principal task for the proletariat was to lead the masses in struggles against imperialism and feudalism, a task that has already been accomplished. What then is the principal contradiction now? We are now carrying on the socialist revolution, the spearhead of which is directed against the bourgeoisie, and at the same time this revolution aims at transforming the system of individual production, that is, bringing about co-operation; consequently the principal contradiction is between socialism and capitalism, between collectivism and individualism, or in a nutshell between the socialist road and the capitalist road. The resolution of the Eighth Congress makes no mention of this question. It contains a passage which speaks of the principal contradiction as being that between the advanced socialist system and the backward social productive forces. This formulation is incorrect.[183]

183 Mao, *SW*, 5.492-93.

It is, of course, Mao's revised formulation just quoted that is now seen in China as incorrect. Right or wrong, however, it was the emphasis on class struggle, against the bourgeoisie and between the "two roads," that was to characterize Mao's thought for the rest of his life. Within this broad orientation, there were, however, to be significant twists, turns and fluctuations during the ensuing nineteen years, both in the vigor and harshness with which Mao Tse-tung promoted class struggle and in his analysis of the existing class relations.

On the eve of the Great Leap, Mao spelled out his view regarding the class structure of Chinese society in rather curious terms, stating that "the reciprocal relations between people" were "determined by the relationship between three big classes": (1) "imperialism, feudalism, bureaucratic capitalism, the rightists, and their agents"; (2) "the national bourgeoisie," by which he said he meant all the members of this class except the rightists; and (3) "the left, that is to say the labouring people, the workers, the peasants." To this last category Mao added, more or less as an afterthought, the parenthetical remark: "In reality there are four classes – the peasants are a separate class."[184]

In his speech of 6 April 1958 to the Hankow Conference, Mao corrected one anomaly – the failure to single out the particular role of the peasantry – but continued to include the "imperialists" among the classes existing in China. On this occasion, he put the matter as follows:

... there are four classes within the country, two exploiting classes and two labouring classes. The first exploiting class consists of imperialism, feudalism, bureaucratic capitalism and the remnants of the Kuomintang, as well as 300,000 rightists. The landlords have now split up, some of them have been reformed, and others have not been reformed. The unreformed landlords, rich peasants, counter-revolutionaries, bad elements and rightists resolutely oppose communism. They are the Chiang Kai-shek and the Kuomintang of the present day, they are the class enemy, like Chang Po-chün. The rightists in the Party are just the same.... If you add up all these people, they come to roughly 5 per cent of the population, or about 30 million.... This is a hostile class, and still awaits reform. We must struggle against them, and at the same time take hold of them.... If we succeed in transforming 10 per cent of them, this can be accounted a success.... After a few years, when they demonstrate a sincere change of heart and are genuinely reformed, their exploiting class hats can be removed.[185]

The second exploiting class, made up of the national bourgeoisie, including the well-to-do middle peasants in the countryside, Mao described as a vacillating and opportunistic class. As for the "two labouring

184 Schram, *Mao unrehearsed*, 112–13.   185 *Wan-sui* (1969), 180–81; *Miscellany*, 85–86.

classes, the workers and the peasants," Mao remarked: "In the past, their minds were not as one, and they were not clear about ideology or about their mutual relations." And he added; "The workers and peasants work and till the land under the leadership of our Party, but in the past we did not properly handle the problem of their mutual relations."

In the aftermath of the Great Leap Forward, Mao's previous approach to the problem of class, which combined objective and subjective criteria, was modified by the addition of a new dimension: the notion that privileged elements among the cadres and intellectuals constituted an embryonic class. This trend was linked to the generational change referred to above, for it had long been understood that, because they were accustomed to a certain standard of living, intellectuals of bourgeois origin must be paid high salaries. This was extensively discussed in the Chinese press in 1956-57, and in January 1957, Mao himself defended what he called "buying over" at a "small cost" the capitalists plus the democrats and intellectuals associated with them.[186] Obviously the same considerations did not apply to the newly trained young people, who did not have such expensive tastes, and who might be assumed to have a higher level of political consciousness.

I have already noted Mao's advocacy, at the Peitaiho meeting of August 1958, of the "free supply system." His speech on this occasion was not, of course, openly published at the time, but much of the substance of his thinking was conveyed in an article by Chang Ch'un-ch'iao reproduced in the People's Daily in October 1958. Chang's article, which had originally appeared in Shanghai in September, did not, in fact, represent simply an accidental convergence between his views and Mao's, but was the result of a clever political maneuver. K'o Ch'ing-shih, the leftist mayor of Shanghai, who was present at the Peitaiho meeting, had read out to Chang Ch'un-ch'iao over the telephone his notes of Mao's speech, and this had provided the inspiration for Chang's piece. Mao's decision, on reading the article, to have it reprinted in Peking was therefore evidence both of his own susceptibility to flattery, and of the functioning, already at this time, of a Shanghai link, if not a Shanghai network.[187]

In the editorial note he wrote to accompany Chang's article when it appeared in the People's Daily, Mao said the views expressed were "basically correct," but he judged the article "one-sided," and "incomplete" in

186 Mao, SW, 5.357.
187 Information regarding the role played by K'o Ch'ing-shih from a conversation of 23 April 1986 with Hu Hua, confirmed by Kung Yü-chih in a conversation of 24 April 1986.

its explanation of the historical process.[188] But even though Mao thought Chang was in too much of a hurry to eliminate the "ideology of bourgeois right" or bourgeois legal norms defined by Marx, the issue evoked by this term remained posed in his speeches and writings from this time forward. In brief, Mao regarded the inequalities resulting from compensation according to work, even under a socialist system, as qualitatively similar to the "bourgeois right" defined by Marx with reference to capitalist society, and it was this that provided the theoretical basis for his view that the Party, because it contained the greatest number of high cadres attached to their privileges, was a nest of bourgeois or bourgeois-minded elements.[189]

I have already stressed the importance of the Lushan Plenum of 1959 as a turning point toward an ever greater emphasis on class struggle. Condemning P'eng and his allies as anti-Marxist "bourgeois elements" who had infiltrated the Chinese Communist Party,[190] Mao declared that the struggle at Lushan had been a class struggle, "the continuation of the life-and-death struggle between the two great antagonists of the bourgeoisie and the proletariat in the process of the socialist revolution during the past decade," and predicted that such struggle would last "for at least another twenty years."[191] (In the event, Mao very nearly saw to it that it did.)

---

188 Chang Ch'un-ch'iao, "P'o-ch'u tzu-ch'an-chieh-chi ti fa-ch'üan ssu-hsiang" (Eliminate the ideology of bourgeois right), *JMJP*, 13 October 1958.

189 For the most authoritative recent Chinese analysis of this trend in Mao's thought, see Shih Chung-ch'üan, "Ma-k'o-ssu so-shuo-ti' tzu-ch'an-chieh-chi ch'üan-li' ho Mao Tse-tung t'ung-chih tui t'a ti wu-chieh" (The "bourgeois right" referred to by Marx, and Comrade Mao Tse-tung's misunderstanding of it), *Wen-hsien ho yen-chiu*, 1983, 405–17, and the revised openly published version of this in *HC*, 11 (1985), 12–22. This article, like many other recently published accounts, asserts unequivocally that Mao played the central role in introducing the concept of "bourgeois right" into Chinese political discourse from the Great Leap onward. The term commonly rendered into English as "bourgeois right" has as its *locus classicus* Marx's "Critique of the Gotha Programme," where he makes use of it in criticizing the notion of a "fair distribution of the proceeds of labour." (Karl Marx and Frederick Engels, *Selected works*, 317–21.) *Recht* means, in German, both right, in the sense of entitlement to the rewards of one's labor (or of human rights), and legal order. Marx is in effect referring, in the passage in question, to both these dimensions, as he makes plain when, after stating that "equal right is still in principle bourgeois right," he goes on to note: "Right by its very nature can consist only in the application of an equal standard." In other words, right (or rights) in the sense of entitlement is defined by a system of legal or quasi-legal norms. The Chinese have further compounded this confusion by rejecting the translation of the term used by Mao, *tzu-ch'an chieh-chi fa-ch'üan* (meaning literally "bourgeois legal rights"), since 1979, in favor of *tzu-ch'an chieh-chi ch'üan-li*, which points rather toward the rights of the individual subject. In any case, Mao's concern was primarily with the fact that, as he saw it, the strict application of the socialist principle of "to each according to his work" failed to take into account the social needs of the individual, and was therefore in some degree heartless, just as the capitalist system of wage labor was heartless.

190 Speech of 11 September 1959 to the Military Affairs Committee, Schram, *Mao unrehearsed*, 147–48.

191 "The origin of machine guns and mortars," 15 August 1959, *CLG*, 1.4 (1968–69), 73.

Discussing Mao Tse-tung's "errors regarding the problem of class struggle" in the period just before the Cultural Revolution, Teng Li-ch'ün has pointed to another source for Mao's increasing radicalism: "In reality, after 1958, he basically paid no attention to economic work. This affected his estimate of the situation regarding classes and class struggle."[192] The above statement should not be taken literally to mean that Mao henceforth took no interest in anything related to the economy. After all, it was in 1960 that he produced his "Reading notes on the [Soviet] textbook of political economy," and Mao is now said to have taken personal charge of the drafting of the "Sixty Articles" on the communes in March 1961.[193] Teng Li-ch'ün's point, therefore, was that although Mao continued to talk about the political and ideological dimensions of the economic system, he took little serious interest in economics or in economic reality. In this sense, Teng's conclusion is undoubtedly justified.

Mao's growing conviction, form 1959 on, that the bureaucratic tendencies which not only he, but also Liu Shao-ch'i and others, had long denounced in the Chinese Communist Party were not simply the result of a defect in "work style," but reflected an incipient change in the class character of the Party and its cadres, was inspired to a significant extent by his observations regarding the Soviet Union. But the comments he made in 1960 regarding the emergence of "vested interests groups" in a socialist society after the abolition of classes, although they occur in his reading notes on the Soviet textbook of political economy, were obviously intended to apply to China as well.

Indeed, there are scholars in China today who take the view that Mao's analysis of Soviet "revisionism" had as its primary purpose the forging of a weapon against those in the Chinese Communist Party who did not share his ideas. That is probably putting it too strongly; Mao undoubtedly did have an acute distaste for Khrushchev's Russia and all it had come to stand for in his eyes. In fact, he even traced the defects in the Soviet system back to its very origins. After the October Revolution, he asserted, the Soviets had failed to deal properly with the problem of "bourgeois right." As a result, a pattern of stratification reminiscent of the tsarist era had emerged; most Party members were the children of cadres, and ordinary workers and peasants had no chance of advance-

192 Teng Li-ch'ün, answering questions about the resolution of 27 June 1981 at an academic discussion held on 11 and 12 August 1981, in the context of a national meeting on collecting materials for Party history, in *Tang-shih hui-i pao-kao-chi*, 145.

193 T'ao K'ai, "K'ai-shih ch'üan-mien chien-she she-hui-chu-i ti shih-nien" (The ten years which saw the beginning of the all-round construction of socialism), in *Hsüeh-hsi li-shih chüeh-i chuan-chi* (Special collection on the study of the Resolution on [Party] history), 121.

ment.[194] He also noted that the Soviets had failed to smash bourgeois freedom, and thereby to promote proletarian freedom; China's political and ideological revolution had been more thorough.[195] Nonetheless, Mao's most acute concern was with the threat that such unwholesome tendencies might take root in China. Already at this time, he attributed to the Chinese bearers of such contagion two traits that were to remain central to his ideas on this theme in later years. On the one hand, they were attached to their privileges, founded in the principle of distribution "to each according to his work" – in other words, to the "ideology of bourgeois right." And at the same time, they behaved like overlords. "This animal, man, is funny," said Mao, "as soon as he enjoys slightly superior conditions he puts on airs."[196]

In January 1962, in a speech mainly stressing the need to continue the struggle against the old reactionary classes (landlords and bourgeoisie), which he said were "still planning a comeback," Mao stated explicitly that in a socialist society, "new bourgeois elements may still be produced."[197] And in August 1962, at a preliminary meeting of the Central Committee in Peitaiho before the Tenth Plenum, Mao declared; "In the book *Socialist upsurge in China's countryside* [which he had himself edited] there is an annotation saying that the bourgeoisie has been eliminated, and only the influence of bourgeois ideology remains. This is wrong, and should be corrected.... The bourgeoisie can be born anew; such a situation exists in the Soviet Union."[198]

As it stands, this statement that the bourgeoisie can be "born anew" leaves open the question, central for our purposes, of whether Mao means the old bourgeoisie can be reborn, or whether he is referring to the reincarnation of the soul or essence of the bourgeoisie in a new form, adapted to the conditions of a socialist society. He probably was talking about the second of these things, in other words about what Djilas and others have called the "new class" – although Mao himself may never have used that term. He seemed unable to make up his mind, however, in the mid-1960s, as to whether these "new bourgeois elements" were merely isolated individuals, corrupted by the advantages drawn from the misuse of their status, or whether *all* cadres, because of the privileges and power they enjoyed, were prone to take on this character.

---

194 *Hsüeh-hsi wen-hsüan*, 305. (Speech of 21 August 1958, in the morning.)
195 Ibid., 311. (Speech of 21 August 1958, in the afternoon.)
196 *Wan-sui* (1967), 192. For an earlier reference to "putting on airs like overlords," see Mao's speech of November 1958 on Stalin's *Economic problems of socialism in the USSR* in *Wan-sui* (1967), 117–18.
197 Schram, *Mao unrehearsed*, 168.   198 *Wan-sui* (1969), 424.

In the early 1960s, he appeared to lean in the first direction, by stressing the corrupting effects of money, and advantages bought with money. Thus, while continuing to acknowledge that material incentives were necessary in Chinese society at the present stage, he argued that they should be subordinated to "spiritual incentives" in the political and ideological domains, and that individual interests should be subordinated to collective interests.[199]

In his speech of 30 January 1962 to a central work conference, Mao related the "five bad categories" to the social origins of the individuals in question: "Those whom the people's democratic dictatorship should repress," he declared, "are landlords, rich peasants, counter-revolutionary elements, bad elements and anti-communist rightists. The classes which the counter-revolutionary elements, bad elements and anti-communist rightists represent are the landlord class and the reactionary bourgeoisie. These classes and bad people comprise about four or five per cent of the population. These are the people we must compel to reform."[200]

At the Tenth Plenum of September–October 1962, Mao put forward the slogan "Never forget the class struggle!" and personally revised the communiqué of the plenum that summed up his thinking.[201] Like his speech five years earlier, at the Third Plenum, and the confrontation at Lushan, this occasion marked yet a further turn toward a policy of promoting "class struggle." The nature and locus of the classes being struggled against remained, however, fundamentally ambiguous. In his speech of January 1962, Mao had referred to "classes and bad people." In other words, although the counterrevolutionaries and other "bad elements" were said by Mao to "represent" the landlords and the reactionary bourgeoisie, they did not necessarily come from these classes. Two passages from speeches by Mao during the period from the summer of 1962 to the spring of 1963, when the Socialist Education Campaign was in the process of taking shape, stress more heavily the class origins of deviations within the Party, but at the same time underscore the continuing importance, in Mao's view, of transformation through education.

In his talk of 9 August at Peitaiho, Mao said:

The composition of Party membership [tang-yuan ti ch'eng-fen] includes a large number of petty bourgeois, a contingent of well-to-do peasants and their sons and younger brothers, a certain number of intellectuals, and also some bad people who have not yet been properly transformed; in reality, [these last] are not

199 Wan-sui (1967), 206, 210. (From Mao's reading notes of 1960 on the Soviet textbook of political economy, now known to be edited versions of his remarks at sessions discussing the Soviet text.)
200 Schram, Mao unrehearsed, 169–70.   201 1981 resolution, annotated edition, 339.

Communist Party members. They are called Communist Party members, but they are really [members of the] Kuomintang.... As for the intellectuals and sons and brothers of landlords and rich peasants, there are those who have been transformed by Marxism [*Ma-k'o-ssu-hua le ti*], there are those who have not been transformed at all, and there are those who have not been transformed to a satisfactory level. These people are not spiritually prepared for the socialist revolution. we have not educated them in good time.[202]

In May 1963, on the eve of the promulgation of the first directive regarding the Socialist Education Campaign (the "Former Ten Points"), Mao defined the class composition of the Party quite differently, but discussed the problem of "transformation" in very similar terms:

With respect to Party composition, the most important class components are workers, poor peasants and farm labourers. Consequently, the main class composition is good. However, within the Party there is a large number of petty bourgeois elements, some of whom belong to the upper stratum of the urban and rural petty bourgeoisie. In addition, there are intellectuals, as well as a certain number of sons and daughters of landlords and rich peasants. Of these people, some have been transformed by Marxism; some have been partly, but not totally transformed by Marxism-Leninism; and some have not been transformed at all. Organizationally they may have joined the Party, but not in terms of their thought. They are not ideologically prepared for the socialist revolution. In addition, during the last few years some bad people have wormed their way in. They are corrupt and degenerate and have seriously violated the law and discipline.... This problem requires attention, but it is relatively easy to deal with. The most important problem is the petty-bourgeois elements who have not been properly reformed. With respect to intellectuals and the sons and daughters of landlords and rich peasants we must do more work. Consequently, we must carry out education, and yet more education, for Party members and cadres. This is an important task.[203]

It is evident from these two quotations that although objective social origins remained important for Mao, personal transformation through political education was likewise a crucial aspect of the problem of class taken as a whole. If anything, the stress on "transformation," that is, on subjective criteria, is greater in 1963 than in 1962.

In May 1964, as the Socialist Education Campaign unfolded, Mao declared, at a meeting with four vice-premiers:

We must definitely pay very close attention to class struggle. The "four clean-ups" in the countryside is a class struggle, and the "five antis" in the cities is also

---

202 *Wan-sui (1969)*, 426.
203 *Tzu-liao hsuan-pien* ([Peking], January 1967), 277. For a conveniently available translation of this whole directive, see Richard Baum and Frederick C. Teiwes, *Ssu-ch'ing: the Socialist Education Movement of 1962–1966*, 58–71. (The passage by Mao is on pp. 70–71.) This text was first openly published in the ninth Chinese reply to the Soviet open letter; see Schram, *Political thought*, 367.

a class struggle.... Class status [ch'eng-fen] must also be determined in the cities. As for how such class lines should be drawn criteria must be formulated when we come to do this work. We cannot take account only of [inherited] class status [wei ch'eng-fen lun]. Neither Marx, Engels, Lenin nor Stalin had working-class family origins [ch'u-shen].[204]

A directive on drawing class distinctions, undated but almost certainly from late 1964, discusses explicitly the relation between subjective and objective criteria:

It is necessary to draw class distinctions.... Of the two, [objective] class status [chieh-chi ch'eng-fen] and the behaviour of the person in question [pen-jen piao-hsien], it is the behaviour of the person in question which is most important. The main thing in drawing class distinctions is to ferret out the bad elements.

We must moreover clearly distinguish between family origins [ch'u-shen] and the behaviour of the person in question. The emphasis must be placed on behaviour; the theory that everything depends on class status alone [wei ch'eng-fen lun] is wrong, the problem is whether you take the stand of your class of origin, or whether you adopt a different class stand, that is, on the side of the workers and the poor and lower-middle peasants. Moreover, we must not be sectarian, but must unite with the majority, even including a portion of the landlords and rich peasants, and their children. There are even some counter-revolutionaries and saboteurs who should be transformed; it suffices that they be willing to be transformed, and we should be willing to have them, one and all.[205]

It can be argued that, in Mao's later years, certain pairs of opposites that had hitherto coexisted in dynamic and creative tension became dissociated, thus unleashing forces that ultimately propelled his thought and action into destructive channels. In several crucial and interrelated respects, this unraveling of the previous synthesis began with the Tenth Plenum in the fall of 1962. Increasingly, Mao came to perceive the relation between the leaders, with their privileges, and the rest of society, as an antagonistic contradiction rather than a contradiction among the people. The consequence that inevitably flowed from this insight was that the Party, considered as an entity that included virtually all of these privileged power holders, must not be simply tempered and purified in contact with the masses, but smashed, at least in large part.

Apart from the relation between the Party, or privileged elements in the Party, and the masses, the very complex process of dissociation or disaggregation of the structure of Mao Tse-tung's thought that took place

204 Miscellany, 351; Wan-sui (1969), 494-95.
205 Miscellany, 351; Wan-sui (1969), 602-3. (For the dating of this text, see the discussion in volume 2 of the index to Mao's post-1949 writings published in 1981 by Kyoto Daigaku Jimbun Kagaku Kenkyūsho [Research Institute of Humanistic Studies, Kyoto University], p. 47.)

beginning in the 1960s involved a number of other polarities. I have already dealt at some length with the interaction between Marxism and the Chinese tradition, and also with the issue of the relation between the Soviet model and Chinese experience.

The Sino-Soviet conflict also played an important role in shaping Mao Tse-tung's philosophical thought by contributing to the context in which the key idea of "One divides into two" emerged. On 26 October 1963, Chou Yang delivered to the Chinese Academy of Sciences a speech entitled "The fighting task confronting workers in philosophy and the social sciences." This speech, which was published, by an altogether too striking coincidence, on Mao's seventieth birthday (26 December 1963), plainly represented Mao Tse-tung's own thinking. In it Chou Yang surveyed the history of the workers' movement from Marx's own day to the present in terms of the axiom "One divides into two."[206]

Mao himself had, in fact, used this expression in a speech of 18 November 1957 at the Moscow meeting, although on that occasion his emphasis was not on divisions within the socialist movement, but on the fact that all societies, including socialist society, "teem" with contradictions, and on the fact that there is good and bad in everyone. "One divides into two," he concluded. "This is a universal phenomenon, and this is dialectics."[207]

Very soon after Chou Yang's speech of 1963, the slogan "one divides into two" came to evoke above all, in Mao's own usage, the need to struggle against "capitalist roaders" in the Chinese Communist Party. In other words, it was, by implication, a call for class struggle. (It was also, as discussed in CHOC, 14. 466–69, the rallying cry for the purge and persecution of Yang Hsien-chen and other partisans of the opposing formulation, "Two combine into one.")

This principle, Mao declared, constituted "the heart of dialectical materialism." He drew from it the conclusion that the electron, like the atom, would ultimately be split.[208] But above all, he was persuaded that social categories and political forces would continue to split, now and forever.

In the last analysis, Mao's conflict with others in the leadership revolved, of course, around the fundamental political and economic strategy that should be adopted for building socialism. The domain of culture

206 PR, 1964.1, 10–27, esp. p. 14; Chinese in HC, 1963.24, 1–30. (The expression *i fen wei erh* appears on pp. 4–5.) On Mao's involvement with this report, see also Schram, *Ideology and policy*, 44–45.
207 Mao, *SW*, 5.516.   208 Strong, "Three interviews," 499–500.

was, however, a crucial battleground as well, In the early 1960s, Mao perceived certain developments in literature and philosophy not only as the expression of unwholesome tendencies, but as weapons for attacking the very foundations of socialism through the agency of the superstructure. It is thus no accident that Mao should have first expressed his anxieties in cogent form precisely at the Tenth Plenum, simultaneously with his call for class struggle:

Writing novels is popular these days, isn't it? The use of novels for anti-party activity is a great invention. Anyone wanting to overthrow a political regime must create public opinion and do some preparatory ideological work. This applies to counter-revolutionary as well as to revolutionary classes.[209]

The clear implication of this statement was that "counter-revolutionary classes" were still at work in China, thirteen years after the conquest of power, seeking to overthrow the dictatorship of the proletariat, and that constant struggle in the realm of the superstructure was necessary in order to keep them in check. There is here present in embryonic form the idea of "continuing the revolution under the dictatorship of the proletariat" that was to loom so large during the Cultural Revolution decade. In view of the ambiguity of Mao's notion of class at this time, this development clearly represents a further manifestation of the accent on the superstructure, and on subjective forces, which had characterized Mao's thought from the beginning.

Just as Mao's call for class struggle at the Tenth Plenum had led to the Socialist Education Campaign, so this statement gave the impetus to a movement for literary rectification, and encouraged Chiang Ch'ing to launch the reform of the Peking Opera. These policies and their consequences have been described and analyzed in *CHOC*, 14, chapter 10. Here it will suffice to mention briefly two directives by which Mao continued to pour fuel on the fire. In December 1963, he complained that the "dead" still ruled in many departments of art, literature, and drama. "The social and economic base has already changed," he declared, "but the arts as part of the superstructure, which serve this base, still remain a great problem today.... Isn't it absurd that many communists are enthusiastic about promoting feudal and capitalist arts, but not socialist art?" In June 1964, his judgment was even harsher. The Chinese Writers Union, he said, "for the past fifteen years had *basically* [Mao's italics] ... not implemented the Party's policy." Instead of uniting with the workers and peasants,

209 Schram, *Mao unrehearsed*, 195. A similar concern with the influence of the media, and with the superstructure as a crucial realm of political struggle, had already been expressed by Mao in his then unpublished "Reading notes" of 1960 on the Soviet textbook of political economy. See *Wan-sui* (1969), 342–43; *Miscellany*, 266.

they had acted as bureaucrats and overlords, going to the brink of revisionism. Unless they mended their ways, they would become another Petrőfi Club.[210] In other words, they would be outright counterrevolutionaries, and would be treated as such.

At the same time, in 1963–64, Mao showed greatly increased skepticism regarding the role of intellectuals in revolution and development. Without carrying his distrust of intellectuals to the point of characterizing them, as would the Gang of Four, as the "stinking ninth category," Mao therefore moved toward education policies infinitely more extreme than those of the Great Leap Forward. "We shouldn't read too many books," he said in February 1964. "We should read Marxist books, but not too many of them either. It will be enough to read a dozen or so. If we read too many we can move toward our opposite, become bookworms, dogmatists, revisionists."[211]

In all of these various domains – art and literature, philosophy, education – Mao attacked leading intellectuals not so much because they were privileged elements exploiting the masses (although he could make a good case to show that they were), but because they failed to share his utopia of struggle, and to obey wholeheartedly his directives.

In the summer of 1964, Mao referred scathingly to material corruption throughout the Party. "At present," he said, "you can buy a branch secretary for a few packs of cigarettes, not to mention marrying a daughter to him."[212]

The reference here to lower-level cadres would suggest that at that moment, shortly before Liu Shao-ch'i produced his "revised later ten points," Mao did not wholly disagree with the view that the Socialist Education Campaign should be directed at the grass roots, as well as at the higher echelons. He was, however, particularly exercised about the attitudes and behavior of the privileged urban elite. In a talk of June 1964 on the 3rd Five-Year Plan, he remarked:

Don't strive for money all the time, and don't spend it recklessly once you've got it.... In accordance with our policy, bourgeois intellectuals may be bought when necessary, but why should we buy proletarian intellectuals? He who has plenty of money is bound to corrupt himself, his family, and those around him.... In the Soviet Union, the high-salaried stratum appeared first in literary and artistic circles.[213]

As discussed in *CHOC*, 14, ch. 7, the final confrontation between Mao Tse-tung and Liu Shao-ch'i took place in December 1964, when

210 These are two of the "five militant documents" on art and literature published in May 1967. For a translation (somewhat modified here) of the directives of 12 December 1963 and 27 June 1964, see *PR*, 1967.23, 8.
211 Schram, *Mao unrehearsed*, 210.   212 Ibid., 217.   213 *Wan-sui* (1969), 498–99.

Mao, dissatisfied with what he perceived as the distortion and watering-down of his original strategy for the Socialist Education Campaign, put forward a new twenty-three–article directive that Liu, Mao later claimed, refused to accept. On this occasion, he made a number of observations regarding the "new bourgeoisie" in which power, rather than money, began to appear as the decisive factor.

It is perhaps worth noting in passing that although the problem of status and wage differentials was obviously of very acute concern to Mao, he displayed toward it even at this time a relaxed and humorous attitude scarcely to be found in the writings of the glum and fanatical ideologists of the Gang of Four. "This business of eating more and possessing more is rather complex!" he declared. "It is mainly people like us who have cars, and houses with central heating, and chauffeurs. I earn only 430 yuan, and I can't afford to hire secretaries, but I must."[214]

It is hard to resist reading this passage in the light of Mao's remark, earlier in the same year of 1964, "Hsuan-t'ung's salary of a little over a hundred yuan is too small – this man is an emperor."[215] One has the impression that for Mao, there existed, in addition to "worker," "poor peasant," "son of revolutionary martyr," and so on, yet another *ch'eng fen*: that of ruler. As for those who did not share this status with him, and with the former emperor, they could not be allowed to grow attached to their privileges.

In a discussion of 20 December 1964, he thus castigated once again those "power holders" among the cadres who were primarily concerned about getting more wage points for themselves, and agreed that the "hat" of "new bourgeois elements" should be stuck on "particularly vicious offenders" among them. He warned, however, against overestimating their number, and said they should be referred to as elements or cliques, not as "strata" – still less, obviously, as a fully formed class.[216] A week later, on 27 December 1964, Mao declared that there were "at least two factions" in the Chinese Communist Party, a socialist faction and a capitalist faction; these two factions thus incarnated the principal contradiction in Chinese society.[217]

Such formulations, and Mao's determination to direct the spearhead of the Socialist Education Campaign against "those in authority taking the

214 Ibid., 587.
215 Schram, *Mao unrehearsed*, 198. (Remarks at the Spring Festival Forum on Education.) Hsuan-t'ung was the reign title of the last Manchu emperor, a boy at the time of his abdication in 1912, and also known as Pu-yi (P'u-i) when he was emperor of the Japanese puppet state of Manchukuo from 1932 to 1945. He was still living in Beijing in 1964.
216 *Wan-sui* (1969), 582–88.   217 Ibid., 597–98.

capitalist road," led, of course, directly to the confrontation with Liu and others in the Party, and to the Cultural Revolution.

THE IDEOLOGY OF THE CULTURAL REVOLUTION

Before addressing the substance of Mao's thinking during the Cultural Revolution, it may be useful to ask ourselves precisely why he launched this movement, and what was the relationship between this decision and the "unraveling" of the Great Leap and post–Great Leap synthesis evoked above. Did he adopt extreme lines of conduct because his thinking had become skewed or distorted, or did he think as he did because he was obsessed with certain existential problems – above all, with the desire to punish and ultimately to destroy his critics?

As I have already suggested, especially in discussing his changing ideas on dialectics, and on class struggle, there were, in my view, elements of both these processes at work, but the predominant factor was the second one. In other words, the political and psychological roots of his ideas were notably more important than the intellectual ones. As a Chinese author has put it, Mao was so thoroughly persuaded that his own views were the only correct exposition of Marxism-Leninism that anyone who failed to agree with him automatically became a revisionist in his eyes. As a result, "The more it proved impossible to put his ideas into practice, the more he saw this as the reflection of class struggle, ... and of the emergence of 'counter-revolutionary revisionist elements' within the Party."[218]

Dictatorship, rebellion, and spiritual transformation

Among the multifarious ideological and policy innovations of the Cultural Revolution, it was the radical calling into question of the Party, and of authority in all its forms (except that of the Chairman), that attracted the most attention at the outset of this upheaval. In retrospect, it is clear that Mao's repudiation of leadership from above was not so sweeping as it appeared at the time. Nevertheless, he did go very far.

In his comments of 1960 on the Soviet manual, Mao had declared: "No

---

218 Wang Nien-i, "Mao Tse-tung t'ung-chih fa-tung 'wen-hua ta-ko-ming' shih tui hsing-shih ti ku-chi" (Comrade Mao Tse-tung's estimate of the situation at the time when he launched the "Great Cultural Revolution"), *Tang-shih yen-chiu tzu-liao*, 4.772. For a more extended discussion of the psychological roots of the Cultural Revolution, see Schram, "Party leader or true ruler?" 221–24, 233–37. Also, Stuart Schram, "The limits of cataclysmic change: reflections on the place of the 'Great Proletarian Cultural Revolution' in the political development of the People's Republic of China," *CQ*, 108 (December 1986), 613–24.

matter what, we cannot regard history as the creation of the planners, it is the creation of the masses."[219] And yet, he had always held, down to the eve of the Cultural Revolution, the view that the masses could exercise this role of making history only if they benefited from correct leadership. As the great confrontation with the Party approached, in December 1965, he went a step farther, proclaiming that democracy meant "dealing with the affairs of the masses through the masses themselves." There were, he added, two lines: to rely entirely on a few individuals, and to mobilize the masses. "Democratic politics," he said, "must rely on everyone running things, not on a minority of people running things." At the same time, however, he called once more for reliance on "the leadership of the Party at the higher level and on the broad masses at the lower level."[220] It was only with the actual onset of the Cultural Revolution in March 1966, that Mao sounded a much more radical note, suggesting that the masses could dispense with centralized Party leadership:

The Propaganda Department of the Central Committee is the palace of the King of Hell. We must overthrow the palace of the King of Hell and set the little devils free. I have always advocated that whenever the central organs do bad things, it is necessary to call upon the localities to rebel, and to attack the centre. The localities must produce many Sun Wu-k'ungs to create a great disturbance in the palace of the King of Heaven.[221]

Two months later, these "Monkey Kings" burst upon the scene, using Mao's own rhethoric, including the slogan "To rebel is justified!" which he had coined in 1939, attributing it – irony of ironies – to Stalin.[222] "Daring to ... rebel is ... the fundamental principle of the proletarian Party spirit," proclaimed the Red Guards of Tsing-hua University Middle School. "Revolutionaries are Monkey Kings.... We wield our golden rods, display our supernatural powers, and use our magic to turn the old world upside down, smash it to pieces, pulverize it and create chaos – the greater the confusion the better! We are bent on creating a tremendous proletarian uproar, and hewing out a proletarian new world!"[223] The "old world" these Red Guards wanted to smash was, of course, that controlled by the Party; they did not propose to rectify it, but to dissolve it in the chaos of the Cultural Revolution, and replace it by a completely new order.

Mao himself never proclaimed such a goal. At a central work confer-

219 Wan-sui (1967), 206.
220 Wan-sui (1969), 630. (Talk of 21 December 1964 with Ch'en Po-ta and Ai Ssu-ch'i.)
221 Wan-sui (1969), 640.
222 MTTC, 7.142; translated in Schram, Political thought, 427–28.
223 JMJP, 24 August 1966; translated in PR, 1966.37, 2–21.

ence on 23 August, he remarked, "The principal question is what policy we should adopt regarding the so-called disturbances [*so-wei luan*] in various areas. My view is that we should let disorder reign for a few months [*luan t'a chi-ko yueh*].... Even if there are no provincial Party committees, it doesn't matter; aren't there still district and *hsien* committees?"[224]

The phrase "for a few months" should probably be taken literally, to mean three or four months, or six at the outside. That in itself would have made the Cultural Revolution more like a conventional rectification campaign. Nevertheless, by accepting the prospect that for a time the Party might survive only in the form of local-level committees, the central organs having been effectively smashed and put out of action, Mao was at the very least taking the risk of destroying the political instrument to which he had devoted more than four decades of his life, in order to purge it of his enemies.

When events moved in such a direction, in late 1966 and early 1967, that the threat to the very existence of the Party became acute, Mao was forced to choose between Leninism and anarchy. He had no hesitation in preferring the former. Speaking in February 1967 to Chang Ch'un-ch'iao and Yao Wen-yuan, Mao noted that some people in Shanghai had demanded the abolition of "heads," and commented: "This is extreme anarchism, it is most reactionary. If instead of calling someone the 'head' of something, we call him 'orderly' or 'assistant,' this would really be only a formal change. In reality, there will still always be heads."[225] Discussing the objections to setting up communes as organs of government, as Chang and Yao had just done in Shanghai, Mao queried: "Where will we put the Party? ... In a commune there has to be a party; can the commune replace the party?"[226] The history of the ensuing nine years made it abundantly clear that in the Chairman's view it could not.

Another contradiction that became acute at this time was the one between Mao's consistently held view that the Party should command the gun and the gun should never be allowed to command the Party, and the increasingly dominant role of the People's Liberation Army in Chinese politics from 1960 on. This trend had begun, of course, as an essentially tactical maneuver on Mao's part to develop a power base in Lin Piao's PLA because he felt the Party to be slipping from his grasp, and not because of any innovation or brusque mutation in his thought. The pursuit of these tactics, however, soon led Mao in directions that, whatever his own original intentions, had major theoretical implications.

224 *Wan-sui* (1969), 653.   225 Schram, *Mao unrehearsed*, 277.
226 *Wan-sui* (1969), 670–71; *Miscellany*, 453–54.

The most important of these developments was the establishment in the course of the "Learn from the PLA" campaign launched in February 1964 (see *CHOC*, 14, ch. 7) of political departments, modeled on that of the army, in industrial enterprises, schools, and other units throughout the country. Not only did the army provide the model for these departments; it also provided the personnel, as Mao himself had decided in advance. On 16 December 1963, he wrote to Marshals Lin Piao, Ho Lung, and Nieh Jung-chen and to General Hsiao Hua, saying in part:

In every branch of state industry people are now proposing to emulate the People's Liberation Army from top to bottom (i.e., from the ministry down to the factory or to the mine), to set up everywhere political departments, political offices and political instructors, and to put into effect the Four Firsts and the Three-Eight work style. I too propose that several groups of good cadres be transferred from the Liberation Army to do political work in the industry ministries.... It looks as though we just can't get by without doing this, for otherwise we will be unable to rouse the revolutionary spirit of the millions and millions of cadres and workers in the whole industrial sector (and commerce and agriculture too).... I have been considering this question for several years.[227]

Such colonization of other organizations by the army rather than the Party was without precedent in the history of the world communist movement. Of equally great symbolic importance was the fact that by 1964 the People's Liberation Army was becoming increasingly the ideological and cultural mentor of the Chinese people. It was the army that compiled and published, in May 1964, the first edition of the "little red book," *Quotations from Chairman Mao*. Moreover, Mao himself, although he is not known to have participated in the work of compiling this breviary, had a share in the authorship of it, for the preface was drawn in large part from a resolution of the Military Affairs Commission of October 1960 that he had personally rewritten and approved at the time.[228] Thus the stage was set for the dialectic between anarchy and military control during the period 1966–72, and for the further and final unraveling of the polarities of Mao Tse-tung's thought.

By no means the least of the paradoxes of the Cultural Revolution period lay in the role of youth. On the one hand, Mao called on the Red Guards, at the outset of the movement, to serve as the vanguard, as he and his own generation of students had burst upon the stage of his-

227 *Tzu-liao hsuan-pien*, 287; translated in Stuart Schram, "New texts by Mao Zedong, 1921–1966," *Communist Affairs*, 2.2 (1983), 161.

228 The resolution of 20 October 1960 is translated in J. Chester Cheng, ed., *The politics of the Chinese Red Army; a translation of the Bulletin of activities of the People's Liberation Army*, 66–94. The passage corresponding to the preface to the *Quotations* appears on p. 70; on p. 33 of the same volume, it is noted that the resolution has been revised "by Chairman Mao himself."

tory in 1919; and yet, on the other hand, the policies of 1966 and after involved downgrading sharply the role of this very educated elite. Part of the explanation is to be found in the undisciplined and self-indulgent behavior of the Red Guards, for which Mao castigated them in the summer of 1968, before sending them to the countryside, beginning in December 1968, to learn "proletarian class consciousness" from the peasants. But this paradox also reflects a deeper ambiguity, in Mao's thinking and policies, regarding the role in building socialism of expertise, and of the highly trained people who are the bearers of expertise.

Theoretically, all these contradictions should have been subsumed in a larger unity under the slogan "Red *and* expert." In fact, the emphasis was shifted so far, in the aftermath of the Cultural Revolution, in the direction of politics as a substitute for, rather than as a complement to, knowledge and skills, that the whole foundation for the enterprise of modernization to which, as we have seen, Mao was committed, was substantially undermined.

The fountainhead for many of these excesses was Mao's directive of 21 July 1968, which reads as follows:

It is still necessary to have universities; here I refer mainly to the need for colleges of science and engineering. However, it is essential to shorten the length of schooling, revolutionize education, put proletarian politics in command and take the road of the Shanghai Machine Tools Plant in training technicians from among the workers. Students should be selected from among workers and peasants with practical experience and they should return to practical work in production after a few years' study.[229]

Mao commented on this text, or perhaps on the talk from which it is drawn, in his conversation of 28 July 1968 with Red Guard leaders. On this occasion, he showed himself less exclusively concerned with technical knowledge for practical purposes, but in some respects even more skeptical about the value of formal education. "Should we continue to run universities?" he asked. "Should universities continue to enrol new students? To stop enrolling new students won't do either. You should make some allowances for [the context of] that talk of mine. I spoke of colleges of science and engineering, but I by no means said that all liberal arts colleges should be closed." Mao then went on, however, to say that if liberal arts colleges were unable to show any accomplishments, they should be overturned. In any case, he argued, courses in senior middle schools merely repeated those in junior middle schools, and those in

229 Schram, *Political thought*, 371. For the example of the Shanghai Machine Tools Plant, see *PR*, 1968.37, 13–17.

universities repeated those in senior middle schools. The best method, he held, was independent study in a library, as practiced by Engels, and by Mao himself in his youth, or setting up a "self-study university" (as Mao had done in 1921). "The real universities are the factories and the rural areas," he concluded.[230]

Some account must be taken, in interpreting these remarks, of the fact that Mao had at the same time a very stern and indeed harsh message to convey to his Red Guard interlocutors, namely that the party was over and the activities in which they had been indulging for the past two years would no longer be tolerated. In these circumstances, it was understandable that he should sweeten the pill by expressing agreement with them on some things. Thus he also went on to say that examinations were a waste of time. "All examinations should be abolished, absolutely abolished. Who examined Marx, Engels, Lenin and Stalin? Who examined Comrade Lin Piao? Who examined me? Comrade Hsieh Fu-chih, call all the students back to school."[231]

The students were indeed to be called back to school, and though the academic discipline of examinations was (for the moment at least) to be abolished, social discipline was to be forcefully restored. Explaining to the Red Guard leaders why he was obliged to put a stop to the bloody internecine conflicts that had already claimed thousands of victims, Mao declared:

The masses just don't like civil wars.... For two years, you have been engaged in the Great Cultural Revolution, that is, in struggle-criticism-transformation, but at present you are neither struggling nor criticizing nor transforming. It's true that you are struggling, but it is armed struggle. The people are unhappy, the workers are unhappy, the peasants are unhappy, Peking residents are unhappy, the students in most schools are unhappy.... Can you unite the realm in this way?

"If you are unable [to handle the problem]," he warned, "we may resort to military control, and ask Lin Piao to take command."[232] That was, of course, exactly what Mao did do, but whatever the Soviets or leftists of various persuasions may think, military dictatorship was not his ideal. He "resorted to military control" because there was no other instrument, apart from the People's Liberation Army, capable of putting down factional fighting conducted not merely with bricks and slingshots, but with rifles and even with mortars and other heavy weapons. As soon as circumstances appeared to permit it once again, he undertook to reestablish the primacy of the Party over the "gun." Justifying this step in

230 *Wan-sui* (1969), 693, 706, 695; *Miscellany*, 475, 488, 471.
231 *Wan-sui* (1969), 714; *Miscellany*, 496.   232 *Wan-sui* (1969), 698, 688; *Miscellany*, 481, 470.

his talks of August–September 1971 with military commanders, he suggested that the PLA was not the best instrument for exercising leadership in complex political and economic matters. "I approve of the army's traditional style of quick and decisive action," he said. "But this style cannot be applied to questions of ideology, for which it is necessary to make the facts known and reason with people." The main thrust of these talks was, in fact, the reestablishment of unified Party leadership, and the subordination of the army to the Party. "Now that the regional Party committees have been established," said Mao, "they should exercise unified leadership. It would be putting the cart before the horse if matters already decided by regional Party committees were later turned over to Army Party committees for discussion."[233]

The Ninth Congress of the Chinese Communist Party in April 1969 was presented at the time, and was widely seen outside China as marking the conclusion of the Cultural Revolution. In retrospect, and despite the symbolic significance of the formal disgrace of Liu Shao-ch'i on this occasion, the overarching continuity of events from 1966 to 1976 was such that it is probably more accurate to speak, as the Chinese have done since the Third Plenum of 1978, of the "Cultural Revolution decade." Nonetheless, the phase inaugurated by the Ninth Congress did see the emergence of significant new themes and formulations in the thought of Mao Tse-tung.

Marx and Ch'in Shih-huang-ti: the ambiguous legacy

Thus far, the term "Cultural Revolution" has served as a convenient label for the period beginning in 1966, without further inquiry into its meaning. Before proceeding in the analysis of the ideological content of the so-called Great Proletarian Cultural Revolution, as it continued to unfold after 1969, let us consider the appropriateness of the expression.

Leaving aside the adjective "great," the force of which is purely rhetorical or emphatic, was it "proletarian"? Was it "cultural"? Was it a revolution? Plainly Mao believed it to be all three of these things. To my mind, it was in truth none of them. The question of why Mao thought it *was* is, however, central to any understanding of his thought during his last decade.

In reality Mao's reasons for attributing to the movement he launched in 1966 each of these three qualities overlap to such a significant extent that they stand or fall together. In other words, either it was proletarian,

233 Schram, *Mao unrehearsed*, 296.

cultural, and revolutionary, or it cannot appropriately be characterized by any of these terms.

If we consider the three attributes in the order in which they are commonly placed, "proletarian" might signify, to begin with, "related to the urban working class." In that sense, the upheaval of 1966 was assuredly not proletarian. As indicated in the next chapter, the shock troops of the movement, during its first and formative stage, were students rather than workers. And though so-called revolutionary rebels among the workers subsequently played a significant role in political events, their intervention scarcely reflected the qualities of discipline, and of orientation toward technological modernization that Marx attributed to the urban proletariat.

The Cultural Revolution might, in a slightly looser sense, be legitimately called "proletarian" if it contributed to industrial development, and thereby to expanding the working class, and laying the material foundations for a society dominated by the proletariat. That was assuredly not the case, either. In December 1968, when Mao issued his directive ordering educated young people to go to the countryside to be reeducated by the poor and lower-middle peasants, this was interpreted to signify that the sons and daughters of urban workers would receive "a profound class education" from the poor peasants in the countryside.[234] And although, as has already been stressed repeatedly, Mao never ceased to call for rapid economic development, arguing even that the policies of the Cultural Revolution would produce economic and technical miracles, he showed increasing anxiety about the consequences of economic development.

In August 1958 at Peitaiho, he had called for the revival of the spiritual heritage of Yenan, but nevertheless, at that time the emphasis was overwhelmingly on economic goals. In April 1969, on the other hand, at the First Plenum of the new Ninth Central Committee, he spoke with nostalgia of the very high proportion of comrades killed during the struggle for power, and went on to say:

For years we did not have any such thing as salaries. We had no eight-tier wage system. We had only a fixed amount of food, three mace of oil and five of salt. If we got 1½ catties of millet, that was great.... Now we have entered the cities. This is a good thing. If we hadn't entered the cities Chiang Kai-shek would be occupying them. But it is also a bad thing because it caused our Party to deteriorate.[235]

234 PR, 1968.52, 6–7.   235 Schram, *Mao unrehearsed*, 288.

Although Mao concludes that it was, after all, right to enter the cities, his sentiments toward the consequences of modernization and economic development were, thus, profoundly ambiguous.

If the Cultural Revolution did not reflect either the role or the ideals of the urban working class, there remains only one sense in which it might qualify as proletarian: by its conformity to "proletarian" ideology as defined by Mao. We have already noted the threefold framework in which Mao Tse-tung had begun to view classes in the late 1950s and early 1960s. During the Cultural Revolution, while objective class origins were never regarded as *irrelevant*, high and generally decisive importance was attributed to subjective factors as the main criterion of class nature.

Lenin, for his part, had written in an orthodox Marxist vein, "The fundamental criterion by which classes are distinguished is the place they occupy in social production." In November 1966, Mao's evil genius, K'ang Sheng, said that Lenin's definition had proved inadequate, for class differentiation also fell under political and ideological categories, and in 1970 K'ang stated more precisely: "The existence of the capitalist class is particularly manifest in relations of economic exploitation. In socialist society, although there are economic contradictions among the various classes, the existence of classes shows itself ideologically and politically."[236]

Leaving aside for the moment the question of just where and how the existence of classes in this sense "showed itself" in China at this period, it is evident that to define class in ideological terms brings, in effect, the matter of the "proletarian" character of the movement launched by Mao in 1966 into the cultural domain. In other words, this "revolution" was proletarian only to the extent that it was also cultural.

The notion, propagated at the time by some naive observers, that the events of 1966 constituted a "cultural revolution" in the same sense as the May Fourth Movement, and indeed as the legitimate continuation of the May Fourth Movement, was altogether absurd. A bitter joke current in China in the years after Mao's death, *Wen-hua ko-ming shih ko wen-hua ti ming* ("The Cultural Revolution was about doing away with culture"), is nearer the mark. This upheaval did grow, nonetheless, as we have seen, out of Mao's reaction to certain cultural phenomena, and from beginning to end it was marked by an overwhelming stress on cultural and psychological transformation.

To mention only a few manifestations of this tendency, which clearly

236 Mao, *SW*, 18–19.

reflects Mao's long-standing conviction that by changing people's attitudes through indoctrination or thought reform, one can change their objective nature, there was the emphasis on a "great revolution which touches people to their very souls." That is to say, the Cultural Revolution was to constitute a process of subjective transformation leading to a new political identity. There was also the whole range of ideas and policies summed up by the slogan "Fight self, oppose revisionism," with the implication that "bourgeois" tendencies were to be found even in the hearts of veteran revolutionaries and proletarian fighters, if not in that of the Chairman himself.

Finally, however violent the resulting struggles, and however frenzied the enthusiasm they unleashed, can these events be called a revolution? Broadly speaking, there are two commonly accepted meanings for the word "revolution"; it may refer either to the conquest of power by a different class, social category, or political faction, or to the use that is made of power, once attained, to transform society. Theoretically, China had, in Mao's view, been carrying out socialist revolution in this second sense since 1949, and especially since 1955. As I have already noted, however, the concrete economic dimension of "building socialism" did not figure very extensively in Mao's scheme of things during his last decade. The transformation of attitudes is, of course, a form of social transformation, but even this came, in the end, to play a relatively limited role. The dominant concern was rather with the "seizure of power" from the "bourgeoisie."

Such an enterprise was possible in a country that had been ruled for seventeen years by a "dictatorship of the proletariat" only thanks to the redefinition of the class enemy from whom power was to be seized as the "bourgeois elements" and "capitalist roaders" in the Party – that is, all those who had ventured to disagree with Mao Tse-tung about anything from material incentives to literature and philosophy. So in the last analysis, the Cultural Revolution was a "revolution" only by virtue of an ideological and cultural definition of its target and goal.

Ironically, the Cultural Revolution, which had opened with manifestos in favor of the Paris Commune model of mass democracy, closed with paeans of praise to that most implacable of centralizing despots, the first Ch'in emperor. This decade saw the rise and fall of Lin Piao and of the influence of the PLA; the fall, rise, and renewed partial eclipse of the Party, in favor of the "Legalist leading group around the emperor (or around the empress)."[237]

---

237 Liang Hsiao, "Yen-chiu Ju-Fa tou-cheng ti li-shih ching-yen" (Study the historical experience of the struggle between the Confucian and Legalist schools), *HC*, 1974.10, 60; *PR*, 1975.2, 11.

Apart from Lin Piao's probable reluctance to accept the renewed subordination of the army to the Party, the reasons for his fall are of little interest here. This affair, though it throws light on the functioning of the Chinese political system, is scarcely relevant to the analysis of Mao Tse-tung's thought. The "Campaign to criticize Lin Piao and Confucius," on the other hand, is not merely a fascinating puzzle for Pekingologists; it also had significant theoretical implications.

One crucial aspect of the campaign in this respect was the veritable cult of Ch'in Shih-huang-ti that developed in 1973–74. It is only an apparent paradox that the "Shanghai radicals" should have propagated such an ideal of centralized rule by an autocratic leader, for anarchy and despotism are two maladies of the body politic which engender one another.

In the Great Leap period, as we have seen, Mao had not hesitated to praise Ch'in Shih-huang-ti and to evoke him as a precursor. But this does not necessarily mean that he took, then or later, the same view of the historical significance of the Ch'in unification of the empire as did the ideologists of 1973–75. At that time, Chairman Mao was said to have expounded, in his speech of 1958, quoted earlier, "the progressive role of revolutionary violence, and exposed the reactionary essence of attacks on Ch'in Shih-huang as attacks on revolutionary violence and the dictatorship of the proletariat."[238] The conclusion, which is never stated outright, but is clearly implicit in materials of the mid-1970s, is that the Ch'in Shih-huang-ti analogy should, as it were, be turned inside out. Lin Piao had criticized Mao as a despot; right-minded people should, on the contrary, see Ch'in Shih-huang-ti as a revolutionary leader and the Ch'in autocracy as a kind of protoproletarian dictatorship.

The analogy obviously requires that there should have been a change in the "mode of production," that is, in the ruling class, and not merely a change in the organization of the state, with the founding of the dynasty. The transition from slaveholding society to feudalism, which Mao himself had earlier placed (in the original version of "The Chinese revolution and the Chinese Communist Party") in the eleventh century B.C., was therefore brought forward to the fifth, or even the third, century B.C. Conceivably, Mao might have changed his mind on this point since 1939, and in any case the views put forward in 1972–74 had long been held by some Chinese historians. It is quite another matter to suggest, however, even if there *was* a change in the ruling class at the end of the third century B.C., that the "new rising landlord class" was consciously reshaping Chinese society, taking Legalist ideology as its guide, in the same sense that the

238 Chin Chih-pai, "P'i-K'ung yü lu-hsien tou-cheng" (Criticism of Confucius and two-line struggle), HC, 1974.7, 32; PR, 1974.33, 11 (and note 2).

Communists, armed with Marxism-Leninism–Mao Tse-tung Thought, are doing so today. Such a view was totally un-Marxist, and historically absurd, and there is no evidence that Mao ever espoused it.

The only justification for this line of argument would appear to reside in a desire to demonstrate that China had revolutionary power, and revolutionary ideology, before anyone else. In other words, in putting forward the Ch'in Shih-huang-ti analogy, Yao Wen-yuan and the other theoreticians of the Gang of Four were, in reality, disciples of Lin Piao, baptizing "class struggle" an exceedingly old-fashioned Chinese view of politics as a succession of palace coups. Mao's position was subtler, and despite his pride in China's cultural heritage, less narrowly nationalistic.

Nevertheless, the mid-1960s had seen, as already stressed, a further unraveling of the polarity between Marxism and the Chinese tradition in Mao Tse-tung's thought, in the context of a general trend toward the dissociation of opposite insights held in creative tension.

As has already been suggested, it can be argued that the changes in Mao's philosophical outlook at this time resulted from the resurgence of Chinese influences in his thinking, and in particular from a drift toward a quasi-Taoist understanding of the relation between opposites in terms of ebb and flow, such that the direction of historical change was no longer built into the structure of the dialectical process. But Mao's pessimism about the prospects for revolution also grew out of his fear of "restoration" in China and the Soviet Union. It was because the pursuit of the more moderate course that he had himself worked out with Chou En-lai only a year or two earlier conjured up once more in his mind the specter of "revisionism" that Mao had endorsed, in 1973, the *P'i-Lin p'i-K'ung* campaign of which Chou was the real target. It was the same bugbear that led him to support wholeheartedly the "campaign to study the theory of the proletarian dictatorship" launched by Chang and Yao in the spring of 1975.[239]

Joseph Esherick draws a distinction between Lenin, who "always identified the primary threat of capitalist restoration with the spontaneous capitalist tendencies of the 'small-producer economy,'" and Mao, who saw the main danger of restoration in the emergence of a new class in the Party and state bureaucracy.[240] This approach leads him to put forward the idea of the new bourgeoisie as a potential hereditary ruling class in a socialist society that has taken the road of revisionism and "restoration." He calls attention to a striking passage in Mao's notes of 1960 on the Soviet textbook regarding the defects of the children of cadres:

239 Liao, "Li-shih ti ching-yen," 147; English in *Issues & Studies* (November 1981), 98.
240 Joseph W. Esherick, "On the 'restoration of capitalism': Mao and Marxist theory," *Modern China*, 5 (January 1979), 57-58, 71-72.

The children of our cadres are a source of great concern. They have no experience of life and no experience of society, but they put on very great airs, and have very great feelings of superiority. We must teach them not to rely on their parents, nor on revolutionary martyrs, but to rely entirely on themselves.[241]

Recalling Mao's disparaging comments in the 1960s, to Snow and others, about the defects of China's youth, Esherick argues that, in Mao's view, these sons and daughters of cadres might inherit the status and privileges of their parents, thus constituting a "vested interest group" that, by perpetuating itself over several generations, would transform itself into a class.[242]

The difficulty with this argument is that it fails to provide any serious analysis of the relation between such a bureaucratic stratum and the rest of society, or any real justification for calling it a class. I do not mean to suggest that an argument cannot be made for focusing on control rather than ownership of the means of production, and treating existing socialist systems as forms of "state capitalism," ruled by a "new class" or "new bourgeoisie" defined in this context. From Djilas to Bahro, a great many people have done just that during the past three decades. Moreover, on the basis of all the available evidence, it appears that Mao himself leaned in this direction in his later years. Not only did he accept K'ang Sheng's view that in a socialist society, classes manifested themselves "ideologically and politically" rather than in terms of relation to the means of production, but he actually did subscribe to the view, put forward in 1975-76, that in China the bourgeoisie was to be found primarily, or decisively, in the Party. Moreover, he accepted the logical conclusion from such a premise, namely, that these "new bourgeois elements" exploited the workers and peasants through the mechanism of the socialist system, that is, of the state apparatus.[243]

Even if we conclude, however, that Mao held such a view in the early 1970s, he did not produce a systematic argument to justify it – indeed, by that time he was probably incapable of doing so. Nor, in my opinion, have those Western scholars who have written on these issues done so on his behalf.[244]

On the problem of the relation between the old and the new bourgeoisie, Chang and Yao, while discussing at considerable length the sel-

241 *Wan-sui* (1969), 351.
242 Esherick, "On the 'restoration of capitalism,'" 66-68.
243 This statement regarding Mao's position during his last years corresponds to the view commonly expressed by responsible theoretical workers, at the Chinese Academy of Social Sciences and elsewhere, in conversations conducted in April and May 1982. See also Liao, "Li-shih ti ching-yen," 135-36; English in *Issues & Studies* (November 1981), 84-85.
244 The study by Richard Kraus, *Class conflict in Chinese socialism*, is a far more important contribution to the subject in general than Esherick's article. On many aspects of the problem of the relation

fish and corrupt behavior of privileged strata among the leading cadres, in terms derived from Mao, treat these "extremely isolated persons" rather as the tools of those remnants of the "overthrown reactionary classes" who desire the restoration of capitalism in the literal sense. If the role of "bourgeois right" and material incentives is not restricted, writes Yao Wen-yuan:

... capitalist ideas of making a fortune and craving for personal fame and gain will spread unchecked; phenomena like the turning of public property into private property, speculation, graft and corruption, theft and bribery will increase; the capitalist principle of the exchange of commodities will make its way into political and even into Party life, undermining the socialist planned economy; acts of capitalist exploitation such as the conversion of commodities and money into capital, and labour power into a commodity, will occur.... When the economic strength of the bourgeoisie has grown to a certain extent, its agents will demand political rule, demand the overthrow of the dictatorship of the proletariat and the socialist system, demand a complete changeover from socialist ownership, and openly restore and develop the capitalist system.[245]

This analysis is likewise ill worked out, and even more difficult to reconcile with reality than that in terms of a new bureaucratic elite controlling the means of production. Was the pre-1949 bourgeoisie really so powerful in China a quarter of a century after the revolution? Above all, how could the "new class elements" within the Party, who reveled in their power and perquisites under the existing order, willingly participate in the restoration of actual capitalism, involving the private ownership of the means of production? Surely they must have realized that, in such a system, they would be very poorly equipped to compete with the "real" capitalists of yore, and would soon lose their privileged position? And yet, both of the perspectives just evoked regarding the role of the "new class" in Chinese society build explicitly on tendencies apparent in Mao's own writings from the late 1950s onward.

To a large extent, Mao's primary concern was with the resurgence in China, after the revolution, of "bourgeois" attitudes such as attachment to money, pleasure, and privilege. Such deviations would, in his view, be encouraged by inequality of material rewards – hence his support, qualified or not, for the campaign of 1975 against "bourgeois right." But in the last analysis he was more concerned with the struggle to transform

between stratification based on class origins, and "class as political behavior," Kraus offers extremely subtle and illuminating analyses. I believe that he errs, however, as does Esherick, in arguing that in his later years, Mao defined class primarily in terms of the privileges, and the control of the means of production, derived by cadres from their relationship to the state.
245 Yao Wen-yuan, *On the social basis of the Lin Piao anti-Party clique*, 7–8.

"hearts" or "souls." If he focused his attention on "bourgeois elements" in the Party, this was partly because such people enjoyed more of the privileges likely to corrupt them, and more of the power and influence that would enable them to corrupt others.

At the same time, it should be stressed that in Mao's view, the source of corruption was not merely the rewards of power, but power itself. In one of the very last directives published in his lifetime, Mao was quoted in May 1976 as saying that revolutions would continue to break out in future because "junior officials, students, workers, peasants and soldiers do not like big shots oppressing them."[246] There is no way of verifying the authenticity of this text, but it sounds very much like the irrepressible Mao. Although he remained committed to the need for leadership, and for a strong state, he was plainly skeptical that anyone – except the emperor himself – could be trusted with power.

I have stressed repeatedly that the remarkable and extreme tendencies in Mao's thought and behavior during his last years were based, to a substantial extent, on his conclusions regarding the measures necessary to ensure the thoroughgoing and systematic realization of Marxist ideals or principles such as struggle against the class enemy, the reduction of the differences between town and countryside, and the creation of a more egalitarian society. But although such ideas of Western origin, however oddly interpreted, remained a significant component of his thought, there is no denying the increasingly large place occupied in Mao's mind, and in the Chinese political system, by Chinese and traditional influences.

Apart from the cult of Ch'in Shih-huang-ti discussed above, a notable manifestation of this trend was the stress on devotion to the Leader and his Thought, symbolized by the value of "loyalty" (*chung*). Not only were "proletarian revolutionaries" such as the Red Guards to learn by heart the "little red book," so they could repeat a suitable saying on every occasion and thereby demonstrate their mastery of Mao Tse-tung Thought. They were also to be "boundlessly loyal to Chairman Mao," and this quality above all others was the touchstone for distinguishing genuine from sham revolutionaries in the China of the late 1960s and the early 1970s.

In the *Tso-chuan*, under the ninth year of Duke Ch'eng, it is written: *Wu ssu, chung yeh*. Loosely translated, this can be taken to mean "He who is selfless is truly loyal [to the ruler]." The Chinese, in Mao's last years, read this equation both backward and forward. On the one hand, he who was genuinely selfless, who was willing to serve the people like Lei Feng as a "rustless screw," was a true and loyal disciple of Chairman Mao and a genuine proletarian revolutionary. But conversely, he who was loyal to Mao Tse-tung and Mao Tse-tung Thought became, by that very fact, selfless and proletarian, and endowed with all the other revolutionary virtues.[247] In this respect, as in the use of the parallel with Ch'in Shih-huang-ti, Mao truly moved, at the end of his life, from expressing Marxist ideas in a language accessible to the Chinese people to a somewhat eclectic position in which traditional values and ideas played an increasingly large part.

CONCLUSION: IN SEARCH OF MAO'S IDEOLOGICAL LEGACY

The term "Mao Tse-tung Thought," or "Mao Tse-tung's Thought," has at least three different meanings. First of all, it can be used to signify what Mao himself actually thought, in the course of his long life, as evidenced by contemporary sources for the writings of each period. Second, it may have the sense given to it in China from the 1950s until Mao's death (or, indeed, until the Third Plenum, in December 1978); that is, it may refer to the orthodox doctrine at any given time, as laid down in the post-1951 edition of the *Selected works* and in other speeches and writings openly published, including the extracts issued during the Cultural Revolution period as "supreme directives." Third, it can be used as the Chinese use it today, to designate that portion of the total corpus of Mao Tse-tung's writings still regarded as correct, complemented by works in which Chou En-lai, Liu Shao-ch'i, Chu Te, and others further developed some of Mao's ideas, but without those writings by Mao reflecting the "errors of his later years."

This chapter has continued the attempt begun in the closing chapter of Volume 13 of *The Cambridge History of China* to trace the development of Mao Tse-tung's thought, in the first sense, from 1917 to 1976. The present chapter has also dealt with the problem of changing patterns of orthodoxy grounded in Mao's writings, which did not exist for the period before 1949 because there was no official canon and no such orthodox interpretation of "Mao Tse-tung Thought." Now, the task remains of summing up the essence of Mao's theoretical contribution, but of doing so on a basis rather different from that currently adopted in China.

It is often suggested that the approach of the present leaders of China

247 For a discussion of the significance of *chung*, and more broadly of the nature of Mao's rule in his last days, see Schram, "Party leader or true ruler?" 223–25, 233–43.

to Mao Tse-tung Thought is altogether arbitrary, manipulative, and cynical – in other words, that they characterize as "correct" those ideas of Mao's which will serve to justify the policies they have laid down on a quite different basis. That seems to be far too simple a view. Apart from the need to adopt enough of Mao's ideological heritage to demonstrate that they are his legitimate successors, those engaged in defining and elaborating Mao Tse-tung Thought today are for the most part veterans of decades of revolutionary struggle under Mao's leadership, who cannot but have internalized and built into their own thinking many ideas and practices from the era of Mao Tse-tung. It is therefore not implausible to accept that the current attempt at a redefinition of Mao's Thought has the aim that is attributed to it, namely, to determine what portions of his heritage are correct, in the dual sense of being good Marxism, and of being adapted to China's needs.

Even if this is so, however, the goals, and therefore the logic and the criteria, of the ongoing Chinese reassessment are different from those of this chapter. Here, our concern is rather with what constitutes the essence of Mao's thinking about problems of socialist development, from 1949 to 1976.

In the past, this chapter's author referred to the substance of Mao Tse-tung's positive contribution to the theory of building socialism as "mainstream Maoism," and suggested that it could be found in the period 1955–65, and more precisely in the early 1960s.[248] In other words, "mainstream Maoism" was defined as the rational kernel of the "Chinese road to socialism" devised by Mao, minus the excesses of the Great Leap and the Cultural Revolution. On further reflection, this usage seems less than satisfactory. As argued, the progression from 1958 to 1966 was in many respects inexorable, and the leftist tide that carried everything before it in the course of both these radical experiments might well be regarded as more characteristic of Mao's last quarter century (if not of his life as a whole) than the relatively prudent and realistic position he adopted in the early 1960s, and again in the early 1970s.

"In all things, one divides into two," said Mao in March 1964. "I, too, am a case of one divides into two."[249] That is, perhaps, the first and most fundamental thing that must be said by way of conclusion. On the one hand, Mao's thought from beginning to end, and especially his thought of the 1950s and 1960s, was an uneasy juxtaposition of disparate ideas and imperatives. And second, the provisional and unstable synthesis he had

248 See in particular Stuart Schram, *Mao Zedong: a preliminary reassessment*, 71.
249 *Wan-sui* (1969), 477; *Miscellany*, 343. (Remarks at a briefing.)

managed to forge between these elements began to unravel and fly apart with the onset of the Cultural Revolution.

If we look at Mao's economic ideas during and after the Great Leap Forward as formulated at the time, we must recognize, in my opinion, that they are far less one-sided and simplistic than they have commonly been made out to be in recent years, in interpretations based on the Cultural Revolution reconstruction of the "struggle between two lines." We find him placing stress equally on moral *and* material incentives, on redness *and* expertise, and on large- and small-scale industry. The policy of "walking on two legs," which was in some respects the heart of his whole economic strategy, was a policy of walking as fast as possible on both legs, and not of hopping along on the leg of small-scale indigenous methods alone.

And yet, there are aspects of Mao Tse-tung's approach to development, even after he had retreated from the extravagant illusions of the summer of 1958, that reflect a fundamental ambiguity toward the implications of industrialization and technical progress. One of these, to which I devoted considerable attention earlier, was his attitude toward the intellectuals. Another was his conception of the political process, and of the relation between the leaders and the masses.

In 1960, discussing the Soviet Constitution, Mao Tse-tung said that this constitution gave the workers the right to work, to rest, and to education, but that it gave the people no right to supervise (*cheng-li*) the state, the economy, culture or education, whereas these were the most basic rights of the people under socialism.[250] A parallel passage in the "Reading notes" uses the term *kuan-li*, instead of *cheng-li*.[251] Although there is a significant nuance between these two expressions, both are relatively ambiguous, and their ambiguity reflects, once again, the contradictions we have already noted in Mao's theory and practice of the "mass line." *Kuan-li*, the term that appears in Mao's own words as reproduced by the Red Guards, may mean "manage," "run," "administer," or "supervise"; *cheng-li*, employed by Liao Kai-lung in his paraphrase, signifies "put in order," "straighten out," or "arrange." The first is obviously more concrete, evoking an organizational context rather than simply a process. Both are equally vague as to whether the workers, or toilers (*lao-tung che*) are intended by Mao essentially to keep track of what is going on, and to make sure that political authority is exercised in accordance with their wishes, or whether he means they should actually *run* things themselves.

250 Liao, "Ch'üan-mien chien-she she-hui-chu-i ti tao-lu," 2.
251 *Wan-sui* (1969), 342–43.

One of the English translations of Mao's "Reading notes" has "run" and "manage" for *kuan-li*; the other has "administer" and "take charge."[252] I have preferred "supervise," which does not imply that the workers, collectively, are all actually taking charge to the same degree, because such a reading corresponds better to Mao's thought in 1960 as I understand it. This choice is, admittedly, arbitrary, but no more so than that of the other translators. The ambiguity is in fact there, in Mao's own language, and in his thought.

Another case in point is the passage of 1965 asserting that democracy means "dealing with the affairs of the masses through the masses themselves" (*ch'ün-chung ti shih-ch'ing yu ch'ün-chung lai kuan-li*).[253] For the character *yu* can mean either *by* the masses, in the sense that they are the effective agents, or *through* the masses, in other words, to mean that the matter is laid before them and they are consulted. Here, it is translated as "through" because the clear statement, in the same text of December 1965, about the need for Party leadership from above confirms that, at the time, Mao still held to the view, which he had clearly and repeatedly stated, that centralism was even more important than democracy. And yet by 1965 his approach to these matters was clearly beginning to shift.

During the period before and after the Great Leap, the emphasis on centralism took the form of an insistence on the crucial and decisive role of Party leadership. As noted in the first section of this chapter, Mao revived the concept of *i-yuan-hua*, or integrated Party control, which had been so much stressed in Yenan.

Generally speaking, Mao's view during the Great Leap period was that integration or *i-yuan-hua* had to be carried out not merely at the national level, but in the localities. Otherwise, even the "small power" referred to in the 1953 jingle could not be dispersed without leading to confusion. And the agent of integration could only be the Party committee at each level. Party control, whether at the center or in the localities, involved, as Mao made clear in 1958, first taking decisions on matters of principle, and then subsequently checking on their implementation.

With the approach of the Cultural Revolution, this whole philosophy was undermined because Mao Tse-tung called into question in theory, and then denied in practice, the legitimacy and political rectitude of the Party that was supposed to exercise the function of "integration." One of the first and most dramatic hints of what was to come is to be found in the famous passage from the Ninth Reply to the Soviets, dated 14 July

252 Mao Tse-tung, *A critique of Soviet economics*, tr. Moss Roberts, 61; *Miscellany*, 266.
253 *Wan-sui* (1969), 630.

1964, stating that if cadres were to be "corrupted, divided, and demoral-ized" by the class enemy (made up of "the landlords, rich peasants, coun-ter-revolutionaries, bad elements and monsters of all kinds"), then "it would not take long ... before a counter-revolutionary restoration on a national scale inevitably occurred, the Marxist-Leninist party would undoubtedly become a revisionist party or a fascist party, and the whole of China would change its colour."[254]

Although Mao reasserted, in his conversations of February 1967 with Chang and Yao, that there had to be a Party as a leading nucleus, and although he continued to strive to combine in some fashion the need for leadership with the anti-elitism and the encouragement of initiative from below that had constituted the justification (if not the principal motive) for the Cultural Revolution, this whole enterprise was distorted and vitiated by the fact that the right of the masses to "rebel" against the Party hierarchy and state bureaucracy was guaranteed only by a figure exercising personal authority of a kind that soon came to be officially likened to that of the first Ch'in emperor.

It is in this light that one must interpret the calls by Wang Hung-wen at the Tenth Party Congress[255] and by Chang Ch'un-ch'iao at the Nation-al People's Congress in January 1975[256] for the "integrated [i-yuan-hua] leadership" of the Party over the state structure, and over everything else. For by this time, neither Chang, nor indeed Mao himself, were so much interested in the relation between organizations as in imposing Mao Tse-tung's personal authority. Henceforth, truth and authority resided not in the Party, but in Chairman Mao, the leader invested by history with the mission of educating the Chinese people and guiding them toward communism.

Throughout his career, from the Ching-kang-shan and Yenan to the 1960s, Mao Tse-tung treated democracy and centralism as two indisso-lubly linked aspects of the political process, one of which could not be promoted without reference to the other. The Cultural Revolution saw the emergence of two quite different concepts. Democracy was replaced by "rebellion"; centralism was replaced by chung, or personal loyalty to the great leader and helmsman. No doubt Mao Tse-tung saw these tendencies as bound together in a dialectical unity, like democracy and centralism, which he had not in principle repudiated. Nevertheless, he allowed a situation to develop in which the "heads," of which he himself acknowledged the necessity, at all levels of society and the economy,

254 HC, 1964.13, 31–32; PR, 1964. 29, 26. (Originally from a note by Mao on a document of 9 May 1963 regarding cadre participation in productive labor in Chekiang.)
255 HC, 1973.9, 22, 27; PR, 1973.35–36, 25, 28.   256 HC, 1975.2, 17; PR, 1975.4, 19.

could not in fact function as heads, because although they were held accountable, they had no power to make decisions. The alliance between the leader and the masses took the form, on the national level, of an unstructured plebiscitary democracy, sadly reminiscent of earlier examples. At lower levels, it produced a mixture of arbitrary rule by ad hoc committees, military control, apathy, and confusion.

The roots of these last developments go back to the 1960s, and in particular to Mao's repeated statements, beginning in 1963, asserting the axiom "One divides into two." For it is only if the Party is in reality symbolized by and incarnated in one man that the two principles of *i-yuan-hua* or "making monolithic," and *i fen wei erh*, or the divisibility of all things (and the propensity of their components to struggle with one another) can coexist. In other words, the Communist Party could split, and yet remain one, capable of carrying out its mission of integration, only if its oneness and integrity were the emanation of Chairman Mao, who (despite his remark quoted earlier) did not split, but remained permanently in charge, even though his thoughts teemed with contradictions.

Another duality central to the interpretation of Mao's thought was, as I have stressed throughout this account, that between Marxism and the Chinese heritage. The fact that, in Mao's later years, the leader had come to be the focus of loyalty and the fount of truth is not in harmony with Marxist theory, or indeed with Mao's own reminder, in 1971, of the words of the "Internationale" denying the existence of "supreme saviours."[257] This does not, in itself, make of his rule a species of oriental despotism, nor does it even signify that the ideology to which he lent his name was primarily Chinese rather than Western. There were, after all, sufficient Western or Westernizing sources for the cult of the leader – including Stalin's red fascism, as well as the original doctrines of Hitler and Mussolini. Moreover, in the complex process of acculturation, if new Western ideas can be made to serve old Chinese goals and values, Chinese forms can also be turned to purposes defined by foreign doctrines.[258] The final balance is therefore not easy to draw up, but the problem merits a few final reflections.

Between the mid-1950s and the mid-1960s, Mao Tse-tung moved from the rejection to the acceptance of Chang Chih-tung's principle "Chinese learning as the substance, Western learning for practical application." In his "Talk to music workers" of August 1956, he adopted the relatively balanced view he had expounded since 1938, namely that China must

257 Schram, *Mao unrehearsed*, 297.
258 On this theme, see Schram, "Party leader or true ruler?"

learn many things from the West, while remaining herself. Marxism, he declared, was a "general truth which has universal application." This "fundamental theory produced in the West" constituted the foundation, or *t'i*, of China's new regime, although it must be combined with the concrete practice of each nation's revolution.[259] In December 1965, at Hangchow, on the other hand, he said in effect that Chang Chih-tung was right: "We cannot adopt Western learning as the substance.... We can only use Western technology."[260]

Even though Mao declared in the same speech, as noted earlier, that he was a "native philosopher," such remarks should not be understood to mean that Mao no longer proposed to take anything from Marxism, or from the West. They were rather an emphatic way of saying that China's revolutionary doctrine today must be rooted in her culture, and in her past, if borrowings from the West were to be put to good use. The problem is not, however, one that can fruitfully be approached in purely intellectual terms, through the dissection of Mao's theoretical formulations. Deep-rooted feelings also come into it, and color even his political or ideological statements.

In March 1958 at Chengtu, Mao declared: "First classes wither away, and then afterward the state withers away, and then after that nations [*min-tsu*] wither away, it is like this in the whole world."[261] Talking to Edgar Snow on 18 December 1970, Mao put the matter as follows:

What is a nation [*min-tsu*]? It includes two groups of people [*liang pu-fen jen*], one group consists of the upper strata, the exploiting classes, a minority. These people know how to speak [effectively], and to organize a government, but they don't know how to fight, or to till the land, or to work in a factory. More than 90 per cent of the people are workers, peasants, and petty bourgeoisie; without these people, it is impossible to constitute a nation [*tsu-ch'eng min-tsu*].[262]

Mao's remarks of 1970 illustrate once again his tendency, in his later years, to see class struggle as a conflict between a small group of "big shots" and the people as a whole. But they also underscore, as does his comment of 1958, the fundamental importance he attached to the nation as a primary form of social organization.

Although Mao quite unquestionably always regarded China as the "central place," and Chinese culture as the "central flower" (*chung-hua*), we should by no means draw from this trait the conclusion, commonly put forward by the Soviets and their supporters, as well as by Trotskyites

---

259 Schram, *Mao unrehearsed*, 85-86.   260 Ibid., 234-35.

261 *Mao Chu-hsi kuan-yü kuo-nei min-tsu wen-t'i* ..., 8.

262 Ibid., 6-7. (This quote is from the official Chinese record of the talks; to my knowledge, Snow never made use of this passage in his own writings.)

and other leftists of various persuasions, that Mao was, after all, nothing but an old-fashioned Chinese nationalist with very little of the Marxist about him.

The fact remains that, during the Cultural Revolution decade especially, the synthesis toward which Mao had been bending his efforts for many decades largely fell apart, at least as regarded his own ideas and attitudes. Moral and political criteria drawn from the *Tso-chuan* and similar sources thus loomed very large in 1976, when Mao, as he put it to Edgar Snow, "saw God," or "saw Marx" (or perhaps both of them), and a new era opened under his successors.

If we look, however, not at these last sad, anticlimactic years but at the soberer elements in Mao's Thought, from 1935 to 1965, it seems to constitute, in the last analysis, rather a revolutionary ideology of Western origin, and a vehicle of Westernization.

No doubt, the crucial link between this Westernizing thrust and Mao Tse-tung's indisputable Sino-centrism is provided by his view regarding what has been called the "dialectics of backwardness." In his "Reading notes" of 1960, one of the quintessential expositions of "mainstream Maoism," Mao devoted a section to the topic "Is revolution in backward countries more difficult?" Needless to say, he concluded that it was not. The poisons of the bourgeoisie were, he said, extremely virulent in the advanced countries of the West, after two or three centuries of capitalism, and affected every stratum of society, including the working class. Lenin's dictum " The more backward the country, the more difficult its transition from capitalism to socialism" was therefore incorrect:

In reality, the more backward the economy, the easier, and not the more difficult, the transition from capitalism to socialism. The poorer people are, the more they want revolution.... In the East, countries such as Russia and China were originally backward and poor. Now not only are their social systems far more advanced than those of the West, but the rate of development of the productive forces is far more rapid. If you look at the history of the development of the various capitalist countries, it is again the backward which have overtaken the advanced. For example, the United States surpassed Britain at the end of the 19th century, and Germany also surpassed Britain in the early 20th century.[263]

This extravagantly optimistic vision has, of course, today been repudiated in China, and emphasis has been placed, rather, on the need to develop the productive forces as a precondition to the transformation of the social system. Mao's view, expressed in the passage just quoted, that in the West (and, by implication, in China, once the economy has been

263 *Wan-sui* (1969), 333–34; *Miscellany*, 258–59.

developed) "the important question is the transformation of the people" (*jen-min ti kai-tsao*) has not, however, been similarly abandoned.

Perhaps, in the end, this vision of China's place in the world and this emphasis on the human and moral dimension of politics will remain among Mao Tse-tung's main contributions to the theory and practice of revolution, because these insights are grounded in a long historical perspective.

CHAPTER 8

A NEW RELATIONSHIP BETWEEN
THE INTELLECTUALS AND THE STATE
IN THE POST-MAO PERIOD

During the Mao Zedong era (1949–76), a number of Western scholars characterized the events of that era as moving from one orthodoxy to another – from the neo-Confucianism of the Qing dynasty to the Marxism-Leninism-Maoism of the People's Republic of China. Describing the intervening period from the fall of the Qing in 1911 through the weak Leninist party-state and watered-down Confucianism of the Republican era (1928–49) as one of cultural and intellectual pluralism, they called these early decades of the twentieth century "an interregnum" between two orthodoxies.[1]

When Deng Xiaoping came to power in 1978 and established a milder form of authoritarianism than the totalitarianism of his predecessor Mao, a number of Western scholars again revised their views of twentieth-century Chinese history. As Deng and his associates loosened the state's economic hold on the economy and relaxed the controls over the intellectuals as well as over people's personal lives, they pointed out that the 1949 divide of the Chinese Communist revolution was not as sharp and as singular a break in modern Chinese history as had been presented. They suggested that the Mao era should be seen as part of an ongoing effort to build a strong Chinese state and modern economy inspired by nationalist pride that had inspired reformers since the late Qing.[2]

Such a characterization may be appropriate for the economic and political spheres, but only in the early years of the Mao era. Beginning with the anti-rightist campaign (1957–59) against 750,000 of China's best and brightest through the Great Leap Forward (1958–60), and then the Cultural Revolution (1966–76), Mao's utopian policies undermined that strong state and modern economy. Furthermore, the blurring of the 1949 divide was not at all appropriate in the intellectual and cultural spheres. Even before 1949, the Chinese Communist Party carried out campaigns in

---

[1] Cyril Birch, "Change and Continuity in Chinese Fiction," in *Modern Chinese Literature in the May Fourth Era,* Merle Goldman, ed. (Cambridge: Harvard University Press, 1977), pp. 385–404.
[2] Conference on "China's Mid-Century Transitions," at the Fairbank Center, Harvard University, Cambridge, September 9–10, 1994.

Yan'an in 1942–44 and in the Northeast in 1948, in which Mao and his colleagues purged intellectual dissenters and sought to indoctrinate intellectuals in the Maoist principle, enunciated in his Talks on Literature and Art in 1942, that all intellectual and creative activity must be conducted under the party's direction.

Consequently, almost immediately after the party took power in Beijing in 1949, party leaders created a party-state with more control over the intellectuals than that of any dynastic ruler, including China's most despotic First Emperor of the Qin dynasty (221–209 B.C.), who supposedly burned the books and buried Confucian scholars alive. Almost immediately after 1949, the relative intellectual autonomy and cultural pluralism that existed in the first half of the century ended abruptly with the imposition of Mao's interpretation of Marxism-Leninism onto intellectual thought and creative arts. All intellectuals were forced into party-controlled professional organizations and subjected to repeated and intensifying campaigns to remold their thinking and actions in criticism and self-criticism sessions in which any individual or dissident ideas were purged.

The more pluralistic intellectual and cultural environment of the twentieth century's early decades returned in the post-Mao era. Even before the Deng Xiaoping regime formally came to power at the Third Plenum of the Eleventh Central Committee in December 1978, some controls had been lifted and others were relaxed over intellectual activity. With Deng's permission, his supposed successor and younger disciple, Hu Yaobang, rehabilitated virtually all intellectuals as well as party officials imprisoned or sent away to do labor reform since the Yan'an days. As these intellectuals came back, some to high positions in the political and cultural hierarchy, there was a revival of some of the ideas that had excited their May Fourth predecessors in the earlier decades, an indication that these ideas had not been totally suppressed despite Mao's repeated campaigns against them. These ideas ranged from individualism to Western Marxism, from Nietzche to Freud, and from existentialism to Christianity. The intellectuals were also able to renew contacts with Western colleagues and friends from whom they had been cut off for almost 30 years. As earlier in the century, China's intellectuals indiscriminately latched onto the newest Western intellectual fades, such as postmodernism and symbiotics, Toffler's concept of "the third wave" of postindustrialism, and humanistic Marxism sweeping Eastern Europe at the time.

As their May Fourth predecessors had rebelled against Confucianism and the traditional political structure, so too did a significant number of intellectuals challenge the ideology and political system in which they they had been indoctrinated since 1949. Their protest was impelled not only by their persecution and that of their families, colleagues, and friends during the Mao era, but also by their belief that the party's Leninist-Maoist policies had not improved the lot of society, but in fact had made it worse. Equally important, they became aware of the failings of the Soviet system, which China had emulated in the 1950s and the movement toward democracy throughout the world, especially among their East Asian ethnic and post-Confucian neighbors, in the last decades of the twentieth century. As the May Fourth period has been described as China's enlightenment, post-Mao China may also be viewed as a time of renewed enlightenment when China's intellectuals once again sought more intellectual and individual freedom.

With some important exceptions, particularly the June 4, 1989, military crackdown on student demonstrators in Tiananmen Square and the persecution of their intellectual supporters in its aftermath, most intellectuals in the post-Mao era enjoyed a privileged status similar to that of the traditional literati and they pursued intellectual and cultural endeavors with relative freedom. In the 1980s, even on sensitive political issues – such as Chinese culture versus Western culture, authoritarianism versus democracy, and the rule of law versus the rule of man – there were wide-ranging debates without the imposition of an orthodox or official view. Relatively open discourse on politics as well as on culture took place in mainstream party newspapers, journals, academic forums, professional meetings, films, theater, and periodically on national television in the 1980s. Though the 1990s did not allow public debate on political issues, such discourse occurred privately among colleagues, at academic meetings, and briefly in 1997–1998 reappeared in the public media. At the same time, China's intellectual life became increasingly more diverse and pluralistic.

The party's withdrawal from most areas of life, except the political arena, opened up public spaces into which entered informal intellectual networks, literary salons, study groups, and in the 1980s semi-official think tanks and in the 1990s, hundreds of semi-official journals and newspapers. These spaces became channels through which various groups of intellectuals could influence officials and public policies. The political scientist Tang Tsou has called these public spaces "zones of indifference," in which intellectuals had a relative degree of freedom.[3] At the same time, however, these zones existed side by side with "forbidden zones" – any political challenge to the party or its leaders – into which intellectuals en-

---

[3] Tang Tsou, *The Cultural Revolution and Post-Mao Reforms* (Chicago: University of Chicago Press, 1986), pp. 3–66.

tered at their peril. Furthermore, these public spaces were not protected by laws, institutions, or a deeply rooted civil society.

Because of factional disputes in the top leadership between Deng's Long March colleagues, the revolutionary elders, and the slightly younger reform leaders, specifically Hu Yaobang and Zhao Ziyang in the 1980s, the Deng era, like that of his predecessor, Mao, oscillated between cycles of relative relaxation and relative repression. The elders wanted economic reforms without political reform; the reform leaders believed that some political reforms were necessary in order to sustain the economic reforms. Nevertheless, the cycles were the reverse of the Mao era. Since the reform leaders were more often in the ascendancy in the 1980s, the periods of relaxation, particularly toward the intellectuals, were far-reaching and longer in duration than the periods of repression, which had predominated in the Mao period. In the 1990s, despite the resurgence of Maoists and Maoist policies toward intellectuals in the aftermath of June Fourth, by the mid-1990s intellectuals were again treated with relative indifference as long as they stayed clear of political issues.

Still, attacks on political dissent continued in the post-Mao era and had some of the features of the Mao campaigns – a small number of intellectuals were singled out as scapegoats in the media and were chosen to represent the values the regime sought to repudiate. Nevertheless, because of the tragic legacy and fears of another Cultural Revolution, these attacks of the post-Mao era were without the fanaticism, mass mobilization, and indiscriminate terror of the Mao years. Moreover, they were limited to a very small number rather than expanding to the whole intellectual community as a class as happened under Mao. Sometimes they extended to one's family, but generally left one's colleagues, friends, and profession alone. Although the scapegoats were briefly silenced, with some important exceptions, they were generally not imprisoned, ostracized, subjected to personal disgrace, nor did they become nonpersons as happened under Mao. In addition, most of their colleagues refused to criticize them as they were forced to do under Mao and most did not participate in the attacks. In some cases, the regime allowed the targets of attack to go into exile abroad, following the methods used by Soviet leaders in the post-Stalin era.

Equally significant, most of those under attack refused to make a self-criticism or they made only a perfunctory one and shortly after the campaign ended, in the 1980s they resumed arguing even more vigorously for the very same ideas for which they had just been criticized. Because of the reluctance of Deng and his colleagues to use the harsh methods of the Mao era, which had brutalized even them, the intellectuals lost the fear that had incapacitated and silenced them during the Mao years. As a result, despite periodic attacks on a small number of intellectuals for dissident political ideas, most intellectuals were able to carry on their intellectual and creative work and some of them held important positions in the media, government, academia, and the professions. Those with technological, economic, and scientific skills in particular were able to rise high in the political hierarchy as advisers to the leadership or find lucrative jobs in the nonstate sector.

The fate of intellectuals outside the political–intellectual establishment was not so fortunate. Within the non-establishment group were ex Red Guards, who would have been intellectuals if not for the fact that Mao's Cultural Revolution had suspended their education. After the height of the Cultural Revolution frenzy in the late 1960s, Mao had dispersed the Red Guard youth to work in factories and to the countryside. There some continued their education on their own; others became disillusioned with Mao and joined those who rebelled against his policies during the April 5, 1976, demonstrations in Tiananmen Square supposedly against the "gang of four," but in reality against the Cultural Revolution and Mao's policies. After Mao's death in September 1976, as ex Red Guards returned to the cities, a small number were able to pass the competitive exams to get into the universities. Some of them and ex Red Guard colleagues who had become workers and participants in the April 5 movement became leaders in the Democracy Wall movement that exploded in Beijing and other cities in late 1978 and early 1979. In this movement, they used the methods they had learned in the Cultural Revolution to express their views against authority: to write wall posters, mimeograph and distribute pamphlets, form groups of like-minded people, make speeches, and engage in debates. Since their demands in the Democracy Wall movement – an end to Mao's destructive policies, dismissal of Maoists in the leadership, pragmatic economic policies, and political reform – initially coincided with Deng's policies at the time, Deng and his reform associates allowed the movement to continue until spring 1979 because it helped to consolidate Deng's hold on power. Even though some of the rehabilitated establishment intellectuals expressed similar demands for political reform as well as for economic reforms, most of them kept their distance from the Democracy Wall movement for fear that they would lose their newly acquired prestige and access to power by associating with ex Red Guard political activists.

Despite minimal contact between them, both establishment and non-establishment intellectuals had a similar view of their role. Like their literati predecessors, both groups saw themselves as the conduit through which the political leaders learned of the defects of their policies and heard the demands of the people. They both emphasized the need for political as well as economic reform in order to avoid another Cultural Revolution.

The establishment intellectuals, however, expressed their ideas less directly and in the mainstream media. Instead of protesting in the streets, writing wall posters, and mimeographing pamphlets, they used their high-level official contacts and published articles in the party newspapers and journals to convey their views. Moreover, as they had given their wholehearted support to the Mao regime in the early days of the People's Republic until they were purged, they similarly gave their full support to the Deng regime in the belief that the modern, humane government which they had been seeking would finally become a reality. They also expected to play a leading political role as their literati predecessors had done through most of Chinese history until the Mao period.

By contrast, a small number of the non-establishment intellectuals were less fully supportive and much more direct in stating their disillusionment with the Leninist political system. They expressed a broad range of views, but virtually all of them demanded political rights and called for China's observance of the UN Charter on Human Rights, echoing their Soviet and East European dissident colleagues. At one end of the Democracy Wall political spectrum was Wei Jingsheng, who directly denounced China's present leadership. His pamphlet, *Exploration (Tansuo)*, in March 1979, prophesized that Deng would turn into a dictator like Mao if the present political system continued.[4] Deng's anger at Wei's personal attack and the consolidation of his power led to Wei's arrest and sentencing to 15 years in prison. It also led to the beginning of the end of the Democracy Wall movement.

While the Democracy Wall political activists were suppressed, intellectuals associated with the party's chairman (general secretary did not come into being until 1982) Hu Yaobang continued to call for political reforms. Since most members of Hu's intellectual network were humanist intellectuals, versed in Marxism, they used ideological persuasion and argument to convince the leadership to reform and used the party media to publicize their views. In the late 1970s and early 1980s, they were especially attracted to Marxist humanism, as interpreted by East European theorists, and tried to make this ideology relevant to China's reforms. Because of the disillusionment with and increasing irrelevance of ideology in the aftermath of the Cultural Revolution, they had Hu's full support. He too sought to revive Marxism as a viable ideology. Another network of younger, more technocratically oriented intellectuals formed another network around Prime Minister Zhao

---

[4] Editorial, "Do we want democracy or new dictatorship?" *Tansuo (Exploration)*, special edition, March 25, 1979, 1–4; Joint Publications Research Service-PRC, no. 73421, May 10, 1979, p. 29.

Ziyang. They sought to learn about the newest Western economic thinking and advised Zhao on economic policies in the 1980s.[5]

In the late 1970s and early 1980s, there was a literary and artistic explosion of stories and art works critical of the violence, injustice, and suffering endured during Mao's rule, especially during the Cultural Revolution. Called the "literature of the wounded," the characters in these works were no longer the socialist realist heroes of the Mao era, but flawed characters, damaged by having been forced to be the victimizers or the victimized. Another new literary form was "misty poetry" *(menglong shi)*. It too diverged from the traditional and socialist realist genres in that it expressed intensely subjective views as a protest against the subordination of the individual to Mao's whims and party policies. Proponents of misty poetry claimed to be totally apolitical and focused on personal feelings and relationships, but in reality their conscious repudiation of politics and assertion of their individuality were political acts in a culture which hitherto had been totally politicized.

In fact, experimentation with styles and genres cut across all art forms as a protest against the imposed socialist realist style of the Mao years. Artists experimented with abstract modernist symbols and new materials. Writers used stream of consciousness and nonlinear time sequences. Some creative works looked back into China's past for inspiration; other works conveyed a sense of alienation from the Chinese present. Initially, most officials welcomed these new art forms because they were in accord with their own desire to expose and repudiate the excesses of the Cultural Revolution in which they too suffered. Although there was some official criticism of the unintelligiblity and inaccessibility of these works, specifically misty poetry, stylistic experimentation was allowed to continue relatively unimpeded.

A revival of Confucianism was another effort to close the wounds inflicted by Mao's class struggle and anti-intellectualism. Party leaders praised the Confucian emphasis on harmonious social relationships, stability, and education. A small number of academics and officials, some of them quite prominent, founded institutes, study societies, and journals devoted to the study of Confucianism. The majority of intellectuals, however, were disinterested in Confucianism and China's traditional values. Some questioned the very nature of Chinese civilization and asked whether such values had been responsible for making China, once the greatest, wealthiest country in the world, into one of the poorest and weakest. They echoed the May Fourth and Communist argument that Confucianism had been a cause

[5] See Joseph Fewsmith, *Dilemmas of Reform in China* (Armonk, NY: M.E. Sharpe, 1994).

of China's stagnation. Nevertheless, Confucianism continued to exert an inchoate influence on intellectuals in their sense of themselves as leaders of society, their feeling of responsibility to speak out against unjust officials, and their efforts to bring social grievances to the attention of the leadership.

The intellectuals also echoed the May Fourth view of science and democracy as the answer to China's present-day problems. While the humanist intellectuals emphasized democracy, the leadership emphasized science and technology as the key to China's modernization. Nevertheless, early on, almost a decade before competitive elections began in the villages, members of scientific institutes were allowed for the first time in the People's Republic to select their own leaders through competitive elections. This practice was encouraged not to promote democratization but to rid the scientific institutes of untutored, obstructive bureaucrats who had assumed leadership of these institutes in the Mao years. The effect of these procedures gradually reintroduced the pre-1949 scientific and professional standards and undermined political criteria for intellectual leadership in the sciences.

Although priority was given to science and technology, the social sciences were not neglected. Such disciplines as sociology, anthropology, political science, and law, which had faded away early in the Mao period, were revived in the belief that they too could help China modernize its economy. The Chinese Academy of the Social Sciences (CASS) was established as early as 1977 and in the 1980s became a think tank for the reform officials. At the same time, tens of thousands of intellectuals and students were sent abroad to study, primarily the sciences and to a lesser degree the nonsciences. Western academics, particularly scientists and economists, were invited to China to teach and advise on reforms. The interaction of China's intellectuals and students with their counterparts beyond their borders in the post-Mao era was on a greater scale than at any other time in Chinese history. Increasing contacts with peers, particularly in the West, further weakened party control, as professionals, intellectuals, and artists began to identify more with their international colleagues, their professions, and specific interests than with their Chinese colleagues and domestic concerns.

Beginning in the later half of the 1980s, well-known intellectuals for the first time in the People's Republic began withdrawing from party-run and government professional organizations to become freelance writers and artists or experts for hire. China's expanding market and internationalized economy made it possible for economists, engineers, scientists, lawyers, and linguists to free themselves from economic dependence on the state. Professionals were generally able to prevail over bureaucrats, primarily in scientific and technological organizations. While in the nonscientific professional organizations, some multicandidate elections were allowed, they continued to be supervised by party bureaucrats. Consequently, intellectuals involved in the sciences, technology, and economics had more freedom to pursue their interests than those involved in the humanities and the arts. Nevertheless, nonscientists and scientists alike enjoyed a degree of freedom in their work that they had not experienced since 1949.

CONFLICTS BETWEEN INTELLECTUALS
AND PARTY LEADERS IN THE 1980S

As intellectuals supported and acted as spokespersons for political leaders in factional and ideological battles in the premodern and Maoist periods, so too did they continue to do so in the Deng era, using some of the same methods. Deng and his disciple Hu Yaobang used Hu's intellectual network to repudiate Mao's ideas, practices, and allies. They launched a campaign-like discussion on "practice is the sole criterion of truth" in spring 1978 even before Deng formally came to power.[6] This campaign was to displace the "whatever faction" of Mao's anointed successor Hua Guofeng and the Maoists still in government. They were called the "whatever faction" because they insisted that whatever Mao said be followed. But as also happened in the past, the intellectuals often went beyond their leaders to make arguments with which their leaders did not necessarily agree. Therefore, once Deng had dispensed with Hua and the Maoists and consolidated his power, he sought to stop the campaign, but members of Hu's network refused to desist.

Despite the similarities in some of their arguments, members of Hu's intellectual network were relatively unaffected by the crackdown on the Democracy Wall activists. Nevertheless, a breach occurred in the coalition between them and Deng at the Theory Conference held from January until early April 1979, which Hu convened to revise the party's ideology. At this conference, members of Hu's network went beyond repudiation of Mao's policies and ideas to call for specific democratic reforms, such as the end of lifelong tenure, limited terms of office for officials, use of institutionalized procedures, and the rule of law. The intellectuals associated with the more conservative of Deng's Long March allies, who also attended the conference, regarded these proposals as efforts to subvert the Leninist political structure and leadership. While the Long Marchers cooperated with Deng in purging the Maoists, they would not sanction any weakening of the Lenin-

---

[6] Michael Schoenhals, "The 1978 Truth Criterion Controversy," *China Quarterly*, no. 126 (June 1991), pp. 243–268.

ist political structure, which was the basis for their power. Deng shared his elderly colleagues' Leninist view and at this time was also concerned by the continuing protests of the Democracy Wall activists. Therefore, in a speech he gave on March 30 at the conference, Deng enunciated the "four cardinal principles," which demanded unswerving allegiance to the Leninist party-state. The speech, drawn up by the elders' conservative spokesman Hu Qiaomu, made it clear that there would be no tolerance of any effort to undermine the party's authority. Nevertheless, despite Deng's speech and the suppression of the Democracy Wall activists, Hu's network continued to call for reform of the political structure and revision of ideology.

Moreover, contradicting his speech at the Theory Conference, Deng in a speech on August 18, 1980, attributed the "mistakes" of the Maoist period to the overconcentration of power in the top leadership and the political system that made that possible, an indirect indictment of the Leninist political structure.[7] And once again, he called for political reforms. Accordingly, in university areas in Beijing, Shanghai, and Hunan, students took Deng at his word and ran for positions on the local people's councils. They ran their own campaigns, wrote campaign platforms, conducted political debates, and established election procedures with little party interference. But when several of those who ran without party approval won these local elections, the party stopped competitive elections in the urban areas in 1980–81.

By mid-1981, the tacit coalition between the reform intellectuals and the party leaders became tenuous. The revolutionary elders, including Deng, became increasingly concerned that China's intellectuals and workers would join in a movement similar to Solidarity in Poland that undermined and eventually brought down the Polish Communist Party and its leadership. Even though several Democracy Wall activists had hailed Solidarity in their pamphlets and posters, there was no similar link-up between intellectuals and workers in China in the 1980s. Nevertheless, there was the historical precedent for such an alliance in the May Fourth movement that led to the overthrow of the existing warlord government and to the establishment of the Chinese Communist Party itself. Consequently, beginning in 1981, campaigns were launched periodically against dissenting elite intellectuals as well as against non-establishment intellectuals who moved beyond intellectual circles to speak directly to a broader public.

The first campaign was against the writer Bai Hua and a film scenario he had written, "Unrequited Love." Despite some resistance from Hu Yaobang, who had promised the intellectuals that never again would they

---

[7] *Selected Works of Deng Xiaoping* (1975–1982) (Beijing: Foreign Languages Press, 1984), p. 310.

be subjected to attacks for their work, in the summer of 1981 Deng approved criticism of the scenario even though the film on which it was based was shown only to small selected audiences. The criticisms of "Unrequited Love" reflected another of the elders' increasing concerns with the more openly blatant attacks on Mao. The scenario ridiculed the "worship of Mao" as superstition. Even more, the elders were upset with the implication in Bai's film that loyalty to one's country was not synonymous with loyalty to the party leader or even to the party. Nevertheless, although this campaign used some Maoist methods such as a nationwide media attack and a demand for a self-criticism, it was qualitatively different. Bai Hua was criticized only for the scenario; his other works were praised, and one even won a prize. Moreover, the campaign petered out because unlike those of the Mao era when fear of reprisal forced most intellectuals to participate, most refused to join in without ill effect. When the campaign ended in late 1981, Bai Hua resumed publishing and speaking out on sensitive subjects.[8]

Another issue that weakened the tacit coalition between the reform intellectuals and the party was the discussion of the existence of alienation in a Communist state. This issue arose in the aftermath of the Cultural Revolution and evoked a call for "humanism" as a way to moderate this sense of alienation. A similar discussion was going on in Eastern Europe at the time, another indication that happenings in Eastern Europe had a profound influence on China in the post-Mao era. The topic of alienation under socialism began to be debated in the press in the late 1970s, particularly in the party's premier official newspaper, *People's Daily,* under its editor-and-chief Hu Jiwei and deputy-editor Wang Ruoshui, both well-known party intellectuals associated with Hu Yaobang's network. While these ideas excited the intellectual community, they infuriated the party elders, who again pressed Deng to stop the discussion. Accordingly, in the fall of 1983, Deng launched another campaign, this time against "spiritual pollution," another euphemism for Western ideas and values seeping into China, along with the influx of Western goods and businesses. The two editors lost their positions, but the campaign formally ended after only six weeks because of pressure from Deng's reformist disciples, Hu and Zhao Ziyang, who warned that such a campaign would frighten away overseas investors, a greater concern to Deng than Western ideas and values.

As the campaign waned, Hu Yaobang, with Deng's support, tried again to move ahead with limited political reforms. At a Chinese Writers Associ-

[8] See Merle Goldman, *Sowing the Seeds of Democracy in China* (Cambridge: Harvard University Press, 1994), Chapter 4, pp. 88–112. Much of the discussion of the post-Mao relationship between the intellectuals and the state in the 1980s comes from the above book.

ation conference, for example, in late 1984–early 1985, instead of its leaders being appointed by the party, for the first time in the People's Republic, they were nominated and voted on by the writers themselves. Furthermore, Hu appointed a genuine writer, Wang Meng, as minister of culture. During his tenure from 1986 until June 4, 1989, one hundred flowers truly bloomed in the creative arts. Even more important, though Deng merely desired administrative reforms, such as the establishment of a civil service system to replace party appointments in the lower levels of the bureaucracy and the separation of the party from the government, the call for political reforms sparked intellectuals in the spring and summer of 1986 to call for more far-reaching political reforms than Deng desired.

At public meetings and in the media in 1986, not only members of Hu Yaobang's network, but intellectuals, young and old, establishment and non-establishment, debated a variety of political reforms that went far beyond administrative reforms, such as making the National People's Congress, a rubber-stamp congress in the Mao era, into a genuine legislature and establishing laws to protect freedom of speech. A small number even proposed going beyond multicandidate elections to multiparty elections.[9] These proposals hitherto discussed privately among elite intellectuals became issues of national discourse in the summer of 1986. A few even repudiated the party's view that rights were determined by a country's history and culture and insisted that rights were universal and inalienable.

Most outspoken on this issue was the astrophysicist, Fang Lizhi, a vice chancellor of the prestigious University of Science and Technology in Hefei, Anhui province, where Hu Yaobang had encouraged him to establish a relatively free liberal arts environment. In the fall of 1986, Fang spoke at a number of universities on the issue of individual rights. At Shanghai's Jiaotong University, for example, he urged students to go out and fight for their rights because, he asserted, rights are not granted from above, "rather men are born with rights." In contrast to the "obedient intellectuals of the 1950s," he encouraged students and intellectuals "to strive for what is one's due." He declared that "It is up to the intellectuals as a class, with their sense of social responsibility, their consciousness about democracy, and their initiative, to strive for their rights."[10]

As discussions of political reform spread to forums of the Communist Youth League and even to the Central Party School, several of the revolutionary elders at the Sixth Plenum of the Twelfth Central Committee in September 1986 demanded an end to public discourse on political reform.

---

[9] Deng Weizhi, "Enhance liberal atmosphere," *Jiefang Ribao* (*Liberation Daily*), May 21, 1986, p. 4.
[10] A transcript of Fang Lizhi's speech was reprinted in the *Washington Post*, January 18, 1987, p. C4.

But instead of the discussions ending, they intensified and expanded further. Aware of mounting opposition and influenced by their vice chancellor, the students at the University of Science and Technology did as Fang had urged. They tried to assert their rights by running in local elections in Hefei just as students at Beijing University had done in 1980. When they were thwarted by local party officials, they began protests in late 1986 that extended down the coast to Shanghai and reached Beijing in early January 1987. The demonstrations spread as students communicated with other university students by phone and news of the protests was reported by Voice of America. Again with pressure from the elders, Deng ordered Hu to suppress the demonstrators, which he refused to do.

Consequently, at an expanded Politburo meeting that included the participation of the elders, on January 16, 1987, Hu was purged as party general secretary. A campaign was then launched against "bourgeois liberalization," another euphemism for Western political ideas and values, and three prominent intellectuals were targeted as the instigators of the student protests. In addition to Fang Lizhi, two well-known writers, Liu Binyan and Wang Ruowang, who had also spoken to large audiences on these issues in 1986, were blamed for the student protests. The common denominator in their selection was that they attracted large, enthusiastic audiences in the student and educated community. Perhaps even more important, all three along with Fang's colleague, Xu Liangying, the translator of Einstein, had been planning a meeting to commemorate the victims of the 1957 antirightist campaign, in which they had suffered grievously for almost 20 years. At Mao's instigation, Deng had led that movement so he took the commemoration as a direct attack on him.

Like the earlier campaign against spiritual pollution, this campaign was also cut short after a few months. In addition to Deng's fear of frightening away foreign investors, China's growing intellectual ties with the outside world was another moderating factor. Foreign friends, colleagues, and merely acquaintances of these three gentlemen, including Nobel prize-winners, as well as Chinese students studying abroad, rushed to their defense with public statements and petitions. Unlike during the Mao period, China's intellectuals had contacts with their international counterparts, whom they could call upon for help. Furthermore, unlike Mao, Deng and his appointed successor to Hu, Zhao Ziyang, cared about China's international image and desired help from abroad intellectually as well as economically. Consequently, the campaign concluded in mid-April 1987.

Unlike the purges of the Mao era, Hu Yaobang retained his position on the Central Committee, but he became politically inactive. This meant that members of his intellectual network no longer had his political protection. Except for the few who joined Zhao Ziyang's network, they began to lose their prominent positions in the intellectual establishment. Despite the fact that the campaigns of the Deng era were shorter and gentler than those during the Mao period, their continuation into the 1980s finally broke the bonds between the politically engaged establishment intellectuals and the party-state. In addition to the erratic, but persistent repression, increasing exposure to the outside world through travel, books, and personal contacts and the democratizing changes underway in East Asia as well as in the Communist world led some intellectuals to reconsider their relationship to the party-state.

Thus by the late 1980s whereas most intellectuals began to define themselves in terms of their professions, the politically engaged intellectuals, particularly those associated with Hu, gradually came to see themselves less as loyal remonstrators in the Confucian tradition and as they had tried to be in the Mao era and more as loyal opponents of the party leadership and the political structure to which they had hitherto committed their lives. By 1988, the coalition between the Deng regime and the politically engaged humanistic intellectuals had been severed beyond repair.

INCREASING AUTONOMY OF THE INTELLECTUALS

Although Zhao Ziyang as party general secretary became Deng's new successor and was not as actively protective of politically engaged reform intellectuals as his predecessor, he was not uninterested in political reform. Moreover, he was very protective of his technocratic network. At the Thirteenth Party Congress in fall 1987, he called publicly for a civil service system and the separation of the party from the government, which Deng also still supported. At the same time, he also established a committee, under his personal secretary, Bao Tong, to study political structural reform. Nevertheless, only a few members of Hu's intellectual newwork allied with Zhao's more technocratic supporters.

One reason they distanced themselves from Zhao was that Zhao and several of his supporters espoused the neo-authoritarian view, supposedly based on the East Asian model, that until China had gone through several decades of rapid economic reform and developed a large middle class it could not proceed to political reform. This view was in opposition to that of some members of Hu's network who believed that political reforms should accompany economic reforms in order to alleviate the social dislocations, corruption, and inequalities evoked by the economic reforms. They also used the Marxist argument that changes in the economic substructure produce changes in the political superstructure. From that they argued that democracy, not the current political system of rule by an elderly oligarchy or the new authoritarian approach, was the best means for maintaining stability during the period of economic change.

A typical example of the transformation in the thinking of the politically engaged intellectuals and specifically of a member of Hu's network can be seen in the ideological evolution of Hu Jiwei, former editor-in-chief of *People's Daily*. A Marxist, obedient party member since Yan'an, who was persecuted in the Cultural Revolution, he admitted that it was not until the discussion on the "practice criterion" and attack on the "whatever faction" in the aftermath of the Cultural Revolution that he questioned the party's policies. He realized that if one "obeyed" the leadership then one committed mistakes and hurt one's "comrades"; if one "disobeyed," then one made fewer mistakes.[11] Under his editorship, the *People's Daily* in the late 1970s and early 1980s had criticized Mao's policies and presented a variety of views. After he was attacked in the 1983 spiritual pollution campaign and purged as director of *People's Daily*, he called for a code of laws to guarantee freedom of the press and for the establishment of a non-official media. Hu Yaobang put him in charge of drawing up a journalism law. His was one of several efforts in the post-Mao era to establish codes of behavior for both journalists and the party in its treatment of the media.

As he became more acquainted with the workings of the Western press, especially through contacts with Hong Kong journalists, Hu's views became more sophisticated. Not only did he argue for laws to protect journalists from government reprisals, but by the late 1980s he concluded that competitive democratic elections were the only way to guarantee the stability so desired by most Chinese. In early 1989, he concluded that "democratic elections may not necessarily choose leaders of the best quality, but they ensure that bad leaders will not be able to remain in power." In addition, he no longer shared the party's definition of democracy as simply "majority rule"; he now recognized that the minority of people who hold different opinions must be respected and protected.[12]

Hu Jiwei was also typical of intellectuals who in the post-Mao era began to look beyond Marxism-Leninism for other ideas on which to base political authority. He looked inward to China's own traditions as a source of inspiration for reform. Although Hu shared the May Fourth negative view of China's traditional culture, he and his colleagues participated in the reevaluation of the relevance of that culture, particularly Confucianism, to

[11] Hu Jiwei, "Obey or disobey," in *Mengxing de shike (The Moment of Awakening)*, Yu Guangyuan, Hu Jiwei et al., eds. (Beijing: Zhongwai wenhua chuban gongsi, April 1989), pp. 246–278.
[12] Hu Jiwei, "Establish Democratic Authority," *Jingjixue zhoubao (Economic Weekly)*, March 5, 1989, p. 5, FBIS, March 17, 1989, p. 16.

China's modernization. Like the leadership, he too was impressed with the accelerating economic dynamism of China's ethnic and post-Confucian neighbors in Asia, but unlike the leadership, he was impressed also by the movement of these countries toward democracy. In fact, the debate about China's traditional culture had become so heated by the mid-1980s that it was termed "cultural fever." While the party elders stressed the authoritarian elements of the tradition, some intellectuals, Hu Jiwei among them, stressed the leading role of intellectuals and importance of morality in governance.

The cultural fever peaked in spring 1988 when it moved beyond intellectual circles to an audience of millions in a television series, called "River Elegy" (*Heshang*). Produced by a group of former Red Guards, this series condemned China's traditional civilization, as symbolized by the Yellow River, the Great Wall, and the dragon, for stifling China's creativity. Through vivid cinematography, "River Elegy" conveyed the sense that China, like the Yellow River, once at the forefront of civilization, had dried up because of its emphasis on stability, isolation, and conservatism. By contrast, it showed flowing blue seas as symbolizing the explorative, open cultures of the West and Japan. The series implied that the present regime represented the dying Yellow River. It also showed film clips of the anti-rightist campaign, Great Leap Forward, and the Cultural Revolution in which the party elders had played leading roles. The elders had the series pulled off the air in fall 1988.

While the cultural fever slowly subsided after this episode, one aspect of "River Elegy" – a critique of the literati for political impotence – continued to provoke heated debate among intellectuals. Because of the literati's economic dependence on the state and their general ideological conformity with the political leadership, the critique asserted that intellectuals were unable to achieve genuine independence which hindered their ability to influence the leadership and policy making. Although most members of Hu Yaobang's network had repudiated tradition, they had hitherto tacitly emulated the literati's dependent relationship on the political leadership. By the late 1980s, however, they began to question this alliance. They had learned from bitter experience in the Deng period as well as in the Mao period that not only could political patrons be purged as happened to Hu Yaobang, but their patrons, whether Hu or Zhao Ziyang, did not carry out the reforms that they advocated nor were they strong enough to protect them from retribution.

Another assumption that they shared with their literati ancestors, which they reconsidered at this time, was that they could speak on behalf of the people or, at least, for the benefit of the people and the party would act accordingly. The party's diminishing response to their demands, in addition to its intermittent repression, led some of them reluctantly to acknowledge that their paternalistic presumption of "speaking for the people" had fallen on deaf ears and had invited retaliation. At such times, their demands had been counterproductive, leading not only to their own persecution, but sometimes to a retreat from the reforms underway.

Consequently, the politically engaged elite intellectuals gradually changed their approach by the late 1980s. They put less stress on ideological revisions and moral persuasion and more stress on the need to establish democratic institutions. As seen with Hu Jiwei, this shift derived not only from their own repression and disillusionment with the Deng leadership from which they had expected so much, but also from a growing understanding of the workings of liberal democracy. Like their May Fourth predecessors, they initially thought that it was only necessary to create a receptive intellectual climate and political reforms would follow. But by the late 1980s, having been subjected to periodic attacks, with few political reforms to point to, some of them concluded that a change in the intellectual and ideological climate was not enough. It may help, but only institutional changes, in which intellectual freedom was guaranteed by law and checks on arbitrary power were established, could produce genuine political reforms as well as protect them as individuals.

They also altered their strategy. Having focused on creating a receptive intellectual climate, like their May Fourth predecessors, they had made little effort in the early years of the Deng leadership to organize to achieve their goals. But with the loss of Hu Yaobang's protection in 1987 and growing distrust of Zhao Ziyang as well as Deng in late 1988, they started to set up their own organizations and journals and link up for the first time with several non-establishment or non-official (*minban,* people run) groups, which also sought to change political institutions. Since the mid-1980s, in an effort to encourage technological advance, the party had allowed the establishment of non-official groups and journals, though, like the official associations, they had to be registered with an official unit. In 1988, for example, members of Hu's network joined with like-minded intellectuals in Shanghai to set up the New Enlightenment group and to publish a book series under the same name. While it was necessary to obtain permission from the party's Propaganda Department to establish a new journal, a book series could be commissioned directly with a publisher. Because of their prominence, however, their series was stopped after only four issues and they were even prevented from meeting in public places.

Therefore, in early 1989, members of Hu's network for the first time started reaching out to non-official as well as semi-official think tanks concerned with bringing about political change. They held seminars with non-establishment intellectuals and with urban and rural entrepreneurs, spawned by the economic reforms. They shared with the emerging middle class, professionals, students, and ex Red Guard political activists the desire to establish laws and institutions that would limit the party's control over their activities and protect them from arbitrary interference. Yet, despite these growing connections, and acknowledgment of the need for a broader social base to achieve political reform, their views and actions still retained the traditional focus on the educated elite.

One manifestation of this shift in strategy was that in the early months of 1989, members of Hu's network joined with intellectuals in semi- and non-officials groups in signing and forwarding a series of petitions to the leadership urging political reform. Fang Lizhi sent the first petition to Deng Xiaoping asking him to pardon Wei Jingsheng and other political prisoners in commemoration of the forthcoming anniversaries of the May Fourth Movement, the French Revolution, and the establishment of the People's Republic. Fang's example sparked the first organized efforts of members of Hu's network, scientists solicited by Fang's older colleague Xu Liangying, the translator of Einstein, and a younger generation of politically engaged non-establishment intellectuals, to confront the party publicly with political demands. In three separate petitions, these groups, in addition to urging the pardon of political prisoners, called for freedom of speech and rule of law.

While sending petitions to the top leadership proposing reform resembles the literati's memorials to the emperor and high officials, the fact that their petitions were signed by a coalition of elite intellectuals, independent writers and artists, scientists, and members of the semi- and non-official think tanks, some led by ex Red Guard activists, made these protests different from the traditional literati memorials and previous pleas of individual establishment intellectuals in the People's Republic. This new political collaboration of disparate social groups, albeit among the educated, resonated more with the political coalitions that were to lead to the 1989 revolutions in Eastern Europe and marked a radical change from the previous elitist, individualistic strategies of influencing government through high-level political contacts and patronage.

EMERGENCE OF A NEW KIND OF INTELLECTUAL IN THE POST-MAO ERA

In the semi- and non-official think tanks that mushroomed in the late 1980s in the People's Republic, a new breed of politically engaged intellectual emerged, who differed qualitatively from the traditional literati and the establishment intellectuals of the Mao era. Representative and perhaps the most prominent of this breed were Chen Ziming, Wang Juntao, and their associates who had come of age in the Cultural Revolution.[13] Both Chen and Wang had participated in the April 5, 1976, demonstration. They were imprisoned for their activities at that time, but were released shortly after Mao's death in September 1976. Although Chen was admitted to the Academy of Sciences and Wang to the physics department at Beijing University, they joined the Democracy Wall movement of late 1978, where they put out the relatively moderate political journal *Beijing Spring* and gathered around them a corps of followers, some from the April 5 demonstration, others from prison, and still others who were "sent-down" youth with Chen in Inner Mongolia.

Their non-establishment activities were not necessarily ones they would have chosen for themselves; they were shaped by their Cultural Revolution experiences. Though from official and intellectual families, Chen and Wang were forced in the Cultural Revolution to fend for themselves. That experience led them to a more independent, more politically activist course in the post-Mao era than the older intellectual elite, who used their high-level contacts and ideological discourse to press for change from the top down, much in the tradition of their literati predecessors. By contrast, Chen, Wang, and their ex Red Guard associates sought to bring about political change from the bottom up, with colleagues and methods they had acquired in the Cultural Revolution. In contrast to their elders, their approach was to form their own groups, journals, and networks to carry out their political agenda.

When Deng suppressed the Democracy Wall movement in 1979, Chen, Wang, and their associates then participated and made possible the relatively democratic elections to the local people's congresses held in university areas in 1980, principally in Beijing and Shanghai. Although the local congresses had little real power, former Red Guards and Democracy Wall activists seized the opportunity to work for political reform by making these local elections competitive. They used the skills of speech making, pamphlet writing, and group mobilization in their election campaigns that they had learned in the Cultural Revolution.[14]

---

[13] For full biographies of Chen Ziming and Wang Juntao, see George Black and Robin Munro, *Black Hands of Beijing* (New York: John Wiley and Sons, 1993); also, Goldman, *Sowing the Seeds of Democracy*, pp. 256–295 and Merle Goldman, "The Emergence of Politically Independent Intellectuals" in *The Paradox of China's Post-Mao Reforms*, Merle Goldman and Roderick MacFarquhar, eds. (Cambridge: Harvard University Press, 1999), pp. 283–307.

[14] See Hu Ping, Wang Juntao et al., *Kaituo-Beida xueyun wenxian (Exploration-Beijing University Student Movement Materials)* (Hong Kong; Taiyuan shuwu, 1990).

The most competitive elections took place in Haidian, the university area of Beijing. Candidates literally nominated themselves. The students, not the party, at Beijing University organized the meetings and debates among the candidates and set the rules for the election. The candidates negotiated the procedures for the debates, and wrote their own platforms. With virtually the entire physics department as his campaign committee, Wang Juntao emphasized the need for political reform to accompany economic reform. Though an eloquent speaker, he lost by a small margin to philosophy graduate student and former Red Guard, Hu Ping, who ran on a platform of freedom of speech, guaranteed by law. Chen Ziming won a seat in the Academy of Sciences area. To Wang and Chen, the process of competitive elections was more important than winning or serving on the local congresses because the congresses had little real power.

When Chen and Wang graduated they were punished for their past political activity by being assigned jobs inappropriate to their training and talents. Although both men held high positions in the Communist Youth League, a sure path to party leadership, they resigned or let their memberships lapse. Such an act was not even contemplated by their intellectual elders who sought to hold onto their party memberships no matter how badly the party treated them. The elite considered party membership and access to the leadership the only way to influence policy making. Although Chen and Wang also sought several times to interest the party leadership in their political ideas – Wang tried to find a university administrator willing to establish a school to train officials; Chen sent numerous reform proposals to Zhao Ziyang – all these efforts were rebuffed. Not only their Cultural Revolution experience, but also the post-Mao leadership's rejection of their proposals led them to put their ideas into practice on their own without official patronage. Unable to find positions in the official institutes and forced to fare for themselves, they tried to function independently of the state.

As the market economy took off in the mid-1980s, Chen and his wife set up a correspondence school to teach administrative skills to new entrepreneurs as well as bureaucrats. With the profits, they established the Beijing Social and Economic Research Institute in 1986, the first non-official political think tank in Beijing. Though Chen sought through economic independence to become politically independent, he was not above using family connections to get his think tank officially registered with the Beijing party government. Most of the researchers in his think tank had endured the travails of the Cultural Revolution, had participated in the April 5, 1976 demonstration, were fellow prisoners, or had been members of the Beijing Spring group during the Democracy Wall movement.

In 1988, Chen bought *Economic Weekly* (*Jingjixue Zhoubao*), a journal that came with an official registration. He hired a former editor of the official *Worker's Daily* as its editor-in-chief, and Wang Juntao became its main columnist. Very quickly, they transformed it from a pedestrian trade magazine into a forum on a broad range of topics that soon rivaled the highly regarded semi-official *World Economic Herald* published under the auspices of the Shanghai Academy of Social Sciences. Whereas the *Herald* was a mouthpiece for the reformist views of Zhao's intellectual network, *Economic Weekly* was not attached to any specific view of reform. It published articles not only by members of both Hu Yaobang's and Zhao's networks, but also by scholars engaged in academic debates on Confucianism, the May Fourth movement, and nonpolitical issues. In addition, they set up a variety of other activities. They established a publishing company that published translations of Western books and those of Chinese political thinkers. They set up their own public opinion polling organization as an alternative to the party's polling services whose results they believed were skewed. They were able to get their results published in the party's mainstream media, including the *People's Daily*. They held seminars that attracted hundreds of professors, students, well-known scholars, and even members of the newly emerging entrepreneurial class.

Chen's and Wang's efforts to establish intellectual institutions outside the control of the party were radical in the Chinese traditional and Communist context. By the late 1980s, like their counterparts in Eastern Europe and the Soviet Union, Chen and Wang had set up a number of independent organizations that appeared to be laying the basis for a civil society similar to those developing in Eastern Europe. Their activities had gained so much prominence that intellectuals who had earlier kept their distance, such as members of Hu Yaobang's network, by early 1989 not only were publishing in *Economic Weekly*, but asked Chen to sponsor journals and projects they wished to establish.

Though their activities were radical, Chen's and Wang's views in the late 1980s were still relatively moderate. Like the establishment intellectuals, they too believed that political reform could be carried out within the existing political system and primarily by intellectuals. They also participated vigorously in the debates on neo-authoritarianism versus democracy of the late 1980s, in which some of their members supported the neo-authoritarian view. Their journal *Economic Weekly*, as well as the *World Economic Herald*, gave coverage to both sides of the debate. The presentation of opposing sides in the same paper was also unprecedented in the People's Republic. The interaction and cooperation of political activists in the nonofficial think tanks with politically engaged establishment intellectuals were other profound changes in the People's Republic. While such interactions occurred most prominently in Beijing and Shanghai, they were going on all over the country by the late 1980s.

Although Chen and Wang believed that politics was primarily the preserve of intellectuals, they differed from the establishment intellectuals in that they demanded a voice in government for those outside the establishment. While their activities had more resonance with their East European counterparts, they differed from them in that they did not see civil society in opposition to the prevailing government, but rather as working with and negotiating with the government for certain rights. Chen described the relationship as one in which "we contend, but not clash and cooperate, but remain independent of each other."[15] His view of civil society was definitely one with Chinese characteristics.

INTELLECTUAL CHANGE AFTER JUNE 4, 1989

When Hu Yaobang died unexpectedly of a heart attack on April 15, 1989, sparking widespread student demonstrations, for the first time in the People's Republic elite intellectuals joined in a student demonstration. Although the intellectual networks of Hu and Zhao had influenced the students' political ideas, none of them had participated in demonstrations until spring 1989. Nor had any of them instigated the demonstrations as the party later charged or played a major role in them. They joined the demonstrations relatively late in mid-May and did little more than sign petitions and march in support of the students. Consequently, they had little influence over the course of events. Neither did they nor the student leaders know how to produce concrete results from the popular support and dramatic symbolism of the spring 1989 demonstrations.

While Chen and Wang may have had more influence over the demonstrations' student leaders than other intellectuals, by the time Zhao Ziyang sent a representative in mid-May to ask them to persuade the students to leave the Square in order to avoid a military crackdown, it was too late. Students were coming into the Square from outside Beijing, who did not know the original student leaders, let alone Chen and Wang, so their ability to influence events in Tiananmen Square at that time was limited. When martial law was announced on May 20, Chen and Wang sought to organize a coalition of all the independent unions formed during the demonstration in order to negotiate a peaceful withdrawal. They even included the Beijing Independent Workers Union, which up until then had

---

[15] Defense Statement of Chen Ziming, *News from Asia Watch*, June 10, 1992, p. 7.

been shunted to the periphery of the Square by the students. Most of the students not only did not want to join with the workers, they also feared a crackdown because of the party's well-known fear of an alliance between intellectuals and workers. It is likely that this emerging alliance, plus shouts of "down with Deng" heard in mid-May, reminiscent of the Cultural Revolution, was a factor in leading Deng to order the troops into Tiananmen Square on June 4, where they indiscriminately killed over 1000 people along the way. The student leaders were arrested, and Chen and Wang received the longest sentences of 13 years for being the "black hands" behind the demonstrations.

The tragic outcome perhaps was pre-ordained when the party's revolutionary elders assumed leadership during the demonstrations. Unaccustomed to negotiating with those with whom they disagreed or whom they perceived as undermining their political authority, they resorted to their usual practice of using force against them. Unlike Gorbachev, who refused to send in troops against those demanding political change in Eastern Europe and Russia, when confronted with a political challenge, China's party elders resorted to military force. Moreover, China still lacked an alternative political organization or leadership group comparable to Solidarity in Poland or Charter 77 in Czechoslovakia with which to negotiate a compromise. Despite all the changes that had occurred since Mao's death, the weakness of the intellectuals' organizational structure and lack of connections with other classes undermined their ability to influence events. Their weakness was largely due to the party's unwillingness to tolerate any political opposition, but it was also due to the fact that elite intellectuals had not even contemplated, with the exception of a few non-establishment groups like that of Chen and Wang, setting up an independent intellectual organization, let alone a political organization, until shortly before the 1989 demonstrations erupted. Although Chen and Wang's think tank and other non-official groups had the potential to become an alternative political organization, these groups were just beginning to lay a foundation for such an alternative. And even they did not join with other social groups until late into the 1989 Tiananmen demonstrations.

Consequently, China's intellectual elite, the ex Red Guard political activists, and the 1989 student demonstrators shook up the party leadership and increased popular awareness of political issues, but were unable to lead to any fundamental change in China's Leninist party-state. Nevertheless, their actions helped inspire the East European demonstrations, which unlike those in China, proved successful in bringing about political reform and change of leadership by the early 1990s. Besides the fact that in contrast to China, Gorbachev refused to send in the military against the demonstrators, these countries, including the former Soviet Union, had already established alternative political organizations and leaders, who had formed coalitions over the years with other social groups, including the rising middle class and workers. Their organized power and broad social support made it possible for them to challenge effectively and in some cases, assume leadership from their nations' weakened Communist parties. China's intellectual elite, because of party repression and their own reluctance to take independent action, and the democratic activists, because they had not been able to build up a strong alternative social base of support, were unable to play such a role in China.

Still, the June 4 crackdown had a profound impact on the student and intellectual community in general. Some opted out of any political engagement in the belief that it would only provoke repression. While others lost faith in the party's legitimacy to rule or ability to rule humanely, they became disillusioned with political activity. The major intellectual players in the 1989 events no longer believed that they could induce change by themselves. A few sought contact with non-establishment intellectuals; a smaller number even sought contact with other social groups, such as the workers. Nevertheless, even they continued to believe that only intellectuals could lead such a coalition and bring about change.

The majority of intellectuals, however, immersed themselves in their professions or in a variety of nonpolitical pursuits. While disillusioned with the regime, most intellectuals and students were not alienated from the political system, which continued to deliver economically for them. After a brief economic downturn in the aftermath of June 4, Deng's symbolic trip south to the Special Economic Zones in 1992 reenergized China's move to the market and its GNP resumed its 9 percent yearly growth. Most intellectuals continued to work in the party-state bureaucracies, academia, and the media. Those participants in the 1989 demonstrations, who were not imprisoned or forced into exile, but were unable to gain a position in the official establishment, joined with others of their generation in going into business (*xiahai*). They along with other new college graduates were attracted to business because it was more lucrative than academic life and, in the Deng era, was more secure than politics. The creation of a market economy and opening to the outside world offered alternatives to government employment, especially in nonstate enterprises, foreign-joint ventures, or private businesses. Unlike the bureaucracy or academia, where they might lose their jobs or salaries for expressing dissident views, these alternatives provided a degree of economic independence that offered some protection from political retaliation.

INTELLECTUALS DURING THE JIANG ZEMIN ERA

In the aftermath of June 4th, Deng appointed Jiang Zemin to succeed the purged Zhao Ziyang as party general secretary. Initially insecure in his leadership role, Jiang allowed Maoists to return briefly to power. A small number of them assumed high positions in the Propaganda Department, the universities, research institutes, and the media in the early 1990s. As Jiang with their help continued Deng's policy of persecuting dissidents in the June 4 aftermath, most intellectuals and students became virtually silent on political issues.

Unlike the Mao period, however, intellectuals as a class, their colleagues and profession did not suffer for the supposed "crimes" of a small number of their associates. Although the campaigns of the early 1990s against "all-out Westernization" and "peaceful evolution" were similar to the attacks on Western values in the campaigns against "spiritual pollution" and bourgeois liberalization in the 1980s, they did not stop the inflow of Western ideas and products. Equally important, as in the 1980s, intellectuals were not forced nor were they willing to participate in political movements.

Jiang also shared Deng's view of the intellectuals as essential to achieving the goal of economic modernization and fulfilling the goal since the late nineteenth century to make China once again "rich and powerful." Consequently, intellectuals involved in the sciences, technology, and economics in particular maintained their elite status as advisers to the government. After Deng's visit south, Jiang continued China's opening to the outside world and move to a market economy. Moreover, China's growing economic and technological international interdependence made it virtually impossible to keep out influences from abroad. Despite the waning of the intellectuals' political influence, by the mid-1990s intellectuals generally worked in an increasingly pluralistic cultural and intellectual environment with even greater access to their international peers than in the 1980s through the new technologies of the Internet. China's large cities, universities, and institutes became gathering places for foreign experts, academics, artists, writers, entertainers, audiences, and visitors, who were allowed to participate in a wide variety of cultural, intellectual, and artistic endeavors, so long as they had no ostensible political content.

The ideological homogeneity of the Mao era gave way in the 1990s to a broad range of intellectual and cultural activities.[16] While the kind of in-

[16] See Orville Schell, *The Mandate of Heaven* (New York: Simon and Schuster, 1994); also Geremie Barmé, *In the Red: On Contemporary Chinese Culture* (New York: Columbia University Press, 1999).

tellectual engagement in public political debates of the 1980s was suppressed through most of the 1990s, the party-state's further retreat from the cultural and intellectual realms in terms of censorship and financial support and its tolerance of diversity and foreign influences sparked an explosion of artistic experimentation, a vibrant popular culture, and nonpolitical intellectual discourse. As long as the content and style of one's intellectual, cultural, and professional work stayed away from politics in a public forum, the party-state tolerated and at times even encouraged an apolitical culture in the 1990s as a diversion from political engagement.

Only a small number of intellectuals on either side of the political spectrum, leftist/conservative and liberal/democratic, expressed dissident political views as China's economic reforms took off again in the 1990s. Although Deng on his southern trip had attacked the "left" as a greater danger than the right, neo-Maoists, led by conservative elder Deng Liqun, led an effort begun in the early 1990s to revitalize Mao's ideas and reindoctrinate the population in Marxism-Leninism. "Mao fever," *(Mao re)* spread to China's major cities with the reappearance of Mao's "Little Red Book," Mao souvenirs, and Mao medallions hanging in taxicabs. While some of this kitsch poked fun at Mao, the fever was also fired by nostalgia for the supposed order and honest officials of the Mao years in contrast to the disorder and corruption of the post-Mao era.

Although the Mao fever subsided by the mid-1990s, the group of neo-Maoists around Deng Liqun persisted in asserting Maoist doctrine. They circulated four successive "ten-thousand word" statements in the 1990s that called for the continued dominance of the state-controlled economy.[17] Their statements warned that the decline of state industries would help capitalism prevail over socialism and would impoverish state workers as well as the party-state. In opposition to Deng Xiaoping's nonideological approach, they persisted in advocating socialism. Though criticized and pushed to the margins once again, as the post-Deng leadership moved in the late 1990s to reform state industries, neo-Maoists continued to warn publicly against the evils of capitalism through several journals that they controlled.[18]

At the same time, the more open political atmosphere following Deng's trip south emboldened a handful of liberal intellectuals, participants in past demonstrations, and released political prisoners to issue publicly a series of petitions in 1993–94 that called for the freeing of political prison-

---

[17] Shi Liuzi, ed., *Beijing dixia "wanyan shu"* (*The Ten Thousand Word and Other Underground Writings in Beijing*) (Hong Kong: Mingjing chubanshe, 1997).

[18] See *Zhong Liu* zazhi she, eds., *Zhong Liu baiqi wencui* (*Collection of One Hundred Issues of Zhong Liu*) (Beijing: Jincheng chubanshe, 1998).

ers, a removal of the designation of the 1989 demonstrations as "counter-revolutionary," and tolerance of diverse political as well as religious views. Once again they used the literati practice of issuing memorial-like petitions to the leadership urging them to reform. This political thaw, however, was short-lived. Some of the political activists were re-arrested or put under surveillance. And by the mid-1990s, all public liberal dissent was suppressed once again. Nevertheless, although both the neo-Maoists and advocates of Western liberal ideas were publicly marginalized, political discourse continued on sensitive issues on both sides of the political spectrum in private, in a limited number of scholarly journals, and among small groups of like-minded people.

The collapse of the Soviet Union and the disorder accompanying Russia's move to democracy were other factors shifting the intellectual discourse in the 1990s away from the humanist and liberal tone of the previous decade. Largely because of the economic and political chaos following the disintegration of the Soviet Union and the move to democracy, the Russian scenario came to symbolize the negative effects of the collapse of the party-state. In addition, a growing number of younger intellectuals reacted against the pro-Western, antitraditional discourse of the 1980s, when disillusionment with Maoism had instilled an unreasoned idealism about Western societies and political life. As these intellectuals and returned students had more frequent and closer contact with the realities of Western countries through travel and study, their idealism waned. Many no longer believed that the Western democratic path would lead China to the stable, harmonious future they were all seeking.

Consequently, in the mid-1990s, a younger generation of intellectuals who came of age in the post-Mao era, some of whom were close to the "princelings," children of the party elders, moved to another extreme, neoconservatism. Like the neo-authoritarians of the late 1980s, they did not refer to Marxism-Leninism, but unlike them, they did not endorse a full-scale move to the market and the development of a middle class that eventually would lead China toward democracy. Rather, some of their neoconservative views overlapped with those of the Neo-Maoists in that they decried the decentralization that had accompanied China's move to the market and urged a retightening of centralized controls over the economic regions and cultural life. They were particularly upset about the destabilizing impact of millions of rural migrants coming into the cities in the 1990s in search of economic opportunities, and urged their return to the countryside.[19]

---

[19] Luo Yi Ning Ge Er, *Disanzhi yanjing kan Zhongguo* (*Looking at China through a Third Eye*) (Taiyuan: Shanxi renmin chubanshe, 1994).

Whereas the neo-Maoists had argued for a reassertion of a recentralized economy in ideological terms, the neoconservatives argued for it in practical terms – a strong central state was necessary to ensure stability and continuing tax revenues.[20] Without a restrengthening of party-state controls, they asserted, the party would be unable to handle the social instabilities caused by the growing economic regionalism, internal migrants, and increasing inequalities unleashed by the economic reforms. Unless the erosion of the party-state's authority were stopped, they warned that chaos, *luan,* the traditional Chinese nightmare, would result. Theirs was an implicit criticism of Deng's reforms for weakening and devolving the central government.[21]

Another important intellectual current in the mid-1990s was a revival of neo-Confucianism. Although its proponents did not refer to Marxism-Leninism, the Jiang leadership found their views more in tune with its goals than the views of either the neo-Maoists or the liberals. The neo-Confucianists asserted that modernization need not mean Westernization. In fact, the seeds of modernization, they argued, could be found in Chinese history and values, specifically in Confucianism. Instead of China's deeply embedded traditional culture being an obstacle to its modernization, as preached by the May Fourth intellectuals and party and intellectual reformers in the 1980s, they insisted that Confucianism was conducive to modernization. Citing the dynamic economies of the post-Confucian-shaped societies of their East Asian neighbors, they asserted that a revived neo-Confucianism, with its emphasis on the group, authority, and education, could provide the intellectual and cultural underpinnings for China's rapid economic development while helping China avoid the immorality and individualism of Western capitalism.[22]

Counter to China's growing involvement with the outside world and growing intellectual pluralism, the post-June 4 leaders and their intellectual spokespersons not only reemphasized ideological unity, they also reenergized a spirit of nationalism, as leaders earlier in the century had done to promote political unity. Furthermore, with the bankruptcy of ideology in the aftermath of the Cultural Revolution, the leadership used nationalism periodically to engender support for the regime. Generally, the younger generation of intellectuals, urban youth, and emerging middle class readily embraced the leadership's reinvigorated nationalism. They needed little prodding. In 1993, they spontaneously protested against the rejection of

[20] Wang Shaoguang and Hu Angang, *Zhongguo guojia nengli baogao* (*Study of China's State Capacity*) (Shenyang: Liaoning renmin chubanshe, 1993).

[21] Luo Yi Ning Ge Er, *Disanzhi yanjing kan Zhongguo* (*Looking at China through a Third Eye*) (Taiyuan: Shanxi renmin chubanshe, 1994).

[22] See the collection of articles translated in *Chinese Studies in Philosophy,* vol. 24, no. 3 (Spring 1993).

China's bid to host the International Olympics in the year 2000, blaming the United States. China's increasingly apparent economic success and reemergence as a player on the world scene had also awakened nationalist pride among these groups. They echoed their leaders' charge that the United States was attempting to contain China's rising power. Their indignation was expressed in such books as *China Can Say No* (*Zhongguo keyi shuo bu*) and the numerous variations on that theme, which became bestsellers in the mid-1990s.

The rising tide of nationalism cut across all schools of thought in the mid-1990s – neo-Maoism, neoconservativism, and neo-Confucianism – with the exception of the virtually silenced liberal school. Despite Deng Liqun and his allies' efforts, Jiang Zemin merely paid lip service to reviving Marxism-Leninism and Mao Thought. He stressed building "socialist spiritual civilization," but this concept had little to do with socialism and ideology. Though urging polite behavior in public places, its major concern was with keeping order and maintaining unity. The leadership agreed with the neo-Confucians that Confucianism was relevant to the present, but stressed its authoritarian, hierarchical values rather than other Confucian teachings, such as the intellectuals' obligation to criticize officials who abused power or engaged in unfair treatment of the population. Nevertheless, like other intellectual currents in post-Mao China, nationalist discourse was contradictory. Its stridency was challenged in articles in relatively liberal journals, such as *The Orient* (*Dongfang*) until it was suspended in May 1996.[23]

The leadership tried to suppress the nationalist upsurge of the mid-1990s. Soon after they appeared, it discouraged such writings as the "China Can Say No" books that were specifically directed against the United States and Japan. In September 1995, it stopped demonstrators from demanding reparations from Japan, fearing that such protests would ignite large-scale destabilizing demonstrations as well as frighten off Japanese investors. With the improvement of relations with the United States, inaugurated by the visits of Jiang to the United States in 1997 and President Clinton to China in 1998, the rise in nationalist sentiment that had permeated the intellectual and student circles in the mid-1990s gradually subsided. When Jiang called for political reforms to go along with the reform of state industry at the Fifteenth Party Congress in 1997, scores of intellectuals, both in and out of the establishment, once again called for the introduction of democratic practices.

[23] For translations, see "Chinese Intellectuals: Selections from *Dongfang*," *Contemporary Chinese Thought*, vol. 29, no. 2 (Winter 1997–98).

At the same time, another group of intellectuals, some of whom had been sent down to the countryside and to factories in the Cultural Revolution and so claimed to be in closer touch with ordinary working people, expressed a moral leftist view. They charged that China's economic reforms and involvement in the global economy had brought increasing inequalities as well as rampant corruption. They expressed a populist dismay at the layoffs of workers due to reform of state industries, the lagging incomes of peasants, and the plunder of state wealth by officials.[24] They also excoriated the consumerism and consumer culture that had accompanied China's move to a market economy. Though they shared some of the social idealism of the Mao era, their criticisms, unlike those of the neo-Maoists, were made without reference to any ideology or any overall solution.

As the post-Deng leadership since the mid-1990s continued to tolerate a number of different, contending intellectual currents, a new political springtime blossomed briefly in late summer–early fall of 1998.[25] Seemingly with the tacit consent of the Jiang leadership, disparate individual intellectuals were emboldened to call for greater freedom of expression and political reforms in public forums. Liu Ji, a vice president of CASS and an adviser to Jiang, sponsored the publication of a series of books which gave Jiang a reformist image and criticized the nationalist, neo-Maoist discourse of the mid-1990s. While Jiang had not spelled out what he meant by political reforms at the Fifteenth Party Congress, several highly placed intellectuals provided the rationale. The economist Dong Fureng, an adviser on state industry reform, publicly pointed out, as did several of his colleagues, the need for political reforms to deal with the rising unemployment, widening income gaps, environmental pollution, and widespread corruption precipitated by the market reforms.[26] A provincial reform official-turned-businessman, Fang Jue, distributed a proposal for democratic reforms based on the Western system of checks and balances and direct elections.[27]

Li Shenzhi, the retired head of the American Studies Institute at CASS, explained in the journal *Reform (Gaige)* that contrary to the leadership's emphasis on economic rights, one could not act as a "citizen" unless one also had political and civil rights. Because China had already made headway in

---

[24] He Qinglian, *Xiandaihua de xianjing: Dangdai Zhongguo de jingji shehui wenti (China's Pitfalls: Contemporary Economic and Social Problems)* (Beijing: Jinri Zhongguo chubanshe, 1998); and the review, Liu Binyan and Perry Link, "A Great Leap Backward?" *New York Review of Books,* October 8, 1998.

[25] Joseph Fewsmith, "Jiang Zemin takes Command," *Current History* (September 1998).

[26] "China: Economist says Market Economy Calls for Political Reform," Zhongguo Xinwen She (Beijing), February 15, 1998, FBIS-CHI-98-056, March 3, 1998.

[27] Fang Jue, "Zhongguo xuyao xinde zhuanbian" (China Needs New Changes), *Beijing zhichun* (Beijing Spring), no. 57 (February 1998), pp. 24–28.

providing people with a basic economic livelihood, he urged that it now provide political and civil rights. Counter to the views of the neoconservatives and some of China's leaders, who insisted that civil and political rights were alien to Asia, Li pointed out that the idea of such rights had been introduced and discussed in China in the early decades of the twentieth century. Therefore, the concept of universal human rights, he asserted, had already become a part of China's history and culture.[28] The fact that Jiang allowed President Clinton to discuss the indivisibility of economic rights and political rights at public meetings and on China's national television when Clinton visited China in June 1998 indicated a tolerance and perhaps tacit approval of public discussion of political reforms at that time.

In the midst of this discussion, a controversial book, *Cross Swords* (*Jiaofeng*), by two journalists from the *People's Daily* became a bestseller. The book attacked the neo-Maoists, and especially the "ten-thousand word" statements sponsored by Deng Liqun, not only for opposing reform of state industry, but also for criticizing China's involvement with the Western capitalist world.[29] But the book provoked a counterattack in the neo-Maoist journal *Dangdai Sichao* (*Contemporary Trends in Ideology*), in which its editors sued the authors for quoting from one of the "ten-thousand word" articles without authorization and distorting its contents. The editors lost the suit.

By late 1998, however, the atmosphere changed precipitously again. A cold wind in late fall froze the few flowers that had just blossomed. A number of different forces were pushing the cold wind: (1) the effects of the Asian economic crisis, slowing economic growth; (2) unemployed worker protests against the reform of state industry and unpaid wages; and (3) rising peasant discontent. These forces not only led to a slowing of state industry reform, they also led to a retreat from the public political discourse. Jiang's liberal adviser, Liu Ji, was "retired" as a vice president of CASS, while an older Maoist propagandist Wang Renzhi remained as an active vice president at the academy. A compilation of articles calling for political reform, *Governing China* (*Zhengzhi Zhongguo*),[30] was not allowed to be reprinted and one of its editors was put under house arrest for a time. Fang Jue, who had proposed a system of Western-style democracy, was arrested, though for an unrelated crime of "fraud."

[28] Li Shenzhi, "Ye yao tuidong zhengzhi gaige" (We Must also Promote Political Reform), *Gaige* (*Reform*), no. 1 (1998), pp. 13–14.

[29] Ma Licheng and Li Zhijun, *Jiaofeng: Dangdai Zhongguo sanci sixiang jiefang shilu* (*Cross Swords: A Record of Three Episodes of Liberated Thought in Contemporary China*) (Beijing: Jinri Zhongguo chubanshe, 1998).

[30] Dong Youyu and Shi Binhai, eds., *Zhengzhi Zhongguo: Mianlin xin tizhi xuanze de shidai* (*Governing China: The Time to Face the Choices of the New System*) (Beijing: Jinri Zhongguo chubanshe, 1998).

Another indication of retreat was reflected in the restrained twentieth anniversary in December 1998 of the launching of Deng's reforms at the Third Plenum of the Eleventh Central Committee. A speech by Jiang Zemin set the parameters of what could be discussed on this anniversary and reasserted Deng's Four Cardinal Principles, in which obedience to the party was paramount. Such restraint in marking this watershed event in the People's Republic revealed the wariness of the Jiang leadership to move forward with further reforms, economic as well as political, for fear of provoking unrest.

This retreat on political discourse was accompanied by a turn inward in spring 1999 as seen in the ferocious reaction to the tragic, but accidental NATO bombing of the Chinese Embassy in Belgrade, in which three Chinese journalists were killed. This event provoked another upsurge in nationalism, partly organized by the state and partly spontaneous. Clearly, there was a latent undercurrent of anti-foreignism, particularly among the youth ready to be incited, whenever the regime desired. In the period leading up to the tenth anniversary of the party's violent crackdown on demonstrators in Tiananmen on June 4, the regime welcomed the opportunity to divert attention onto foreign adversaries and away from itself. Though initially using the anti-American demonstrations for its own political purposes, by late May the leadership tried to rein in the nationalist fervor lest it turn into xenophobia sparking further demonstrations that could not only antagonize countries with which China sought trade and investment, but also be turned against the regime itself for its own inadequacies and oppressiveness.

NON-ESTABLISHMENT POLITICAL ACTIVISTS

Other forces silencing the public political discourse in the late 1990s were the actions of democratic activists emboldened by President Clinton's visit to China and China's signing of the U.N. Covenant on Civil and Political Rights in 1998 and its signing a year earlier of the U.N. Covenant on Social and Economic Rights, which sanctions independent labor unions. The National People's Congress ratified the latter covenant, but without sanctioning labor unions, in 2001. A number of non-establishment intellectuals tested the leadership's commitment to the covenants by attempting to set up political organizations and independent labor unions. Among the organizers were again some of the same ex Red Guards, survivors of the 1978–79 Democracy Wall movement, and participants in the spring 1989 demonstrations. One group sought to establish the first opposition party in the People's Republic, the China Democracy Party, at the time of Clinton's trip to China. By late 1998, several of its leaders were charged with seeking to overthrow the government and given long prison sentences, ranging from 11 to 13 years. All their efforts to register their party legally were thwarted and the organizers detained or arrested.

Another association, the China Development Union, established ostensibly to deal with environmental problems and hold seminars on political issues, was also disbanded, ostensibly because it was registered in Hong Kong rather than in Beijing, but primarily because of the party's fear that such an organization would also become politically active. Although supposedly over 1 million nongovernmental organizations were established in China by 1998, a large number of which dealt with intellectual, social, and cultural issues, none were allowed to engage in political activities and none came close to carrying on the political activities of the relatively independent think tanks of the 1980s.[31] Nevertheless, the effort to establish the China Democracy Party was unprecedented in that it was the first attempt to set up a public political opposition party in the People's Republic. Moreover, the efforts were not confined just to Beijing and Shanghai; the activities were carried out all over the country.

The party's arrest of the leaders of the China Democracy Party and other political dissidents in the late 1990s revealed another new approach used by China's dissident intellectuals. The party also confiscated computers, fax machines, beepers, and cellular phones. These technologies, especially the Internet, had transformed the means of political communication in China in the 1990s. They had the potential to become China's equivalent to the Soviet *samizdat*, the underground typewritten literature that ultimately helped to bring down the Soviet Union and the Soviet Communist Party. Even more threatening, despite the party's efforts to censor these technologies, they had the potential for organization that the party had not encountered before. In December 1998, the party sentenced to two years the owner of a computer software company, who had supplied thousands of email addresses to Chinese dissident publications in the United States, thus enabling them to communicate through the Internet with thousands back in China. Whereas the party had no trouble closing down the Democracy Wall in Beijing in 1979, it remains to be seen whether it can similarly control the Internet, which has been called China's "virtual Democracy Wall."[32]

Another group that the Jiang government severely repressed was the

---

[31] Tony Saich, "Negotiating the State: The Development of Social Organizations," *The China Quarterly*, no. 161 (March 2000).

[32] He Xintong, wife of Xu Wenli (since sentenced to 13 years), in talk at the Fairbank Center, Harvard University, August 1998.

families of those students and citizens who were killed or imprisoned on June 4. The families have persistently sought a reversal of the negative verdict on the 1989 Tiananmen Square demonstration. Ding Zilin, a retired professor at Chinese People's University, whose only son was killed in the crackdown, has led the effort to compile a list of those killed on June 4 and to distribute funds sent by overseas Chinese to the families of the victims. In addition, former officials, such as Zhao Ziyang, who was placed under house arrest in 1989, and Zhao's personal secretary, Bao Tong, who had been imprisoned for defending the students, also asked for a reevaluation of the "counter-revolutionary" designation of the 1989 demonstrations. On each June 4 anniversary or on the occasion of a visit from a prominent foreign leader, members of this group have been detained by the government or put under a form of house arrest for fear that they might stir up a protest that would gain popular support.

Another reason for the party's harsh repression of non-establishment intellectuals in 1999 was its confrontation with the qigong meditation group Falun Gong, which held a silent demonstration of 10,000 of its followers in front of the party-state headquarters in Zhongnanhai on April 25, 1999. Members of this movement were mostly middle-aged unemployed workers, some party members, and just a small number of intellectuals. Nevertheless, the leadership was most concerned that the non-establishment intellectuals who had joined with disaffected workers in attempts to set up independent labor unions may also join with this meditation movement, which had millions of followers all over the country and abroad.

As the bankruptcy and reform of state industries provoked growing and widespread workers' demonstrations in the late 1990s, the party's fear of an alliance between disaffected workers and intellectuals became palpable. So far, however, there is lack of concrete evidence and detail on these underground unions. It is difficult to estimate the number and size of such alliances and unions. All that is known is that those engaged in such activities are being arrested in cities from Xi'an to Wuhan and from Heilongjiang to Shenzhen. Some of these people are ex Red Guards, who might have been establishment intellectuals had it not been for the suspension of their educations in the Cultural Revolution; others wrote in the journals of the 1978–79 Democracy Wall movement; and still others participated in the 1989 demonstrations. Yet, the party regards this relatively small number of marginal intellectuals as having the potential to spark widespread social unrest.

Whereas the party-state moved swiftly and harshly against such intellectuals helping to organize labor unions and political organizations, it was more cautious toward the demonstrating workers and pensioners, particularly in China's rust belt – Sichuan, Shaanxi, the Northeast, and Hubei. In many cases, local officials stepped in to pay the back wages and pensions in order to stop the demonstrations.[33] The greater caution toward the workers reflected the party-state's fear that a violent crackdown on workers could ignite social unrest into a conflagration that would spread quickly and be difficult to contain. Ever since the Polish Solidarity labor union developed into a political movement in 1980 with the help of Poland's intellectuals that overthrew the Polish Communist Party, China's leaders have feared a similar development in China. They have reason for concern. The first half of China's twentieth-century history was marked by instances of intellectuals and workers joining in political movements that destabilized regimes and caused profound changes, as witnessed in the May Fourth movement and, most important, the establishment of the Chinese Communist Party itself.

Like the efforts to control the Internet, it is unlikely that the party-state will succeed in totally suppressing efforts of non-establishment intellectuals to join with other social groups. Those leading these efforts came of age during the Cultural Revolution. They became workers or were sent-down youth when their education was interrupted during the Cultural Revolution. Having been forced to labor in factories and fields, they have contacts with ordinary working people, which their intellectual predecessors and the younger intellectuals did not have. Moreover, having become totally disillusioned with their political leaders and the political system during the Cultural Revolution, this generation tends to question accepted practices. Consequently, they express more independence than other generations of Chinese intellectuals. While most intellectuals and students in the 1990s appear to have become apolitical or more interested in making money, the politically engaged intellectuals of the Cultural Revolution generation have been the most active in joining with other social groups in common cause and seeking political change.

CHINA'S INTELLECTUALS AT THE END
OF THE TWENTIETH CENTURY

Although the Jiang leadership tolerated a variety of voices in the 1990s, it did not let any of those voices organize into political associations. Moreover, it only briefly tolerated public political discourse. Still, political ideas, ranging from conservative to liberal, from neo-Maoist to moral leftist, continued to be discussed internally among elite intellectuals and in

[33] Dorothy Solinger, "The Potential for Urban Unrest," in *Is China Unstable?* David Shambaugh, ed. (Washington, DC: Sigur Center for Asian Studies, George Washington University, 1998).

policy-making circles. Perhaps as the price for continuing these discussions, members of the intellectual establishment have stayed clear of any contact with non-establishment political and labor activists. At the same time, the Jiang leadership appeared willing to tolerate political discourse among establishment intellectuals that did not directly challenge its authority or move beyond establishment circles or into the public sphere.

China's zigzag, contradictory treatment of intellectuals in the 1990s reveals that while some leaders, including Jiang,[34] may agree with some intellectuals on the need for political reforms to deal with problems produced by the economic reforms, they are hesitant to move actively in this direction. They fear and warn not only of social unrest, but of a Soviet-style scenario in which both they and the Leninist party-state would be replaced and chaos would ensue. Consequently, though the party's controls weakened further in the 1990s due to accelerating market reforms, growing involvement with the outside world, and the party's continuing withdrawal from most areas of daily life, the party continued to suppress any action that it considered a political threat.

Though confronted with persistent Falun Gong protests at the turn of the century, the Jiang government has not been confronted with massive student demonstrations, which it has not sanctioned. Except for flare-ups of nationalism, not only have students become more politically quiescent since June 4, the Jiang government has preempted political protests by detaining or arresting potential instigators. It has also equipped the People's Armed Police with nonlethal weapons so that it will be able to deal with demonstrations more effectively than was the case in 1989 and, therefore, not need to send in the military. The party-state has been successful so far in suppressing any intellectual and student challenges on sensitive anniversaries or during visits by Western leaders, by putting controversial intellectuals and students under surveillance, house arrest, or detention and preventing students from gathering outside their universities. The party-state's precautions and increased ability to suppress protests may lessen their threat.

The party-state's major concern about intellectuals in the late 1990s was to prevent underground intellectual–worker alliances that might surface as a political movement that could ultimately overthrow the regime. Despite the small number of marginal intellectuals engaged in such activities and the government's precautions, the potential for demonstrations, led by intellectuals, that might spread to disaffected workers and other groups such as the Falun Gong is real. China's leaders appear to have not yet learned

---

[34] Jiang Zemin, "Hold High the Great Banner of Deng Xiaoping Theory," report delivered at the 15th National Congress of the CCP on September 12, 1997, *Beijing Review* (October 6–12, 1997), pp. 10–33.

the lesson from June 4: the gradual building of political institutions – a genuine legislature, competitive elections above the village level, independent unions, rule of law, and a free press – can provide disaffected elements, such as laid-off workers, their former Red Guard associates, restive students, politically engaged intellectuals, and even non-official meditation groups, with less destabilizing means to express their grievances and seek redress than through demonstrations and mass protests.

Despite the stifling of public debate on political issues in the 1990s, the cultural and intellectual pluralism of the late twentieth century, while in a different context, was comparable to that of the May Fourth period. When China's modern intellectual history is viewed from the perspective of the century's close, the Mao era rather than the May Fourth period appears to have been the interregnum between the lively intellectual and cultural scene of the early decades and the late decades of the twentieth century. Like their May Fourth predecessors, intellectuals in the post-Mao period also discovered that intellectual pluralism does not necessarily lead to democracy, though it might be the precondition for democracy. After June 4, those intellectuals who stayed out of the forbidden zones of politics continued to enjoy relative freedom in their personal lives, professional work, and intellectual enquiries; those who continued to venture into the political realm continued to be suppressed. An apolitical, increasingly cosmopolitan, and popular culture not only survived, it thrived.

Deng and his successor Jiang Zemin's approach to intellectual and cultural endeavor resembled that of the Republican era. The Guomindang's weak Leninist party-state and watered-down ideology left intellectuals alone as long as they did not challenge the leadership or party politically. Guomindang leaders may have wanted to impose tighter controls over intellectual life, but they had neither the will nor the capacity to do so. Their governments censored dissent after it appeared and repressed a small number of politically engaged intellectual dissidents. Likewise the Deng-Jiang regimes imprisoned and silenced those intellectuals whom they regarded as direct political threats. Nevertheless, both before and after the Mao era, waning ideology and weakening party controls allowed more room for intellectual exploration and creativity without reference to any ideology or political directive.

Therefore, despite episodes of repression and the arrest of scores of intellectuals who directly challenged the regime, the cultural and intellectual pluralism of the post-Mao era looked more like the norm in the twentieth century than the Mao era. Though not as brilliant nor as original as the urban cultural explosion of innovative literary and art works in the 1920s and 1930s, the openness and vibrant popular culture of the last decades of the twentieth century had not been seen since the early decades of the century. Most Chinese intellectuals and students in the 1990s enjoyed more individual and intellectual freedoms, access to their foreign counterparts, and a more pluralistic cultural environment than at any other time in the history of the People's Republic.

Yet, while China's cultural environment at century's end may resemble that of its early decades, it appears to be moving in a different direction because of very different political and international contexts. The May Fourth Movement, reacting to the chaos caused by the warlord conflicts and threat of Western imperialism, sought to build a more powerful state. The Deng era, reacting to the Maoist period in which the unlimited power of the leader and state had caused so much damage, sought to lessen the state's power and reach. Therefore, while both cultures, early and late in the century, tended to be critical of the state, their concerns were very different. The former culture created an intellectual atmosphere conducive to building a strong state; the later culture sought to limit the controls of the state over society, the economy, and the individual.

Equally important, the impact of the outside world was even greater at the end of the twentieth century than in the early decades. At that time Western culture was indiscriminately absorbed by China's urban intellectuals, but it did not extend much beyond the cities along the eastern coast and lower Yangzi. The inner provinces and traditional cities had little knowledge or contact with the West, let alone its culture. At the beginning of the twenty-first century, an international culture was pouring into China from all over the world and flooding not only its seacoast cities, but its countryside through television, film, phone, fax, Internet, email, music, and travel. While strict controls remained on reporting on political issues, even the official press was increasingly governed by the market and its content determined more by the public than by the government. Furthermore, the media's space for nonpolitical news – economic, social, cultural, entertainment, and international – expanded at a rapid rate. Therefore, while the audience for the official media such as the *People's Daily* was shrinking, that for nonparty media was growing.[35] Thus, a worldwide popular culture, which was seeping into all areas and all classes, was gradually transforming China. It subverted the party's controls and promoted values that were alien to the mainstream traditional Chinese and Marxist-Leninist emphasis on obedience and conformity.

A similar process as well was transforming the intellectuals' traditional

---

[35] Li Xiguang, Xinhua editor, unpublished paper given at the Kennedy School, Harvard University, May 1999.

role as leaders of Chinese society. Even in the Mao period when they were so persecuted, part of the reason for their persecution was the persistent traditional view of intellectuals as the nation's leaders. In the post-Mao era, on the one hand, intellectuals have played an important role not because of a strong institutional base or because of their symbolic leadership role, but because of their skills in helping China modernize its economy, science, and technology. On the other hand, however, China's intellectual pluralism and spread of popular and international culture undermined their position as China's cultural, moral, and political standard-bearers. At the same time, because of increasing market opportunities for their talents and expertise, a growing proportion of China's intellectuals became less dependent on the state and were changing from their traditionally close relationship with government to a relationship of increasing autonomy.

Even those politically engaged elite intellectuals, who in the late 1980s had established their own journals, think tanks, and networks, used these institutions to influence society, though most intellectuals continued to work through the political leadership as they had done traditionally. Due to their failure in the past to influence political leaders, even those whom they initially supported, another major change in the post-Mao era was the intellectuals' growing realization that an intellectual elite, acting alone, could not bring about political change. It was necessary to join with other social groups in political action to be effective. Evidence of this change in view appeared briefly during the martial law period from May 20,1989 until June 4, when some of the intellectuals' and workers' independent unions, formed during the demonstration, joined in a coalition to bring about a peaceful resolution to the stand-off between the students and party. This coalition was attempted again briefly at the end of the century, when a small number of intellectuals tried to help workers form independent labor unions and establish an alternative political party, the China Democracy party. Once more, the party thwarted this effort by arresting the party's leaders.

Even though the intellectuals involved still believed that they should lead these coalitions, their actions resembled more those of their intellectual counterparts in Eastern Europe, especially in Poland and Czechoslovakia, just before the overthrow of the Communist party-states than their literati predecessors. Instead of using ideological revisions and political contacts to press for change from above, a small number of intellectuals began to organize among themselves and join with other social classes to achieve specific political aims. Similar efforts began during China's May Fourth period and continued until the 1949 revolution. But until the post-Mao era, intellectuals in the People's Republic were either in the establishment or if they were dissidents, labeled "rightists" and pushed to the margins of society. The party's weakening controls, the move to the market, and openness to the outside world made possible the emergence of an increasingly independent intellectual class. Most of them in the 1990s were no longer at the center of political power, except for a small number of technocrats. The majority carried on their professional activities or business relatively unconcerned with political matters. Those intellectuals in the establishment who tried to push political reform in the 1980s were silenced or pushed out of the establishment. The non-establishment intellectuals in the 1990s, who tried in conjunction with other social groups, particularly workers, to promote political change in China were in prison or were sent away to labor-reform camps.

Thus, while intellectuals in the last decades of the twentieth century may resemble their counterparts in the early decades of the century, they are undergoing a radical transformation in terms of their relationship with the state. Instead of becoming advisers or officials in the government as they had done through most of Chinese history even during the Mao era, the majority choose, for the first time in Chinese history, to be relatively unengaged in political activities. At the same time, a small number on the margins continue political activities in alliance with other social groups. If these trends continue into the next century, then the close, but essentially subservient relationship of the intellectuals to the state may gradually change.

Likewise, the intellectuals' status as the political pace-setters and moral leaders of Chinese society may also change. As the intellectuals lose their singularity and become one among a number of social groups and political actors, they may help produce a more pluralistic society and build new institutions, but they also will help shape a society in which they are no longer the symbolic leaders of the country. Perhaps that is the price China's intellectuals may have to pay for political change.

BIBLIOGRAPHY

A built-in ambiguity haunts any bibliography of Chinese writings: Entries that are immediately intelligible to the reader of English, like *Central Daily News* or *Liberation Daily,* are not directly clued to the Chinese characters in which the originals are written (*Chung-yang jih-pao, Chieh-fang jih-pao*). Yet, on the other hand, an entry like *Chin-tai shih yen-chiu-so,* though more accurate in the esoteric script of romanization, may be translated variously as Modern History Institute or Institute of Modern History. In this situation we have put romanized accuracy ahead of English-translated intelligibility, but with occasional cross-references.

Another problem is that large compilations of documents are usually edited by committees, departments, or other institutional organs, so that listing such works by compiler or editor would confront the reader with many words but little information. In such cases we prefer to list by title. Compilers and editors are then cited in the body of the entry.

Footnote notation systems, like romanization systems, may appeal only to certain people. Yet they are necessary and have to be arbitrary. The sole test is their accuracy and economy. Numbers of issues within volumes of periodicals we unite with a period. (If pages are within a volume only, they are united with its number by a period: e.g., Mao, *SW,* 5.27.) For journals that use the year as the volume number, the year is treated as a volume number: The citation therefore appears as, say, 1981.4, 17–21.

Materials such as speeches, reports, and articles of and about the Chinese leadership are normally cited with reference to their place of origin in the press or published collections, but a certain number of such materials are listed independently in the bibliography.

A great part of Chinese publications is put out by the People's Publishing House, Jen-min ch'u-pan-she, which we abbreviate Jen-min. We have similarly abbreviated the names of most other publishing houses by omitting ch'u-pan-she.

A Ying. *Wan-Ch'ing hsiao-shuo shih* (A history of late Ch'ing fiction). Peking: Tso-chia ch'u-pan-she, 1955. Hong Kong reprint: T'ai-p'ing shu-chü, 1966.

A Ying. *Wan-Ch'ing wen-i pao-k'an shu-lüeh* (A brief account of late Ch'ing literary journals and newspapers). Shanghai: Ku-tien wen-hsueh ch'u-pan-she, 1958.

Abrams, M.H. *A glossary of literary terms.* New York: Holt, Rinehart & Winston, 3rd ed., 1971.

[Ai Ssu-ch'i]. *Ai Ssu-ch'i wen-chi* (Ai Ssu-ch'i collected works). Peking: Jen-min, 1981.

Ai Ssu-ch'i. *Che-hsueh yü sheng-huo* (Philosophy and life). Shanghai: Tu-shu sheng-huo, 1937.

Ai Ssu-ch'i. *Ta-chung che-hsueh* (Philosophy for the masses). Shanghai: Tu-shu sheng-huo, 1936.

Alitto, Guy S. *The last Confucian: Liang Shu-ming and the Chinese dilemma of modernity.* Berkeley: University of California Press, 1978.

Bastid, Marianne. *Aspects de la réforme de l'enseignement en Chine au début de XXᵉ siècle. D'après des ecrits de Zhang Jian.* Paris and the Hague: Mouton, 1971.

Bauer, Wolfgang. *China and the search for happiness: Recurring themes in four thousand years of Chinese cultural history.* Trans. from the German by Michael Shaw. New York: Seabury Press, 1976.

Baum, Richard, and Teiwes, Frederick C. *Ssu-ch'ing: The Socialist Education Movement of 1962–1966.* Berkeley: Center for Chinese Studies, University of California, 1968.

Bernal, Martin. 'Chinese socialism before 1913,' in Jack Gray, ed. *Modern China's search for a political form,* 66–95. London: Oxford University Press, 1969.

Bernal, Martin. *Chinese socialism to 1907.* Ithaca: Cornell University Press, 1976.

Bernal, Martin. 'The triumph of anarchism over Marxism 1906–1907,' in Mary Wright, ed. *China in revolution: The first phase 1900–1913,* 97–142.

Berninghausen, John, and Huters, Ted, eds. *Revolutionary literature in China: An anthology.* White Plains, N.Y.: M. E. Sharpe, 1977. First published in *Bulletin of Concerned Asian Scholars,* 8.1–2 (1976).

Bien, Gloria. 'Baudelaire and the Han Garden,' paper presented at the Chinese Language Teachers Association panel, Modern Languages Association annual meeting, New York, Dec. 1976.

Bien, Gloria. 'Shao Hsun-mei and the flowers of evil,' paper presented at the Association for Asian Studies annual meeting, Chicago, April 1978.

Bing, Dov. 'Sneevliet and the early years of the CCP.' *CQ,* 48 (Oct.–Dec. 1971) 677–97.

Birch, Cyril. 'Change and continuity in modern Chinese fiction,' in Merle Goldman, ed. *Modern Chinese literature in the May Fourth era,* 385–406.

Birch, Cyril. 'English and Chinese meters in Hsu Chih-mo.' *Asia Major,* NS 8.2 (1961) 258–93.

Birch, Cyril. 'Lao She: The humourist in his humour.' *CQ,* 8 (Oct.–Dec. 1961) 45–62.

Brown, Edward J. *Russian literature since the revolution.* New York: Collier, 1963; rev. ed., 1969.

Calinescu, Matei. *Faces of modernity: Avant-garde, decadence, kitsch.* Bloomington: Indiana University Press, 1977.

Cambridge history of China, The (CHOC). Vol. 1. *The Ch'in and Han empires, 221 B.C.–A.D. 220,* ed. Denis Twitchett and Michael Loewe (1986). Vol. 3. *Sui and T'ang China, 589–906, Part I,* ed. Denis Twitchett (1979). Vol. 7. *The Ming Dynasty, 1368–1644, Part I,* ed. Frederick W. Mote and Denis Twitchett (1988). Vol. 10. *Late Ch'ing 1800–1911, Part 1,* ed. John K. Fairbank (1978). Vol. 11. *Late Ch'ing 1800–1911, Part 2,* ed. John K. Fairbank and Kwang-Ching Liu (1980). Vol. 12. *Republican China 1912–1949, Part 1,* ed. John K. Fairbank (1983). Vol. 13. *Republican China 1912–1949, Part 2,* ed. John K. Fairbank and Albert Feuerwerker (1986). Vol. 14. *The People's Republic, Part 1: The emergence of revolutionary China 1949–1965,* ed. Roderick MacFarquhar and John K. Fairbank (1987). Vol. 15. *The People's Republic, Part 2: Revolutions within the Chinese revolution 1966–1982,* ed. Roderick MacFarquhar and John K. Fairbank (1991). Cambridge: Cambridge University Press.

Carrère d'Encausse, Hélène, and Schram, Stuart R., comps. *Marxism and Asia: An introduction with readings.* London: Allen Lane, 1969.

CB. See U.S. Consulate General, *Current Background.*

CFJP. See *Chieh-fang jih-pao.*

Chan, Agnes. 'The Chinese anarchists.' University of California, Ph.D. dissertation, Berkeley, 1977.

Chan, Wing-tsit. *Religious trends in modern China.* New York: Columbia University Press, 1953.

Chang Ching-lu, ed. *Chung-kuo chin-tai ch'u-pan shih-liao* (Historical materials on modern Chinese publications). *Chia-pien* (Part I), 1953; *Erh-pien* (Part II), 1954. Peking: Chung-hua.

Chang Ching-lu, ed. *Chung-kuo ch'u-pan shih-liao* (Historical materials on Chinese publications). *Pu-pien* (Supplement), 1957. Peking: Chung-hua.

Chang Ching-lu, ed. *Chung-kuo hsien-tai ch'u-pan shih-liao* (Historical materials on contemporary Chinese publications). *Chia-pien* (Part I), 1954; *I-pien* (Part II), 1955; *Ping-pien* (Part III), 1956; *Ting-pien* (Part IV), 1959, 2 vols. Peking: Chung-hua.

Chang Chün-mai. 'Jen-sheng kuan' (Philosophy of life), in *K'o-hsueh yü jen-sheng kuan,* prefaces by Hu Shih and Ch'en Tu-hsiu. Shanghai: Ya-tung shu-chü, 1923.

Chang Ch'un-ch'iao. 'P'o-ch'u tzu-ch'an-chieh-chi ti fa-ch'uan ssu-hsiang' (Eliminate the ideology of bourgeois right). *JMJP,* 13 October 1958.

Chang Jo-ying, ed. *Hsin wen-hsueh yun-tung shih tzu-liao* (Materials concerning the new literary movement). Shanghai: Kuang-ming shu-chü, 1934.

Chang Man-i *et al. Hsien-tai Chung-kuo shih-hsuan, 1917–1949* (Modern Chinese poetry: An anthology, 1917–1949), 2 vols. Hong Kong: Hong Kong University Press and the Chinese University of Hong Kong Publications Office, 1974.

Chang Ping-lin. 'Chü-fen chin-hua lun' (Progress as differentiation). *Min-pao,* 7 (5 Sept. 1906) 1–13.

Chang Ping-lin. *Ch'iu shu* (Book of raillery). Shanghai, 1904; Taipei, photolithographed reprint: Chung-kuo Kuo-min-tang tang-shih shih-liao pien-tsuan wei-yuan-hui, 1967.

Chang Ping-lin. *Kuo-ku lun-heng* (Critical essays on antiquity). Shanghai, n.d.; Taipei, photolithographed reprint: Kuang-wen shu-chü, 1971.

Chang Ping-lin. 'Po shen-wo hsien-cheng shuo' (Against 'soul' as a foundation for constitutional government). *Min-pao*, 21 (10 June 1908) 1–11.

Chang Ping-lin. 'She-hui t'ung-ch'üan shang-tui' (Discussion of the history of politics). *Min-pao*, 12 (6 March 1907) 1–24.

Chang Ping-lin. 'Ssu-huo lun' (On four delusions). *Min-pao*, 22 (10 July 1908) 1–22.

Chang Ping-lin. 'Wu-wu lun' (The five negatives). *Min-pao*, 16 (25 Sept. 1907) 1–22.

Chang Tung-sun. 'Yü chih K'ung-chiao kuan' (My view of Confucianism). *Yung yen*, 1.15 (July 1913) 1–12.

[Chang Wen-t'ien]. *Chang Wen-t'ien hsuan-chi* (Selected works of Chang Wen-t'ien). Peking: Jen-min, 1985.

Chang, Hao. *Liang Ch'i-ch'ao and intellectual transition in China, 1890–1907.* Cambridge, Mass.: Harvard University Press, 1971.

Chang, Parris. *Radicals and radical ideology in China's Cultural Revolution.* New York: Columbia University Press, 1973.

Chao Shu-li. *Li-chia-chuang ti pien-ch'ien* (Changes in Li village). Shansi: Hua-pei hsin-hua shu-tien, 1946.

Ch'en, Jerome, ed. *Mao papers: Anthology and bibliography.* London and New York: Oxford University Press, 1970.

Ch'en Pei-ou. *Jen-min hsueh-hsi tz'u-tien* (People's study dictionary). Shanghai: Kuang-i shu-chü, 2nd ed., 1953.

Ch'en Po-chün. 'Lun k'ang-Jih yu-chi chan-cheng ti chi-pen chan-shu: Hsi-chi' (On the basic tactic of the anti-Japanese guerrilla war: The surprise attack). *Chieh-fang*, 28 (11 Jan. 1938) 14–19.

Ch'en Tu-hsiu. 'Ching-kao ch'ing-nien' (A call to youth). *Hsin ch'ing-nien*, 1.1 (Sept. 1915) 1–6 (sep. pag.).

Ch'en Tu-hsiu. 'K'ung-tzu chih tao yü hsien-tai sheng-huo' (Confucianism and modern life). *Hsin ch'ing-nien*, 2.4 (1 Dec. 1916) 1–7 (sep. pag.).

Ch'en Tu-hsiu. 'Tui-yü Liang Chü-ch'uan [Liang Chi] hsien-sheng tzu-sha chih kan-hsiang' (Impressions of the suicide of Mr. Liang Chü-ch'uan). *Hsin ch'ing-nien*, 6.1 (15 Jan. 1918) 19–20.

Cheng Chen-to *et al. Chung-kuo hsin wen-hsueh ta-hsi tao-lun hsuan-chi* (Selected introductory essays to *Comprehensive compendium to China's new literature*). Hong Kong: Ch'ün-i ch'u-pan-she, 1966.

Cheng, Ch'ing-mao. 'The impact of Japanese literary trends on modern Chinese writers,' in Merle Goldman, ed. *Modern Chinese literature in the May Fourth era*, 63–88.

Cheng, J. Chester, ed., with the collaboration of Ch'ing-lien Han *et al. The politics of the Chinese Red Army: A translation of the Bulletin of Activities of the People's Liberation Army.* Stanford, Calif.: Hoover Institution Press, 1966.

Cheng-chih chou-pao (Political weekly). Peking, 1924– .

Ch'eng Chi-hua *et al. Chung-kuo tien-ying fa-chan shih* (A history of the development of Chinese cinema). 2 vols. Peking: Chung-kuo tien-ying, 1963.

Ch'i Pen-yü. 'Comment on Li Hsiu-ch'eng's autobiography,' *LSYC,* reprinted as 'How should we look at the surrender of Li Hsiu-ch'eng?' *JMJP* and *KMJP,* 23 August 1963.

Ch'i Pen-yü and Lin Chieh. 'Comrade Chien Po-tsan's outlook on history should be criticized.' *HC,* 4 (24 March 1966) 19–30, *JPRS,* 35,137, 23–43.

Chiang Ch'ing. 'Do new services for the people.' *Tung fang hung* (The east is red), 3 June 1967, *SCMP-S,* 192, 7.

Chiang K'ang-hu. *Hung-shui chi: Chiang K'ang-hu san-shih-sui i-ch'ien tso* (Flood tide: Collection of writings by Chiang K'ang-hu before the age of thirty). n.p. Title page dated Sept. 1913.

Chieh-fang jih-pao (Liberation). Published at approximately weekly intervals in Yenan by the CCP Central Committee, from May 1937 to July 1941; thereafter became *Liberation Daily.*

Chien-she (Construction). Shanghai, Aug. 1919– .

Ch'ien Chih-hsiu. 'Shuo t'i-ho' (On adaptation). *TFTC,* 10.7 (1 Jan. 1914) 1–4 (sep. pag.).

Chih Ta. 'Nan-tao nü-ch'ang chih Shang-hai' (Shanghai, where men are robbers and women are whores). *T'ien-i,* 5 (10 Aug. 1907) 95–7.

Chin Chih-pai. 'P'i-K'ung yü lu-hsien tou-cheng' (Criticism of Confucius and two-line struggle). *HC,* 7 (1974), 23–34. Trans. in *PR,* 32 (1974) 6–10, 12, and 33(1974) 8–12.

Chin, Steve S. K. *The thought of Mao Tse-tung: Form and content.* Hong Kong: Centre of Chinese Studies, University of Hong Kong, 1979. [Preface to Chinese edition dated 1976.]

China Quarterly, The. Quarterly. London: Congress for Cultural Freedom (Paris), 1960–8; Contemporary China Institute, School of Oriental and African Studies, 1968– .

Chinese Law and Government: A journal of translations. Quarterly: Armonk, N.Y.: M. E. Sharpe, 1968 – . [Before 1977 published by IASP.]

Chinese studies in history: A journal of translations. (Formerly *Chinese studies in history and philosophy.*) Quarterly. Armonk, N.Y.: M.E. Sharpe, 1967– .

Chinese studies in philosophy: A journal of translations. Quarterly. Armonk, N.Y.: M. E. Sharpe, 1969– .

CHOC. See *Cambridge history of China, The.*

Chou En-lai. 'On literature and art.' *Wen-i pao* (Literary gazette), February 1979. Trans. in *PR* (30 March 1979) 9.

Chou Tso-jen. 'Jen ti wen-hsueh' (A humane literature). *Hsin ch'ing-nien,* 5.6 (Dec. 1918) 575–84.

Chou Yang. 'Kuan-yü kuo-fang wen-hsueh' (Concerning national defence literature), in Lin Tsung, ed. *Hsien chieh-tuan ti wen-hsueh lun-chan,* 31–8. Shanghai: Wen-i k'o hsueh yen-chiu-hui, 1936.

Chou Yang. 'Kuan-yü Ma-k'o-ssu-chu-i ti chi-ko li-lun wen-t'i ti t'an-t'ao' (An exploration of some theoretical questions of Marxism). *JMJP,* 16 March 1983.

Chou Yü-tung. (Old and new text classical learning). Shanghai: Commercial Press, 1926.

Chow Tse-tsung. *The May Fourth movement: Intellectual revolution in modern China.* Cambridge, Mass.: Harvard University Press, 1960.

Chu Hsi-chou, ed. *Lin Ch'in-nan hsien-sheng hsueh-hsing p'u-chi ssu-chung* (The life and works of Mr. Lin Shu, four records); (Works from the Ch'un-chueh study), 1.17 (*see Lin Ch'in-nan*).

Ch'u Min-i [Min]. 'Wu-cheng-fu shuo' (On anarchism). *Hsin shih-chi,* 31–47 (25 Jan.–16 May 1908).

Ch'ü Ch'iu-pai. 'Chi-an ti ch'ü-te ho sang-shih' (The conquest and loss of Chi-an). *Shih hua* (True words) (Shanghai), 2 (9 Dec. 1930) 3–4.

Chung-kung tang-shih yen-chiu (Research into the history of the CCP). Peking: Chung-kung chung-yang tang-hsiao, 1988–. Replaced *Tang-shih yen-chiu.*

Chung-kung yen-chiu (Studies on Chinese communism). Monthly. Taipei: 1967– . Cited as *CKYC.*

Chung-kuo ch'ing-nien pao (China youth news). Peking: 21 April 1951 (suspended August 1966, resumed October 1978) – .

Chung-kuo hsien-tai wen-hsueh shih ts'an-k'ao tzu-liao (Research materials on the history of modern Chinese literature), ed. by Pei-ching shih-fan ta-hsueh Chung-wen hsi hsien-tai wen-hsueh chiao-hsueh kai-ko hsiao-tsu (Peking Normal University, Chinese literature department, Contemporary literature teaching reform group). 3 vols. Peking: Kao-teng chiao-yü, 1959.

Chung-kuo hsien-tai wen-i tzu-liao ts'ung-k'an ti-i chi (Sources of modern Chinese literature, first series), ed. by *Shang-hai wen-i* pien-chi pu (Editorial department of *Shanghai Literature*). Shanghai: Shang-hai wen-i, 1962.

Chung-kuo hsin wen-hsueh ta-hsi (A comprehensive compendium of China's new literature), general ed. Chao Chia-pi. 10 vols. Shanghai: Liang-yu t'u-shu kung-ssu, 1935–6; Hong Kong reprint, 1963.

Chung-kuo jen-min chieh-fang-chün cheng-chih hsueh-yuan hsun-lien-pu t'u-shu tzu-liao kuan, *Mao Tse-tung chu-tso, yen-lun, wen-tien mu-lu* (A list of Mao Tse-tung's works, utterances, and telegrams). Peking: February 1961.

Chung-kuo Kuo-min-tang ch'üan-kuo tai-piao ta-hui hui-i-lu (Minutes of the National Congress of the Kuomintang of China). Reprinted, Washington, D.C.: Center for Chinese Research Materials, 1971.

CKYC. Chung-kung yen-chiu.

CLG. See Chinese Law and Government.

Cohen, A. *The communism of Mao Tse-tung.* Chicago: University of Chicago Press, 1964.

Compton, Boyd, trans. and intro. *Mao's China: Party reform documents, 1942–44.*

Seattle: University of Washington Press, 1966 [1952]; Westport, Conn.: Greenwood Press, 1982 [1952].

CQ. See *China Quarterly, The.*

Current Background. See U.S. Consulate General, *Current Background.* Cited as *CB.*

Day, M. Henri. *Mao Zedong 1917–1927: Documents.* Skriftserien für Orientaliska Studier no. 14. Stockholm, 1975.

Dirlik, Arif. *Revolution and history: Origins of Marxist historiography in China 1919–1937.* Berkeley: University of California Press, 1978.

Dolezalová, Anna. *Yü Ta-fu: Specific traits of his literary creation.* New York: Paragon, 1971.

Dolezelová-Velingerová, Milena. *The Chinese novel at the turn of the century.* Toronto: University of Toronto Press, 1980.

Dolezelová-Velingerová, Milena. 'The origins of modern Chinese literature,' in Merle Goldman, ed. *Modern Chinese literature in the May Fourth era,* 17–36.

ECMM. See U.S. Consulate General. *Extracts from China Mainland Magazines.* 1955–1960.

Egan, Michael. 'The short stories of Yü Dafu: Life through art.' University of Toronto, Ph.D. dissertation, 1979.

Egan, Michael. 'Yü Dafu and the transition to modern Chinese literature,' in Merle Goldman, ed. *Modern Chinese literature in the May Fourth era,* 309–24.

Eighth National Congress of the Communist Party of China. Peking: FLP, 1956.

Eighth National Congress of the Communist Party of China. Vol. 1: *Documents.* Vol. 2: *Speeches.* Peking: FLP, 1981.

Esherick, Joseph W. "On the 'restoration of capitalism': Mao and Marxist theory." *Modern China,* 5.1 (Jan. 1979), 41–77.

Esherick, Joseph W. *Reform and revolution in China: The 1911 Revolution in Hunan and Hubei.* Berkeley: University of California Press, 1976.

Fang, Achilles. 'From imagism to Whitmanism in recent Chinese poetry: A search for poetics that failed,' in Horst Frenz and G.A. Anderson, eds. *Indiana University conference on Oriental-Western literary relations,* 177–89. Chapel Hill: University of North Carolina Press.

FBIS. See Foreign Broadcast Information Service.

Feng Hsueh-feng. *Hui-i Lu Hsun* (Reminiscence of Lu Hsun). Peking: Jen-min wen-hsueh, 1952.

Feng Yu-lan. 'Criticism and self-criticism in discussion about Confucianism,' *Che-hsueh yen-chiu* (Philosophical research), 1963. 6 in *Chinese Studies in History and Philosophy,* 1.4 (Summer 1968), 84.

Feuerwerker, Yi-tsi Mei. *Ding Ling's fiction: Ideology and narrative in modern Chinese literature.* Cambridge, Mass.: Harvard University Press, 1983.

Feuerwerker, Yi-tsi [Mei]. 'The changing relationship between literature and life: Aspects of the writer's role in Ding Ling,' in Merle Goldman, ed. *Modern Chinese Literature in the May Fourth era,* 281–308.

Feuerwerker, Yi-tsi [Mei]. 'Women as writers in the 1920s and 1930s,' in Margery

Wolf and Roxane Witke, eds. *Women in Chinese society*, 143–68. Stanford: Stanford University Press, 1975.

Fitzgerald, John. 'Mao in mufti: Newly identified works by Mao Zedong.' *Australian Journal of Chinese Affairs*, 9 (Jan. 1983) 1–16.

FLP. Foreign Languages Press.

Fokkema, Douwe W. 'Lu Xun: The impact of Russian literature,' in Merle Goldman, ed. *Modern Chinese literature in the May Fourth era*, 89–102.

Foreign Broadcast Information Service. Washington. D.C.: U.S. Department of Commerce, 1941– . Cited as *FBIS*. The *Daily Report* of this agency has appeared in sections designated for specific regions but the names of these regions have been changed from time to time in a manner that makes it difficult to construct a precise genealogy. These designations have been used at various times: Asia and Pacific; China; Communist China; East Asia; Eastern Europe; Far East; People's Republic of China, USSR; USSR and Eastern Europe. *FBIS* is discussed in *CHOC*, 14.557 et passim.

Foreign Languages Press. Cited as FLP.

Friedman, Edward. *Backward toward revolution: The Chinese Revolutionary Party*. Berkeley: University of California Press, 1974.

Fung Yu-lan. *Hsin shih lun* (New culture and society). Changsha, 1941; 3rd printing. Shanghai: Commercial Press, 1948.

Furth, Charlotte, ed. *The limits of change: Essays on conservative alternatives in Republican China*. Cambridge, Mass.: Harvard University Press, 1976.

Furth, Charlotte. *Ting Wen-chiang: Science and China's new culture*. Cambridge, Mass.: Harvard University Press, 1970.

Gasster, Michael. *Chinese intellectuals and the Revolution of 1911: The birth of modern Chinese radicalism*. Seattle: University of Washington Press, 1969.

Giles, Herbert A., ed. *A history of Chinese literature*. Reprint. New York: Frederick Ungar, 1967; 1st ed., 1901.

Glunin, V. I. 'The Comintern and the rise of the communist movement in China (1920–1927),' in R. A. Ulyanovsky, ed. *The Comintern and the East*, 280–344. Moscow: Progress, 1979.

Goldblatt, Howard. *Hsiao Hung*. New York and Boston: Twayne, 1976.

Goldman, Merle. *Literary dissent in Communist China*. Cambridge, Mass.: Harvard University Press, 1967.

Goldman, Merle, ed. *Modern Chinese literature in the May Fourth era*. Cambridge, Mass.: Harvard University Press, 1977.

Goodman, David S. G. *Centre and province in the People's Republic of China: Sichuan and Guizhou, 1955–1965*. Cambridge and New York: Cambridge University Press, 1986.

Graham, Angus. *Chuang-tzu. The seven inner chapters and other writings from the book 'Chuang-tzu'*. London: Allen & Unwin, 1981.

Graham, Angus. *The book of Lieh-Tzu*. London: John Murray, 1960.

Grieder, Jerome B. *Hu Shih and the Chinese renaissance: Liberalism in the Chinese revolution, 1917–1937*. Cambridge, Mass.: Harvard University Press, 1970.

Grigoriev, A. M. 'The Comintern and the revolutionary movement in China under the slogan of the soviets (1927–1931),' in R. A. Ulyanovsky, ed. *The Comintern and the East,* 345–88. Moscow: Progress, 1979. Evidently a translation of L. P. Deliusin, ed. *Komintern i vostoki.*

Guide Weekly, The. See *Hsiang-tao chou-pao.*

Gunn, Edward Mansfield, Jr. 'Chinese literature in Shanghai and Peking (1937–45).' Columbia University, Ph.D. dissertation, 1978.

Gunn, Edward Mansfield, Jr. 'Chinese writers under Japanese occupation (1937–45).' Report on research in progress, Columbia University, Sept. 1976.

Gunn, Edward Mansfield, Jr., ed. *Twentieth-century Chinese drama: An anthology.* Bloomington: Indiana University Press, 1983.

Gunn, Edward Mansfield, Jr. *Unwelcome muse: Chinese literature in Shanghai and Peking, 1937–1945.* New York: Columbia University Press, 1980.

Hanan, Patrick. 'The technique of Lu Hsun's fiction.' *Harvard Journal of Asiatic Studies,* 34 (1975) 53–96.

Harding, Harry. *Organizing China: The problem of bureaucracy, 1949–1976.* Stanford, Calif.: Stanford University Press, 1981.

HC. See *Hung-ch'i.*

Historical experience of the dictatorship of the proletariat, The. Peking: FLP, 1959.

History of the Communist Party of the Soviet Union (Bolshevik): Short course. Moscow: Foreign Languages Publishing House; New York: International Publishers, 1939.

HMHHTL. See *Hsin-min hsueh-hui tzu-liao.*

Ho Chen. 'Lun nü-tzu tang chih kung-ch'an-chu-i' (On why women should know about communism). *T'ien-i,* 8–10 (30 Oct. 1907) 229–32.

Ho Chen. 'Nü-tzu fu-ch'ou lun' (On women's revenge). *T'ien-i,* 3 (10 July 1907) 7–23.

Hofheinz, Roy, Jr. *The broken wave: The Chinese communist peasant movement, 1922–1928.* Cambridge, Mass.: Harvard University Press, 1977.

Hou Chien. *Ts'ung wen-hsueh ko-ming tao ko-ming wen-hsueh* (From literary revolution to revolutionary literature). Taipei: Chung-wai wen-hsueh yueh-k'an she, 1974.

Hou Wai-lu. *Chin-tai Chung-kuo ssu-hsiang hsueh-shuo shih* (Interpretive history of modern Chinese thought). Shanghai: Sheng-huo, 1947.

Howe, Irving, ed. *The idea of the modern in literature and the arts.* New York: Horizon Press, 1967.

Hsia, C. T. 'Obsession with China: The moral burden of modern Chinese literature,' in his *A history of modern Chinese fiction,* 533–54.

Hsia, C. T. 'The fiction of Tuan-mu Hung-liang,' paper delivered at the Dedham conference on modern Chinese literature, Aug. 1974.

Hsia, C. T. 'The travels of Lao Ts'an: An exploration of its art and meaning.' *Tsing Hua Journal of Chinese Studies,* NS 7.2 (Aug. 1966) 40–66.

Hsia, C. T. 'Yen Fu and Liang Ch'i-ch'ao as advocates of new fiction,' in Adele A. Rickett, ed. *Chinese approaches to literature from Confucius to Liang Ch'i-ch'ao,* 251–7.

Hsia, C. T., ed. *A history of modern Chinese fiction.* New Haven: Yale University Press, 2nd ed., 1971.

Hsia, C. T., ed. *Twentieth-century Chinese stories.* New York: Columbia University Press, 1971.

Hsia Tseng-yu. *Chung-kuo li-shih chiao-k'o-shu* (Textbook on Chinese history).

Hsia, Tsi-an. *The gate of darkness: Studies on the leftist literary movement in China.* Seattle: University of Washington Press, 1968.

Hsiang-tao chou-pao (The Guide Weekly). Shanghai: 1922–1927.

Hsiao Hung. *Two novels of northeastern China: The field of life and death and Tales of Hulan River.* Trans. by Howard Goldblatt and Ellen Yeung. Bloomington: Indiana University Press, 1979.

Hsiao, Kung-chuan. *A modern China and a new world: K'ang Yu-wei, reformer and utopian 1858–1927.* Seattle: University of Washington Press, 1975.

Hsiao Sheng and Chiang Hua-hsuan. 'Ti-i-tz'u Kuo-Kung ho-tso t'ung-i chan-hsien ti hsing-ch'eng' (The formation of the first Kuomintang-Communist united front). *LSYC*, 2 (1981) 51–68.

Hsi-lo-k'e-fu [Shirokov] *et al.*, trans. by Li Ta *et al. Pien-cheng-fa wei-wu-lun chiao-ch'eng* (Course of instruction in dialectical materialism). Shanghai: Pi-keng-t'ang shu-tien, 15 May 1933.

Hsin ch'ing-nien (New youth). Sept. 1915–July 1926. Reprinted Tokyo: Daian, 1962.

Hsin-min hsueh-hui tzu-liao (Materials on the New People's Study Society), ed. by Chung-kuo ko-ming po-wu-kuan. Hu-nan sheng po-wu-kuan (Chung-kuo hsien-tai ko-ming shih tzu-liao ts'ung-k'an). Peking: Jen-min, 1980. Cited as *HMHHTL.*

Hsu, Chieh-yu [Hsu Kai-yu]. *Hsin-shih ti k'ai-lu jen–Wen i-to* (A trail blazer of the new poetry–Wen i-to). Hong Kong: Po-wen shu-chü, 1982.

Hsu, Kai-yu, trans. and ed. *Twentieth-century Chinese poetry: An anthology.* Garden City, N.Y.: Doubleday, 1963; New York: Anchor, 1964; Ithaca: Cornell University Press, 1970.

Hsu, Kai-yu. *Wen I-to.* Boston: Twayne, 1981.

Hsueh Fu-ch'eng. *Ch'ou-yang ch'u-i* (Preliminary proposals on foreign affairs, 1886); partially reprinted in Yang Chia-lo, comp., *Wu-hsu-pien-fa wen-hsien hui-pien* (Documentary collection of the 1898 reform movement), 1.151–61.

Hsueh-hsi wen-hsuan (Documents for study). 1967.

Hu Chin-ch'üan. *Lao She ho t'a-ti tso-p'in* (Lao She and his works). Hong Kong: Wen-hua sheng-huo ch'u-pan-she, 1977.

Hu Feng. *Min-tsu chan-cheng yü wen-i hsing-ko* (The national war and the character of literature). Chungking: Hsi-wang she, 1946.

Hu Hua. *Chung-kuo she-hui-chu-i ko-ming ho chien-she shih chiang-i* (Teaching materials on the history of China's socialist revolution and construction). Peking: Chung-kuo jen-min ta-hsueh, 1985.

Hu Hui-ch'iang. 'Ta lien kang-t'ieh yun-tung chien-k'uang' (A brief account of the campaign to make steel in a big way). *Tang-shih yen-chiu tzu-liao*, 4 (1983) 762–5.

Hu, John Y. H. *Ts'ao Yü.* New York: Twayne, 1972.

[Hu Shih]. *Hu Shih wen-ts'un* (Collected works of Hu Shih). 4 vols. Taipei: Yuan-tung t'u-shu kung-ssu, 1953.

Hu Shih. 'Pi-shang Liang-shan' (Forced to the Liang mountain), in his *Ssu-shih tzu-shu* (Autobiography at forty), 91–122. Shanghai, 1933; Taipei reprint: Yuan-tung t'u-shu kung-ssu, 1967.

Hu Shih. *The Chinese renaissance.* Chicago: University of Chicago Press, 1934.

Hu Shih. 'Wu-shih-nien-lai Chung-kuo chih wen-hsueh' (Chinese literature of the past fifty years), in *Hu Shih wen-ts'un*, 2.180–260.

Huang, Philip. *Liang Ch'i-ch'ao and modern Chinese liberalism.* Seattle: University of Washington Press, 1972.

Huang, Philip C.C. 'Mao Tse-tung and the middle peasants, 1925–1928.' *Modern China*, 1.3 (July 1975) 271–96.

Hung-ch'i (Red flag). Peking: 1958–88. Cited as *HC.*

IASP. International Arts and Sciences Press. See *Chinese Studies in Philosophy* and *Chinese Studies in History.*

Issues & Studies. Monthly. Taipei: Institute of International Relations, 1964– .

I-ta ch'ien-hou (Before and after the First Congress), ed. Chung-kuo she-hui-k'o-hsueh-yuan hsien-tai shih yen-chiu-shih and Chung-kuo ko-ming po-wu-kuan tang-shih yen-chiu-shih (Chung-kuo hsien-tai ko-ming shih tzu-liao ts'ung-k'an). Peking: Jen-min, 1980.

Jen-kung [Liang Ch'i-ch'ao]. 'Lun ch'iang-ch'üan' (On power). *Ch'ing-i pao,* 31 (1899) 4–7.

Jen-min ta hsien-chang hsueh-hsi shou-ts'e (Handbook for the study of the great people's constitution). Shanghai: Chan-wang chou-k'an, November 1949.

Jen-min ta hsien-chang hsueh-hsi tzu-liao (Materials for the study of the great people's constitution). Tientsin: Lien-ho t'u-shu, 1949.

JMJP. Jen-min jih-pao.

Joint Publications Research Service (*JPRS*). Washington, D.C.: U.S. Government. Various series. See Peter Berton and Eugene Wu, *Contemporary China: A research guide.* Stanford, Calif.: Stanford University Press, 1967, 409–30, and M. Oksenberg summary in *CHOC*, 14.557–8. Includes regional, world-wide, and topical translations and reports. Published periodically. The following items are cited in footnotes:

JPRS. Bibliography-index to U.S. JPRS research translations. See Kyriak, Theodore.

JPRS. China Area Report (*CAR*). 1987– . Cited as *CAR.*

JPRS. China Report: Political, sociological and military affairs. 1979–1987.

JPRS. China Report: Red Flag. Monthly. Continues *Translations from Red Flag.*

JPRS. China/State Council Bulletin (*CSB*). 1987– . Cited as *CSB.*

JPRS. Miscellany of Mao Tse-tung Thought. See Mao Tse-tung, *Miscellany. . .*

JPRS. Translations on Communist China political and sociological information. 1962–1968.

JPRS. Translations on international communist developments.

K'ang Yu-wei. 'Chung-hua chiu-kuo lun' (On China's salvation). *Pu-jen tsa-chih,* 1 (March 1913) 21–2.

K'ang Yu-wei. *Ta-t'ung shu* (Book of the Great Commonwealth). Shanghai: Chung-hua, 1935.

K'ang-chan ta-hsueh. Organ of the Anti-Japanese Military-Political University, Yenan, 1937– .

Kikuchi Saburo. *Chūgoku gendai bungaku shi* (History of contemporary Chinese literature). 2 vols. Tokyo: Aoki, 1953.

Kinkley, Jeffrey C. 'Shen Ts'ung-wen's vision of Republican China.' Harvard University, Ph.D. dissertation, 1977.

KMJP. Kuang-ming jih-pao.

KMWH. See *Ko-ming wen-hsien* (Documents of the revolution).

Knight, Nick. 'Mao Zedong's *On contradiction* and *On practice:* Pre-liberation texts.' *CQ,* 84 (Dec. 1980) 641–68.

Knight, Nick. *Mao Zedong's 'On contradiction': An annotated translation of the pre-liberation text.* Griffith Asian Papers Series. Nathan, Queensland: Griffith University, 1981.

'Ko min-chu tang-p'ai lien-ho hsuan-yen' (Joint declaration of the Democratic Parties). *JMJP,* 4 November 1950.

Ko-ming wen-hsien (Documents of the revolution), comp. by Lo Chia-lun *et al.* Taipei: Central Executive Committee of the Chung-kuo Kuo-min-tang, many volumes, 1953– ; cited as *KMWH; KMWH* printed in vols. 10–21 excerpts from Ch'en Hsün-cheng, *Kuo-min ko-ming-chün chan-shih ch'u-kao.* Taipei: Wen-hai chu-pan-she, 1972.

K'o-hsueh yü jen-sheng kuan (Science and the philosophy of life). Prefaces by Hu Shih and Ch'en Tu-hsiu. Shanghai: Ya-tung, 1927.

Kraus, Richard Curt. *Class conflict in Chinese socialism.* New York: Columbia University Press, 1981.

Krebs, Edward. 'Liu Ssu-fu and Chinese anarchism 1905–15.' University of Washington, Ph.D. dissertation, Seattle, 1977.

Kuan Feng and Lin Yü-shih. 'Some problems of class analysis in the study of the history of philosophy.' *Che-hsueh yen-chiu* (Philosophical research), 6 (1963) in *Chinese Studies in History and Philosophy,* 1.4 (Summer 1968) 66.

<*Kuan-yü chien-kuo-i-lai tang-ti jo-kan li-shih wen-t'i ti chueh-i*> chu-shih-pen (hsiu-ting) (Revised annotated edition of the Resolution on certain questions in the history of our Party since the founding of the People's Republic). Peking: Jen-min, 1985.

Kuang-ming jih-pao. Cited as *KMJP.*

Kung Wen-sheng. 'Sun Yeh-fang's theory is a revisionist fallacy.' *JMJP,* 8 Aug. 1966, *SCMP,* 3766, 17.

Kung Yü-chih. "Fa-chan k'o-hsueh pi-yu chih lu – chieh-shao Mao Tse-tung t'ung-chih wei ch'uan-tai 'Ts'ung i-ch'uan hsueh t'an pai-chia cheng-ming' i wen hsieh ti hsin ho an-yü" (The way which the development of science must follow – presenting Comrade Mao Tse-tung's letter and annotation relating to the republication of 'Let a hundred schools of thought contend' viewed from the perspective of genetics). *KMJP,* 28 Dec. 1983.

Kung Yü-chih. "'Shih-chien lun' san t'i" (Three points regarding 'On practice'), in *Lun Mao Tse-tung che-hsueh ssu-hsiang* (On Mao Tse-tung's philosophical thought), 66–86. Peking: Jen-min, 1983.

Kung-ch'an-tang (The Communist Party). Shanghai, Nov. 1920– .

Kwok, D. W. Y. *Scientism in Chinese thought 1900–1950.* New Haven and London: Yale University Press, 1965.

Kwok, Sin-tong E. 'The two faces of Confucianism: A comparative study of anti-restorationism of the 1910s and 1970s,' paper presented to the Regional Seminar on Confucian Studies, University of California, Berkeley, 4 June 1976.

Kyoto Daigaku Jimbun Kagaku Kenkyusho (Research Institute of Humanistic Studies, Kyoto University). *Mo Takuto chosaku nenpyo* (Chronological table of Mao Tse-tung's works). Vol. 2. *Goi sakuin* (Glossary and index). Kyoto: Kyoto Daigaku Jimbun Kagaku Kenkyusho, 1980.

Kyriak, Theodore, ed. *Bibliography-index to U.S. JPRS research translations,* vols. 1–8. Annapolis, Md.: Research and Microfilm Publications, 1962– .

Lan Hai. *Chung-kuo k'ang-chan wen-i shih* (A history of Chinese literature during the war of resistance). Shanghai: Hsien-tai, 1947.

Lancashire, Douglas. Translation of Li Po-yuan: *Wen-ming hsiao-shih* (A little history of modern times), in *Renditions: A Chinese-English translation magazine,* 2 (Spring 1974) 128.

Lang, Olga. *Pa Chin and his writings: Chinese youth between the two revolutions.* Cambridge, Mass.: Harvard University Press, 1967.

Lao She. *Camel Xiangzi.* Trans. by Shi Xiaoqing. Bloomington: Indiana University Press; Peking: FLP, 1981.

Lao She [Shu Ch'ing-ch'un, She Yu]. *Rickshaw boy,* by Lau Shaw. Trans. from the Chinese by Evan King [Robert Ward]. New York: Reynal and Hitchcock, 1945.

Lao She. *Rickshaw: The novel Lo-t'o Hsiang-tzu.* Trans. by Jean M. James. Honolulu: University of Hawaii Press, 1979.

Lao, D. C. *Mencius.* Harmondsworth: Penguin Books, 1970.

Lardy, Nicholas R., and Lieberthal, Kenneth, eds. *Chen Yun's strategy for China's development: A non-Maoist alternative.* Trans. by Ma Fong and Du Anxia; introduction by the editors. Armonk, N.Y.: M.E. Sharpe, 1983.

Lau, Joseph S.M. *Ts'ao Yü: The reluctant disciple of Chekhov and O'Neill, a study in literary influence.* Hong Kong: Hong Kong University Press, 1970.

Lau, Joseph S.M., Hsia, C.T., and Lee, Leo Ou-fan, eds. *Modern Chinese stories and novellas, 1919–1949.* New York: Columbia University Press, 1981.

Le Gros Clark, and Cyril Drummond. *The prose-poetry of Su Tung-p'o.* Shanghai: Kelly & Walsh, 1935.

Lee, Leo Ou-fan. 'Genesis of a writer: Notes on Lu Xun's educational experience, 1881–1909,' in Merle Goldman, ed. *Modern Chinese literature in the May Fourth era,* 161–88.

Lee, Leo Ou-fan. 'Literary trends I: The quest for modernity, 1895–1927.' *CHOC,* 12.451–504.

Lee, Leo Ou-fan. 'Literature on the eve of revolution: Reflections on Lu Xun's leftist years, 1927–1936.' *Modern China*, 2.3 (July 1976) 277–91.

Lee, Leo Ou-fan. *The romantic generation of modern Chinese writers.* Cambridge, Mass.: Harvard University Press, 1973.

Legge, James, trans. *The Chinese classics.* 5 vols. Reprinted Hong Kong: Hong Kong University Press, 1960 [1866].

Lenin, V. I. 'Conspectus of Hegel's *Science of Logic,*' in his *Collected Works*, 38.85–238. Moscow: Foreign Languages Publishing House, 1961.

Levenson, Joseph R. *Confucian China and its modern fate.* 3 vols. Berkeley: University of California Press, 1958–65.

Levenson, Joseph R. *Liang Ch'i-ch'ao and the mind of modern China.* Cambridge, Mass.: Harvard University Press, 1953.

Lewis, John Wilson, ed. *Party leadership and revolutionary power in China.* Cambridge: Cambridge University Press, 1970.

Leyda, Jay. *Dianying: An account of films and the film audience in China.* Cambridge, Mass.: MIT Press, 1972.

Li Ho-lin. *Chin erh-shih-nien Chung-kuo wen-i ssu-ch'ao lun* (Chinese literary trends in the recent twenty years). Shanghai; Sheng-huo, 1947.

Li Ho-lin *et al. Chung-kuo hsin wen-hsueh shih yen-chiu* (Studies on the history of new Chinese literature). Peking: Hsin chien-she tsa-chih she, 1951.

Li Ho-lin, ed. *Chung-kuo wen-i lun-chan* (Literary debates in China). Hong Kong: Hua-hsia, 1957.

Li Jui. *The early revolutionary activities of Comrade Mao Tse-tung.* Trans. by Anthony W. Satiti, ed. by James C. Hsiung, intro. by Stuart R. Schram. White Plains, N.Y.: M.E. Sharpe, 1977 (Trans. of Li Jui, 1957).

Li Jui. "Ch'ung tu Chang Wen-t'ien ti 'Lu-shan ti fa-yen'" (On rereading Chang Wen-t'ien's 'Intervention at Lu-shan'). *Tu-shu,* 8 (1985) 28–38.

Li Jui. 'Hsueh-sheng shih-tai ti Mao Tse-tung' (Mao Tse-tung during his student period). *Hsin-hua wen-chai* (1984) 175–81.

Li Jui. *Lun San-hsia kung-ch'eng* (On the Three Gorges project). Changsha: Hunan k'o-hsueh chi-shu, 1985.

Li Jui. *Mao Tse-tung ti ch'u-ch'i ko-ming huo-tung* (The early revolutionary activities of Mao Tse-tung). Peking: Jen-min, rvsd. ed., 1980.

Li Jui. *Mao Tse-tung ti tsao-ch'i ko-ming huo-tung.* Changsha: Hu-nan jen-min, 1980; rev. ed. of Li Jui, 1957.

Li Jui. *Mao Tse-tung t'ung-chih ti ch'u-ch'i ko-ming huo-tung* (The early revolutionary activities of Comrade Mao Tse-tung). Peking: Chung-kuo ch'ing-nien ch'u-pan-she, 1957.

Li Mu. *San-shih nien-tai wen-i lun* (On the literature and arts of the 1930s) Taipei: Li-ming, 1973.

Li, Peter. *Tseng P'u.* New York: Twayne Publishers, 1978.

Li Po-yuan. *Wen-ming hsiao-shih* (A little history of modern times). Shanghai, 1903. Reprinted Peking: T'ung-su wen-i ch'u-pan-she, 1955.

Li San-pao. 'K'ang Yu-wei's iconoclasm: Interpretation and translation of his earliest writings 1884–87.' University of California, Ph.D. dissertation, Davis, 1978.

Li Shih-tseng [Chen]. 'San-kang ko-ming' (Revolution against three bonds). *Hsin shih-chi*, 11 (31 Aug. 1907) 1–2.

Li Ta-chao. 'Chin' (Now). *Hsin ch'ing-nien*, 4.4 (15 April 1918) 307–10.

Li Ta-chao. 'Ch'ing-ch'un' (Spring). *Hsin ch'ing-nien*, 2.1 (1 Sept. 1916) 1–12 [sep. pag.].

Li Ta-chao. 'Hsin chi-yuan' (A new era). *Mei-chou p'ing-lun* (15 Jan. 1919).

[Li Ta-chao]. *Li Ta-chao hsuan-chi* (Selected works of Li Ta-chao). Peking: Jen-min, 1962.

Li Ta-chao. 'Ya-hsi-ya ch'ing-nien ti kuang-ming yun-tung' (The luminous Asiatic youth movement), in Li Ta-chao, *Li Ta-chao hsuan-chi*, 327–9.

Li Ta-chao. 'Yen-shih hsin yü tzu-chueh hsin" (On misanthropy and self awareness). *Chia-yin* (The tiger), 1.8 (10 Aug. 1915).

Liang Ch'i-ch'ao. 'Chung-kuo shih hsu-lun' (Introduction to Chinese history, 1901). *YPSWC, ts'e* 3.1–12.

Liang Ch'i-ch'ao. 'Chung-kuo tao-te chih ta-yuan' (Fundamentals of Chinese morality). *Yung-yen*, 1.2 (Dec. 1912) 1–8; 1.4 (Feb. 1913) 1–8 (sep. pag.).

Liang Ch'i-ch'ao. 'Fu-ku ssu-ch'ao p'ing-i' (Critique of the restorationist thought tide). *Ta Chung-hua*, 1.7 (20 July 1916) 1–10 (sep. pag.).

Liang Ch'i-ch'ao. 'K'ai-ming chuan-chih lun' (On enlightened despotism). *Hsin-min ts'ung-pao*, 73–75 (25 Jan.–23 Feb. 1906); reprinted in *YPSWC, ts'e* 6.13–83.

Liang Ch'i-ch'ao. 'Kuo-chia ssu-hsiang pien-ch'ien i-t'ung lun' (On similarity and difference in alterations in national thought, 1901). *YPSWC, ts'e* 3.12–22.

Liang Ch'i-ch'ao. 'Kuo-hsing p'ien' (Essays on the national character). *Yung-yen*, 1.1 (Jan. 1913) 1–6 (sep. pag.).

Liang Ch'i-ch'ao [Jen-kung]. 'Lun ch'iang-ch'üan' (On power). *Ch'ing-i pao*, 31 (1899) 4–7.

Liang Ch'i-ch'ao. 'Ou yu hsin-ying lu chieh-lu' (Reflections on a trip to Europe), in *Yin-ping-shih ho-chi, chuan-chi, ts'e* 5, 1–162. Shanghai: Chung-hua, 1936.

Liang Ch'i-ch'ao. 'Pao-chiao fei so-i tsun-K'ung lun' (To 'save the faith' is not the way to honour Confucius). *Hsin-min ts'ung-pao*, 2 (22 Feb. 1902) 59–72.

Liang Ch'i-ch'ao. 'Shuo-ch'ün hsu' (Preface to groups, 1896). *YPSWC, ts'e* 2.3–4.

Liang Ch'i-ch'ao. 'Shuo tung' (On dynamism, 1898). *YPSWC, ts'e* 2.27–40.

Liang Ch'i-ch'ao. 'Wu-nien-lai chih chiao-hsun' (Lessons of the past five years). *Ta Chung-hua*, 2.10 (20 Oct. 1915) 1–5 (sep. pag.).

Liang Ch'i-ch'ao. *Yin-ping-shih ho-chi* (Combined writings from the Ice-drinker's Studio) in 40 vols. (*wen-chi*, 16 vols.; *chuan-chi*, 24 vols.). Shanghai: Chung-hua, 1936; reprint Taipei: Chung-hua, 1960.

Liang Ch'i-ch'ao. *Yin-ping-shih wen-chi* (Collected essays from the Ice-drinker's Studio). Shanghai: Chung-hua, 1936; Taipei: Chung-hua, 16 vols., 1960. Note that this is also published as part of the preceding item. Cited as *YPSWC*.

Liang Hsiao. 'Yen-chiu Ju-Fa tou-cheng ti li-shih ching-yen' (Study the historical experience of the struggle between the Confucian and Legalist schools). *HC*, 10 (1974) 56–70.

Liang Shu-ming. *Tung-Hsi wen-hua chi ch'i che-hsueh* (Eastern and Western civilizations and their philosophies). 1922; reprinted, Taipei: Hung-ch'iao shu-tien, 1968.

Liao Kai-lung. *Ch'üan-mien chien-she she-hui-chu-i ti tao-lu* (The road to building socialism in an all-round way). *Yun-nan she-hui k'o-hsueh*, 2 (March 1982) 1–8, and Peking: Chung-kung chung-yang tang-hsiao, 1983.

Liao Kai-lung. "Kuan-yü hsueh-hsi 'chueh-i' chung t'i-ch'u ti i-hsieh wen-t'i ti chieh-ta" (Answers and explanations regarding some questions which have been posed in connection with the study of the 'Resolution [of 27 June 1981]'). *Yun-nan she-hui k'o-hsueh*, 2 (March 1982), 101–10.

Liao Kai-lung. 'Li-shih ti ching-yen ho wo-men ti fa-chan tao-lu' (The experience of history and the path of our development). *CKYC*, 9 (Sept. 1981) 101–77.

Liao Kai-lung. 'She-hui-chu-i she-hui chung ti chieh-chi tou-cheng ho jen-min nei-pu mao-tun wen-t'i' (The problem of class struggle and of contradictions among the people in socialist society), in Liao Kai-lung, *Ch'üan-mien*, 229–83.

Liao Kai-lung. *Tang-shih t'an-so* (Explorations in Party history). Peking: Chung-kung chung-yang tang-hsiao, 1983.

Lin Ch'in-nan hsien-sheng hsueh-hsing p'u-chi ssu-chung (The life and works of Mr. Lin Shu, four records), ed. by Chu Hsi-chou; includes 'Ch'un-chueh chai chu-shu chi' (Works from the Ch'un-chueh study). 3 *chüan*. Taipei: Shih-chieh shu-chü, 1961.

Lin, Julia C. *Modern Chinese poetry: An introduction.* Seattle: University of Washington Press, 1972.

Lin Kuo-chün. 'Meetings of Immortals drive the intellectuals forward in self-remolding.' *JMJP*, 16 May 1961, *SCMP*, 2513, 11.

Lin, Yü-sheng. *The crisis of Chinese consciousness: Radical anti-traditionalism in the May Fourth era.* Madison: University of Wisconsin Press, 1978.

Lin Yun-hui. 'Lüeh lun Mao Tse-tung t'ung-chih tui Li-san lu-hsien ti jen-shih ho ti-chih' (A brief account of Mao Tse-tung's understanding of, and resistance to, the Li-san line). *TSYC*, 4 (1980) 51–9.

Ling Yü. 'Mao Tse-tung t'ung-chih ho Li-san lu-hsien ti kuan-hsi t'ao-lun tsung-shu' (A summary of the discussion regarding Comrade Mao Tse-tung's relationship to the Li-san line). *TSYC*, 3 (1982) 78–80.

Link, E. Perry. *Mandarin ducks and butterflies: Popular urban fiction in early twentieth-century China.* Berkeley and Los Angeles: University of California Press, 1980.

Link, E. Perry. 'The rise of modern popular fiction in Shanghai.' Harvard University, Ph.D. dissertation, 1976.

Link, E. Perry. 'Traditional-style popular urban fiction in the teens and twenties,' in Merle Goldman, ed. *Modern Chinese literature in the May Fourth era*, 327–50.

Li-shih yen-chiu. (Historical research). Monthly. Peking, 1954–66, 1975– . Cited as *LSYC*.

Liu Hsin-huang. *Hsien-tai Chung-kuo wen-hsueh shih-hua* (Discourse on the history of modern Chinese literature). Taipei: Cheng-chung, 1971.

Liu I-chang. 'Ts'ung k'ang-chan shih-ch'i tso-chia sheng-huo chih k'un-k'u k'an she-hui tui tso-chia ti tse-jen' (The responsibility of society toward writers; A view based on the writers' impoverished lives during the war years). *Ming-pao yueh-k'an* (Ming-pao monthly), 13.6 (June 1978) 58–61.

Liu Shao-ch'i. *Lun tang* (On the party). Dairen: Ta-chung shu-tien, 1947.

[Liu] Shih-fu. [Shang-hai wu-cheng-fu kung-ch'an-chu-i t'ung-chih she kung-pu] [Manifesto of the Shanghai anarchist-communist fellowship]. 'Wu-cheng-fu kung-ch'an-tang chih mu-ti yü shou-tuan' (Goals and methods of the anarchist-communist party). *Min-sheng* (Voice of the people), 19 (18 July 1914).

Liu Shih-p'ei. 'Jen-lei chün-li lun' (On the equalization of human powers). *T'ien-i*, (10 July 1907).

Liu Shih-p'ei. "Lun hsin-cheng wei ping-min chih-ken' (On why the new politics injures the people). *T'ien-i*, 8–10 (30 Oct. 1907).

Liu Shih-p'ei and Ho Chen. 'Lun chung-tsu ko-ming yü wu-cheng-fu ko-ming chih te-shih' (On the strengths and weaknesses of racial revolution as opposed to anarchist revolution). *T'ien-i*, 6 (1 Sept. 1907).

Liu Shou-sung. *Chung-kuo hsin wen-hsueh shih ch'u-kao* (A preliminary draft history of modern Chinese literature). 2 vols. Peking: Tso-chia ch'u-pan-she, 1956.

Liu Ya-tzu. *Nan-she chi lüeh* (A brief account of the Southern Society). Shanghai: Kai-hua shu-chü, 1940.

Lo Chia-lun. See *Ko-ming wen-hsien*.

Lotta, Raymand, ed. *And Mao makes 5: Mao Tse-tung's last great battle.* Chicago: Banner Press, 1978.

LSYC. See *Li-shih yen-chiu*.

Lu Hsun. *Fen* (Graves). Shanghai: Ch'ing-kuang shu-chü, 1933.

[Lu Hsun]. *Lu Hsun ch'üan-chi* (Complete works of Lu Hsun). 20 vols. Peking: Jenmin wen-hsueh ch'u-pan-she, 1973.

Lu Hsun. 'Mo-lo shih li shuo' (On the power of Mara poetry, 1907), in *Fen* (Graves) 53–100.

Lu Hsun. *Na-han* (A call to arms). Reprint from *Lu Hsun ch'üan chi*, 1938 ed. Hong Kong: Hsin-i, 1967.

Lu Hsun. 'No-la ch'u-tsou hou tsen-yang' (What happens after Nora goes away), in *Fen* (Graves). Reprint from *Lu Hsun ch'üan-chi*, 1938 ed., 141–50. Hong Kong: Hsin-i, 1967.

Lu Hsun. *P'ang-huang.* Reprint from Lu Hsun ch'üan-chi, 1938 ed. Hong Kong: Hsin-i, 1967.

Lu Hsun. 'Wen-hua p'ien-chih lun' (On the pendulum movement of culture), in *Fen* (Graves) 36–52.

Lu Hsun. *Yeh-ts'ao* (Wild grass). Reprint from *Lu Hsun ch'uan-chi*, 1938 ed. Hong Kong: Hsin-i, 1967.

Lyell, William. *Lu Hsun's vision of reality.* Berkeley: University of California Press, 1976.

Ma Nan-ts'un [Teng T'o]. *Yen-shan yeh-hua* (Evening talks at Yenshan). Peking: Pei-ching ch'u-pan-she, 1963 and 1979.

MacFarquhar, Roderick. *The origins of the Cultural Revolution, 1: Contradictions among the people, 1956–1957.* London: Oxford University Press; New York: Columbia University Press, 1974.

MacFarquhar, Roderick. *The origins of the Cultural Revolution, 2: The Great Leap Forward, 1958–1960.* London: Oxford University Press; New York: Columbia University Press, 1983.

Mantici, Giogio. *Pensieri de fiume Xiang.* Roma: Editori Riuniti, 1981.

Mao Chu-hsi kuan-yü kuo-nei min-tsu wen-t'i ti lun-shu hsuan-pien (Selections from Chairman Mao's expositions regarding problems of nationalities within the country). Peking: Kuo-chia min-tsu shih-wu wei-yuan-hui ti-san ssu (Third Department of the State Commission on Minority Affairs), Oct. 1978.

Mao Chu-hsi tui P'eng, Huang, Chang, Chou fan-tang chi-t'uan ti p'i-p'an (Chairman Mao's criticism and repudiation of the P'eng, Huang, Chang, Chou anti-Party clique). Peking: n.p., 1967.

Mao Chu-hsi wen-hsien san-shih p'ien (Thirty documents by Chairman Mao). Peking: Special Steel Plant, 1967.

Mao Chu-hsi wen-hsuan (Selected writings by Chairman Mao). n.p., n.d.

Mao Tse-tung. *A critique of Soviet economics.* Trans. by Moss Roberts. New York: Monthly Review Press, 1977. [A translation of Mao Tse-tung, "Tu 'cheng-chih ching-chi-hsueh'. . .".]

Mao Tse-tung. 'Cha-tan pao-chü' (A brutal bomb attack). *Hsiang River Review,* 1 (14 July 1919) 3.

Mao Tse-tung che-hsueh ssu-hsiang (chai-lu) (Mao Tse-tung's philosophical thought [extracts]). Compiled by the Department of Philosophy of Peking University. Peking, 1960.

Mao Tse-tung chi (Collected writings of Mao Tse-tung), ed. by Takeuchi Minoru. 10 vols. Tokyo: Hokubosha, 1970–2. Cited as *MTTC.*

Mao Tse-tung. 'Chung-kuo nung-min ko chieh-chi ti fen-hsi chi ch'i tui ko-ming ti t'ai-tu' (Analysis of all the classes of the Chinese peasantry, and their attitudes toward revolution). *MTTC,* 1.153–9.

Mao Tse-tung. 'Chung-kuo she-hui ko chieh-chi ti fen-hsi' (Analysis of all the classes in Chinese society). *MTTC,* 1.161–74.

Mao Tse-tung. *Four essays on philosophy.* Peking: FLP, 1966.

Mao Tse-tung. *Hsuan-chi* (Selected works) 5 vols. Peking: Jen-min, vols. 1–4, 1960; vol. 5, 1977. Cited as *MTHC.*

Mao Tse-tung. 'Kai-ko hun-chih wen-t'i' (Problems concerning the reform of marriage customs). *MTTC, pu chüan,* 1.149.

Mao Tse-tung. 'Lien-ai wen-t'i – shao-nien-jen yü lao-nien-jen' (Problems of being in love – the youth and the elderly). *MTTC, pu-chüan,* 1.161–3.

[Mao Tse-tung]. *Mao Tse-tung chi, pu chüan,* 1 (supplementary volumes, 1). Tokyo: Sososha, 26 Dec. 1983. Six volumes out of nine projected were issued up to October 1984. Cited as *MTTC, pu chüan.*

Mao Tse-tung. 'Min-chung ti ta lien-ho' (The great union of the popular masses).

Hsiang River Review, 2–4 (July–Aug. 1919). Trans. by S. Schram in *CQ*, 49 (Jan.–Mar. 1972) 76–87; reprinted in *MTTC*, 1.57–69.

Mao Tse-tung. *Miscellany of Mao Tse-tung Thought (1949–1968)*. 2 vols. Arlington, Va.: *JPRS*, Nos. 61269–1 and -2, 20 February 1974 [Trans. of materials from *Mao Tse-tung ssu-hsiang wan-sui!*].

Mao Tse-tung. *Selected readings*. Peking: FLP, 1967. Trans. of an earlier, and substantially different, version of *Mao Tse-tung chu-tso hsuan-tu*. Peking: Jen-min, 1986.

Mao Tse-tung. *Selected works of Mao Tse-tung* [English trans.]. Peking: FLP, vols 1–3, 1965; vol. 4, 1961; vol. 5, 1977. Cited as Mao, *SW.*

Mao Tse-tung shu-hsin hsuan-chi (Selected letters of Mao Tse-tung). Peking: Jen-min, 1983.

Mao Tse-tung ssu-hsiang wan-sui! (Long live Mao Tse-tung Thought). Peking: n.p., 1967. Cited as *Wan-sui* (1967).

Mao Tse-tung ssu-hsiang wan-sui! Peking: n.p., 1969. Cited as *Wan-sui* (1969).

Mao Tse-tung ssu-hsiang wan-sui! Peking: n.p., 1967. Supplement. Cited as *Wan-sui* (Supplement).

Mao, *SW.* See Mao Tse-tung, *Selected Works.*

Mao Tse-tung. 'Talks at the Yenan Forum on literature and art,' in Mao Tse-tung, *Mao Tse-tung on literature and art.* Peking: FLP, 1967.

Mao Tse-tung t'ung-chih lun Ma-k'o-ssu-chu-i che-hsueh (chai-lu) (Comrade Mao Tse-tung on Marxist philosophy [extracts]). Urumchi, Sinkiang: Ch'ing-nien, 1960. Compiled by the Office for Teaching and Research in Philosophy of the Party School under the Chinese Communist Party Committee, Sinkiang Uighur Autonomous Region.

Mao Zedong. *Une étude de l'éducation physique.* Ed. and trans. by Stuart R. Schram. Paris: Mouton, 1962.

Mao Tse-tung. 'Wei Te ju hu ti Fa-lan' (France fears Germany as if it were a tiger). *Hsiang River Review*, 3 (28 July 1919).

Marx, Karl. 'Critique of the Gotha Programme,' in Karl Marx and Friedrich Engels, *Selected works*, 311–31. London: Laurence & Wishart, 1970.

Masson, Michel. 'The idea of Chinese tradition: Fung Yu-lan, 1939–1949.' Harvard University, Ph.D. dissertation, 1978.

McDonald, Angus. *Hogaku kenkyu*, 46.2 (1972) 99–107.

McDonald, Angus. *Ronin* (Tokyo), 14 (Dec. 1973) 37–47.

McDonald, Angus W., Jr. *The urban origins of rural revolution: Elites and masses in Hunan province, China, 1911–1927*. Berkeley: University of California Press, 1978.

McDougall, Bonnie S. *Mao Zedong's 'Talks at the Yan'an conference on literature and art': A translation of the 1943 text with commentary*. Ann Arbor: Center for Chinese Studies, University of Michigan, 1980.

McDougall, Bonnie S., trans. and ed. *Paths in dreams: Selected prose and poetry of Ho Ch'i-fang*. Queensland, Australia: University of Queensland Press, 1976.

McDougall, Bonnie S. *The introduction of Western literary theories into modern China, 1919–1925*. Tokyo: Centre for East Asian Cultural Studies, 1971.

Mei-chou p'ing-lun (Weekly review). Ed. by Li Ta-chao *et al.* Peking, 22 Dec. 1918–31 Aug. 1919.

Meisner, Maurice. *Li Ta-chao and the origins of Chinese Marxism.* Cambridge, Mass.: Harvard University Press, 1967.

Meserve, Walter, and Meserve, Ruth, eds. *Modern drama from Communist China.* New York: New York University Press, 1970.

Metzger, Thomas A. *Escape from predicament: Neo-Confucianism and China's evolving political culture.* New York: Columbia University Press, 1977.

Mills, Harriet C. 'Lu Hsun: 1927–1936, the years on the left.' Columbia University, Ph.D. dissertation, 1963.

Mills, Harriet. 'Lu Xun: Literature and revolution – from Mara to Marx,' in Merle Goldman, ed. *Modern Chinese literature in the May Fourth era,* 189–220.

Min-sheng (People's voice), 1–29 (Aug. 1913–June 1921). Reprinted by Lung-men shu-tien, Hong Kong, 1967.

Mi-ting (M. Mitin) *et al.* Trans. by Ai Ssu-ch'i *et al. Hsin che-hsueh ta-kang* (Outline of the new philosophy). Shanghai: Tu-shu sheng-huo ch'u-pan-she, 1936.

MTHC. See Mao Tse-tung. *Hsuan-chi* (Selected works of Mao Tse-Tung).

MTTC. See *Mao Tse-tung chi.*

MTTC, pu chüan. See *Mao Tse-tung chi, pu chüan.*

NCNA. See New China News Agency.

New China News Agency. *Daily News Release.* Hong Kong: 1948– . Cited as NCNA.

Ortega y Gasset, José. 'The dehumanization of art,' in Irving Howe, ed. *The idea of the modern in literature and the arts,* 83–96.

Osaka Tokushi. *Chūgoku shin bungaku undō shi* (History of the new literature movement of China). 2 vols. Tokyo: Hosei daigaku, 1965.

Pai-chia cheng-ming – fa-chan k'o-hsueh ti pi-yu chih lu. 1956 nien 8 yueh Ch'ing-tao i-ch'uan hsueh tso-t'an hui chi-shu. (Let a hundred schools contend – The way which the development of science must follow. The record of the August 1956 Tsingtao Conference on Genetics). Peking: Commercial Press, 1985.

'Pei-ching ta-hsueh-t'ang chih kuo-hsueh wen-t'i' (The problem of national learning at Peking University). *Hsin-min ts'ung-pao,* 34 (July 1903) 61–2.

Peking Review. Weekly. Peking: 1958– . (From January 1979, *Beijing Review*). Cited as *PR.*

Pickowicz, Paul G. 'Ch'ü Ch'iu-pai and the Chinese Marxist conception of revolutionary popular literature and art.' *CQ,* 70 (June 1977) 296–314.

Pickowicz, Paul G. *Marxist literary thought in China: The influence of Ch'ü Ch'iu-pai.* Berkeley: University of California Press, 1981.

Pollard, David E. *A Chinese look at literature: The literary values of Chou Tso-jen in relation to the tradition.* Berkeley: University of California Press, 1973.

PR. See *Peking Review.*

Price, Don C. *Russia and the roots of the Chinese Revolution, 1896–1911.* Cambridge, Mass.: Harvard University Press, 1974.

Prusek, Jaroslav. 'A confrontation of traditional oriental literature with modern

European literature in the context of the Chinese literary revolution.' *Archiv Orientalni*, 32 (1964) 365–75.

Prusek, Jaroslav. 'Lu Hsun's "Huai-chiu," a precursor of modern Chinese literature.' *Harvard Journal of Asiatic Studies*, 29 (1969) 169–76.

Prusek, Jaroslav. 'Subjectivism and individualism in modern Chinese literature.' *Archiv Orientalni*, 25.2 (1957) 261–83.

PTMT. See Schram, Stuart R. *The political thought of Mao Tse-tung.*

Ragvald, Lars. "The emergence of 'worker-writers' in Shanghai," in Christopher Howe, ed. *Shanghai: Revolution and development in an Asian metropolis*, 301–25. Cambridge: Cambridge University Press, 1981.

Ragvald, Lars. *Yao Wen-yuan as a literary critic and theorist: The emergence of Chinese Zhdanovism.* Stockholm: University of Stockholm, 1978.

Rankin, Mary Backus. *Early Chinese revolutionaries: Radical intellectuals in Shanghai and Chekiang, 1902–1911.* Cambridge, Mass.: Harvard University Press, 1971.

Rankin, Mary Backus. 'The emergence of women at the end of the Ch'ing: The case of Ch'iu Chin,' in Margery Wolf and Roxane Witke, eds. *Women in Chinese Society*, 39–66. Stanford: Stanford University Press, 1975.

Resolution on certain questions in the history of our Party since the founding of the People's Republic of China [27 June 1981]. NCNA, 30 June 1981; *FBIS Daily Report: China*, 1 July 1981, K1–38; published as *Resolution on CPC History* (1949–1981). Peking: FLP, 1981.

Reynolds, David. "Iconoclasm, activism and scholarship: The tension between 'spontaneity' and 'obligation' in the thought of Fu Ssu-nien," paper presented at the Regional Seminar on Confucian Studies, Berkeley, 4 June 1976.

Rickett, Adele, ed. *Chinese approaches to literature from Confucius to Liang Ch'i-ch'ao.* Princeton: Princeton University Press, 1978.

Roy, David. *Kuo Mo-jo: The early years.* Cambridge, Mass.: Harvard University Press, 1971.

Scalapino, Robert A., and Yu, George. *Modern China and its revolutionary process.* Vol. I: *Recurrent challenges to the traditional order, 1850–1920.* Berkeley and Los Angeles: University of California Press, 1985.

Scalapino, Robert A., and Yu, George. *The Chinese anarchist movement.* Berkeley: University of California Press, 1963.

Schneider, Laurence A. *Ku Chieh-kang and China's new history.* Berkeley: University of California Press, 1971.

Schneider, Laurence A. 'National essence and the new intelligentsia,' in Charlotte Furth, ed. *The limits of change: Essays on conservative alternatives in Republican China*, 57–89.

Schram, Stuart R. "Chairman Hua edits Mao's literary heritage: 'On the ten great relationships'." *CQ*, 69 (March 1977), 126–35.

Schram, Stuart R., ed. *Chairman Mao talks to the people: Talks and letters, 1956–1971.* New York: Pantheon, 1975. See also Schram, Stuart R., ed. *Mao Tse-tung unrehearsed: Talks and letters, 1956–1971.*

Schram, Stuart [R.]. 'Decentralization in a unitary state: Theory and practice 1940–1984,' in Stuart Schram, ed. *The scope of state power in China*, 81–125.

Schram, Stuart [R.]. *Documents sur la théorie de la 'révolution permanente' en Chine.* Paris: Mouton, 1963.

Schram, Stuart [R.], ed. *Foundations and limits of state power in China.* London: School of Oriental and African Studies, and Hong Kong: The Chinese University Press, 1987.

Schram, Stuart R. "From the 'Great Union of the Popular Masses' to the 'Great Alliance'." *CQ*, 49 (January–March 1972), 88–105.

Schram, Stuart [R.]. *Ideology and policy in China since the Third Plenum, 1978–1984.* London: School of Oriental and African Studies, 1984.

Schram, Stuart. *Mao Tse-tung.* Harmondsworth, Eng.; Baltimore, Md.: Penguin Books, 1967, 1974.

Schram, Stuart [R.]. 'Mao Tse-tung and the theory of the permanent revolution, 1958–1969.' *CQ*, 46 (April–June 1971) 221–44.

Schram, Stuart R. ed. *Mao Tse-tung unrehearsed: Talks and letters, 1956–71.* Middlesex, Eng.: Penguin Books, 1974. Published in the United States as *Chairman Mao talks to the people: Talks and letters, 1956–1971.* New York: Pantheon, 1975.

Schram, Stuart [R.]. *Mao Zedong: A preliminary reassessment.* Hong Kong: The Chinese University Press, 1983.

Schram, Stuart R. 'Mao Zedong and the role of the various classes in the Chinese revolution, 1923–1927,' in *Chūgoku no seiji to keizai* (The policy and economy of China—the late Professor Yuji Muramatsu commemoration volume), 227–39. Tokyo: Toyo Keizai Shinposha, 1975.

Schram, Stuart [R.]. 'New texts by Mao Zedong, 1921–1966.' *Communist Affairs*, 2.2 (April 1983) 143–65.

Schram, Stuart R. "On the nature of Mao Tse-tung's 'deviation' in 1927." *CQ*, 27 (April-June 1964) 55–66.

Schram, Stuart [R.]. 'Party leader or true ruler? Foundations and significance of Mao Zedong's personal power,' in Stuart R. Schram, ed. *Foundations and limits of state power in China*, 203–56.

Schram, Stuart R. 'The great union of the popular masses.' *CQ*, 49 (Jan.–March 1972) 88–105.

Schram, Stuart [R.]. "The limits of cataclysmic change: Reflections on the place of the 'Great Proletarian Cultural Revolution' in the political development of the People's Republic of China." *CQ*, 108 (December 1986) 613–24.

Schram, Stuart [R.]. 'The Marxist,' in Dick Wilson, ed. *Mao Tse-tung in the scales of history*, 35–69.

Schram, Stuart R. *The political thought of Mao Tse-tung.* Rev. ed. New York: Praeger, 1969. Cited as *PTMT.*

Schram, Stuart [R.]. ed. *The scope of state power in China.* London: School of Oriental and African Studies, and Hong Kong: The Chinese University Press, 1985.

Schultz, William. 'Lu Hsun: The creative years.' University of Washington, Ph.D. dissertation, Seattle, 1955.

Schurmann, Franz. *Ideology and organization in Communist China*. Berkeley: University of California Press, 1968 [1966].

Schwartz, Benjamin. *In search of wealth and power: Yen Fu and the West*. Cambridge, Mass.: Harvard University Press, 1964.

Schwartz, Benjamin, ed. *Reflections on the May Fourth movement: A symposium*. Cambridge, Mass.: Harvard East Asian Monographs, 1972.

Schwartz, Benjamin. 'Some stereotypes in the periodization of Chinese history.' *Philosophic Forum*, 1.2 (Winter 1968) 219–30.

SCMM. See U.S. Consulate General, *Selections from China Mainland Magazines*.

SCMP. See U.S. Consulate General, *Survey of China Mainland Press*.

Shadick, Harold, trans. *The travels of Lao Ts'an*. Ithaca: Cornell University Press, 1966 [1952].

Shaffer, Lynda. *Mao and the workers: The Hunan labor movement, 1920–1923*. Armonk, N.Y.: M.E. Sharpe, 1982.

Shaffer, Lynda. 'Mao Ze-dong and the October 1922 Changsha construction workers' strike.' *Modern China*, 4 (Oct. 1978) 379–418.

Shang-hai wen-hsueh (Shanghai literature). Monthly. (Superseded *Wen-i yueh-k'an*.) Shanghai, October 1959–December 1963.

Shih Chung-ch'üan. "Ma-k'o-ssu so-shuo-ti 'tzu-ch'an-chieh-chi ch'üan-li' ho Mao Tse-tung t'ung-chih tui t'a ti wu-chieh" (The 'bourgeois right' referred to by Marx, and Comrade Mao Tse-tung's misunderstanding of it). *Wen-hsien ho yen-chiu*, 1983, 405–17.

Slupski, Zbigniew. *The evolution of a modern Chinese writer: An analysis of Lao She's fiction with biographical and bibliographical appendices*. Prague: Oriental Institute, 1966.

Snow, Edgar. *Red star over China*. London: Gollancz, 1937; New York: Random House, 1938; 1st rev. and enlgd. ed., Grove Press, 1968.

Snow, Edgar. *The long revolution*. London: Hutchinson, 1973.

Socialist upsurge in China's countryside. Peking: FLP, 1957; and General Office of the Central Committee of the Communist Party of China, ed. Peking: FLP, 1978.

Stalin, Joseph. *Economic problems of socialism in the USSR*. Peking: FLP, 1972.

Strong, Anna Louise. 'Three interviews with Chairman Mao Zedong.' *CQ*, 103 (September 1985), 489–509.

Su Shao-chih. *Tentative views on the class situation and class struggle in China at the present stage*. Peking: Institute of Marxism-Leninism-Mao Zedong Thought, Chinese Academy of Social Sciences, 1981.

Su Wen, ed. *Wen-i tzu-yu lun-pien chi* (Debates on the freedom of literature and art). Shanghai: Hsien-tai, 1933.

Summary of World Broadcasts. Daily and weekly reports. Caversham Park, Reading: British Broadcasting Corporation, Monitoring Service, 1963– . Cited as *SWB*.

Su-wei-ai Chung-kuo (Soviet China). Moscow: Izdatel'stvo Inostrannyky Rabochikh (Foreign Workers Publishing House), 1934.

SWB. See *Summary of World Broadcasts*.

Ta Chung-hua (Great China). Shanghai (Jan. 1915–Dec. 1916).

Tagore, Amitendranath. *Literary debates in Modern China, 1918–1937.* Tokyo: Centre for East Asian Cultural Studies, 1967.

Tai Yih-jian. 'The contemporary Chinese theater and Soviet influence.' Southern Illinois University, Ph.D. dissertation, 1974.

Takeuchi Minoru, ed. *Mao Tse-tung chi* (Collected writings of Mao Tse-tung). 10 vols. Tokyo: Hokubosha, 1970–72; 2nd ed., Tokyo: Sososha, 1983. See also *Mao Tse-tung chi.* Cited as *MTTC*.

Takeuchi Minoru, ed. *Mao Tse-tung chi, pu chüan* (Supplements to the collected writings of Mao Tse-tung). 10 vols. Tokyo: Sososha, 1983–86. Cited as *MTTC, pu chüan.*

T'an Ssu-t'ung. 'Chih shih p'ien' (Essay on public affairs), in Yang Chia-lo, comp. *Wu-hsu pien-fa wen-hsien hui-pien* (Documentary collection of the 1898 reform movement), 3.83–92.

T'an Ssu-t'ung. 'Jen hsueh' (On humanity). *Ch'ing-i pao,* 2–14 (2 Jan. 1899–10 May 1899).

[T'an Ssu-t'ung]. *T'an Ssu-t'ung ch'üan chi* (Complete works of T'an Ssu-t'ung). Tokyo, 1966.

Tang-shih hui-yi pao-kao-chi (Collected reports from the Conference on Party History). Ch'üan-kuo tang-shih tzu-liao cheng-chi kung-tso hui-yi ho chi-nien Chung-kuo kung-ch'an-tang liu-shih chou-nien hsueh-shu t'ao-lun-hui mi-shu-ch'u (Secretariat of the National Work Conference on Collecting Party Historical Materials and the Academic Conference in Commemoration of the Sixtieth Anniversary of the Chinese Communist Party), eds. Peking: Chung-kung chung-yang tang-hsiao, 1982.

Tang-shih yen-chiu. (Research on Party history). Peking: Chung-kung chung-yang tang-hsiao, 1980– . Also see *Chung-kung tang-shih yen-chiu.* Cited as *TSYC.*

Tang-shih yen-chiu tzu-liao (Research materials on Party history). Chengtu: Szechwan jen-min (for the Museum on the History of the Chinese Revolution), 1980– .

T'ao K'ai. 'K'ai-shih ch'üan-mien chien-she she-hui-chu-i ti shih-nien' (The ten years which saw the beginning of the all-around construction of socialism), in Chung-kung tang-shih yen-chiu-hui, ed., Hsueh-hsi li-shih chueh-i chuan-chi. Peking: Chung-kung tang-hsiao, 1981.

T'ao Meng-ho [T'ao Lü-kung]. 'Lun tzu-sha' (On suicide). *Hsin ch'ing-nien,* 6.1 (15 Jan. 1918) 12–18.

Teng T'o. See Ma Nan-ts'un, Wu Nan-hsing.

TFTC. See *Tung-fang tsa-chih* (The eastern miscellany). Shanghai, 1904–48.

T'ien Chun [Hsiao Chün]. *Village in August.* Trans. by Evan King, intro. by Edgar Snow. New York: Smith & Durrell, 1942.

T'ien Han, Ou-yang Yü-ch'ien *et al. Chung-kuo hua-chü yun-tung wu-shih-nien shih-liao chi, 1907–1957* (Historical materials on the modern Chinese drama movement of the last fifty years, 1907–1957). Peking: Chung-kuo hsi-chü, 1957.

T'ien-i (Natural morality), 3–19 (10 July 1907–15 March 1908); reprinted in *Chung-kuo tzu-liao ts'ung-shu,* series 6 *Chung-kuo ch'u-ch'i she-hui-chu-i wen-hsien chi,* no. 2. Tokyo: Daian, 1966.

T'ien Yuan. 'Tsai lun Mao Tse-tung t'ung-chih tui Li-san lu-hsien ti jen-shih ho ti-chih' (More on Comrade Mao Tse-tung's understanding of and resistance to the Li-san line). *TSYC*, 1 (1981) 65–71.

Ting I. 'Chung-kuo tso-i tso-chia lien-meng ti ch'eng-li chi ch'i ho fan-tung cheng-chih ti tou-cheng' (The founding of the League of Left-wing Writers and its struggle against reactionary political forces), in Chang Ching-lu, ed. *Chung-kuo hsien-tai ch'u-pan shih-liao i-pien*, 35–49.

Ting Ling *et al. Chieh-fang ch'ü tuan-p'ien ch'uang-tso hsuan* (Selected short works from the liberated areas). 2 vols. n.p., 1947.

Ting Miao. *P'ing Chung-kung wen-i tai-piao tso* (On representative works of Chinese Communist literature). Hong Kong: Hsin shih-chi ch'u-pan-she, 1953.

Ting Wei-chih and Shih Chung-ch'üan. 'Ch'ün-chung lu-hsien shih wo-men tang ti li-shih ching-yen ti tsung-chieh' (The mass line is the summation of the historical experience of our Party). *Wen-hsien ho yen-chiu*, 1983, 420–28.

Ts'ai Ho-sen wen-chi (Collected writings of Ts'ai Ho-sen). Peking: Jen-min, 1980.

Ts'ai Yuan-p'ei. 'Wu-shih-nien-lai Chung-kuo chih che-hsueh' (Chinese philosophy in the past 50 years). *Shen pao* anniversary issue, *Tsui-chin wu-shih-nien* (The last 50 years), 1–10 (sep. pag.). Shanghai: Shen pao, 1922.

Ts'an-k'ao tzu-liao. See *Chung-kuo hsien-tai wen-hsueh shih ts'an-k'ao tzu-liao*.

Ts'ao Chü-jen. *Wen-t'an san i* (Three reminiscences of the literary scene). Hong Kong: Hsin wen-hua, 1954.

Ts'ao Chü-jen. *Wen-t'an wu-shih-nien hsu-chi* (Sequel to 'Fifty years on the literary scene'). Hong Kong: Hsin wen-hua, 1969.

Ts'ao Yü. *Jih-ch'u* (Sunrise). Shanghai: Wen-hua sheng-huo, 1936.

Ts'ao Yü. *Sunrise.* Trans. by A. C. Barnes. Peking: FLP, 1960.

Ts'ao Yü. *The Wilderness.* Trans. by Christopher C. Rand and Joseph S.M. Lau. Hong Kong and Bloomington, 1980.

Ts'ao Yü. *Thunderstorm.* Trans. by A. C. Barnes. Peking: FLP, 1958.

Tso-lien shih-ch'i wu-ch'an-chieh-chi ko-ming wen-hsueh (Proletarian revolutionary literature in the period of the Left-wing League), ed. by Nan-ching ta-hsueh Chung-wen hsi (Department of Chinese, Nanking University). Nanking: Chiang-su wen-i.

Ts'ung Wei. "Yang Hsien-chen and the 'Identity of thinking and existence.'" *KMJP*, 11 December 1964, *SCMP*, 3380, 5.

Tsun-yi hui-i wen-hsien (Documents of the Tsun-yi Conference). Peking: Jen-min, 1985.

TSYC. See *Tang-shih yen-chiu*.

Tung-fang tsa-chih (The eastern miscellany). Shanghai, 1904–48. Cited as *TFTC*.

Tzu-liao hsuan-pien (Selected materials). Peking: n.p., Jan. 1967.

U.S. Consulate General. Hong Kong. *Current Background.* Weekly (approx.). 1950–1977. Cited as *CB*.

U.S. Consulate General. *Extracts from China Mainland Magazines.* 1955–1960. Cited as *ECMM*. Title changed to *Selections from China Mainland Magazines*, 1960–77.

U.S. Consulate General, *Selections from China Mainland Magazines.* 1960–77. Cited as *SCMM*. Formerly *Extracts from China Mainland Magazines*.

U.S. Consulate General, *Survey of China Mainland Press*. 1950–1977. Cited as *SCMP*.

Van Slyke, Lyman P. *Enemies and friends: The united front in Chinese Communist history*. Stanford: Stanford University Press, 1967.

Vohra, Ranbir. *Lao She and the Chinese revolution*. Cambridge, Mass.: East Asian Research Center, Harvard University, 1974.

Wakeman, Frederic, Jr. *History and will: Philosophical perspectives of Mao Tse-tung's thought*. Berkeley: University of California Press, 1973.

Wang Che-Fu. *Chung-kuo hsin wen-hsueh yun-tung shih* (A history of the new literary movement in China). Hong Kong: Yuan-tung t'u-shu kung-ssu, 1965.

Wang Chi-chen, ed. *Stories of China at war*. New York: Columbia University Press, 1947.

Wang, C. H. 'Chou Tso-jen's Hellenism.' *Renditions*, 7 (Spring 1977) 5–28.

Wang Nien-i. "Mao Tse-tung t'ung-chih fa-tung 'wen-hua ta-ko-ming' shih tui hsing-shih ti ku-chi" (Comrade Mao Tse-tung's estimate of the situation at the time when he launched the 'Great Cultural Revolution'), in *Tang-shih yen-chiu tzu-liao*, 4 (1983), 766–74.

Wang P'ing-ling. *San-shih-nien wen-t'an ts'ang-sang lu* (Changes on the literary scene in thirty years). Taipei: Chung-kuo wen-i-she, 1965.

Wang Shu-pai and Chang Shen-heng. 'Ch'ing-nien Mao Tse-tung shih-chieh kuan ti chuan-pien' (The transformation in the world view of the young Mao Tse-tung). *LSYC*, 5 (1980) 47–64.

Wang T'ao. 'Pien-fa' (Reform), reprinted in Yang Chia-lo, comp., *Wu-hsu-pien-fa wen-hsien hui-pien* (Documentary collection of literature of the 1898 reform movement), 1.131–5.

Wang Yao. *Chung-kuo hsin wen-hsueh shih-kao* (A draft history of China's new literature). 2 vols. Shanghai: Hsin-wen-i ch'u-pan-she, 1953.

Wan-sui (1967) (1969). See *Mao Tse-tung ssu-hsiang wan-sui!*

Watson, Andrew, ed. *Mao Zedong and the political economy of the border region: A translation of Mao's 'Economic and financial problems.'* Cambridge: Cambridge University Press, 1980.

Wei shih-mo yao cheng-feng? (Why do we want to rectify?). Editorial. *JMJP*, 2 May 1957.

Wellek, René. *Concepts of criticism*. New Haven: Yale University Press, 1963.

Wen Chi-tse. 'Mao Tse-tung t'ung-chih tsai Yenan shih-ch'i shih tsen-yang chiao-tao wo-men hsueh che-hsueh ti?' (How did Comrade Mao Tse-tung teach us to study philosophy during the Yenan period?), in *Ch'üan-kuo Mao Tse-tung che-hsueh ssu-hsiang t'ao-lun-hui lun-wen hsuan* (Selected essays from the national conference to discuss Mao Tse-tung's philosophical thought), 68–82. Nanning: Kuang-hsi jen-min, 1982.

Wen-hsien ho yen-chiu (Documents and research). Peking: Chung-yang wen-hsien yen-chiu-shih, 1983– .

Wen-i pao (Literary gazette). Peking, 1949– .

Wile, David. 'T'an Ssu-t'ung: His life and major work, the Jen Hsueh.' University of Wisconsin, Ph.D. dissertation, 1972.

Wilson, Dick, ed. *Mao Tse-tung in the scales of history: A preliminary assessment.* New York: Cambridge University Press, 1977.

Witke, Roxane. *Comrade Chiang Ch'ing.* Boston: Little, Brown, 1977.

Wittfogel, K.A. 'Some remarks on Mao's handling of concepts and problems of dialectics.' *Studies in Soviet thought,* 3.4 (Dec. 1963) 251–77.

Wright, Mary Clabaugh, ed. *China in revolution: The first phase, 1900–1913.* 'Introduction,' 1–63. New Haven: Yale University Press, 1968.

Wu Chiang. "Pu-tuan ko-ming lun-che pi-hsu shih ch'e-ti ti pien-chang wei-wu lun-che' (A partisan of the theory of permanent revolution must be a thoroughgoing dialectical materialist). *Che-hsueh yen-chiu,* 8 (1958) 25–28.

Wu Chih-hui. *Chih-hui wen-ts'un* (Wu Chih-hui's writings), 1st collection. Shanghai: Hsin-hsin Book Store, 1927.

[Wu Chih-hui]. 'T'an wu-cheng-fu chih hsien-t'ien' (Casual talk on anarchism). *Hsin shih-chi,* 49 (30 May 1908) 3–4.

[Wu Chih-hui]. 'T'ui-kuang jen-shu i i shih-chieh kuan' (On curing the world through the extension of medical care). *Hsin shih-chi,* 37 (7 March 1908) 3–4.

Wu Chih-hui. *Wu Chih-hui hsien-sheng ch'üan chi* (Complete works of Mr. Wu Chih-hui). 18 vols. Comp. by Chung-kuo Kuo-min-tang chung-yang wei-yuan-hui tang-shih shih-liao pien-tsuan wei-yuan-hui, Taipei, 1969.

Wu Nan-hsing (Wu Han, Teng T'o, and Liao Mo-sha). *San-chia ts'un cha-chi.* (Notes from a three-family village). Peking: Jen-min wen-hsueh ch'u-pan-she, 1979.

Wu Tung-hui. "Destroy the black backstage manager of 'The three-family village'." *KMJP,* 18 June 1967, *SCMP,* 3977, 14.

Wu Wo-yao. *Vignettes from the late Ch'ing: Bizarre happenings eyewitnessed over two decades.* Trans. by Shih Shun Liu. Hong Kong: The Chinese University of Hong Kong, 1975. A translation of *Erh-shih-nien mu-tu chih kuai-hsien-chuang.*

Wu Yueh. 'Wu Yueh i-shu' (Wu Yueh's testament). *T'ien t'ao: Min-pao lin-shih tseng-k'an* (Demand of heaven: Min-pao special issue), 25 April 1907.

Wylie, Raymond F. *The emergence of Maoism: Mao Tse-tung, Ch'en Po-ta, and the search for Chinese theory, 1935–1945.* Stanford: Stanford University Press, 1980.

Ya Hsien, ed. *Tai Wang-shu chüan* (Collected works of Tai Wang-shu). Taipei: Hung-fan, 1970.

Yang Ch'ao. *Lun Mao Chu-hsi che-hsueh t'i-hsi* (On Chairman Mao's philosophical system). 2 vols. Hsi-yang ti-ch'ü yin-shua-so, 1978.

Yang Ch'ao. *Wei-wu pien-cheng-fa ti jo-kan li-lun wen-t'i* (Some theoretical problems of materialist dialectics). Chengtu: Szechwan jen-min, 1980. [Rev. ed. of *Lun Mao Chu-hsi che-hsueh t'i-hsi.*]

Yang Ch'üan. 'Chung-kuo chin san-shih-nien-lai chih she-hui kai-tsao ssu-hsiang' (Social reform thought in China in the last thirty years). *TFTC,* 21.17 (10 Sept. 1924) 50–6.

Yang, Gladys, ed. and trans. *Silent China: Selected writings of Lu Xun.* Oxford: Oxford University Press, 1973.

Yao Hsin-nung. *The malice of empire*. Trans. of *Ch'ing kung yüan* and intro. by Jeremy Ingalls. Berkeley: University of California Press, 1970.

Yao Wen-yuan. *On the social basis of the Lin Piao anti-Party clique*. Peking: FLP, 1975. Also in Raymond Lotta, ed., *And Mao makes 5*, 196–208.

Yen Chi-ch'eng. 'Shao-nien Chung-kuo tsung-chiao wen-t'i hao p'i-p'ing' (Critique of the special issue on religious questions in the *Young China* magazine). *Min-to*, 3.2 (1 Feb. 1922) 1–12.

Yen Fu *et al*. 'K'ung-chiao-hui chang-ch'eng' (The programme of the Society for Confucianism). *Yung-yen*, 1.14 (June 1913) 1–8.

Yen Fu. 'Lun shih-pien chih chi' (On the speed of world change, 1895), reprinted in *Yen Chi-tao shih wen ch'ao* (Essays and poems of Yen Fu, preface 1916), 1.1–5. Taipei: Wen-hai 1969.

Yen Fu. *Yen Chi-tao hsien-sheng i-chu* (Posthumous works of Mr. Yen Fu). Singapore: Nan-yang hsueh-hui, 1959.

Yen Yuan. 'Ts'un hsueh,' in Yen Yuan, *Ssu ts'un pien*, 40–106. Peking: Ku-chi ch'u-pan-she, 1957.

YPSWC. See Liang Ch'i-ch'ao, *Yin-ping-shih wen-chi*.

Yung-yen (Justice), 1.1–2.6 (Jan. 1913–June 1914); reprint Taipei: Wen-hai, 1971, 10 vols.

INDEX

Advance Morality Society (Chin-te hui), 85
adventurism: campaign against, 429, 432
aesthetics, in Mao Tse-tung's Yenan talks, 255, 265–6
agricultural producers' co-operatives (APCs), 420, 428–9, 435; see also collectivization; cooperativization
agriculture, 403, 413; Mao on, 410–11, 416; socialization of, 412, 418; Soviet, 412; twelve-year development plan, 415; socialist transformation of, 419; see also collectivization; communes
Ah Q, 176–7
Ai Ch'ing, 237
ai-mei (students who loved the theatre), 238
Ai Ssu-ch'i, 250–4; Mao's debt to, 317; Yang Hsien-chen attacked by, 385, 386; on science, 393
Ai Wu, 229
Alitto, Guy, 133
All-China Federation of Literary and Art Circles, 365, 390, 392
All-China Resistance Association of Writers and Artists, 241–2, 261
'Alley in the rain' (poem), 235
Americans, 410, 421; 'ugly American,' 451
Analects, 340; influence on Mao, 270–1
'Analysis of all the classes in Chinese society' (Mao), 292
anarchists, Chinese, 42, 65, 68–87; and

European revolutionary socialism, 67–8; and revolutionary nihilism, 68–70; Paris group, 70, 71–2; anarcho-communist movement, 70–1, 83–4; Tokyo group, 72–3; contribution of, 81–2; post-revolutionary, 82–7, 93
anarcho-syndicalism, 108
Andersen, Hans Christian, 165
Andreev, Leonid, 182, 188
Anfu (Anfu Clique): relations with Japan, 98
anti-capitalism, 105
anti-imperialism, 13, 38; of neo-traditionalists, 45; in battle of the 'two slogans,' 217
anti-Manchu movement, 46–7, 65; Chang Ping-lin on, 107–8
Anti-Rightist Campaign, 389, 390, 426–7, 432; effect on intellectuals, 349, 352
ao-fu-he-pien (aufheben), 198
Aristotle, 183
army, CCP: dominant role in revolution, 297–9, 300; see also New Fourth Army incident; People's Liberation Army (PLA)
Arnold, Matthew, 183, 206
arts: Mao on, 381, 382, 472–3; artists, 426; in post-Mao era, 505
Artzybashev, 188
Asiatic mode of production, 139
assassination, validation as history-making, 69, 90

Association for Literary Studies, 164–6, 173

Association of Chinese Writers and Artists, 215, 218

Auden, W. H., 236

autocracy, and Mao Tse-tung's exercise of political power, 347, 348

autonomy: anarchists on, 78; see also anti-imperialism

Autumn Harvest uprisings, 297, 300

A Ying (Ch'ien Hsing-ts'un), 152, 200, 203, 209, 210, 248

Babbitt, Irving, 206, 128, 183; influence on Critical Review, 129, 162

backsideism, 399

Bacon, Francis, 115; inductionism of, 131

Bahro, Rudolf, 487

Bai Hua, 508–9

Baker, Professor, 238

Balzac, Honoré de, 185, 262

banditry: and warlords, 194

Bao Tong, 532

Barbusse, Henri, 186, 187

base areas, 407, 414, 418, 454; Mao on importance of, 301

Basic tactics (Mao), 307

Baudelaire, Charles Pierre, 186, 187, 189, 193, 234, 236

Bebel, August, 84

Beckett, Samuel, 189, 193

Beijing Independent Workers Union, 520

Beijing Social and Economic Research Institute, 518

Beijing University, 511, 517, 518; see also Peking University (Peita)

Bergson, Henri, 61, 64, 91, 121, 130, 197

Berninghausen, J., 260

Birch, Cyril, 185

birth control, 424

'bloc-within' strategy, 285; Mao's work for, 296; possible revival of, 334

Bolshevik Revolution, 93, 94, 120; Chinese response to, 121

Book of raillery (Chang Ping-lin), 47

Book of rites, 361

Book of the expulsion (Li Shih-p'ei), 47

Border Region government: Mao on centralization and dispersal in, 342

bourgeoisie, 418, 425, 467, 484, 487–8, 497; Mao on, 292; challenge to feudalism by, 329–30; Marx on role of, 330; as possible leaders of revolution, 332–3; Mao on function in Anti-Japanese War, 335–7; in 'people's democratic dictatorship,' 344; concepts of denigrated, 350; radical intellectuals on, 374; corrosive ideas of, 388; national, 401, 418–19, 423, 463; petty, 401, 418; see also petty-bourgeoisie; social class

Brotherhood of the Peach Garden Oath, 69

Bucharest Conference (1960), 458

Buddhism, 23, 46, 111; Mahayana, 15, 102, 109, 130; cosmology of, 32; wei-shih, 50, 60; as alternative to Confucianism, 52; Liang Shu-ming on, 60; Yogacara, 102; Buddha, 457

bureaucracy: blamed by Pa Chin, 356; state, 486–7; bureaucratic elite, 488

bureaucracy, cultural: Mao's 1963-1964 criticisms of, 380–2; position of, 382–3; targets of, 383–6; response to 1964 rectification, 389–91

bureaucratism: and ideological class struggle, 368

Butterfly fiction, 152–5, 157, 185

Byron, George Gordon Lord, 107, 117–18, 165; legend of, 181, 182

cadres, 402, 415; managerial, 421; technical, 421, 426; privileges of, 467, 488–9; children of, 486–7; see

also Seven Thousand Cadres
Conference
Calinescu, Matei, 190
campaigns, 447; Anti-Rightist, 389,
390, 426–7, 432; Hundred Flowers,
418, 421, 426, 458; against
counterrevolutionaries, 424; against
adventurism, 429, 432; Socialist
Education, 446, 468, 469, 472, 473,
474; Resist America, Aid Korea, 449;
Learn from the People's Liberation
Army, 478; P'i-Lin p'i-K'ung
(Criticize Lin Piao, criticize
Confucius), 486; to study theory of
proletarian dictatorship, 486
Canton: as literary center, 242
capitalism: Chinese reformers on, 33–4,
105; part of rational technocracy,
105; attacked by Marxists, 139;
national capitalists, 399; Mao on,
413; contradictions in, 418, 424;
elimination of, 419
Central Committee (CCP), 402, 405,
406, 407; in democratic centralism,
398; on classes leading revolution,
412, 429, 447; on intellectuals, 415;
on APCs, 429; assessment of Stalin,
453; see also Plenums, Central
Committee
centralization: vs. provincial autonomy,
171–2; and dispersal, Mao on, 341;
relationship between localities and
center, 403–9, 476–7;
decentralization I, 405–6;
decentralization II, 405–6; small
power (localities), 406, 407, 408,
477, 493; Mao emphasis on, 408,
447, 493; see also nationalization
Central work conferences: 1962, 468;
1966, 476–7
Ch'a-hua nü (La dame aux camélias),
181, 237
Chang Ai-ling (Eileen Chang), 193,
249, 263, 265

Chang Chi, 69, 84
Chang Chih-tung, 433, 495–6; and
'national learning,' 46
Chang Ch'un-ch'iao, 464–5, 477,
486–8, 494; and radical intellectuals,
372–3; supporter of Mao, 373
Chang Chün-mai (Carsun Chang), 62;
on science and metaphysics, 63;
debate on science and human life,
130–5
change (i): factor in relativized world,
15–16; Chang Ping-lin on, 50;
reformers as agents of, 67; anarchists
on, 81, 86–7; see also I ching (Book
of Changes)
Chang Hen-shui, 156
Chang Hsueh-ch'eng, 101
Chang Hsueh-liang: on cooperation
against Japan, 314
Chang Ping-lin, 47, 48, 102; opposition
to K'ang Yu-wei, 48; attack on New
Text school, 49–50; philosophy of,
50–2; and Taoism, 51–2; on trial, 65;
anti-Manchuism of, 107–8;
mysticism of, 109; journalism of, 144
Chang Po-chün, 463
Changsha: Mao at school in, 269; Mao's
retreat from, 306
Chang Shih-chao, 162
Chang T'ien-i, 171, 185, 220, 223;
short stories by, 227; regional work
of, 229
Chang Tung-sun: on Confucianism, 58;
on science and metaphysics, 63
Chang Tzu-p'ing, 165, 173
Chang Wen-t'ien, 436
ch'ao-chueh (transcendence), 60
Chao Shu-li, 257, 262, 386, 391
Chao yen-wang (play), 238
Chao Yuan-ren, 232
Chaucer, Geoffrey, 158
Chekhov, Anton, 262
Chekiang, 446
Ch'en Ch'ao-nan, 155

Ch'en Chung-fu: see Ch'en Tu-hsiu
Ch'eng, Duke, 489
Cheng Chen-to, 99, 127, 164
Cheng-chih chou-pao (political weekly),
    289, 290, 296
Cheng-ch'i ko (play), 263
Chengchow: First Conference, 432;
    Second Conference, 432
Ch'eng Fang-wu, 114, 165, 166, 173,
    197; on literature and revolution, 198
ch'eng-fen (class status), 470, 474
Ch'eng-hsin ju-i (play), 248
cheng kuei-hua (regularization), 431
cheng-li (supervise), 492
cheng-li kuo-ku (reorganize the national
    heritage), 114
Cheng Po-ch'i, 168, 203
cheng-t'i (form of government), 54,
    400, 401
Chengtu Conference, 429, 432, 457, 496
Ch'en Huan-chang, 57
Ch'en I: on relaxation after GLF, 352–3;
    on thought reform, 356–7; and mass
    line, 398
Ch'en Meng-chia, 234–5
Ch'en Pai-ch'en, 248
Ch'en-pao (Morning news, Peking), 163
Ch'en Po-ta, 219, 250, 254, 372, 374,
    384, 443, 444; on Confucianism,
    327; and Cultural Revolution, 394
Ch'en T'ien-hua, 107, 150
Ch'en Tu-hsiu, 129; editor of New
    Youth, 87, 88, 111, 157, 167; 'A call
    to youth' essay, 89–90; philosophy of,
    89–91, 115; and First World War,
    93; at Peita, 97; and New Culture,
    117; in debate on science, 124, 131;
    and literary revolution, 156, 158,
    159–60, 161, 163; realism of, 184;
    on individualism, 273; on the bloc-
    within, 285, 286
Ch'en Yuan, 164, 205
Ch'en Yun (CC vice-chairman), 416; on
    decentralization, 405–6

Chen Ziming, 517, 518, 519, 520
ch'i (material force), 23
Chia (novel), 226
Chia-ching, 381
ch'iang-chien t'uan (rape brigade), 281
Chiang Ch'ing, 258, 310, 382, 383; and
    Mao, 372, 374, 394; and radical
    intellectuals, 372, 374; and K'o
    Ch'ing-shih, 373; and Peking Opera,
    373, 377–80; biography, 377–8; on
    cinema, 388; on cultural rectification,
    390–1; and Cultural Revolution,
    394; and Peking Opera, 472
ch'iang-ch'üan (coercive power), 77
Ch'iang-hsueh hui (Study Society for
    Self-Strengthening), 14
Ch'iang-hsueh pao (Self-strengthening
    News), 144
Chiang Kai-shek, 458; and Liang Shu-
    ming, 133; on military unification,
    138; Mao on, 297, 313–14, 333,
    449, 463, 482; see also Kuomintang;
    Nationalist government
Chiang K'ang-hu, 83–4
Chiang Kuang-tz'u, 137, 181, 197,
    220; proletarian literature of, 201–2,
    227
Chiang T'ing-fu, 136
Ch'iao (play), 239
chia-tsu chu-i (familism), 53
Chia-yin (Tiger magazine), 162
Chicago, University of, Hu Shih's
    lectures at, 158
chi-chung (centralized), 342
chi-chung ling-tao, fen-san ching-ying
    (centralized leadership and dispersed
    operation), 341
chieh (boundaries), 74, 79
chieh-chi ch'eng-fen (class status), 470
Chieh-fang jih-pao (Liberation Daily),
    339
chieh-shou ta-yuan (confiscation
    tycoons), 263
ch'ien (primary hexagram), 24

Ch'ien Chung-shu, 249, 262, 265
Ch'ien Hsing-ts'un (A Ying), 200, 203, 209, 210, 248
Ch'ien Hsuan-t'ung, 114, 163, 175; on use of classics, 159
Chien Po-tsan, 370–1, 375, 376
chien-tan t'an-tao (only just referred to it), 454
ch'ien-tse hsiao-shuo (fiction of social criticism), 148
ch'ih (madness), 152
chih-chueh (intuition), 61
Ch'ih-jen shuo-meng chi (novel), 150
Chih-mo ti shih (Chih-mo's poetry), 232
chih t'ien-hsia (rule the country as a whole), 272
chi-kan (leader and backbone), 334
ch'in (to immerse), 147
China Daily (Chung-hua jih-pao), 165
China Democratic League, 389
China's destiny (Chiang Kai-shek), 348
China Youth News, 393–4
Ch'in dynasty (221-206 B.C.): unification of empire, 485
Chinese Academy of Sciences, 471; radical group in, 372–3, 375
Chinese Communist Party (CCP), 400, 402, 404, 431, 437, 438, 447, 448, 449, 465, 466, 472, 484; leaders as anarchists, 86; answer to Leninist dilemma, 122; and urban working class, 137; and League of Left-wing Writers, 203, 214–15; use of writers for propaganda, 242; at end of Japanese War, 261; early decisions on armed forces for revolution, 297–9; Soviet directives to, 302–4; agreements with KMT, 313–14, 333–4; debate over conditions of united front, 313–15; Mao on relation to Moscow, 322–3; Mao on leadership in united front, 335–6; Mao on unifying role of, 342; and relaxation after GLF, 354–7; on thought reform, 356–7; meetings of the immortals, 357; view of peasants contradicted, 366; rectification (1964-1965), 380–94; Mao's displeasure with cultural rectification, 394; theory and leadership methods of, 398; social composition of, 399; leading role of, 401, 408, 411, 434, 445, 470, 475–6, 493, 494; and ministries, 405; coordinating role of, 406–7, 495, 496; rural experience of, 411; class composition of, 412, 420, 468–9; drive to recruit workers into, 412, 420; contradictions in, 417–18; and Hundred Flowers, 421; municipal secretaries, 423; provincial secretaries, 423; revisionists and right deviationists in, 426; ghosts and monsters opposed to, 427; resolutions of, 445; relations with Communist Party of the Soviet Union, 448–9; and Great Leap Forward, 458; Khrushchev meddling in, 458; nationalities policy, 460; Mao on need to smash, 470; 'capitalist roaders' in, 471, 484; factions in, 474; hsien committees of, 477; and PLA, 480–1, 485; regional committees established, 481; effect of cities on, 482–3; new class in, 486, 487, 488; see also Congresses, Chinese Communist Party; Li Ta-chao; Mao Tse-tung; Propaganda Department of the CCP
Chinese Eastern Railway, 450
Chinese language: see also Ch'en Tu-hsiu; Hu Shih; Liang Ch'i-ch'ao; pai-hua; and study of popular culture, 128–30; Hu Shih on, 158; phonetic scheme for, 213–14; Mao's attempt to reform, 258
Chinese revolution: Mao on nature of, 299; misunderstood by Soviets, 305–6

Chinese Revolution and the Chinese
    Communist Party (Mao), 328, 332,
    335, 337, 485
Chinese Socialist Party (Chung-kuo she-
    hui tang), 83, 84
Chinese Students Quarterly, 159
Chinese Writers Union, see Writers
    Union
Chinese Youth, 390
Ch'ing dynasty, 107–8, 362; late Ch'ing
    literature (1895-1911), 143–55
ch'ing-i (moralistic views), 37
Ch'ing-i-pao (Political commentary),
    144
Ching-kang-shan, 397, 430, 494; Mao's
    experience in, 301, 306; Mao's report
    on, 308
Ch'ing-kung yuan (play), 248; made
    into film, 263
Ching-ling school, 222
Ch'ing-nien (Youth), 156
ching-shen (spirit), 30, 41, 61
ching-shih (practical statecraft), 49
Ch'in-Han era, 17, 47
Chinkiang, 150
Ch'in Shih-huang-ti: Mao compared to,
    396, 494; Mao on, 447, 485–6, 490;
    and Marx, 481–90; cult of, 485, 489
Chin-te hui (Society to Advance
    Morality), 85
Chin-wei kuei (Nine-tailed turtle), 152
chi-pen-ti (basic), 424
Ch'i Pen-yü, 377; as radical intellectual,
    373, 375–6; on historical analogies,
    376
chi-tse, 30
Ch'iu (novel), 246
Ch'iu Chin, 70, 107
Chiu-ming ch'i-yuan (The scandalous
    murder case of nine lives), 150n
ch'iung-kuang-tan (paupers), 290
ch'i wu (equality of things), 51
Chou Ch'üan-p'ing, 165
Chou dynasty, 36, 46, 49

Chou En-lai, 352, 413, 416–17, 486,
    490; on united front, 314; on
    freedom of speech, 353; on
    intellectuals, 353; and mass line, 398;
    and Mao, 416–17; and Great Leap
    Forward, 431–2
Chou Ku-ch'eng, 389, 392
Chou Kuei-sheng, 145
Chou Li-po, 258, 262, 386
Chou Shih-chao, 279, 280
Chou Shou-chüan, 156
Chou Shu-jen, see Lu Hsun
Chou Tso-jen, 113, 163, 164, 166, 189,
    212, 222, 234, 249; translations by,
    180, 182
Chou Yang, 204, 212, 214, 219–20,
    245, 258, 366, 388, 441–2, 471; one
    of 'four heavies,' 204, 218; on
    national defence literature, 215, 217;
    Feng Hsueh-feng on, 219; on Mao's
    dicta, 250–1, 254; on literature of
    GLF, 351; in 1961-1962 relaxation,
    359; and Propaganda Department,
    364–5, 373; on university courses,
    368–9; in cultural rectification,
    381–2, 386–7, 390–3; in campaign
    against Shao Ch'üan-lin, 386–7; final
    report on campaign, 393
Chow Tse-tsung, 160
Christianity: and New Text
    Confucianism, 56
chuan-cheng (dictatorship), 346, 402
Ch'uang-tsao chi-k'an (Creation
    quarterly), 165
Ch'uang-tsao chou-pao (Creation
    weekly), 165
Ch'uang-tsao jih (Creation day), 165
Ch'uang-tsao she (Creation Society), 164
Chuang-tzu, 51, 79, 109, 269, 375, 447
ch'üan-li (rights), 29
Chu Chih-hsin, 121
Chu Ching-wo, 200
Ch'ü Ch'iu-pai, 99, 127, 140, 163, 301;
    on revolutionary literature, 204;

rebuttal of 'third category' by, 209–10; on partiinost, 211; on mass language, 212–13; essays of, 221

Chu Hsi, 124, 130, 132, 134–5, 269–70, 271; on Confucius, 327

Chu Hsiang, 235

Chu Kuang-ch'ien, 246

Ch'u Min-i, 81, 82

ch'ün (group), 30, 100, 148

chung (loyalty), 489, 494

Chung Ching-wen, 127

Ch'ung-ch'u yun-wei ti yueh-liang (novel), 220

chung-hsin (central), 293

chung-hua (central flower), 496

Chung-hua jih-pao (China Daily), 165

Chung-hua min-tsu (Chinese people), 279, 288

Chungking: as literary center, 243; theatre in, 247–8; at end of Japanese War, 261

Chung-kuo ch'ing-nien (Chinese youth journal), 197

Chung-kuo ch'üan-kuo wen-i chieh k'ang-ti hsieh-hui (All-China Resistance Association of Writers and Artists), 241–2, 261

Chung-kuo hsien-tai ch'u-pan shih-liao (Historical materials on contemporary Chinese publications), 182

Chung-kuo hsin wen-hsueh ta-hsi (A comprehensive compendium of China's new literature), 182

Chung-kuo li-shih chiao-k'o-shu (Textbook on Chinese history), 58

Chung-kuo she-hui tang (Chinese Socialist Party), 83

Chung-kuo wen-i chia hsieh-hui (Association of Chinese Writers and Artists), 215, 218

Chung-kuo wen-i kung-tso che hsuan-yen (Declaration of Chinese literary workers), 215

Chung-shen ta-shih (play), 238

ch'ün hsueh (sociology), 26

chün li (uniform distribution of power), 80

Ch'un-liu she, 237

Ch'un she (The Collective), 85

chün-tzu (superior man), 273

ch'u-shen (family origins), 470

chu-tao (leading), 320

Chu Te, 306, 311, 313, 490

ch'u-tsou (going away), 169

Chu Tzu-ch'ing, 163, 222, 234, 261

chu-tzu pai-chia (one hundred schools), 46

cinema, campaign against 'middle character' in, 388

civil rights: Hu Shih on, 119; see also ch'üan-li (rights)

civil service: civil servants, 399

civil war, 399, 449

class, social: anarchists on, 74, 85; see also bourgeoisie; elite; gentry; merchants; peasants; working class

class consciousness: of revolutionary writers, 199; Mao on, 252; in films, 263–4

classicism, in literature: rebellion against, 157–60; equated with tradition, 183

class struggle: lack in older China, 106, 123; and nationalism, 107–8; growth of, 121; Mao on, 294, 310–11; role of peasants in, 294, 310–11; as armed struggle, 336–7; and literature, 365; resistance to, 367–72; vs. class reconciliation, 371, 384; emphasis on ideological, 374; and Peking Opera, 378–9; Mao on, 384, 409, 417–26, 439, 453, 457, 462–75, 485, 496; in countryside, 419; Stalin on, 452

Cohen, Arthur, 318, 320

collectivization, 416, 418, 430

college: Mao on, 479; see also education; students; universities

Comecon (Council for Mutual Economic
    Assistance), 461
commerce, 413; shopkeepers, 399;
    Soviet transformation of, 419
common people: and National Essence
    movement, 43–4; anarchists on, 86;
    Li Ta-chao on, 94; idea of mass
    mobilization of, 123; Mao on, 128;
    see also popular culture
communes, 429–31, 435–6, 452, 456,
    477; called mistake, 371; Khrushchev
    ridicule of, 456–8; Mao on criticism
    of, 457–8
communism: as meaning anarchism, 86;
    defined by Ch'en I, 353; see also
    Chinese Communist Party (CCP)
Communist, The: Mao's introduction in,
    335, 336, 337
Communist International (Comintern),
    401, 450; Chinese strategy of,
    302–13, 312; 'sinification' a reaction
    to, 323
Communist Manifesto, The, 72
Communist Party of the Soviet Union
    (CPSU), 454; History of the CPSU,
    438; Communist Party, 449, 455;
    Twentieth Congress (1956), 453,
    455; Mao on, 459, 466–7
Communist Youth League, 394, 428,
    510, 518
compradors: Mao on, 294, 295
concession theory, 370–1
Concise philosophical dictionary, on
    Mao Tse-tung's theory of
    contradictions, 318–19
Confucianism: survival of, 16; New
    Text, 19–20, 48; T'an Ssu-t'ung on,
    23–4; Yen Fu's relation to, 27; and
    Liang Ch'i-ch'ao, 30; on value of
    assemblies, 35; rejected by new
    radicals, 41, 71; adaptation to
    modern needs, 43–5; heterodox views
    of, 45, 47–8; and Buddhism, 52; as
    religion, 56–62, 111; attacked in

New Youth, 68, 91, 111; on family,
    75–6; relativization of, 101; as state
    religion, 111; and neo-traditionalism,
    129; Mao on, 269–71, 327, 340;
    Mao's attack on values of, 348;
    revived in criticism of GLF, 360,
    369–70; in post-Mao era, 505–6,
    526, 527
Confucius, 375, 437, 443–4; on
    naming, 23; authenticity of canon,
    44–5; Confucian classics, 426, 444;
    Confucianism, 444, 445, 446;
    Confucian scholars, 447
Congresses, Chinese Communist Party:
    Seventh (1945), 410; Eighth (1956),
    420, 421, 462; Second Session of
    Eighth (1958), 433, 436, 445, 447;
    Ninth (1969), 481; Tenth (1973),
    494; see also Plenums, Central
    Committee
Conscience Society (Hsin she), 83, 84–5
constitutionalism: ideal of 'public'
    government, 35–6; campaign for
    religious clause, 57
Constitutions: PRC state, 402, 409,
    410, 421–2, 445; Chinese
    Communist Party (CCP), 420
Contemporary Review (Hsien-tai p'ing-
    lun), 205, 212; poetry in, 234–5
contradictions: Mao and, 315–38, 347,
    396, 417–18, 422, 443, 462, 470,
    471, 474, 477, 495; among the
    people, 397–427, 453, 454; non-
    antagonistic, 417; theory of, 424
cooperativization, 414, 415, 432
Copernicus, 354
counterrevolutionaries, 410, 447,
    453–4, 468, 470, 472, 473, 475;
    Mao on, 422, 426; campaign against,
    424
CPSU, see Communist Party of the
    Soviet Union (CPSU)
Creation Society (Ch'uang-tsao she), 81,
    113, 199; as Marxist intellectuals,

137; activities of, 164–7; fiction of, 173; hero worship of, 181; and Crescent Moon, 205; see also Ch'uang-tsao she

creativity and social crisis, 220–41; essay, 221–3; fiction, 223–31; poetry, 231–7; drama, 237–41; issue of individual, 249; literature on eve of revolution, 261–6

Crescent Moon (Hsien yueh), 205, 212; and Lu Hsun, 205, 206–7, 208; manifesto of, 205; criticisms of Lu Hsun in, 206–7; poetry of, 234–5

Critical Review (Hsueh heng), 129; opposition to literary revolution, 162

cultural policy: and Chou Yang, 364–5; and Chiang Ch'ing, 378–9

Cultural Revolution (Great Proletarian Cultural Revolution), 399, 420, 443, 461, 462, 466, 472, 480, 481, 485, 490–4; ideological basis of, 374, 376, 475–90; Mao's disappointment with cultural rectification, 394; mass line in, 397; Mao on, 414; origins of, 441–2, 448; ideology of, 475–90; and youth, 478–9; decade, 481, 497

culture: depoliticization urged, 365; Mao on, 379–80; Mao and Chinese, 396, 436–48, 471–2, 496; cultural organs, 406; level of, 425; Mao and cultural policy, 483; see also rectification

Culture, Ministry of: and Chiang Ch'ing, 378; attacked by Mao, 379; and Peking Opera, 379; and 1964 thought reform, 383, 390; and PLA, 391

Dairen: conference at, 366, 390

dame aux camélias, La (Ch'a-hua nü), 237

Dante, 158, 183

Darwinian biology, 16, 24, 26, 33, 109; refuted, 74; see also Social Darwinism

decentralization: Ch'en Yun on, 405–6

'Declaration of Chinese Literary Workers' (Chung-kuo wen-i kung-tso che hsuan-yen), 215

democracy: reformers' view of, 31–2, 34–6; and New Youth, 95; Dewey on, 115; Mao on, 397, 408–9, 476, 487, 493; people's, 397–427; New, 402; parliamentary, 409; mass, 484

Democracy Wall movement, 503, 517

democratic centralism: Lenin on, 122–3, 397; Mao and, 398, 401, 402, 408

Democratic League, 140

Deng Liqun, 524, 527, 529

Deng Xiaoping, 516, 524, 535, 536; as successor to Mao, 499; and Hu Yaobang, 500, 504, 507, 508–10, 511, 513, 515; and Tiananmen Square student demonstrations, 521; and Jiang Zemin, 523

Desire under the elms (O'Neill), 239

determinism: growth of, 40; Chang Ping-lin's protest, 51; Chang Chün-mai on, 63

deviations: backsideism, 399; tailism, 399; dispersionism, 406; subjectivism, 408; adventurism, 429, 432; individualism, 431

Dewey, John, 64, 124, 131, 276, 290; influence on Hu Shih, 94, 115–16, 119, 136; on education, 116, 120; in China, 119

Dialectical Materialism (Mao), 318–22; versions of, 318

dialectics, 319–20, 438–43, 455, 471, 475, 494, 497

Diary of Lei Feng, The, 387

Dickens, Charles, 180, 181, 182, 262

dictatorship, 402, 410, 475–81; 'Scientific,' 136; people's democratic, 344, 400, 401, 411, 418, 468; people's, 400, 412; revolutionary-democratic, of workers and peasants,

dictatorship *(continued)*
   401; autocracy, 402, 425; military,
   480; Oriental despotism, 495
dictatorship of the proletariat, 400, 401,
   422–3, 453, 472, 484–5, 486
dispersionism, 406
Djilas, Milovan, 467, 487
Doll's House (Ibsen), 114, 169, 238,
   239; problems raised by, 169–70
Dong Fureng, 528
Dostoevsky, Feodor, 262
Dowson, Ernest, 181, 188
Doyle, Conan, 150
drama, 237–8, 472; wartime, 220, 248;
   before 1930, 237–9; by Ts'ao Yü,
   238–41; in war of resistance, 242;
   folk, 256–8; second to film, 263;
   Chiang Ch'ing on, 377, 378–80; Mao
   on Peking Opera, 379
Dreisch, Hans, 64
dual rule, 434
Dumas fils, 181, 182, 237
dynamism (tung-li), 28

East China Drama Festival (1963-1964),
   379
Eastern and Western civilization and
   their philosophies (Tung Hsi wen-hua
   chi ch'i che-hsueh), 60, 63, 132
Eastern Europe, 451, 452, 461
economics: conclusions of, after GLF,
   354–5; profit motive in, 371
Economics Institute of the Chinese
   Academy of Sciences, 371
Economic Weekly, 519
economy: Mao on political economy of
   development, 346–7; development
   strategy, 404; Mao's policies, 412–13;
   policies of late 1950s, 430;
   development strategy, 434
education, 473; urged by anarchists, 83;
   influence of Dewey on, 116, 119; use
   of fiction for, 146; aftermath of Great
   Leap, 364; educational organs, 406;

secondary, 424; policy, 473; Mao on,
   479–80; examinations, 480; see also
   schools
Education, Ministry of: on pai-hua, 162
egalitarianism, 431, 489
eight-legged essay, 147, 158
Einstein, Albert, 354
Eliot, T. S., 189, 236
elite class: changes in, 13–14; see also
   bourgeoisie; bureaucracy; gentry;
   intellectuals
Emerson, Ralph Waldo, 121
Emperor Jones (O'Neill), 240
encirclement campaigns, 306–7
Endeavour (Nu-li chou-pao), 119
Engels, Friedrich, 309, 330, 370, 440,
   443, 454, 470, 480
engineering: slighted in GLF, 350
enterprises, 406; large-scale, 405;
   factory managers, 407; one-man
   management in, 407; industrial, 478
Esherick, Joseph, 486–7
Esprit des lois (Montesquieu), 150
essays (tsa-wen), 221–3; by Lu Hsun,
   221–2; personal, 222–3
ether: as unitary material of all living
   things, 23; and dynamism, 28
Eucken, Rudolph, 64, 130
Europe: model for Chinese anarchists,
   67; nihilists in, 69; socialism of, 86;
   see also West, the; individual
   countries by name
Evolution and Ethics (Huxley), 19
evolutionary cosmology: external source,
   16; creators of, 17–31; K'ang Yu-
   wei's version, 18–22; T'an Ssu-t'ung
   on, 22–5; Yen Fu on, 25–8; Liang
   Ch'i-ch'ao on, 28–31; contribution of
   Western science to, 32; shift to
   naturalism from, 41, 42, 64; and
   anarchism, 68–82; and New Youth,
   87–94; Marxism as final state, 94–5;
   summarized, 95–6
evolutionary naturalism: emergence of,

42; defeat of, 64; of radicals, 69; in Chinese literature, 183; combined with subjectivism, 185; see also Social Darwinism

evolutionism, 13–41; of K'ang Yu-wei, 18–22; of Spencer, 25, 28; of Yen Fu, 25–8, 100; of Liang Ch'i-ch'ao, 28; and West as identified with future, 36; erosion of faith in, 38–41, 55; and New Youth, 87–96; see also Social Darwinism

examination system, impact of end, 110, 112

fa-chan k'o-hsueh pi-yu chih lu (the way which the development of science must follow), 422

factionalism, 474

Falun Gong, 534–5

familism (chia-tsu chu-i), 22; vs. Western hedonism, 53; crticized in New Youth, 88

family system: K'ang Yu-wei on, 22, 75; anarchists on, 75; T'an Ssu-t'ung on, 76; later utopians on, 76–7; and feminism, 77; role of sexuality in, 77; abolition of, 83, 84

fang-chen (orientation), 421

fang-jen (non-interference), 72

Fang Jue, 528

Fang Lizhi, 510, 516

Fang Wei-te, 235

fan-shen (turn over), 264

Fei-leng ts'ui ti i-yeh (poetry collection), 232

feminism, 77

Feng Chih, 220

Feng Hsueh-feng, 211, 214, 220, 254; on Chou Yang, 219; liaison man, 219; target in Anti-Rightist Campaign, 373, 390

Feng Nai-ch'ao, 203, 204

Feng Ting, 389, 390

Feng Yuan-chün, 169

Feng Yu-lan, 14, 62, 134–5, 360, 369, 371; criticized, 375, 376

feudalism, 419, 446, 462, 485; blamed by radicals, 67, 68; Marxism on, 139; in literature, 257; of landlords, 293, 306; dates of, 328; Mao on breakdown of, 329–30; Marx on, 330

Feuerwerker, Yi-tsi, 169, 171

fiction: in late Ch'ing writing, 145, 180–1; new, theories, 145–8; growth of political novels, 146; novels of sentiment, 148, 151–2; new, practice, 148–52; short stories, 172–80; translations of, 180–90; by Mao Tun, 223–5, 246; 1928-1937, 223–31; by Shen Ts'ung-wen, 225; by Lao She, 225–6, 229; by Pa Chin, 226–7, 240, 262; by Chang T'ien-i, 227–8; by Wu Tsu-hsiang, 227–9; regional writers, 228–31; after Yenan talks, 258–60; see also literature; new literature

films, 388; wartime, 247–8; from 1945-1949, 262–4; directors of, 263–4; themes of, 263–4; message of revolution in, 264; urban nature of, 265–6

First Prison of Chekiang Province, 446

First World War: effect on evolutionary cosmology, 55; effect on image of West, 63; anarcho-communism after, 70; expectations aroused by, 93

Five Antis, 419, 469–70

five bad categories, 468

Five-Man Group, on cultural reforms, 383

five-year plans (FYP), 413, 419; lst (1953-1957), 413, 419, 451

Flaubert, Gustave, 183, 185, 262

Fokkema, D. W., 188

folk art: as 'national form,' 250, 255; novels and stories, 256; poetry, 256; woodcuts, 256; dance and drama, 256–8

foreign policy: 'leaning to one side,' 449–50, 456; self-reliance in, 451; 1958 crises, 457; Khrushchev's attempt to dictate Chinese, 457
foreign study: Mao on, 279–80
Former Ten Points, 469
Four books, 269
four-class bloc, of Stalin, 345
Four Clean Ups, 469
Four Firsts, 478
'four heavies' gang (ssu-tiao han-tzu), 204, 218
Fourier, Charles, 71
France: work-study programs in, 85; literature of, 181–2, 184, 186
France, Anatole, 186, 187
Franklin, Benjamin, 393, 427
free men (tzu-yu jen), 208–12
French Revolution, 117, 125, 167
'From Kuling to Tokyo' (Mao Tun), 201
Front Line (Ch'ien-hsien), 360
fu-ch'iang (increasing the wealth and power of the state), 269
fu-k'an (supplement), 144
Fung Yu-lan, see Feng Yu-lan
Furth, Charlotte, 99, 131
Fu-shih (novel), 246
Fu Ssu-nien, 80–1, 115, 163; on popular culture, 126
Fu Tung-hua, 262

Galsworthy, John, 182
Gang of Four: analogy, 486
Garibaldi, 147
Garshin, 188
General Office, of CC, 383
gentry: patriotic, 399
Germany, 98, 497; Mao on, 277, 278
Ghosts (Ibsen), 239
GLF, see Great Leap Forward (GLF)
Goethe, 181, 183
Gogol, Nikolai, 188
Goncourt, 185
Gone with the Wind (Mitchell), 262

Gorky, Maxim, 262, 264, 428
government: 'public,' 35–6; patterns of rule, 397–410; coalition, 399; system of, 400, 401, 402; legislative powers, 409; state structure, 409; parliamentary road, 422; see also Nationalist government
Graham, Angus, 447
grain, 410; output, 434
Grammar of Science (Pearson), 131
Great Harmony, 402, 412
Great Leap Forward (GLF), 346, 347, 355, 384, 409, 417, 451, 452, 461–4, 473, 475, 491, 492, 493; denigration of intellectuals during, 349–52; intellectual relaxation after, 352; critique of, by Peking Party Committee, 359; centralism and democracy in, 406; Mao and, 408, 410, 414, 425, 427–38, 444; theory of, 427–36; criticism of, 436; Moscow's reaction to, 455–6, 458
guerrilla warfare: Mao on, 298, 306
Gunn, Edward, 248
Guomindang, 535

Haggard, Rider, 180, 181, 182
Hai Jui, 363, 377
Hai-shang fan-hua meng (novel), 152
Hanan, Patrick, 178, 188
Han Fei-tzu, 445
Hangchow, 82; Conference, 443, 496
Han-hsueh (school of Han learning), 48
Hankow: Conference, 463
Han learning (Han-hsueh), 108; on Confucius, 46
Hanlin Academy, 14
Han people v. Manchus, 108, 111
Han-yeh (novel), 227, 246, 262
Han Yü, 180
Han-yuan chi (The Han garden), 235–6
Hao-chao (appeal), 272
Harding, Harry, 406
Hardy, Thomas, 181, 182

Hauptmann, Gerhart, 182
Hegel, Georg Wilhelm Friedrich, 121, 319
Hegelianism, 438, 440, 441
hei-mu (black screen), 153
Hei-nu yü-t'ien lu (Uncle Tom's Cabin), 237
Hen hai (novel), 151
Higher Party School, 386
history: new ideas of, 101; Li Ta-chao's concept of, 121–2; Marxist concept of, 138; Mao interpretation, 327–30; Confucianism in interpretation of, 369–70; place of class struggle in, 370, 375–6; analogies from, 376–7
History of modern Chinese fiction (C. T. Hsia), 223
History of Socialism (Kirkup), 84
History of the CPSU, 438
Hobbes, Thomas, 77
Ho Chen, 72; on women's rights, 73, 74, 77
Ho Ch'i-fang, 235, 236–7
Ho Lung, 478
Ho Tan-lin, see Feng Hsueh-feng
Hou Wai-lu, 15
Hsia, C. T., 142, 167, 168, 174, 223, 227, 231, 246, 249, 258, 262; on modernity, 194; on 'moral burden,' 266
Hsia, T. A., 216, 219, 260
Hsiang-chiang p'ing-lun (Hsiang River Review), 275–6, 277
Hsiang Ching-yü, 279, 280, 281
hsiang-tang ch'ueh-fa (relatively deficient), 439
Hsiang-tao (The Guide), 288
hsiang-t'u (local color), 229
hsiang-yueh (imperial edict), 446
hsiao-ch'üan (small power), 406, 493
Hsiao Chün, 230, 251, 254
hsiao hsiao shuo (a short short story), 225
Hsiao Hsü-tung, 282

Hsiao Hua, 478
Hsiao Hung, 230
hsiao-jen (little people), 273
hsiao-k'ang (lesser order), 111
hsiao-p'in wen (personal essay), 222; decline of, 222–3
hsiao-shuo ('fiction'), 145
Hsiao-shuo lin (Forest of fiction), 125
Hsiao-shuo yueh-pao (The short story monthly), 157, 164, 165, 174, 185
Hsia Tseng-yu, 58, 145
Hsia Yen, 203, 238, 364, 377, 378, 391; one of 'four heavies,' 204, 218; films of, 388; removed from office, 390
hsieh-ch'ing hsiao-shuo (sentimental novel), 148
Hsieh Fu-chih, 446, 480
hsieh-hui (study societies), 35
Hsieh Ping-hsin, 165, 171, 173
hsien (county), 444; Party committees, 477
hsien-chang chih-tu (constitutional system or instruments), 445
Hsien-tai (Contemporary), 186
Hsien-tai p'ing-lun (Contemporary review), 164, 205, 212, 234
hsin (mind), 25
hsin (new), 191
Hsin-ch'ao (New tide), 163
Hsin ch'ing-nien (La jeunesse, New youth), 68, 87–96, 97, 111, 156
hsin chi-yuan (new era), 93
Hsin Chung-kuo wei-lai chi (The future of new China), 150
hsing (nature), 53
Hsin-hsiang hsiao-shuo (Illustrated Fiction magazine), 145
Hsin hsiao-shuo (New fiction magazine), 145, 146, 151
hsin-hsueh (new learning), 13
hsin-li (psychic energy), 25
hsin-min (new people), 29, 148, 191
Hsin-min ts'ung-pao (New People miscellany), 65, 144

Hsin shih-chi (New Century journal),
71–2
Hsin-wen-pao, 263
Hsin-wen pao (News tribune), 156
Hsin-yueh she (Crescent Moon Society),
164
hsiu-cheng-chu-i t'ung-chih hsia ti Su-
lien (the Soviet Union under
revisionist domination), 460
Hsiung Shih-li, 45, 132; in neo-
traditional movement, 134
hsiu-ts'ai (intellectuals), 444–5
Hsuan-t'ung Emperor, 474
Hsu Chen-ya, 152–3, 156
Hsu Chih-mo, 164, 168, 181, 205, 233,
234; on poetry, 187; poetry
collections, 232
Hsu Ch'in-wen, 165
Hsueh Fu-ch'eng, 14, 17
Hsueh heng (Critical review), 129; on
vernacular, 162
hsueh-hui (study societies), 35
Hsu Hsing, 73, 74
Hsu Mou-yung, 217–18
hsun (to incense), 147
Hsun-tzu, 269, 375
Hsu Ti-shan, 164, 165
hsu to jen (a large number of people),
454
Hua-chü (spoken drama), 237
'Huai chiu' (Recollections of the past),
174
Huang Chen-hsia, 208
Huang Chieh, 46, 47
Huang Hsing, 271
Huang Lu-yin, 165, 169, 173
Huang Mo-hsi, 145
Huang shu (Yellow book), 47
Huang Yen-p'ei, 419, 422
Huang Yuan, 215, 218
Huan-hsiang jih-chi (Diary of returning
home), 264
Hua-yueh hen (Vestiges of flowers and
moonlight), 152

Hu Ch'iao-mu, 363
Hu Ch'iu-yuan, 209–10, 212, 220;
rebuttal of, 210
Hu Feng, 214–15, 217–18, 220, 254,
352, 373, 388, 389, 391; on wartime
literature, 245, 250–1
Hugo, Victor, 181
Hu Han-min, 121
Hu Hsien-su, 162
Hu Hua, 315
Hu Jiwei, 513–14, 515
Hu-lan ho chuan (short story), 230
Hunan: Mao's participaton in autonomy
movement, 278; Mao on reform of,
280–1; Self-Study University in, 284;
Mao's work with peasants of, 288;
Mao report on peasants of, 295, 310
Hundred Flowers Campaign, 389, 417,
421, 426, 427, 439, 458;
Confucianism beginning in, 349;
criticism by intellectuals during,
349; compared to relaxation after
GLF, 352, 354, 355–8, 365;
Khrushchev and, 458
Hundred Schools, 421, 422, 439
Hung (novel), 223–4
Hungary, 454; Hungarian revolt (1956),
382, 422, 423, 451, 453
Hung-chu (poetry collection), 232
Hung Hsiu-ch'üan, 365
Hung-kuang (Szechwan), 429
Hung Ling-fei, 203
Hung-lou meng (Dream of the red
chamber), 109, 146, 152
Hung Shen, 238, 239, 240, 263
Hung-shui (Deluge), 165
Huo-tsang (novel), 246–7
Hu Ping, 518
Hu-shang ti pei-chü (play), 238
Hu Shih, 64, 94, 112, 122, 148, 152;
role in linguistic reform, 97; higher
criticism of, 114, 115; and New
Culture, 115–17; influence of May
Fourth on, 119, 136, 155; political

proposals of, 119–20; on problems and '-isms,' 124–6; on popular culture, 126; in debate on science, 131; and the literary revolution, 155, 157–62, 163; eight principles of, 158–9, 167; translator of Ibsen, 169; poetry of, 187; drama of, 237–8; influence on Mao, 273, 275–6, 280, 290

Huters, Ted, 260

Hu Tieh, 263

Huxley, T. H.: translation of, 19, 26, 147

Hu Yaobang, 500, 504, 507, 508–10, 511, 513, 515, 519, 520

Hu Yeh-p'in, 168

i (change), see change (i)

Ibanez, Vincente Blasco, 186

Ibsen, Henrik, 114, 169–70, 238, 239, 262

I ching (Book of Changes), 24, 58, 60

i-ching chi-pen shang chieh-chüeh le (already been basically resolved), 422

ideinost (ideology), 255

ideology, 447, 481, 491; of Cultural Revolution, 374, 376, 475–90; Mao's ideological legacy, 490–8

i fen wei erh (one divides into two), 471, 491, 495

i-ko chieh-fang yun-tung (a liberation movement), 455

i ku fei chin che tsu (Those who make use of the past to disparage the present should be exterminated together with their whole families), 447

illiteracy, 425, 430

imperialism, 422, 431, 461; reformers' attitude towards, 37; Leninist theory of, 121, 137; and Lincheng Incident, 182–3; use of landlords by, 294; Mao on war against, 296, 306; Mao on, 411, 456; extermination of, 419; see also anti-imperialism; autonomy; West, the

Independent Critic (Tu-li p'ing-lun), 136

India: Soviet neutrality in border conflict, 384

individual: emphasis of literary revolution on, 167; self-definition of women writers, 168–9; issue of creativity in wartime, 249; Mao on initiative of, 270

individualism, 431; Yen Fu on, 25, 103; of anarchists, 68, 74–5, 77–8, 81, 90; of terrorism, 69; New Youth move away from, 89–90; of Mao, 273–4

inductionism, dominant in China, 130–1

industrialization, 33; social costs of, 34; see also modernization

industrial proletariat, Lenin on mass mobilization of, 122; see also labor; working class

industry, 435; nonferrous metal complexes, 402; in coastal areas, 403, 416; heavy, 403, 405, 451; in hinterland, 403, 416; light, 403; Mao attitude toward industrialization, 410–13, 433; Mao on, 411, 413; handicrafts, 413; socialist transformation of, 419

inflation: wartime, 243

initiative, individual (tzu-tung): Mao on, 270

intellectuals, 99, 399, 445, 446, 447, 464, 468–9, 473, 492; vs. politicians, 112; scientific, 120; and the masses, 123–4; spread of Marxism among urban, 137–8; alienation in 1930s, 202–3; in novels of Mao Tun, 224; politicized by war, 244; and Yenan, 250; urban nature of intelligentsia, 264; denigrated in GLF, 349–51; relaxation after GLF, 351–9, 366–7, 394; criticism of Mao's policies by

intellectuals *(continued)*
   officials, 358–9; officials of Peking
      Party Committee, 359–62, 377;
      resistance to Mao's ideological class
      struggle, 367–72; radical, 372–7;
      Mao's 1964 attacks on, 381; Mao on,
      415, 420, 425–8, 473; bourgeois,
      420, 426; pre-1949, 421;
      communist, 444;
      counterrevolutionary, 447; as
      'stinking ninth category,' 473; in
      post-Mao era, 499–538;
      nonestablishment, 503–4, 532–3,
      538; dissident, 531–2; see also elite;
      students
International Anarchist Congress, 83
Internationale, 495
internationalism: of K'ang Yu-wei,
   19–20; of anarchists, 73; phase in
   Mao's thought, 281–2
Internet, 531
Ionesco, 189
I Pai-sha, 157
I-pu-sheng chu-i (Ibsenism), 169
irrigation, 428, 429
Irving, Washington, 181
'-isms' (Hu Shih), 124
Italy, recognition of PRC by, 400
i-te wo-lo-chi (ideology), 198
i-yuan (public assemblies), 35
i-yuan-hua (integrate), 342–4, 407–8,
   493, 494, 495
i-yuan-hua ling-tao (integrated
   leadership), 460

James, William, 58
Japan, 421; Shantung awarded to, 98;
   mediator of Western influence, 108;
   fiction of, 146; naturalism in, 185;
   effect of war on literature, 221; war of
   resistance against, 241
jen (goodness, love, benevolence), 19,
   21, 24, 28, 29, 30, 56, 60, 61, 369
Jen-chien-shih (Human world), 212

jen-ch'ing (human sentiments), 76
Jen hsueh (On humanity), 18, 19, 25, 56
jen-ko (moral personality), 54
jen-min min-chu chu-i ti-chih-tu
   (people's democratic system), 400
jen-sheng kuan (point of view based on
   living experience), 63
Jevons, Stanley, 33
Jiang Zemin, 523, 526, 527, 528, 529,
   531, 533–4, 535
Jih-ch'u (play), 239–41
Johnson, Dr. Samuel, 206
journalism: creation of reformist literati,
   143–4; newspapers, 144; magazines,
   145
Journal of the new people, 65
Jou Shih, 202
Juichin, 214
Ju-lin wai-shih (The scholars), 148
Jun-t'u, 178
ju yü ch'i chung (getting inside of
   things), 278

K'a-fei tien chih i-yeh (play), 238
kai-ko (reform), 281
Kajin-no-kigu (novel), 146
k'ang-chan (war of resistance), 241–4
K'ang Pai-ch'ing, 187, 231
K'ang Sheng, 339, 372, 420, 443, 444,
   483, 487; and radical intellectuals,
   374; and Chiang Ch'ing, 377, 378,
   383; in Five-Man Group, 383
K'ang Yu-wei, 14, 38, 101, 148, 402;
   analysis of theories of, 18–22; use of
   Western science by, 32–3, 34; and
   new cosmology, 44, 110; opposed by
   national essence school, 44, 48, 52;
   on New Text tradition, 48–9, 100,
   114; on Confucianism as a religion,
   56–7, 62, 67, 88, 110–11, 197; on
   personal autonomy, 75; on family, 76,
   77; as 'socialist,' 104, 105;
   newspapers founded by, 144; Mao on,
   272

Kant, Immanuel, 64, 131, 271
k'ao-cheng (empirical research), 114
Kao Ch'ien-ta (Ou-yang Shan), 262
Kao I-han, 157
Kao Kang, 407
Kao T'ien-mei, 153
Kato Hiroyuki, 28
Kawakami Hajime, 197
Keats, John, 181, 182, 232
Ke-chueh (fiction), 169
k'en-ting fou-ting ti-kuei-lü (law of affirmation and negation), 440
Ke-yao chou-k'an (Folksong weekly), 127
Khrushchev, Nikita, 422, 452, 454, 456, 457, 458, 461; and Mao, 422, 449, 455–8, 466; secret speech, 454; on communes, 456–8; on Middle Eastern crises (1958), 457; meddling in China's internal affairs, 458; and P'eng Te-huai, 458
Kiangsi, 302, 304, 311, 398; school of poetry, 160
Kierkegaard, Soren Aabye, 189
King of Heaven, 476
King of Hell, 476
kingship, cosmology of, 110
Kirkup, Thomas, 84
Kita Ikki, 72
K'o Ch'ing-shih, 464; supporter of Mao, 374; on need for new drama, 380
K-o-erh-ch'in ch'i ts'ao-yuan (novel), 231
ko-hsing (individuality), 348
k'o-i shuo chiu shih Chung-kuo wen-ming (could be said to be Chinese culture), 280
ko-jen tu-tuan (arbitrary or dictatorial decisions of an individual), 406–7
K'o Ling, 263
ko-ming (modern revolution), 66
Ko-ming chün (Revolutionary Army), 106
Kotoku Shusui, 72

ko yü-chun wu-chih ti ming (revolution to do away with stupidity and ignorance), 415
Kropotkin, Peter, 71, 73, 74, 81, 83, 85, 124; source of Chinese knowledge of socialism, 86; on mutual aid, 109; contrasted with Marx, 274–5
Kuan-ch'ang hsien-hsing chi (Exposés of officialdom), 149, 150
Kuan Feng: and radical intellectuals, 373, 375; philosophy of, 375; criticisms of Wu Han, 377
Kuang-ming jih-pao (Enlightenment Daily), 349, 422; on scientists, 354
Kuan-li (supervise), 492, 493
Ku Chieh-kang, 99, 114, 115; on popular culture, 126
ku-ch'ui (preached or advocated), 340
kung (commonality), 34
Kung-an school, 222
kung-ch'an chu-i (communism), 86
kung-ch'an p'ai, 286
kung-ch'an ti sheng-huo (communist life), 280
K'ung I-chi (story), 176
kung-li (natural law), 28, 50
kung-tao chen-li (natural morality), 77
kung-t'uan chu-i (syndicalism), 283
K'ung-tzu kai-chih k'ao (Confucius as reformer), 18
kuo (going too far), 327
kuo-chia (nation), 288
kuo-hsing, see national character (kuo-hsing)
kuo-hsueh (national learning), 46
Kuo-hsueh pao-ts'un hui (Association for the Preservation of Classical Chinese Learning), 46
Kuo-ku lun-heng (Critical essays on antiquity), 48
kuo-min (citizens), 288
kuo-min hui-i (national convention), 172

Kuo-min jih-pao (National People's
Daily), 144
kuo-min ko-ming (national revolution),
288
Kuomintang (KMT), 399, 402, 418,
436–7, 460, 463, 469; relation with
writers, 203, 208, 210; Mao's work
for, 296–7; Mao's break with, 297;
Mao on role of against Japan, 333–4;
and intellectuals, 360
Kuo Mo-jo, 102, 113, 137, 197, 233,
237; in Creation Society, 165, 167;
and Marxism, 165; poetry of, 167,
187; writing of, 167, 173, 187, 238;
hero worship by, 181, 193; on
literature and revolution, 197–8; in
May Thirtieth incident, 197–8; on
national defence literature, 216, 219;
drama of, 238; head of Political
Department, 242; on 'national forms,'
251
Kuo Shao-yü, 164
Kuo Sung-t'ao, 14
kuo-t'i (state system), 54, 400
kuo-ts'ui, see National Essence (kuo-
ts'ui) movement
Kuo-wen pao (National news), 144;
fiction in, 145
Kuo-yü lo-ma-tzu (system of
romanization), 214
kuo-yü ti wen-hsueh (a literature in the
national language), 161
Kuriyagawa Hakuson, 187
Ku-t'ien Resolution (1929), 398
Kweilin, 243; theatre in, 248

labor, reform through, 446
labor unions, 530–1
land: Ting Ling on redivision of, 259
landlords, 425, 469; Mao on, 293
Lao She, 185, 220, 223, 243, 401;
fiction of, 225–6; as regional writer,
229; in war of resistance, 241; on use
of old forms, 245; wartime work of,

246–7, 257–8; work adapted to film,
263
Lao Ts'an yu-chi (Travels of Lao Ts'an),
149, 154, 155
Lao-tsu, 28, 36, 109
lao-ts'u (uneducated people), 415
lao-tung che (workers, toilers), 492
Lao-tzu, 447
lao-tzu shih ko-ming ti (I'm a
revolutionary), 415
late Ch'ing literature (1895–1911),
143–52; growth of literary
journalism, 143–5; place of fiction in,
145; theories of 'new fiction,' 145–8;
practice of 'new fiction,' 148–52;
Butterfly fiction, 152–5, 157, 185;
see also New Literature
Latinization, 213–14
Lau, Joseph, 239
leadership: Mao on, 341–2; Mao's
slogans, 341–2; and i-yuan-hua,
342–3
leadership of CCP: and intellectuals,
349; divisions in during cultural
rectification, 392
League of Left-wing Writers: and
Marxism, 140; leadership of, 203–4;
official documents, 204; emphases of,
204–5; Lu Hsun and Crescent Moon,
205–8; in free men dispute, 208–10;
functions of, 211–12; domination of,
212; dissolution of, 214–15
Leavis, F. R., 206
Lee Ou-fan, Leo, 99, 114
leftists, 423; see also League of Left-
Wing Writers
Left-wing Cultural Coalition (Tso-i
wen-hua tsung t'ung-meng), 203
Legalism, 16, 446, 484, 485–6
Lei Feng, 387, 490
Lei-yü (play), 238–40
Lenin, Vladimir I., 137, 309–10, 315,
385, 386, 395, 400–1, 415, 423,
433, 437, 438, 453, 455, 459, 470,

480, 483, 497; and the 'Leninist dilemma,' 103, 106, 112, 122; Sun Yat-sen's interest in, 120, 224; theory of imperialism, 121; on mass mobilization, 122–3; use of theory by, 139; Mao's understanding of, 283; on class consciousness, 300, 325; on unity of opposites, 319; on voluntarism, 321; on revolution in backward lands, 330, 345; Leninism, 385, 402, 411, 446, 456, 459, 477; Mao compared to, 385, 399, 446, 454, 486; on democratic centralism, 397, 398; see also Marxism-Leninism

Lermontov, Mikhail, 188, 237

Levenson, Joseph, 15, 102, 122, 128, 130

li (norms), 21, 23, 27, 130, 135

Liang Chi, 132

Liang Ch'i-ch'ao, 18, 33, 58, 63, 82, 100, 101, 122, 191; on Social Darwinism, 19, 104–5; on evolutionary change, 28–31, 36, 105; on Western science, 33–6; on democracy, 36; erosion of faith in reform utopianism, 38–40, 93; as neo-traditionalist, 44, 62, 68; defense of tradition by, 53, 88–9; 'Reflections on a European journey,' 55, 63, 129; journal of, 65; opposition to Sun Yat-sen, 66; on reform vs. revolution, 66–7, 68; and 'new citizen,' 103; on kingship, 110; on need for religion, 111; use of fiction by, 113, 157; influence on Hu Shih, 115; reassessment of Western civilization by, 129–30; journalism of, 144, 145; on political fiction, 146–8; novels of, 150; influence on Mao, 275

liang-chih (intuitive knowledge), 63

Liang mountain (band), 69

Liang Shih-ch'iu, 220, 253; and Crescent Moon, 205; theory of literature, 206, 246

Liang Shu-ming, 45, 63, 123, 132; intuitionist, 59–62; on national essence, 129; in neo-traditional movement, 132, 134; politicized, 140

Liao Kai-lung, 492

Liao Mo-sha, 360; and Three Family Village, 391–2

liberalism, 140; Yen Fu's translation of, 25–6

Liberation Daily (Chieh-fang jih-pao), 339

Li Chi, 262

Li-chia chuang ti pien-ch'ien (novel), 262

li-chih (establishing the will), 271

Li Chin-fa, 220; poetry of, 234

Li Chin-hsi, 271

Li Ch'u-li, 200

lien-ai tzu-yu (freedom to love), 169

Li Hsiao-feng, 163

li-hsing (intuitive reason), 62

Li Hsiu-ch'eng, 365, 376

Li-hun (novel), 226

Li Jui, on Mao Tse-tung's thought, 273, 275, 284

Li Kuang-t'ien, 235

Li Kung-p'u: on cultural front organizations, 203; strategy of, 302–3, 305–6; divergence from Moscow, 303–4; on role of cities vs. countryside, 303–4; in agreement with Mao on world revolution, 305

Lin-chia p'u-tzu (Lin family shop), 388

Lin Chieh, 373, 375–6; criticism of Wu Han by, 377

Ling Shu-hua, 171, 193

Link, E. Perry, 153–4

Lin Mo-han, 373, 391

Lin Piao, 477, 478, 480, 484, 485; Mao's letters to, 301, 304, 308; P'eng Te-huai replaced by, 383; criticism of Mao as a despot, 485

Lin Ping, 250

Lin Shu, 14, 107, 152; on literary revolution, 162; translations by, 180
Lin Tsai-p'ing, 63
Lin Yü-sheng, 110
Lin Yü-shih, 373, 375
Lin Yutang, 212, 220; magazine of, 212, 222–3
Li-pai-liu (Saturday), 153
Li Pao-chia, 145, 149, 151, 155
Li San-ts'ai, 362
Li Shenzhi, 528–9
Li Shih-tseng, 73, 85; on family, 76–7
Li Ssu, 447
Li Ta-chao, 165, 274, 281; and New Youth, 88, 91–2; Marxism of, 94–5; response to Bolshevism, 121; on problems and '-isms,' 124–6; influence on Mao, 274, 290; on China as proletarian nation, 278
literary criticism: and Marxist materialism, 199; of Liang Shih-ch'iu, 206
Literary Gazette (Wen-i pao), 390; on writers, 355; self-criticism of, 391
literary revolution, 157–63, 215; role of New Youth in, 157; Hu Shih's proposal, 157–9; Ch'en Tu-hsiu's response, 159–60; opposition to, 162–3; new writers of, 163–7; romanticism vs. emancipation, 167–71
Literary Studies, Association for (Wen-hsueh yen-chiu hui), 164; supposed realism of, 165; writings of, 173
literature, 421, 443, 472, 473, 484; as belles lettres, 113; and New Culture, 113–14; inclusion of 'vernacular,' 126–7; proletarian, 139; themes of, 142–3; late Ch'ing (1895-1911), 143–55; May Fourth era (1917-1927), 155–95; literary revolution, 157–63; emergence of new writers, 163–7; romanticism and emancipation, 167–71; short stories,

172–80; impact of foreign writing, 180–90; quest for modernity, 190–5; of 1930s, 196–203; polemics of, 203–20; creativity and social crisis, 220–41; of war and revolution, 241–4; Communist, 261–2; during GLF, 350–1; socialist realism in, 351, 355; tsa-wen of Peking Party Committee intellectuals, 360–3; Chou Yang and, 364; of May 4th writers in Party Propaganda Department, 364–5; revival of 1930s, 365–6; 'middle characters,' 366; literary rectification, 472; in post-Mao era, 505; see also literary revolution; New Culture movement; New Literature; novels; tsa-wen (informal essay)
Liu Binyan, 511
Liu Chieh, 370
Liu Chih-jen, 256
Liu Ch'iung, 263
Liu E (Liu T'ieh-yun), 155, 172
Liu Hsiang, 361
Liu Hsin, 49
Liu Hu-lan, 262
Liu Ji, 528, 529
Liu Shao-ch'i, 368, 372, 376, 413, 466, 473, 481, 490; on nationalization of Marxism, 323; at Seventh Congress, 323; on Mensheviks, 339; force behind 1961-1962 relaxation, 352, 359, 366–7; on Mao's criticisms, 382; on decentralization, 406; on classes leading revolution, 412; number one capitalist-roader, 421
Liu Shih-fu (Liu Ssu-fu), 69, 83, 84, 85
Liu Shih-p'ei, 46, 47, 77; in Tokyo group, 72–3; on social class, 73–5; on family, 77; on self-liberation and equality, 78, 80; on cultural heritage, 108, 109, 111, 128
Liu Shou-sung, 204
Liu Ta-pai, 187

liu ts'ai-tzu (Six talented men), 152
Liu Wu-chi, 248
Liu Ya-tzu, 108, 128, 155
Li yun (Evolution of the Rites), 20
Lo Chen-yü, 46
Lo Chia-lun, 163
Logic (J. S. Mill), 33, 131
Lo-t'o Hsiang-tzu (novel), 225
love, as focus of literary rebellion,
    168–70
Lo-yin (poetry collection), 237
lü hou (concern for posterity), 53
Lu Hsiao-man, 168
Lu Hsun, 81, 99, 113, 163, 197, 241,
    250, 253, 266; and New Culture,
    115, 118, 132; writing of, 118, 176,
    177–8, 188, 221–2; and popular
    culture, 126; on Marxism-Leninism,
    138, 140; on kinds of fiction, 148; on
    A Doll's house, 169, 171; and the
    short story, 172–80; translations by,
    180; poetry of, 188–90, 193; on
    literature and revolution, 198–9;
    rebuttal of revolutionary writers, 200,
    201–2; and League of Left-wing
    Writers, 203, 210, 265; and 'four
    heavies,' 204, 218; vs. Crescent
    Moon, 205–8; defence of translations
    by, 207–8; on romanization, 214; and
    dissolution of League, 214–15; on
    national defence literature, 216–17;
    and battle of the 'two slogans,'
    217–19, 220; creative work of, 220;
    essays of, 221–2; leading writer of
    1920s, 223; on the personal essay,
    223; on Hsiao Chün, 230; Mao on,
    253; commemoration of, 261; on
    individualism, 274; tsa-wen of, 360
Lu Hsun Academy of Arts, 377
Lukacs, Georg, 191
Lu-kou-ch'iao (Marco Polo Bridge),
    241, 245
Lunacharsky, Anatoli V., 202, 206
lun-chan (polemic), 64

Lun-yü (Analects), 212
Lü-sheng, 150
Luther, Martin, 56, 158
Lu Ting-i, 256, 388, 428; on
    intellectuals, 349; in 1960-1961
    relaxation, 359; on Five-Man Group,
    383; minister of culture, 391
Lu-Wang, 15, 63
Lysenko, Trofim, 422

MacArthur, Douglas, 476
Mach, Ernst, 362
Machinery: agricultural, 415; Mao on
    machine tools, 433
Ma Feng, 386
magazines, reformist, 144–5; see also
    journalism
Ma-k'o-ssu-hua le ti (transformed by
    Marxism), 469
Malatesta, Errico, 71
Mallarmé, Stéphane, 186, 234, 236
Manchuria: refugee writers from,
    229–31
Mandarin Duck and Butterfly School
    (Yuan-yang hu-tieh p'ai), 152, 157;
    Perry Link on, 153–4; popularity of,
    155; attacks on, 185
Mao-ch'eng chi (novel), 225
Maoism, see thought of Mao Tse-tung
Mao Tse-tung, 105, 131, 137; as
    anarchist, 86; on ta-t'ung, 94; on
    popular culture, 128; and Liang Shu-
    ming, 134; in Yenan period, 137,
    140–1, 195; on proletariat, 204; on
    the language of the masses, 214;
    Talks on Literature and Art, 249,
    250–81, 364; on leadership, 293; on
    class struggle, 294, 310–11, 367,
    384, 409, 417–26, 439, 453, 457,
    461–75, 485, 496; on Hunan
    peasants, 310; on contradictions,
    315–16, 317, 396, 417–18, 422,
    438, 443, 462, 470, 471, 474, 477,
    495; and mass line, 340–2, 397–9,

Mao Tse-tung (*continued*)
408; on 'people's democratic dictatorship,' 344–8, 400, 401, 411, 418; on literature, 351; and intellectuals, 352, 353, 354; on relaxation after GLF, 353–4; criticized in relaxation of 1961-1962, 358–9, 361–2; personality cult attacked, 361; and Hai Jui, 363; and GLF, 366; resistance to his ideological class struggle, 367–72; and Chiang Ch'ing, 372, 378, 379; and radical intellectuals, 372–7, 392, 394; on cultural rectification, 380–2, 384, 388, 389, 391–2, 393–4; and Hundred Flowers, 389; and Chinese culture, 396; and Westernization, 396; on democracy, 397, 408–9, 476, 489, 493; on democratic centralism, 398, 401, 402, 408; on economics, 403, 404, 408, 409, 410, 412–13, 416, 471, 482, 483, 492; on centralization and decentralization, 403–9; death of, 404, 490; administrative philosophy during Yenan period, 407, 408; and Great Leap Forward, 408, 425, 427–36; increasing radicalism, 409; on agriculture, 410–11; on modernization, 410–12; on industrialization, 410–13; on industry, 411; vision of Chinese revolution, 412; on building socialism, 413–16; on intellectuals, 415, 425–8; rural policies of, 419; on Khrushchev's ideas, 422; on masses, 427, 428; search for Chinese road, 427–48; on co-operativization, 429; rural utopian dreams of, 430–2; role as chairman, 447; visit to Moscow (1957), 455; on education, 479–80; and Red Guards, 479–80; Western scholars on, 487; ideological legacy of, 490–8; see also thought of Mao Tse-tung
Mao Tun, 164, 165, 166, 171, 200–1,

237, 241, 243, 364, 388, 391; on realism, 174, 185–6; on symbolism, 187; on mass language, 213; on national defence literature, 216, 218, 219, 245–6; creative writing of, 220, 223, 239; works of, 223–5, 246; as regional writer, 229
Marco Polo Bridge incident (Lu-kou-ch'iao), 241, 245
marriage, 460; anarchists on, 77–8; Mao on, 280
Marriage (Shih T'o), 262
martial spirit, Mao's emphasis on, 269–70, 308–9
martyrs, tradition of, 107
Marx, Karl, 93, 124, 309, 325, 370, 437, 465, 480, 497; vs. Kropotkin, 274–5; on stages of society, 330; on nature of Communist Party, 399; Mao compares self to, 454; and Ch'in Shih-huang-ti, 481–90; on role of urban proletariat, 482
Marxism, 42, 64, 74, 369, 374, 397, 400, 402, 411, 419, 454, 458, 462, 469, 471, 473, 483, 486, 489, 490, 491, 495, 496, 497; vs. socialism, 86; and New Youth, 88, 93, 94–6; after First World War, 93; of Li Ta-chao, 95; in debate on science, 124, 131; ascendancy of, 135–41; in debate on social history of China, 139; in literature, 140; and literary criticism, 199, 207, 209; Mao on, 250; absent in early Mao writing, 274–5; Mao's partial understanding of, 282, 291–2, 295; Mao begins study of, 315; 'sinification' of, 322, 323; Mao's adaptation of, 323–7, 346, 395, 396; Mao's divergence from, 346; not applicable to Chinese history, 370; of Yang Hsien-chen, 384, 385; Sinification of, 396; theorists of, 426; and Chinese tradition, 436–48
Marxism-Leninism, 105, 349, 365, 393,

395, 423, 437, 444, 446, 449, 458, 459, 469, 475, 495; introduction, 121–4; urged on writers, 252–3; Mao on 'standpoint' of, 325, 326; on 'methodology' of, 325, 326–7; principles applied to China, 325; and New Democracy, 330; 'Mao's thought' as form of, 339; political education in, 353, 357; as transmitted to Mao, 386

masses: language for, 213, 214; Mao on literature for, 254; Mao's early emphasis on, 273

mass language (ta-chung hua), 212–14; proposed by Ch'u Ch'iu-pai, 212–13; rebutted by Mao Tun, 213

mass line, 299–300, 340–2, 397–9, 408, 492

mass mobilization: Lenin on, 122–3; criticism of, 358

mathematics, influence on Chinese thought, 32, 131

Maupassant, Guy de, 182, 184

Mayakovsky, Vladimir, 247

May Fourth movement, 97, 400, 483; student role in, 87–8; description of incident, 98–9; themes characterizing period of, 100–2; 1911 Revolution as forerunner of, 110–18; consequences of, 118–21, 143; and introduction of Marxism-Leninism, 121–4; problems and '-isms,' 124–6; popular culture, 126–8; two-traditionalism, 128–30; debate on science and human life, 130–5; and ascendancy of Marxism, 135–41; literature of, 155–95; literary revolution, 157–61; quest for modernity, 190–5; literature of, 196, 197, 200, 213, 231–2; in fiction, 224, 226–7; echoed in drama, 238–9; legacy of, 244; attacks on literature of, 250–1, 252–4; relation of Mao to, 267–8; dividing line between old and new democracy, 331; Communist

rejection of, 348; intellectuals of, 356, 364–7, 369; later echoes of, 360; attacks on writers of, 373, 388; period, 443–4

May Thirtieth incident, 197

Mazzinni, Giuseppi, 147

McDougall, Bonnie, 183, 236; on symbolism, 186; on avant-garde, 192

media: journalists, 426

meetings of the immortals, 357

Mei-chou p'ing-lun (Weekly Critic), 92, 124, 275

Mei Kuang-ti, 128, 134, 162

Meisner, Maurice, 121

Mencius, 20, 25, 82, 133, 444; reformers' view of, 36; criticisms of, 73, 74

Meng-hu chi (Fierce Tiger poetry collection), 232

Mensheviks, 339

merchants: Mao on role of, 286–7

metaphysics: science and, 63–5

Metzger, Thomas, 134

Miao, 127

'middle character,' 366, 370, 378, 385, 386–7, 388, 391; vs. heroic figures, 378–9, 386–7

Middle East: conflict (1958), 457

middle schools: junior, 479; senior, 479–80

Midnight (novel), 185, 201, 223, 224, 239

militarism: of Chiang Kai-shek, 138

military: copying Soviet advisers on, 452; dictatorship, 480

Military Affairs Commission (MAC), 478

Mill, J. S., 19, 26, 33, 115, 131, 147

min-ch'üan (people's rights), 29

Min-chung chü-she (Popular Drama Society), 238

ming-chiao (doctrine of names, Confucian moral code), 23

Ming dynasty, 46, 107, 158, 360, 362, 363, 381
ming-fen (rank), 53
ming-liao kai-nien (clear concept), 280
Ming-mo yi-hen (play), 248
Ming-yu chih ssu (play), 238
Ministries, central, 405, 407
Min pao (People's journal), 28, 65, 70
Min sheng (Voice of the people), 85
min-sheng chu-i (Sun Yat-sen concept), 66
Min-su chou-k'an (Folklore journal), 127
min-tsu (Chinese nation), 47, 329, 496
min-tsu chu-i wen-hsueh (nationalist literature), 208, 209
min-tsu ko-ming chan-cheng ti ta-chung wen-hsueh (mass literature of national revolutionary war), 217
min-tsu ko-ming wen-hsueh yun-tung (national revolutionary literary movement), 215
min-tsu tzu-wei wen-hsueh (national self-defence literature), 215
missionaries: use of science by, 32
Miyazaki, Toten, 271
mo (bewitchedness), 152
modernity: quest for, 142, 190–5; literary, 183
modernization: Chinese optimism on, 33; of Yen Fu, 103–4; of K'ang Yu-wei, 104; Mao attitude toward, 396, 410–12, 433, 479, 483; Marx on, 482; see also industry; nationalization
monarchy: plans for, 110–11
Monkey King, 476
Montesquieu, Baron de, 19, 26, 150
Moscow: as source of inspiration, 137; 1957 Conference, 455, 456, 471; Mao 1957 visit to, 455; 1960 Conference, 458; see also Russia; Soviet Union
mo-teng (modern), 168, 193
Mo-tzu, 15

Mou Tsung-san, 134
Mussolini, Benito, 495

Nanking government: wartime repression of, 244
Nanning: Conference, 429, 432
Nan she (Southern Society), 155–6
Napoleon Bonaparte, 147
narodnost (Soviet national character), 255
national character (kuo-hsing), 44; Liang Ch'i-ch'ao on, 44, 53–5, 88
national defence literature (kuo-fang wen-hsueh), 215, 218, 219, 245–6; Chou Yang on, 216; Lu Hsun on, 216–17
National Essence (kuo-ts'ui) movement, 38, 41, 43–4, 73, 111, 128; Chang Ping-lin, 47–52; on Confucian humanism, 49–50; opposition to K'ang Yu-wei, 50–2; significance of, 52; neo-traditionalism of successors to, 128–9
nationalism: and Social Darwinism, 19; and populism, 27–8; of neo-traditionalists, 36–8, 45; and progress, 100–6; organic cultural vs. iconoclastic, 107–9, 111; role in Leninist imperialism, 121–2; Mao's early concern for, 268; as independent variable in Marxism, 325–6; see also autonomy; imperialism
Nationalist government: efforts of neo-traditionalists to influence, 136; attitude toward writers, 243; see also Kuomintang; Nanking government
nationalist literature (min-tsu chu-i wen-hsueh), 208; attacks on, 209
nationalization: of land, 66; see also centralization
National Military Council, Political Department, 242
National People's Congress (NPC), 445, 494

national resistance saga, 241–4;
literature of 'patriotic gore,' 244–9;
Yenan Forum, 250–6; Yenan
literature, 256–60; on eve of
revolution, 261–6
'National revolution and the peasant
movement' (Mao), 293–6
naturalism: in Chinese fiction, 185,
224; see also evolutionary naturalism
Natural Morality (journal), 72, 74; on
radical feminism, 72–3; on Tolstoy,
73; on self-liberation to equality, 80
negation of the negation: Soviet work on
concept of, 317, 319; abandoned by
Mao, 319
Nehru, Jawaharlal, 458
Nei-chou p'ing-lun (Weekly Review),
275
neo-Confucianism, 15; K'ang Yu-wei's
version of, 21; shift towards, 64;
Liang Ch'i-ch'ao on, 130; of Hsiung
Shih-li, 134; in post-Mao era, 526,
527
neo-Maoists, 525–6, 529
neo-realism, of Fung Yu-lan, 134
neo-romanticism, 185
neo-traditionalism: alternative to
evolutionary cosmology, 43, 46;
currents of, 43–4; national essence,
43–52; national character, 53–5;
Confucianism as religion, 54–62;
science and metaphysics, 63–5; as
reaction to reform modernization, 65;
as reaction to May Fourth movement,
128–30
New Century (journal), 71–2, 81, 83,
84; on Kropotkin, 73; on social class,
74; on role of sexuality, 77; on
dissolving of barriers, 79; after 1915,
85
New China News Agency (Hsin-hua
hsin-wen-she), 383
'new citizen': of Ch'en Tu-hsiu, 89; ideal
of, 89, 103–4, 107

New Culture movement, 42, 87, 193–4;
separate from politics, 54, 112; and
1911 Revolution, 110–18; fiction,
113; 'Creation' group, 113–14;
higher criticism, 114; search for
Chinese roots, 115, 142; Hu Shih,
116–17; Ch'en Tu-hsiu, 117; Lu
Hsun, 117–18
New Democracy, 402
New Fourth Army incident, 246
New Literature, 113, 145; use of fiction
in, 113, 153–4; romanticism in,
113–14; higher criticism, 114;
discovery of past vernacular literature,
115; popularization of, 154, 155;
tenets of, 199–200; critics of, 200–1;
readers of, 201; pai-hua of, 213;
attacked by Mao, 250; urban nature
of, 264; see also literary revolution;
literature
New People's Study Society, 281, 282
newspapers: reformist, 144;
supplements to, 144–5; and Southern
Society, 156; see also journalism
New Text school, 18, 19, 26, 48–9; on
Confucianism as religion, 49, 56;
syncretism of, 56
Newton, Isaac, 354
New Youth (Hsin ch'ing-nien), 68, 80,
87–92, 175; early stage of, 87;
vehicle for Marxism, 88; philososphy
of Ch'en Tu-hsiu, 88–90; on suicide,
90–1; and New Culture, 111;
revolution in literary content
sponsored by, 157; and literary
revolution, 157–63; Lu Hsun's essays
in, 221; drama in, 238; influence on
Mao, 267–8; Mao's first article in,
268
Nieh-hai hua (A flower in a sea of
retribution), 149, 150
Nieh Jung-chen, 478
Nietzsche, Friedrich Wilhelm, 81, 109,
117, 182, 189

nihilism, 68–70, 90

Ni Huan-chih, 174

Niu T'ien-tz'u chuan (Biography of Niu T'ien-tz'u), 226

Northern Expedition, 137

novels, 472; sentimental, 148, 151–2; social, 148–51; vs. short stories, 172; by Yeh Shao-chün, 173–4; foreign, translations of, 180–2; effect of wartime on, 221; by Mao Tun, 223–5; by Shen Ts'ung-wen, 225; by Lao She, 225–6, 229; by Pa Chin, 226–7, 240, 262; by regional writers, 229–31; of wartime, 246; folk, 258; from 1945-1949, 262; see also New Literature

Nu-li chou-pao (Endeavour), 119

Nung-chen ch'eng-chia (play), 248

October Revolution, 120, 395, 414, 436–7, 452, 453, 454, 466

'On contradiction' (Mao), 315–16, 317, 318, 384, 417–18, 438

'On dialectical and historical materialism' (Stalin), 438

O'Neill, Eugene, 239, 240

'One into two, two into one,' 384, 390

On Liberty (J. S. Mill), 26

On New Democracy (Mao), 331, 332, 400, 401

'On practice' (Mao), 274, 315, 317, 318

On protracted war (Mao), 307

'On reading Ni Huan-chih' (Mao Tun), 200–1

'On the correct handling of contradictions among the people' (Mao), 384, 409, 417, 423, 439

'On the ten great relationships' (Mao), 402–5, 416, 421, 452, 453

'On the unification of party leadership...', 1942 resolution of Politburo, 342–3

operas: Yang-ko, 253, 256–7; Peking, 257, 377–80, 472

'Opposing adventurism' editorial, 416

Ou-yang Ching-wu, 102

Ou-yang Hsiu, 113

Ou-yang Shan, 258, 262, 389, 391

Ou-yang Yü-ch'ien, 238, 239, 263

Overseas Chinese: reformism of, 65

Pa Chin, 215, 220, 223, 350, 364; fiction of, 226–7, 240, 262; wartime work of, 246; article on writer's courage and responsibility, 355–6; attacks on, 373

pai-hua (vernacular), 97; Hu Shih on use of, 97, 157–8; growing use of, 160–1, 213–14; see also Chinese language

Pai-mao nü (opera), 256–7

Pai Yang, 263

Pa Jen, 373

pan kung-jen chieh-chi (semi-working class), 412

Pao Ching-yen (Pao P'u-tzu), 72–3

Pao-feng tsou-yü (novel), 262

Pao T'ien-hsiao, 156

Paris Commune, 484

Paris group, 70, 71–2, 82

Paris Peace Conference (1919), 55, 98

Paris students, 434

partiinost (party spirit), 211, 255, 407; and battle of the 'two slogans,' 218

party-building: Mao on, 337–8

Paulsen, Friedrich, 273

Pa-yueh ti hsiang-ts'un (novel), 230

Peach Garden Oath, 69

Peasant Movement Training Institute, 289

peasants, 417; Mao's early lack of emphasis on, 276; Mao's later emphasis on as center of revolution, 289, 329; classes of, 290; and mass line, 299–300; in 'people's democratic dictatorship,' 344–5; emphasis on education of, 345–6; idealized, 350; mass writings of, 351;

Shao Ch'üan-lin on reality of, 366; and concession theory, 370–1; rebellions of, 370–1, 375–6, 384; and concept of 'middle character,' 386, 387; political role of, 395, 401; role in Chinese society, 395, 411, 415; role of, 395, 401; influence on Mao's thought, 395–6, 411, 430; education of, 412, 415; poor, 412, 420; and Great Leap Forward, 414; middle, 419, 420, 425

Pei-ching-jen (play), 239

Pei-ching wan-pao (Peking evening news), 360, 362

Peita, 97; see also Peking University

Peitaiho: meetings, 429, 430, 445, 464, 467, 468, 482

'Pei-ying' ('Shadow' essay), 222

Peking, 430; literary scene in, 163–4; in novels of Lao She, 225, 229

'Peking coup d'état and the merchants' (Mao), 287–8

Peking Daily (Pei-ching jih-pao), 360

Pekingology, 485

Peking Opera, 472, 257; reform of, 377–80; Chiang Ch'ing on revolutionizing, 378–80; Mao on, 379–80

Peking Party Committee, 358, 359, 373, 377; intellectuals of, 359–64; and Mao's ideological class struggle, 368; not openly criticized, 376; and 1964 thought reform, 383

Peking University (Peita), 14, 370; work-study programs at, 86; role in May Fourth incident, 97; see also Beijing University

penal system: First Prison of Chekiang Province, 446

P'eng Chen, 360; evaluation of GLF by, 359; supposed disparagement of Mao, 359; on Five-Man Group, 383; and Three Family Village, 392

P'eng P'ai, 137

P'eng Te-huai, 383; defense of, 358, 359, 362, 363, 376; possible reference to in drama, 363, 365; criticism of GLF, 436; confrontation with Mao at Lushan, 457; and Khrushchev, 458

pen-jen piao-hsien (behavior of the person in question), 470

pen-yuan (basic principles), 272

People's Daily, 373–4, 383, 392, 413, 422–3, 425, 453, 464, 509, 513, 519, 529; on thought reform, 357; Teng T'o as editor of, 360; on literature, 365

'people's democratic dictatorship' (Mao), 344–8, 400, 401, 411, 418, 468

People's Liberation Army (PLA), 420, 431, 460; and Party rectification, 383; Propaganda Department of, 387; increasing political encroachment of, 391; as power base for Mao, 477; colonization of other organizations by, 478; and Mao, 480–1; relationship to CCP, 481, 485; rise and fall of influence of, 484; control over country, 495

People's Republic of China (PRC), 400, 401, 420, 437, 438; road to convergence with Soviet Union, 395; Chairman of, 410; Mao's leadership of, 410, 447; tenth anniversary celebration, 458

Petöfi Club, 188, 382, 473

petty-bourgeoisie: and revolutionary literature, 201–2; peasantry lumped in, 336; 'people's democratic dictatorship,' 344–5; see also bourgeoisie; social class

Phèdre (Racine), 239

P'iao: Gone with the Wind translation, 262

Pien Chih-lin: poetry of, 236

pien-fa (institutional reform), 20

P'i-Lin p'i-K'ung (Criticize Lin Piao, criticize Confucius) campaign, 486

p'ing (equality), 80

Ping Hsin, 171, 173, 231

p'ing-min (common people), 29, 277

P'ing-she (Equality Society), 85

p'ing-teng (equality), 78

ping wei chin-hsing keng to ti lun-cheng (without providing any sort of further demonstration), 441

p'in ming kan (desperate efforts), 431

Pi shang Liang-shan (Driven to join the Liangshan rebels), 257

PLA, see People's Liberation Army (PLA)

plans, 403, 434, 435, 476

plays, see drama

Plekhanov, Georgi V., 138, 202, 206, 209, 210

Plenums, Central Committee: Mao 1938 report on role of KMT, 333–4; Third Plenum of Seventh CC (1950), 418, 419; Sixth Plenum of Seventh CC (1955), 419; Second Plenum of Eighth CC (1956), 422, 453; Third Plenum of Eighth CC (1957), 406, 462, 468; Sixth Plenum of Eighth CC (1958), 434–5; at Lushan (1959), 436, 457, 465, 468; Ninth Plenum of Eighth CC (1961), 354; Tenth Plenum of Eighth CC (1962), 367, 458, 467, 468, 470, 472; First Plenum of Ninth CC (1969), 482; Third Plenum of Eleventh CC (1978), 481, 490, 500

poetry, 231–7; wartime, 247; from 1945-1949, 262

Poland, 422–3, 451, 453, 508, 521, 533

p'o li chih-ch'i (to some extent established his will), 271

Politburo (CCP), 416, 417, 421, 460; 'On the unification of party leadership...', 1942 resolution of

Politburo, 342–3; April 1956 meeting, 403–5

political departments, 242, 478

political parties: of anarchists, 86; see also individual parties by name

politics: and intellectuals, 112, 244, 358–62, 377; and literature, 203–20, 245–6, 255, 260; Mao on power of, 283; on exercise of authority in, 347–8; in GLF, 349; in relaxation after GLF, 352–4, 356–7, 367, 368–9; and science, 393; in command, 434; Mao on democratic, 476; traditional view of, 486

popular culture: new field for study, 115; as theme, 126–8; sensational fiction, 153

Popular Drama Society (Min-chung chü she), 238

popularization: Mao on, 254–5

populism: of anarchists, 74; of Yen Fu, 106

'Position of the Chinese Communist Party in the national struggle' (Mao), 250

positivism, condemned by Confucianists, 63

power, political: Hu Shih's failure to solve, 125; Liang Shu-ming's rejection of, 133; inability of neo-traditionalists to use, 136

pragmatism: Mao on, 276

problems and '-isms' (Hu Shih), 124

Problems of strategy in China's revolutionary war (Mao), 306–7

production brigades, 435

production teams, 435

progress, 26; linked to nationalism, 16, 100–6; New Youth on, 87

proletarian dictatorship, 400, 401, 422–3, 453, 472, 484–5, 486

proletariat, 401, 418; industrial, and imperialism, 137; literature for, 199–200, 204–5, 206, 210; poetry of, 237; Mao on class stand of, 252; Mao on literature for, 254; Mao's early attitude toward, 279, 282, 284; linked in revolution with peasants, 302; 'viewpoint' in Mao's Marxism, 325; Mao on revolutionary role of, 330, 332; in pre-capitalist revolution, 330; vanguard of, 395; party of, 399; semiproletariat, 412

propaganda: literature as, 199, 208, 245–6, 255; and CCP, 242; in war of resistance, 242

Propaganda Department (KMT Central Executive Committee), Mao head of, 296

Propaganda Department of the CCP, 375, 377; and relaxation of 1961-1962, 358–60; May Fourth Writers of, 364–7; and Mao's ideological class struggle, 368, 376; and 1964 thought reform, 383, 388; campaign against Hu Feng, 388; films criticized by, 388; in post-Mao era, 515

provinces, 444

Prusek, Jaroslav, 143, 149, 189, 192; on the short story, 172

psychic energy (hsin li), 25; Yen Fu on, 25–6; and dynamism, 28

'public' government, 35–6

pu chi (not going far enough), 327

pu hsu (this must not be), 277

p'u-t'ung-hua (commmon idioms), 213–14

quality, transformation of quantity, 319

Questions of strategy in the anti-Japanese guerrilla war (Mao), 307

Quotations from Chairman Mao, 478, 489

race, Liang on concept of, 29–30

Racine, Jean Baptiste, 239

radical intellectuals, 372–7; as China's

New Left, 374; on class struggle, 374–6; outwardly scholarly debates of, 376–7; in campaign for cultural rectification, 383, 387; criticism of, 392; and Cultural Revolution, 394

'Reading notes on the [Soviet] textbook of political economy' (Mao), 466, 492, 493, 497

realism: urged for literary revolution, 160, 166; in literary evolution, 182–3; translations of European, 183; as concern for society, 184, 185; as Lu Hsun, 188–90; in fiction of 1930s, 228–9; dictated by war, 244; and debate over art forms, 251; socialist, 255, 258; of Ting Ling, 259–60

Reclus, Elisée, 71

Reclus, Paul, 71

rectification: campaigns, 250, 251, 380–94, 477; and May Fourth literature, 252–3; and Ting Ling, 259; Mao's thought as basis for, 339; limited nature of, 388–93; in science, 393–4; Mao's displeasure at, 394

Red Army, 298, 301–2; Mao on operational principles of, 306–8; in united front, 313

Red Guards, 476, 478–80, 489, 492; Peking rallies, 447; rustication, 479, 482; Peking, meeting of Mao and, 479–80; and Democracy Wall movement, 503; in post-Mao era, 503, 516, 521, 532

reform movement: native sources for thought, 13; new cosmology basic to, 14; erosion of evolutionary optimism, 38–41; turn to evolutionary naturalism, 41, 64; vs. revolution, 65–6; revolutionary movement outgrowth of, 65–6; Mao's early lack of interest in subject, 269; see also revolution

regional literature: by Hsiao Chün, 228; in 1930s, 229; political significance

regional literature *(continued)*
of, 229–30; by Hsiao Hung, 230; by
Tuan-mu Hung-liang, 231
religion: lack of Chinese term for, 56;
Confucianism as, 56–62; as problem,
59–60; Liang Shu-ming on, 59–62;
need for state religion, 111; see also
Buddhism; Christianity;
Confucianism; Taoism
Remarque, Erich Maria, 238
Resistance Association, 244
'Resurrection of the phoenixes' (poem),
167
revisionism, 382, 389, 391, 484;
peasants unprepared for, 366, 370–1;
criticism of, forbidden, 376; in CCP,
446; modern, 453–61; Soviet, 458,
459, 466–7; semi-revisionists, 459;
Mao on, 475, 486
revolution: impact of concept of, 65–6,
106–18; vs. reform, 66–7; Chinese,
Mao's vision of, 329, 412, 433,
450–1; industrial, 412; new
democratic, 412; socialist, 412;
permanent, 432, 442; Stalin on
China's, 449, 450, 453; see also
Revolution of 1911
revolutionaries: anarchists, 42, 68–9;
outgrowth of reforms, 66
'revolutionary-democratic dictatorship'
(Lenin), 337, 345
revolutionary nihilism, 68–70
revolutionary rebels, 482
revolutionary romanticism, 351, 354
revolutionary writers: tenets of, 199;
radical orientation of, 200–3; League
of Left-wing Writers, 203–8; and
nationalist literature, 208, 209; free
men vs. 'third category' of writers,
209–12; mass language vs.
Latinization, 212–14; battle of the
'two slogans,' 214–20
Revolution of 1911: legacy of, 40; and
New Culture movement, 110–18

rightists, 445; see also Anti-Rightist
Campaign
rights: Liang Ch'i-ch'ao on, 29, 39; of
women, 72–3, 77; 'bourgeois,' 465;
see also civil rights
Rimbaud, Arthur, 186
Rolland, Romain, 165, 181, 186, 187,
262
romanticism: of Creationists, 113, 137,
162; and emancipation, 167–71; and
women's status, 168–71; translations
of European, 183; reaction of
modernity against, 191; in national
defence literature, 216; reaction
against, 234; in poetry, 236
Rousseau, Jean-Jacques, 47, 150, 182,
196, 206, 386
rural areas: in fiction, 225, 228–9; shift
of literature from city to, 265;
vagabonds, 399; 'high tide' of
socialism, 416; fundamental
cleavages, 419; infrastructure, 429;
society, 430
rural reconstruction movement: Liang
Shu-ming on, 133; Maoist use of,
133, 136; see also Yen Yang-ch'u
(James Yen)
Russell, Bertrand, 64, 197, 282
Russia, 401, 497; revolution a model for
Chinese, 68–9, 88; early influence on
Mao, 282, 283; 'ugly Russian,' 451;
move toward democracy, 525; see also
Soviet Union

Sa-fei nü-shih jih-chi (short story), 170
sai (obstruction, stoppage), 23
Saint Simon, Count de, 71
san-ko hao-chieh (three worthies), 282
San-ko p'an-ni ti nü-hsing (plays), 238
san-shih nien-tai wen-hsueh (literature
of the thirties), 196
Sato Haruo, 188
Schneider, Laurence, 111, 114
schools: PLA in, 478

School-teacher Ni Huan-chih (Yeh Shao-chun), 223
Schopenhauer, Arthur, 60, 109
Schram, Stuart, 443
Schurmann, Franz, 405–6
Schwartz, Benjamin, 192
science, 422; Chinese view of, 31, 36, 95, 131; contributions of Western, 32; Yen Fu on, 33; and religion, 59; and metaphysics, 63–5; and New Youth, 87; Ch'en Tu-hsiu on, 89, 117; and democracy, 115; and human life, 130–5; slighted under GLF, 350; and reaction to cultural rectification, 393–4; scientists, 415, 420, 426, 427; genetics, 422; Mao on colleges of, 479; see also evolutionary naturalism; Social Darwinism
scientism: of radicals, 68, 71
scientists: wooed by CCP, 354
Scott, Sir Walter, 181
Second International, 83
Selected Works (Mao), 411, 418, 490
Selected Works (Teng Hsiao-p'ing), 400
self-awareness (tzu-chueh): Mao on, 270
self-government, local: and kung, 34
self-strengthening, 14, 144
Self-Study University (Tzu-hsiu ta-hsueh), 280, 284, 290
Seven Thousand Cadres Conference, 354, 459
Shakespeare, William, 183, 262
Shanghai, 464, 477; reformist journalism in, 144, 165; in fiction, 153; May Thirtieth incident, 197; refugee writers in, 229; wartime drama in, 248; Mao's early work in, 288; literature of, 365–6; Chiang Ch'ing in, 376; economic development of, 416; Machine Tools Plant, 479; radicals, 485
Shanghai Party Committee: Propaganda Department of, 372, 373; on drama, 379

Shantung, 133
Shao Ch'üan-lin, 243; on 'middle character,' 366, 386–7; attacks on, 386–7, 389, 390
Shao Hsun-mei, 186
Shao Yung, 101
Sha Ting, 229
Shelley, Percy Bysshe, 181, 182, 232
sheng (life), 60
sheng-ch'an tui (production team), 435
Sheng-kuan t'u (play), 248
Sheng-ssu-ch'ang (novelette), 230
sheng-yuan (lowest-level graduates of the imperial examination system), 445
Shen-pao (Shanghai newspaper), 156
Shen Ts'ung-wen, 99, 127, 185, 223; autobiography Ts'ung-wen tzu-chuan, 225; fiction of, 225; as regional writer, 229; on wartime literature, 246
Shen Yen-ping, see Mao Tun
Shen Yin-mo, 163
Shih (novel), 223–4
Shih (poetry journal), 164
Shih Chih-ts'un, 234
Shih-ching, 444
Shih Hui, 263
Shih-pao (Shanghai newspaper), 144, 156
Shih she (Truth Society), 85
Shih T'o, 262
Shih-tzu hou (The lion's roar), 150
Shih-wu pao (Current affairs, The China Progress), 18, 144
shizen (nature), 185
Shorter Dictionary of Philosophy, 439
short stories: by women writers, 169–71; of Lu Hsun, 172–80; of Mao Tun, 201, 224–5; of Chang T'ien-i, 227; of Wu Tsu-hsiang, 227, 228; of Chao Shu-li, 257
Short Story Monthly (Hsiao-shuo yueh-pao), 157, 164; Manifesto in, 164–5

shu (reciprocity), 53, 76
Shuang-yeh hung ssu erh-yueh hua
    (novel), 246
Shui-hu chuan (The water margin), 146
Shui-pien (play), 239, 248
Sian incident, 314
Sienkiewicz, Henry, 188
Sikiang, 460
Sinclair, Upton, 199, 200
sinification, 348; applied by Mao to
    Marxism, 322, 323–7; 'methodology,'
    325, 326–7; 'viewpoint,' 325;
    'standpoint' of Marxism applied to,
    325–6
Sino-American relations, 459
Sino-Indian border: dispute, 458
Sino-Soviet relations, 427, 448, 451–2,
    459, 461, 462, 471; split, 395, 424,
    448–75; joint-stock companies, 410;
    split, 448–75; Party conference, 458;
    dispute, 459
Sino-Soviet Treaty of Friendship,
    Alliance, and Mutual Assistance, 449,
    450
'Sixty articles on work methods' (Mao),
    406, 432, 440, 441, 442, 445, 466
Skinner, G. William, 447
Smiles, Samuel, 271
Smith, Adam, 19, 26, 103; Yen Fu on,
    105
Snow, Edgar, 289, 315, 322, 448, 487,
    496, 497
social class: and literature, 201, 206,
    210; Mao on, 292, 335–6; in
    'people's democratic dictatorship,'
    344–5
Social contract (Rousseau), 150
Social Darwinism, 19, 26, 51, 84, 131;
    Liang Ch'i-ch'ao on, 28, 89;
    condemned, 63, 112; implications of,
    100, 104–5; and nationalism, 100
socialism: in Chinese thought, 34, 105;
    revolutionary Western, 67; Chinese
    debate on, 83, 105–6; of CCP, 83–4;

anarchist, 86; capitalism evaluated by,
    105; Mao on lack of, in arts, 381;
    Mao on, 400, 403, 413, 414, 416,
    423, 427, 458, 491; Mao's conception
    of socialist development, 412; road
    to, 413, 432, 451–2; peaceful
    transition to, 422; socialist
    transformation, 425, 432
Socialist Education Campaign, 368,
    446, 468, 469, 472, 473, 474;
    intensification of class struggle
    questioned, 371
socialist realism and literature of GLF,
    351, 355
social utopia, as background for May
    Fourth, 65–96; see also anarchists;
    New Youth (Hsin ch'ing-nien); Paris
    group; revolutionary nihilism;
    socialism; Tokyo group
society, Chinese, 485; peasantry in, 395,
    411; atmosphere of, 414; class
    structure of, 463
Society for the Recovery of Women's
    Rights, 72
Society to Advance Morality, 85
South China Society (Nan-kuo she), 238
Soviet Union, 435, 480; literary
    influence of, 197–8, 255; Mao on
    Chinese revolution vs. Soviet, 299;
    Mao's debt to, 345; literary influence
    of, 351; withdrawal of advisers, 351;
    as model for China, 395, 402, 412,
    413, 436–7, 448, 451, 452, 471;
    agriculture, 412; compared to China,
    414, 424, 453–4; de-Stalinization in,
    422, 453–61; criticism of experience
    of, 423, 452, 473; differences with
    China, 424; and transition to
    communism, 435; PRC competition
    with, in Great Leap Forward, 436;
    and China's foreign policy, 449–50,
    458; agriculture in, 452; assistance to
    PRC, 456; Mao calls for overthrow of
    existing regime in, 459; revisionism

in, 459–60, 466–7, 486; Mao on
standard of living in, 461;
Constitution of, 492; disintegration
of, 525; see also Sino-Soviet relations
so-wei luan (so-called disturbances), 477
Spencer, Herbert, 19, 40, 71, 84, 131;
Yen Fu on, 25, 28, 147; refuted, 74
Spring and Autumn period, 421
Spring Festival on Education (1964),
381, 393, 444
Spring Willow Society (Ch'un-liu she),
237
ssu-hsiang (thought), 272, 276
Ssu-ma Ch'ien, 180
Ssu shih-t'ung-t'ang (novel), 247
ssu-shu (private school), 273
Ssu-shui (Dead water poetry collection),
232–3
ssu-t'iao han-tzu ('four heavies'), 204,
218
Stalin, Joseph, 136, 423, 433, 437, 441,
443, 470, 480, 495; on sian incident,
314–15; Mao's debt to, 321; on
Marxism, 321, 325–35; on revolution
in backward lands, 330; on armed
struggle in China, 337; and
Sinification of Marxism, 396; Mao
compared to, 399, 454; on four-class
bloc, 401; de-Stalinization, 422,
453–61; Mao criticism of, 438–9,
452, 454, 455, 457; Mao and, 449,
450; on Chinese revolution, 450, 453
standard of living, 425, 460
State Council, 405, 445
steel, 410; backyard production, 431,
435; competition with United
Kingdom in, 456
Stevenson, Robert Louis, 188
Stowe, Harriet Beecher, 237
Strong, Anna Louise, 435, 461
struggle: as instrument of revolution,
310
students, 420, 482; and New Youth,
87–8; in May Fourth Incident, 98;

Mao's early emphasis on, 276;
university, 425
study abroad, 85–6; and knowledge of
the West, 14; in post-Mao era, 506
study societies, 14, 18; T'an Ssu-t'ung
on, 35
subjectivism, 408
suicide: New Youth on, 90–1
Su Man-shu, 181
Sun Ch'uan-fang, 125
Sun Fu-yuan, 163, 164
Sung Chih-ti, 248
Sung dynasty, 64, 158
Sung Liang, see Sun Yeh-fang
Sun Society, 137, 199, 209; and
Crescent Moon, 205
Sun Tzu, 307–8
Sun Wu-k'ung, 476
Sun Yat-sen, 106, 111, 136, 449; and
T'ung-meng hui, 65; on land reform,
66; 18th century ideas of, 106;
organic nationalism of, 108; after
May Fourth, 120–1, 122; and KMT,
138; Mao on, 272, 332
Sun Yeh-fang, 338, 371–2
Su-pao (Kiangsu daily), 144
superstructure, 396, 424, 472
supply system: free, 430–1, 464
Supreme State Conference, 404, 421
Su Tung-p'o, 321
Su Wen (Tai K'e-ch'ung), 209, 210, 212
symbolism: vs. neo-romanticism, 186;
of Lu Hsun, 188; symbolist poetry,
233–5, 236, 237
syncretism, in New Text school, 56
Szechwan, 429

Ta-chiang (novel), 231
ta chiang-shan (contending for the
country), 301–2
ta-ch'üan (great power), 406
ta-ch'üan tu-lan (great power is
monopolized), 406–7
Ta Chung-hua (Great China), 44

ta chung hua (mass language), 212
ta fang (big way), 410
Tagore, Rabindranath, 165, 181
t'ai-chi (Great Ultimate), 58
Tai Chi-t'ao, 121
Tai Li, 244
Tailism, 399
Taine, Hippolyte Adolphe, 228
Taiping Rebellion, 365, 376
T'ai-tung, 165
Tai Wang-shu, 186, 220; poetry of, 234
T'ai-yang Society, 137
ta i-yü (spiritual will), 60
T'ai-yung chao-tsai Sang-kan ho shang
    (novel), 259–60
ta-ku (beating the drum while telling a
    story), 245
Ta-kung-pao (Shanghai newspaper),
    239; film supplement of, 263; Mao's
    reply to article on strikes, 284–5
Talks on Literature and Art (Mao), 249,
    250–81, 364; enforced by Chou
    Yang, 364
Talk to music workers (Mao), 495–6
t'a-men na-i-t'ao (their stuff), 445
T'a na-ko tung-hsi kao-ti pu-hao (He
    didn't deal with this matter well at
    all), 454
T'ang Chün-i, 134
tang-hsing (party spirit), 407
tang-yuan ti ch'eng-fen (composition of
    Party membership), 468
T'an Ssu-t'ung, 18, 19, 28, 51, 82, 89,
    91, 100, 148, 275; analysis of
    writings of, 22–5; use of Western
    science by, 32, 34; on study societies,
    35; on democracy, 35–6; on
    imperialism, 37; on Confucianism as
    religion, 56, 60–1, 68; on family, 75,
    76; on women's rights, 77; on history
    as moral drama, 104
t'an-t'uo (inquire into), 441
T'ao Hsing-chih, 123, 133
T'ao Hsi-sheng, 139–40

Taoism, 15, 24, 109, 439–40, 447, 486;
    of Chang Ping-lin, 50, 51–2; and
    Confucianism, 58, 80; revival of, 102,
    104; attack on, 111; influence on
    Mao, 317
Taoism-Buddhism, 121, 131
t'ao lao p'o, t'ao lao kung (get an old
    lady, get an old man), 425
ta-pen-yuan (basic principles): Mao on,
    272
ta-she (big co-ops), 429–30
Ta-ti ti hai (novel), 231
ta-t'ung (Great Harmony), 20, 30, 51,
    65, 273, 345–6, 402, 412; as native
    utopian ideal, 31, 34, 36; Confucius
    on, 49; anarchism as modern version,
    67, 86; seen as old-fashioned, 94
Ta-t'ung shu (The book of the great
    commonwealth), 18, 19; sources of,
    20–1; philosophy of, 21–2; on family,
    75–6; mystical element in, 104
teachers, 426, 428; after GLF, 369
technicians, 415, 420
technology: Chinese acceptance of, 32,
    33; mastery of as goal, 103
Teng Hsiao-p'ing, 394; and 1961–1962
    relaxation, 359; Report to Eighth
    Congress, 420–1
Teng Li-ch'ün, 466
Teng Shih, 46
Teng T'o, 367; evaluation of GLF by,
    359; tsa-wen of, 360–2; 'The royal
    way and the tyrant's way,' 361
Terrien de la Couperie, 47
terrorism, 69
Textbook on Chinese History (Chung-
    kuo li-shih chiao-k'o-shu), 58
textbooks: translated from Russian,
    rewriting of, 350
themes dominating May Fourth period:
    progress and nationalism, 100–6;
    revolution, 106–9
'third category' of men (ti-san-chung
    jen), 208–12, 216, 219

Third International, 449
thought of Mao Tse-tung, 349–50, 383; strains of anarchism, 86; development of, 267, 344; from student movement to peasant movement (1917-1927), 267–96; nationalism in, 268–9; 1917 article in New Youth, 268–73; martial spirit in, 270; emphasis on will, 271; early political ideas, 272; theme of practice, 273; 1919 article, 274–6; 'The great union of the popular masses,' 275; on Hunanese autonomy movement, 278–9, 280; on marriage, 280; study of Marxism, 282, 291–2, 295, 315–16; in peasant period (1925-1927), 283, 288–96; on political power, 283; during workers' period in Hunan (1921-1922), 283–5; as 'organization man' (1923-1924), 283–8; on party, army, and masses (1927-1937), 296–315; influence on CCP use of armed force on, 298–9; on national and social contradictions (1937-1940), 315–38, 347; on relation between CCP and Moscow, 322–3; adaptation of Marxism, 323–7, 346, 395, 396; on 'sinification' of Marxism,' 323–7; on art of statecraft, 326–7; on interpretation of Chinese history, 328–30; on 'New Democracy,' 330–2; on role of classes in revolution, 335–7; chronology of ideas and events, 338–9; triumph of (1941-1949), 338–9; on mass line, 340–2; on party's unifying role, 342; on people's democratic dictatorship, 344–8, 400, 401, 411, 418, 468; later trends already implicit in, 346–8; reduced stress on in universities, 368–9; radical intellectuals' use of, 374; influence of peasantry on, 395–6, 411; from 1949-1976, 395–498; patterns of

rule, 397–410; from people's democracy to contradictions among the people, 397–427; patterns of development, 410–17; people, classes, and contradictions, 419–27; Chinese and Marxist elements in, 436–48, 471, 486, 495; radicalization of, 462, 470, 489; defined, 490
thought reform campaigns: after GLF, 357; 1964, 383, 388–9; see also Anti-Rightist Campaign; rectification
'three ages' doctrine, 20, 24
Three Antis, 419
Three-Eight work style, 478
Three Family Village group, 360, 391–2
Three Gorges, 429
Three People's Principles, 108, 139, 296, 334
three worthies (san-ko hao-chieh), 282
t'i (to uplift), 147
Tiananmen Square student demonstration, 501, 520–2, 532
Ti Ch'u-ch'ing, 144
T'ien-an men (Gate of Heavenly Peace), 98
T'ien Chien, 237; wartime poems of, 247
T'ien Han, 183, 204, 364, 377, 390, 391; one 'four heavies,' 204, 218; plays of, 237, 238; films of, 263
t'ien-hsia (all under heaven), 19, 73, 149, 272
T'ien-i (natural morality), 72
Tientsin: in fiction, 151
T'ien-yen lun (Evolution and ethics, Huxley), 26
Ting Ling, 165, 168, 169, 170, 243, 373; on women in Yenan, 251–2, 254; writings in Yenan, 258–60, 262; target of Anti-Rightist Campaign, 389, 390, 391

Ting Wen-chiang (V. K. Ting), 119,
    122, 125, 141, 470; in debate on
    science, 131; after May Fourth, 136
ti-san-chung jen ('third category' of
    men), 208
Ti-san tai (novel), 230
Tito, Joseph Broz, 449
Tokyo group, 70, 72, 82
Tokyo Imperial University, 165
Tolstoy, Leo, 73, 165, 181, 182, 184,
    262
tou mei-yu tui-k'ang hsing-t'ai ti ts'un-
    tsai (none of these exist in
    antagonistic form), 417
traditionalism: attacked by May Fourth
    writers, 167; of late Ch'ing novel,
    172; see also neo-traditionalism
translation: and knowledge of the West,
    14; by Lin Shu, 14, 107, 181; by Yen
    Fu, 14, 19, 33, 147; of Mill, 33; of
    novels, 147; by Association for
    Literary Studies, 164; impact of,
    180–90; idealization of Western
    writers, 182; numbers of, 182–3; Lu
    Hsun's of Russian, 206–8; of Western
    authors, 262
treaty ports: journalism of, 143–5, 155
Trotsky, Leon, 199, 209; on revolution
    in backward lands, 330
Trotskyites, 139, 496–7
Ts'ai Ho-sen, 278, 281–2
ts'ai-tzu chia-jen (talent-beauty) novels,
    152
Ts'ai Yuan-p'ei, 14, 86, 162; president
    of Peita, 97
Tsang K'o-chia, 237, 243; wartime
    work of, 247
Ts'ao Ts'ao, 447
Ts'ao Yü, 220; plays of, 238–41, 248;
    films of, 263
tsa-wen (informal essay), 362–3, 201,
    221–3, 253; by Lu Hsun, 360, 361;
    by Wu Han and others, 360; by Teng
    T'o, 360–2

Tseng Kuo-fan (Tseng Wen-cheng):
    Mao's admiration for, 272
Tseng P'u, 149, 151, 155
Tsing-hua University, 428; Middle
    School, 476
Tsingtao, scholarly conference in (1956),
    422
Tso-chuan, 489, 497
Tso-i wen-hua tsung t'ung-meng (Left-
    wing Cultural Coalition), 203
Tsou Jung, 106
Tsou-p'ing (county, Shantung), 133
Tsou Tang, 501
tsu-ch'eng min-tsu (constitute a nation),
    496
tsung-chiao (religion), 56
Tuan-mu Hung-liang, 231
tu-li (autonomy), 78
Tu-li p'ing-lun (The independent critic),
    136
tung (dynamism), 28
t'ung (pervasiveness, permeability,
    circulation, communication), 23, 28,
    34
T'ung-ch'eng (school of philosophy), 160
Tung-fang tsa-chih (The eastern
    miscellany), 39
Tung Hsi wen-hua chi ch'i che-hsueh
    (Eastern and Western civilizations
    and their philosophies), 60
t'ung-i (to unify), 342
tung-li (dynamism), 28
Tung-lin scholars, 362–3
T'ung-meng hui (Revolutionary
    Alliance), 65; reform gradualism
    attacked by, 38; and anarchists, 71;
    literary society of, 156
t'un t'un t'u t'u pien-cheng-fa (dialectics
    of hemming and hawing), 439
Turgenev, Ivan, 182
tu-ts'ai (autocracy), 345, 347, 402
t'u-ts'ai chu (local moneybags), 290
tu-tuan (arbitrary or dictatorial
    decisions of an individual), 406–7

Twenty-one Demands (1915), 98
Twenty-Six-Country Drafting
    Committee, 458
two-party system: Mao on, 409
'two slogans' battle, 204, 205, 214–20
tz'u (to prick), 147
tzu-chu (autonomy), 75
tzu-chueh (self-awareness), 270
Tz'u-hsi Empress Dowager, 38
Tzu-hsiu ta-hsueh (Self-Study
    University), 280, 284
Tzu Jen: pseudonym of Mao Tse-tung,
    292
tzu-li keng-sheng (slogan of self-
    reliance), 347
tzu li wei kuo (independent country),
    280
tzu pen chia (capitalists), 282
tzu-tung (individual initiative), 270
Tzu-yeh (novel), 185, 201, 223, 224,
    239
tzu-yu (freedom), 78
tzu-yu jen (free men), 208–12

U.N. Charter on Human Rights, 504
U.N. Covenant on Civil and Political
    Rights, 530
U.N. Covenant on Social and Economic
    Rights, 530
Uncle Tom's Cabin, 237
united front, 402, 418; first (1923-
    1927), 285–6, 333, 337; second
    (1933-1941), 215, 217
United Kingdom, 433, 456, 497
universities: after GLF, 368–9;
    professors, 426; Mao on, 479–80;
    self-study, 480
urban areas: popular fiction of, 127,
    153; writers of, 200, 202; depicted
    by Mao Tun, 224; in 1930s fiction,
    227; writing moved from, 245; films
    as medium of, 264–5; Mao's early
    emphasis on, 287–8; later
    downgraded by Mao, 291–5; goal of

encirclement of from countryside,
    301; residents resettled in country,
    350
utilitarianism: of literature, 210
utopia: K'ang Yu-wei's vision of, 21,
    105; Liang Ch'i-ch'ao on, 29, 39; in
    antiquity, 36; social, and May Fourth
    movement, 64; defined by radicals,
    71; of Paris group, 71; of Tokyo
    group, 72; and family system, 75–6;
    without barriers, 79; and individual
    emancipation, 80; in Chinese novels,
    150

vagabonds, in Red Army, 308
Valéry, Paul, 186
Verlaine, Paul, 186, 187, 234, 235
vernacular: as vehicle for literature, 115,
    157–9; Hu Shih on development of,
    126, 160–1; see also Chinese
    language
Versailles, Treaty of, 93, 98, 121
Vijnanavada school of Buddhism, 109
villages: new, promoted by Mao, 290;
    shift away from, 345
Voronsky, 209

wages: system of, 430–1; Soviet eight-
    grade system, 431; differentials, 474
wai-hang ling-tao nei-hang (for the
    layman to lead the expert), 445
Wakeman, Frederic, Jr., 443
Wang Chi-chen, 243
Wang Ching-wei, 69
Wang Juntao, 517, 518, 519, 520
Wang Kuo-fan cooperative, 414
Wang Kuo-wei, 109
Wang Meng, 510
Wang P'ing-ling, 208
Wang Renzhi, 529
Wang Ruoshui, 509
Wang Ruowang, 511
Wang Shih-wei, 254; on Yenan, 251–2
Wang T'ao, 14, 18

Wang Tu-ch'ing, 173–81
Wang T'ung-chao, 164, 165
Wang Yang-ming, 131, 134; centrality of thought of, 132; influence on Mao, 273
Wang Ying-hsia, 168
war, 241–9; Mao on role of, 269–70, 308–9; effect in mid-1930s, 311–12; see also revolution
war literature: fiction, 245–6; weaknesses of, 245–6; poetry, 247; drama, 247–9
warlords: Mao on, 294
Warring States period: Confucianists vs. Taoists in, 51; and Hsu Hsiang, 73; contending philosophies, 421
Warsaw: Conference, 458
Washington, George, 147
Water Margin, The, 257, 308
Watt, James, 393
Wealth of Nations (Smith), 103–4
Weekly Critic (Mei-chou p'ing-lun), 92, 275; debate on problems and '-isms,' 124
Wei-ch'eng (novel), 249, 262, 265
wei ch'eng-fen lun (everything depends on class status alone), 470
wei-chiao (encircle and anihilate), 458
wei-hsin (reform), 151
Wei Jingsheng, 504, 516
Wei-shih (consciousness only) Buddhism, 60
Wen-hsuan school of prose, 160
Wen-hsueh chou-pao (Literature weekly), 164
Wen-hsueh hsun-k'an (Literature thrice-monthly), 164
wen-hsueh ko-ming (literary revolution), see literary revolution
wen-hsueh ti kuo-yü (a literary national language), 161
Wen-hsueh yen-chiu hui (Association for Literary Studies), 164–6; fiction of, 173

wen-hua ko-ming shih ko wen-hua ti ming (the Cultural Revolution was about doing away with culture), 483
Wen-hui pao, 262
Wen I-to, 220, 247; poetry of, 232–3; assassination of, 244, 262
wen-i tsai-tao (literature to convey the Confucian way), 159
wen-i t'ung-hsun yuan (literary reporters), 241
wen-jen (man of letters), 113, 167
wen-ming (enlightenment), 38
Wen T'ien-hsiang, 263
wen-t'i ko-ming (stylistic revolution), 158
wen-yen, 213
wen-yen (classical style), 158, 162, 174, 181
West, the, 421, 458, 497; China's discovery of, 14–31; Chinese view of, 31–2, 36–7; and neo-traditionalists, 63; anarchists in, 67, 68, 70, 100; view of after First World War, 93–4; revolution as 18h century idea, 106; Liang Ch'i-ch'ao's re-evaluation of, 129–30, 132; imitation in fiction, 181–2; translations of works of, 182–4; and China's search for modernity, 193; on literature, 205–6, 212, 233, 250–1; on Ts'ao Yü, 239–41; on Mao, 271, 272, 275; Mao on study abroad, 279–80; impact on feudalism, 329–30; and rejection of Chinese values, 348; criticism of learning from, 349; revival of values in criticism of GLF, 360; influence on Chou Yang, 364–5; teachers trained in, 369; history of vs. Chinese, 370; Mao and Westernization, 396, 437; ideas of, 409, 489, 495–6; standard of living in, 425; wealth of, 430; Western scholars on Mao, 487;

Westernization, 497; see also imperialism; specific countries by name

Western Han, 49, 58

Western Hills faction, KMT, 292

Westernization: views concerning, 14–17; K'ang Yu-wei on, 22; 'national learning' as opposition to, 44; advocated in New Youth, 89

'Where do correct ideas come from?' (Mao), 385

White Cloud Monastery, 83

Whitman, Walt, 187, 193

Wilson, Edmund, 206, 244

Wilson, Woodrow, 93

Winckler, Edwin, 447

Wittfogel, Karl August, 298

Wo che i pei-tzu (novelette), 263

women: and 'freedom to love,' 68–9; rights of, 72–3, 77; emancipation urged by anarchists, 77; New Youth on, 90; as writers, 169–71, 173; in Yenan, 251; Mao's early emphasis on, 276, 310

Women and socialism (Bebel), 74

Wordsworth, William, 232

worker-peasant: alliance, 418

workers, 417, 420, 482, 493; idealized in GLF, 350; writings of, 351; office workers, 399, 420; recruitment into CCP, 412; urban, 412

working class, 497; and Marxism, 137; Mao on, 293; in 'people's democratic dictatorship,' 344–5; leadership, 411–12, 419; semi-, 412; intellectuals, 426; see also proletariat

World Economic Herald, 519

world revolution: Mao on China's place in, 331–2

writers: wartime conditions of, 243; moved into country, 244–5; teams of, 245; latitude for after GLF, 355; shift from individuals to committees, 387; see also fiction; literature; poetry

Writers Union, 386, 472; during GLF, 350–1

wu (non-existence), 81, 102

wu-ch'an chieh-chi (propertyless class), 282

Wuchang, 434

wu-cheng-fu chu-i (anarchism), 68

Wu cheng-fu chu-i t'ung-chih she (Society of Anarchist Comrades), 85

Wu Chih-hui, 64, 71, 79, 82, 85; in debate on science, 131; on vernacular, 162

Wu Ching-tzu, 148, 149

Wu Ch'uan-ch'i, 373

Wu Ch'ung-ch'ing (play), 248

Wu Han, 360, 367, 376–7; tsa-wen by, 360, 377, 378; articles on Hai Jui, 373, 377

Wuhan: newly founded government, 137; as literary center, 242–3

Wu Leng-hsi: in Five-Man Group, 383

Wu Mi, 128, 162

Wu Nan-hsing (pen name of Wu Han, Teng T'o, and Liao Mo-sha), 360

Wu P'ei-fu: and Chihli government, 120

wu-ssu (five-four) movement, 97; see also May Fourth movement

Wu-ssu-wen-hsüeh (May Fourth literature), 196; see also May Fourth movement

Wu Tsu-hsiang, 185, 220, 223; short stories by, 227, 228–9

Wu Wo-yao (Wu Yen-jen), 145, 149, 155, 172; on novel of sentiment, 151–2

Wu Yü, 88, 157

Wu Yüeh, 70, 107

Xu Liangying, 511, 516

Yang (short story), 230

yang-ch'ang (foreign mall), 151

Yang Ch'ang-chi, teacher of Mao Tse-tung, 271, 272, 275

Yang Ch'ao, 442
Yang Chiang, 248, 265
Yang Han-sheng, 204, 364, 365, 376,
    377, 391; one 'four heavies,' 204,
    218; films of, 263; films directed by,
    388; removed from office, 390
Yang Hsien-chen, 471; target of Party
    rectification, 383–5, 389, 390;
    Marxism of, 384–6; attacked by Ai
    Ssu-ch'i, 385; removed from position,
    386
Yang Hu-ch'eng, 314
yang-ko (rice-sprout song), 256
Yang Shang-k'un: in Five-Man Group,
    383
Yang Tu-sheng, 69
Yangtze River, 429
Yang Wen-hui, 102
yang-wu (foreign affairs), 150, 151
Yao K'o, 248
Yao Wen-yuan, 477, 373, 486, 487–8,
    494; on cultural rectification, 387;
    criticism of, 392
Yeats, William Butler, 236
Yeh Shao-chün, 200, 163, 164, 165;
    short stories of, 173–4; novel of,
    223
Yeh tien (Night lodging), 264
Yeh-ts'ao (Wild grass), 189
Yellow Emperor, 47
Yellow History (Huang Chieh), 47
Yenan, 364, 397, 399, 408, 409, 441,
    449, 482, 493, 494; communists in,
    128, 136; Chiang Ch'ing in, 377–8;
    heritage, 396, 398; period, 407;
    model, 430
Yenan Forum on Literature and Art:
    Mao's talks published, 339
Yenan Forum on literature and art, 214,
    250–1, 252–60, 339; debate on
    'national forms,' 250–2, 255; four
    problems raised, 252; Mao's attack on
    May Fourth literature, 252–4; new
    Marxist aesthetic, 254, 265; and 'the

party line,' 254–5; literature of,
    256–60, 339
Yen Fu, 275, 14, 17, 51, 100, 107, 110,
    122, 129, 141, 192, 277; translations
    by, 19, 131, 147; philosophy of,
    25–8, 71; on Western thought, 33;
    on imperialism, 37; contrasted with
    K'ang Yu-wei, 101–3; on social
    Darwinism, 104–5; populism of,
    106, 158; on a state religion, 111;
    influence on Hu Shih, 115;
    newspapers founded by, 144; on place
    of fiction, 145–6
Yen-i pai-hua pao (Paraphrased news in
    vernacular), 147
Yen Tu-ho, 156
Yen Yang-ch'u (James Yen), 123, 133
Yen Yuan, 15, 269
yin (causes), 61
yin i jen, chi to chiu i jen (one more
    person saved), 280
youth: revolt of, 87–8; as cutting edge
    of change, 91; in Cultural
    Revolution, 478–9; Mao's view of,
    487
yu (existence), 81
Yuan Chün (Chang Chün-hsiang), 261
Yuan dynasty, 158
Yuan Shih-k'ai: on state religion, 57;
    attacked by New Youth, 87–8;
    monarchial movement of, 110; Mao
    on, 272, 333–4
Yuan Shui-p'o, 391
Yuan-yang hu-tieh p'ai (Mandarin Duck
    and Butterfly School), 152–5, 157,
    185
Yuan-yeh (play), 239, 240
Yü-chou feng (Cosmic wind), 212
Yueh-yueh hsiao-shuo (Monthly fiction),
    145
Yugoslavia, 405, 449, 456, 459
yu-hsiu (warrior heroes), 107
Yü-li hun (Jade pear spirit), 153, 155
yü-lu (records of conversation), 158

yu-min (éléments déclassés), 399

yung (courage): Mao on, 270

yung-jen hsing-cheng (employing people in the administraton), 327

Yung-yen (Justice), 44, 53, 54

yun hui (a cosmic-historical process of change, turning-point of destiny), 17

Yun Tai-ying, 197

Yü P'ing-po, 222

yu-shih (times), 320

Yü-ssu (Threads of talk) weekly, 163, 164, 221

Yü Ta-fu, 113, 114, 165, 167, 168, 197; short stories of, 173, 174; and foreign literature, 181; on neo-romanticism, 187; poetry of, 188

Yü-wai hsiao-shuo chi (Stories from abroad), 180

Zhao Ziyang, 502, 504, 512, 514, 515, 518, 520, 523, 532

Zhdanov, Andrei, 351

Zola, Émile, 185

Lightning Source UK Ltd.
Milton Keynes UK
UKOW06f1157070116

265968UK00009B/262/P